SMEAR!

Wilson and the Secret State

STEPHEN DORRIL and ROBIN RAMSAY

FOURTH ESTATE · London

First published in Great Britain in 1991 by
FOURTH ESTATE LIMITED
289 Westbourne Grove
London W11 2QA

A catalogue record for this book is available from the British
Library

ISBN 1-872180-68-X

Typeset by York House Typographic Ltd, London
Printed in Great Britain by Hartnolls, Bodmin

CONTENTS

Contents

INTRODUCTION

Parapolitics. A system or practice of politics in which accountability is consciously diminished. Generally, covert politics, the conduct of public affairs not by rational debate and responsible decision-making but by indirection, collusion, and deceit. Cf. conspiracy. The political exploitation of irresponsible agencies or parastructures, such as intelligence agencies.
PETER DALE SCOTT
Notes for an Unwritten Future Dictionary

IN THE SUMMER of 1990, amidst the great explosion of information on the Soviet satellites, a former KGB officer remarked that much of the KGB's intelligence on America was acquired simply by reading the American press, which published a great deal of information. This was not the case in Britain however, he said. He was right, of course: for the most part the areas which the British state does not want examined are still left alone by our serious papers. Throughout the entire period from 1987 to date there has not been a single journalist whose brief was to pursue the Colin Wallace/Peter Wright Affair. If there is a correspondent working full-time on, for example, the British nuclear industry, the funding of the Conservative Party, the secret state (even the non-secret state) – the list could be extended greatly – we are unaware of them.

The convention in this country that 'politics' means the Houses of Parliament works very nicely for the state (and secret state), which is left in peace to get on with running things. Peter Wright said in *Spycatcher* that within MI5 they say 'Politicians may come and politicians may go but the Security Service goes on forever.' So do the Treasury, the Home Office, the Foreign Office . . . all of them protected from effective political or journalistic scrutiny by this country's secrecy laws and our largely supine media. Even so – and this is one of the major themes in this book – there actually is a great deal more information available about this society and this state than is generally acknowledged. By American standards, even by the standards of some of the Soviet bloc these days, things are bad; but they are not impossible.

This book really began in 1985 when Stephen Dorril went down to Southend to meet the former military intelligence officer, Fred Holroyd, who had been forced out of the British Army in the mid-1970s, one victim of the internecine intelligence war there. Holroyd took Dorril to Lewes prison to meet Colin Wallace, then serving a 10-year sentence for manslaughter. Dorril came back with what were then mind-boggling allegations about covert intelligence operations in Northern Ireland and mainland Britain. Five months and a crash course on contemporary British politics later, we put out issue 11 of our journal, *Lobster*, with the first attempt to explain in detail what Wallace was saying about the covert operations of the British secret state.

Colin Wallace is the most important defector from the British secret state in this country since the war, and his insider's information confirmed to us that the previously largely unexplored role of the intelligence services on British politics amounted to a new agenda for post-war British political history. Somehow most British contemporary historians and political scientists had managed not to notice that their accounts of our history and our society encompassed everything except who was actually running much of it. At the beginning of his book, *Whitehall*, Peter Hennessy tells the reader that he does not propose to discuss the security and intelligence services: and they do not appear at all in Jeremy Paxman's recent *Friends in High Places: Who Runs Britain?*

This book is centrally concerned with the impact of the secret state on the Labour governments of Harold Wilson – and their aftermath. It is an attempt to write contemporary history incorporating the activities of the secret state. It also goes some way towards providing a revisionist account of the Wilson governments, and particularly of Harold Wilson. One of the few things the left and right in Britain now agree on – though for different reasons – is that the Wilson governments failed. Looking at the Thatcher era it would not be difficult to make a case that Labour's 'failure' in the sixties and seventies has been grotesquely exaggerated. But even if, for the sake of argument, we accept the failure thesis, we would argue that they did not fail so much as they were defeated; and the methods used to defeat them were often covert, conspiratorial – what we would call parapolitical. In many of the key incidents in the Wilson governments there was a significant covert input. How far Wilson was aware of this at the time is unclear.

Throughout this book we use two terms frequently: secret state and permanent government. By 'the secret state' we mean what have now become widely known as the security services; and in particular by that term we mean the security service, MI5, Special Branch and the secret intelligence service, MI6. By 'the permanent government', the term introduced by Anthony Verrier, we mean the secret state plus Cabinet Office and upper echelons of Home and Foreign and Commonwealth Offices, the Armed Forces and Ministry of Defence, the nuclear power industry and its satellite ministries; and the so-called 'Permanent Secretaries Club', the network of very senior civil servants – the 'Mandarins'. In addition to this network of 'servants of the Crown' – more accurately, perhaps, 'servants of the state' – there are its satellites, including:

- MPs, particulary Tory MPs;
- 'agents of influence' in the media, ranging from actual agents of the security services, conduits of official leaks, to senior journalists merely lusting after official praise and, perhaps, a knighthood at the end of their career;
- former security services personnel;
- front companies of the security services; nominally 'private' security firms comprised of former secret state employees used to provide 'deniability' for the security services and Ministry of Defence;
- the many think tanks and opinion-forming bodies such as the Ditchley Foundation, Royal Institute for International Affairs, Royal United Services Institute and so forth.

The whole ramified network is integrated and co-ordinated at the executive level in the traditional British manner by other, informal networks centred round the clubs of London, especially Whites, Brooks, Army and Navy, Carlton, Travellers and Special Forces.

This (by no means exhaustive) list has four outstanding characteristics: these institutions and organisations are almost entirely composed of men; with a handful of individual exceptions, they are the exclusive preserve of the Conservative Party, still unpenetrated by the Labour (or indeed Liberal Democrat) Party; all of these bodies escape democratic accountability or control; and, until very recently, none of them have been taken seriously by the Labour Party – or, as suggested above, by this society's analysts and commentators.

The first outstanding post-war exception to the rule that this power structure has been ignored by the Labour Party was Harold Wilson. (More recently, of course, there has been Tony Benn.) This may explain why, in the words of Wilson's friend Lord Goodman, 'They saw a really dangerous threat to their well-being.' It is a measure of Wilson's isolation in his unequal struggle with this largely uncharted network, that many of his Cabinet colleagues found him increasingly paranoid after 1966: his 'persecution complex' and 'obsession with the newspapers' have become part of the received vocabulary of the Wilson years. Yes, he did get somewhat paranoid round the edges, sometimes seeing plots where none existed; but mostly he was spot on. They *were* plotting against him; they *were* running smear campaigns against him. (Though who 'they' were precisely, he never really found out.)

This book is laden to the gunwales with footnotes. This is not only unavoidable, it is central to the activity. The real political world is extremely complex and showing that complexity means showing the documentation. Without it there would be mere assertion. Because of the complexity of the material it is impossible to construct a single continuous chronological narrative that would be intelligible. We have therefore organised the book in sections of chapters dealing with single subjects, in an overall chronological framework.

In writing this book we owe a good deal to certain people, notably the journalists Barrie Penrose and David Leigh, who were extremely generous with their own, unpublished, research: and without Colin Wallace and Fred Holroyd it would never have been written. Our other sources and other debts will be found in our notes.

On a personal level we would like to thank Christopher Potter, our editor at Fourth Estate, Stephanie Smith, who read through the unedited chapters and contributed valuable criticism, and our literary agent, Andrew Lownie.

Huddersfield and Hull, June 1991

PROLOGUE

Smear – Daub or stain with greasy or sticky substance; (seek to) discredit or defame.
POCKET OXFORD DICTIONARY

IN LATE 1986 we were engaged on the fringe of the London media hunt for information on 'the Wilson plots', when word first leaked out of the existence of the 'Henry Worthington' file, apparently the code-name of the key MI5 file on Harold Wilson. What was in the file? At that time no journalist in London knew (though one or two camped out near Peter Wright in Australia probably did). Six months later another dribble of information landed on the British journalists. The file did *not* contain the evidence that Wilson was a communist, or that the Labour Party had been funded by Soviet bloc money, or that Wilson had been sexually compromised on a trip to Moscow, or that he had had affairs with Marcia Falkender, and/or Barbara Castle, and/or Marcia Falkender's predecessor as his Private Secretary – all of which had then been floating around for more than twenty years. No, said this rumour, the only piece of genuine dirt in the file was something else entirely.

What was the status of this particular rumour? As usual, it was impossible to track it back to its source(s); nor was it possible to decide if it was intended to be helpful to Wilson (by dismissing the more common rumours), or meant to be just another smear, given a ring of authenticity by the claims that the 'Worthington' file contained nothing else of substance. Our guess is the latter, for this 'revelation' had its antecedents. In 1977, a biography of Wilson by the American journalist Andrew Roth, *Harold Wilson: the Yorkshire Walter Mitty*, was withdrawn after Wilson issued a writ against it. The offending passage obliquely referred to this 'Henry Worthington' rumour.

The point of all this is not to denigrate Lord Wilson, merely to illustrate the extraordinary lengths to which Lord Wilson's political opponents, within and without the British secret state, have gone to find something – anything – with which to attack him. We do not know or care if this 'Henry Worthington' rumour is true or false; nor should anyone else. It was just another smear, and, as far as we are aware, the last substantial smear about Lord Wilson.

In this book you will come across a great many others, about Lord Wilson, Lady Falkender and dozens of other Labour Party (and, indeed Liberal and Conservative Party) politicians and supporters. Almost all of them were false, and known to be false by their originators. In writing an account of these disgraceful smear campaigns we are unable to avoid repeating the content of the smears. We can only hope that, like us, their victims think the exposure of the smear campaigns justifies the repetition of their contents.

PART ONE

1916–64

I

'THE BOY WONDER'

Too clever by half.
BRENDAN BRACKEN

JAMES HAROLD WILSON was born on 16 March 1916 in a small terraced house in Milnsbridge on the outskirts of the northern industrial town of Huddersfield. The family were lower middle class, and regular church goers – radicals who supported the Liberal Party. His father was a works chemist, his mother a teacher. Like many of his generation, after the First World War his father's political allegiance moved from the Liberals to the rising force in British politics, the Labour Party. Although never himself poor, the young Harold saw real poverty and the reliance on charity all around him. For a clever young man in his position there was one obvious route up the social ladder – education.

The family instilled in Harold an austere view of life. Each member was a 'self-contained, self-sufficient person, disinclined to display feelings'. Harold learned that anxieties and problems were best kept under personal control. He was to become an intensely loyal, warm man but a lonely figure with few friends to whom he could relate his feelings. Years later, when he had a particular political problem, Harold would often walk along Mullion Cove in Cornwall alone in contemplation. 'If there was a solution, it was certain to occur to him there. Conversely – as occasionally happened – if no solution occurred there, he felt that none could exist.'[1]

His natural gifts plus hard work won him a scholarship to Oxford. At university, Wilson was Treasurer of the Liberal Club, a member of the Fabian Society and the Student Christian Movement. At a time when some of his later Labour Cabinet colleagues were flirting with the Communist Party, Wilson was active in reviving liberalism. Just after becoming Prime Minister, he said: 'I felt that the Oxford Labour Club wasn't for the likes of me . . . certainly I never had any common cause with the public school Marxist.' Even as a student, Wilson was interested more in the hard realities of economic and social affairs than in theory, and was gradually to evolve into a Keynesian 'socialist'. At this stage, however, 'Jimmy' Wilson's main ambition was a first-class degree in Politics,

3

Philosophy and Economics, and this he achieved in 1937 with what was possibly the best of its kind this century. At twenty-one years old, he became an Oxford don, an accomplishment 'said to have been unequalled since the time of Cardinal Wolsey'.[2]

But for the intervention of the Second World War, Wilson might have remained an Oxford don, which would have suited his quiet, rather shy wife, Mary (née Baldwin), the daughter of a Congregational Minister. His marriage to her in 1940 was a supremely private affair with few concessions to his political career or public life. In March that same year, he joined the Ministry of Supply. On being drafted into the civil service, Wilson would have been negatively vetted by MI5; a procedure which consisted simply of checking his name against security files to see if there were any negative 'traces'. It seems that there were none. A few years later, he was allowed to undertake secret work on supply problems for the second front.[3]

Wilson quickly moved to the Cabinet Office Secretariat, on the recommendation of his old tutor Sir William Beveridge, to head the Manpower, Statistics and Intelligence section at the Ministry of Labour. So began his admiration of the British civil service, one which was to influence him for much of his time as Prime Minister. 'His respect for the hierarchy', says Dr Bernard Donoghue, 'with the Cabinet Secretary sitting at the peak, was established for life', though he did retain a dislike of the 'wily and dominating ways of the Treasury' and the way they 'played their little tricks'.[4]

In the summer of 1941, Wilson was posted to the Mines Department of the Board of Trade (later the Ministry of Fuel and Power), where he began the mammoth task of sorting out complicated shift allowances and wages for the miners ('Wilson's work on coal statistics is regarded throughout the civil service as one of the most brilliant statistical achievements in civil service history'). Wilson was chosen for the task by Hugh Gaitskell, the man who was to become his main political rival over the next twenty years.[5]

Wilson realised, as did others such as Michael Foot, that the right place for Keynesians like himself was in the Labour Party. In September 1944, he resigned from the civil service after securing selection as the Labour candidate for Ormskirk in Lancashire. Former Liberal friends were staggered to discover that Wilson had been elected a socialist at the 1945 General Election. But his talents were being quickly noted. The *Daily Telegraph* commented: 'At 28, Mr Wilson is looked on by socialists as a coming President of the Board of Trade or Chancellor of the Exchequer.'[6]

A rising star in the first Attlee Government, Wilson was appointed Parliamentary Secretary at the Ministry of Works. In early 1947, he was made responsible for Overseas Trade at the Board of Trade under Sir Stafford Cripps. Cripps – a strong believer in Christianity, science and bureaucratic socialism – was to influence Wilson more than any other politician; something which may have not gone unnoticed at MI5. Roger Hollis, then responsible for Communist Affairs within MI5, was anxious about the 'Communist sympathies of people in high places, like Stafford Cripps.' Wilson later complained that the security services

4

were incapable of telling the difference between a social democrat and a communist.[7]

The *Telegraph*'s prediction was fulfilled when, in 1947, Wilson was appointed President of the Board of Trade (BOT); at thirty-one, the youngest Cabinet minister this century. At the BOT Wilson came into his own with his attention to detail, resourcefulness and hard work. Few within the Labour Party considered Wilson to be anything other than a right-wing technocrat; an efficient minister but no rebel. He was known as 'the man who gets things done'. The BOT was the biggest department within the civil service and he earned the respect of civil servants.[8]

Even so, Wilson had enemies in the Party. Hartley Shawcross, who replaced him at the BOT, spoke of 'some highbrows educated beyond their capacity.' It was at the BOT that the security services and the Conservative Party right-wing began to take note of Wilson. The Cold War had begun and the war-time sympathy within the Labour movement for the Soviet Union was evaporating. Wilson's trips to the Soviet bloc on government business aroused their curiosity.[9]

The BOT ran a series of quasi-governmental control bodies, the largest of which was Timber Control. 'In the case of Timber', Wilson told the House of Commons, 'as in many more, it took a socialist Minister to make free enterprise free and enterprising.' The state was desperate for timber to meet the demands of their vast rebuilding programme. Searching for timber to import, Wilson went to see Freddie 'Bomber' Smith, a senior Ministry of Works official, who put him in touch with Tom Meyer, the son of Montague Meyer. The Meyers were émigrés, socialists, personal friends of the Foreign Secretary Ernest Bevin, and owners of one of the largest timber firms in Britain.[10]

There were two main sources of timber imports, the United States and the Soviet Union. US timber could be bought only with dollars, which were in acute shortage in the immediate post-war years. But Soviet timber could be had on a barter basis. Acting on the advice of his friend Meyer, Ernest Bevin took up the question of timber with Stalin, and Wilson found himself en route to Moscow on his first trip to the Soviet bloc as the head of a small team of civil service negotiators. His opposite number was Anastas Mikoyan, Deputy Premier and Minister of Foreign Trade, a tough and astute negotiator. They would meet many times over the next twenty years. Wilson returned in June and again in December 1947 trying to secure deals on timber and grain. He took with him his Parliamentary Secretary Tom Cook, a former electrician. 'I had already made considerable use of the bugs which I knew would have been planted in my suite', Wilson recalls, 'though as I did not know their exact location I had to speak loud and clear. Tom was sent to find them and achieved considerable success.' At the last encounter, after seventeen hours of hard bargaining, Wilson clinched the deal. Though acting with the full agreement of the Cabinet – and Foreign Secretary Bevin – Wilson was singled out as the man who did trade deals with the Communists.[11]

Wilson met many businessmen at the BOT and he was not always complimentary about their achievements. In his first book, *New Deal for Coal*, for the émigré publisher George Weidenfeld, he accused some of wasting accumulated profits 'in riotous living when it should have been spent on a vigorous and urgent programme of modernization, mechanization and new development'. He attacked the cosy boardrooms dominated by family ties. Instead, he passionately advocated the idea of taking the 'merchant venturer spirit into the markets of the world', in the process 'pursuing maximum efficiency'. The merchant venturers of his day were the East–West traders who were opening up new markets and, like himself, had few ties to the out-dated Establishment which was holding back Britain. These 'venturers' were often émigrés from Eastern Europe, many of them Jews. Like the Yorkshire-born Wilson, they were all outsiders. Despite Hitler's war, anti-semitism was still commonplace in post-war Britain, and a group of Jews trading with the Bolsheviks was anathema to the 'patriots' in the City, the security services and the Conservative Party.[12]

The Secret Intelligence Service (MI6), which collected information on the Soviet bloc, happened to employ officers who were émigrés and who had strong ties to the timber trade. The then head of R-5, the Counter-Espionage Directorate which included the Russia desk, was Brigadier Douglas Roberts. His deputy was a future head of the service, Maurice Oldfield. In the thirties, Roberts had been employed by E. and A. Harriman in Russia buying and selling timber. It is highly likely that MI6 had infiltrated Montague Meyer. One of the ironies of the security and intelligence game is that while MI6 exploited the East–West traders for intelligence purposes, MI5 – responsible for monitoring subversion – issued warnings about trade with the Communists. As so often is the case, the right hand of the British secret state did not know what the left hand was doing.[13]

The complexities of the intelligence game in the arena of East–West trade are well illustrated by the example of Robert Maxwell, the current owner of Mirror newspapers. Maxwell was a Labour MP in Wilson's first Government and subjected to an MI5 smear campaign due to his connection to the Wilson circle of East–West traders. At the end of the Second World War, the merchant banker Sir Charles Hambro, formerly head of the Special Operations Executive (SOE), was given the task by MI6 of acquiring technical intelligence from the scientific community in occupied Germany. Physicists and scientists selected by Hambro, and an MI6 team lead by Eric Welsh, were debriefed at a special centre in England known as Farm Hall. One of those interrogating German scientists in Germany was Robert Maxwell. In November 1945, Maxwell, a Czechoslovakian Jew, worked in Germany for British Intelligence as an Interrogation Officer. As part of his duties, Maxwell visited the Russian sector – he spoke Russian, a rare skill in the British Army of 1945. These visits gave rise to the first rumours about his patriotism.

In 1946, flooded with a mass of scientific papers, the British Government set up a Scientific Advisory Board which included top British scientists. Hambro, a Board member, and another MI6 officer, Count Van den Heuvel, persuaded the publishing company Butterworths to enter the field of scientific publishing. (Two of Butterworth's directors, Hugh Quennell and John Whitlock, had worked in the SOE during the war.) The editor of the proposed journal was Dr Paul Rosebaud, an MI6 agent run by Eric Welsh in Nazi Germany. In effect, the Board was an MI6 front. Meanwhile, Maxwell had moved to the Press and Publicity Branch of the British Information Service in Berlin where he came into contact with the German scientific publishers, Springer Verlag, whose fortunes were at a low ebb. While still working in the Control Commission, Maxwell became a director of a firm which later offered to distribute Springer's journals. Springer's scientific adviser in the thirties had been Paul Rosebaud.[14]

Butterworth Scientific Publications failed to prosper and in 1948 a joint company was created – Butterworth–Springer. With Rosebaud as editor of the journals and Maxwell as Managing Director, the company would in 1951 evolve into Pergamon Press. Financial backing came from Hambro, who was introduced to Maxwell by the Board of Trade. By coincidence, in May 1949, Wilson announced that the 'progressive banker' Hambro was providing the BOT with financial advice. Pergamon eventually moved into the publication of Soviet scientific journals and quickly became the world's leading authority on Soviet bloc publishing. Maxwell had realised the potential of East–West trade but, as we shall see, his break from the traditional markets in Europe and the Commonwealth brought him many enemies.[15]

On 26 March 1947, the Chiefs of Staff of the Armed Forces issued a 'Top Secret' memorandum compiled by MI5 which set out their objections to East–West trade: Soviet trade delegations were likely to be used as cover for Russian intelligence officers. In this respect, MI5 were particularly worried about 'the Russian Wood Agency concerned with timber exports and the Soviet trade delegation itself ', which, the Chiefs believed, should be refused visas to Britain. Many items available for export should be put on a 'secret list' and embargoed for export.[16]

The Chiefs were annoyed by the decision of the President of the BOT, Cripps, and Attlee – against the advice of the Cold War advocates – to sell the Soviets twenty Rolls Royce Nene and Derwent jet engines. Wilson played absolutely no part in this decision. They were more angry at the offer of jet aircraft as bargaining chips in Wilson's search for timber and grain supplies in the Soviet Union. Foreign Secretary Ernest Bevin, the most strident anti-communist minister in the Government, led the attack on the proposed sale. 'He had not been party to the original decision to let these engines go out of the country', Cabinet minutes noted. He was worried lest Britain had lost 'certain secret manufacturing processes'. In fact, in an era of rapidly developing technology, the engines were already obsolete and export licences were denied for the latest versions.[17]

A myth soon grew, particularly in the Foreign Office and the security service, that Wilson had been personally responsible for the proposed sale. The story went that 'the Soviet Union wished to buy jet aircraft engines which had strategic uses – the turbine blades were made of a secret steel called "Mnemonic 80" '; 'that the Foreign Office "fought like cats" to prevent this, but the Board of Trade believed that exports were more important than ideology; that the minister approved the idea in the absence of Ernest Bevin in Moscow; and the engines were subsequently copied in the new MIG fighters used by the Russians.'[18]

With Britain desperate for American aid in the form of the Marshall Plan, Foreign Office officials had to issue a categorical statement, in April 1948, that 'no aircraft had been sold to Russia since the end of the war, and that no engines on the secret list had been or were going to be supplied'. American politicians were not as easily persuaded. One Republican Senator alleged that 'jet planes which Russia is supposed to be turning out by mass production are copies of jet planes sold to Russia by England'. Conservative MPs were fed information, some from intelligence sources, to keep the disinformation mills grinding. Labour politicians were accused of 'Socialist treachery' for putting 'a deadly weapon in the hands of our deadliest enemies'. MIG–15 fighters used in the Korean War were said to be 'powered by engines which are copies of the Nene'. Twenty-five years later, MI5 circulated this conspiracy theory with the clincher that the sale took place 'in 1947, the year in which Wilson had become responsible for all overseas trade'. None of the 'facts' were true but they later let it be known to right-wing journalists that 'the Americans had been worried about Wilson since the late 1940s or early 1950s when a Congressman had wanted Wilson charged because he was trading with the enemy'. It was true that certain 'isolationist' Congressmen backed by the right-wing Hearst press had used the announcement of Wilson's trips to the USSR and subsequent trade agreements as the basis for an attack on the idea of aid to Britain.[19]

In 1949, shortly after the founding of NATO, the West set up COCOM, the Co-Ordinating Committee for Multilateral Export Controls, which drew up a list of goods which could not be exported to the Eastern Bloc. These were materials which ostensibly were judged to be of possible military use to the Soviet Union, but in reality they covered a wide range of items. Although not binding, the US Battle Act of 1951 made observance of the embargo a condition of the receipt of American military and financial assistance. This caused tremendous strains on the relationship between the two countries. 'It was notorious, too, that Americans were slightly more hysterical about communism, and Britain and the West European allies were expected to pay for American fears.' Some of that hysteria was shared by the 'ultras' in MI5 – and the Tory Party – who targeted East–West traders as 'fellow-travellers' and hence open to recruitment by Soviet intelligence.[20]

On his return from the Soviet Union, Wilson was attacked by the Conservatives as an 'appeaser' and a 'Russia man'. It was the owner of the *Financial Times*, Brendan Bracken, who led the critics with the jibe that the Soviets were to get priority over Britain's true friends. Bracken was the first to describe Wilson as 'too clever by half ', a phrase which stuck for many years.[21]

During rationing Wilson regulated much of British industry through quasi-governmental control bodies on individual product areas. It appeared as a form of Soviet-style state socialism and thus brought him into conflict with the 'free enterprise' faction in the Tory Party led by Bracken, who was helping to set up and fund right-wing free enterprise groups such as the Institute of Directors, which sprang up in the late forties. In the Commons, Wilson was continually barracked by a group of Tories known as 'The Harriers'. They included Bracken, Quintin Hogg, Oliver Lyttelton, David Eccles and Peter Thorneycroft – the last three, past and future Presidents of the BOT.

From 1947 until the 1950 general election, Wilson was under attack more by innuendo than by any frontal assault. Attlee warned Wilson about the double-standards of British politics: 'A Tory minister can sleep in ten different women's beds in a week. A Labour minister gets it in the neck if he looks at his neighbour's wife over the garden fence.' Two scandals blew up which, though barely connected to Wilson, were used against him. First there was the so-called Groundnuts scandal, then the Lynsky Tribunal.[22]

In 1948 John Strachey, Minister of Food, and the United Africa Company – with the support of the Tories – proposed solving the the post-war shortage of oil and fats by growing groundnuts on a massive scale in Tanganyika. It ended with losses of £30 million. Although it was never the national catastrophe portrayed by the Tory press, it was a personal and political disaster. Wilson was not involved, but Strachey, a former communist, apppointed Wilson's closest friend Dick Plummer, Assistant General Manager of the *Daily Express* group, as Chair of the Board to oversee the project.

Plummer was a controversial choice. In the thirties, he was regarded as a committed socialist, perhaps a communist. At the time of the Nazi–Stalin pact, he had exclaimed to Tom Driberg: 'You can count me out as a friend of the Soviet Union.' After the war, Plummer turned to a more moderate position and joined the Labour Party in 1950. He became a powerful figure in the London area. Another old left-wing friend of Strachey's, Lord Victor Rothschild – a financial supporter of *Tribune* – was appointed scientific adviser to the scheme, while timber was supplied by Wilson's new friend Montague Meyer. Strachey was subjected to a smear campaign by the Tory press – Beaverbrook was the instigator – and the Groundnuts 'scandal' was used to attack Labour competence. As late as the 1964 General Election, Wilson was occasionally being heckled at meetings by people shouting 'What about the groundnuts!'[23]

The Lynsky Tribunal began after Wilson was told by a Permanent Secretary of alleged corruption in the Board of Trade. Wilson, the Board's President, called in the police and immediately informed the Prime Minister, Clement Attlee. The Government then set up the inquiry under Judge Lynskey in October 1948. The alleged corruption involved a football pool promoter, Harry Sherman, who had exceeded his paper ration, and a firm importing fun-fair machinery. It centred around a 'spiv' and 'fixer' Sidney Stanley, a Polish Jewish émigré, who claimed to be friendly with John Belcher, MP and Parliamentary Secretary to Wilson.

This tale of black market racketeers in ration-bound Britain was headline news in the Tory press for several weeks, and at one stage threatened to become a major political problem for the Labour Party. But when the dust settled, nothing of real consequence was discovered, though Belcher did resign. Over the years, there were rumours about Wilson's role, but at no point was Wilson actually implicated. He had acted with the utmost probity and speed in pursuing the case. At the Lynsky Tribunal, Hartley Shawcross, Attorney General, conducted exhaustive cross-examinations.[24]

In 1974, at the height of the smear campaign against Wilson, Shawcross wrote to *The Times* about 'knowledge which came to me when I was President of the Board of Trade'. It 'caused me a good deal of anxiety in regard to one individual occupying a far more exalted position than the comparatively small fry in recent cases . . . In the absence of a power of interrogation I could do nothing.' He had been advised, Shawcross said, to keep silent, 'and the evil-doers continue to flourish'. *The Times* talked of 'the profoundly disturbing revelations' hinted at. Many people assumed Shawcross had been referring to Wilson, his predecessor at the BOT. The following day Shawcross issued a statement that the the person was 'long since dead' but rumours concerning Wilson continued to circulate. Chapman Pincher talked to Shawcross and says that he disposed of the rumour. In fact, Pincher's report in some ways made it even more damaging. He mentions that the case involved paying 'large bribes to provide export credit guarantees to firms and people trading behind the Iron Curtain.' Shawcross had hinted 'at one politician who had "sailed near the wind" in connection with it'. He also alleged that a senior Board of Trade civil servant, unconnected with Wilson himself, was bribed by an aircraft company in the hope of getting export licences to sell planes to an unidentified communist country. This seems too close to the problems Wilson encountered over the sale of aero-engines to the Soviet Union to be a mere coincidence.[25]

In early 1951, Hugh Gaitskell, Chancellor of the Exchequer, prepared the Budget. Even though the economy was still in a precarious state, Gaitskell proposed nearly to double Britain's defence budget to support the Americans in their war in Korea – guns before butter. Gaitskell also proposed introducing charges for National Health Service spectacles and teeth. The left, and Aneurin Bevan in particular, saw the proposal as an attack on the concept of a free National Health Service. Bevan, Wilson and John Freeman all resigned over the issue. Wilson later claimed that he had supported a big increase in defence expenditure but 'felt that the £4,000 million programme was physically beyond our capacity . . . it was a practical problem. Nye saw it more as an issue of principle.' Time was to prove Wilson correct; Britain never did meet the target.[26]

One interpretation of his resignation was given by John Junor at Express newspapers. 'He is', Junor wrote, 'a young man and he sees quite clearly that in the right-wing of the socialist Party there is no room for him to expand. For Mr Gaitskell, who resembles Mr Wilson in so many respects, is taking up all the room.' Wilson's resignation is the key to his political character. Wilson was interested in what was achievable; he was a politician.[27]

The resignation made Wilson a darling of the activists on the left but it created difficulties in his Huyton constituency where 80 per cent of the voters were Catholics. At the October 1951 General Election, the Roman Catholic Bishop of Leeds, John Heenan, denounced the 'crypto-communists' in the Labour Party, whom he identified as the Bevanites. His Conservative opponent said Wilson was a Bevanite, implying he was an extreme left-winger and supporter of the communists. Wilson accused his opponent of spreading 'poisonous slime to try to discredit me.' This was the first of many personal attacks on Wilson. At the height of the Cold War Wilson was unwilling to make the simplistic choice – the Soviet Union or the United States.[28]

II

'NYE'S LITTLE DOG'

*[The Bevanites] . . . Extreme left-wingers . . . some with outlooks soured
and warped by disappointment of personal ambitions, some highbrows
educated beyond their capacity.*
HARTLEY SHAWCROSS

*[Denis Healey] is a strange person. When he was at Oxford he was a
communist. Then friends took him in hand, sent him to the Rand
Corporation of America, where he was brainwashed and came back very
right-wing.*
HAROLD WILSON

THE RESIGNATION of Bevan, Wilson and John Freeman, in April 1951,
turned out to be 'the first shot in a prolonged war of intense bitterness inside the
Labour Movement – a war that continued up to the death of Aneurin Bevin in
July 1960 – and indeed beyond that to the death of Hugh Gaitskell in 1963. It
was a struggle for the soul of the Labour Movement.' So bitter was the struggle
that members of the National Executive Committee of the period have spoken of
throwing up in the toilets before NEC meetings.[1]

The struggle did not simply reflect the polarisation of the Cold War, though it
was that in part. The anti-communism of the major union leaders was a stick
with which to beat anything which resembled a rank and file movement. The
charismatic leader of the left, Aneurin Bevan, was a potential leader of the party
who wished 'to distinguish Labour's domestic and foreign policies from those of
the Tories.' Arthur Deakin, the leader of the movement's biggest union, the
Transport and General Workers' (TGWU), realised that such polarisation
'required an activist Party programme and activist Leader', something Deakin
would not tolerate. In the fifties, the union block vote sustained a right-wing
Parliamentary leadership which was always in danger of losing touch with the
more radical membership of the Labour Party. Activism was detested by the
right because it posed a threat to their control of the Party. Around Bevan was
gathered a group of Labour MPs who had not abandoned the idea that between
the Soviet Union and America there was the possibility of finding a 'third way'.[2]

The so-called Bevanites, what would nowadays be called a Bevanite Tendency, were centred around the papers *Tribune* and *New Statesman* and the parliamentary group Keep Left. Prominently associated with the group were Tom Driberg, Barbara Castle, Dick Crossman, Michael Foot, Ian Mikardo, George Wigg and Harold Wilson. Wilson was well aware of the 'communist' smear. 'There were indeed undercurrents of which one had to be wary', he said looking back on this period. 'Those who were supporting Nye Bevan had to be very careful not to become tainted by their company in the eyes of the right-wing of the Party.' Where the Keep Left group had been an exclusive club, after the resignations of Bevan, Wilson and Freeman the left opened up, and began organising beyond the confines of the Parliamentary Party.[3]

The group achieved national prominence and their publications were highly successful, with print runs up to 100,000. The popularity of the Bevanites promoted the right to take action. In March 1952, 57 Labour MPs defied the Labour whip over the Conservative Government's Defence White paper. With the support of 100 MPs, Deakin called for the expulsion of Bevan and his closest associates including Wilson, Michael Foot, Jennie Lee, Tom Driberg, John Freeman and others. Rather than expulsion, the Party imposed Standing Orders, rules of behaviour, on MPs for the first time since 1945. The nature of the Bevanite struggle changed. 'Held in check by the standing orders in the Commons the Bevanites concentrated on extra-parliamentary activity', wrote Leslie Hunter, 'and so came into head-on collision with the leaders of the big trade unions.' These leaders condemned the Bevanites as 'a party within a party'.[4]

The leaders of the big three unions, Deakin, Will Lawther (National Union of Miners) and Tom Williamson (General and Municipal Workers' Union), looked for a Parliamentary spokesman. They found an articulate anti-Bevan voice in Hugh Gaitskell, the former Chancellor of the Exchequer. So began a period of 'counter-organisation' during which 'exhortation, threats and cajolery' were used against the Bevanites. In an infamous speech at Stalybridge in October 1952, Gaitskell, the rising star of the right, called for the isolation of the Bevanites, referring to them as a 'group of frustrated journalists', a coded reference to Michael Foot (*Tribune*), Crossman (Odhams Press), Driberg (*Reynolds News*) – and, perhaps, to Wilson, who wrote editorials for the *Sunday Express*. Gaitskell alleged that many of the speeches and resolutions at Conference had been 'Communist-inspired' and that 'about one-sixth of the constituency party delegates appear to be Communists or Communist-inspired'. The general view on the right was that 'the Left was infiltrated and dominated by the Communists and that the Bevanites were their catspaws'.[5]

'Inevitably, the leadership acted against it [the Bevanite group]', recalled Fenner Brockway. 'It was ordered to dissolve by a majority in the Parliamentary Party.' The Bevanites went through the motions of dissolution, but carried on meeting clandestinely – ironically, thereby becoming the conspirators the right believed them to be. They adapted to the new conditions by operating a 'first eleven' of well-known parliamentary figures, such as Wilson, and a 'second eleven', comprising the more activist members who engaged in extra-parliamentary activity, which increased after the ban. Throughout 1954, the second eleven attempted to create a rank-and-file base in secret, developing links with the Co-operative Party, which had long been a legitimate 'party within a party', and the Union of Democratic Control.[6]

Eventually the National Executive Committee decided to take action against the 'second eleven', and began a long, rancorous series of investigations. A minor witch-hunt took place with those found guilty required to sign loyalty oaths. A number of Trotskyists were expelled, often on evidence supplied by their main enemies, the Stalinist Communist Party of Great Britain (CPGB), but they were a side-show to the real target, which remained the Bevanites. On the NEC, Edith Summerskill, on the hard right of the party, demanded further measures. 'I mean expelling those who are suspected of fellow-travelling', she told Richard Crossman. 'This was said with her eyes fixed on Ian [Mikardo] who I think is the most hated of the Bevanites.'[7]

The crunch came in March 1955 when Bevan and 62 Labour MPs abstained on a vote over the construction of the H-Bomb. In the House of Commons debate, Bevan appeared to attack his own leadership. On 7 March, the Shadow Cabinet voted 9–4 in recommending the withdrawal of the whip from Bevan, with a clear inference that expulsion from the Party would follow. Deakin and Gaitskell were willing to risk splitting the Party in order to rid themselves of the Bevanites. The Shadow Cabinet, with George Brown and Hartley Shawcross prominent, threatened to resign if the Parliamentary Labour Party voted against their decision. It did not.

Richard Crossman accused Gaitskell 'of merely being a stooge for big forces outside'. The jibe provoked Gaitskell into a moment of candour. 'Bevanism', he retorted, 'is and only is a conspiracy to seize the leadership for Aneurin Bevan. It is a conspiracy because it has three essentials of conspiracy, a leader in Bevan, an organisation run by Mikardo and a newspaper run by Foot.' He went on: 'It's got to be cleaned up. There are extraordinary parallels between Nye and Adolf Hitler. They are demagogues of exactly the same sort.'[8]

This was as classic an example of psychological projection as we could hope to see. If anyone was seriously conspiring inside the Party it was Gaitskell, who was no stranger to the world of covert politics. During the war he worked in the shadowy Special Operations Executive. 'Mr Gaitskell', wrote the historian M. R. D. Foot, 'had worked as one of the three bright men employed by [Hugh] Dalton, on the French system, to go sniffing round the department looking for points of friction: an un-English arrangement that helped to give SOE its black name in Whitehall'. Gaitskell held a series of secret meetings at the Russell Hotel, where he planned the expulsion campaign with Sam Watson, the leader of the Durham miners. Also in attendance was the Labour Attaché at the American Embassy in London, Joe Godson. One of the most important post-war events in the Labour Party's internal affairs was overseen by an American spook.[9]

If some of the Labour left were 'fellow-travellers' in the sense of being naive believers in the Soviet model of society and the economy, the right was at least as naive about America. If there is any evidence of Soviet involvement in the

Labour Party in the fifties, we have never seen it; and, given the enthusiasm with which such information would have been sprayed around, had it existed, we conclude that there was none. The endless cries of 'Moscow gold' hurled against the left – none of which has ever been found other than in the Soviet subsidies to the CPGB's paper *Daily Worker* – concealed the fact that it was Washington gold that was shaping the face of British politics.

During the Cold War the United States (and to a much lesser extent the UK) engaged in what have been called 'robust' methods, i.e. covert operations, bribery, propaganda and the occasional assassination. From 1947 onwards State Department and CIA money and personnel flooded out across the European political scene. In some places, such as Italy, US intervention was massive and barely hidden, but behind such fire-brigade operations were quieter, long-range operations to shape the political development of Europe. Under Thomas Braden, head of the Agency's International Department, and 'with the support of Allen Dulles and Frank Wisner, the CIA began its covert support of the non-Communist political left around the world – trade unions, political parties, and international organizations of students and journalists'. Into this great ocean of money swam many on the right of the Labour Party.[10]

The history of US involvement in post-war Labour politics has yet to be written and is beyond the scope of this book. We shall only lightly skim across the surface. Joe Godson was the US Government's main, semi-overt link with the Labour Party in the fifties and was based in Britain from 1953 to 1959 as US Labour Attaché at the London Embassy. His obituary in *The Times* in September 1986, headed 'Determined champion of Anglo-American relations', noted that: 'He was a friend of many leading members of the social democratic parties and trade unions in Western Europe.' Godson was the friend of the social democratic wing – in effect, the anti-socialist wing – of the Labour Party, and had a hand in making that wing the dominant faction. Curiously missing from *The Times'* list of Godson's friends is the most important of them all, Labour Party leader Hugh Gaitskell.[11]

Godson's close, covert ally was Irving Brown, head of an anti-communist grouping within the US American Federation of Labour (AFL) called the Free Trade Union Committee. This grouping, which was the link to the British Labour movement, was funded by CIA dollars, distributed by Brown. Brown's role in the CIA is now well documented. His CIA case officer was Paul Sakwa, who handled Brown's annual budget of nearly $300,000. While Godson and Brown 'befriended' Labour and union leaders, Sakwa was placed under cover as the Assistant Labour Attaché at the US Embassy in Brussels, from where all the CIA's European labour operations were controlled. According to Jack Anderson and Drew Pearson, 'few labor attachés are appointed to American embassies abroad without Lovestone's okay'. Jay Lovestone was an asset of the CIA.[12]

A number of leading anti-socialist intellectuals within the Party, who would later be called Gaitskellites, became involved in the Congress for Cultural Freedom (CCF) – one of the CIA's covert operations in the 1950s. The liberal faction within the CIA recognised that in Europe the best opponents of the socialist and communist movements were going to be the social democrats

15

within the European Labour movement. Funds for the CCF came from the CIA via Lovestone; something alleged by the Soviet media at the time but not believed.[13]

The CCF began spawning journals – in Britain, in co-operation with MI6, it launched the magazine *Encounter*. The CCF's flagship publication, which began in 1953, became the major outlet for the 'revisionist' thinking of the younger intellectuals around Gaitskell, such as Douglas Jay, Patrick Gordon Walker and Anthony Crosland. Crosland and Gaitksell were regular guests at CCF conferences: Crosland's CCF role in the fifties as member of the International Council, says one CIA officer, was 'encouraging sympathetic people' to attend CCF conferences.[14]

Parallel to the growth of *Encounter* was that of *Socialist Commentary* as a vehicle for the anti-socialists in the Labour Party. This had begun life post-war as the journal of a group of refugee German social democrats but by the early 1950s had been absorbed by the right wing of the Labour Party. In 1953 a 'Friends of *Socialist Commentary*' group was set up – Gaitskell became its Treasurer, raising money for the paper through his contacts with the unions. Denis Healey had written widely for *Socialist Commentary*'s American counterpart, *New Leader*, which was funded by the CIA. Unwittingly, a tiny part of Healey's income in the late forties and early fifties came indirectly from the CIA, but – and in this Healey is representative of other social democrats – it was the exposure through the columns of magazines like *Encounter* and *New Leader* which mattered: careers were assisted, status acquired, ideas spread. These days we should perhaps write of the creation of an intellectual hegemony. For the most part the Labour Party members who were cultivated by the Americans were people comfortable within the British ruling circles, natural successors to the Conservatives: Oxbridge, clever, educated, middle-class men, élite members, many with war-time experience of the secret services – all except Wilson, who had never had any connection with this secret world.[15]

In the early 1950s Gaitskell, George Brown, Patrick Gordon Walker, Anthony Crosland, Douglas Jay, Denis Healey, John Strachey and Michael Stewart all found their way across the Atlantic. Their trips were paid for by a variety of foundations and trusts set up to show sympathetic foreign politicians the wonders of America. Jay went in 1954 with Gaitskell. He came away surprised by the shared understanding of the world. 'At its strongest, naturally, among Washington officials and Harvard academics, this similarity struck me as permeating far wider and deeper than I had been led to expect.' These social visits were supplemented by personal contacts. Gaitskell was friendly with Joe Godson, George Brown with two CIA London station chiefs, Chester Cooper and Archie Roosevelt.[16]

At one level sponsorship was a cheap way for the Americans to educate an alternative team of élite managers and bind the two Anglo-American groups together into the Atlantic community. But is that all? How would it look from inside the CIA? One of its former senior covert operations officers, Richard M. Bissell, described the Agency's political operational method as 'the identification of allies who can be rendered more effective, more powerful, and perhaps wiser through covert assistance.' He added that 'many of the "penetrations" don't take the form of "hiring" but of establishing a close or friendly relationship (which may or may not be furthered by the provision of money from time to time).' Would the Agency's operations with the Labour right not look like this in Langley, the CIA's headquarters?[17]

One major American target was the leader of the Durham miners, Sam Watson, Gaitskell's main supporter on the NEC. In the Labour Party machine of the fifties Watson formed a powerful alliance with two other key right-wingers: Harry Crane, the long-serving Chairman of the conference machinery, known as the Arrangements Committee; and Sara Barker, first assistant and later National Agent. Watson had a close understanding with 'the velvet steamhammer' Crane and 'shaped the latter's definition of what would be a good outcome from the compositing meetings on foreign and defence policy'. Not only did Watson influence the intended motions, but also the NEC response. 'I used to have regular contact with the Security Services', Crane later admitted. 'Whenever I got information about anybody from them, I would pass it on to Sara Barker.'[18]

Wilson was never sucked into the Atlanticist infrastructure. He was his own man, with his own support base outside and inside the Labour movement. After his resignation from the Government in 1951 he accepted the part-time post of economic adviser on foreign tax laws and exchange rates with Montague Meyer, the timber importers. This gave him a degree of financial independence and enabled him to travel abroad and develop contacts. There was a great deal of adverse comment on his appointment for accepting the fruits of private enterprise. Out of office, Hartley Shawcross called Wilson a Communist 'fellow-traveller' and regarded his industrial contacts with 'distain'.[19]

An indication of how far out on a limb Wilson had gone by his support for East–West trade was shown in the spring of 1952. That year the Soviet Union sponsored an Economic Conference on international trade in Moscow. The Labour Party leadership denounced those Labour MPs who attended – Emrys Hughes, Sidney Silvermen and Harold Davies – as 'fellow-travellers'. Despite that, and despite the fact that the Korean War was still in progress, Wilson produced a *Tribune* pamphlet, *In Place of Dollars*, which objected to American interference with East–West trade. It proposed fewer strategic controls on exports to the Soviet Union and other Communist countries. He alleged that American policy had consistently created difficulties for Britain. This view was shared by a number of Labour politicians who claimed that the most natural market for Britain was in the East, but none were as visible in their support as Wilson.[20]

In May 1953, Wilson returned to the Soviet Union. It was his first visit since the Board of Trade days, six years before, and the first by a senior Western politician since the beginning of the Cold War, when an embargo had been imposed following the Berlin Crisis. He stole the headlines with an interview with the Soviet Foreign Minister Molotov, arranged by his old friend Mikoyan. Relations between the two remained warm: it was Mikoyan who organised Wilson's visas to the USSR. Even though he had cleared the trip with Prime

Minister Winston Churchill, and was debriefed on his return by Churchill and the Foreign Office, his visit caused fury on the Tory right.[21]

Wilson was never a communist sympathiser and 'he was never one of the left-wing Labour MPs who received unsolicited compliments from Communist front organizations and newspapers, and the Communists never took him for more than a conventional labour politician'. Yet Wilson did admire the Soviet Union's economic achievements. In the light of the USSR's current plight that may appear somewhat naive, but in the fifties, considering the destruction caused by the war, the successes looked considerable. Just a few years later the Soviets would beat the United States into space.[22]

In September 1953, Wilson claimed that strategic controls, which restricted the sale of materials and technology which might be of military use to the Soviet Union, were out of date and were probably more harmful to Britain than to the USSR. Paradoxically, the embargoed list included materials which the Soviet Union were happy to export to the West. The Co-Ordinating Committee for Multilateral Export Controls (COCOM) list was often used by the United States as an economic weapon to keep its monopoly on supplies and protect particular industries like machine tools. The embargo created tensions within the Anglo-American alliance principally because Britain adhered strictly to the list whilst other allies were more circumspect. In March 1954, the 'inexhaustible Harold Wilson' cited the absurdity of some of the cases. 'By stringently applying the strategic controls', he said, 'Britain was losing good business'. Many in the Government agreed with him – there were good orders in the pipeline – and Britain had recently informed the Americans that it intended to reduce the COCOM list.

After the return to London of a group of businessmen who had been to Moscow, Prime Minister Winston Churchill said: 'I do not suggest that at the present time there should be any traffic in military equipment, including certain machine tools such as those capable only or mainly of making weapons. But a substantial relaxation of the regulation affecting manufactured goods, raw materials and shipping . . . would undoubtedly be beneficial in its proper setting.' Churchill and the President of the Board of Trade, Peter Thorneycroft, soon came under intense pressure from the Americans. A major diplomatic effort was launched by President Eisenhower to rein Britain in, on the basis that 'the very short United Kingdom list will cause unmanageable repercussions in the United States'. There were veiled threats of withdrawal of loans and the danger of splitting the alliance but the lists of forbidden export items were pruned.[23]

One businessman who had to deal with the restrictions on trade with the Soviets, and who suffered because of the suspicions which this aroused in the American and British security agencies, was the publisher Robert Maxwell. His interest in East–West trade was extended when in the spring of 1952, John Whitlock, who was later indentified as an MI6 agent, introduced him to Dr Kurt Waller. A German-Jewish refugee, Waller was heavily involved in bartering and East–West trade. He believed that trading with the East, which included chemicals, could involve him in serious trouble with the American authorities.

There was some substance in this view. The COCOM list imposed severe restrictions on exports to communist countries. 'His relationship with Maxwell', argued the *Sunday Times* in a profile of the publisher, 'makes sense only if it is understood that – rightly or wrongly – he really did believe Maxwell could protect him from trouble with various secret services.' Maxwell clocked up millions of miles on his travels and spent a great deal of time in the Eastern bloc meeting Communist officials to build up his deals. It appears that he never had any problems with MI6 but he certainly did with MI5.[24]

In 1954, Maxwell's secretary Anne Dove, a former Special Operations Executive employee, was invited by MI5 for a discreet chat in the War Office. They wanted her to vouch for Maxwell's loyalty, which of course she did. Although there were absolutely no grounds for suspicion, according to Peter Wright, MI5 continued to be concerned about Maxwell.[25]

Despite this general atmosphere of suspicion, Wilson continued to lead the attack on the COCOM list. In 1958, he argued in the House of Commons that full employment in some British industries depended on the Soviet trade. He said the American belief that 'these restrictions retarded Soviet development was ridiculous'. However, as the tension between the two super-powers eased in the late fifties with the appointment of Khruschev in the Soviet Union and the promotion of his co-existence policy, the United States agreed to reduce the embargo list. By 1958, the COCOM list of strategic exports contained only 120 items that were totally embargoed. As contacts with the Soviet bloc became easier, the East–West traders were able to extend their commerce. This, however, brought them into conflict with MI5, who continued to see any contact with the Soviets as the first stepping stone to recruitment by the KGB. MI5 later released to Chapman Pincher case studies of sexual entrapment operations – 'honeytraps' – run against British businessmen in the Soviet bloc which he subsequently published in the *Daily Express*. MI5 attempted to turn these entrapments to their advantage by recruiting among the Eastern European émigré groups and East–West traders in Britain as many 'double agents' as possible. This was a throw-back to the counter-espionage 'double-cross' operations used successfully by MI5 against German intelligence during the Second World War. In this instance, MI5 hoped to ensnare a KGB officer; however, as Peter Wright reveals, these revived operations 'were a time consuming charade'. MI6, with their requirement to collect information, saw things differently and, abandoning the strict policy of not operating on British soil, began 'to exploit the rich field of opportunities provided by the thaw in relations between East and West'.[26]

According to the spy George Blake, conscious that they lacked reliable information on the communists, the London based Controller of Production Research in MI6 was transformed into an 'agent-running organisation'. The new head was Dickie Franks, a hardliner and later chief of the Service. Blake was his deputy and in his memoirs reveals that they began to recruit businessmen, journalists and academics on a massive scale – anyone who might be able to supply intelligence on the Soviet bloc or came into contact with Soviet officials who might be recruited. One target group was the East–West traders. MI6 agents, often in the guise of interpreters, were attached to all British trade delegations to the Soviet Union.[27]

Another indication of the differing attitudes to links with the Soviet bloc and change of policy within a section of the British intelligence community was their response to the acceptance by the Notley Advertising firm of the East German account in October 1960. The East Germans were trying to secure diplomatic recognition and mounted a public relations exercise at Westminster in pursuit of it. The account had first been offered to Brigadier Terence Clarke, a Director of the PR firm Voice and Vision, but because of his company's links to the Conservative Party, Clarke declined. However, Clarke, together with another Tory MP, Barnaby Drayson, became 'consultants' to Notley. Both were heavily involved in East–West trade. In particular, Drayson represented the biggest trader, Rudi Sternberg, at Notley. Sternberg came to Britain as a student from Germany in 1935 aged eighteen. He joined the army at the beginning of the war and was invalided out in 1942. By 1946, he was importing and selling raw materials from Eastern Europe. Turnover grew to nearly £30 million and he was well regarded as 'British industry's ambassador-at-large' in the East. 'I'm merely practising what Churchill preached', was his response to criticism. Sternberg was seen by MI5 as a security risk but, given our current knowledge of his true allegiance, as discussed later, this whole episode looks like an MI6 operation – perhaps, the product of the Production Research department.[28]

The process of gradual relaxation continued until 1961 and the Berlin Wall crisis. Almost immediately, heavy pressure was put on US firms trading with the Soviet bloc; they were discouraged from attending the Leipzig trade fairs in East Germany. The change in the political climate had the effect of throwing suspicion on to the East–West traders. Edward Heath, Lord Privy Seal, warned MPs that it would be better if they did not attend as the East Germans were only interested in securing sympathetic support in the West. He was ignored. Furthermore, the House of Commons was informed that the 'British Council for the Promotion of International Trade is a Communist-controlled organisation and business firms should consider very carefully whether to become associated with it'. The President of the Board of Trade added that it was 'initiated by the World Peace Council, one of the principal agencies of international communism.'[29]

A right-wing Labour MP, Desmond Donnelly, with the backing of Hugh Gaitskell, said: 'MPs should not accept Communist hospitality in the present state of international relations, nor act as entrepreneurs in the Cold War for personal gain. I have also felt deeply at the sight of British MPs being used as vehicles for Communist propaganda such as the East German campaign for recognition.'[30]

Security and diplomatic concerns about an 'East German connection' centred on the role of Sternberg. Initially, the press had been friendly towards him and his activities. On 3 August 1961, the *Evening Standard* profile headed 'Salesman Sternberg makes a killing in the East' was sympathetic, with only a passing reference to 'gossip regarding the connection between MPs and companies trading with Iron Curtain countries'. Ten days later, the Berlin Wall was built and within days two of Notley's directors resigned. Nine months later, after the Berlin crisis and subsequent deepening of the Cold War, the mood changed. The *Daily Mirror* front page was titled 'Red Fair MPs and the Amazing Rudi'. With other businessmen and MPs, Sternberg had been photographed with the East German leader, Walter Ulbricht; they toured the fair together, earning them the nickname 'Sternberg's Circus'. Sternberg, who had been trading with East Germany since 1950, told the press that: 'We have always experienced this sort of animosity during our experience of East–West trade.'[31]

Most of the MPs who had accompanied Sternberg were Conservatives who encountered few problems with their involvement in East–West trade and were even able set up a backbench committee on the subject. Labour MPs Ian Mikardo, his secretary Jo Richardson, Arthur Lewis, Will Owen, John Stonehouse and Wilson's friend Leslie Plummer, were also traders but all were subjected to smears. Both Lord Boothby, chair of the all-party East–West Trade committee and a director of one of Sternberg's companies, and Tory MP Commander Anthony Courtney, were targeted with sex smears. The publisher Robert Maxwell was another victim.

During the 1959 General Election, and again in 1964, when Maxwell was elected as a Labour MP, there was a 'whispering campaign' about his origins and trips behind the Iron Curtain. Maxwell was also the target of anti-semitism. Suspicion extended into the Labour Party. For MI5 it was enough that Maxwell was an émigré, Jewish and traded with 'the enemy'.[32]

For the moment Wilson escaped being linked in the press with the 'East German connection' – though later MI5 would ensure that the press did make the connection. Wilson had left his consultancy with Montague Meyer in 1959 and was no longer directly involved in trading. However, his consistent championing of East–West trade, his criticism of COCOM and his refusal to give *carte blanche* endorsement to US foreign policy had not endeared him to the Americans. According to one commentator on the Anglo-American alliance, 'much of American opinion had been taught by American press reportage to regard him as the leader of the neutralist, if not of the fellow-travelling, wing of the party.'[33]

III

REDS

Twinkle, twinkle, little Hugh,
How I wonder how you knew,
Who was red and who was not.
Mass Observation on the spot.
          TRIBUNE, 1955

IN 1959, Wilson was appointed Chair of the House of Commons Public Accounts Committee. His appointment, Wilson reveals, was 'the only agreeable transaction I had with Hugh Gaitskell during the difficult year that followed'. Gaitskell had been badly shaken by losing the 1959 General Election and 'now a further crisis, or rather a series of crises, arose between us'. The Gaitskellites blamed the left for the defeat and, according to Wilson, 'the atmosphere in the Party became uncomfortably divisive and exclusive'.[1]

Largely by accident, Wilson had assumed the leadership of the Party's left wing from Bevan. The expulsion campaign against Bevan had not been pursued to its final conclusion, and the middle-class intellectuals of Bevanism such as Wilson and Crossman had already begun to draw away from their former leader. Crossman met Gaitskell in secret where he confided, 'that there was now a left of centre emerging which was not merely his [Bevan's] stooge'. Quietly and covertly, the Gaitskellites moved to split the left. Sam Watson went to see Bevan with 'a bottle of whiskey and ten little bottles, five of gin and five of soda'. Watson told Crossman, 'by the end of the evening Nye wasn't noticing whether it was gin or soda.' The next day, Bevan conducted an 'intellectual somersault' and reversed his position on the burning question of the Bomb. He now saw himself in the role of world statesman and representative of the world's mineworkers. Gaitskell appointed him Shadow Foreign Secretary and encountered few problems thereafter. Bevan died of cancer in 1960.[2]

Under Gaitskell's leadership, the Labour Party had again lost a General Election and now the struggle between the socialists in the Party – mainly among the ordinary grass-roots membership – and the anti-socialists centred round

Gaitskell, became intense. The leaders of the Gaitskell faction in the Parliamentary Labour Party (PLP) – Tony Crosland, Douglas Jay, Roy Jenkins and Patrick Gordon Walker – began to reorganise the Party so as to marginalise the left. An informal 'policy review' began among Gaitskell's Hampstead set to 'modernise' the Party. Ideologically, the focus of their attention became 'Clause 4' of the constitution – in real political terms, the committment to nationalisation. Jay caused an uproar when he wrote a piece for *Socialist Commentary* expressing the wish to repeal Clause 4.

The Gaitskell faction dominated the PLP leadership and most union leaders supported them. However, they had serious socialist opposition at grass-roots constituency party level, in some of the unions and from the left in Parliament. In the eyes of the Gaitskellites the grass-roots socialism led by the second eleven Bevanites 'represented a political outlook, that was, on the whole, alien to the traditions of British social democracy.' Crossman sensed the change. 'I get the impression that the right-wing of the Party is really getting desperate at the feeling that their support in the constituencies is slipping ever further away and that more and more MPs are being accused by their constituency parties of betraying Socialism. This, they feel, is all due to some terrible secret Mikardo organisation.'[3]

A left-wing organisation, Victory for Socialism (VFS), was working steadfastly in the constituencies. It 'questioned whether the Labour Party had enough socialist drive to effect the transition from capitalism to Socialism' and appealed to 'convinced Socialists who are prepared to live and work for Socialism' to join the group. The VFS was formally set up in February 1958, when former Bevanites, including MPs, candidates, trade unionists and Party members, joined the group. The new Chair, Stephen Swingler, made it clear in *Tribune* that the VFS was not an alternative to the Labour Party. 'The Communist Party is discredited. Because it reproduced Russia's vices without the solid achievements of Soviet virtues, it has been reduced to a tiny faction.' There were two main issues before the movement: firstly 'a clear stand against the Bomb' (the Communist Party at this stage opposed unilateral nuclear disarmament); secondly, the need to win the Labour Party over to a total commitment to common ownership. 'We intend', he continued, 'to recruit thousands of active Labour Party members, form branches, stimulate fresh discussion about the application of Socialist principles, and above all, inspire renewed faith in the power of democratic action.' The group came under instant attack from Labour's hierarchy. 'The emergence of Victory for Socialism', Crossman noted, 'has switched all trade unionists and right-wingers back into their mood of intolerance of any discussion and into their feelings that one must be either for them or against them.'[4]

In this divisive atmosphere Wilson had drawn away from the Bevanites and moved to the centre of the Party. It was no longer wise to be too closely associated with the supporters of extra-parliamentary Bevanism. By 1960, Crossman had finally cut his ties to the activists. 'I took another look at the list of names. Did I want to be in with [Konni] Zilliacus, Emrys Hughes, Stephen Swingler, Julius

Silverman and Sydney Silverman? Reluctantly, but rather definitely, I ditched them.'[5]

The Party leadership had been covertly working against the left for most of the decade, often in co-operation with the secret state. General Secretary, Morgan Phillips, had his well-thumbed files in which were marked out unacceptable 'fellow-travellers'. Mrs Marcia Williams had been Phillips' secretary 'until she changed sides and came over to Harold with all her files and secrets'. There were other more sinister secret dossiers. 'What we didn't know at the time', Ian Mikardo recalls, 'was that our leaders were using the National Agent's Department in Transport House and the Regional Organisers out in the country to compile MI5-type dossiers on us'. Mikardo discovered their existence by chance when he worked with Sara Barker at an Elections Sub-Committee meeting to consider candidates. Barker, who 'looked as if she ought be selling toffees in a village shop, [was] vested instead with all the dank, meaningless and mindless power of a great machine'. She immediately proposed ditching Konni Zilliacus and Ernie Roberts. When Mikardo raised objections, Barker produced her files. 'They were', says Mikardo, 'an eye opener. No MI5, no Special Branch, no George Smiley could have compiled more comprehensive dossiers. Not just press-cuttings, photographs and document-references but also notes by watchers and eavesdroppers, and all sorts of tittle-tattle.' He was convinced there was intelligence input, possibly from Joe Godson, the Labour Attaché at the American Embassy.[6]

The sources for these dossiers have now been documented. The Regional Organisers obtained information from their own private intelligence network of agents, Party officials, union officials and ex-communists. Additional material was prepared by the trade union anti-communist front, the Industrial Research and Information Service (IRIS). Party Agents forwarded reports to the National Agent based on information supplied by Special Branch. There was also, as Mikardo had suspected, input from MI5 and the flow of information went both ways.[7]

While the Party machine could deal with individual rebels, it lacked an organised grass-roots faction supporting the policies of the leadership of the Party. What was to become the Campaign for Democratic Socialism (CDS) began in February 1960 when William Rodgers, Secretary of the Fabian Society, organised a letter of support to Gaitskell from 15 prospective parliamentary candidates. The origins of the letter lay in a meeting between Rodgers and Crosland, who 'agreed that there was inadequate contact and co-ordination between those in the Party who wished to preserve Gaitskill's leadership on the one hand and multilateralism on the other'. Shortly after, a steering committee was set up with Rodgers as chairman. A report of these events in the *Observer* written by one of the participants, Ivan Yates, omitted the names of Jenkins, Gordon Walker, Jay and Crosland – at their request. The CDS was to be a 'grass-roots' campaign: to reveal the participation of this Gaitskell inner group at this stage would have given the game away immediately. So the CDS was formed in deception.[8]

Harold Wilson was the only recognisable leader of the PLP who was not a member of Gaitskell's faction. 'The division between Hugh's heavy squad and me', says Wilson, 'was a simple one. I wanted to fight to work for Party unity, including Gaitskellites and erstwhile Bevanites. He wanted to divide. I was against "fight, fight, fight"; he was determined on it.' It was to be Wilson's major achievement that he held the two wings of the Party together from 1964 onwards. At this stage Wilson was still weak, with guaranteed support only on the left of the Party. However, events were to push him on to centre stage.[9]

Victory for Socialism openly demanded that Gaitskell resign as leader of the Party. The left-winger Anthony Greenwood, a CND member and leading unilateralist, 'let it be known that if I did not contest the Leadership, he would'. Very reluctantly, Wilson agreed to stand 'for the unhappy reason that if Hugh was unopposed, he would claim an undeniable mandate to act against a substantial number of the loyal members of the Parliamentary Party . . . Hugh's intimates were putting it about that the Leader had decided that the unilateralist issue had to be pushed to finality, even if he had to expel fifty or sixty MPs.' Wilson states that 'it was the most miserable decision I have ever had to take'. As he dithered, he displayed some of the paranoia which later became a trademark. He became defensive. 'I was not in any way exercised by the argument that in standing against Hugh I would be indentified again with the Marxists in the Party as the Bevanites had been ten years earlier. I had taken charge of Party organization and neutralized their influence effectively. A number of my public speeches had been patently anti-Russian.' But more importantly, 'I knew it would be a mucky election, not because I thought Hugh would fight dirty, but because some of his friends were determined to do so.' Wilson's paranoia, as so often in later years, was entirely justified.[10]

Crosland's notes and letters on this period are rather revealing. On 21 October 1960, he writes to Gaitskell: 'These are my immediate reactions to the Wilson decision [i.e. to contest the leadership of the Party]. Object. In the next 10 days, we have one single over-riding object: to make sure that his vote is as low as possible, and yours as high as possible. Our possibilities over the next 12 months will depend entirely on this; and to achieve this we must resort to any degree of chicanery, lying etc etc.'[11]

So began the long personal smear campaign against Wilson, instigated initially not by MI5 but by the Gaitskellites. One of those helping to spread the smears was Kenneth Younger, MP for Grimsby, whose seat was passed on to Crosland. Younger was a former senior member of MI5 and it is possible that it was through his endeavours that the security service began its 'Worthington' file on the Wilson circle. One of the smears which circulated referred to Wilson's wife Mary and her alleged affair in the forties with a Polish academic. The main gossip concerned a supposed liaison between Wilson and Mrs Marcia Williams, who was then in the process of divorcing her husband.

Mrs Williams joined Wilson in October 1956 as his political secretary and assistant at Montague Meyer. She was politically devoted to her new boss but that was all. They spent long hours together, often working into the night when the House of Commons was sitting late. This helped to fuel rumours about their relationship, added to which there was resentment by colleagues about the way she, like any good personal assistant, controlled access to Wilson. Her devotion to Wilson – someone she knew was going to the top – caused strains in her own marriage. Her husband Ed, who already felt neglected by his wife, was offered a job with Boeing in the United States in 1957 on a two-year contract. He went without his wife, partly because they hoped to raise enough money for a house from his highly-paid job. The enforced separation also caused strains between Wilson and Mrs Williams. Wilson was once late for a meeting with Crossman 'because he had just been with his secretary, who had just had a nervous breakdown. He had spent twenty minutes on the phone with her husband. All this was really endearing, since afterwards, he said, "Take my mind off her, for God's sake, by discussing pensions".'[12]

By the end of the two years, Ed Williams had met a woman in Seattle he wished to marry and in 1959 he sought a divorce from his wife. In January 1960, while on a lecture tour of the United States, Wilson stopped off in Seattle with Mrs Williams to see her husband. Gossip was already current about Wilson and Mrs Williams and although they might have hoped to postpone the divorce until after Wilson's bid for the Party leadership, Ed insisted on pursuing it. On 1 November 1960, divorce proceedings began in King County, Washington State, and the final decree nisi was granted on 7 April 1961. To help quash rumours, the Wilson campaign had to organise 'a semi-public tea party in which Harold and Mary were joined by Marcia and her presumed husband' – in reality Marcia's brother.[13]

In the event, Gaitskell won the leadership contest by a two to one majority – 166 votes to 81. Wilson was depressed by the result but Crossman, his 'psychological warfare adviser', saw it as the turning point. Wilson had established himself as the 'Unity Candidate' and all they needed now was 'only one or two little heaves to finish the job'.[14]

Within the Party, the left was organising around the issue of unilateral nuclear disarmament. In *Encounter*, October 1960, just before the Labour Party annual conference, Crosland named the central point: if Gaitskell won narrowly on defence it might be worse than defeat. If Gaitskell lost decisively: 'We should have then, for the first time in the party's history, a direct confrontation of the Parliamentary group and conference. From the resulting crisis and confusion there might, eventually, emerge a much-altered radical Labour party attuned to the reality of the 1960s.' If he lost narrowly the opposition – Crosland calls them 'Left-wing constituency militants' (i.e. socialists) – would just do it all again.[15]

For the first time since the war the left was in a position to exert its influence. The Labour movement was moving to the left after a decade of right-wing control. The issue of the Bomb had become the central issue of socialism. The unilateralists won a narrow victory in October 1960 when the TGWU voted at conference to support unilateral nuclear disarmament principally because Frank Cousins had replaced Arthur Deakin as its head. During the debate Gaitskell made his famous 'fight, fight and fight again' speech. But it was another section of his speech which caused the real uproar. 'Do you think we can simply accept a decision of this kind?' Gaitskell asked. 'Do you think that we can become overnight the party of pacifists, unilateralists and fellow-travellers.' (He omitted from the prepared text the word communists.) The rest of the speech was drowned out by booing and shouting.

Cousins, who became Minister of Technology in Wilson's first Cabinet, had become the new hate figure for the Gaitskellites. His wife Nancy refused to acknowledge Gaitskell at the traditional post-conference dinner. 'Her explanation for her behaviour', Geoffrey Goodman writes, 'is that she could not forgive Gaitskell for his slur about "fellow-travellers". She claims that this was a clear implication directed towards Frank, insinuating that he was fellow-travelling with the Communists and, she suspected, an imputation about her own earlier association with the Communist Party.' Indeed, Gaitskell wrote in his diary: 'I could not help thinking of her Communist past.' His conspiratorial view was fed by Deakin, who 'frequently tried to pin a specific charge of membership of the Communist Party on Cousins, not because he ever had any valid evidence of this, but because the rebellious Cousins would consistently be found opposing Deakin's policies.'[16]

The result of the debate had an electric effect on both wings of the Party. The VFS immediately called a meeting to discuss further penetration of the trade unions and the constituency parties. This was a move that did not go unnoticed and was one of the reasons which underlay the establishment of the CDS, which Crossman described as a 'Croslandite anti-Victory for Socialism group'. A report in *The Times* made it clear that its own aim was to counteract the VFS, which Gaitskell described as 'a dangerous, malicious, underground conspiracy'. Revealingly, CDS was initially going to be called Victory For Sanity, an explicit reference to its role in combating Victory for Socialism.[17]

On 24 November, following Gaitskell's narrow defeat, the Crosland/Rodgers group announced itself officially as the Campaign for Democratic Socialism, with Rodgers as Chair and John Diamond as fund-raiser. The CDS campaign had the support of 45 MPs. According to a sympathetic chronicler: 'The whole Central Leadership of the Party in Parliament, with the single exception of Wilson, were Campaign sympathisers.' There have been unresolved questions of how this large, expensive operation with a permanent staff and headquarters was funded. Some people, looking at the Congress for Cultural Freedom connections, have assumed it was funded by the CIA. There has never been any evidence for this view. In mid-November 1960, 'Rodgers reported to the steering committee that many small donations had been received, together with a large sum from a source who wished to remain anonymous'. As it turned out, the source was the head of Trust House Forte, Charles Forte: THF not CIA.[18]

To change Labour Party policy then, as now, meant changing union policy. In 1961 policy reversals were achieved in two unions, the shop-workers' union (USDAW) and the Amalgamated Engineers' Union (AEU), in effect guaranteeing the Gaitskell line at that year's Labour Party conference. Most commentators attribute this change in policy to the CDS. A different view is that of Labour MP and Wilson Cabinet minister Charles Pannell. To the American academic Irving Richter, Pannell 'described his close relationship with the General Secretary of the AEU, Mr Hallett, and their combined efforts to defeat the Left in the industrial and political wings of the movement, by building "IRIS cells".' (IRIS was the aforementioned trade union anti-communist black-listing group, Industrial Research and Information Service.) The work he and Hallett performed through IRIS cells, Pannell felt, did 'more than any single thing to reverse the direction of the AEU, the pivotal union, when the left-wing was about to throw Hugh Gaitskell to the wolves.' Conceeding the importance of the Campaign for Democratic Socialism in leading the conflict against the left wing, Pannell 'seemed to feel that both he and Hallett, as well as the Trade Union Group (of MPs), had not been given enough recognition for Gaitskell's victory in the great Labour Crisis of 1959–61.'[19]

IRIS had links to the Americans through its parent body Common Cause, and had very close relations with the Trade Union Group of MPs whose leading member was George Brown. In 1955, the group invited Irving Brown, 'Mr Labour' for the CIA, to address them. Pannell told Richter that 'Irving Brown's work was valuable in fighting the "Communist conspiracy" . . . comparable with the work of the IRIS cells.'[20]

In November 1960, Crosland wrote to Gaitskell about the next steps to be taken to defeat the socialists in the Party. 'Every party must have its extremist wing . . . But our left is clearly too numerous . . . generally it makes the Party virtually ungovernable.' Whilst Crosland thought the *New Statesman* and ex-ILP left 'could constitute a perfectly normal Left wing', there was a group of '20 hard-boiled extreme Left . . . This is the crucial group which must be expelled.' Correspondence followed between Gaitskell, Gordon Walker and Woodrow Wyatt, an ex-member of Keep Left and future right-wing maverick. A number of options were considered.[21]

Gaitskell's biographer claims that the Labour leader never intended a purge. 'At the height of the unilateralist battle he had privately thought that the hard core of VFS might end up in the wilderness, perhaps by their own choice, but had still hoped the line could be "drawn so as to keep as many people as possible in the Party".' The chair of the VFS home policy committee, Ian Mikardo, was closer to the truth when he claimed that the leadership's 'one and only concern is to break the unilateralists into pieces . . . and to get out their disciplinary broom and sweep the pieces out of the party and out of sight.' In March 1961, at Brown's instigation, the whip was withdrawn from five MPs: Michael Foot, William Baxter, S. O. Davies, Emrys Hughes and Sydney Silverman; Zilliacus was suspended from the Party. All were members of the VFS. Ironically, the VFS had already started to disintegrate. Brown had Gaitskell's full support. He thought Brown was the kind of person 'with whom you can safely go tiger-hunting', and the pair were now off the leash, hunting for Reds.[22]

IV

LOOKING OVER HIS SHOULDER

The outstanding unrecognised and unrecorded feature of the Left versus the Right struggle within the Labour Party is that the Right is always much better organised than the democratic Left.
IAN MIKARDO

THE CAMPAIGN for Democratic Socialism set up a number of secret committees to organise against the socialists in the Party, the wider Labour movement and CND. They were co-ordinated by Patrick Gordon Walker, who acted as 'general liaison officer'. Prompted by a letter from Crosland in July 1961, a three-man committee of Gaitskell, Brown and Gordon Walker set out to investigate those MPs thought to be 'crypto-communists'. A list of fifteen MPs was drawn up. 'The hard core is made up – let us face it because there is no point in mincing words', *Socialist Commentary* thundered in October, 'of many who would, almost certainly, belong to the Communist Party if Communism had any chance of political success in this country. Not only are their political attitudes indentical with the Communists, in that they are perpetually fighting the cold war on the side of the Soviet Union, but they pursue the same strategy and use the same methods.'[1]

Who was on this list? We know from published sources that Tom Driberg, Konni Zilliacus (died 1967) and S. O. Davies – the last two were members of the Victory For Socialism (VFS) group – were included. From studying the comments and smears of Gaitskell and his colleagues about 'fellow-travellers' and 'crypto-communists' we can guess at the others. Julius Silverman, Tom Braddock, Barnett Stross (died 1967), Leslie Plummer (died 1963), John Baird (died 1965) and William Warby (resigned 1966) seem likely. Members of VFS included Ian Mikardo, Harold Davies (Joint Parliamentary Secretary Ministry of Pensions, 1965–6), Stephen Swingler (Joint Parliamentary Secretary at the Ministry of Transport, 1964–7), Judith Hart (Joint Parliamentary Secretary for Scotland, 1964–6), Robert Woolf, Frank Allaun (PPS to Secretary of State for the Colonies 1964–5), Walter Monslow (died 1966), Albert Oram (Parliamentary Secretary Ministry of Overseas Development, 1964–9) and Ben Parkin (a

29

close friend of Wilson). Many of these MPs were to be subjected to smear campaigns.[2]

The investigating committee with its background in intelligence work was well suited to its task. Gordon Walker had been active before the war at Oxford in anti-communist circles with Christopher Mayhew. During the war, Gordon Walker served with the Psychological Warfare Executive at the BBC and later with Richard Crossman in propaganda work at SHAEF (Supreme Head-quarters Allied European Forces). Gaitskell had his own back-channels to the security service and had known its Director-General at Oxford. As Shadow Defence Minister, George Brown had contact with the CIA and MI6. It is rather odd, therefore, given this background and the known security service links with the right wing of the Labour Party, that George Brown should see the journalist Chapman Pincher about securing access to MI5 and MI6. The real purpose seems to have been for Pincher to publish the results of their enquiries. Pincher was an obvious choice. A well known defence correspondent with intelligence contacts, in 1960 he was contacted by Michael McCaul, an MI5 officer responsible for counter-intelligence, and asked to help in an attempt to compromise a KGB officer.[3]

Brown met Pincher on 1 August 1961, when the Labour Deputy Leader told him that the committee was 'aimed at exposing the communists who were fraudently posing as socialists and expelling them publicly from the party'. That way, as Brown put it to Pincher, 'they could go into the next election "clean of crypto-communists" '. The committtee was looking for concrete evidence including 'records of tapped telephone conversations, bank payments from Soviet bloc contacts' and 'the names of subversive Iron Curtain contacts in touch with the British crypto-Communists'.[4]

Brown and Gaitskell had been largely responsible, through Parliamentary action, for the setting up of the Radcliffe Committee, following the arrest of the Soviet spy in the Admiralty, John Vassal. The Gaitskellites had a direct input into the Committee through the presence of the former Labour Minister Kenneth Younger who had once worked for MI5 running agents in communist organisations. Radcliffe's brief was to review security procedures and practices. The organisation from which they received their information, and to whom they were addressing their final comments, was, of course, MI5. The principal threat to security ascertained by the Radcliffe Committee was from the KGB (and off-shoots) and, secondly, 'subversive organisations in this country, of which, in current conditions, the most formidable is the Communist Party of Great Britain, with its fringe of associated bodies and sympathisers'. This was some-thing which the Gaitskell/Brown committee was happy to see made official and public. Their view of the world and MI5's coincided.[5]

Since 1929, the Labour Party had dealt with such CPGB 'associated bodies' by use of the Proscribed List. The main grounds for inclusion of an organisation in the List was its alleged status as a Communist front. Transport House, which collated the information, had no mechanism for monitoring communist-inspired or pro-Soviet groups and they had to rely on outside resources. The List was substantially enlarged in 1953, based on information from 'the Foreign Office and Special Branch', with additional material from Common Cause, the parent body of IRIS. The Information Research Department, IRD, was undoubtedly the Foreign Office department responsible and their source was likely to have been MI5. The Chair of the Party's International Committee responsible for compiling the List was Sam Watson, who told Conference that these societies were agents for 'destruction of social democracy and the propagation of international Communism'.[6]

The Radcliffe Committee's predecessor, the 1956 Conference of Privy Councillors, noted: 'One of the chief problems of security today is thus to identify the members of the British Communist Party, to be informed of its activities and to identify that wider body of those who are both sympathetic to Communism, or susceptible to Communist pressure and present a danger to security.' As if by magic, within a matter of months, MI5 obtained the entire 'secret' CPGB membership list in an operation called Party Piece. According to Peter Wright, the operation was masterminded by Hugh Winterborn, following the discovery of a secret hiding place in the Mayfair flat of a wealthy Party member. MI5's A2 branch were called in to burgle the flat and copy the files. If we are to believe Wright – he only formally joined MI5 after the operation – 'In all, 55,000 files were copied that weekend, and the result was a priceless haul of information about the Communist Party'.[7]

Operation Party Piece, insists Wright, 'gave MI5 total access to the Party organisation . . . the material also contained the files of covert members of the CPGB . . . These were people in the Labour Party, the trade union movement . . . who had gone underground largely as a result of the new vetting procedures.' Wright goes on to claim, 'the CPGB was never again in a position to seriously threaten the safety of the realm. From then on, MI5 was able to locate every single active Party member, particularly the covert ones, and monitor their activities . . . The Party Piece material remained of enormous assistance right up until the early 1970s.' Is it possible that 55,000 files could be copied in a weekend, using the photographic technology of the mid-1950s? This sounds implausible and the assistant general secretary of the Communist Party for that period, George Mathews, was contemptuous of Wright's claim. 'We had not had 55,000 members since the final years of the war. At most we had half that number. We never had centralised records and there was no list of secret members because there were no secret members.' It is more likely that 'Party Piece' was collated from Special Branch and MI5 files on alleged members, which had been collected since the end of the war – the product of surveillance, telephone-taps, monitoring meetings, the use of secret informers, rumour and gossip. The story of Operation Party Piece was a simple piece of disinformation, a cover story for other clandestine methods.[8]

Wright has alleged 'the Communist Party's underground membership included thirty-one MPs serving under the guise of Labour Party membership'. There were indeed ex-communists serving as Labour MPs, but they included people like Denis Healey and John Strachey, firmly on the right of the Party and determined anti-communists, and Edmund Dell, elected in 1964 and appointed a junior minister at the Ministry of Technology, who later joined the SDP. This

figure of thirty-one has been bandied about by many anti-communist writers –
Pincher and Richard Deacon for example – and is similar to that of Labour MP
John McGovern. 'In my estimation', McGovern said in 1959, 'there were
twenty-six Communist under-cover agents or fellow-travellers, and if we took it
to a wider field the number would increase to seventy-nine, who I considered
would, if the Kremlin was winning the world struggle for Communism, throw off
their democratic masks and join the Communist world.' This was the kind of
conspiracy theory which appealed to people like Peter Wright.[9]

In January 1962, some five months after the initial approach, George Brown
called to see Roger Hollis about the results of the Labour leadership's inquiry.
He was to be disappointed. Prime Minister Macmillan and the Home Secretary
had ordered that the inquiry be curtailed. There appear to have been a number
of reasons for this decision. Firstly, Macmillan was concerned at the political
damage that would ensue if news of the inquiry leaked. This probably suited
Hollis, who disliked embroiling the security service in political squabbles (as
happened later during the Profumo Affair). Secondly, Hollis was concerned
about revealing sources and methods. He had recently listed CND as a
'subversive organisation' which automatically provided justification for the
opening of files and the surveillance of Labour members of the campaign. The
final reason has been given by Wright. 'Everybody in MI5 was opposed because
it would have blown all (our) sources inside the Labour Party.' The irony was that
one of MI5's main sources had been Tom Driberg MP, who had been recruited
by MI5 before the war. A Bevanite, Driberg was also on the Gaitskell/Brown list
of crypto-communists. However, during those five months an investigation had
been carried out and files had been built up. Later, much of the material
gathered would be deliberately leaked as part of a smear campaign.[10]

Brown was thrown one morsel. MI5 had uncovered 'an agent of Soviet bloc
Intelligence in a high position in the Labour Party machine at Transport House'.
This supposed agent was Arthur Bax, since 1946 the Party's Press and Publicity
Officer. It was said that he had received money from Czech agents and records
existed of telephone conversations, photographs and bank statements. The
American FBI had also allegedly informed the Special Branch that Bax was a
communist. Since the only information Bax had in his possession was internal
Labour Party material he could not be prosecuted under the Official Secrets
Act.[11]

Brown persuaded Bax to leave his post. According to Pincher, who was told
the details by Brown, 'Bax had denied the charges but confessed when faced
with the evidence that he had been passing on information for at least four years
and was allowed to resign on the grounds of ill health'. Bax is now dead but his
wife told us that 'the evidence was completely fabricated'. Her husband had
dealings with a number of foreign journalists (who were something of a curiosity
at the time) and he sometimes received money for articles. She pinpoints the
problems with MI5 to her husband's meetings with Antonin Buzwk, a Czech
'correspondent'. Bax helped Buzwk set up a branch of a news agency in London,
the Czech Press Agency. He 'did this quite openly' and lent his name to the
venture. It was this which did not go down well with the authorities, who saw

such agencies as possible cover for intelligence operations. According to Mrs Bax, 'Arthur was an innocent in these matters. He didn't have any idea that the Czechs had anything to do with intelligence.'[12]

When Bax saw Brown, 'he was frightened and upset that he may have damaged the Party'. He was under a lot of pressure from MI5. Mrs Bax was so angry about what had happened that she stormed into MI5 headquarters in Curzon Street. Forcing her way past the security guard, she demanded of the stunned officers what evidence there was against her husband. She says, 'MI5 conducted an investigation. They cleared him. They were like snakes in the grass, horrible people'.[13]

The leadership's drive against the left in the Party then hit a snag: Gaitskell fell ill. The first symptoms developed in early 1962 when rheumatic pains returned in his shoulder. That summer, he was taken ill and briefly blacked out. On 4 December 1962 Gaitskell, then aged 56, returned to London from France feeling unwell. He claimed to have 'picked something up in Paris' but worked on until the 15th, when he was admitted to the Manor House Hospital in Hampstead and found to be suffering from viral pneumonia. He was discharged after treatment on 23 December and his doctor pronounced him fit enough to travel to Moscow to see the Soviet leader, Khrushchev, on 1 January 1963. Gaitskell had an immediate relapse with symptoms of full-scale immunological collapse. On 4 January, he entered Middlesex Hospital and died three days later. The cause of death according to his death certificate was pulmonary oedema (fluid in the lungs), carditis (inflammation of the heart) and kidney failure.

In Wright and Pincher's view, the disease responsible for these symptoms was not viral pneumonia but Systematic Lupus Disseminata Erythematosis, a complaint caused by the victim's own antibodies. Rare in temperate climates, particularly in males over 40, only two or three cases are reported each year, and Gaitskell had not been to the tropics. From whom did the story about Lupus emanate? None of the doctors treating Gaitskell told MI5. Nor did MI5 have any contact with him while he was ill. So who fed the story about Lupus to them? Probably someone close to Gaitskell. Gaitskell's chief doctor in this period, Walter Somerville, recalled that someone in Gaitskell's entourage 'feared a pill may have been dropped in his coffee while on a visit to Poland. They hadn't seen this happen – they were speculating.' The fiction that a doctor was the source of the Lupus story protects the real source.[14]

The post-mortem on Gaitskell was carried out on 18 January 1963. It showed that Gaitskell was not suffering from Lupus; no Lupus cell had been found in his body. 'It was a condition like Lupus. What he actually had was what was called an immune complex deficiency. His immune system broke down as the cells degenerated.' Never a group to let the facts spoil a good story, as we shall see, the anti-Wilson faction in MI5 developed a convoluted conspiracy theory based on the events surrounding Gaitskell's death.[15]

Gaitskell's death lead to a no-holds barred leadership battle between Wilson, Brown and James Callaghan. It was a dirty campaign with all the anti-Wilson smears resurrected by the Gaitskellites. Most centred on Mrs Marcia Williams. George Thomas was accosted by a right-wing colleague, Percy Holman, who was hostile to Wilson. 'Holman asked me if I had ever seen Wilson's wife, commenting that it was strange that she was never with him.' A Wilson supporter, Thomas asked him what he was driving at: 'There was no reply.' Thomas went to see Wilson who told him Mary was shy and was not happy mixing with crowds. 'When Mary hears this', Wilson told him, 'she will come with me tomorrow to the Abbey for Hugh Gaitskell's memorial service.'[16]

In the first round of the leadership contest Callaghan received 41 votes and was eliminated. In the second, Wilson triumphed over George Brown by 144 votes to 103.

Although the approach by the Party leadership to the security services had failed, the bitter internal factional battle continued. In March 1963, the local CDS group in Putney complained to Transport House about their constituency party, which had taken part in the Aldermaston March with CND. The National Agent, Sara Barker, and Ray Gunter MP, Chair of the Organisation Sub-committee, used this as the pretext to investigate the Putney party and question the endorsement of the Parliamentary candidate, Hugh Jenkins. They were also concerned about Ann Kerr, a local left-wing activist, a member of CND and its direct action off-shoot the Committee of 100, which was under surveillance by the Special Branch and MI5. In 1960, she had married Russell Kerr, a former bomber pilot in the Royal Australian Air Force. Anne became Labour MP for Rochester in 1964 and Russell MP for Feltham in 1966. In January 1989, a Conservative MP, Sir Richard Body, told Parliament that an MI5 officer had informed him that telephone calls by the Kerrs were regularly intercepted. Both Tam Dayell and Michael Foot confirmed that Russell Kerr 'believed that he had been mistreated by the Security Services'.[17]

Hugh Jenkins, who had replaced CDS member Dick Taverne as Putney's candidate, was Chair of the VFS and an executive member of CND. Jenkins had been to the left of the Bevanites and was marked down as a 'fellow-traveller' by the Gaitskellites. As a member of Equity – as was Kerr – in the late forties and early fifties, Jenkins had experienced the McCarthy-like campaign by the right against the left in the union. There is little doubt that these credentials, coupled with his activities in the Union of Democratic Control, which had links with the Bevanite 'second eleven', gave him a bulky file at MI5.[18]

Another Jenkins, Clivé, General Secretary of the white-collar union ASSET (later ASTMS), had been proposed as a Labour Party candidate for Shoreditch. He was soon the target of a dirty tricks operation, probably set up by one of the 'IRIS cells'. The former Communist Party member was a founder member of the VFS and a close friend of Ian Mikardo, who organised the ASSET Parliamentary Committee, which contained a number of left-wingers. Wilson was eligible for ASSET membership because of his work for Montague Meyer on trade questions and had been recruited to the committee. In the late fifties, when Jenkins was involved in discussions with the Soviet aviation company Aeroflot, he naturally had contacts with the head of the International department of the Soviet Trade unions, Boris Averyanov, who was described in the right-wing press as 'a full colonel in the KGB': another black mark in Jenkins' MI5 personal file.[19]

At the 1963 Trade Union Conference a smear sheet was distributed accusing Clive Jenkins of being the leading Trotskyist in the country, dedicated to the violent overthrow of British democracy. The 'scurrilous document' had been distributed by 'Big' Jim Mathews, the national industrial officer of the National Union of General and Municipal Workers (NUGMW) and a member of the National Executive Committee of the Labour Party. Mathews was on the advisory board of Common Cause, the controlling body of IRIS, and later a 'staff consultant' for Securicor. The Chair of the NEC in 1963 was Bessie Braddock, who 'spent a lot of time telling [Tony Benn] about the secret anti-Communist intelligence digest to which she subscribes'. Jenkins discovered that the 'anonymous letter which had been mailed to every member of the [constituency] selection committee came from a man who was seemingly a member of the CIA and operating under cover of a petty news agency'. Jenkins lost the nomination for Shoreditch to Ron Brown, brother of George.[20]

Wilson as the 'unity' leader managed to keep the Party together on the thorny problem of rebellious left-wingers, though George Brown, with responsiblities for candidates, ensured that seats went predominantly to the Gaitskellites. Wilson took the initiative on the Putney case and called for a truce between the CDS and the VFS. Hugh Jenkins' candidacy was endorsed. Wilson would later appoint him Minister for Arts. The Rebel Five, Foot, Davies, Baxter, Silverman and Hughes, who had lost the whip in 1961, were reinstated. Left and right wings in the party called a truce until after the approaching general election.[21]

It would seem that Wilson had some inkling of the Brown/Gaitskell approach to the security services in 1961 and he appeared to know that there had been some infiltration of the Party during the bitter factional struggles over nuclear disarmament in 1960–2. He also knew that as late as July 1963 his deputy, George Brown, was still in contact with MI6 and its head 'C'. Wilson had 'become convinced that the Security Service's interest in the Party factions and their arguments went way beyond the requirements of National Security'. This contributed to Wilson's belief that MI5 'was staffed by people who could not tell the difference between a democratic socialist and a communist'.[22]

When Wilson won the leadership contest on 14 February 1963, George Thomas was one of the first to congratulate him. Thomas asked him how he felt. Wilson expressed relief; he had defeated his enemies 'I will no longer have to look over my shoulder.' The reality was that Wilson had to spend the next thirteen years doing just that.[23]

V

'SICK THINK'

*The effect of Golitsyn was horrendous. The greatest disaster to Western
security that happened in twenty years.*
CHIEF OF THE CIA'S SOVIET BLOC DIVISION

IT IS ALMOST CERTAIN that in his eight years as Prime Minister, Wilson
never once heard the name Anatoliy Golitsyn. Yet few people were to have as
much influence as this shadowy figure in creating the image of Wilson as a Soviet
'agent of influence'. It was Golitsyn who legitimised the absurd story that
Gaitskell had been assassinated by the KGB in order to facilitate the rise of their
agent, Harold Wilson. Peter Wright points out in his book *Spycatcher*: 'Much has
been written about Harold Wilson and MI5, some of it wildly inaccurate. But as
far as I am concerned, the story started with the premature death of Hugh
Gaitskell in 1963.'[1]

Thirty-five-year-old Lieutenant-Colonel Anatoliy Golitsyn was a middle-
ranking KGB counter-intelligence officer working in Helsinki. Under his alias
'Klimov', Golitsyn began his defection to the United States on 15 December
1961 when he walked into the US embassy office of CIA station chief Frank
Friberg. Although he claimed to have planned for this day for five years, Golitsyn
turned up without any documents. He appears to have been very much in the
standard mould of defectors who had become frustrated in their careers. In the
late fifties, another defector, Peter Deriabin, had mentioned Golitsyn to the CIA
as a possible recruit, having noticed that his former colleague had an overblown
notion of his expertise and was unpopular with his fellow officers. 'What struck
me above all about Golitsyn', Deriabin recalls, 'was that he seemed to be the
perpetual student rather than a practical operator. He had a big mouth and
tended to invent stories which would make him look important . . . he was always
full of plans, plans to re-organize everything.'[2]

Golitsyn's debriefing was handled by Donald Jameson and began in earnest in
February 1962 at a heavily guarded compound in Maryland known as 'the
Farm'. Jameson dealt with Golitsyn until August 1962, during which time,
according to one inside account, he revealed only a 'meagre network of facts'

which produced only limited results. There were immense problems with his debriefing. Golitsyn refused to speak Russian and everything was told in his fractured English, which made the information often frustratingly vague. He distrusted all officers who spoke Russian and was suspicious of anyone with any Russian elements in their background.[3]

'Golitsyn is a very suspicious, very withdrawn, very difficult man', says one CIA officer who dealt with him. 'He saw his information as his only capital in the West.' Among defectors there is often the attitude that 'the West is a great opportunity, and they think they have this chunk of gold, and every time they tell something they are cutting another piece off from it, and they feel when they finish they'll be thrown away. Golitsyn from the beginning was bargaining about information'. Golitsyn quickly tired of the extensive sessions and became unco-operative with a whole series of case officers, who he insisted were idiots.[4]

In March 1962, two senior British counter-intelligence officers were sent to Washington to see the defector. MI5's Arthur Martin had been head of D1 (Soviet counter-espionage) since 1960, the same year that Geoffrey Hinton was appointed head of CI4, the Soviet espionage section of MI6. Golitsyn gave Martin and Hinton three leads. He told them about a 'Ring of Five' Soviet agents but nothing at all about Kim Philby. He aroused suspicions about possible Soviet penetration of the Admiralty but was not able to identify spy John Vassall. They also extracted 'various items of circumstantial evidence which suggested the existence of a Soviet mole inside MI5'. This material became known as the 'ten serials' and was regarded by MI5 as the 'best proof of Soviet penetration'. However, another commentator reveals that in his first debriefings with the CIA Golitsyn 'made clear that there was no high level penetration of MI5'. Golitsyn's 'information' was very much in the eye of the beholder.[5]

'The subject of how Golitsyn was handled by the CIA and ourselves is a thorny one. His relationships with the CIA in 1962 were stormy', says Stephen de Mowbray, a head of Soviet counter-intelligence in MI6. 'I don't think anyone in the CIA would deny that they had never handled a case like this and that mistakes were made on both sides.' According to a senior CIA officer who dealt with Golitsyn: 'The trouble was he got out of the control of people who knew how to handle Russians and got higher and higher. In consequence, he got into the position of bargaining about information . . . after a while he came to realize he didn't necessarily have to tell the truth in order to get attention. His later information, from the fall of 1962, lacked an element of veracity. It was about that time that [CIA Counter-Intelligence head James] Angleton took over, apologized to him for the behaviour of people who tried to get him to straighten up a little bit, and Golitsyn at that point realized he had a nice situation he could control, and he's travelled with it ever since.' After his initial debriefings by the CIA's Soviet Bloc Division, Golitsyn had grown increasingly aloof, refusing to deal with anyone but James Angleton or his assistant, Raymond Rocca, in the Counter-Intelligence Division. This was, experts agree, 'contrary to all normal practice'.[6]

A literary scholar and expert on orchids, James Jesus Angleton was a man afraid of his own shadow. Only a handful of people had ever seen him, yet he was probably the most powerful person in the CIA in the fifties and sixties. In 1954, he set up the CIA's counter-intelligence staff under the new Director, Allen Dulles. Its remit was to organise a unit which would guard against Soviet deception operations such as those that had destroyed operations against the Soviet bloc. It had three main tasks: liaison with allied counter-intelligence, determining which defectors were *bona fide* sources and, the most controversial, 'provid[ing] the highest form of counter-intelligence; a picture of the enemy's thinking'. The problem was that 'Angleton had a special view of the world', says former colleague Hank Knoche. 'You almost have to be 100 per cent paranoid to do that job. You always have to fear the worst. You always have to assume, without necessarily having the proof in your hands, that your own organization has been penetrated and there's a mole around somewhere. And it creates this terrible distrustful attitude.'[7]

Golitsyn did not have the proof but he was able to supply a world-view which supported Angleton's own. 'With the single exception of Golitsyn', says staff member Clare Edward Petty, 'Angleton was inclined to assume that any defector or operational asset in place was controlled by the KGB.' According to John Hart, who conducted an extensive review of the agency's handling of defectors, Golitsyn's warnings 'centred around the idea that the KGB had vast resources which it was using to deceive not only the U.S. government but other Western governments. This plot was masterminded by something called the KGB Disinformation Directorate, and [it] was able to deceive the West . . . because of the fact that it had penetrations at high levels, both within the intelligence sevices of these countries, including our own, but also in high places in the governments of various countries'. This was the 'wilderness of mirrors' of Angleton's fertile brain – 'the strategies, deceptions, artifices and other devices of disinformation which the Soviet bloc and its co-ordinated intelligence services use to confuse and split the West'. This schizophrenic view of the world became known in the CIA by detractors of Angleton as 'sick think'.[8]

In late 1962, as he continued to abuse his debriefers, Golitsyn indicated to Raymond Rocca that he wanted to resettle abroad under a new identity. 'The way that Golitsyn went to the UK', says one CIA officer, 'was very unusual.' Simply going out was a tremendous ordeal for Golitsyn who was 'very much afraid of everything'. According to a fellow defector, who knew him well in this period, 'He was just paranoid'. Although his information was extremely vague, Golitsyn was invited to Britain by Arthur Martin, who told him that 'his help would receive the recognition that the Americans were so reluctant to give'. This included being paid £10,000 per month and, in a typical piece of British flattery, being made an honorary Commander of the British Empire. The Soviet Bloc Division of the CIA went along with the request, believing it had 'squeezed' him dry, but with an agreement being made whereby it would be possible for them to question him at a later date. He was given permission to leave for England where 'Golitsyn was almost solely in Arthur Martin's custody'. Amazingly, while in Britain Golitsyn was allowed to fend for himself, touring the country, staying in hotels and making contact with Martin only every few days to arrange a debriefing session. The 'safe houses' were arranged by Alec MacDonald, a future head of D branch.[9]

Golitsyn turned up in London on the day Kim Philby defected to the Soviet Union. 'Gollywog', as Golitsyn was known by the British, was not, according to De Mowbray, 'merely another defector. He was, as far as British intelligence was concerned, probably the most important defector in recent history.'[10]

Golitsyn's 'ten serials' confirmed what some officers already saw as proven: namely, that MI5 had been penetrated by the KGB. Martin had narrowed the field of potential spies down to two people, initially the Deputy Director, Graham Mitchell, and later the Director-General, Roger Hollis. Martin went to see Dick White, Chief of the rival service MI6, who proposed a secret inquiry. Hollis agreed to the setting up of the inquiry codenamed 'Peters' and the seconding of an MI6 officer, Stephen de Mowbray, to head a secret group of 'Watchers'. Meanwhile, the Chief of MI6 put pressure on Hollis to agree to 'technical facilities' being made available, which included Peter Wright joining the team.[11]

Wright, who admits to having been a 'fervent admirer of Golitsyn', believes the defector was badly handled when he came to London. 'He was allowed to think himself too important . . . Right from his first visit . . . we opened up to Golitsyn, and I was responsible for that as much as anyone.' Much of his information was of little use. 'It often appeared true as far as it went, but then faded into tantalising obscurity, and part of the problem was his clear propensity for feeding the information out in dribs and drabs.' Golitsyn knew that MI5 were hunting a high-level spy. 'In the tense and almost hysterical months of 1963, as the scent of treachery lingered in every corridor, it is easy to see how our fears fed on his theories.'[12]

It was at this point that Arthur Martin introduced to Golitsyn the idea that Hugh Gaitskell had been assassinated, with its rider that the beneficiary of this good fortune had been Harold Wilson. Golitsyn heard Martin and Wright talking about Gaitskell and the mysterious death. The defector enquired, 'Could Gaitskell have been assassinated?' He then produced for the first time his story that the chief of KGB operations in Northern Europe, General Rodin, had once told him of a plan to kill 'a Western leader'; it was never anything more precise than that. According to his boss Alec MacDonald, Wright 'was all for believing it'. Golitsyn said: 'Your best leader on the socialist side . . . Gaitskell was eliminated.' MacDonald was certain that 'he didn't suggest that he was to be replaced by anybody else'. Martin then asked for more details and told him that they were investigating a particular case. 'Between the three of them, they soon convinced themselves that it could have been Gaitskell.'[13]

As we have seen in Chapter IV, someone close to Gaitskell and the security services speculated that Gaitskell had died of Lupus because 'a pill may have been dropped in his coffee'. The 'pill' theory was a current conspiracy theory within MI5 and Wright himself believed that the operation possibly happened when Gaitskell visited the Soviet consulate to obtain a visa for his proposed visit to Russia. Arthur Martin asked Wright to investigate the matter further at the Microbiological Research Establishment at Porton Down. Wright saw Dr Ladell, and asked his advice. 'He said that nobody knew how one contracted

Lupus. There was some suspicion it might be a form of fungus and he did not have the foggiest idea how one would infect someone with the disease.' Martin contacted the British Medical Association and spoke to a virus specialist who told him that although the Soviets had worked on the disease it was in fact impossible to develop a Lupus poison. Once more, Golitsyn offered additional information. 'He pointed out that the chief of Department 13 was a man called General Rodin, who had been in Britain for many years and had just returned on promotion to take up the job, so he would have had good knowledge of the political scene in England.' Head of MI5, Roger Hollis, dismissed the inquiry but the head of Counter-Espionage, Martin Furnival-Jones, 'remained concerned about the circumstances of Gaitskell's death and the long-term consequences'.[14]

Golitsyn helped feed other fears. He insisted that Oleg Penkovsky, the GRU (Soviet Military Intelligence) Colonel who had supplied the CIA and MI6 with top-level secrets during the Cuban Missile Crisis, was really a KGB plant. This found favour with Wright, Martin and Angleton who had doubted Penkovsky's bona fides. The possibility was put to Golitsyn by the Wright/Martin axis in MI5 that the political split between the Soviet Union and China was a fake. They also suggested that a Soviet agent, Agent 19, recently discovered in recorded Second World War radio traffic, was possibly the renowned American statesman, Averell Harriman.[15]

In his final interrogation by MI5, Golitsyn 'suggested that he had demonstrated to the CIA that it had also been penetrated'. However, he claimed that 'the CIA's Soviet Division had never zeroed in on his leads'. Golitsyn assumed his CIA case officers were 'either incompetent or unwilling to find a mole in the CIA'. After listening to his story of CIA incompetence, Arthur Martin telephoned his American counterpart, James Angleton, who agreed that 'the Soviet Division had not got the full story from Golitsyn'. Angleton wanted his prize catch back in the United States and so Golitsyn's presence in England was deliberately leaked by the CIA to the *Daily Telegraph*'s Washington correspondent. The paper's Editor, Sir Colin Coote, then used his considerable contacts in the Conservative Government to force confirmation. On 12 July 1963, only days after it was confirmed that Philby was in Moscow, an article appeared in the paper headlined 'Soviet Spy gets British Asylum'. It was sufficient for the paranoid Golitsyn to catch the next plane back to the United States.[16]

Golitsyn was Angleton's prize defector. According to Peers de Silva, Chief of Operations of the Soviet Bloc Division, 'Angleton made a career out of Golitsyn. He built his whole position on Golitsyn'. This was in the face of John Hart's assessment that Golitsyn's information was 'quantitatively and qualitatively much smaller' than from other defectors. Without Angleton's backing Golitsyn's warnings would never have been taken seriously. 'Angleton was the only officer who possessed the command of fact, the strength of personality, the force of conviction needed to overcome the disbelief that traditionally greeted warnings about Soviet plots.' Golitsyn had been diagnosed by a psychiatrist as a 'paranoid'.[17]

Back in the United States, Golitsyn 'produced no new concrete evidence. His "case" was based entirely on deductions drawn from the matrix of his philosophy – namely that the KGB had penetrated every nook and cranny of the Western alliance'. The effect, according to MI6's Deputy Chief, George Young, was corrosive and destructive. 'Jim Angleton – a gullible soul who saw himself as a Machiavelli – had been completely under Philby's influence and sought to whitewash himself by finding KGB agents in every British department and agency'. Maurice Oldfield, MI6's Chief of Station in Washington and incidentally a wine lover, later told Chapman Pincher: 'The first pressings from a defector almost always have the most body. The third pressings are suspect.' The third pressings took place in the United States.[18]

Golitsyn told an eager Angleton that the recent rupture between China and the USSR was a fraud. He claimed it was a massive disinformation campaign designed to lull the West into a false sense of security. Golitsyn was allowed to put his theory to a panel of experts on Sino-Soviet affairs, who 'agreed unanimously that his thesis had no basis in fact'. He then suggested that Averell Harriman, former Ambassador to Britain, was recruited by the KGB in Moscow in the 1930s.[19]

Golitsyn convinced Angleton that the KGB had poisoned Gaitskell in order to promote the new leader of the Labour Party, Harold Wilson. Angleton commissioned a thorough search of Russian scientific literature for published material on Lupus. He discovered that three papers had been published with the information that Soviet medical researchers had undertaken experiments in which they administered a chemical substance to animals which produced the fatal symptoms of the disease. In particular, a 1956 article mentioned a proprietary drug called hydralalzine which had been found to produce Lupus-like effects in rats.

The information was passed on to Wright, who for the first time went to see Gaitskell's doctor, Walter Somerville. He told Wright that 'there was nothing new in what they were saying. The side effects of hydralalzine had been well known in the West for ten years.' The 'pill in the coffee theory' was untenable according to Somerville. It would require that Gaitskell took the pill repeatedly. Wright took Angleton's find to Ladell at Porton Down, who thought the scenario unlikely though the Soviets might have produced a 'one shot drug'. Somerville says: 'They clearly did believe there was something in this theory that Gaitskell had been poisoned, and they were reluctant to let go of it.'[20]

Angleton ran a 'trace' on General Rodin, the man Golitsyn claimed had told him about the assassination plot. He was identified as a senior officer in the KGB's Department 13, believed to be responsible for political assassinations. 'Even more disturbing to Angleton, Rodin was, at the time of Gaitskell's visit to the Soviet Consulate, stationed in London'. Rodin had used the pseudonym 'Korovin'. There was a Nikolai Korovin at the Soviet Embassy who controlled the Portland spy-ring and the Admiralty spy, John Vassall, but he left in 1961, over a year before Gaitskell visited the Embassy. It is also true that the Politburo had by this time abandoned assassination by the KGB outside the Soviet Union.[21]

Golitsyn suggested that 'the KGB would carry out such an intervention [as the

Gaitskell 'assassination'] in only two circumstances: first, if Wilson was their man, or, second, if someone in Wilson's entourage was their man.' However, even if Wilson were the KGB's man, the assassination theory seems unlikely, for good reasons. First, East–West détente was still a possibility and Khruschev would not want to upset it. More importantly, Gaitskell's most likely opponent, and hence successor, was not Wilson but George Brown, a noted anti-communist and no friend of the Soviets.[22]

Golitsyn told Angleton that Harold Wilson was a 'Soviet asset'. He had been informed, presumably by MI5, that Wilson had made frequent trips to the Soviet Union during the 1950s, on behalf of Montague Meyer, the timber merchants. That was all he needed to know. Wilson, Golitsyn argued, 'must have been at least propositioned by the KGB during these visits and might well have been recruited'. Within the Wright/Martin circle in MI5 this analysis was accepted and Wilson's time in Moscow became known as the 'lost weeks'.[23]

The acceptance by the Angleton/Wright/Martin axis of the conspiracy theories of Golitsyn had created a nightmare at the heart of the counter-intelligence world. MI6's liaison officer with the CIA in Washington, Maurice Oldfield, reportedly said, 'the situation here is much more like *Alice in Wonderland* than anything Lewis Carroll could have thought up. There must be several candidates for the role of Mad Hatter.' Over the following ten years, a bitter factional dispute took place within the CIA which crippled the Agency's work against the KGB. In the opinion of one chief of the CIA's Soviet Bloc Division, 'if you take the thesis of the KGB dispatching a defector to carry out a disinformation programme and tie the CIA into knots, the classic operation would be Golitsyn'. These suspicions reached a climax in late 1973, when both Angleton and Golitsyn were placed under surveillance by CIA officers. A former colleague of Angleton's in the Counter-intelligence Division, Clare Edward Petty, then submitted a long exhaustive study – one of the CIA's most important secrets – concluding that 'Golitsyn was a "sent agent" whose primary mission was to disrupt the Western services with disinformation'.[24]

Did the KGB send Golitsyn to Angleton? One could just as easily substitute MI5 for KGB. Golitsyn was involved in what is known as 'spinning' – telling ever more astounding stories in order to remain the centre of attention. Perhaps, by design, Golitsyn's supporters in MI5 had set up a deception operation known by Angleton as 'the Loop'. This consisted of 'two lines of communications that hooked up rival intelligence services – one perpetuating the deception; the other the victim of it. The deceiver uses one set of lines to pass messages to its opposition. In practice, this means that its intelligence service must establish channels, whether human or electronic, that connect it to its adversary's intelligence service. And these must be channels that the victim relies on for its secret information.' In this case, Golitsyn was a two-way channel to Angleton and MI5, both of whom relied on him for their secret information. MI5 fed Golitsyn stories – Gaitskell, Wilson, Harriman, Sino-Soviet split – which he then relayed to Angleton as his own secret information.[25]

According to Angleton's own conception of 'the Loop', for perfect deception two further conditions were necessary. First, 'the victim's leadership has to be in a state of mind to want to accept and act on the disinformation it receives from its own intelligence.' This was easy, Angleton himself was still in shock from the defection of Kim Philby, the man who taught him much of what he knew about intelligence work. Second, 'the victim has to be in a state of mind in which he is so confident of his own intelligence that he is unwilling to entertain evidence, or even theories, that he is or can be duped.' This fits Angleton perfectly. He accepted Golitsyn with absolute certainty. Leonard McCoy, who worked with Angleton, says he was unshakeable in his belief of Soviet domination and 'he certainly would not admit you had information or logic superior to his own'.[26]

The CIA Chief of Station in London, Archie Roosevelt, was not happy about the fact that Angleton and his friends were controlling Golitsyn. 'It did affect us all in further poisoning the atmosphere.' MI5 Director-General Roger Hollis referred to the small coterie of Golitsyn's supporters inside MI5's counter-intelligence branch as the 'Gestapo'. Peter Wright was 'adored' by those officers who believed in Golitsyn. 'He was', says a female officer, 'always going on about Soviet misinformation and what he called "agents of influence". That was his passion.' According to one of their senior colleagues, 'the Gestapo' had been 'swept away by all sorts of theories of espionage which became more and more elaborate. Eventually, they ceased to have anything to do with reality.' Before he died, Angleton admitted as much when he suggested: 'In peacetime, disinformation might be the chief job of an intelligence agency.'[27]

A 'Gestapo' section of MI5, a handful of officers in its sister agency MI6 and, perhaps, the most important person in the CIA believed that Harold Wilson was a Soviet 'agent'. A group of élite counter-intelligence officers had willingly swallowed Golitsyn's conspiracy theory and were happy to promote it and let it seep into the body politic as part of their attempt to discredit the leader of the Labour Party.

C
O
Py

30 November 1964

MEMORANDUM FOR: Mr. McGeorge Bundy
Special Assistant to the President
The White House

SUBJECT: Rumors Current in London Regarding Prime
Minister Harold Wilson's Secretary

1. I have summarized below our existing information concerning the
rumors current in London of the impending divorce of Harold Wilson's
personal secretary and its possible political implications.

2. On 5 March 1964, Mrs. Barbara McCorqudale (Barbara Cartland,
the novelist) speaking at a small local meeting in Hertfordshire was highly
irritated by questions from the floor on the Profumo case by pro-Labor
members of the audience. Mrs. McCorqudale was so stung by these
remarks that she lashed out with the charge that Harold Wilson for the past
eighteen months had been having an affair with his secretary. This statement caused an uproar at the meeting which was later covered in a front
page story in the London Sunday Telegraph of 15 March (copy attached).
This newspaper story carefully omitted the nature of Mrs. McCorqudale's
statements for libel law reasons.

3. A personal contact of one of our | officers on the
editorial staff of the Daily Herald, confirmed 16 March that Mrs.
McCorqudale had made the statement and that it had caused a furor at Labor
Party headquarters. He added his personal comment that many had long
suspected that Mr. Wilson was having an "affair" with his secretary, but
this was the first time to his knowledge that a public charge had been made.

4. On 8 October, Hailsham Hogg in a campaign speech referred to
"adulterers on the front bench of the Labor Party." This created a furor
and demands for parliamentary censure of Mr. Hogg. In commenting on
Hogg's statement;   stated that the rumors concerning
Wilson and his secretary were now "common gossip" in London circles.

5. On 2 November, a London solicitor who is a partner in a highly
reputable London law firm informed one of our   officers that Wilson's

RELEASE   1975

secretary's divorce was to come before the courts in November. On 5 November, one of our [   ] officers attended a small dinner at which several prominent London lawyers were present. Several of these lawyers were discussing the possibility of a political crisis arising from Wilson's secretary's contemplated divorce and their interest was apparently not one of gossip, but rather of politics. They all seemed agreed that a divorce was to take place and one added the note that the secretary's husband was a "card-carrying member of the British Communist Party." Circumstances of the dinner were such that our officer was in no position to follow up on the basis for such an allegation. We have no information to confirm such an allegation and, due to the obvious sensitivity of the situation, are in no position to check back through our normal liaison with the British Security Service.

6. Of the foregoing, the only hard facts are (a) Mrs. McCorqudale's statements and the resultant furor; (b) the existence of fairly widespread London "gossip" on this subject; and (c) the apparent probability of the impending divorce of Wilson's secretary. In the aftermath of the Profumo scandal, much of London "gossip" can be rapidly dismissed as trash and this story could well be in that category. However, if there is any truth at all in these rumors this situation could lead to future serious political embarrassment for Mr. Wilson personally and for the Labor Government.

7. A copy of this memorandum has been sent to The Honorable Llewellyn Thompson, Deputy Under Secretary for Political Affairs, Department of State.

> Richard Helms
> Deputy Director for Plans

VI

SMEAR!

No other statesman has ever been subjected to such a stream of scurrilous rumour.
CHAPMAN PINCHER

IN THE RUN-UP to the 1964 General Election a series of smear campaigns were launched against Harold Wilson and his private secretary, Mrs Marcia Williams. The true extent of these campaigns is unknown: many Labour Party members from that era are reluctant to discuss the subject. Even if the reported instances are all there is and not the tip of an iceberg – and we have reason to believe it is the latter – it is still a considerable catalogue; and one that makes intelligible Wilson's sensitivity to press sniping at Mrs Williams and speculation about their relationship.

Throughout 1963 the rumours which had first appeared during the leadership campaign continued to surface. Tariq Ali had just joined the Oxford University Labour Club, where 'the two cult figures of the Oxford Right after Gaitskell's death were William Rodgers and Brian Walden, who regularly addressed the Club and kept their followers supplied with anti-Wilson gossip.' The security services had at one point considered recruiting Walden as an informant but the proposal was rejected when they discovered 'an adverse trace' against his (first) wife. These two leading members of the Campaign for Democratic Socialism were rewarded with junior ministerial posts in the first Wilson Government.[1]

Similar anti-Wilson gossip was to be heard across the road at the Oxford Conservative Association, where Col. Douglas Dodds-Parker had been wrongly informed that 'Harold Wilson had had sexual relations with his left-wing parliamentary colleague, Barbara Castle, when they were both on a visit to Canada', also that 'Wilson had had an affair with his secretary, Mrs Marcia Williams'. During the war, Dodds-Parker had been a senior member of the Special Operations Executive; in the fifties, he was a Conservative MP and a Parliamentary Under-Secretary in the Foreign Office responsible for liaison with MI6. According to Kim Philby, he chaired the Psychological Warfare Consultations Committee. Better known as the Dodds-Parker Committee, it 'carried on . . . psychological operations against any peace movements . . . and planned Intelligence Service operations against progressive organizations in England.' When Dodds-Parker lost his seat in 1959, the well-connected former Intelligence officer with experience in the art of black propaganda moved to Conservative Central Office, returning to Parliament in 1964.[2]

George Wigg, Wilson's watchdog, on the lookout for possible scandals, showed Chapman Pincher 'documentary proof that there could not be any possible truth in the [Marcia Williams] story. It was a copy of the proceedings under which Williams had divorced Marcia in King County, Washington, USA back in 1960 before Wilson had ever become leader of the Labour Party.' This did little to quell the interest of Conservative Central Office or, more importantly, the security services. The involvement of Dodds-Parker put the distribution of the smears on to a higher level of importance. He had apparently known of them 'by the autumn of 1960', very early on in their genesis, suggesting that his source was a Gaitskell supporter. Dodds-Parker had an extra piece of the story; the affair between Wilson and Marcia Williams had 'taken place, so the story went, in Moscow, while they were travelling on behalf of Montague Meyer'.[3]

This added twist to the story was not part of the smear campaign at the 1964 General Election, but this tale of Soviet interest with its hints of possible blackmail was one which MI5 was later to promote assiduously. During the fifties, MI6 had been collecting material for its files on Wilson's trips to the Soviet Union from its agents amongst the East–West traders. This is not to suggest that the stories were true, but the security services were in a position to be creative with the information in their possession. Wilson's eleven trips to the Soviet Union were common knowledge during the election campaign but no one – except MI5 – considered them of any great importance. Dodds-Parker's extra snippet of disinformation indicates that the security services had entered the fray and were beginning to dish the dirt.[4]

In the end, this particular smear concerning Wilson and Mrs Williams in Moscow reached the public only in 1975. Auberon Waugh wrote a thinly veiled account of the story in *Private Eye*: 'I have never attempted to disguise my belief that Harold Wilson [was] recruited in Moscow and London in 1956/8.' A year later he wrote in the *Spectator*: 'The affair only lasts a comparatively short short time – about two years – but he makes the mistake during this time of taking his lady friend to Russia with him, where he is visiting on business, not once but three times. During the first of these visits, they are photographed in compromising circumstances by agents of the Soviet security police at a hotel where they are both staying.'[5]

There were various attempts by the Conservatives to launch anti-Wilson smears in the press. In January 1964, Tory MPs planted derogatory information – presumably about Wilson's relationship with Marcia Williams – on the *Daily Telegraph*. H. B. Boyne, then its chief political correspondent, wrote of 'some rather unworthy attempts to find skeletons in Mr Wilson's cupboard' and of 'Conservative MPs who have whispered in my ear'. In her book on Prime Minister's wives, Diana Farr says, 'that whispering campaign, [was] started by one of the foremost, younger members of the Conservative Party'. The MP, later a Cabinet Minister, was a member of the Bow group and one of the organisers in October 1963 of the Conservative leadership bid by Quintin Hogg (Lord Hailsham). Randolph Churchill, a Hogg supporter, predicted that in the forthcoming General Election 'the whole character of the Socialist party will be under close scrutiny. Mr Quintin Hogg has rendered a great service to the country by reminding it of the number of unpatriotic communists and fellow-travellers who have infiltrated the [Labour] party and who scheme and agitate against the interests of Britain in every part of the world.'[6]

In the autumn of 1964, *Private Eye* referred to a 'Tory sex-smear campaign against Wilson which has been operating as a secret weapon in the constituencies for at least three months . . . It was in the early spring that the Tories decided, after opinion-polling on the vote-effects of Profumo, that a sex smear was a good thing to have.' A bizarre operation then began over one weekend in June. 'Suddenly at key spots all over the country, men turned up in pubs talking about an alleged intimate relationship between Marcia Williams and Harold Wilson. The following Monday, Labour MPs converged on Westminster to discuss the outbreak of what some thought was Conservative-inspired "black propaganda".'[7]

According to one story, which was given to the *Daily Mirror* – and subsequently denied – Conservative Central Office were well prepared for the campaign. The Chair of the Conservative Party, Lord Blakenham, had 'hired a posse of private detectives to pursue George Brown during the 1964 Election'. Pincher reveals that this had been running for some time. 'Scotland Yard's Special Branch was also in the surveillance programme. I [have] established the identity of an outside agent who was employed by Special Branch to follow Wilson around on one occasion in 1963 and who tailed George Brown for a whole week.'[8]

Brown came under further pressure in the summer of 1964. The convicted fraudster Ernest Shinwell, son of the Labour Peer Emmanuel Shinwell, claims he came across evidence linking George Brown to corruption. Shinwell alleges he saw documents indicating Brown 'had been receiving money in exchange for helping a company secure important defence work'. This involved a 'network of corruption among several highly-placed figures'. On 23 June, Shinwell went to see George Wigg, no friend of Brown, who tried to persuade him to report the details to Scotland Yard. Wigg took the case seriously but Shinwell, not the most trustworthy of characters, was not prepared to inform the police unless he had help to fight a forged shares case in which he was involved. 'I knew that Wigg would have thrown me to the wolves, once I had given him the evidence against Brown. He was only interested in getting hold of the documents I had seen and, at that stage, had access to.' There was no deal and, in February 1965, Ernest was found guilty of deception. He was at the time also involved in a shady deal with the Kray twins.[9]

In July, the Conservative Party tried to 'surface' smear stories in France. *Private Eye* reported that 'A missionary from Tory Central Office spent time and money in Paris last week trying to peddle alleged feelthy (sic) stories about

Labour leaders to the French newspapers . . . We had a story 'linking the name' of Harold Wilson with those of various female fellow-workers. Another stating that a Labour MP was having an affair with the wife of a leading Tory. Etc Etc.' After describing at some length the kinds of difficulties presented by launching such stories about an abstemious person like Wilson, the *Eye* commented: 'The choice was now between a young socialistically idealist girl debauched by . . . No, no, no. It just won't do. So she's a married woman. Well? Well she's not only a married woman but, I say look here, her husband's madly jealous and he's going to bring a divorce action and cite Wilson as co-respondent? Or . . . or . . . hold it . . . the husband isn't so much jealous as he's a blackmailer, by George you've got it, he's a man who realises the terrific hold he has over Wilson in election year and he's holding him up . . . He's forcing him to pay out somehow or other not to bring the action . . . Not until after the election.'[10]

This was a creative use of the circumstances surrounding the marriage and divorce of Mrs Williams. Chapman Pincher noted in *Inside Story*, 'rumours which crystallized into the wide-spread belief, just before the 1964 General Election, that Marcia's husband, Edmund Williams, had been paid a large sum by wealthy supporters of Wilson to withdraw a divorce action which could have been embarrassing.' *Private Eye* further reported in October that the Tories 'have actually laid on a man who, for a reasonable sum in cash is standing ready and willing to start some kind of court proceedings . . . There is certainly enough in the kitty to meet whatever minimal legal costs might be incurred'. The money had been garnered by 'a group of anti-socialist businessmen'. An *Evening Standard* reporter was sent to ask Mrs Williams about the breakdown of her marriage but, according to Andrew Roth, Wilson 'sent the reporter off with a flea in her ear'. The papers continued to pursue the story. 'Another newspaper considered urging Ed Williams to return to Britain to divorce his wife, only to discover belatedly that he was already divorced.'[11]

Various smears referred to 'an ex-secretary, or a research worker closely associated with Wilson at some time or another' and a 'third woman'. One story concerned Mrs Elsie Cannon, Wilson's first secretary at Montague Meyer. 'A tall, dark girl, who was photographed with him when he visited the ancient monastry of Zagorsk' in the Soviet Union, she was subjected to a stream of sexual smears and falsehoods. A second rumour involved Mrs Willliams; a third, a revival of the Castle story heard by Dodds-Parker. It was alleged that in May 1947 Wilson had slept with Barbara Castle, his Parliamentary Private Secretary at the Board of Trade, when the two were part of a trade delegation to Canada. It was untrue but variations of the story persisted for many years on the 'cocktail circuit' finding their way into print in only 1987. 'It was an open secret', according to an obscure left journal, 'that Harold Wilson and Barbara Castle were bonking away behind the Cabinet doors late at night in a torrid affair.' Tom Driberg passed on a variation on the same story to his 'contact' at MI5, a 'delighted' Peter Wright. Years later, Castle heard the story and 'found it so bizarre that I realise I was always out of my depth with him [Driberg]'.[12]

Private Eye noted of the Conservative Central Office campaign that 'every newspaper in Fleet Street has been telephoned about it at some time or other during the past few weeks'; and later commented on 'an extraordinary comic opera of varying versions of the smear which are current in different districts and constituencies' passed to them by national newspapers. In the context of this campaign the outburst by Quintin Hogg MP during the 1964 Election campaign was, as *Private Eye* commented at the time, 'a collector's piece . . . of political deception'. At a public meeting on 13 October, Hogg was heckled with shouts of 'What about Profumo'. Irritated, he replied: 'If you can tell me there are no adulterers on the front bench of the Labour Party you can talk to me about Profumo.' Hogg had used this line before. Pincher reports that: 'After the Profumo affair Quintin Hogg had made a front-bench speech about adultery which was so pointed that Wilson went out of his way to assure a private meeting of the Parliamentary Labour Party that his secretary was "as white as snow".' Pincher's informant was George Caunt, a minor official at Transport House who turned against Wilson and was recruited by MI5.[13]

The romantic novelist Barbara Cartland made a similar speech to Hogg's at a local meeting of the Women's Institute. Wilson's friend, John Junor, recalled 'that the speech was pointed in a way which clearly made it a personal attack on Harold Wilson. And, unusually for a Barbara Cartland speech, a copy of it was sent by the Press Association to every newspaper office in London.' The papers, wary of Britain's libel laws, decided against publishing, but the Cartland speech was picked up by the FBI representative in London who passed it on – along with 'dirt' on George Brown – to Washington. Hogg's intervention backfired. London University students gave him a noisy and violent reception at one meeting, chanting 'Smear, smear, smear . . . Profumo . . . Ferranti . . . Rachman . . . We want Wilson.'[14]

On the night he was elected Leader of the Labour Party, Wilson was asked what he would do if he had only a small majority following the General Election. Wilson shrugged, 'Oh, we don't discuss nightmares like that . . . ' As late as eleven-thirty on the day after voting, Wilson was predicting a defeat by one seat. The count on 16 October was a cliff-hanger. It was late in the day when the results finally confirmed that Labour had won with a slim majority of four. Wilson had become the third Labour Prime Minister, at the age of 48, the youngest since Lord Roseberry in 1894; and, until the election of John Major, the youngest this century. Wilson had won power but he had inherited a divided party and a majority which limited his room for manoeuvre. Added to which, the 'secret state' was lined up to thwart his every move.

VII

THE SPECIAL RELATIONSHIP

There was deep-seated hostility in the US intelligence community to the accession to power of Harold Wilson and the Labour Government in 1964.
PETER WRIGHT

BEFORE THE SECOND WORLD WAR, the description of US–UK foreign policies as embodying a 'special relationship' accurately described a network centred around the 'think tanks' (as they later came to be known), the Council on Foreign Relations in the United States and the Royal Institute of International Affairs in the United Kingdom. These two foci were in turn linked to the various regional institutes spread across the (white) Commonwealth. The special relationship was at its firmest during the Second World War, and then declined as US economic interests began moving in on the remnants of the British Empire. The Suez débâcle of 1956 finally showed, even to British supporters of the relationship, that Britain was the junior partner: the US administration started a run on the pound and Eden's expeditionary force simply came to a halt.[1]

During the fifties, Labour became the Party with closest links to the Americans. The Tories were the imperial party, resentful of British decline and of the constant American incursions into her lost Empire: the Labour left was simply 'anti-American'. For the Gaitskellite wing of the Labour Party, however, an alliance with America, especially with the post Cold War generations represented by the Kennedy administration, was seen as being a progressive development. This is cruelly captured in a letter to Arthur Schlesinger from the American historian and part-time foreign policy adviser Richard Neustadt, dated 22 March 1962: 'Hugh Gaitskell talked to St. Antony's [College, Oxford] the other night about his Washington visit, in terms of such warmth, appreciation, even admiration, towards the President and others in Washington, as I rarely dare use hereabouts, for fear of being tagged a propagandist.'[2]

At the heart of the US–UK relationship were the intelligence and military treaties secretly negotiated in the late forties by the British state and approved by the politicians with minimal understanding. The agreements extended the war-

49

time Anglo-American alliance, principally in the area of information exchange; however, increasingly it was the Americans who supplied the hardware because only the USA had the economic surplus to enable its government to spend between 30 and 50 per cent of its tax revenues on its military-nuclear-intelligence expenditure.[3]

In 1957, Conservative Defence Minister Duncan Sandys announced the results of a defence review which committed Britain to a reliance on nuclear weapons for its defence – primarily because nuclear weapons are cheaper than conventional forces ('More bang for a buck'). As usual, policy lagged some way behind reality. Sandys announced the new policy at a time when doubt was growing among strategists about the efficacy of the existing nuclear strategy. The doctrine of the time was 'massive retaliation' of nuclear bombs and missiles on the Soviet Union in response to any Soviet conventional military attack. This made sense as long as the US had the only long-range delivery systems, missiles and bombers based around the Soviet Union, many of which were in Britain (Airstrip 1). However, Sputnik's appearance and the success of the USSR's rocket technology heralded the threat of a Soviet inter-continental ballistic missile (ICBM).

As chance would have it, Sputnik was launched during the meeting of the Bilderberg group, a secretive Anglo-European–American discussion group set up to promote European unity at the onset of the Cold War. The Americans present, reports Denis Healey, were 'flabbergasted at the news'. With Soviet possession of ICBMs, 'massive retaliation' would cease to make sense at all. In effect, such a policy became the 'threat' of US suicide – and in defence of Europe. The dawning Soviet ICBM capability meant that the US military could no longer base their strategy of 'containment' on the central notion of fighting the Red Army to the last European (or Arab or Asian). Some way had to be found to make the NATO deterrent 'threat' credible again. In 1956, Healey, more or less in parallel with Henry Kissinger, co-authored one of the first attempts to produce the theory then known as 'graduated deterrence or response'.[4]

Sandys' policy of reliance on nuclear weapons was not popular with a number of UK military chiefs. More nuclear weapons meant fewer ships and tanks, and theoretical doubts about the usefulness of nuclear weapons fuelled inter-service rivalries for (relatively) limited UK defence funds, causing 'Whitehall battles of a ferocity unknown since the Second World War'. Of the three Chiefs of Staff, Mountbatten and Templer, heads of the Navy and Army respectively, were against the independent British deterrent, with the head of the RAF, whose bombers would deliver the British bomb, in favour of it. The conflict even began to surface in public. On 4 November 1959, General Sir John Cowley, on active service as Comptroller of Munitions, delivering a lecture at the Royal United Services Institute, 'took aim at the entire concept of the British independent deterrent'. For the last time something approaching a rational debate about the direction of defence policy was held in public in Britain.[5]

The manifestly absurd notion that the United States would engage in a mutually destructive nuclear exchange with the Soviet Union in response to *any* kind of Soviet conventional attack reinforced the uncertainty in Conservative minds about the reliability of the US 'nuclear umbrella'. The Tories' determination to retain an independent nuclear deterrent was always based, in part, on mistrust of the United States. But was it conceivable that Britain would ever use – or threaten to use – its nuclear forces without the Americans? Lord Mountbatten, appointed Chief of the Defence Staff in 1958, thought not: 'To use it in retaliation for an attack on Western Europe would surely be to commit national suicide immediately.'[6]

Prompted by the 1957 Sandys defence review, the Labour Party began an internal debate on its defence policy. At its centre were the pro-nuclear Shadow spokesman on Defence, John Strachey, and the anti-nuclear George Wigg. The new nuclear strategic thinking in NATO was being carried into the Labour Party by Denis Healey and Strachey. Strachey had come a long way. Before the war he had been a communist and had later been denounced as a crypto-communist by the Americans. Like Healey, in the late fifties Strachey stayed at the Rand Corporation in the United States. In March 1958, Richard Crossman recorded in his diary an informal discussion on defence which took place in Gaitskell's office. Healey, the Party's defence intellectual, and Strachey, the Shadow Defence Secretary, outlined the new, post 'massive retaliation' thinking. 'The proper sharp division is no longer between conventional and nuclear weapons, but between controllable weapons, including conventional and atomic tactical on the one hand, and uncontrollable thermo-nuclear on the other. According to them, there is a whole range or spectrum of nuclear weapons, from a rifle bullet to a large Hiroshima bomb and John Strachey's theory of graduated deterrence is obviously their accepted doctrine.' This was not, however, a doctrine accepted either by Wigg, who saw the nuclear programme gradually eating away at Britain's conventional forces, or by the left in the Party, who were beginning to see in the newly-formed Campaign for Nuclear Disarmament the focus for their hostility towards the Americans, NATO and weapons of mass destruction.[7]

Although the realities of the 'special relationship' had been exposed at Suez, Harold Macmillan contrived to resuscitate it with the Anglophile John Kennedy, who had taken office in 1960 with a foreign policy administration dominated by east coast Anglophiles. Though Kennedy got on well with Macmillan, the 'special relationship' during those three years was largely based on Kennedy's friendship with the British Ambassador, David Ormsby-Gore, whom Kennedy had known since the war. During the Cuban Missile Crisis Ormsby-Gore actually sat in on National Security Council discussions. His successful penetration of the White House resulted in what Henry Kissinger later described as 'a pattern of consultation so matter-of-factly intimate that it became psychologically impossible to ignore British views. They evolved a habit of meetings so regular that autonomous American action somehow came to violate club rules.'[8]

In the end, diplomatic skills could not substitute for actual power. However fine the social dressing, the real substance of the Anglo-American relationship had become intelligence and nuclear power. The price of the unequal nuclear exchange was paid in diplomatic terms. At its most favourable this could be expressed thus: 'Britain was able to offer in return for US technology her invaluable diplomatic support in a number of contemporary international crises such as those over Quemoy and Matsu, Berlin, the Congo and Laos.' More realistically, the UK became the fig-leaf for American imperialism as well as remaining 'the unsinkable aircraft carrier'. Useful though this was, by 1961 some in the Kennedy administration had concluded that Britain had little to offer in the way of nuclear weapons information, that the minor British nuclear force was little more than a strategic irritant, and that it was no longer in US interests to sustain British nuclear pretensions.[9]

The British had a strategic problem concerning their choice of a delivery system for its warheads. While the US and USSR were developing missiles, British nuclear weapons were entrusted to the so-called V-bomber force, which was almost obsolete by the mid-fifties. In search of a British missile the government turned down an American offer of the Polaris in 1959 (largely because the Navy did not want it) and decided to develop the Blue Streak rocket. The *Evening News* carried a headline in February 1959: 'Blue Streak wins. Go-ahead for 3000 mile missile. Now Macmillan will talk from strength.' Less than a year later the Blue Streak was abandoned: declining Britain could no longer afford the level of arms expenditure required to remain an independent nuclear power. The British state then asked the United States for the Skybolt missiles, at that time being developed for the USAF.[10]

By this time, however, development difficulties had begun to surface with Skybolt. Dean Acheson headed an inquiry into its development for Kennedy. The 1961 report concluded: 'it would be desirable for the British, in the long run, to phase out of the nuclear deterrent business. If the development of Skybolt is not warranted for US purposes alone, the United States should not prolong the life of the V-bomber force by this or other means.' Skybolt was duly cancelled, leaving Britain with an ageing, near obsolete nuclear capacity. Inside the State Department, were a group of 'Europeanists', led by Under Secretary of State George Ball, who opposed Britain's retention of the independent deterrent. They believed that the 'special relationship' had led the US into a series of decisions favouring Britain which were a hindrance to better, more equitable relations with France, Germany and the EEC. The time had come for Britain to relinquish her notional nuclear independence. In May 1962 Defence Secretary Robert McNamara condemned national (i.e. outside NATO control) nuclear forces as 'dangerous' and 'lacking in credibility', stressing the need for the Europeans to provide conventional forces for the 'flexible response strategy'.[11]

Yet despite the opposition within the American administration, at the Nassau meeting in 1962, Macmillan persuaded Kennedy to promise to provide the Polaris missile on condition that it be consigned to NATO control – except under conditions of 'supreme national emergency'. Such an emergency was undefined (and probably undefinable). This was 'a form of words, a concession to British national susceptibilities, and that there were no imaginable circumstances – and no possible way – in which Britain would, in strategic nuclear matters, act independently from America.' Another view is Denis Healey's that Kennedy 'thereby wrecked not only his defence policy, but also a major objective of his foreign policy – to get Britain into the Common Market. For the Polaris deal made it certain de Gaulle would veto Britain's entry.' There were reports that

Macmillan had given the Americans cause for concern during the negotiations for British entry into the EEC by hinting that Britain would be prepared to transfer nuclear weapons design information to the French as the price of British entry. Harold Wilson made this charge in the Commons on 31 January 1963.[12]

Through all this, Wilson pursued a middle way which might hold together the anti- and pro-nuclear wings of his Party. From 1960 onwards he argued that Britain should please the Americans by abandoning the notional 'independence' of the deterrent by beefing up its conventional forces. This was something which the US wanted; the US standing army in Western Europe was very expensive. In Wilson's view, Britain could remain 'Airstrip 1' for the USAF and continue to provide anchorage for the US Navy. In the Blue Streak debate in April 1960, Wilson stated: 'Like so many other rather pathetic individuals whose sense of social prestige outruns their purse, he [Sandys] is left in the situation at the end of the day of the man who dare not admit that he cannot afford a television set and who knows that he cannot afford it and who just puts up the aerial instead. That is our situation, because without an independent means of delivery, the independent nuclear deterrent, the right hon. Gentleman's cheap, short cut to national greatnesss, is an empty illusion.'[13]

On becoming Party leader in 1963, Wilson along with his Shadow Foreign Minister, Patrick Gordon Walker, posed as the friends of America: the extraordinary popularity of John F. Kennedy could make the President a very useful electoral ally. Labour proposed re-negotiating the Macmillan–Kennedy agreement signed at Nassau in 1962 which promised Britain delivery of the Polaris missiles, implying (but not stating) that the British deterrent might be abandoned. On US visits Wilson (April 1963 and March 1964) and Patrick Gordon Walker (February 1964) both reiterated that, under Labour, Britain's defence priorities would be re-ordered, away from nuclear weapons towards conventional expenditure. In April 1963, on his first visit to Washington as leader of the Opposition, Wilson told the National Press Club: 'Every American pressman I meet asks whether a Labour government would repudiate the Nassau Agreement. I don't like the word "repudiate" which implies breaking faith with a partner, and I have my doubts about the enthusiasm with which the US Administration approached the Nassau Agreement. My answer is that a Labour government's first task would be to survey the defence position we inherit, to survey the shambles, some say, then to enter into discussions with our American partners about Nassau and about our broader approach to NATO. In view of our policy on deterrents, we should then renegotiate, I have the heard the word "denegotiate", the agreement.'[14]

How convincing this posture of Wilson's looked to the Americans is unclear. Britain's Ambassador in Washington wrote to Macmillan: 'Unfortunately those who had already met him dislike him, and those who have not distrust him.' As we have seen, sections of the US intelligence community had been persuaded by the KGB defector Golitsyn on his return from a visit to MI5 in July 1963 that Wilson might be a Soviet 'asset'. In September 1963 Golitsyn saw John McCone, the Kennedy-appointed head of the CIA. What Golitsyn told McCone is in dispute. In one version he claimed Wilson was an 'agent' and that he believed Hugh Gaitskell had been killed by the KGB. McCone wondered why he had heard nothing from MI5 about this and asked London for background. MI5 head Roger Hollis wrote back telling McCone that there was nothing to it. Head of CIA Counter Intelligence James Angleton, was not prepared to let the matter drop. 'At the behest of some eight to ten agency counter-intelligence officers, John McCone went to see President Kennedy in 1963.' This was a significant section of the CIA's counter-intelligence staff and McCone, new to the post, could hardly ignore them. According to McCone's staff officer, Walter Elder, the CIA chief in fact did not hear the 'KGB killed Gaitskell' theory but did hear of 'unease about [Wilson's] relationships through the International Socialist movement'. This would make bureaucratic sense. Angleton did not have enough to go on to take the 'Wilson-is-KGB' story to McCone but wanted action. The 'International Socialists' was a semi-legitimate cause for concern: it was the Cold War; the US Government was spending nearly half its annual tax income on it. McCone could take that to the President. John Kennedy, who had been a dilettante student at the London School of Economics before the war and knew something of British socialists, appears not to have taken it seriously. 'If you have specific proof, you pursue leads . . . In the meantime, as President of the US, I will deal with Wilson if he becomes Prime Minister of the UK. And let's hear nothing more about it until something crops up.'[15]

Wilson had high hopes of John Kennedy and saw a similarity in their positions: young men taking over from the stuffy old ones. Prime Minister Harold Macmillan watched Wilson address the 1963 Labour Party Conference: 'A very brilliant and effective "key-note" speech . . . a "new vision" is developed in a Jack Kennedy sort of style. It was excellently done, if fundamentally dishonest.' There were some fairly silly attempts – some by Wilson himself – to extend the analogy: Wilson's first 100 days, etc. The assassination at Dealey Plaza on 22 November 1963 ended those fantasies and after only two months of being leader of the Labour Party, Wilson was faced with President Lyndon Baines Johnson, a man who had spent his career in pork-barrel domestic politics and had little experience of foreign affairs.[16]

In the house journal of the US foreign policy élite, *Foreign Affairs*, in April 1964, Shadow Foreign Secretary Patrick Gordon Walker made a renewed pitch for Britain to remain the superpower's special friend: 'We do not wish simply to cancel it [the Nassau Agreement]. We want to negotiate a far-reaching new arrangement with Washington . . . We want to participate fully, intimately and without limit in the formulation of the ideas, policy and strategy that together make up the doctrine upon which any particular decision of the President must depend. This would be to ask a lot from America. But in exchange we would recognize and support the ultimate nuclear monopoly of the United States in the West.'

Quite what Gordon Walker meant, let alone whether or not such a policy could be sold to the Parliamentary Labour Party, was never tested. As the election loomed the entire complex of issues boiled down to whether or not Labour would abandon the independent nuclear deterrent. The key word was 'independent'. Just before the 1964 General Election, the *Economist* noted:

'One's guess nowadays is that if the Labour Party came to power next month it might well decide to go ahead and build Polaris submarines (if they could not be converted into hunter killers) and then try to solve the problem by putting the submarines under some joint allied command.'[17]

Following Labour's election triumph, the Cabinet met at Chequers on 21 and 22 November, a meeting described in the tabloid press as 'the weekend of the crunch'. Against building the Polaris submarines were George Wigg, Lord Chalfont and George Brown. Lord Chalfont, former *Times* Defence Correspondent Alun Gwynne-Jones, had taken the anti-nuclear side during the debates of 1958–60. He had been knighted by Wilson to enable him to sit in the Lords and thus be Minister for Disarmament.[18]

Wigg was for more conventional forces, and opposed to the new NATO doctrine of controlled escalation which Healey was promoting within NATO. The 'antis' were 'overwhelmed by Healey and the professional advisers'. More accurately, perhaps, they were overwhelmed by the news that, as Wilson put it in his 1971 account, 'the production of the submarines was well past the point of no return; there could be no question of cancelling them except at inordinate cost'. Three and half years later, in Cabinet, Barbara Castle's (unchallenged) recollection was 'that *we had been told* the cost of cancelling the four Polaris would be as great as keeping them on, so all we could do was abandon the fifth, which we readily did' (emphasis added). In one variant the financial bind is attributed to Conservative machinations, 'in order to thwart Labour's policy . . . [they] made contractual agreements so inflexible that compensation costs would exceed any political savings from cancellation'. Despite wide and continuing circulation, this version of events is false.[19]

'In fact the Treasury had been holding back on authorising new expenditure during 1964 until the election was over. By the time Labour came to power, £40 million had been spent and another £270 million had been committed on all aspects of the programme. The net cost of foreclosing would have been £35–40 million . . . this was not prohibitive.' The truth was that on getting the official figures 'it soon became clear to Healey and Harold Wilson that the Polaris deal had been a good one'. As Healey admitted later, 'the Polaris force was tremendous value for money *in political terms*' (emphasis added). However, for political reasons this could not be revealed. And so, according to Healey, Wilson came up with the idea of telling the Cabinet that the Polaris deal was 'past the point of no return'. The Cabinet was 'bounced' by its leaders.[20]

The Cabinet was misled by Wilson, Healey and Gordon Walker, but it hardly mattered. With a parliamentary majority of 4 behind them, and a sizeable chunk of the Parliamentary Labour Party being pro-nuclear, the Labour Cabinet were never going to vote for a non-nuclear policy. Told that cancelling Polaris would be too expensive, they took the sign-posted way out, cancelling one of the submarines to placate the left of the Party. '[N]obody at senior levels in Whitehall really expected the Wilson Government to turn Britain into a non-nuclear power.'[21]

Nuclear weapons provided leverage not with the Soviet Union but with the Americans. Wilson confirmed this to Peter Hennessy after he retired. 'We might need to restrain the Americans . . . And it also helped us in our general negotiations with America on other things not in the field of foreign affairs but in economic co-operation or something of that sort you see? In order that they could get us to agree to some of the things they wanted, we got them to agree to a few things we wanted, like money.'[22]

By constantly reiterating that the deterrent was not independent, and by the symbolic cancellation of one of the Polaris submarines, Wilson persuaded the left of the Party not to make waves. Looking for Britain to give up the British deterrent, the left were persuaded by Wilson that to give up pretending that it was independent would be nearly as good.

Two weeks after the decision to buy four of the five submarines Wilson, Healey and a mixed crew of top British military brass went to Washington. Another London package of disinformation about Wilson winged its way across to President Johnson. The London FBI liaison officer with MI5 and Special Branch, Charles Bates, had been active during the Profumo Affair checking possible American leads to the story. MI5 or Special Branch – Bates can no longer remember which – passed him stories about Wilson and Marcia Williams. At first Bates refused to believe them but his British contacts insisted that he pass them across the Atlantic to J. Edgar Hoover. 'I'd sent him some information on Harold Wilson right after he came in about him and Marcia. Hoover said, "That was terrific".' Hoover then passed the smears to the President.[23]

One of the great exponents of the politics of bribe and smear, L.B.J. had a serious taste for sleaze. The Wilson–Williams story was the kind of information he was familiar with. He asked Hoover – who asked Bates – for more. Bates did not believe the stories but, 'My thinking was, when you get into negotiations with anybody, if you know more than they know, you're in a damned good position.' On 30 November 1964, the President's Special Assistant, McGeorge Bundy, had also received a summary of the Wilson smears from Richard Helms, the CIA's Deputy Director of Plans (covert action). The document contained details of the Barbara Cartland and Quintin Hogg speeches and gossip from several prominent London lawyers. An informant on the *Daily Herald*, one of the few newspapers to support the Labour Party, had also offered information to his CIA contact. How far these stories affected L.B.J.'s perception of Wilson is hard to ascertain. But when Wilson, Healey and the military brass arrived for their crucial first visit in November 1964 to discuss Polaris and the rest of the main nuclear agenda, L.B.J. found Wilson 'too ordinary, too much like other politicians with whom L.B.J. had dealt, and took an almost instant dislike to him'. Mrs Williams subsequently found herself unwelcome in America. The Prime Minister's Principal Private Secretary, Derek Mitchell, insisted she could accompany Wilson only provided she travelled as Mrs Wilson's maid. Johnson then refused to allow her to attend restricted meetings.[24]

In Washington there were conflicting views about the new Labour Government. Within the nuclear establishment, for example, there was suspicion of the Government's intentions which resulted in a 'temporary breakdown in Anglo-American [nuclear] technical exchanges'. Sections of the CIA and the east coast foreign policy networks had become very familiar and comfortable with the

Gaitskellite wing of the Labour Party in the 1950s and preferred that version of the Party to the Conservatives. However, even amongst the liberal wing of the US secret state there must have been some irritation that having so comprehensively penetrated and co-opted the anti-socialist wing of the Labour Party, the Party had fallen into the hands of someone who had avoided these covert postwar US operations, who had been been travelling east rather than west during the Cold War. The hostility was personal, largely specific to Wilson; and largely to be found among the US intelligence community's right-wing extremists, mostly – as in Britain – within the counter-intelligence sections who in 1964 opened a file on Wilson code-named 'Oatsheaf'.[25]

PART TWO

1964–70

VIII

WILSON AND THE SPOOKS

In the bitter Labour Party struggles over nuclear disarmament in the early 1960s, Wilson had become convinced that the Security Service's interest in the party factions went some way beyond the requirments of National Security.

SUNDAY TIMES, 'INSIGHT', 1977

WILSON WAS NOT an intelligence 'insider'. He had no direct experience of the world of 'spooks'. His closest contact with the intelligence agencies had been in the forties when as President of the Board of Trade he received security briefings. When he finally did enter the secret corridors of Whitehall, meeting the Chief of MI6, Dick White, Wilson put on the vestments of secrecy like a true patriot.

In July 1963, a security row blew up when it was announced that Kim Philby, formerly 'attached to the Foreign Office', had defected to the Soviet Union. Wilson requested an appointment with the then Prime Minister, Harold Macmillan, and in one of those arcane rituals common to the British state, a meeting was arranged 'behind the Speaker's Chair' on Privy Council terms. This meant that the contents of the conversation could not be passed on to Wilson's colleagues. Macmillan reveals in his diaries that he asked Dick White to give Wilson 'the whole facts'. 'While what was public knowledge could not have justified the manifest failure of the Secret Service to keep Philby under control, one simple fact I was given made sense of the story. I was satisfied and felt it my duty to say so in the House without giving any reason, and to ask my Hon. Friends to let it go.'[1]

To ensure completely that the Opposition leader shared his views on the 'national interest', Macmillan convened a second meeting on 11 July. 'I had an hour with Harold Wilson', Macmillan wrote in his diary, 'and tried to explain to him how the so-called Security Services really worked. It seemed to me right to do so, and he took it quite well.'[2]

One Labour backbencher, Niall MacDermot, knew all about Philby and his true importance as a defector. MacDermot had served in MI5 and met MI6's

61

then head of Section V during the war. When MacDermot began to raise the matter in the House of Commons, Wilson cut him off by suggesting that there were 'issues which cannot be discussed across the floor of this House'. Next day, Macmillan recorded how grateful he was for Wilson's 'high sense of responsibility'.[3]

The slim knowledge which Wilson did possess regarding the intelligence world was filtered through George Wigg. Colonel Wigg had served in the Army for eighteen years and had been the Parliamentary Private Secretary to a Labour Minister of War. As a backbencher, Wigg was known as the Army's watchdog in the House of Commons. Although he had never actually been in the intelligence game and was really an amateur, he did possess a high degree of experience in the defence field and held strong views on security and patriotism.

The Philby affair reinforced Wigg's contempt for MI6, views which were encouraged by Henry Kerby, a maverick Tory MP who had served in MI6 during the war. Kerby believed the secret service had been deeply penetrated by the KGB. MI6 was doing nothing about it, he suggested, because the service was run by 'unfrocked dons, misfits, oddities, queers and drunks' and the 'Foreign Office boys' who were 'rogering their own rectums'. Kerby trusted Wigg's patriotism more than he did that of his own party and the gossip he gave him encouraged Wigg towards a sympathetic view of MI5. What Wigg did not know was that Kerby was being run as an 'agent' within the House of Commons by MI5.[4]

A former defence correspondent and backbench colleague of Wigg, Ray Fletcher, says that Wigg saw the difference between MI5 and MI6 'as a class thing'. Wigg told him: 'Some of the MI5 boys had been to Secondary schools but the MI6 lot were all Oxbridge types.' Fletcher believes that while Wigg was not perfect, 'he did an honest job but was later the victim of MI6 smears'. This is an early example of the recurring battle between MI5 and MI6, one of the themes dominating British intelligence.[5]

Not long after the 1964 General Election, Labour's campaign manager, George Caunt, informed Wilson that MI5 were recruiting within the Party. 'Some of these were MPs and others were insinuated into Transport House.' Caunt revealed that the previous year he himself had been approached as a possible 'sub-agent' by a Party official who was already working for MI5. 'I knew it!', Wilson replied. A Permanent Secretary responsible for the security services, Sir Dennis Greenhill, later confirmed that 'one of our best men was working at Transport House'.[6]

The Labour leader was ignorant of how exactly MI5 was controlled, but then so were most people. In June 1963, during the debate on the Profumo Affair, Wilson asked, before the Denning Report, 'did anyone believe that the Home Secretary was the Minister responsible for security?' As the scandal unfolded, MI5 became increasingly concerned about Wilson's sharp criticism of their role. In the House of Commons, Wilson pointed out that 'the first the security services knew or even guessed about this very big security risk was when a Sunday newspaper told them a few months ago. If this is true this would imply that the £60 million spent on these services under the right hon. Gentleman's Premiership have been less productive in this vitally important case than the security services of the *News of the World*.'[7]

When Labour took power, 'MI5 was in a state of morale-sapping crisis'. As well as the legacy of the Profumo Affair and other security scandals, the internal inquiries into the Deputy Director-General, Graham Mitchell – codenamed 'Peters' – and into the Director-General, Roger Hollis, were at their peak. There was a strong belief among some senior members of the security service that MI5 had been penetrated at a high level by Soviet Intelligence. Mitchell and Hollis became the chief suspects. Although Macmillan had been briefed, Hollis had no intention of informing the new Prime Minister about the molehunts taking place inside MI5. The feeling within the office was that 'had the operation led to a confession it would have compromised the entire organisation and the Cabinet would probably have been obliged to disband MI5, if only to restore the confidence of the Americans'.[8]

The secret state had never been on the Labour Party's agenda in the post-war period. In the mid-fifties a small group of left-wingers, notably Benn Levy, had tried to initiate a debate about the security services but failed to arouse much interest. The Party as a whole knew nothing and cared not at all. The idea that the permanent government existed, let alone that it was hostile to Labour, would have produced incredulity in 1964 in all but a handful of the Parliamentary Labour Party. The notion prevailed that the civil service was a politically neutral machine which would do the Party's bidding. In any case, Wilson had a tiny majority and was in no position to do anything radical – even if he had wanted to. Although Wilson's suspicions about MI5 are well documented, at that time he didn't realise how big this area would turn out to be.[9]

The Denning Report on the Profumo Affair had discreetly lifted the veil on one small section of the secret state. It published, for the first time, the 1952 Maxwell-Fyfe directive, issued by Conservative Home Secretary, David Maxwell-Fyfe, which set out the relationship between the security service and the Government. Wilson thought Denning's Report showed that there was 'still too much laxity in the operation of security procedures, with all too obvious confusion of where responsibility lay'. Wilson, like many commentators, had been surprised to learn that the Director-General of MI5 'was personally responsible to the Home Secretary. The Security Service is not, however, a part of the Home Office.' An additional directive issued by the previous Cabinet Secretary, Lord Normanbrook, revealed that the Director-General could 'turn to a senior Permanent Secretary for advice and assistance on the policy aspects of his work'. However, on 'matters of supreme importance and delicacy, the Head of the service should always be able, at his initiation, to arrange a personal interview with the Prime Minister.'[10]

The Principal Private Secretary at No. 10, Derek Mitchell, who had special duties in the security field, told Wilson that he had not known of this instruction – confirming Wilson's perception of the British state as being run with 'nonchalant amateurism in a world of ruthless professionalism'. Wigg, who knew nothing of the molehunts within MI5, told his friend Chapman Pincher, 'he had been assured that some of MI5's apparent failures in the past had really been due to

Whitehall delays in acting on its warnings'. Someone, possibly Kerby, had had a quiet word in Wigg's ear. Wigg passed this on to Wilson and criticism of MI5 was quietly replaced by criticism of the civil servants.[11]

Wilson attacked the cosy relationship between civil servants and MI5 during the debate on the Denning Report. He also commented on Macmillan and the Government's lack of knowledge of Profumo's affair with Christine Keeler: 'Why was there no approach to the Prime Minister on the matter, which, it cannot be denied was a matter of "supreme importance and delicacy"?' Defending himself, Home Secretary Henry Brooke told the Commons: 'frankly, if the Security Service . . . pick up any information about Parliamentary private lives, I do not want them to come and tell me, if it is the fact that in their considered judgement there is no security interest involved.' Wilson, however, did not trust the 'considered judgement' of the amateurs: and he had a point. The Conservative Government had fallen partly because Brooke had been kept in ignorance of the facts.[12]

The Profumo Affair had begun in the summer of 1961 when War Minister, John Profumo, met a 'call-girl' Christine Keeler. Unfortunately for Profumo, she was also friendly with a Soviet intelligence officer, Eugene Ivanov, who was the subject of a 'honeytrap' operation run by MI5. Concerned that their operation could be undermined by the appearance of Profumo, MI5 warned the War minister about his involvement with Keeler. In July 1961, MI5 consulted Normanbrook, the Cabinet Secretary, who then failed to pass the information about Profumo's affair on to the Prime Minister. Wilson had stumbled on a crucial secret, namely the fact that the Cabinet Office, not the Prime Minister's Office, had overall control of the security service and, crucially, the flow of information to the Prime Minister. The Normanbrook directive had placed control firmly in the hands of the civil servants and the permanent government and, as one writer commented in 1965, 'The Maxwell-Fyfe directive of 1952 has, in the end, done little to alter the pre-1952 position.'[13]

The third person seen by a new Prime Minister when he takes office is the Director-General of MI5, 'who arrives and departs discreetly, after, equally discreetly, leaving a dossier on the background of some Parliamentary colleagues which the new PM might like to read before making final ministerial dispositions'. According to former intelligence officers: 'In the months before a General Election, the Security Service always calls up and reviews its files on existing and likely new MPs. Peers are also kept under the same, usually passive, surveillance.' The dossier contains the results of this surveillance, which is always maintained over political leaders and MPs of all parties. Much of the information is tittle-tattle, regularly passed on about the personal life and politics of all potential appointees to ministerial office. This, as Duncan Campbell points out, does 'place MI5 in a particularly powerful position to influence events.'[14]

Wilson found distasteful this intrusion into colleagues' private lives and the paranoia it created amongst them. Only ten days after the election, Tony Benn and a member of the Political Office at No. 10, John Allen, agreed that they both felt weighed down by the security side. 'We all had the feeling our letters were being opened and our telephones bugged – though we suspected the security people were as inefficient as the government departments over which we had some control.'[15]

Although he was not prepared to undertake a root and branch reform, the Prime Minister did attempt to corral MI5 in one crucial area – surveillance of Members of Parliament. Wilson told Hollis that 'he must seek his personal approval before making any investigations involving any member of either the Commons or the Lords'. MI5 was specifically forbidden to carry out any form of surveillance including 'telephone tapping, the opening of letters, examination of bank accounts and the other routine procedures applied to suspects'.[16]

Wilson knew that there 'had been tapping of MPs' telephones up to the time Labour came into office; second, that this had covered members of more than one party'. He found the tapping of MPs' phones – mostly from the Labour Party – 'undesirable'. Wilson inherited the rules about telephone tapping recommended by the 1957 'Committee of Privy Councillors appointed to Inquire into the Interception of Communications': namely, 'A Member of Parliament is not to be distinguished from an ordinary member of the public, so far as the interception of communications is concerned'. Wilson sought Wigg's advice 'on reviewing the practice about tapping Members' telephones when we came into office. He therefore shares such responsibility as I can take for the present arrangements.' Wilson argued that 'there is always a difficult balance between the requirements of democracy in a free society and the requirements of security . . . I decided on balance – and the arguments were very fine – that the balance should be tipped the other way'.[17]

Wilson is said to have warned Hollis that he would not accept the evidence of defectors as a basis for any investigations of MPs. According to Pincher: 'These restrictions, which were partly conditioned by Wilson's belief that MI5 was anti-Labour and over-zealous to identify any left-wing Labour Parliamentarian as pro-communist, were confirmed to Hollis in writing and made known to the MI5 staff.'[18]

Finally, having learned from the Profumo episode that 'ministerial responsibility was blurred', Wilson issued 'a new directive'. Using the language of the Normanbrook directive, in cases of 'supreme importance and delicacy' the Prime Minister, not just the Permanent Secretary, would be informed. On such matters, in future, the head of MI5 should deal directly with the Prime Minister or with Wilson's final innovation, his security adviser, George Wigg.[19]

Taken together, Wilson's decisions amounted to a serious attempt to protect his Government against an embarrassing fiasco like Profumo and against MI5's search for dirt on the Parliamentary Party. The formulation of security policy by a democratically elected Prime Minister, and not by the permanent government in the shape of the Cabinet Secretary, was a radical break with the past and was not well received by either MI5 or the civil service. 'They weren't a bit happy', says Charles Bates, the London based FBI liaison officer with MI5. 'It restricted their movements and the cases they were handling.' It was felt to be 'too much of a political intrusion into the operation of the Security Service'.[20]

Unfortunately, Wilson's attempts to curtail MI5's activities did not work.

IX

WIGGERY-POKERY

'You know that I have good sources . . . '
GEORGE WIGG

THE APPOINTMENT of George Wigg as Paymaster General, special assistant to the Prime Minister with 'a wide-ranging brief, to interfere in a great variety of ad hoc matters', was a 'bombshell' to Government Whips Edward Short and Herbert Bowden. It was, says Short, 'a recipe which set all our alarm bells ringing'. Wilson appreciated that the new post would create difficulties. He told the Chief Whip that 'a formula would have to be drafted to define his duties . . . because he anticipated a good deal of Tory interest in the appointment – and how right he was.'[1]

According to Wilson, Wigg's 'remit, which I put in writing and circulated to all the departments concerned, was not to cut across departmental responsibilities, but nevertheless it charged him with the duty of keeping me fully informed, and at the earliest moment, of any developments of which I ought to know.' He was to have special responsibilities in the field of security, acting as linkman between the Prime Minister and MI5.[2]

Wigg's appointment was not received well within the civil service. Wigg later admitted: 'My arrival at No. 10 was neither understood nor accepted by the Private Office.' He did make an effort to learn their ways but the 'No. 10 Civil Servants showed their displeasure at his appointment by allocating him a private secretary who was a higher executive officer – a very lowly rank for a minister's secretary.' They also shunted him off into a small inconvenient room away from the Cabinet Office. He had to fight to get back in – in fact, by the back door.[3]

Wigg was called 'security overlord' and 'spymaster' but what did he actually do? Wigg himself was suitably anodyne in his memoir: 'He [Wilson] wanted me to assist him in a personal capacity on a range of subjects connected with public and Parliamentary business, and to help him with security matters.' Wigg was given a number of official jobs, including acting as Government co-ordinator on Party publicity and as Chair of the Liaison Committee with Transport House, and he played an important role as a member of Wilson's Political Office. 'It was valuable', Short believed, 'to have at least one of the Prime Minister's confidants who possessed a good deal of down-to-earth political nous.'[4]

Wigg's role as security link-man entailed giving Wilson 'the earliest possible warning of any imminent security scandals so that they could be eliminated, if possible. Failing that, the Prime Minister would be able to assure Parliament that he had not been ignorant of the position, as Macmillan had been with Profumo.' Wigg added that 'both he and Wilson were convinced that the Tories, who were enraged about their part in the Profumo case, would do all they could to exact revenge, preferably finding a security case involving a Labour Minister or MP.'[5]

It was a sensible assessment. In July 1963, the *Spectator* – owned by one of Quintin Hogg's supporters – thundered that McCarthyism 'in its occasional collapses into political squalor, had never exhibited anything so despicable as the spectacle of Mr Harold Wilson leading his entire following away from serious matters to shuffle and jostle round the dirty linen of Miss Christine Keeler's various beds in the hope of finding some easy way to power'. Described as 'that industrious garbage collector', Wigg took out a writ for libel.[6]

The campaign against Wigg continued throughout his period in office with the occasional question about his activities tossed into the House of Commons arena by a Tory backbencher. 'It got off to a muted start', says Short, with accusations that Wigg was 'in many ways a very unsatisfactory character'. In fact, Colonel Wigg was a patriot of whom the Conservatives could be proud. He once told Alec McDonald, MI5's head of counter-espionage, 'the one thing he couldn't stand was traitors, and if he had his way, he'd kick them off Beachy Head.'[7]

Wigg's appointment was partly a response to the security scandals, such as that of the homosexual Admiralty Clerk, John Vassall, which revealed a laxity in security in the civil service and reflected badly on the Government. In an attempt to prevent this happening to the new Labour Government, Wigg deployed his talents 'to strengthen security measures'. Wilson told him that 'he was to satisfy himself, and me, that departmental procedures were adequate for the task laid on them; Wigg said that his 'task was to see a Minister and, with his approval, discuss security arrangements with those of his officials responsible for the Department's security' – that is, with the department's in-house MI5 personnel. Richard Crossman, with his war-time experience in Intelligence, backed Wigg to the hilt. The implications alarmed Tony Benn. 'Dick is a fierce security man and said that, as a Minister, he would think it right that his phones should be tapped and all his letters opened.'[8]

The truth is that Wigg was side-tracked into the relatively unimportant and – from MI5's point of view – harmless area of protective security. In carrying out his tasks in this field, Wigg liaised with the Director of C Branch of MI5, Anthony Simkins, a future Deputy Director-General, and, after 1965, Michael Hanley, a future Director-General. 'The Security Service,' the 1971 Franks Committee on the reform of Official Secrets Act revealed, 'plays a very considerable part in giving advice to Government Departments on the measures they ought to take for the protection of secrets.' Hanley informed the Committee that protective security covered 'regulations which regulate the behaviour of those who have access to security information, vetting, education in security, rules for handling classified information and the physical protection of information, locks and safes, guards etc.' Wigg's mundane work explains Pincher's comment that though his appointment was 'ill received at first, the Security Service was grateful for his attentions as nobody had taken much interest in it before', and Wigg's that 'we steadily built up the status and quality of the Security Service'.[9]

Lord Radcliffe's Committee Report of 1962 on 'Security Procedures' had recommended that 'the team of Security Advisers should be strengthened', which meant an increase in the size of C Branch. The élite counter-intelligence officers in MI5 regarded the lowly C branch with disdain but the recommendation was well received by Hollis who 'was particularly sensitive about this issue having served as the post-war Director of C Division [Branch]'. Wigg had found an ally – 'a real professional'.[10]

The old soldier Wigg thus spent most of his time not looking over people's shoulders at MI5 headquarters but stalking his natural home, the corridors of the Defence Departments. 'Both the security services, and the departments, especially Defence', wrote Wilson, 'welcomed his intervention, and a lot of necessary changes were made and procedures brought up to date.' Wilson wrote 'with some pride' that his security overlord 'had discovered about 3,000 airmen who had not been positively vetted when they should have been'. Wigg, says Edward Short, 'was responsible for major improvements, particularly in the Army.'[11]

It was all run-of-the-mill stuff; however, there was one sensitive area in C Division. Though the vetting process itself was carried out by the Ministry of Defence Personnel Security Investigating Unit (PSIU), which is responsible for vetting civil servants throughout Whitehall, MI5 supplied information and collated the files. Negative vetting is solely concerned with political allegiances and membership of subversive organisations, whereas positive vetting looks at 'character defects'. The 1955 Conference of Privy Councillors listed these 'failings' as 'drunkenness, addiction to drugs, homosexuality or any loose living'. As Wigg and Wilson had consistently said, Profumo's relationship with Christine Keeler was a security issue since it opened him up to the possibility of blackmail. This was the background for later claims of Tory MPs such as Jonathan Aitken that 'the Security Service would no longer engage in dubious fishing expeditions of the kind that Mr George Wigg persuaded the service to indulge in when he was in some way in charge of the Security Service in the 1960s with results that were at times unfair to some of his colleagues in this House.'[12]

Although swimming in these murky waters was bound to lead to problems, Wilson and Wigg thought it necessary. They knew that the Tories were watching and waiting to pounce on any indiscretion by a Labour Minister. However, Wilson was not prepared to go as far as Wigg in bringing MI5 into the process. He had little trust in their integrity. 'Wigg wanted Ministers to be positively vetted too', Benn learned, 'but Harold Wilson had refused.' There were practical difficulties. 'The main reason for the immunity of Ministers to positive vetting is that the process takes too much time.'[13]

Wilson thought that there was little need for positive vetting of Ministers. Most senior Cabinet Ministers are made Privy Councillors before they achieve high office through service in junior appointments and, according to Pincher, 'the oath they take when achieving that honour is sufficient security cover'. The oath, dating back to 1250, states that Councillors 'have a responsibility to be true and faithful servants of her Majesty, to defend all pre-eminences against foreign prelates, potentates and so on.' It concludes: 'I will keep secret all Matters committed and revealed unto me', from which, as Peter Hennessy points out, 'Like the Mafia's system of omerta, only the grave can bring release.' Benn had the Oath of Office administered to him when he became a minister. 'You do nothing except stand there with your hand raised while it is read to you. You don't even have to assent. But, with the Lord President being present, it apparently constituted a binding oath.' The former Labour Cabinet minister, David Owen, revealed that: 'It has been agreed with the Americans over many decades that they accept people who are members of the Privy Council as having been, in effect, positively vetted. That was the compromise achieved when we had the problem of dealing with security information between the United States and ourselves and there was a refusal of positive vetting for Members of Parliament.'[14]

Instead of the positive vetting process, 'every minister on first appointment is briefed by a senior MI5 officer about the ever-present threat of espionage and the Whitehall system of protective security opposing it.' The Foreign, Home and Defence Secretaries were seen by Hollis. Benn was briefed by Dick Thistleth- waite, a senior officer who had been the MI5 link-man with the FBI at the time of the Burgess–Maclean affair. 'He went through all the material that is in the security services' book, *Their Trade is Treason* [sic: *Treachery*].' The fifty-nine- page classified book, prepared by Thistlethwaite, warned that KGB 'spies are with us all the time. They are interested in everything – defence secrets, scientific secrets, political decisions, economic facts – even people's characters, in order to recruit more spies.' Benn found the briefing 'a most unattractive hour and a half. This man, though very intelligent, was deep in the heart of the James Bond world and whatever else one may think about espionage and counter- espionage there is no morality in it either way.' Thistlethwaite went on to head MI5's counter-subversion F Branch.[15]

Wigg acted as the watchdog, sniffing out potential scandals before the Tories got a whiff of them. Although he did, on occasion, use the services of MI5 and, in one particular instance, discussed below, in a disgraceful manner, most of his information came by his own efforts through his old contacts and links with the Whips' office. This was an excellent source of information as the Chief Whip is 'aware of almost everything in the lives of his fellow MPs'. He is automatically entitled to a peerage and membership of the Privy Council and hence subject to its oath of absolute secrecy. 'This is because', revealed former Chief Whip John Silkin, 'the secrets with which they have been entrusted, and which none of them has ever divulged, put them in an unique position – even, in some cases, giving them knowledge that even Prime Ministers do not share.' When Ted Short became Chief Whip in 1964, he discovered the Conservative Whips' 'dirt book' which contained 'unsavoury personal items about Members'. Short 'gave strict instructions that no such book was to be kept in future.' Not only that, according to John Silkin, 'Short's first action as Chief Whip was to burn it.'[16]

Some of the gossip which Wigg picked up centred on the Tory Party, though there is little evidence that he used it. In 1965, when Edward Heath was elected Leader of the Conservative Party, Wigg was fed a smear by his Tory MP informer, Henry Kerby. Kerby told him that Heath was a homosexual who had in the past had an affair with the Third Secretary at the Swedish Embassy. Wigg told Peter Shore, a member of the Kitchen Cabinet, 'I could destroy Heath given three hours.' Shore asked him what he meant: 'George replied he could destroy anyone within three hours including Peter.' David Leigh says the story 'was duly fed to MI5, whose members recalled it later when Heath became Prime Minister and showed distaste for MI5's style of work.' It is more probable that MI5 had already fed the story to their 'agent' Kerby.[17]

'We had no security or indeed any governmental scandals when he [Wigg] was in office', says Edward Short. 'I know that he headed off a number of both varieties by scenting them before they materialised and taking the appropriate action.' One potential problem involved a Labour MP with strong Middle East interests who 'had inadvertently become caught up in an international plot to assassinate the Shah of Iran . . . a plot to assassinate a powerful and friendly head of state was out of my league. I decided that it was made to measure for the Paymaster General . . . [and] it was dealt with solely by George Wigg with great skill and discretion.'[18]

Though there was a certain legitimacy in the Paymaster General nosing into the private lives of his colleagues, 'his interest in one, who had a regular mistress, aroused the animosity even of Tory MPs'. Leading Tories induced Wigg to 'desist under threat of exposure in the House' and Wilson had to privately apologise to the Cabinet Minister whose 'love life had been the subject of over-zealous police prying'. The minister was Fred Peart, who was responsible for Agriculture, Fisheries and Food. Peart, who died in 1988, was involved in an extra-marital affair with a full-time Labour Party worker. Word of the affair spread and Wigg became increasingly worried about the risks he was running. When warnings failed to finish the liaison, Wigg took matters further. According to a reliable source, Wigg, whose interest was horse-racing, took Peart's young lady to the races. It is alleged that on the same day MI5 burgled her flat and stole a batch of love letters between the two lovers. Peart was presented with the evidence and warned that he had to stop the affair.[19]

The actions of Wilson and Wigg in this period were almost entirely the result of their experience during the Profumo Affair. It had been Wigg's dogged pursuit of Profumo which had brought the affair into the open. The scandal had nearly brought down the Conservative government and had helped pave the way for Labour's election success the following year. They learned then the damage security scandals could cause and resolved to prevent them happening to Labour. Unfortunately, they did not know enough about the British secret state to make their bureaucratic changes effective. Issuing directives is one thing; ensuring that they are followed up is another matter. Their success during the Profumo Affair with their own private intelligence operation gave them a self-confidence which was not justified.

X

THE KITCHEN CABINET

*Unremitting press comments, including unwarrantable invasions of
personal and family privacy have been addressed uniquely, to my
appointees.*
HAROLD WILSON

THE PRIME MINISTER'S Political Office, people whose loyalty was to the
Party and the leader, not to the Crown or Parliament, was an important and
unpopular innovation. It was vigorously opposed by the civil service and, to a
lesser extent, by Wilson's closest adviser, George Wigg. According to Marcia
Williams, Wigg 'wanted the Civil Service to carry on all the work that was
necessary and give all the advice needed. Yet what would have happened without
the creation of a Political Office?' Wilson would have been left to the mercy of
civil servants, 'mostly very senior men almost completely out of touch with
Labour politicians and the Labour government after thirteen years of uninter-
rupted Conservative government'; and, presumably, in Wigg's vision, himself.[1]

Hostility to the Political Office began before the General Election. Tim Bligh,
Macmillan's Principal Private Secretary, saw Mrs Williams and made it clear to
her that 'the Civil Service considered that there was no place for me, or my office
colleagues, at No. 10'. Bligh's successor, Derek Mitchell, carried on the
campaign against Mrs Williams. 'Mitchell's first objective', Edward Short
reveals, 'had been to keep her out of No. 10 altogether.' Mitchell had a secret
meeting in No. 12 with Herbert Bowden under the auspices of Freddie Warren,
the Chief Whip's Principal Private Secretary and the terror of every Whitehall
Private Office, with the object of 'keeping Marcia in her place'. Bowden, the
Opposition Chief Whip until the Election, was supposed to approach Wilson and
tell him to keep Mrs Williams out but the Prime Minister would have none of it.
The civil service hit back by causing problems over her vetting and allocating her
out-of-the-way accommodation, an old waiting room – a situation resolved only
after a bruising battle.[2]

From the start the civil service raised questions 'about the security aspects of
enlisting people to do political work within No. 10'. Wigg agreed, and as a

precaution Wilson wanted them to be both negatively and positively vetted. As we have seen, however, the Prime Minister was a reluctant advocate of the process. 'From the day he moved into Number 10 in 1964 his relations with the security services – MI5 in particular – were prickly', one political commentator recalls. 'For example, he was angered by the way they dealt with Marcia Williams' positive vetting', as was Mrs Williams. According to Edward Short, 'she took great umbrage at some of the questions she was asked, particularly about her divorce. In my opinion her anger was justified.'[3]

The security-conscious Wigg went on the rounds of his colleagues instructing them to co-operate fully with the vetters. He said that they should reveal to MI5 any potentially damaging secrets. Through this action Wigg would be in a position to protect them and be ready to head off any looming scandal. One of the No. 10 political advisers proposed Tony Benn for a character reference. An MI5 man visited Benn: 'The chap was a real pudgy flatfoot police type, and very friendly. But it is an odious business being asked to answer personal questions such as drinking habits, sexual deviations and private life.' Wigg naively trusted MI5, he admired Hollis as 'a real professional and patriot'. But what of the faction which was gunning for Wilson, the 'Gestapo' as Hollis called them? The reality was that MI5 were being handed all the dirt on a plate.[4]

Whether Wigg told MI5 about the one skeleton in his own cupboard is not known, but he certainly did fail to inform the Prime Minister. Wilson stumbled on his secret at a lunch party given by Richard Crossman. Wigg had been invited but did not attend. Wilson asked Crossman where George was. Crossman is reported to have said, 'Oh, George has gone to see his son.' Wilson looked quizzically: 'But, George hasn't got a son.' Crossman, to Wilson's amazement, revealed that Wigg had one and that he was illegitimate. Wigg had a steady mistress for a number of years.[5]

There was more trouble over the positive vetting of the 'Hungarian twins', economic advisers Thomas Balogh and Nicholas Kaldor, which went on for weeks. News of the vetting problem soon leaked and right-wing Tory back-benchers put down questions in the House of Commons. Dame Irene Ward suspected that there had been a change of policy in the 'rules governing the access of foreign persons to secret information'. She worried about the interference with security and 'their responsibility to deal with anyone who has any contact with Communist or other organisations which are antagonistic to this country.' Niall MacDermot, the Financial Secretary for the Treasury, who dealt with civil service matters, replied for the Government. Revealing that he had worked in 'security' for six and half years, MacDermot accused Mrs Ward of indulging in 'a particularly un-English activity', a veiled reference to McCarthyism.[6]

Life was made difficult for Balogh and Kaldor. They received much critical press for their apparent stranglehold on economic policy (much exaggerated) and were 'never fully integrated in the team'. Balogh, like Wigg and Mrs Williams, suffered problems over accommodation in the Cabinet Office and was excluded by the civil service from the inner sanctum. 'It was often almost impossible', Mrs Williams has said, 'for Thomas to receive all the Cabinet papers which he needed to read in order to be fully informed about what was going on'. Clive Ponting recognised this as 'an old but effective Civil Service device.' Wilson was furious at the way in which his political advisers were treated: 'That was not the case with the appointees of Harold Macmillan. Unremitting press comments, including unwarrantable invasions of personal and family privacy have been addressed uniquely, to my appointees.'[7]

The press attacks were directed against the 'Kitchen Cabinet'. Wilson was portrayed as isolated and paranoid, surrounded by a bunch of dubious cronies. 'To understand this picture it is necessary to identify Wilson as the loneliest of all the Prime Ministers, a man bedevilled by a great sense of insecurity. He had no friends as the rest of us know, personal and family friends and so, in his solitude, his political entourage assumed a greater importance in his life than would otherwise have been necessary.' Susan Crosland believes he should have taken on board the views of Ministers, but 'more and more he seemed influenced by his cronies – the "Kitchen Cabinet" whom he trusted. It wasn't evident that he trusted many people.' His over-reliance on the Kitchen Cabinet, in James Margarch's view, 'prevented his becoming a Prime Minister of substance'.[8]

There is an element of truth in this statement, but who could Wilson turn to? His Cabinet, dominated by Gaitskellites, had never wanted him as leader and was willing to plot against him at every turn. He saw himself 'running a Bolshevik Revolution with a Tsarist Cabinet', staffed by 'bitterly hostile and suspicious, miserable creatures'. His insecurity and paranoia were not the product of character but the recognition of the reality around him.[9]

There was, for example, a great deal of leaking to the press going on. Plugging leaks was a task carried out by Wigg on behalf of the Prime Minister. Wilson was 'a voracious newspaper reader and each morning he's busy guessing which of us has given the particular piece of poison to which he takes objection and George Wigg feeds him in his hatred'. The 'Kitchen Cabinet' would pore over the first editions of the newspapers looking for smear stories, leaks and the source of the information. On a number of occasions the Lord Chancellor was asked to conduct investigations into particularly damaging leaks. 'As he always failed to find the culprit the Whips office created their back-room machinery which was similar to that set up by Wigg.'[10]

A major target of the smears was Marcia Williams, the Prime Minister's Personal and Political Secretary. Her post largely entailed keeping in touch with the Parliamentary Labour Party and Wilson's constituency, as well as dealing with the large quantity of correspondence which arrived at No. 10. There were many, both inside and outside of the Party, who felt Mrs Williams went beyond this remit and had an undue influence over the Prime Minister. Chief Whip Edward Short believes that, in the early days at least, her alleged power was exaggerated. 'It is probably untrue that Marcia influenced ministerial appointments to any great extent.' In fact, Short saw her as being a rather isolated figure. 'In spite of her claim to an encyclopaedic knowledge of the Parliamentary Labour Party it was almost entirely second-hand. She was virtually unknown to the majority of Members of Parliament apart from the small circle who haunted

Harold's office when he was Leader of the Opposition. Of these the most prominent was George Wigg with whom Marcia was very friendly at that time.'[11]

It was her role as Wilson's friend that gave Mrs Williams such influence as she had. Wilson was not a socialiser and had few intimates. Beattie Plummer, wife of Sir Leslie Plummer until his death in 1963, was one of his 'few close friends'. She was often invited to the 'left-wing clan' which occasionally met for informal talks at Chequers, the PM's country residence. Mrs Williams' most important role was as a sounding board for Wilson. At the end of a long day, Wilson would sit down with Wigg and a few other close advisers in the 'Kitchen Cabinet' to mull over problems. Wigg knew Wilson well enough 'to understand the need for somebody near him who would speak fearlessly and would hold up a mirror from time to time. He did not want a crony. He wanted a colleague and trusted friend linking him with the outside world with which all Prime Ministers inevitably lose touch.' At the start, it was Wigg who was the closest colleague but both he and Mrs Williams acted as a counter-weight to the official advice which the Prime Minister received and it was often Mrs Williams who tried to keep Wilson to the Party's manifesto. Tony Benn thought her 'the most able, loyal, radical and balanced member of Harold's personal team'. Short believed that Mrs Williams debunked the Prime Minister. 'Marcia never stood in awe of him, but always told him in plain, often rough, language what she believed he should be told – as opposed to what he often wanted to believe.'[12]

The fact that Wilson valued her advice, mostly on party matters, was increasingly resented by Wigg, who wanted a monopoly on Wilson's ear. Wigg did not share her distrust of the (all-male) civil servants. Looking back, she wrote: 'He was the one among us who at first, but less later, got on extremely well with the civil servants in No. 10 and elsewhere. This seemed to me to be because he was a military man and thus respected the Civil Service system which is so similar.' He was also an 'old Soldier and anti-feminist' who could not come to terms with a woman close to the centre of power.[13]

There were times when Wigg was correct in his criticisms. It did seem to some close to Wilson that Mrs Williams' personal problems occasionally took precedence over the official agenda. Soon after Wilson became leader of the Labour Party, John Allen joined his staff as a political and economic researcher. He was separated from his wife. In the early months of the Government, Allen and Marcia Williams had an affair. According to George Caunt, 'he was the first person to take her and all her problems seriously'. In 1965, Allen proposed marriage to the divorced Marcia Williams. However, he quickly changed his mind and withdrew his offer, causing traumas in the No. 10 camp which took years to subside. There were a series of intense meetings in No. 10 at which Williams, Wilson, Joseph Kagan and Lady Plummer tried to persuade the vacillating Allen to sort himself out. Later in the year, Allen left for Swaziland to prepare a report on African development. There he allegedly received a note from Wilson to the effect that he 'should sort out his problems while he was away. The decision he arrived at would make a difference to his employment on his return.' The affair finished and Allen stayed in the 'Kitchen Cabinet' until the 1970 General Election. Wilson was later to tell him half-jokingly, 'Do you realise I've spent more time on your private life than I have on the Vietnam war?'[14]

Richard Crossman was willing to forgive Marcia Williams these distracting personal problems because of her other qualities. 'She is really quite important since she is still the most influential person in Harold's life. So it is of the greatest importance that she should not feel isolated. She is gradually being ejected from No. 10 by the Civil Service.' In early 1965, Tony Benn had lunch with Mrs Williams and another of Wilson's personal secretaries, Brenda Dew. 'They hate Derek Mitchell. We discussed at length how these men operate, why their loyalty is to each other rather than to the Government, the techniques they use for evaluating the standing of Ministers and their power to undermine them and influence events.' Six months later, Crossman realised that the civil servants were still working against Mrs Williams. 'Marcia has been fighting to get a glimpse of Cabinet papers, but is still no nearer to achieving it; and she and Tommy [Balogh] cling to their place in Harold's life, well aware that they are in danger of being thrust out.' Tony Benn picked up a 'little bit more about Derek Mitchell's attempt to get Marcia Williams out. There is a big tussle going on.'[15]

Things came to a head. Edward Short discovered that 'Marcia, after a disagreement with Derek Mitchell . . . downed tools and walked out'. Tommy Balogh had to go and persuade her to come back, 'which she did in her own good time'. The row over the right of the political advisers, and more especially Mrs Williams, to see classified documents remains a matter of some controversy. 'In fact, no member of my Political Office ever had access to classified documents', Wilson has written. He noted with anger: 'That was not the case with the appointees of Harold Macmillan.' Others disagree.[16]

'Marcia, in her role as political secretary, saw classified documents', Chief Whip Edward Short states. In turn, Andrew Roth writes of Wigg being 'against allowing her to be privy to secrets to which she was not entitled'. Years later, still bitter, Wigg wrote: 'As Mrs Williams said in 1967: "Who does George Wigg think he is? I've known more secrets than he'll ever know". I was, however, a Member of the Government and a Member of the Privy Council; I saw Cabinet papers and a wide range of sensitive documents. The inference was that Mrs Williams saw and heard everything.'[17]

This disagreement provided the context within which the *Sun* was able to publish what purported to be extracts from the forthcoming memoir by another of Wilson's retinue in the 1960s, George Caunt. On 22 February 1977, the newspaper revealed a 1965 'minute' from Mitchell to Wilson. 'You said you would like Marcia to see in future all the Cabinet and Cabinet Committee papers which you now see. As a result of this I would like to suggest that Marcia should see Secret and Confidential papers dealing with domestic issues only.' As it was, Mrs Williams never did get to see the full range of Cabinet papers. Highly classified papers never found their way to her at all and she was placed on the bottom of the distribution list so that by the time the papers reached her the information was already out of date.

The relationship between Wigg and Mrs Williams, Short acknowledged, 'quickly disappeared in government and degenerated into near hostility'. Mrs

Williams saw herself 'more and more as a political adviser rather than a personal secretary'. Wigg believed her influence on Harold was 'not always exercised with wisdom or discretion'. Short thought he was better placed than most to know. 'My criticism of her', he writes, 'was not that she lacked wisdom or discretion but that she was ill-informed on matters on which she felt singularly well-equipped to give advice'. She tended, to 'interfere in matters which were not her concern'. The whips did not like the fact that for the first time a non-minister, Mrs Williams, was to be present at the daily meeting between the Chief Whip and the PM.[18]

As always, Wilson stood loyally by his close friends and the loser in this instance was Mitchell. 'Probably because of his attitude towards Marcia, a note of estrangement crept into the relationship between the Prime Minister and his Principal Private Secretary from the start.' In April 1966, Mitchell was replaced by Michael Halls, whom Wilson had worked with at the Board of Trade. The Civil Service was not pleased but Wilson insisted on the appointment.[19]

Following the March 1966 General Election the amosphere in No. 10, according to Edward Short, changed. 'Marcia was much more in evidence and seemed more relaxed than she had been before the General Election.' Relations had improved due to the appointment of Halls. 'Marcia's star was clearly in the ascendency in Downing Street . . . it marked the beginning of George Wigg's estrangement from Harold, to whom he had up to now given almost dog-like devotion.'[20]

XI

WILSON AND THE BANKERS

The choice was effectively made on the day after the Election by three people; the Prime Minister, Jim Callaghan and George Brown. While other Ministers were assiduously linking up with their Permanent Secretaries, the three met at No. 10 on Saturday 17th October to 'open the books', and decided that a Labour government must not be once again associated with devaluation as it had been in 1949.

BARBARA CASTLE

THE BRITISH ESTABLISHMENT – and it makes sense to talk of such a thing in 1964 – had many reasons to distrust Wilson, but the most important facet of his character from their point of view was his hostility to the City of London and his support for the domestic manufacturing economy. This distaste for the money-lenders was expressed early on. Campaigning for the young Elizabeth Longford in 1950, Wilson said in a speech: 'The rate of bankruptcies has fallen under this government. Industries and commerce are buoyant. All except the money-lenders. And we have never promised, in any of our manifestos, to put money in the usurers' pockets.'[1]

His 'contempt for the makers of money' had initially made enemies for him during the Bank Rate affair of 1957 and 1958. The 'affair' was simple enough. The Bank of England was planning to raise what would now be called the minimum lending rate. A number of the City's first division international money-lenders – Lazard's, Pearson's, Matheson's of Hong Kong, 'old money', a slice of the true core of the City, in effect – were alleged to have got wind of the news in time to unload large amounts of government securities. (As interest rates rose the relative returns on these bonds declined.) In other words, some losses were avoided in an entirely routine part of City business. The 'old boy' network operated with its usual, discreet efficiency. An inquiry was set up into allegations that the news of the raising of the Bank Rate had been leaked – 'insider trading'.[2]

At the heart of this business was a man called William Keswick, a director of Matheson's, and also a part-time Director of the Bank of England. With his Bank of England hat on he was informed by letter, by the Deputy Governor of the Bank, that a rise in the Bank Rate was 'being discussed'. (The Deputy Governor also suggested Keswick burn his letter.) Wearing his Matheson's hat he then unloaded about £1 million worth of government paper. (This sum then was equivalent to roughly £20 million today – serious money.) Paul Ferris reported that 'Lord Cobbold, Governor of the Bank of England, admitted to the Tribunal that a director might be under strain at times when he had to keep his Bank of England knowledge in a watertight compartment. But this sort of thing, he said, happened in banking and accountancy and the law.' As Andrew Roth noted, the Tribunal led to 'many interesting aspects of City and Conservative activity [being] uncovered . . . [and] made public property for the first time.'[3]

It was Wilson who made the running on the issue for the Labour Party front bench. In February 1958, after the Tribunal, to nobody's great surprise, had whitewashed everything, Wilson spoke in the House of Commons of its 'valuable insight into . . . the essentially amateurish way in which vital decisions affecting our whole economic well-being are taken – the "old boy" network, the grouse moors.' This unaccustomed exposure made the City and the Conservative Party extremely unhappy. The *Sunday Times* noted that Wilson 'had cast himself as the enemy No. 1 for the Tories. Long after the issues of the case are forgotten, the Tories will be after his scalp.' Wilson had gone beyond the pale for the City, the English ruling élite. A Labour Government led by anyone who wanted to do anything was going to be attacked by the City in 1964. But with Wilson as leader, the attack was also personal.[4]

Throughout 1964 the Labour Party knew that they were likely to win the coming General Election. They also knew that with the keys to 10 Downing Street would be acquired the large (by the standards of the day) balance of payments deficit being accumulated by the Tories under Chancellor of the Exchequer, Reginald Maulding, in his 'dash for growth', the 'glittering prize' of 'expansion without inflation, the end of stop-go and a break-out from the constrictions of the past'.[5]

As the election approached, Wilson began to warn the Labour Party and the trade unions not to raise their expectations: the balance of trade deficit – estimated at perhaps £500 million, although it turned out to be £800 million, roughly £7.5 billion today – would shackle the Government. In Edinburgh he said: 'You cannot go cap in hand to the central bankers as they [the Conservatives] have now been forced to do, and maintain your freedom of action, whether on policies maintaining full employment here in Britain or even on social policies. The central bankers will before long be demanding that Britain put her house in order.' To the Trades Union Congress he hinted at his solution to this problem – and its price. 'This does not mean we are necessarily facing a crippling run on sterling. We can borrow . . . but don't then talk about an independent foreign policy or an independent defence policy.' He was telling the delegates – and his party, mainly, perhaps, its left wing – that if they borrowed from the Americans, the Americans would have power over the Government.[6]

In his memoir, Maudling argues that the economic situation he had left for the incoming Labour Government was less serious than economic commentators claimed and the Wilson Government believed. 'The facts seem to me to speak for themselves. Whatever the deficit, there were, in Mr Wilson's own words, reserves and facilities more than adequate to cover it. The trade position was already dramatically on the mend. The figures of the current balance quarter by quarter speak for themselves, second quarter 1964 minus £63 million, third quarter minus £192 million, fourth quarter minus £101 million; first quarter 1965 minus £35 million, second quarter minus £8 million. The trend was definite, and as we had predicted . . . Confidence in sterling *until Mr Wilson took charge of it* had remained high. A great opportunity for Britain which the Conservative Government had created had been destroyed by Labour's loss of nerve' (emphasis added).[7]

This is largely true, in economic terms, but it fails to take into account the *political* realities of the time. Despite the fact that it was carrying out economic policies chosen from the same options presented by the Treasury as would have been available to Maudling had the Tories won the election, the Labour Government suffered a sustained assault by Maudling and his friends – and subsequent employers – in the City. 'Labour's loss of nerve' had nothing to do with it.[8]

From the evening of Wilson's appointment, 16 October 1964, 'The American banks started and spread the most alarmist rumours about the future of the British currency. There was talk of devaluation, floating, nationalisation of merchant banks, a tax on capital, controls on capital, import quotas and the closure of the gold market. Several merchant banks seriously considered leaving Britain.' The Labour Government's first budget in November 1964 produced the first sterling crisis.[9]

In *Modernisation Frustrated*, Newton and Porter argue that 'unprepared for the scale of the inherited external deficit, Labour had made no assessment of its implications for the modernisation strategy. Indeed, there were no plans to deal with it at all. The new government was thus in an extremely weak position when it came under pressure from the City and the Bank of England, in the person of the governor, Lord Cromer, as well as from the Treasury, to take orthodox measures which would satisfy the international financial community, and so leave confidence in the currency intact.'[10]

This may be true, in that there were no briefing documents from the Party telling the Parliamentary Labour Party what to do. But Wilson had already decided that the way out was the orthodox Keynesian method of borrowing dollars – and he was under no illusions about what this meant. Wilson and Shadow Chancellor James Callaghan were snuggling up to the American bankers throughout 1964 as they prepared to take power. The US Government was told about Chancellor Callaghan's first budget before his Labour Cabinet colleagues were. Clive Ponting is correct, from one point of view, in saying that 'the overwhelming impression of the first few months of the new government is that it actively sought to increase British dependence on the United States and develop its relationship with the American administration into the central pillar of its policy in the strategic, foreign, defence and economic fields.' However, it would be more accurate to say that, depending upon the Americans for economic support, Wilson had no alternative but to support American diplomatic and strategic objectives. What was the alternative, the Bank of England?[11]

In the event, with a Parliamentary majority of 4 at the Party's back, and with something like an O-level understanding of economics, James Callaghan became Chancellor. In authentic *Yes, Minister* fashion, 'An immense brief was thrust before him. Pinned to its cover and staring at him monstrously was a sheet of paper with the latest forecast of the balance-of-payments deficit for 1964 – £800 million. "Unless we take action." ' But what 'action'? Devaluation of the pound, one of the three options presented by the Treasury, was 'not really available to us because, well ahead of the election, an understanding had been reached on behalf of the Labour Opposition with Alfred Hayes, President of the New York Federal Reserve Bank, which is part of the Federal Reserve system in the United States, that if we became the Government, we would not devalue the pound. In return we received a promise of massive American support for sterling if it should be needed.'[12]

Edward Short is the first person to reveal this pre-election deal which *by itself* entails rethinking the received perception of the Wilson Government as the incompetent inheritors of the Tory Party's trade deficit. This deal with the New York Federal Reserve Bank must have been an intense irritation to Lord Cromer, the Governor of the Bank of England, for it meant, ultimately, that the English money-lenders could not completely control the Labour Government. In January 1966, for example, Cromer threatened to resign when he learned that, without consulting him, Chancellor Callaghan had invited the Vice President of the New York Federal Reserve over for talks.[13]

By going to the Americans before the election, Wilson escaped part of the trap set by the Bank of England. However, this did not stop Cromer, the City's major mouthpiece, from *trying* to dictate government policy. Wilson 'had to listen night after to night to demands that there should be immediate cuts in government expenditure, and particularly in those parts of government expenditure which related to the social services. It was not long before we were being asked, almost at pistol-point, to cut back on expenditure, even to the point of stopping the road-building programme, or schools which were only half constructed.'[14]

If Wilson had to listen to this, thanks to the Americans he did not actually have to comply fully with the demands. In the ensuing game of political poker, which climaxed on 26 November 1964, Wilson, in his own account (and that, for example of Henry Brandon), out-bluffed Cromer and the international financial community which was speculating against the pound. The then editor of the *Guardian*, Alastair Hetherington, records Wilson's account of the meetings with Cromer. 'He went on to tell me – with great relish – about a meeting on Tuesday night . . . he was sure no Governor in this century had been talked to like that. As soon as the Governor was in the Cabinet room Wilson had asked why the Bank was not operating in the forward market. Lord Cromer had given his reasons, which to the Prime Minister had seemed poor . . . the country could elect whomsoever it liked so long as it was a Conservative Government . . . he would go to the country on this issue . . . he would come back with a huge majority. The Governor, he said, was horrified. The Prime Minister had added that during the election sterling would be on "floating" rates, which Lord Cromer said would wreck not only sterling but the whole European system. Wilson replied that it was the City's choice, not his.'[15]

These threats by Wilson apparently did the trick. The next day Cromer announced that a $3 million loan had been secured for the Government. 'Sir Alec Douglas Home accompanied by Reginald Maudling visited Downing Street oozing bonhomie and promising Wilson all support in a coalition Government in the nation's hour of crisis. Wilson wiped the smiles off their faces with news of his massive loan. Home and Maudling left, still in Opposition.'[16]

Cromer had to work with the Americans to organise loans to support the pound. At the same time, however, he and the Bank of England were working against the Government. Fred Hirsch noted in his 1965 study that 'the most significant event in the week following the 1964 autumn budget was that such suggestions – i.e. alarm over the government's actions and competence is shared by the Bank of England – spread far beyond the tiny circle that is normally privy to such rarified gossip. Specifically it got to be known that the Bank of England was recommending an increase in the Bank Rate and when this was refused for the second Thursday running the speculative crisis broke.' The speculative attack was, at least in part, generated by the Bank of England.[17]

The key decision was that of maintaining the value of the pound at $2.80. The Americans wanted this because it was cheaper for them to defend the value of sterling than it was to defend the dollar, which they believed would come under attack next if the pound collapsed. This problem had arisen under the Conservatives. 'In September 1963 Harold Macmillan, then on an official visit to Washington, told John F. Kennedy very clearly that if there were not an increase in the dollar price of gold or a devaluation of the dollar, the pound itself would have to devalue and the whole Bretton Woods system [the post-war monetary system agreed by Anglo-American bankers] would be threatened. At the time it was sacrilege even to offer such a threat. Kennedy, terrified that it might be known he had even heard such words, had all trace of this conversation expunged, even down to the notes of his own assistants.'[18]

Of Wilson's agreement to maintain the $2.80 rate with the pound, one of President Lyndon Johnson's economic advisers noted: 'If he [Wilson] makes an absolute objective of $2.80 – then, of course we are in the saddle and can impose whatever terms we wish when he comes for help.' The truth is more complex – and more interesting – for the deal cut both ways. Wilson had to *appear* to be absolutely wedded to maintaining the value of the pound until he had called another election. Wilson was nothing if not a politician. With a majority in Parliament of 4, then 3, sometimes 2, top of the Wilson agenda was – had to be – increasing this majority. As soon as he had done this, in 1966, the Americans discovered that Wilson began dumping his agreements with them.[19]

In the first week of December 1964 Wilson went to America as Prime Minister for the first time. In his diary entry for 11 December, Richard Crossman gave his version of Wilson's report back to Cabinet. 'President Lyndon Johnson had shown himself deeply concerned about our situation and virtually promised us all aid short of war.' We know now for sure that there was a deal done, presumably to supplement that struck before the Labour Party became the Government. Though the 'deal' was secret from the majority of the Cabinet, the *quid pro quo* emerges in fragments recorded by the diarists. On 11 February Crossman talked of the defence package: 'The tremendous decision to buy American . . . has put us temporarily completely in the power of the Americans . . . [Wilson] has shown a solid determination to recreate the Anglo-American axis . . . we are cutting back the British aircraft industry in order to concentrate on maintaining our imperial position East of Suez. And we are doing that not because we need these bases ourselves but because the Americans can't defend the Far East on their own and need us there.'

This deal – or rather some of the implications of it – was whizzed through a Cabinet already tired by a two-hour row about government expenditure. 'We turned exhausted to the proofs of the Defence White Paper', Barbara Castle records. 'I hadn't even read it. Frank Cousins was the only one who raised a murmur. He protested that he had received his documents last night and had not had adequate time to study such a detailed defence policy.'[20]

Head of the Mirror Group, Cecil King, noted in his diary, after a leak from George Brown: 'In spite of Wilson's categorical statement at the Labour Party conference that there had been no deal with the US – trading financial support for the pound against military support on S.E. Asia – this is exactly what was done.' Indeed, the nature of the deal is visible, even in Wilson's own memoir.[21]

The discovery of this deal throws an interesting light on an apparent discrepancy between Wilson's version of events and that of the Governor of the Bank of England. 'Cromer says', recalls King, 'he [Wilson] did not get categorical promise of support from Johnson . . . Cromer's and Wilson's picture of the situation are so different as to be irreconcilable'. Cromer is wrong, Wilson telling the truth. 'Categorical support' – i.e. support at a price (categorical does not mean unconditional) – is precisely what Wilson had negotiated; and it was done by the Government, not the Bank of England. Some of Cromer's hostility towards Wilson may have been generated by the simple fact that he had been out-manoeuvred by Wilson's deal with the Americans. In 1965, King, a Wilson-appointed member of the 'court' of the Bank of England, reported in his diary: 'our reserve figures are faked, thanks to the co-operation of the Americans'. These 'fake' figures became one of King's central themes in the years that followed.[22]

Wilson turned to the US because the price in foreign policy commitments demanded by the US for support of the pound was less damaging than the deflationary price demanded for a nod of 'confidence' from the City and the Bank of England. However, there were some things which Wilson knew he could not get away with – notably overt material Labour support for the war in Vietnam. This could not be delivered, as McGeorge Bundy told Johnson in September 1964: 'The one thing which he [Wilson] was apparently trying to avoid was a liability in Vietnam'.[23]

The Bank of England's Cromer had not conceded defeat. On 1 February 1965 he began to say in public what he had been saying to ministers in private – that the Government had to entrench more, cut back on overseas defence spending and defer the 'attractive amenities at home so extensively being provided by local authorities.'[24]

Although the threat to domestic social spending angered Labour MPs, it was the call for cuts abroad which stung Wilson. He wrote to Cromer 'it would be politically irresponsible and economically useless to abandon our bases.' Wilson knew better than this, of course. Staying east of Suez was part of the deal with the Americans.[25]

In fact, the American administration was divided on this. Merchant banker and Labour supporter Siegmund Warburg told Wilson that the real problem was spending on defence programmes, Britain's imperial pretensions. In so doing he was reporting the view of a section of the US Administration. As well as being a director of the élite Wall Street bankers Koehn-Loeb, and a member of the Bilderberg Group, Warburg was a friend of George Ball, the US Secretary of State, and knew that the economists advising L.B.J., 'such as Dillon, Rosca and Martin, feared that this spending would inevitably lead to a devaluation of the pound, then to that of the dollar. They therefore thought that the pound must be defended, and that in order to do this, British military spending abroad must be reduced'. This view, however, had lost the argument to those, such as McNamara and Rusk, who wanted Britain to remain East of Suez and provide a political fig-leaf of 'international' cover for US intervention in South East Asia.[26]

On 10 February 1965, a week after Cromer's speech, Barbara Castle reported in her diary that there had been rumours of the formation of a 'National Government' – after just three months of the Labour Government. She talked with Chancellor Callaghan: 'He told me that Lord Cromer had not approached him about the formation of a national government. Although he had heard the rumour, he had nothing with which to substantiate it. But undoubtedly Lord Cromer had been pressing for stiff deflationary measures and would continue to do so. At one point he [Callaghan] was faced with the threat of his resignation though that was later withdrawn.' This campaign for a 'national government' reached its climax with the so-called 'Cecil King Coup Plot' of 1968 which we discuss below (Chapter XXIV).

Cromer repeated his call for cuts in government domestic spending a fortnight after the speech of 1 February, again referring to the need for 'deferment of the level of public services they would like to have'. This time the Labour movement as a whole noticed what he was saying. For Crossman this was an 'astonishing speech' and he 'wrote a minute to the Prime Minister asking him what steps would be taken to shut up this one-man May Committee'. Wilson's victory of 25 November 1964 over Cromer had been only round one.[27]

The struggle continued throughout that year. One of its peaks occurred in August 1965. On 5 August, Cecil King talked with Lord Cromer: 'A gloomy session at the Bank . . . it is not thought that any further deflationary gestures would produce any effect [i.e. on speculation against the pound]. The Governor thinks the only card left to play is a wage and price freeze.' Later that evening Cromer saw Wilson and once again raised the idea of a 'National Government'. According to Henry Brandon's account of the meeting: 'The Governor . . . was clearly worried . . . that if nothing new and decisive was done sterling would be in danger of collapse. Would this of necessity lead to the formation of a National Government? In any event was this not a propitious time for National Government?'[28]

Wilson's own account of this meeting makes no mention of National Government but it does show him outflanking Cromer. 'The governor was in his gloomiest mood and clearly felt that the financial end of the world was near. More speculation, more trouble for the pound could only mean the collapse of the world monetary system, the dollar would be engulfed: it might even go first. I said again, as I had said nine months earlier, that in that case, perhaps the rest of the world might take a hand in curbing the speculators.'

Cromer persisted, he demanded to see Edward Heath and Jo Grimond to explain the gravity of the situation. This Wilson refused to allow. Instead, he called Cromer's bluff, threatening him with the 'American card': 'I said that if the issue was as bad as he thought, then I would be ready to fly to America for talks with the President and the Federal Reserve authorities there because, obviously, we were all in it together. I went so far as to have a call put through to the President on a contingency basis and to make provisional arrangements to have a plane ready to pick me up.' At this point Cromer gave up and rather publicly went off on holiday – a gesture intended to show confidence on his part in the economy. It seems to have worked. The 'crisis' dematerialised.[29]

Defending the pound for its own reasons, the US Government worked with the rest of the international (European) money-lenders to tie a long-term bail-out package to policies of its choosing. American insistence on an incomes policy was one such condition. This was also the policy adopted by Cromer. The incomes policy was prepared at the Treasury; the Americans were consulted. The problem was how to make any such proposals stick with the wider Labour Party and the trade unions? George Brown was the man who drew the short straw and had the job of cajoling the leaders of the CBI and TUC in August 1965. There is an amusing account by Brandon of Brown grandstanding at the joint CBI–TUC meeting on these proposals, announcing at one stage that 'he had just heard from Washington over the transatlantic telephone that President Johnson had authorised US participation in the vital support operation, based on the "package" proposal which included the new assurances about Britain's incomes policy'. Whether or not those present found this performance interesting is unrecorded. At any rate, the TUC and CBI delegates agreed to a form of words; and, against the odds, Brown managed to get the TUC General Council to accept the proposals on 2 September.[30]

This 'agreement', spurious though it may have been in reality – there is little evidence that the trade unions leaders took it seriously – was enough to satisfy the US bankers (who had little choice but to bail the pound out anyway) and on 10 September an announcement of more support for the pound was made.

Wilson eventually got rid of Lord Cromer in early 1966: he was not reappointed when his term as governor came to an end. Cromer must have known that this was going to happen and had one last crack at nobbling the Wilson Government. In 1966, just at the beginning of the General Election campaign, he tried to get the Bank Rate (base lending rate) raised. In the climate of the time that would have sparked another bout of speculation against the pound – as well as being unpopular through its effect on hire-purchase, and money-lending generally. It would have been a nice valedictory blow, but the Government would not buy it.[31]

Having got his increased majority in 1966, Wilson began backing out of the deal with the Americans. Just after the election, Wilson ordered a new defence review. It seems that the Americans were aware of this, for in February 1967 they proposed a massive loan to fund the sterling balances, stabilise the pound at its existing level and create a joint sterling–dollar area to protect both currencies and the position of gold. This US deal was the equivalent of a personal loan that pays off all the other loans you have.

The US offer never had the slightest chance of being taken seriously. In April 1967, the Cabinet was discussing pulling out of some of the Far Eastern areas – precisely what the Americans did not want. Wilson and Brown were leaned on during visits to America in 1967, but resisted. They were extricating themselves from their American ties. This was possible because, with a large majority, Wilson could now contemplate devaluation – the obvious escape route from domestic deflation – which he had been unable to do previously with a majority of four or less.

XII

'RHODESIAN DISTRACTIONS'

The success of UDI in Rhodesia in the sixties was due in part to MI6 misreading the situation there. Their intelligence was so bad for so long that, when I was Paymaster-General, I had to organize a private team to get the right answers.
GEORGE WIGG

IN 1965, SOUTHERN RHODESIA issued a Unilateral Declaration of Independence (UDI) thereby rejecting the authority of the British Crown. This move followed the refusal by the white minority to approve a modest step toward black voting rights. In his 1971 account of his governments, 'Rhodesian distractions' was Harold Wilson's dismissive description of the problems generated by UDI. In the sense that the major concerns were the economy – the balance of payments deficit, speculation against sterling and Wilson's war with the City – Rhodesia was indeed a distraction. Nevertheless, it was important. Not only did it take up much Cabinet time, it was the occasion for Wilson's first serious encounter with the British secret state and the Whitehall information machine. It was here that he discovered what a hostile intelligence system can do.

The 'rebellion' by the Rhodesian Front would have presented a peculiarly difficult problem to any British government in 1965. It had been staged by whites, not the blacks, browns and yellows of previous post-war 'colonial difficulties' – and by super-patriotic, hard-line anti-communist, God-fearing whites, at that. Bristling with the symbolism of polite British racism, 'kith and kin', 'civilisation versus savagery' – the conceptual baggage of Empire – this anomalous, white settler regime was a very tricky problem. At the start of 1965, as mentioned in the previous chapter, Labour's priority was getting a bigger majority; another General Election, sooner rather than later, was certain. If the left of the Parliamentary Labour Party (in the Cabinet, notably Barbara Castle) did not seem to appreciate this, seeing Rhodesia as an issue of principle, the permanent government in Whitehall understood the political realities very clearly and proceeded to misinform and disinform the Wilson Cabinet, ensuring that its room for manoeuvre was as limited as possible.[1]

The threat of Rhodesian UDI had been in the air ever since the break-up of the Central African Federation and the Macmillan Government had begun preparations for it in February 1961. Their contingency planning included military action against Rhodesia. What the military plans were remains a secret, but 'fourteen days after Smith became Prime Minister . . . British troops were on instant stand-by in Aden to fly in to Salisbury if there was a UDI.' If any sense of this was communicated to the new Labour Cabinet, it has not been recorded in the accounts written by Cabinet members. What they *were* told was recorded by the Lord Elwyn Jones, then the Attorney General: 'Rhodesia had her own well-equipped army and air-force under the command of the regime's authorities. *We were advised* [emphasis added] that a British military assault would be resisted. Our army would have to be supplied through Tanzania and Zambia, and the aerodrome at Lussaka in Zambia would have been put out of action easily. Many South Africans would help Rhodesia with soldiers, money and arms.'[2]

The Ministry of Defence's detailed version of the difficulties that they would face in Rhodesia was reported by William Gutteridge in *The World Today*, journal of the Royal Institute of International Affairs. In the MOD's picture, despite a white population only the size of Stoke-on-Trent, Rhodesia was depicted as presenting a fearsome obstacle to the British, then still possessing the third or fourth most powerful armed forces in the world. Suddenly in 1965, the British military was revealed as incapable of fulfilling what had previously been its major post-war role – maintaining British overseas assets. Almost all of this information, including that recorded by Lord Elwyn Jones, was false or exaggerated.[3]

The evidence, basically, is that the Rhodesian armed forces would *not* have resisted. The Commander of the Rhodesian Army, Major-General Sam Putteril, and his counterpart in the Rhodesian Air Force, Air Vice Marshal Harold Hawkins, had made it clear to the Rhodesian Government that they were not prepared to issue 'illegal or unconstitutional' orders: to order their forces to oppose British troops would be a breach of their oath of allegiance to the Crown. What is more, says Ken Flower, the head of the Rhodesian Central Intelligence Organisation (CIO) at the time, 'the British Intelligence Service [i.e. MI6] knew it.'[4]

There were also rumours that the British military would refuse to carry out the Government's instructions. Denis Healey, Minister of Defence, 'heard there had been some mutinous muttering among senior army officers about our policy on Rhodesia'. Anthony Verrier, with extensive contacts in the permanent government, and MI6 in particular, tells us that on the one hand 'the Chiefs of Staff in London had indicated with sufficient clarity to the government that if there was one place in Africa where intervention was not only strategically impossible but politically unacceptable it was Southern Rhodesia.'[5]

Was this 'mutinous muttering' anything more than that? The Rhodesian Government believed so. A month *before* UDI, the minutes of the Rhodesian Security Council for 19 October 1965 recorded that 'all three services in the United Kingdom had confirmed that there would be no military intervention'. This intelligence came from the Rhodesian High Commissioner in London, ex-

Sandhurst Brigadier Andrew Skeen. Skeen 'had it categorically from [Chief of the General Staff] Sir Richard Hull and others . . . [that] most of the Commanders would refuse to fight against Rhodesia'. Military intervention in Rhodesia, he was told, was 'politically unacceptable' to them.[6]

This is very hard to believe. The British military take the concept of loyalty to the Crown very seriously indeed and would refuse orders from an elected government only if they had the support of the Crown in so doing. (This is a recurring feature of the various abortive coup plans during Wilson's years.) UDI was, literally, a rebellion against the Crown. There is anecdotal evidence to support this view. The sociologist John Rex spoke at a meeting of British Army Northern Command just after UDI and 'found no evidence of any potential refusal in the army to carry out orders to restore constitutional rule in Rhodesia; indeed, many officers found the suggestion of such a refusal offensive'.[7]

On the other hand, in 1977, a former MI6 officer, Anthony Eaton, told reporters that in 1965 or early 1966 'a small band of top-ranking officers had actually approached Queen Elizabeth, the Queen Mother, with their plan for a coup'. If it had succeeded, 'South Africa would have returned to the Commonwealth'. Eaton said that the plan was known in military circles at the time. A number of prominent, mostly Scottish peers with interests in Rhodesia had been involved in the plot, including the Duke of —, the Earl of Cromartie and a top official with the Joint Intelligence Bureau which had important links with the MOD. Also supporting the coup was a 'minor member of the Royal Family'. The Queen Mother had declined to give it her blessing and the plan was aborted.[8]

Marcia Williams had heard fragments about this 'coup'. She had 'gained the impression that other meetings had taken place in the mid-1960s, one of them at the Defence Department [sic] itself. She had heard there was a map of the United Kingdom and people present went over the move for a coup with a pointer . . . plans had been discussed for the way a possible coup would be started'. In a later, fuller version of the story, Penrose and Coutiour added that Lady Falkender had actually alleged that Lord Mountbatten had been involved.[9]

Back in Rhodesia, from his own sources, Rhodesian intelligence chief Ken Flower concluded that Skeen was telling the Rhodesian Front politicians what they wanted to hear, told them so – and was ignored. In Flower's view, both the Rhodesian and British Cabinets were symmetrically misinformed about the future actions of each other's armed forces: the British that the Rhodesians would fight, the Rhodesians that the British troops would not. This made British military intervention less likely and gave the Rhodesians confidence.

As UDI threatened, the issue of British military intervention was resolved on 1 November 1965 when Wilson stated in the House of Commons that the British Government would not use force: 'If there are those who are thinking in terms of a thunderbolt hurtling from the sky and destroying their enemies, a thunderbolt in the shape of the RAF, let me say that thunderbolt will not be coming, and to continue in this delusion wastes valuable time, and misdirects valuable energies.' It was here, in Ken Flower's view, that Wilson killed off any chance of forcing Smith to strike a deal. Yet with a majority of four (two, in effect, because two Labour MPs, Reginald Paget and Frederick Bellinger, opposed the Government's policy), and with another General Election on the horizon, Wilson's decision is unsurprising. The spectre of white, neo-Brits being killed by the British armed forces (or British by neo-Brits) raised by the British state was enough to ensure that the Cabinet would baulk at the military option. With all the other pressures on the Government – especially the economic pressures – the chances of the Cabinet voting to support a military invasion were slim. The misinformation from the permanent government on the military situation sealed the argument.[10]

Even then, the Rhodesian Front take-over might have been avoided. Just after UDI was declared a group of Rhodesian soldiers went to the Governor, Sir Humphrey Gibbs, and said: 'Sir, if you will provide us with a warrant for the arrest of Mr Smith as a rebel against the Queen, we will do our duty.' But Sir Humphrey refused.[11]

The visible focus of the Government's efforts became negotiations with the Rhodesian regime and economic sanctions. Would sanctions work? What advice was the Cabinet given? Although our information on this is fragmented, it seems clear that different branches of the permanent government were giving conflicting advice. As early as 17 November 1965, the Cabinet were given a 'completely negative' report by the Ministry of Fuel and Power and the Foreign Office on the possibilities of oil sanctions. They would not work, and should be introduced only 'for whatever marginal effects it would have on the Rhodesian regime and as a diplomatic device with the Africans'. At this meeting Wilson said that 'it was no longer a question of "whether" but "when". We could not possibly veto oil sanctions and the UN would certainly insist on them as a minimum.' Here is Wilson outlining the *political* reality: oil sanctions were inevitable; the UN and the black members of the Commonwealth would insist on them. However, Wilson added that 'he doubted if either South Africa or Portugal [would] want to run foul of the UN for their own reasons – nor would the private oil companies.'[12]

The source of this advice to Wilson is unclear; everyone subsequently denied giving it. Though this was completely false, it was not wholly unintelligible at the end of 1965. South Africa's initial response to the Smith regime had been cautious. In his study of Anglo-South African diplomacy, Berridge notes that, initially, 'South Africa had, indeed, warned Smith against UDI, failed subsequently to extend official recognition to his regime and from the beginning adopted a policy of what was at least nominally "neutrality" in the dispute between London and Salisbury'.[13]

Crucially, Wilson was initially advised that a UN oil boycott would be respected by the oil companies and Rhodesia's neighbours. Therefore, sanctions would work. It must have been clear from even the most cursory look at a map of Africa that the success of economic sanctions against land-locked Rhodesia rested entirely upon the co-operation of Rhodesia's neighbours with coastlines, South Africa and Portugese-controlled Mozambique. Without their co-operation and without a complete naval blockade – an impossibility for the British Navy – sanctions were bound to fail.

As we now know, *before* UDI both the Portugese and South African governments had promised to continue 'business as usual' with the Rhodesians, and the oil companies, including BP, nominally controlled by the state by virtue of the state-owned majority (51 per cent) of its shares, had promised continuation of supplies. In his biography of Tiny Rowland, head of the former Rhodesian mining concern and now multinational company Lonrho, Richard Hall says that 'Rowland's argument was, and always would be, that by giving secret assurances in advance of UDI to supply Rhodesia, the oil companies made Smith's rebellion possible . . . As early as 1967, when I was still editing the *Times* of Zambia, there had been talk of a lawsuit by Lonrho against Shell/BP, on the grounds that they had contracted to send fuel into Rhodesia only by way of the Mozambique pipeline, but after UDI had reneged and were using the railways from South Africa instead.' When the decision was taken, on 17 December 1965, to introduce an oil embargo, the Order in Council that the Queen was given to sign specifically did not mention overseas subsidiaries of British companies. Through this loophole the British companies poured oil. Presumably, the Order had been drafted by civil servants in the Cabinet Office who then obtained the signature of a minister without informing him of the details. The fix was in from the beginning but the Cabinet did not know this in late 1965.[14]

For Cabinet colleague Denis Healey, 'Wilson's illusions about sanctions were shared and encouraged by officials who should have known better'. They indeed should have known better or did know better and deliberately misinformed Wilson that 'the oil sanctions and the closure of the Beira pipeline would bring the Rhodesian economy to a halt', and 'in weeks not months' – a prediction he offered to the Commonwealth Conference in Lagos, Nigeria, on 12 January 1966.[15]

Who produced the notorious 'weeks not months' estimate? The Commonwealth Relations Office (CRO), Foreign Office and Ministry of Power denied being responsible. The Department of Economic Affairs was blamed by one source; Oliver Wright, then Wilson's Private Secretary, who had made a discreet visit to Rhodesia, by another. The CRO were certainly running a similar line. The day before Wilson's Lagos prediction, *The Times* quoted a CRO spokesman's prediction that sanctions would reduce Rhodesia to submission by March or April. Wilson's confidence in the 'weeks not months' estimate did not last long. In the weeks following the Commonwealth Conference, 'Wilson was beginning to doubt the information he had received from the Commonwealth Relations Office and other sources'; and in the middle of April 1966 he purged the top of the CRO – suggesting that this department was the major source of the poor advice he was getting. How would the CRO draw up its assessment? From its own sources and, presumably, from the intelligence services. Which service though? Chapman Pincher, with his contacts in MI6, says flatly, ' "Weeks rather than months" was the considered view of MI6 and Wilson had every reason to rely on it.' This may be true but there is no evidence on the subject. However, it should be noted here that the major intelligence (or security) organisation in Central Africa was MI5. MI6 did not begin surveillance of oil traffic into Rhodesia by road from South Africa until 12 January, the day of Wilson's speech in Lagos.[16]

Later in the year, better information was being received by the Cabinet. After going through the files of the Ministry of Power on the subject, Brian Sedgemore discovered that in late 1966 'Foreign Secretary, George Brown, anticipated sanctions busting by the subsidiary companies of BP, Shell and others. And so did his civil servants. So he proposed making the main companies criminally liable for breaches of sanctions busting by their subsidiaries.' In Cabinet, however, Brown's only support came from the Minister of Technology, Tony Benn. So the Cabinet, eager to impress the Commonwealth countries and the United Nations, decided in 1966 on a policy to stop oil getting into Rhodesia which a few key ministers knew would not work. By then, however, the damage was done, the policy decisions made, the loophole in the Sanctions Order offered to the UK oil companies and the sanctions busting underway.[17]

The received view is that all this was a failure of intelligence. Anthony Verrier, as apologist for MI6, points out that Rhodesia was, more or less, the responsibility of MI5; that MI6 were very late into Rhodesia; and that, anyway, MI6 showed their political masters the nature of reality and they – basically Wilson – preferred their delusory fantasies: 'Wilson knew, at UDI, oil-refinery capacity at Beira had been increased [in 1964] to meet an expected surge in Southern Rhodesian requirements; that oil products were also reaching Southern Rhodesia from South Africa.'[18]

We know, however, of no evidence to support this account of 'what Wilson knew' at the time of UDI – and Verrier offers none. Kenneth Young blames the Commonwealth Relations Office – 'some of its personnel were not of the highest calibre' – and the fact that 'the High Commissioner in Salisbury, and his staff, including the Intelligence members, moved largely in Opposition circles, their informal contacts with the governing party being almost nil.'[19]

The 'failure of intelligence' story is trotted out as if Rhodesia were as difficult an intelligence target as, say, Albania, requiring 'penetration', 'acquisition of assets' and so forth. This is absurd. The British state, its military and intelligence organisations, and British business, were all closely integrated with Rhodesian society and institutions. This was *a colony*, not some hostile foreign power. Rhodesian pilots flew alongside British in some of the British state's 'little foreign difficulties'. Joint planning took place between the Rhodesian and British military establishments. The received version, that somehow the British secret state just got it wrong – about Portugese attitudes, South African attitudes, Rhodesian political attitudes, Rhodesian military attitudes, the plans of the oil companies – is manifestly nonsense. There was no need to 'penetrate' Rhodesia. Britain and Rhodesia were inter-penetrated – and particularly so in the intelligence field.[20]

In 1971, Wilson claimed that he had been 'misled'. Ken Flower supports this judgement. 'CIO [Rhodesian Central Intelligence Organisation] was aware, for example, that Britain had been *deliberately misadvised* that the closure of the pipeline would prove effective and that Portugal would not challenge United Nations action.' Wilson's experience over the Rhodesia problem gradually led to concerns 'about interruptions in the flow of vital information between civil servants and politicians', and the whole area of relations between the Prime Minister's office and the secret services.[21]

Looking back at these events, it is hard to resist the conclusion that the permanent government misinformed the Cabinet about the military position, misinformed the Cabinet about the economic situation, and deliberately issued an Order in Council on sanctions which enabled the UK oil companies to fulfil their pre-UDI pledge to maintain oil supplies. By the time this had become clear, in late 1966, the opportunity for swift, decisive action was gone.

XIII

WAR BY OTHER MEANS

For heaven's sake, let's keep some grip on reality. It's quite possible that
what the PM calls the will-o'-the-wisp of Rhodesian independence will be
a fact long after the Labour Government is thrown out of office.
RICHARD CROSSMAN

IN THE ABSENCE of overt military conflict in Rhodesia, a covert propaganda
and intelligence war developed. During the lead up to UDI, security and
intelligence in the Commonwealth had been essentially the responsibility of
MI5, and there was extensive co-operation between British, colonial and South
African military and intelligence forces in southern Africa.[1]

Until the formation of the Central African Federation in 1953, security and
intelligence in Southern Rhodesia had been the sole responsibility of the British
South African Police (BSAP). With the establishment of the Federation, the
Federal Security and Intelligence Bureau (FSIB) was formed, headed by Bob de
Quehen, who had served in BSAP but came to the Federal Bureau from MI5.
His 'appointment as Director of FSIB made it clear that liaison between BSAP
and MI5 was an essential part of his function'. In 1960 Welensky, Prime
Minister of Northern Rhodesia, had asked for an SIS officer and got 'the son of a
well-known Southern Rhodesian politician . . . [who] had served in the Special
Air Service (with David Stirling) during the Second World War'. On the
dissolution of the Federation in December 1963, Ken Flower was asked to set
up a new security and intelligence organisation for (Southern) Rhodesia, and
went off on a tour of various forces – including the British – to see how to do it.[2]

Although the *de facto* integration of the Federation's forces into MI5's empire-
wide ambit had ceased, relations between the new Rhodesian Central Intelligence Organisation (CIO) and its London counterparts remained very close –
and continued so through the first year after UDI. In the immediate pre-UDI
period 'it suited the British to apprise CIO of every possible consequence of
taking UDI and the wealth of information conveyed via British Intelligence from
British military, political and economic sources helped me to compile as
complete a picture of the Anglo-Rhodesian jigsaw as if I was getting direct access

94

to the sources.' After UDI, Rhodesian intelligence chief Flower 'saw no need to let the politicians' squabbles affect the liaison between British Intelligence and CIO'.[3]

A month after Wilson, in the Commons, had apparently ruled out the use of force, Richard Crossman noted in his diary on 28 November 1965: 'George Wigg said to me one morning "By the way, about psychological warfare, have you time to talk about it and tell me who could help us?" I mentioned Hugh Carleton Greene and Sefton Delmer [both had worked with Crossman during the war in various psychological warfare departments] . . . I then remarked "What the hell George, surely you started thinking about psychological war before now?" George said "Don't get angry, Dick, but that's the situation. The Prime Minister is now beginning to wonder whether we oughtn't to use it." '[4]

Wigg's search for a 'black propaganda' expert led in the end to Harold Robins, who had worked with Delmer and Crossman during the war and who was then with the Information Research Department, the psychological warfare outfit which operated in the no-man's land between the Foreign Office, to which it was officially responsible, and MI6, with which it worked. A radio station was built at Francistown, in Botswana, with security arranged through another member of Wilson's informal network, the Chief Constable of Lancashire, Eric St Johnston. The station was actually a cover for a BBC monitoring station, the Central Africa Unit. However, the operation was not a success: Rhodesia's CIO jammed the station's output. In 1967, a new transmitter was provided to the Zambian Broadcasting Company at Livingstone. The broadcasts from Zambia brought protests from the British right who alleged that the station was broadcasting information on sabotage techniques.[5]

Of the British propaganda efforts, only fragments are known. One anti-Rhodesian propaganda operation, Interform, was based in Geneva. Interform was created after the Commonwealth Prime Ministers' Conference in September 1966, to 'launch a secret political and propaganda campaign to create "liberal opinion" against the Smith regime and make mandatory sanctions effective'. CIO learned of the plan after documents referring to it were stolen from an African diplomatic mission in London. CIO gave the story to the *Daily Telegraph*, which was sympathetic to the Smith regime, and the paper 'blew' Interform's cover in December 1966.[6]

The *Telegraph* was also used by Rhodesia's CIO to publicise another British operation. In 1966, reports Ken Flower, 'We learnt from friends of friends in Britain that there was a threatening build-up of British troops on Malta. My Deputy flew to the island to check personally on British paratroopers being trained at Luqa airport and found they were engaged in simulated practice for dropping on Salsbury airport.' In March, CIO gave the story to Ian Colvin at the *Telegraph*. This led to an editorial 'What next in Rhodesia?': 'the Rhodesian authorities believe Mr Wilson considered using military force against them even without the excuse of internal disorders or an invitation from the Governor . . . Mr Wilson should renew his pledge and say that we will not send British troops into Rhodesia if sanctions fail to achieve their object.' Flower comments: 'That did the trick.'[7]

Despite Wilson's apparent ruling out of military actions, a part of the British state's psychological warfare campaign was a series of rumours of British preparations for invasion which 'came in to CIO, emanating from British, American, South African and other sources'. These fooled no-one, however, and were so inept that CIO dismissed the idea that they were coming from MI6, assuming instead that the likely origin was 10 Downing Street, the Foreign Office or the Commonwealth Relations Office in Whitehall.[8]

Flower's assumption that the conflict between Britain and Rhodesia should not affect his friendly relations with his British (MI6) counterparts is revealing of a certain contempt for politics wide-spread among senior intelligence personnel. At the time, CIO was running covert intelligence gathering operations in Britain, working with the Tory right against the Government's policy – and running smears against Wilson. Although Rhodesia's operations in Britain are completely missing from his memoir, just before his death in 1987, Flower admitted to a South African newspaper that the CIO had run a smear campaign against the Wilson Government – and Wilson in particular. Flower said that his agents planted disinformation in the international press, including the suggestions that Wilson was pro-communist and was sexually involved with Marcia Williams.[9]

Concerning the smear campaign, we know of one document about Wilson's relationship not with Mrs Williams but with her predeccesor, which was 'given wide circulation to MPs, the Archbishop of Canterbury and other public figures'. Where would the Rhodesians get such material? Flower told Australian historian Ian Hancock, that: 'We got the information from London, and used our London contacts to insert the story where we knew it would hurt.' Flower later added that 'there were some British information sources determined to get Wilson out of office'. Another CIO effort was the distribution of leaflets attributed to something called the Tudor Rose Society during the 1966 by-election in Hull, urging a vote against the Labour Government.[10]

Part of the political operation run by the Smith regime in London was propaganda directed at the British public and media. The first attempt had been the Friends of Rhodesia, created by the Rhodesian High Commissioner in 1964, but which had never got off the ground. This was replaced by the Anglo-Rhodesian Society, initially funded by the Rhodesian Government and provided with information by them. In Rhodesia, the Tory right was to find the cause which they had been seeking.[11]

Most remarkable of all, CIO penetrated the Wilson Cabinet Office, using 'agents' who had been placed in the UK before UDI. In 1960, John Fairer-Smith, a former sergeant in Rhodesian Special Branch, arrived in the UK to organise infiltration of exile groups supporting the nationalists in Rhodesia. At this stage, Rhodesian security forces were a British colonial force and this operation in Britain must have been sanctioned by the British state. Fairer-Smith then left Britain in 1965, just before UDI. He returned to the UK in 1966, under business cover as an 'export manager' and 'ran a secret Rhodesian intelligence set-up in London'. One of his London agents was Norman Blackburn.[12]

Blackburn joined the Rhodesian Army in 1960, becoming Fairer-Smith's bodyguard in 1963, and came to the UK in 1965. He recruited informants at Fairer-Smith's direction; claiming to have ten such informers in South African and Rhodesian nationalist exile groups in the UK. That same year, British gang-leader Charles Richardson was recruited by South African intelligence to carry out burglaries of the exiled groups – including ZAPU. In 1966, the Blackburn network was passed from Fairer-Smith to a 'controller' within South Africa House, a 'Mr Kruger'. The reason for the hand-over has never been disclosed. In 1967, now under South African control, Blackburn recruited a typist in the Cabinet Office, Helen Keenan, who passed him Cabinet papers on discussions of the Rhodesian question. Keenan and Blackburn were arrested in May 1967 and Blackburn was jailed for five years, serving four. This short sentence for stealing Cabinet papers is indicative of the ambiguous view of the 'rebellion' of the Smith regime held by sections of the British ruling élite. Astonishingly, Fairer-Smith was allowed to continue working as a 'private' intelligence agent in the UK.[13]

Although only fragments of these operations have surfaced, it is clear that there were fairly large-scale intelligence operations in Britain by the Rhodesians and South Africans which were rarely hindered by MI5 – and more rarely brought to the attention of the Wilson Government. It was left to a couple of Labour backbenchers, Paul Rose and James Wellbeloved, to try to expose these intelligence networks in 1971. This exposure did not, apparently, lead to any action by the British security forces against either Rhodesian or South African intelligence personnel in the UK. To all intents and purposes, they were ignored – and sometimes given support by their British counterparts. Although Matthew Nkoana alleged, in 1971, that in 1966 'British intelligence took over and the Fairer-Smith organisation was smashed', it seems more likely that Fairer-Smith received a warning and, before leaving the country, handed over his network to South African intelligence.[14]

More than a decade later, as we shall see, in the aftermath of his Commons statement alleging South African interference in British political life, Harold Wilson steered reporters Penrose and Courtiour back towards Norman Blackburn.[15]

Eventually, the intelligence and propaganda war stymied Flower's attempt to maintain a friendly relationship with his British counterparts in Salisbury. Following the failure of the negotiations on board HMS *Fearless* between Wilson and Smith, Flower says that 'the entire basis of the connection with British Intelligence changed to one bedevilled by numerous obstacles, rendering the relationship unfriendly even antagonistic. The last British Intelligence representation in Salisbury had been withdrawn in 1966.'[16]

His failure to stay 'on net' with his British contacts was brought home to him when the British High Commissioner, Jack Johnson, leaving Rhodesia in 1966, told Flower that he expected sanctions to have removed the Smith regime inside three months. 'You must be joking!' Flower replied. His comments speak volumes: 'directing my glance more at the British Intelligence Officer present than at Johnson himself, "If you really believe that, we've been wasting our time in liaison all these years".' If the British intelligence personnel had failed to educate the resident diplomat, it is no wonder that the Labour Government in London understood so little.[17]

Flower puzzles over the revealed ignorance of British politicians: 'From our checks and cross-checks with British Intelligence we knew that they [i.e. MI6] had all the right answers, but it seemed their views were subordinated within a system that did not permit them direct access to the Prime Minister'. This, too, is nonsense. The Chief of MI6 has direct access to the Prime Minister – if it is desired. If MI6 were submitting accurate reports – and on this there is no evidence – they were being blocked either at the Joint Intelligence Committee, or within the Cabinet Office.[18]

In 1967, still seeking a clear intelligence picture, Wilson and Wigg decided to obtain the intelligence themselves. They turned to Wigg's friend, the Tory MP Henry Kerby. Kerby went on what he thought was a secret mission to Rhodesia. In fact, the Rhodesians had been tipped off about his visit. Not that it mattered, Ken Flower of CIO was only too happy for the British government to get a clear picture of conditions in the country.[19]

Even if the British state had not comprehensively misinformed and disinformed the Cabinet, we doubt if Wilson's behaviour (or that of HMG) would have been radically different. Most of the major props in the drama were already fixed in place. The British economy's need for trade with South Africa, the nuclear establishment's dependence on uranium from Namibia and the Americans' dependence on gold from South Africa meant that the sanctions against South Africa were out. Had such a proposal reached the United Nations, the United States would have vetoed it. Thus, no real pressure could be brought on South Africa when it assisted 'rebel' Rhodesia, as it obviously had always intended to do.

Even though the Wilson Government's room for real manoeuvre was tiny, the permanent government still reacted with hostility and disinformation. The use of force – urged by a minority of the Labour left and Jeremy Thorpe – was out. Wilson needed another General Election. The political system as a whole was expecting one in 1966 after UDI had been declared in November 1965. The use of military power, the possibility of (white) Rhodesians being killed by British troops, *would* have been politically damaging. Even the idea of British force against our 'kith and kin' was scotched by Wilson – the politician Wilson – as soon as it was raised by the Conservatives. Ian Smith understood this. Returning from talks with Wilson just after UDI, he remarked to Ken Flower that military intervention 'wasn't practical politics'. Practical politics with a Commons majority of four begins and ends with getting a bigger majority. At the beginning of 1966, the Rhodesian 'distraction' was just a question of damage limitation in a General Election year.

Also on Wilson's mind was the effect that Rhodesia was having on the Conservative Party. With an election coming, Wilson was looking at a Tory Party which was split three ways. In the Commons, the Imperial right, led by Julian Amery, mustered 50 votes against oil sanctions; the official Opposition line was abstention; and 31 Tories voted with the Labour Government in favour of them. As Roth commented, only a former Chief Whip like Heath could really appreciate what a defeat this was – and what trouble the issue could cause in the future. One of the really significant effects of Rhodesian UDI was on the development of the Tory right wing, which found in the issue the cause they had been seeking around which they could mobilise. In 1967, Kenneth Young predicted that: 'Future historians of the Conservative Party may discover that upon its heart in the 1960s "Rhodesia" was indelibly graven.'[20]

XIV

BLUNT

In that cloak and dagger world it is terribly difficult to know what MI5 are thinking. They like to be mysterious about it all . . . my main concern was what we should say if it all leaked out.

SENIOR CIVIL SERVANT

THE IMMUNITY DEAL given to the fourth man, Anthony Blunt, by the British state, and the ensuing cover-up, were sanctioned by a Conservative Government. During the period of the Wilson Governments, the Prime Minister was kept in ignorance of the Blunt problem and, although Tory Prime Minister Edward Heath had been 'obsessed' with the damage to the Establishment that exposure of Blunt's homosexual past might create, it was Wilson's ministers whose careers and reputations were ultimately to be destroyed. Dick White and Roger Hollis, in what appears to have been a bureaucratic move, had shunted malcontents such as Peter Wright into the relative backwaters of the molehunts and the Blunt debriefings. Unfortunately, Wright used the opportunity to plough unrestrained through the agency's files in an effort to find dirt on the Labour Party and its supporters. In the process, he found little of substance but enough to create a conspiracy theory which would poison the atmosphere during the two Wilson administrations of the 1960s. It all began when an honourable man, who was later to regret the damage caused, suffered a pang of conscience.

Michael Straight was one of many children of the east coast American élite to have been radicalised by the depression and the rise of fascism. He had been at Cambridge in the 1930s, a fringe member of the university's left, and was recruited into the Cambridge 'cell' which included Guy Burgess and Anthony Blunt. Straight had never been a wholly committed member and during the war had moved from the left to being a routine rich liberal, trying to forget about his youthful flirtation with communism. All went well until June 1963, when the Kennedy Administration offered him the chair of the Advisor Council on the Arts. He was told that his appointment would have to be ratified by Congress and the FBI, who would routinely look into his background.

Straight decided to unburden himself. He went to the FBI and told his tale of pre-war, left-wing intrigue to William Sullivan, the FBI's Deputy Director, responsible for counter-espionage. 'The debriefing with Sullivan's men lasted for most of June 1963 but it was not until January 1964 that British Intelligence learned an American had provided the long-awaited final piece of evidence needed in order to force Sir Anthony Blunt into admitting that he had been a member of the Burgess spy ring.' Although MI5 Director-General Roger Hollis took personal charge of the case, it was Arthur Martin, head of the élite D1 section of D Branch, which monitored Soviet covert activities in Britain, who met and debriefed Straight. Even with Straight's new information, it was unclear whether the evidence existed to secure a conviction of Blunt. Martin agreed with Hollis that the Surveyor of the Queen's Pictures, had to be 'recruited as a source . . . The only way to secure a detailed confession . . . was to offer Blunt immunity from prosecution and a guarantee that there would be no publicity.'[1]

For the secret state, the issue was the necessary absence of publicity. If total immunity was the price, then so be it. Coming so soon after Philby's defection and other security scandals such as the Profumo Affair, the exposure of Blunt threatened a tidal wave of bad publicity. Peter Wright says: 'Hollis and many of his senior staff were acutely aware of the damage any public revelation of Blunt's activities might do to themselves, to MI5, and to the incumbent Conservative Government [and] realized only too well that a scandal on the scale that would be provoked by Blunt's prosecution would surely bring the tottering Government down.' The solution, of course, was a cover-up.[2]

In March 1964, Home Secretary Henry Brooke agreed to authorise the immunity offer: in April, the Queen's Private Secretary, Michael Adeane, was informed. Arthur Martin saw Blunt on 23 April 1964, at the Courtauld Institute, where, after informing him of the Straight confession, he offered Blunt total immunity in exchange for a confession. Martin saw Blunt approximately ten times between April and November 1964 (when he was transferred to MI6).[3]

The Labour Government was elected in October 1964. Hollis did not inform the incoming Home Secretary, Frank Soskice, or the new Attorney General, Elwyn Jones, or George Wigg, the security 'watchdog' appointed by Harold Wilson precisely to keep an eye on such potential embarrassments, about Blunt. Andrew Boyle's sources told him that following the change of power there were anxious deliberations inside MI5. 'When, if ever, would it be appropriate to inform Elwyn Jones, the new Attorney General? The secret consensus was that the Wilson administration deserved to be left severely alone to its pressing economic and political tasks. With a slender working majority of only four seats in the Commons, the new Government would surely not last. So Hollis decided to hold his fire and wait.' Both Charles Cunningham, the Home Office liaison with MI5, and Maurice Crump, the deputy Director of Public Prosecutions who handled the immunity case of Blunt, remained in post until 1966. Neither told their political masters of the Blunt affair.[4]

It was not until March 1966, with the election of the second Wilson Government by a large overall majority, that 'second thoughts began to circulate fitfully in the security directorate. Perhaps it would be advisable to confide in the

Labour Minister responsible for the security services? These second thoughts did not prevail.' In fact, 'no Labour Attorney General was invited to review the case of Anthony Blunt until Sam Silkin reviewed the case in 1974 and concluded that a prosecution of Blunt could not be launched'. Silkin pointed out in the House of Commons that while the Conservative Governments were informed in 1964 and 1970, Elwyn Jones, the Labour Attorney General in the middle, was never told. This was in part because 'there were some Labour Ministers, especially in junior posts, whom MI5, in its received wisdom, looked down on as "security risks". Nor did they care for the nosey George Wigg, Wilson's security adviser.' More specifically, MI5 had doubts about the Lord Chancellor Gerald Gardiner and Elwyn Jones.[5]

Elwyn Jones had had problems with MI5 before and was undoubtedly the subject of a substantial MI5 file. He travelled to Vienna, in March 1934, to give legal help to the prisoners and detainees as the Social Democratic Party was being suppressed. In 1941, he was interviewed at the War Office 'about the possibility of serving in Intelligence, presumably because of my pre-war connections with the underground anti-Nazis, particularly in Germany and Austria. I heard no more about it – whether because of my earlier political activities or the limitations of my French or German I know not.' Post-war, he maintained close links with the British–Polish Society and became Chairman of the Union of Democratic Control, an organisation formed to campaign for open instead of secret diplomacy, which, in the 1920s had been the first pressure group to ask questions about the secret state. MI5 kept files on the group. The UDC had been on the Labour Party's Proscribed List as a number of alleged communists and 'fellow-travellers' were involved. Elwyn Jones was also a founder member of the pressure groups Justice and Amnesty International, both targets of the security services.[6]

Gerald Gardiner, Wilson's Lord Chancellor, also had an MI5 file. He was a pacifist, joining the Peace Pledge Union in 1936. He was also an initial sponsor of the Campaign for Nuclear Disarmament and a leading campaigner for the abolition of the death penalty. Gardiner, the highest legal officer in the land, later confessed that he suspected that his telephone was tapped by MI5. He believed that his office was unsafe. 'When I really had to speak to the Attorney General in confidence, I took him out on one or more occasions in the car because I knew the driver, and I knew that she would never have allowed the car to be bugged without my knowledge.'[7]

On becoming Lord Chancellor, Gardiner asked to see his MI5 file. This was refused. He was told that he would have to see the Home Secretary. However, 'Frank Soskice was embarrassed and said that he couldn't agree and he wasn't allowed to see the files either. When they wanted to show him anything, they photographed a page and gave it to him but he never saw the complete file. He was so upset about it that I just let it drop.' Gardiner told Tony Benn that he had heard that someone who had insisted on seeing his complete file had been informed that it had been destroyed the day before. This was true. Sidney Bernstein, the theatrical and television impressario, who was himself on the MI5 suspects list, heard the tale from Herbert Morrison, Minister of Home Security in the Second World War. 'Sidney asked Morrison if he had seen his files when he took over the department. Morrison replied that he had certainly asked to see the personal files they held on himself and Ellen (Wilkinson), but that a civil servant had replied smoothly: "Minister, they were destroyed yesterday." Morrison cited this as an example of British probity; what amazed Sidney was that he actually seemed to believe the civil servant.' Benn commented that 'it was a direct confirmation of what one suspects: that there is no political control whatsoever over the security services.'[8]

The man who took over the interrogation of Blunt, following Arthur Martin's departure to MI6 in November 1964, was Peter Wright. Although he had helped Martin with technical assistance when Blunt was being debriefed, Wright had no real qualifications for this post. Yet the novice counter-intelligence officer was turned loose. Why did the generally cautious Hollis give him the go-ahead? Was he hoping to shunt 'the Gestapo' down a blind alley? If so, it was a grave mistake because Wright was to turn what was research of purely historical interest – Blunt had left the service twenty years before – into a means of attacking the Establishment and specifically the Labour Party.

Wright began his new career as a counter-intelligence officer already suspicious that a mole lurked in the security service. Almost immediately, his paranoia was fed by a secret report written by Anne Glass, wife of Charles Elwell, another counter-intelligence officer. The report was a catalogue of allegations of Soviet penetration. 'There were literally dozens and dozens of allegations. Many of them fanciful – off-hand comments drawn from agents' reports; but others were more concrete.' Many of them dated back to the period before and during the war when Maxwell Knight was running agents in Britain. Wright must have felt a Cassandra-like kinship with Knight. Both had tried to warn their superiors about the dangers of communist infiltration into public life; both had been ignored. After studying the Glass document, Wright left the office, his head 'humming' with what he had learned. He sprang into action, plunging back into the forgotten files of MI5's Registry in search of other spies outside of the service.[9]

By the time that Wright took over the interrogations from Martin in the spring of 1965, Blunt had given as much as he was going to give. Wright was the 'B team', left with the titbits of minor significance. Blunt was obviously intelligent, highly sophisticated and more than a match for the 'technician'. What seems apparent from the evidence we have is that the Blunt interrogations conducted by Wright were a peg on which Wright was able to hang many of his prejudices. As he admits, 'politicians and successive managements in MI5 were terrified that intensive inquiries might trigger further defections or uncover unsavoury Establishment scandals, and that was considered an unacceptable risk during the 1950s'. However, in the sixties with a Labour Government it was deemed acceptable to allow Wright to go after the 'Oxford Comintern' – his long presumed, though never seen, equivalent of the Cambridge Comintern. According to one MI5 officer, Anthony Motion, who was dispatched to Oxford to dig through the files on the 1930s, his 'inquires had thrown up a few "minor spies" '.[10]

The members of the 'Oxford Comintern' were often people who in the 1930s had campaigned against fascism and whose commitment to the cause had sometimes led them to join the Communist Party. Most had left at the time of the Stalin–Hitler Pact and had subsequently joined the Labour Party. A few were now junior ministers in the Labour Government. They had little sympathy for the Soviet Union, some could hardly be described as left-wing, and they had no contact with Soviet bloc intelligence services. However, Peter Wright and his cronies inside MI5, digging through the dusty old files, began to piece together an intricate conspiracy theory in which these ministers and other Labour Party sympathisers were treated as potential 'spies'.

XV

SPOOKS TWO

*The Security Service that Hollis passed on to his successor, Martin
Furnival-Jones, was an organisation almost paralysed by self-doubt.
Relations with the Americans had been throughly undermined by the
destructive molehunts.*

NIGEL WEST

'WE HAD NO SECURITY or indeed any governmental scandals when he
was in office', says Edward Short of the security watchdog, George Wigg. Short's
comment illustrates how far removed senior Cabinet Ministers were from the
intelligence game. In fact, there were many security scandals to which only the
secret state was privy. Across the Atlantic, the American intelligence community
believed British security to be in deep crisis. Charles Bates, FBI liaison officer at
the American Embassy in London, was deeply disillusioned with MI5. 'I will
never forget going to see Hollis one time. I said, "Roger, you guys haven't come
up with anything since World War II." He said, "Oh, sure we have," I said, "No
you haven't. We gave you almost everything, either us or the CIA." ' J. Edgar
Hoover had long believed MI5 was 'hopelessly unreliable' and, in 1958, ordered
Bates to carry out a secret review of Britain's security at her nuclear facilities.
Bates found that it was 'non-existent'. MI5 was 'full of inexperienced "old
school-tie" men who feared probing supects because of possible political rows'.
The American intelligence community which provided Britain with money,
hardware and information began to suspect that MI5 'amateurism', especially in
the counter-intelligence field, might be compromising their own sources and
security. It therefore became important for MI5 to show the Americans that it
was now a professional service.[1]

The first known operation with Wigg as 'Security Watchdog' was a complete
disaster and confirmed the poor regard in which the Americans held MI5. 'Air
Bubble' began in January 1964 when the Belgian Sûreté d'Etat informed MI5
that a double agent, Paul Soupert, was receiving details of certain manufacturing
processes from two Kodak employees, Alfred Roberts and Godfrey Conway.
Soupert, a Brussels-based retired chemical engineer, had been recruited by the

East German security service, HVS, as part of Operation 'Brunhilde' which trawled the West for industrial secrets and, in particular, details of the joint Anglo-French Concorde project. Arrested by the Belgians in 1964, Soupert had then been 'turned' to work for the West. Attorney General Elwyn Jones later told the Commons that MI5 were involved in operations 'with other allied security services for the purpose of breaking up a hostile spy ring controlled by the East German intelligence service'. One of the industrial agents whom Soupert 'blew' was an East German engineer called Herbert Steinbrecher. 'It was initially thought', Elwyn Jones revealed, 'that Soupert might be involved in the collection of defence secrets in this country.' Roberts, Conway and Soupert were put under surveillance by MI5. However, 'the security authorities came to the conclusion that Soupert's interest in this country was in obtaining trade or industrial secrets. At that stage, the matter passed from the hands of the authorities into the hands of the police.' This was an industrial espionage case and, therefore, technically outside the remit of MI5. But the Attorney General was misled. Roberts was a Communist Party member and Vice-President of the trade union ACTT and 'had been of interest to [MI5's] F Branch for years'. MI5 involved themselves because of 'the allegation of subversion: a CPGB member selling a trade secret'.[2]

On 28 November 1964, Steinbrecher was arrested in Paris in possession of technical film on Concorde. The following night, Special Branch officers arrested Conway and Roberts on a trumped-up charge of receiving a stolen roll of felt. A few days later, they were actually charged under the Prevention of Corruption Act. At a Magistrates' hearing on 14 January 1965, evidence was given by two MI5 'watchers' who said that they had seen Conway and Roberts meeting Soupert. In what looks like a deliberately organised leak, on 28 February 1965 Sunday newspapers revealed that Steinbrecher, 'an East German agent', had 'recruited two British employees of a London photographic firm to help him . . . to collect secret data on the Concorde supersonic airliner.' Kodak had microfilmed many of Concorde's technical drawings but Roberts had no access to this material; and although Steinbrecher was imprisoned for twelve years for industrial espionage, Roberts and Conway were found not guilty at the Old Bailey.[3]

The case against Roberts and Conway collapsed when the prosecution gave the defence a letter which showed that Kodak had agreed to pay Soupert the sum of £5,000 to travel to Britain to give evidence – a month before their arrest. It was also revealed that Soupert's passport had been doctored by Belgian and British Intelligence. Soupert's various allegations were shown to be false and 'Air Bubble' became a personal disaster for Hollis who had decided to pursue it. Confidence on both sides of the Atlantic in the abilities of the Director-General and MI5 to protect aviation secrets hit a new low.[4]

A further case during Wigg's tenure involved right-wing Tory MP, Anthony Courtney. Although this had none of the reverberations of the Profumo Affair, there were aspects of it which Wigg found disturbing and it continues to be something of an enigma. Commander Courtney worked in Naval Intelligence during the war and was posted to Moscow. Leaving the Navy in 1953, he set up an East–West export consultancy, ETG (Eastern Trading Group) Counsultancy Services. As a security precaution, he retained links with MI5 and MI6. As an MP Courtney specialised in security matters, being particularly concerned about the large number of KGB officers posing as diplomats at the London Embassy. Although an anti-communist, Courtney also made many speeches in the House of Commons on improving East–West relations through trade.[5]

The year 1961 was traumatic for Courtney. In March, his wife died of a heart attack. In May, he attended the first British Industrial Exhibition held in Moscow where he had an affair with an Intourist guide, Zina Volkova. In August 1964 Courtney's second wife informed him by letter, while he was on a business trip to Moscow, that the marriage was not working. In January and again in March 1965, anonymous letters were sent to Courtney, his stepson and the leader of the Conservative Opposition, Alec Douglas-Home, accusing Courtney's wife of being unfaithful and urging that 'he should resign as our MP before there is a further public scandal.' In the light of what was to happen later, it is interesting to note that the source 'appeared to be very well-informed about [his] wife's private life'. During March, Courtney returned to the Soviet Union on business. In the first week of August, sexually compromising pictures were sent to MPs, the head of Kodak (whose factory was in his constituency) and to the *News of the World*. They were headed: 'I'm not a Profumo, But . . . (A story in photographs) 1959. Why not try to become an MP to combine business with pleasure and to conduct shady business while "Defending public interests"?' Courtney could not identify the woman but assumed 'that it must be Zina Volkova'. He assumed the smear sheet was a KGB operation. Both H. Montgomery Hyde, a former MI6 officer, and Courtney himself suspected the photographs were faked. Unidentified 'experts', presumably MI5, said the photographs were composites with some indication of faking and re-touching.[6]

Courtney went to see 'an old personal friend', Roger Hollis. Although MI5 could find no similar on-going Soviet operation – and there was no hint of blackmail – they were reasonably certain that the operation was a Soviet 'instrument of character assassination'. Courtney then saw an 'excited' George Wigg who had received a hand-delivered copy of the smear sheet. There was a second meeting in September with Wilson, at which Wigg asked, 'What I want to know is – who are they getting at? They are cracking the whip at someone, and I want to know who that someone is. This may be just the tip of the iceberg.' Ten years later, Wigg was convinced that since Courtney was not a significant figure, the KGB's real motive in distributing the pictures, was to warn 'somebody in a high position'.[7]

Except for a well-informed article in *Private Eye*, the scandal was given little press coverage. Even so, Courtney received no sympathy from his constituency party and in 1966 lost his seat. He and his wife divorced in 1968 and his business collapsed. The smear operation had succeeded but it is not proven that the KGB were behind his fall; it remains speculation. Although Courtney was an anti-communist, it does seem perverse of the Soviets to have ruined one of the small group of East–West traders; the Soviet Union had few friends. On the other hand there were many people in the British intelligence community who disliked commercial contacts with the Eastern bloc and were prepared to undermine such trade agreements. Nearly all the East–West traders were subjected to smear operations, Lord Boothby being the most prominent.[8]

The Courtney smear fed Wigg's general paranoia about security. MI5 were beginning to focus their attention on Downing Street and, for a time, Wigg went along this false trail. In 1977, Wigg told Andrew Wilson of the *Observer* that he had 'become increasingly convinced that someone inside Number Ten during his time as security chief was in fact a deep-cover Soviet intelligence agent and that another highly placed occupant was being blackmailed'. This gave rise to speculation, which Wigg did nothing to curtail, that he was referring to Wilson. However, this was the view of an embittered old man who had been out of office for a decade, who was 'highly wrought' and was said 'by security colleagues to have kept in touch with security circles'.[9]

The next security problem led to a major confrontation with the Americans. It had begun in 1962 with the recruitment by the Americans of two high-ranking Soviet intelligence officers, code-named TOP HAT and FEDORA, who were serving at the United Nations. According to the Soviet sources, TOP HAT – Col. Dmitri Polyakov – passed to the Americans details on nuclear weapons doctrine, civil defence and diplomatic codes. FEDORA – identity still uncertain – gave information to the FBI about an ideological agent in a British Atomic Energy Authority research establishment. The information was filtered by MI5 and led them to an Italian scientist, Dr Giuseppe Martelli, working at the Culham Laboratory in Oxfordshire. Although he had been in contact with Russian intelligence officers, Martelli had not had access to nuclear secrets and when the case came to court in July 1963 it quickly fell apart. Against the advice of its own lawyers, the case had been pursued by MI5 in the hope of improving relations with the FBI's J. Edgar Hoover.[10]

In late 1964, Polyakov – TOP HAT – told the Americans that 'the Soviet Union was obtaining vital information about guidance systems for United States nuclear weapons from a source in Britain'. Once again, they passed the information on to MI5. The source was Frank Bossard, working in the Naval Guided Weapons Branch of the Ministry of Aviation, where he was able to witness highly secret missile tests. Bossard had not been positively vetted for some time, as the documents he saw were classified only 'Secret' or less. More importantly, the Ministry did not know that Bossard – who spied for money rather than ideology – had been convicted for fraud. He was arrested in March 1965 by Special Branch officers and sentenced, in May, to twenty-five years' imprisonment.[11]

A Security Commission report on Bossard, issued in June 1965, revealed serious failures of security procedures in the Ministry of Aviation. However, it 'went out of its way again to exonerate MI5 from any blame whatever'. The report was 'unprecedented in naming certain civil servants whom it considered as deserving of criticism for departmental failures to prevent the espionage, and the Whitehall mandarins – the so-called Permanent Secretaries Club – reacted with alacrity'. Pincher says that Wigg, who had been the 'arch-ferret demanding information from the government . . . quickly became the protector, going to great lengths in his efforts to suppress the names of civil servants who might be held to blame for security lapses'. The Prime Minister was persuaded to set up an independent inquiry under a former mandarin, Sir Henry Wilson Smith, whose White Paper 'exonerated the civil servants and overruled the Commission'.[12]

Senior MI5 officers had doubts about the credentials of FEDORA and TOP HAT because they had supplied information on the Profumo Affair which MI5 believed to be false. In the poisoned atmosphere of the time, any defector from the Soviet Union was treated as an intelligence 'provocation'. They were 'already half-convinced that FEDORA was a fake defector who might have planted the information for mischievous purposes'. MI5 subsequently concluded that TOP HAT had turned over Bossard in 'an inept attempt to damage relations between MI5 and the CIA'.[13]

Whether or not these fears were justified, relations between MI5 and the CIA were damaged. Bossard was the last straw: a convicted criminal had been allowed access to sensitive information; the vetting system had failed. 'The CIA was furious.' Not only was the information flow all one way, from the US agencies to MI5, the information they supplied was mishandled. Tired of MI5's excuses, in the summer of 1965 President Johnson commissioned a secret review of British security from the President's Foreign Intelligence Advisory Board. Two highly experienced National Security advisers on the Board, lawyer Gordon Gray and former FBI agent Patrick Coyne, were sent to London to review the Anglo-American intelligence relationship. 'No one in British intelligence was told that the review was taking place', says Peter Wright. 'Most of Gray and Coyne's material was supplied by Cleveland Cram, the CIA officer in charge of liaison in London with MI5. Cram was a brilliant and level-headed CIA officer . . . Cram brought Gray and Coyne into Leconsfield House and MI6 headquarters on a number of occasions, introducing them merely as colleagues. At this time CIA officers had open access to all British Intelligence establishments.'[14]

Following the Bossard case, one obvious target of the American investigation was the Ministry of Aviation, which was absorbed into the new Ministry of Technology after the March 1966 General Election. The Ministry's security department was responsible for 'policing about five hundred defence firms which handle classified information and [their] employees'. Some time later, Tony Benn, Minister of Technology at the time, was inadvertently told about the Gray/Coyne inquiry by his security officer. 'The Americans had inspected our security system and were satisfied by it. It was an interesting and extraordinary revelation. Here was I, Minister of a British Department, hearing from one of my own officials that another country had inspected our security arrangements and I had never been told about it.'[15]

As the Gray/Coyne report covered counter-intelligence and espionage, a copy went to James Angleton at the CIA, who 'was thrilled by the report', telling Wright that it 'would form the basis of a new relationship between British and American counter-intelligence'. He went on: 'Everything'll change now, we're going to have a beefed-up London CIA station, and half those officers are going to work directly inside MI5.' Though very critical of MI5 himself, even Wright was unhappy about this American intrusion into British affairs and blew the Gray/Coyne operation to MI5. Deputy Director, Martin Furnival-Jones and Hollis then went to see the Foreign Secretary, Michael Stewart, to protest at what they saw as a blatant abuse of the UK–USA agreement on intelligence co-operation.[16]

The Gray/Coyne review took place during a wider Whitehall review of Britain's defence and foreign policy role. It is highly likely that both the reviews were linked and that each side – at the highest levels of the permanent government – knew of the other. The year 1965 saw the final emergence of an integrated Defence Intelligence Service within the Ministry of Defence and a review of signals intelligence initiated by the the Cabinet Secretary and conducted by Stuart Hampshire. There were also changes in MI6 and the Foreign Office's secret propaganda unit, the Information Research Department (IRD).

Within MI6 the review introduced 'a new era of strict financial control, and the first of a series of station amalgamations which served to eliminate certain stations judged to be relatively unproductive'. MI6 was trimmed by the Foreign Office 'to reflect Britain's status as a small debtor nation, with a scaled down army, manoeuvering to join the EEC'. Stations were closed in South America, but MI6 was allowed to move into new areas, such as Africa, where the service took over responsibilties for some of the former colonies like Nigeria. MI5's E Branch, traditionally responsible for internal security in the colonies and Africa, 'withered on the vine'. This gradual run-down of MI6's overseas representation 'changed the nature of the new relationship with the CIA and emphasized the trend towards acceptance of GCHQ's product which, thanks to technical breakthroughs in the data-processing field, was proving both reliable and cost-effective.' GCHQ began to dominate the intelligence output to the Joint Intelligence Committee 'with the result that more weight was given to SIGINT analysis'. Agents in place and human resources were being downgraded, which satisfied the Foreign Office bureaucrats but displeased the MI6 professionals.[17]

The general financial squeeze was also applied to the Foreign Office's secret propaganda unit, IRD. It was initially cut down when the Labour Party took office in 1964, again in 1968 and, following an economy drive the next year, 'slashed' in 1970. Around this time IRD was told to 'stop concentrating so heavily on communism and promote other British interests'. As far as is known, during the Wilson Governments in the sixties no new IRD 'front' agencies were created. It is probable, in our view, that the CIA's expansion in 1965 of the London-based propaganda front, Forum World Features, which was 'run with the knowledge and co-operation of British Intelligence', was a response to the political and financial pressure on IRD. As a result of the cut-backs Britain's intelligence agencies had to rely increasingly on the support of the Americans for resources.[18]

Hollis had been so enraged by the Gray/Coyne review that 'he refused to speak to Helms, the CIA chief, thereafter. The more diplomatic-minded [CIA] officers in the London station persuaded Helms to drop the idea of direct political intervention in British affairs. Instead they argued, why not wait for

Hollis to retire at the end of the year?' Due to retire in December 1965, Hollis had recommended his deputy, Martin Furnival-Jones, as his replacement but 'initially Wilson was determined to override Hollis's advice and appoint an outsider – another "honest copper" in the shape of Sir Eric St Johnston, who he knew personally and admired. Sir Eric, Chief Constable of Lancashire, had been helpful to Wilson who held the Lancashire seat of Huyton.' St Johnston had liaised closely with MI5 during the war when they were based at Blenheim and had met Hollis who he 'did not think very bright'. Wilson had 'wanted someone from outside whom he could trust'. Sir Eric told Pincher 'that he would have been unable to resist the offer. In the event the approach was never made because of the intervention of George Wigg, Labour's Paymaster-General.'[19]

Wigg confided in Pincher that 'after listening to "professional advice" inside MI5 he had been convinced that the previous "honest copper", Sir Percy Sillitoe, had almost wrecked MI5 by introducing police methods and attitudes. He had also, incidentally, set back everybody's promotion prospects for several years, as would St Johnston, who was only fifty-three.' The 'proposal was vehemently and successfully opposed by . . . the Home Office'. The nominal controller of MI5, Home Secretary Frank Soskice, was easily persuaded by his officials. An 'impossibly reactionary man', in the opinion of Tony Benn, Soskice was no stranger to MI5, having served in the Special Operations Executive during the war as a security officer. However, he was a weak Home Secretary 'entirely in the hands of his civil servants'.[20]

Wilson called in the new Director-General and asked him, 'Are you running any MPs as agents?' Furnival-Jones, who knew about Henry Kerby, stalled by answering, 'If we are, I will stop it.' Kerby, who enjoyed his role by all accounts, was disappointed and his apparent change of sides – from reporting to MI5 to reporting to Wilson and Wigg – seems to have occurred at this point. Or was this simply a cover, the appearance of changing sides, feeding Wilson and Wigg 'chicken feed' while continuing as an agent for MI5? Pincher suggests that the 'MI5 management had been trying to use Kerby to discover what Wigg was saying about them and what he might intend to do'.[21]

Furnival-Jones was an acceptable 'hawk' to the US and UK intelligence community who could be relied on to make MI5 counter-intelligence much more powerful. Peter Wright says that Furnival-Jones 'was a determined man who believed he faced one major problem – the scale of the Soviet assault, in terms of numbers of Russian intelligence officers in London, relative to his own pitiful forces. His tenure as Director-General was marked by his campaign to expand MI5 and reduce Soviet diplomatic personnel. He had some success with the first, and eventually with the second.' The new Director-General 'struggled to get the Treasury to agree to an expansion of MI5's counter-espionage capability, but they were always reluctant'. In 1971, Furnival-Jones took a side-swipe at Wigg's promotion of the expansion of C Branch at the expense of the counter-intelligence D Branch. He told the Franks Committee, he had wanted to reduce 'the area in which protective security operates . . . I think Clausewitz was right, that concentration of force is one of the principles of warfare, and it is one of the principles of security.' Protective security, he added, was 'basically non-productive'. Furnival-Jones achieved a certain amount by re-directing internal resources so that 'D Branch had first call on all the resources'.[22]

Shortly after Furnival-Jones took over as Director-General, the molehunting team inside MI5 made their report recommending further investigation into their candidates for Soviet spies. In November 1964, as a result of claims by Soviet defector Anatoliy Golitsyn that British Intelligence was heavily penetrated, the two counter-espionage officers who had de-briefed him, Arthur Martin and Christopher Hinton, approached their respective heads, Roger Hollis and Dick White. They concluded that a joint MI5/MI6 investigative committee – later code-named FLUENCY – be set up to look at Golitsyn's claims. Not long afterwards, following a series of internal rows, Martin was transferred to MI6 counter-intelligence staff where he served as the MI6 representative on FLUENCY. Hollis deferred to MI6 Chief, Dick White, who was regarded as his senior, and Peter Wright was made Chair of the new committee.[23]

This small coterie of Golitsyn supporters, whom Hollis had dubbed the 'Gestapo' and others the 'Guardians', were now off the leash, searching for notional 'moles' inside MI5 and MI6. Stephen de Mowbray, described by Wright as 'hot-headed and over impressionable', was a FLUENCY member until he left to take up the MI6/CIA liaison post in Washington in 1966, where, according to one CIA officer, 'he was never out of Angleton's office'. De Mowbray had replaced the popular Christopher Phillpotts, another Angleton enthusiast, who was regarded as de Mowbray's mentor and protector within the service. Both Phillpotts and de Mowbray were committed Golitsyn supporters, which made them many enemies. In 1966, Phillpotts replaced Hinton as head of MI6 counter-intelligence and began a molehunt within the secret service. Pursuing Golitsyn's hypothetical master-spy, Phillpotts helped ruin the careers of a number of innocent officers and wasted enormous energy. It was all highly destructive.[24]

One consequence of the 1965 Gray/Coyne review was that in 1967, without consulting the politicians, this pro-Golitsyn group of officers in MI5, MI6 and the CIA initiated the CANZAB (Canada, Australia, New Zealand, America and Britain) counter-intelligence conferences. At the CANZAB meetings, Angleton and his acolytes 'conducted doom-laden future scenarios' and promoted their global theory – that the KGB were everywhere and every agency was penetrated. Within a decade Labour governments in Australia, New Zealand and the United Kingdom were to experience varying forms of destabilisation from their domestic security and intelligence services – with American assistance.[25]

XVI

MI5 AND THE WILSON CIRCLE

No one should be allowed to become Prime Minister who made twelve trips to Moscow!
PETER WRIGHT

For those of us who know the backgrounds of a number of influential Tory MPs, the natural intimacy between the secret services and the Conservative Party is remarkable. If a Labour government were elected, the secret services would be cuddling up with the Conservative Party in exile day and night, you may be sure of it.
JOHN LE CARRÉ

UNDER PRESIDENT KENNEDY, CIA counter-intelligence chief James Angleton had been allowed to do no more than 'pursue leads' with regard to Harold Wilson. However, with Kennedy's death and the election of an American President who disliked the British Premier, Angleton was in a position to take the matter further. The file opened on Wilson at the CIA, code-named 'Oatsheaf', soon filled with more names, as did its companion file, code-named 'Worthington', held by MI5. Angleton now began to probe what was known as the 'Wilson circle'.[1]

Angleton told journalist Edward J. Epstein that he 'concentrated on the activities of Wilson's close associates, who had made frequent business trips to Moscow. He found out, through his liaison with the National Security Agency (NSA), that when these men were in Moscow, some of their telephone conversations . . . had been routinely intercepted. An analysis of these intercepts showed that they had been in contact with well-known KGB case officers. This connection was not in itself incriminating, since Soviet officials put in contact with important Western visitors are often KGB recruiters. But two of these businessmen had become part of Wilson's entourage.'[2]

Angleton passed the 'Oatsheaf' file to MI5 Director-General Roger Hollis, but masked the source of his alleged information, believing that British Intelligence was deeply penetrated by the KGB. (Angleton would not want to jeopardise his privileged position as the CIA's liaison point with the NSA.) Wright says Angleton 'was clearly worried any action would blow his source'. What was Hollis to do? According to Wright, he 'consulted the Cabinet Secretary, then Burke Trend, and they decided to take no action'. Instead, the matter was raised with the Prime Minister in a roundabout way. Wilson was asked by MI5 'if the KGB had ever made a pitch at him and he said, categorically, that they had not'. An account later confirmed by Wilson to Pincher.[3]

During the first security briefings which Wilson received in office, MI5 warned him about some of his personal friends and MPs. MI5 refused 'to clear certain friends for regular access to Number 10', which is reported to have been 'the root cause of his dislike and distrust of the organisation'.[4]

MI5 investigations had begun while Wilson was still in opposition; something confirmed in 1981 by the *Sunday Times*' Insight Team, who revealed that 'MI5 first became interested in [Joseph] Kagan before Wilson became Prime Minister'. MI5 investigated the suspicion that the Lithuanian born manufacturer of Gannex raincoats 'had been sent to Britain in 1946 as a Soviet agent.' Wright says that MI5 'had been suspicious of Kagan for years . . . We became very concerned when it became very clear that Kagan was courting Wilson's friendship and patronage.' Wilson disliked the way that they were 'automatically suspicious of Kagan because he had managed to escape from the Soviet zone after the war.' Other Wilson 'friends' who were pre-election targets included '[Rudi] Sternberg and his East European friends and Maxwell of Pergamon. We were very suspicious about these people and warned Wilson repeatedly about the risks.' Wilson continually rebuffed MI5, he 'deeply resented routine inquires that MI5 made about those who happened to be involved with East–West trade, which he wanted to encourage.' The pre-1964 election investigation of Kagan apparently reached no conclusion and appeared to be left 'in the air'.[5]

MI5, however, did not leave matters entirely unresolved. They began to compile a subject file code-named 'Worthington', an MI6-generated dossier which 'contained material about Wilson's friends and his journeys behind the Iron Curtain in the 1950s . . . one report came from the Anglo-US GCHQ–NSA code-break . . . it referred to Wilson speculatively as a Soviet "asset".'[6]

With Hollis in control the investigations continued but on a low level. There was a sub-text to the investigations. According to a security source in *The Times*, 'the MI5 investigation was intensified when the Prime Minister tried to appoint an outsider as head of MI5 instead of the usual inside candidate.' We know from Peter Wright's memoirs and other published evidence that the first reaction of MI5 when there was any bureaucratic fight going on which threatened their independence and power was to smear the opposition and create a bogus security threat. For example, when Wilson appointed Michael Cudlipp to investigate and reorganise the government information services in Northern Ireland in 1975, 'Intelligence officers considered creating false "traces" to block his appointment on the grounds that he was a security risk.' And the tactic usually worked.[7]

Hollis retired in November 1965, to be replaced by his heir apparent Furnival-Jones, who had in effect been in control for the last few months. Much to the pleasure of the MI5, 'Gestapo' pressure on Wilson and his circle was increased. The new Director-General's top priority, according to Peter Wright, was Russian counter-espionage, and 'once he took over, the whole approach to the problem changed'. Wright and his friends were given support 'unreservedly' by Furnival-Jones in their investigations. This would appear to have included investigations of the 'Wilson circle'. Arguments over the nature of this 'official' investigation are at the root of allegations of MI5 plotting against Harold Wilson.[8]

In 1965, Angleton made a special trip to England to see Furnival-Jones about Wilson. Relations between President Johnson and the new British Prime Minister were distinctly cool. Johnson wanted greater UK support – preferably a token British ground force – for the war in Vietnam, which Wilson refused to give. Johnson knew of the concerns about Wilson and there was nothing now to stop Angleton taking a more aggressive lead with his information. Also, the Johnson Administration were pushing for changes inside MI5 for a more aggressive counter-intelligence stance. The Americans believed, correctly, that Furnival-Jones would be more sympathetic towards their security concerns than had Hollis.

Angleton, Wright has written, 'said he would give us more detailed evidence and information if we could guarantee to keep the information inside MI5 and out of political circles'. He told MI5 that the CIA had evidence from a defector-in-place behind the Iron Curtain that Wilson was 'assisting the Soviets'. He insisted that to protect the contact, who was in a most sensitive position, MI5 should take no action without first consulting the CIA. 'Not surprisingly the management of MI5 were deeply disturbed by the manner in which Angleton passed this information over.'[9]

Of course, there was no 'defector-in-place': Angleton's source had been the defector Anatoliy Golitsyn. Angleton's 'new material' was the scraps about two of Wilson's friends based on alleged telephone contacts picked up by the NSA, discussed above. What Angleton wanted from MI5 was 'additional material on these two advisers. He expected a discreet investigation into the backgrounds of these two associates of Wilson.' Their indentity has not been revealed but we have a fairly good idea whom he was interested in.[10]

Angleton's mission caused ructions within MI5. He found a security service which was 'out of control'. 'Some MI5 officers', according to Angleton's mouthpiece, Epstein, 'demanded that he be put under surveillance. Others were appalled at the idea that British intelligence would spy on a Prime Minister.' There were moderates, suspicious of Wilson but not prepared to do anything treasonable, and the 'ultras', such as Wright, who believed Wilson was an 'agent of influence'. Angleton was told that 'MI5, after going through this crisis, rejected the proposed investigation'. If this was formally true – and Epstein is the only source so far on this – then the investigation continued unofficially.[11]

One of the 'moderates' was former Indian policeman, Alec MacDonald, head of D Branch with responsibilites for counter-espionage. Before he died in 1988, he told a journalist: 'Wilson had some dubious friends. Even the Labour Party were getting exercised about it, Wigg especially. I was asked to find out about Wilson's friends, which I did. There was nothing very sinister about it. We took it from there.' MacDonald was contemptuous of those like Wright but he still sought to protect the reputation of MI5. He shifted the blame to Wigg.[12]

'Almost reluctantly and certainly sadly', Wigg told Richard Deacon, 'I could never get Harold on his own to warn him of the background of these people.' This is hard to believe because Wigg saw Wilson every day and certainly more than any other Labour figure did. This is a case of chicken and egg. Wigg's concerns were most probably generated by MI5's interest in these people; they were expressed *after* the investigation had already begun.[13]

Via another MI5 defender of the investigation into the Wilson circle we know that MI5 had 'a *theory* that the Communists had a key agent within the Treasury' (our emphasis). They believed 'the source of the high-level leaks was within No. 10 itself'. The Treasury agent had supplied 'the KGB with details of Top Secret economic decisions concerning defence, foreign and domestic policy'. There is, as far as we are aware, no mention of these leaks in any memoir of the period, which makes it of particular interest. Did it in fact exist?[14]

Although MI5's role in protective security embraced the prevention of leaks, Furnival-Jones made it clear to the Franks Committee that he had no specific responsibility for investigating such disclosures, because, 'if there is a leakage of information from that Department the Minister has responsibility, and he cannot push it off on to me'. Further, MI5 involved themselves in leak inquiries only 'where a hostile intelligence service is involved'. The 'discovery' of the Treasury leak thus became highly convenient. It seems that MI5 simply created a 'loop' by inventing a 'trace' which would lead back to a hostile intelligence agency. By this means MI5 could 'legitimately' start an investigation of the Wilson circle after the Prime Minister had vetoed the idea.[15]

The 'trace' connected to John Diamond, Chief Secretary at the Treasury. Six months before the 1964 General Election, Diamond had been the subject of a surveillance operation by MI5, who regarded him as a 'womaniser'. The innocent Diamond was photographed in Venice in the company of two Yugoslav women in what MI5 suggested was a KGB 'honeytrap' operation. On the basis of their theory, MI5 mounted 'a highly secret investigation to track down the suspected No. 10 spy'. This 'centred on "twin targets": Harold Wilson's personal and political staff – and the Treasury.' Reportedly, 'counter-espionage officers maintained surveillance over Downing Street staff. People they met out of office hours were checked.' This source also claims that 'some telephone "intercepts" were authorised. Most of them were domestic telephones.' The purpose of this admission is to suggest that this is how 'the No. 10 "bugging" legend began'. By this means MI5 managed to circumvent Wilson's strictures on the telephone-tapping of MPs.[16]

Other investigations centred on a supposed 'Communist agent of sympathy' at No. 10. A member of Wilson's 'Kitchen Cabinet', George Caunt, confirmed that Beattie Plummer was 'a major cause of security concern in his [Caunt's] day' – the first years of Wilson's administration. According to Richard Deacon:

'Because of her links with business circles behind the Iron Curtain and her frequent calls at No. 10, she was the subject of some suspicion in security circles as a possible source of leakages of Treasury . . . classified information. MI5 were alarmed by her close contacts with Sternberg and her close friendship with, and influence on, Harold Wilson.' By creating Plummer a Peeress in 1965, Wilson demonstrated that not only did he not take the stories about her seriously, neither did the British state (or it would have blocked the honour). He made her a member of the Independent Television Authority in 1966 at the height of MI5's campaign.[17]

The other person investigated was the 'notorious' Rudi Sternberg. The Foreign Office and the security service had been suspicious of his East–West trading activities since the furore over the 1961 Leipzig Trade festival. Although Sternberg's name has been repeatedly linked with Wilson's, the two men hardly knew each other and, in fact, Wilson appears to have avoided associating with him. Wilson was far too canny to open himself up to the smear of guilt by association in such an obvious way. He once posed with a Soviet General on a trip to Moscow. He told a TV producer afterwards: 'You notice that I didn't smile.' He was well aware whom not to be seen smiling with. Security fears about Sternberg were passed on to Deacon: 'Some leakages of information were traced to Sir Rudi and it was then discovered that Lady Plummer had acted as courier for him and passed on the intelligence to officers in East Germany.'[18]

Tory MP James Scott-Hopkins was invited by Sternberg to one of the trade fairs at Leipzig in East Germany. 'Of course, I informed MI6 and they asked me to keep an eye on him . . . MI6 didn't know who Rudi was working for. That's what they wanted to know.' He reported back that Sternberg appeared to be on friendly terms with 'everyone in the Politburo.'[19]

Sternberg, like Plummer, was a member of the British Agricultural Exports Council and from 1968 its Chair. In recognition of his efforts the Agriculture Ministry had on a number of occasions put his name forward for a knighthood. The requests had been blocked by Furnival-Jones, who warned Wilson that there were 'security concerns' about Sternberg. According to Marcia Williams, 'Wilson had at first heeded MI5's warnings, and refused on two or three occasions to recommend Sternberg for an honour, saying, "He's a spy." But finally he ordered a full security check.'[20]

It was this security check, routine for all knighthoods and peerages, which enabled MI5 later to claim that the 'checking out' of Wilson's friends had been 'conducted with the approval of Mr Wilson'. However, the security check did not turn out in the way that MI5 imagined it would. It was discovered that, far from being a spy, 'Sternberg was using his Iron Curtain contacts in a way that was helpful to Western Intelligence.' According to one source: 'Sternberg had always willingly briefed the Foreign Office and MI6 about his impressions of Soviet Bloc officials he had met, including Khrushchev.' And this was on file at MI5. Sternberg received his knighthood.[21]

Towards the end of 1965, Scott-Hopkins was asked by the Tory leader, Sir Alec Douglas-Home, to look for proof for the gossip surrounding Wilson. The former Prime Minister told the MP that Wilson may have 'laid himself open to blackmail' and was possibly a 'security risk'. Douglas-Home 'was certainly aware of all the gossip about Wilson, both about his marriage and the Soviet trips'. Scott-Hopkins believed that 'Alec had been told about MI5's concern about Wilson when he was Foreign Secretary for Macmillan'. That is entirely possible, for Douglas-Home was a hardline anti-communist and a strong supporter of the security service. He also had a back channel to MI5 through his life long friendship with J. C. Masterman, Chair of the Double-Cross Committee during the war, who remained active as a trainer and recruiter for the service.[22]

Scott-Hopkins was also working for MI6. He had been recruited by Chief of MI6 Sir Stewart Menzies while working for Military Intelligence in 1947. In the fifties, he supplied information on people during his trips abroad and continued to do so when elected to Parliament in 1959. Throughout his year-long inquiries he heard, but failed to find any evidence of, the full range of Wilson gossip. This included allegations of an affair with Barbara Castle in 1949, and the claim that Mrs Williams' husband had finished up with a financial settlement of £30,000, for which wealthy friends had raised money, and that he had stayed out of Britain resisting all demands that he be interviewed. Scott-Hopkins' inquiries continued until March 1966, when he lost his seat in the Commons. Between the General Election and winning a by-election in November 1967, more inquiries continued, this time, with MI6 as his paymaster, concentrating on Wilson's relationship with the East–West traders.[23]

It was this last aspect which also troubled Dodds-Parker. In a section of his autobiography he writes about the alleged increase in KGB activity in the UK between 1966 and 1971. 'Mr Wilson, had always taken a deep interest in Soviet affairs, helping through commercial channels . . . he believed that trade could be of mutual benefit to both countries. A considerable expansion had taken place . . . of which the KGB had taken undue advantage.'[24]

There is some evidence that also under investigation was Wigg's Tory informant and another East–West trader, the Russian speaking Henry Kerby. Pincher was told, presumably by Wright, that Kerby 'seemed to be friendly with so many Russians that there were some fears inside MI5 that he might be operating as a double' – i.e. a KGB agent. This soon leaked, Kerby told Richard Deacon that 'he had been denounced as a KGB man by (a Tory "wet") to the Conservative Chief Whip.'[25]

In the end, MI5 officers 'found no spies in No. 10' and so 'switched to the only alternative – The Treasury. Possible suspects were narrowed down to one, ideally placed official.' According to this scenario, the spy was actually discovered, but conveniently the 'official remained in place because there was not enough evidence for a trial'. The alternative security source story was that the 'Government decided not to prosecute the spy as a trial might reveal that MI5 once suspected that Mr Wilson had innocently introduced a Communist agent into No. 10'.[26]

It cannot be a coincidence that MI5 were at the time harrying two Labour ministers in the Treasury. One was John Diamond, discussed above. The other was Niall MacDermot, a junior minister at the Treasury, who came to Chief Whip Edward Short's attention in the autumn of 1965: 'We had a sad personal problem involving one of our most able ministers', wrote Short in an oblique reference to MacDermot. 'Simple adultery was one thing, but if the lady concerned was Russian and the adultery was alleged to have taken place on the Continent, that was quite another matter. And, of course, if he was sued for divorce, the adultery would become public knowledge.'[27]

In 1940, MacDermot married Violet Maxwell, a fellow member of an obscure political sect called the New Britain Group. He joined the Labour Party in the mid-fifties and was soon elected as member for Lewisham North and later for Derby. In 1954, MacDermot fell in love with a half-Italian, half-Russian woman called Ludmila Benvenuto. She was at the time learning English in Richmond on Thames in the hope of securing a translator's job with the United Nations in Geneva. In 1961, after a series of temporary appointments, she secured a permanent contract. Miss Benvenuto's father, the son of a well-known Russian writer, had been denounced by the Bolsheviks as a 'capitalist'. In 1938, the 18-year-old Ludmila and her Italian mother, who attended Leningrad University, were expelled from the Soviet Union as 'foreigners'. They subsequently found exile in Italy. All of Ludmila's Russian relatives died during the Great Patriotic War or as the result of Stalinism.

MacDermot's affair with Ludmila blossomed but he decided to remain married at least until his son had finished school. Not long after the 1964 General Election, MacDermot sought a divorce from his wife. She agreed and he informed the Prime Minister. The Leader of the House of Commons, Herbert Bowden, and the Chief Whip, Edward Short, 'were of the opinion that the risk to a Labour Government was such that at the first indication of divorce proceedings, our unfortunate colleague must be asked to resign'. There were security implications and MacDermot offered his resignation. During his meeting with MacDermot, the Prime Minister asked: 'Is she anti-Soviet, then?' MacDermot replied: 'No – from time to time she goes to Russia. Ludmila was never a communist, of course. She went through enough not to be.'[28]

'Wilson would hear nothing of me resigning', recalls MacDermot. 'He brushed it all aside and said I could carry on – "There'll be talk, but never mind. It'll be a nine-days wonder".' It turned out to be more than that. According to Short, 'Harold, as magnanimous and loyal to his friends as ever, was quite unwilling to make up his mind.' The Prime Minister was under pressure from his Party managers to seek MacDermot's resignation. Three months later, the Housing Minister, Richard Crossman, wanted MacDermot as his new Minister of State. 'Ah', Wilson told him. 'Niall's only staying in Parliament another twelve months because he is marrying again.' Crossman thought it showed 'Harold's very amiable tolerance of private life'. In August 1966, the couple finally got married. The papers splashed the 'Minister's secret wedding' across their pages.[29]

Deciding to wait until after the expected General Election, Wilson turned down Crossman's request and kept MacDermot on at the Treasury. In 1967, it was hinted to MacDermot, a respected barrister, that he might get the post of Solicitor General. It was not to be. Eight years later, the Attorney General, Elwyn Jones, let his Cabinet colleague Tony Benn into a secret. 'One of our ministerial colleagues in the last Government had his whole career ruined by security . . . MacDermot's Italian wife was investigated by the Security Services and was suspected of being a security risk.' Wilson saw MacDermot in July 1967 when he told him: 'MI5 have received reports . . . there are allegations from abroad.' MI5 made it clear that they wanted to interview his wife. Wilson was optimistic but the secret state was about to exact its revenge for MacDermot's attempt to expose Philby.[30]

In the events described in this chapter are the foundations of the MI5 plots against Wilson. Obviously, MI5 see it very differently. In May 1987, in what was clearly an official capacity, a senior MI5 source broke silence to present the security service's side of the story. He explained that: 'Far from seeking to de-stabilise the Wilson government, the so-called "plotters" were carrying out their security service duties by "checking out" some members of the then Prime Minister's circle . . . The aim was to warn the Prime Minister that his security was being endangered by some of the company he was keeping. It was essentially an operation to stabilise the Government, not the opposite.'[31]

This repeats the defence put out in 1977 when Wilson's suspicions about MI5 were first raised publicly. According to another anonymous MI5 officer: 'The operation was aimed at protecting the government from damage by subversive elements.' MI5 had become increasingly concerned about the background and motives of some members of the Wilson circle. They believed that it had been penetrated by 'people who were at least sympathetic to the KGB. These people used their connections to seek information at the highest levels about what was going on inside the Government of this country.' Security fears of KGB infiltration extended to 'the clutch of personal and political advisers, staff – and friends – which Labour's then Prime Minister brought into Downing Street.'[32]

The 1987 MI5 source further alleged that they did not want 'to suggest in any sense at all that Harold Wilson *was* a security threat.' However, MI5 did believe that 'he lacked judgement and allowed a chain of events which, in turn, created circumstances in which there could be legitimate grounds for concern over security.' To most of us, 'could be legitimate grounds for concern' would lead to an empirical question and investigation to find out if there were or were not. But in MI5's curious view of the universe 'could be' is interpreted as meaning the same as 'were'. MI5 had no evidence that Mrs MacDermot actually was a 'security risk', merely that she 'could be' one. As far as MI5 was concerned – and this applied especially to Labour Ministers – they were all guilty unless proven innocent. The slightest whisp of a connection with the Soviet bloc, no matter how far removed, became 'legitimate grounds for concern over security'. In an imprecise and imperfect world, it suited MI5's politics to apply to the Labour Government this preposterous absolute standard. (Concerning their own members – the most famous example being Philby – these absolute standards are conspicuously not applied.) Since Wilson 'could have been a security risk', MI5 treated him as one. The result of this *Alice in Wonderland* thinking was that as early as 1967 MI5 personnel were putting it around that they had '*absolute proof*' that Wilson was a Soviet agent.[33]

XVII

POLITICAL PLOTS

*When I was young and naive many years ago, I asked you, Harold, at
Chequers what we should do if you were run over by a bus and you said,
'Find out who was driving the bus.'*
TONY BENN

THERE IS A FAMOUS CARTOON of Harold Wilson facing both ways at
once – only a slight parody of his role as leader of the Labour Party. Neither
Gaitskellite nor Bevanite, Wilson had emerged as leader after Hugh Gaitskell's
death precisely *because* he could face in both directions simultaneously. With left
and right wings far more pronounced than they are today, no leader of the
Labour Party then could have done otherwise without serious in-fighting;
Gaitskell had demonstrated this in his battles with the left during the fifties. But
being in the middle means catching flak from both sides.

As Prime Minister, Wilson was attacked by the British state, the City and their
allies in the media. As leader of the Parliamentary Labour Party, he was attacked
by the right and left of the Party: the rhetoric of technology and getting Britain
moving again did not paper over the conflicts for long. While the Parliamentary
left protested, abstained and carried on in the Bevanite tradition, the right,
essentially the Gaitskellites, organised against him. The Gaitskellite wing had
not really accepted his legitimacy as leader of the Party. Adored by the liberal–
social democrat centre of the British political and media establishment, Gaitskell
had been cheated of his rightful turn at the top of the greasy pole. Little wonder
that the joint CIA/MI5 rumour, that Gaitskell had been murdered by the KGB
to let Wilson in, was so freely circulated.

Although the Gaitskellite Campaign for Democratic Socialism (CDS) had
apparently disbanded in 1963, Wilson was convinced that it was still operating
inside the Party. His suspicions were correct, the CDS parliamentary members
carried on as the 1963 Club, a 'dining club'. (His recorded hatred of the CDS
was partly based on his suspicion that it was they who had first circulated the
rumours about his relationship with Marcia Williams.) [1]

In Government, Gaitskellite plotting against Wilson began in July 1966 when the Labour Government was into its third 'sterling crisis'. Although the Labour Party had then recently won a resounding General Election victory, there were other problems: the deadlock in Rhodesia continued, and Wilson had just made his notorious remarks about the 'politically motivated' men – the CPGB – alleged to be controlling the seamen's strike (which had aggravated the balance of payments, reducing financial 'confidence', putting more pressure on the value of the pound). Always, there was the pound.[2]

The Chancellor of the Exchequer, James Callaghan, was ill-equipped to resist the conventional wisdom of deflation demanded by the London financial establishment. A minority within the Cabinet, notably George Brown, then at the Department of Economic Affairs (DEA), the putative Whitehall arm of manufacturing, favoured devaluation of the pound – or floating it, which came to the same thing. Others favouring devaluation were the leading Gaitskellites – Roy Jenkins and Anthony Crosland, and on the left, Barbara Castle and Richard Crossman. Their position was intelligible: no deflation, no cuts in government programmes; let the currency take the strain: the domestic economy would *not* be sacrificed in the interests of the overseas, sterling lobby. Nevertheless, after a debate in the Cabinet the devaluation lobby was defeated and deflationary measures were introduced. In the midst of this 'crisis' there was the alleged 1966 'July plot'.[3]

There is now a widespread consensus which says there was, in fact, no plot – it was just the first major manifestation of Wilson's paranoia, misreading political discussions among colleagues as cabals. In 1971, the political commentators David Butler and Michael Pinto-Duschinksy concluded that over the critical mid-July weekend, when Wilson was out of the country, 'key members of the cabinet were widely dispersed . . . it was thus impossible to organise a cabal, and while there were a number of consultations by telephone, the later talk of a plot was clearly exaggerated'. This simplisitic view is, in our opinion, wrong. [4]

On 8 July the *Tribune* column 'Francis Flavius' noted that 'some members of the right-wing of the PLP [Parliamentary Labour Party] are getting extraordinarily bold . . . it has decided that it cannot really trust Mr Wilson and what will finally be needed is a Right-wing leader of the Labour Party'. A week later, Wilson told Barbara Castle: 'There was a great plot on by George and Jim to get rid of him [Wilson]. "You know what the game is: devalue and get into Europe. We've got to scotch it".' The next day, Saturday 16th, Wilson flew to Moscow.[5]

On the 25th, following his return, Wilson told Castle: 'it was all a plan to get us into the Common Market. But the real threat is Jim . . . he has been seeing a lot of Cecil King.' Barbara Castle believed in this 'plot' sufficiently to brief Mathew Coady of the *New Statesman*, who duly reported on 29 July: 'What he [Brown] appears to have wanted was devaluation . . . and a rapid move to join the European Economic Community . . . There were unexpected forces at work in the inner councils of Whitehall and what took place amounted to an attempt to hustle Britain into Europe on the back of the economic whirlwind.' This is certainly one of the things which Brown wanted, as we show below, but of the 'unexpected forces in Whitehall' there was apparently no sign. Nor was there any media follow-up of this tantalising titbit: the story disappeared from public view.[6]

However, inside the Cabinet, the rumblings continued. On 6 August, Benn talked to Peter Shore, who reported on a meeting with Marcia Williams: 'Apparently the events of the last few weeks have absolutely shaken Wilson to the core. He is convinced that a deliberate plot was conceived to get rid of him . . . Roy Jenkins and his gang decided to get rid of George Brown and to make Jim Callaghan No. 2 with a view to getting Roy in as No. 1.' On 12 September, Callaghan told Tony Benn that 'Harold had told him that this [conspiracy] had been organised while he, Harold, was in Moscow, that Roy Jenkins and Tony Crosland were behind it and that I [i.e. Benn] had fallen for it along with the Left who were very naive.'[7]

Wilson returned to this theme on 7 October, the last day of the Labour Party conference, complaining to Barbara Castle about 'Ministers who went a-whoring with society hostesses'. He was 'livid with Tommy Balogh for coming down specially to attend Pamela Berry's dinner'. Mrs Berry's husband owned the *Daily Telegraph*, which was no friend of the Labour Party. 'Mrs Ian Fleming is another one', he said 'darkly' to Castle. Although she was politically naive, the wife of the late novelist held court to a number of political figures. She was prone to anti-semitic statements. ' "If any of you knew your job you would find out who attended that weekend meeting at her place last July when I was in Moscow . . ." ' He knew what the plot was – to make Jim Callaghan Prime Minister, Roy Jenkins Chancellor and form a coalition government.'[8]

Over the four months from July to October the story had altered more than once. Version one had George Brown and the mandarins of Whitehall trying to bounce the Government into the EEC on the back of a devalued pound. Version two saw Callaghan and Jenkins in place as Prime Minister and Chancellor of the Exchequer respectively. Version three had Callaghan and Jenkins as part of a coalition government.

These Prime Ministerial rumblings eventually surfaced in the press on 9 October 1966 when the *Mirror*'s Anthony Shrimsley wrote of 'a curious story being mulled over and exaggerated by Labour MPs'. Shrimsley talked to some fans of Jenkins and their idea that the leader of the Party should be Callaghan, but added: 'there is no reason to believe that either Mr Callaghan or Mr Jenkins joined in this "contingency planning" ', and concluded that 'Mr Wilson seems to have given The-Plot-That-Never-Was greater significance than it deserved.'

In the *Daily Mail* the next day, Walter Terry, the lover of Wilson's Private Secretary, Marcia Williams, responded with what is manifestly No. 10's version. The idea, according to the source, was to make Callaghan PM, Jenkins Chancellor and 'bring in several outriders of respectability into the government as a demonstration of national unity . . . the rebels supposedly had their main meeting in a Kent country house on Saturday July 16th . . . That night these conspirators, whose hostess is well known outside the political orbit, began a series of discussions of how to be rid of Harold and introduce Jim as PM.' Wilson, reported Terry, 'has had the fullest inquiries into the meeting . . . remnant figures who once supported the Campaign for Democratic Socialism.'[9]

However, Wilson's version failed to carry the day. A broad consensus emerged: that there had never been a 'plot'. The *Statist* and the *Sunday Mirror*, both owned by Cecil King, wrote of 'The Plot that Never Was'. Desmond Donnelly, the first of the many Labour MPs to resign between 1966 and 1979, was clear in his thin 1968 *apologia*: 'In fact there was no plot.' In his memoir, George Wigg, at the time a kind of one-man counter-intelligence unit for Wilson, commented: 'despite all the idle chatter, there was no real dissension in the cabinet'. This statement is, of course, absurd. Plot or no plot, there certainly was major dissension in the Cabinet – and Wigg knew all about it. On 19 July, while Wilson was out of the country, he phoned Crossman: 'You know, I have very good sources. I know what everybody is doing.' Callaghan blamed 'some highly impressionistic information conveyed by George Wigg to the Prime Minister on his return [from Moscow]'. But as the quotations from Barbara Castle show, Wilson was mindful of the situation *before* he left for Moscow.[10]

What had really happened that July weekend after Wilson flew to Moscow on the Saturday? 'By Sunday night', acknowledged Susan Crosland, widow of Tony, Secretary of State for Education and Science, 'at least a score of meetings had taken place in London between certain Ministers and economic advisers. The agenda: could Callaghan at last be persuaded to devalue or float the pound?' Perhaps because she is American and thus accustomed to political-plotting-as-normal-politics, Mrs Crosland acknowledges – obliquely, if not obscurely – that there was a plot at this point. After the 1966 March General Election, 'Roy Jenkins . . . became the hero of the liberal press. Older Right-wingers in the PLP and a number of young revisionist backbenchers looked to Roy as the only Cabinet Minister who could replace Wilson . . . Apart from the Prime Minister, it was very unusual for a Cabinet Minister to have a personal public relations officer. Not only did Roy Jenkins have one: John Harris was far more adroit in dealing with the press than was the PM's PRO . . . Harris' press campaign was poisoning relationships . . . the Prime Minister by this time had reason to believe people were plotting against him.' Tony Crosland 'privately . . . made clear his aversion to plotting against a colleague and was particularly irritated by conspirators who had supported Wilson for the leadership'.[11]

In 1973, the *Observer*'s political correspondent, Nora Beloff, reported that Wilson's 'spies correctly informed him' about that weekend, when a group of 'former Gaitskellites', including Crosland, had been 'convened by George Brown' at Roy Jenkins' country cottage. Jenkins denies this. 'Nora Beloff is unusually inaccurate. George Brown was in Durham that weekend, Tony Crosland was I believe in London, I was staying in Wiltshire, i.e. not at East Hendred. The three of us were broadly agreed, but we had no meeting.'[12]

Roy Jenkins spent Saturday evening and night at Mrs Ian Fleming's house. Susan Crosland writes: 'in moments of crisis people are caught in characteristic poses. Roy is at a great country house.' On the Sunday afternoon he arrived at the Croslands'. Anne Fleming's letters show that she was on intimate terms with the leading Gaitskellites (and Lord Goodman, Wigg's close friend). In a letter on 24 October 1966, she is ambiguous regarding the plot. She reports 'an amazing scandal . . . it seems that Mr H. Wilson imagined or was wrongfully informed that I was entertaining Callaghan, Crossman (some say Crosland) and Jenkins, hatching a plot to uncrown Wilson and crown Callaghan . . . I was first told by Arnold Goodman . . . he had been asked by a Wilson go-between if it could be true . . . [m]alice *or a germ of truth somewhere?*'[13]

Richard Crossman's diary reveals another strand. 'In so far as there was [a plot] it was Roy Jenkins and Tony Crosland and Tony Wedgwood Benn and me who were implicated in it, along with George Brown.' Crossman's 'cabal' (his word) was a series of meetings that been held to discuss devaluation of the pound while Wilson was in the Soviet Union: 'Roy, Tony Crosland, Tony Benn, Barbara Castle and myself all firmly committed to opposing a new package of cuts except as a preparation for floating off the pound.' However, Crossman's meetings began on Monday 18 July – after the weekend's events.[14]

Independent of both the Gaitskellites and Crossman, George Brown was doing the rounds. On that Saturday Brown was at the Durham Miners' Gala with Tony Benn: 'in a state of tension . . . he intended to resign from the Government tonight . . . has only told Harold Wilson, Roy Jenkins and me . . . his resignation would become effective on Wednesday when the economic statement was made.' He tried to persuade Jenkins to go with him. Jenkins declined the offer. Off went Brown to the diarists Crossman and Castle – Wilson loyalists. Brown was all over the place, telling Crossman in one conversation on the 18th 'that he wasn't going to take part in any kind of conspiracy': then 'talking about a coup against him [i.e Wilson] in the last resort'; asking Crossman if he would support Brown 'if Harold had to resign'; finally 'imply[ing] that there were other people prepared to go with him . . . Harold had to be replaced in order to float the pound.' Brown went to Castle on the same day. 'We've got to break with America, devalue and go into Europe . . . this is what Pompidou said to us: devalue as we did and you're in' – precisely what Wilson had told her the plot was about a week before. Would Castle have him as leader? She would not.[15]

Brown had been in touch with Wilson in Moscow. He complained to Castle: 'He can't budge. Why? Because he is too deeply committed to Johnson . . . what did he pledge? I don't know: that we wouldn't devalue and full support in the Far East?' Brown had revealed the secret understanding between Wilson and L.B.J. which was an extension of the agreement made with the American bankers in 1964. It was a secret not shared with the Cabinet; Brown had been tipped off by Leslie O'Brien, the Governor of the Bank of England. The day before Brown's weekend of canvassing against Wilson, Brown met O'Brien, who later told Cecil King that 'it was clear that George was hoping to use this occasion to oust Wilson'. The next day, the 16th, Cecil King – a director of the Bank of England at this point as well as head of Mirror newspapers – had the British Treasury Representative in Washington, John Stevens, to dinner: 'He said Johnson has made it clear to Wilson that the pound was not to be devalued and no drastic action east of Suez was to be undertaken until after the American election in November. In return the pound would be supported by the Americans to any extent necessary.'[16]

Wilson's secret agenda contained a second item, which was to join the Common Market. In his autobiography, the anti-EEC (and anti-Wilson) Douglas Jay makes much of Wilson's supposed great change of mind, between March and October 1966, from anti- to pro-EEC. He attributes the change to Wilson being pushed by George Brown and Cecil King. Jay notes that 'there was no visible sign of Wilson's somersault until Brown arrived at the Foreign Office at the end of June'. In fact, six months before, King recorded in his diary that Brown had brought forward their lunch 'in order to tell me that Wilson is deciding to enter the Common Market.' All the evidence suggests that Wilson's attitude to the EEC had been ambiguous: 'on the right terms' is suitably politic.[17]

Wilson's secret agenda was under terrible strain. He could hardly tell his Cabinet colleagues of the deal with President Johnson. There would have been uproar from the left-wing at the idea of a Labour Prime Minister manipulating the British economy in the interests of a US President, especially with this one's Vietnam policies. At the beginning of that weekend in July Wilson had this central dilemma: how to fend off the pressure for devaluation until November, when he could not explain why he had to do so?[18]

His agreements with Johnson at stake, Wilson had to be against devaluation or floating the pound (which was the same thing: with a balance of trade deficit it would float down; that was the point of the float), and anti-EEC (a precondition of entry into which was thought to be devaluation of the pound, the forbidden subject, 'the Unmentionable'). His first recorded reference to plotting was two days after 13 July, when he heard that Callaghan was considering 'The Unmentionable' – devaluation.[19]

The assessment of Jenkins and Alexander is accurate: 'There had, it appeared, been two plots: one among a few of the younger Labour MPs to replace the Prime Minister with Jenkins, or in some versions, Callaghan; the other, a separate plot by Conservative Central Office and the city to form a national government.' This latter theme was alluded to by Desmond Donnelly in a speech during that climactic weekend and reported by the *Observer*: 'There is talk in Westminster corridors about a coalition.' In reporting such talk – formation of a coalition government was a part of Wilson's third 'plot' – Donnelly was not alone. Right-wing Labour MP John Mackintosh wrote in his book *The British Cabinet*: 'in one form spread by the City, talk was of a coalition government led by Mr Callaghan . . . in the other form . . . it was an attempt at a Cabinet coup.'[20]

Just before the 'plot week' in 1966, Cecil King had begun to show an interest in a 'national government' (discussed in more detail in Chapter XXII). In August, King discussed a 'national government' with George Brown and then with *The Times*' editor, Denis Hamilton, who told him that 'both Macmillan and Rab Butler forsee a National Government'. King commented then that 'there seems to be a current of opinion leading to a National Government of non-politicians rather than a government with a Labour PM and some non-politicians participating'. This was the origin of the 'businessman's government', the theme which King was to pursue from here right through to 1968 and which was hinted at in the Walter Terry story in October 1966, cited above.[21]

It is clear that Brown was trying to organise something during the July weekend – but not with the Gaitskellites. There were machinations that weekend by the Gaitskellites – substantially hinted at by Susan Crosland – but Brown went off on his own, probably 'messing things up'. Brown was never a serious candidate: Jenkins was the man whom the Gaitskellites (and sections of the media judiciously courted by Jenkin's PR man, John Harris) really wanted. Callaghan had not been included: refusing to accept devaluation, he was the immediate problem; of his involvement there is no evidence.

Wilson was apparently never seriously worried that he would lose the vote in Cabinet and thus he could afford to fly to Moscow, leaving the mice to play. In the crucial vote in Cabinet after his return devaluation was rejected 16 to 8, with Crossman, Jenkins, Castle and Crosland in the latter group. The significant element in Wilson's reported allegations is his anxiety about Callaghan, who was indeed the threat. Brown was unacceptable to the Parliamentary Labour Party as a potential Prime Minister: his drinking was hardly a secret. Jenkins did not have the support of the PLP. Wilson would 'read' all this routinely. Callaghan, an important contact man with the unions and the wider Party, was the only serious threat. Wilson, of all people, understood the significance of Callaghan's role within the party machinery: this was how Wilson had established himself in the mid-fifties. Wilson got his retaliation in quickly. Mathew Coady of the *New Statesman* was briefed against Brown in July by Barbara Castle. In October Walter Terry ran the revised version, pointing the finger at Callaghan.[22]

Wilson's Governments are now almost universally regarded as an enormous failure, a wasted opportunity. Much of the blame for this has been laid at the door of Wilson himself, who, it is now said, grew increasingly paranoid seeing non-existent political plots against him everywhere. In fact, such plots did exist.[23]

XVIII

'RED PLOT': THE SEAMEN'S STRIKE

Ray Gunter 'seemed to find Communist-Trotskyist agitators under the bed of every strike'.
JACK JONES

We have had during this week the destruction of the Wilson myth in the public eye. It's amazing how his luck ran up to a certain point – the day he listed the nine Communists in the seamen's union and pulled off the end of the strike the next morning. That was the apex of his luck. Since then catastrophe after catastrophe.
RICHARD CROSSMAN

IN LATE 1965, the right-wing magazine *Time and Tide* headlined a strange, rambling article 'Mr Wilson's government likely to fall in eight weeks'. This piece concluded that the Communists had fastened on to the trade unions: 'Industries vital to export or to power supply can be crippled in a day. Some of the unofficial strikes are trial runs. And to Mr Wilson, who boasts of his many friends in Russia, they are the most dangerous threat. Even more surely than Mr Callaghan's squeeze, or the treatened revolt on both right and left wings in the Labour Party, the Communists could bring him down'. Clearly intended as a smear, this nonsense did oddly foreshadow forthcoming events.[1]

Like most centrist Labour politicans, Wilson dreamed of an incomes policy, a general corporatist settlement which would remove the messy and economically damaging business of strikes from the scene. This was a particularly pressing issue in 1965 because of Wilson's determination to defend the value of the pound with the economy in trade deficit. Industrial disputes not only reduced 'confidence' in sterling among the international money-lenders, they also reduced output, exports and threatened the balance of payments. This, in turn, led to selling of the pound and pressure to increase interest rates to keep the world's floating liquidity in sterling. Higher interest rates then damaged the manufacturing economy, threatening to further reduce output, exports – and so the trade balance.

128

The difficulty was that a pay policy was unacceptable to large sections of the wider Labour movement. In February 1966, Richard Crossman commented in his diary that the proposed Prices and Incomes Bill – the 'anti-trade union bill' as he called it – would cause serious trouble within the Party. The seriousness of this group of related problems for the Labour Government cannot be exaggerated.[2]

In early 1966, Labour attempted to maintain a 'pay norm' of 3.5 per cent – a challenge to every left-leaning trade unionist which would inevitably lead to a show-down. In January 1966, the *Economist*, which had consistently urged action against trade unions, advised that 'the only way to achieve an incomes policy in 1966 is going to be by outfacing the trade unions in some big national wages struggle'. But a show-down with whom? Improbably, the challenge came from the National Union of Seamen (NUS), which had not organised a national strike since 1911.[3]

The NUS wanted an improvement in its 1965 agreement, which, if met – and the employers were willing to do this – would be equivalent to a rise of 17 per cent. The Government decided that maintaining the 'norm' was more important than the possible damage to Britain's trade which would be caused by a seamen's strike. Following long and fruitless talks with various members of the Government, the NUS executive called an official strike in May 1966. Crossman noted at the time that 'the people [in the Cabinet] who were talking about fighting it out and the impossibility of giving way were uneasily aware that standing firm was going to ruin us'.[4]

Attempts to mediate failed: the recommendation by an official inquiry of a settlement roughly equivalent to half of what the NUS sought was rejected by the union. After a month, Wilson played the card which haunted him for the rest of his career. On 20 June 1966, Wilson made his infamous speech claiming that the strikers were being manipulated by 'this tightly knit group of politically motivated men who, as the last General Election showed, utterly failed to secure acceptance of their views by the British electorate . . . Some of them are now saying very blatantly that they are more concerned with harming the nation than with getting the justice we all want to see.' The speech caused a sensation in the press and 'consternation on the [Labour] backbenches'. Wilson was accusing the Communist Party of direct interference in the strike. The following day, Wilson told the Cabinet that the strikers would go back were it not for 'outside pressures'. The Cabinet reacted 'in pretty non-committal silence', according to Barbara Castle. 'I asked if we could be given more details of the conspiracy, to which Harold replied ponderously that there were some things which were better not revealed, even to the Cabinet'. Castle thought this showed 'shades of Wigg'.[5]

Initially, no evidence was given by Wilson to back up his claim, though it was obvious that he had been instructed to leak selective information. Journalist Stephen Fay went to see George Wigg, who told him about an 'ugly plot' which Fay dismissed as nonsense. The *Daily Mail*'s editor, Michael Randall, was offered the evidence but refused to publish what he thought were, at best, 'exaggerated half-facts'. The *Sunday Times* dismissed the claims, though the

Guardian did say that 'There are allegations of telephone calls to branches from other union offices and from one or two provincial universities which are known to have militant left-wing groups.' Wigg's final visitor was Eric Clarke of the *Observer*. On 26 June, the *Observer* published a major article entitled 'The Plot behind the Strike'. The paper named Communists – Norris, Coward, Gollan, Ramelson and Goodwin – and stated that the paper had also been in contact with the anti-union blacklisting agency, the Economic League. The *Observer* referred to 'information placed before the Prime Minister', though not to the fact that it had obviously come from MI5 or Special Branch.[6]

With these names out in the open and, perhaps, feeling the pressure of the surrounding scepticism, Wilson now gave the House of Commons some of the details. On 29 June, in the debate on the emergency powers deemed necessary for combatting the seamen's strike, he provided more information of meetings, dates, times and details of the alleged Communist conspiracy. Wilson's naming of the Communists, records Tony Benn, 'made me sick and reminded me of McCarthyism'. Nor did Wilson get the support he expected from the Leader of the Opposition, Edward Heath. At a meeting with Heath 'behind the Speaker's chair', Wilson produced the head of MI5's F Branch, Dick Thistlethwaite, and the operative responsible for 'bugging' the seamen's union's headquarters. Heath responded by tabling a motion demanding that Wilson produce more public information. In his memoir Wilson contrasts Heath's unwillingness to support him on this issue to his (Wilson's) compliance with Macmillan's request for silence and support over Philby. Wilson had a valid point. Heath had, in effect, rejected MI5's analysis of the situation. Wilson was being 'the patriot' – and still getting criticised; and from quarters which knew better.[7]

It has been widely assumed that it was Wigg who organised the use of MI5. In fact, the major impetus for the anti-communist line within the Government came from Minister of Labour, Ray Gunter, a hard-line anti-communist trade unionist of the old school. Gunter sat on the Labour Party's Organisation Sub-Committee, sniffing out infiltration from the left, often on the basis of official security reports. He was part of the anti-communist Common Cause–IRIS (Industrial Research and Information Service) network and joined the Board of Directors of IRIS shortly after the seamen's strike. As NUS headquarters was then the home of IRIS it cannot have been difficult for the union's officials to co-operate with Special Branch in keeping 'an eye on its own dissidents'. As Minister of Labour, Gunter was regularly furnished with security reports on the trade unions by MI5. His successor, Barbara Castle, commented in her diary that her Permanent Secretary 'doesn't take these Security boys seriously'. Castle was also unimpressed. 'The more I read these reports the less confidence I have in our intelligence . . . Altogether, I really wonder what we pay these people for.' Gunter did believe these fact-sheets, which were 'designed to help ministers and officials judge the political dimensions of industrial disputes'.[8]

A major strike by a strategically important union such as the NUS, with the added *frisson* of Communist Party of Great Britain involvement, would of itself have produced a massive MI5 operation with or without Labour Government approval. To date only fragments have emerged of this. In his memoir, Wilson acknowledges that the penetration of the strike leadership was so good that 'we could predict the exact line the group would take at the next meeting'. Pincher refers to 'records of bugged conversations and photographs of intercepted documents.' According to one report, penetration of the union at the time of the strike 'was apparently so complete . . . that one of the NUS's committees consisted entirely of the Special Branch'. At the time, senior members of the union were convinced that 'one of the so-called "moderates" on the Executive' was an informer. Eventually, Wilson actually met the MI5 officers running operations. Mrs Williams says: 'The people on the ground came to tell him of their work and how they bugged everybody and how they got tape-recordings.' This was an unusual event and suggests that Wilson needed some persuading of the truth of the reports being relayed from MI5 by Gunter.[9]

The simple truth behind the use of the security machine appears to be that, in defence of their pay policy, the Labour Cabinet had decided to break the seamen's strike. The account of the Cabinet debates in Crossman's diaries make it clear that this was accepted as necessary by the majority of the Cabinet. It was distasteful to them, but they felt that there was no choice. It tends to be forgotten that Wilson held back for a month before playing the anti-communist card. Though it was certainly true that (along with the rest of the British left) the Communist Party did want to wreck the Government's attempt to establish a pay policy, the actual significance of the CPGB's input into the strike remains unclear, despite Wilson's use of the product of MI5/Special Branch operations. Whatever the CPGB's influence, however, the strike was overwhelmingly supported by the union's members.

Wilson remained unapologetic. In his memoir of the period he used three and half pages to reproduce part of his Commons statment on the 'communist threat'. His use of the anti-communist card should not have been quite the shock to the Parliamentary Labour Party that it was. The fact that he conspicuously stood aside from the witch-hunting of the fifties did not mean that he had any sympathy towards the extra-parliamentary left. He knew the Communist Party tried to exploit industrial disputes in the furtherance of class struggle: that was accepted on all sides. As Tony Benn wrote in his diary on the day of Wilson's notorious speech: 'In a sense Harold said nothing that was new, since every trade union leader knew it.' The fatal error was his decision to make public his use of the secret state's activities; and it is quite clear that he eventually went much further on that line than he had wanted to. Ted Short seems to blame Ray Gunter, 'who had personal problems at the time', because he did not have 'either the ability or the flexibility to deal with [the strike].' The original tactic was clearly the ambiguous Commons statement hinting at CP involvement, followed by the Wigg-orchestrated campaign of press revelation. This back-fired when, first, the majority of the press and then Edward Heath refused to play ball. This major political error took the gloss off Wilson for many in the Labour Party. Until then, he had been perceived as having something of a magic touch – he had just led Labour to an overwhelming General Election victory – and had massive support across the Party. On this occasion, having to choose between his economic policies and the goodwill of the Labour movement, he chose the former. Short believes Wilson's disappointment with the lack of support that his prices and incomes policy received 'marked the beginning of his disillusion with high office'.[10]

By late 1966, Wilson should have learned to be extremely cautious when dealing with the British secret state. MI6's prediction that the sanctions against Rhodesia would work in 'weeks not months' had returned to haunt him; and his involvement with MI5's operations during the seamen's strike had alienated a chunk of the Labour movement. Undeterred, he proceeded to embroil himself with the secret state again.

It all began when a 'minor harouche had blown up about telephone-tapping' after reports in the *Daily Express*. 'Four back-bench Labour MPs headed by Russell Kerr told the *Express* that they knew their phones were being tapped and wanted Questions asked.' The *Express* suggested that the Labour Party was 'involving itself in a sense of conspiracy. And one Minister – Mr George Wigg, the Paymaster-General – is not far from the scene. Truth or lies, fact or fiction, it is becoming believed by too many Labour MPs that Mr Wigg is keeping a close watch on either themselves or members of the Government.' Wilson was prepared for this and arranged to have the questions transferred to him.[11]

Wilson told the Commons that 'there is no tapping of the telephones of hon. Members, nor has there been since this Government came into office'. Prompted by a question from Tom Driberg, Wilson revealed that 'there had been tapping of MPs' telephones up to the time Labour came into office [and] that this covered members of more than one party'. The Conservative front bench responded with what *The Times* called an 'uncomfortable silence'. And so it blew over – or so Wilson thought at the time. In fact, this was the overture to what became known as the D-Notice affair, described by Mrs Williams as 'the real watershed'.[12]

XIX

THE D-NOTICE AFFAIR:
WILSON FIGHTS BACK

*Without question there had been a full-blown Whitehall conspiracy to
conceal the truth.*
CHAPMAN PINCHER

*This whole affair, which began as a serious matter affecting the security of
this country, has degenerated into an acrimonious public debate in which
personalities have begun to obscure the real issues.*
LORD CHALFONT, 1967

'NATIONAL SECURITY' has always been a problem for the Labour Party.
When a scandal involving security has arisen with the Labour Party in opposition, its leaders have often found it difficult to raise the legitimate 'national
security' questions, let alone exploit the situation to their advantage. Labour
Leader Neil Kinnock found this out to his cost during the Peter Wright Affair in
1987 when his office was accused (sic) by the Conservative Government of
talking to the lawyers acting for Peter Wright in the case resulting from the
attempt by the British Government to suppress the publication of *Spycatcher* in
Australia. With a General Election on the horizon, and afraid that he would be
portrayed in the press as a less than avid supporter of 'national security', Kinnock
quickly wrapped himself in the Union Jack, and declined to ask how the
Government and media knew the contents of telephone conversations between
his office and Wright's legal team on the other side of the world.

When in government, protecting and defending 'national security', Labour is
often portrayed as engaging in Big Brother activities. Lacking the knowledge of
intelligence operations and the black arts of smearing and disinformation,
second nature to a section of the Conservative Party, Labour Party leaders
usually stay well clear of this area. Harold Wilson was unusual. In the 1967 D-
Notice Affair, perhaps encouraged by his skilful handling of the Profumo Affair,
he made the last serious attempt by a senior Labour politician to take on the

133

spooks – with disastrous results. Wilson described this episode in his account of February and March 1967: 'There were problems. One of these, the D-Notice affair, I can only describe as self-inflicted, in personal terms one of the costliest mistakes of our near six years in office.'[1]

Although Wilson had grown increasingly sensitive about leaks to the press through 1966, until the D-Notice Affair the media had been reasonably sympathetic towards the Labour Government. After the D-Notice débâcle, relations became strained, even antagonistic. 'What I should have foreseen', Wilson noted, 'was the almost unanimous press attack which followed . . . at least it could be said that I had succeeded in uniting the press – though not on my side.'[2]

However, Wilson has never revealed the real background to this own-goal. We can now see that it was the consequence of an attempt by the Prime Minister – and George Wigg, Wilson's main ally in this and the Profumo Affair – to hit back at the smear campaigns which had been operating since the 1964 election. Unfortunately, if not surprisingly, the whole thing back-fired.

On 16 February 1967, a young man named Robert Lawson visited the offices of the *Daily Express* in Fleet Street where he saw the paper's defence correspondent, Chapman Pincher. He informed Pincher that while working as a telegraphist in the offices of Commercial Cables and Western Union he had discovered that all copies of overseas cables were collected daily and taken to the Ministry of Defence offices at the old Admiralty building. Lawson understood that within a period of forty-eight hours the cables were vetted by the security service (MI5) – interesting cables being photographed and examined before being passed back to the cable companies. Lawson believed that the practice had been going on for at least two years.

Intrigued by the information that *all* cables, not just the odd few, were 'routinely' vetted, Pincher began to make inquiries. A friend, Turlough O'Brien, Director of Public Relations at the Post Office, told him, in confidence, that in substance the story was true, but that 'only those specially selected went for thorough scrutiny by the security authorities'. Pincher then called a friend of fifteen years' standing, Colonel L. G. 'Sammy' Lohan, secretary of the press watchdog on security matters, the D-Notice Committee. Set up by government, the committee contains both press and Ministry of Defence personnel, and issues guidance in the form of D-Notices on what is thought permissible to publish in the areas of security and defence. It is a voluntary form of self-censorship by the media which works remarkably well to the state's benefit. Pincher sought confirmation of the story and wanted to know if it was covered by a particular D-Notice which would prevent him from publishing it. Pincher believed that Lohan had said there was no such notice, and on 21 February the *Daily Express* splashed its front page with the banner headline, 'CABLE VETTING SENSATION'.[3]

Lohan has often been portrayed as a kind of drunken blimp, a buffoon. In fact, before heading the D-Notice Committee he had been Deputy Director of Public Relations for the British Army, a substantial position. Secretary of the D-Notice

Committee was a very important post from where the state was given early warning of trouble ahead.[4]

Reaction by the other newspapers, except the *Daily Mail* which had been given the story by Robert Lawson but declined to print it, was muted, and it might have ended there. However, that afternoon, by coincidence, a question was asked in the Commons about the D-Notice system and, in answering it, Wilson attacked the *Daily Express*. 'Unfortunately, the confidence and trust, which are the basis of the whole system, have been called into question by the action of one newspaper in initiating this morning a sensationalised and inaccurate story purporting to describe a situation which, in fact, the powers and practice have not changed for well over forty years.'[5]

Pincher's article had been cleverly put together mixing the then current concern on telephone-tapping with 'This "big brother" intrusion into privacy.' The former editor of the *Sunday Telegraph*, Donald McLachlan, who was well experienced in the Intelligence world, wrote: 'The presentation of facts was to my mind misleading. The link-up with telephone tapping, the suggestion that the Government might be obtaining 'advance information of trade negotiations . . . a story that, in fact, had to do with external intelligence . . . was presented as having to do with the misuse by Government of the Security Service. By mixing up espionage and counter-espionage the writer was well wide of the mark.'[6]

The day after Wilson's Commons attack, the *Daily Express* published a refutation of the Prime Minister's statement. There was now a complete conflict between the PM's account and that of Pincher and the *Express*: Pincher said there was no D-Notice; the Government said there was. The press was not sympathetic to Wilson. Prodded by Opposition leader, Edward Heath, and seeking vindication, Wilson set up an inquiry into the affair by three senior Privy Councillors under the chairmanship of Lord Radcliffe. The Committee's report, however, failed to confirm the Prime Minister's account and showed some sympathy for Pincher.

In retrospect, this was the central move in the Affair. At this point it passed out of the hands of Government and into the state machinery. Edward Heath had made the call for such an inquiry. Wilson initially refused it and, in Crossman's words, 'referred it to a committee from which the editor of the *Daily Mirror* has now resigned, rather than handle it, and so the PM has had to give in and concede the Committee of Privy Councillors'. Crossman's 'committee' was, in fact, the D-Notice Committee itself. Wilson, following traditional Labour Party procedure, had 'referred it back to the committee'.[7]

We should not hurry past Crossman's sentence. In early 1967, Cecil King, head of the Mirror Group, was well advanced in his plotting to remove Wilson (discussed below). King says in his diary that 'we' – by this he appears to mean himself and Hugh Cudlipp – 'by the resignation of Lee Howard [*Mirror* editor] from the D-Notice Committee, *forced* [our emphasis] Wilson to appoint a tribunal.' King is therefore claiming the credit for this move which led to the initial inquiry – and thus to all the subsequent trouble for Wilson.[8]

A member of the Radcliffe Committee trio was veteran MP Manny Shinwell, an old friend of George Wigg. This led *Private Eye*'s anonymous correspondent on the story (by far the best informed) to assume that Shinwell was appointed as a friend of the Government. In her account of Wilson's Political Office's post-mortem on the Affair – from which they had been excluded at the time – Marcia Williams comments that 'it was slightly comical too that almost everybody seemed to have welcomed the choice of Emmanuel Shinwell as one of the Privy Councillors conducting the inquiry . . . at a time when he had just lost the chairmanship of the Parliamentary Party, embittered too by the events of the year, particularly what he regarded as the growing indiscipline of Labour MP's, struck me as naive.'[9]

When the Radcliffe Committee failed to find in his favour, Wilson, against the advice of almost everyone around him, refused to cut his losses and let it go. Bizarrely, the Government then issued a White Paper which dissented from the conclusions of its own inquiry. Coupled with long acrimonious debates on the affair in both houses of Parliament, which gave the Tory press a field day, the D-Notice Affair became a major embarrassment for the Prime Minister.

In retrospect, one of the odd things is that even those close to Wilson in the Cabinet, Richard Crossman, for example, do not seem to have ever wondered what this obsession of Wilson's was really about. Looking back at this period a decade later, Marcia Williams hinted at a still hidden sub-text to the affair: 'Both newspapers were playing with something far bigger than they knew because there was more to the story than could be revealed. No doubt thirty years from now the full story will be given and the whole thing set in its proper perspective.' Fortunately, we do not have to wait that long. An examination of some of the surrounding security events and issues shows that two of the major parties to the Affair had hidden agendas which they were working through. It also illustrates the kind of difficulties any Labour Government – or politician – has to face when the 'enemy within' are those who proclaim their patriotism the loudest.[10]

When Pincher began making inquiries into the cable vetting story, the Ministry of Defence, after a briefing by an unnamed MI5 officer, had informed him 'that the story was undoubtedly untrue'. This was the answer of the civil service. They had denied the story 'on the basis that it was factually incorrect, no telegrams were sent to the Ministry of Defence'. Responsibility lay elsewhere. Official response to the story was being co-ordinated by the Foreign Office. A high-powered conference was organised by Christopher Ewart-Biggs, head of the Permanent Under-Secretary's department at the Foreign Office. It 'was the Foreign Office that wanted to suppress the Pincher story'. In the inquiry that followed, and in the mass of newspaper articles which reported the Affair, no-one asked why the Foreign Office, which held a brief for external affairs, was involved. Simple logic might have drawn the conclusion that the FO was responsible for a hitherto unknown department which undertook the cable vetting operation. Further inquiries would have revealed that Ewart-Biggs was more than a FO civil servant. A slightly comical figure with a monocle, later assassinated by the IRA, Ewart-Biggs liaised with MI6 and, more importantly, with the then still secret electronic surveillance service, Government Communications Headquarters (GCHQ) at Cheltenham. It was GCHQ which had ultimate responsibility for running the cable-vetting operation, yet it was never mentioned by the press.[11]

During the First World War, Britain's intelligence services conducted the first systematic surveillance of every letter and telegram delivered in or out of the country. The 'vetting' covered the national Post Office and the two main cable companies, Commercial Cable and Western Union. The practice carried on after the war when the two companies were instructed to send copies of all overseas telegrams to Naval Intelligence at Admiralty House. Admiralty vans picked up the sacks of ten-day-old telegrams which were scrutinised overnight and returned to the cable offices the next morning. The President of Western Union revealed this to a shocked US Senate sub-committee in December 1920.[12]

Although the American company had tried to end their involvement in this surreptitious activity, British Government pressure had ensured its continuance. At first the Government denied that any such practice took place, but at the same time it added an all-embracing amendment to the 1911 Official Secrets Act giving powers to demand from a telegraph company the production of 'the originals and transcripts, either of all telegrams, or of telegrams of any specified class or description, or of telegrams sent from or addressed to any specified person or place, sent or received to or from any place outside the United Kingdom'. Until Pincher's article the vetting operation had remained unnoticed for nearly fifty years. The only major change was that the operation had been taken over by GCHQ. By 1967, telegrams were not of great importance, but the revelation of the operation could have been very embarrassing as the surveillance had been extended to all forms of electronic communication from telephone to the telex.[13]

Following the example of the British, the Americans had instructed the cable companies to do likewise and all traffic was secretly supplied to their own code-breaking organisation, the so-called 'Black Chamber', which eventually grew into the National Security Agency (NSA). In 1947, the NSA and GCHQ concluded an intelligence pact called BRUSA–UKUSA under which the two agencies agreed to share the fruits of the intercept trawls. All cables in and out of Britain went not only to GCHQ but also to their American counterparts. This was one aspect of the operation which Pincher did not know of, or report, though the authorities may have been worried that he might. Despite the fact that as Lohan told Pincher (and Wilson told the Commons) 'it had been going on since 1920 . . . a continuing operation', it was a window into other operations whose exposure would have been embarrassing for the Americans – and nothing makes our secret state so nervous as embarrassing their much bigger and richer 'cousins'. An MI5 officer told Lohan, the D-Notice Committee Secretary, that 'the Foreign Office attaches the greatest importance to killing the story'. Keeping GCHQ – and thus the NSA – and their operations out of the story was the top priority for the permanent government.[14]

Pincher's article appeared while an argument was going on in the permanent government and Intelligence community about the growing cost of GCHQ and the use of its facilities by the Americans. This debate had been triggered by the

June 1965 establishment of the first satellite link between the United States and Europe through the launch of the Early Bird satellite by the International Telecommunications Satellite Organisation, INTELSAT, which provided a transatlantic telephone and television service. It also provided a unique opportunity for the NSA–GCHQ intelligence partnership to extend its surveillance operations. In 1967, the field of operations was further extended when the second series of satellites, capable of handling all forms of communications simultaneously, from telephone to facsimile, was launched.

A key link in the INTELSAT system was the signals earth station at Goonhilly Downs on the north Cornwall coast, then only one of five such stations in the world. In 1967, the planners of GCHQ and NSA proposed building a pair of satellite dishes at Morwenstow which would eavesdrop on all the INTELSAT communications developed by Goonhilly. The Ministry of Defence, which co-financed GCHQ, provided a cliff-top site at Sharpnose Point, near the village of Bude, seventy miles north of Goonhilly. The Treasury, the other co-financier, questioned whether the intelligence gained was worth the estimated £500,000 outlay. A classic Treasury versus 'spending Ministry' conflict ensued at a time when the other British Intelligence services were facing cuts in their budgets.[15]

In 1965, concerned about the escalating costs involved in the new satellite intelligence programme, Wilson instructed Cabinet Secretary Burke Trend to set up a secret review of GCHQ. Advised by MI6 Chief Sir Dick White, Trend asked the philosopher, Stuart Hampshire, to conduct the inquiry. Hampshire was familiar with GCHQ, having worked for one of its predecessors, the Radio Security Service, during the war. Peter Wright, who liaised closely with GCHQ and had some contact with Hampshire during this period, knew of the inquiry: 'Hampshire's inquiry lasted the best part of a year, during which time he had full access to GCHQ, as well as a six-week visit to NSA. There were a number of fundamental issues raised in Hampshire's report. The first was whether, in the light of growing costs, Britain could afford to maintain its share of the UK–USA agreement, which guaranteed so much exchanged information from the Americans. The second, more immediate issue, was whether Britain should opt in with the Americans on a new generation of spy satellites.' The report concluded that although Britain could not afford to lose the UK–USA exchange, it did not necessarily have to fund every technical development on the same level as the Americans.[16]

The report supported the Treasury case. All the British traffic could be monitored – and presumably was – by other stations in Britain. The internal dispute was finally resolved when the Director of GCHQ, Leonard Hooper, played the American card, telling the Treasury that a refusal to sanction the project would put the SIGINT (signals intelligence) agreements between the two governments in jeopardy. Heavily dependent upon US support for sterling, the Treasury had a good idea of what American pressure could mean and capitulated. The new facility at Bude, called the Composite Signals Organisation when it opened in 1971, was packed out with American supplied computers and communications terminals linked to other NSA shadowing stations in the United States at Etam, Virginia and Brewster Flats in Washington. Two years later, Hooper explained to his opposite number at the NSA, the retiring Lieutenant General 'Pat' Carter, how he had used the threat of American pressure: 'I know that I have leaned shamefully on you, and sometimes taken your name in vain, when I needed approval for something at this end. The aerials at Bude ought to be christened "Pat" and "Lou".'[17]

The Morwenstow facility and the corresponding financial row were ultra secret but *The Times* was getting close in February 1967: 'Communications specialists from Cheltenham have visited Goonhilly to study the methods there for handling telephone traffic. This will be the type of message coming by way of the Bude station.' Was *The Times'* article part of the Treasury/GCHQ row? Though most writers on the subject would accept Pincher's 1978 assessment that 'Britain is totally dependent on the USA for intelligence . . . dependence is so great and co-operation so close . . . that the security and intelligence chiefs would go to any lengths to protect the linkup', others, less pro-American among the intelligence services, may have felt other HUMINT (human as against electronic) forms of intelligence-gathering would have to pay for the continued expansion of GCHQ. To what lengths would they go? [18]

It was against this (secret) background that Robert Lawson stepped into the *Daily Express* offices after 'hawking round a rather odd circuit that included the *Daily Mail*, the Manchester *Evening News*, an "American press agency", and the London University magazine *Sennet*'. Curiously, when the subsequent inquiry into the D-Notice Affair was undertaken the only evidence which was not published was Lawson's, the man who had started the whole farce. Our knowledge of what Lawson was saying is limited to reports from those outside the committee who talked to him. One was Labour MP Ray Fletcher, a former Defence Correspondent and a close colleague of George Wigg. Fletcher told the House of Commons: 'One comment which Mr Lawson made was that Chapman Pincher has a political axe to grind, and made it quite clear in the course of the interview.'[19]

A fellow Labour MP, David Ensor, concurred. He had also interviewed Lawson, and quoted him as saying that 'If it could be proved to me that cable vetting was essential to the security of the country, then I would not have divulged the circumstances surrounding such an operation. But although Colonel Lohan was well aware of my physical whereabouts, no such offer was made.' (This, if true, is a very important point. As we discuss below, it seems clear that to begin with Lohan did not know about the GCHQ/NSA sub-text to the story. The fact – if true – that he failed to contact Lawson supports this view.) Ensor thought Lawson to be 'a gentleman who is so obviously unreliable and who must so obviously have been unreliable to Mr Chapman Pincher that it would be absolutely fantastic to believe one word that he said'. We now know that Lawson was telling the truth, which makes Ensor's subsequent remarks all the more 'fantastic'. He continued: '[Lawson] told me a story which was in the realms of fantasy and beyond belief. He told me that at one time he was involved with Russian espionage. He told me in the same breath that he was involved with our own espionage, whatever that may be. He told me that he had been involved in a rather unpleasant murder case in Cyprus as a result of his espionage. He told me that he had given evidence to Scotland Yard which had resulted in several arrests in connection with a bullion robbery. He told me that he had sent a telegram to the Prime Minister about another matter which had resulted in the murder of his best friend.' Fantasist or not, Lawson warranted a fuller investigation. No one in an official position seemed to want to touch Lawson. Certainly he was never prosecuted or investigated under the Official Secrets Act, and has never surfaced since.[20]

Pincher's story had certainly hit a raw nerve in the leader of the Labour Party. Marcia Williams' account reveals an intense crisis, and one from which she was excluded. 'The Prime Minister's discussions on it were limited to a few people . . . this was the only period when the door between my room and the Cabinet Room remained locked for long stretches at a time . . . the meetings on it were so numerous that it was impossible for the Private Office to keep up with the locking and unlocking of the door, and it gradually became the case that the door remained locked.'[21]

Crossman went to the House of Commons for the debate: 'We had speeches from Manny Shinwell and Ray Fletcher, who had obviously been briefed by George Wigg, trying to divert the attack off Harold [Wilson] on the unfortunate Colonel Lohan, though the one thing we had all agreed in Cabinet when Harold asked our advice was that Lohan must not be the fall-guy, and the Government mustn't look as though it were throwing him to the wolves in order to protect the higher civil servants.'[22]

But attack Lohan the Prime Minister did, hinting in the process at other dimensions of the affair. 'The question of the relationship between Colonel Lohan and Mr Chapman Pincher was a matter of concern in the lifetime of the *previous* [our emphasis] Government. Early in 1964 [before Labour won power], preliminary consideration was given to the suitability of the Secretary for the post he held. That led to a decision, in the autumn of 1964, to make specific inquiries, one of a number of questions for examination being over-close association with journalists and especially with Mr Chapman Pincher. Finally, I was asked – and I will answer it – whether Colonel Lohan had been given full positive vetting clearance. The answer is that he has not.' Crossman noted: 'It was a fatal mistake, since it almost certainly means that the press campaign will continue and the D-Notice case will not be closed, as I hoped it would be, by this debate.'[23]

Indeed, the press campaign did continue and a separate debate on Lohan was held a week later. The Conservative Sir Richard Glyn, who had served with the Special Operations Executive during the war, asked the Prime Minister a number of questions about Lohan's 'suitability'. Wilson dropped more clues: 'Specific inquiries had been conducted in March 1966 when very senior officials dealing with these matters placed on the record their conclusion that they were all satisfied that there were no grounds on which they could question Colonel Lohan's reliability.' Wilson added that 'the matter was opened up again during the winter [1966] . . . The matter came to a head in later January or early February [1967], but, because of the newspaper article and everything that followed, the matter was held over.' The debate was full of innuendo and exactly what the specific inquiries were was never made plain. All that was clear was that the 'over-close' relationship between Colonel Lohan and Pincher had been a recurring source of worry since before the election of the Labour Government in 1964.[24]

The state's disquiet at the Lohan–Pincher relationship was quite widely known. The Defence Correspondent of *The Times*, Charles Douglas-Home, observed: 'There seems no doubt that the Government as a whole intend if possible to stop up Mr Pincher's sources and are taking extraordinary measures to deal with him . . . The Government have widely questioned civil servants and politicians in their search for the source of leaks to Mr Pincher and they now believe they have indentified the prime source.' Ray Fletcher had no doubts as to the identity of the 'prime source'. 'I have spoken to three defence correspondents and at the moment Fleet Street is buzzing with rumours to the effect that Colonel Lohan has been the source of many of Chapman Pincher's stories in the *Daily Express* in the past.' The writers of the only book on the Affair commented: 'Mr Pincher's assiduousness, resource and ingenuity in digging up exclusive stories were a growing irritation to the Government. Trip wires had been laid for him. He had always managed to evade them. It was no secret that his old friend Mr George Wigg, Paymaster-General and grey eminence of Downing Street, was thirsting for his professional blood.'[25]

In July, Lohan wrote in the *Spectator*: 'Chapman Pincher is poison to Whitehall. Some idiot somewhere must have formulated the theory that I actually conspired with him . . . To support this stupid and untruthful theory my reputation had to be ruined.' However, there was a real conspiracy and Wigg had indeed laid a 'trip wire'. Wilson had dropped a clue in his attack on Lohan: 'The matter came to a head in later January or early February [1967].'

Pincher, who knew nothing of the GCHQ–NSA aspect of the story as late as 1978 when he published his account of the Affair in *Inside Story*, had himself first thought that the basis of the attack was Wilson's perception of a smear campaign in the press against Marcia Williams (and thus himself). The *Observer*, in what looks like a semi-official briefing, noted: 'the Prime Minister's judgement seems to have been affected by justified anger at the teasing tactics of the Beaverbrook newspapers. The *Daily Express* and the *Evening Standard* have for some while been publishing snide little non-political references and photographs of his political secretary, Mrs Williams. These manoeuvres – they are not an open campaign – appear to be atavistic and quite unworthy. Mrs Williams, by all accounts a serious character in a serious job, is being treated quite inexcusably.'[26]

Just before the Affair began, reading the Sunday papers on 15 January, Crossman noted in his diary: 'Politics is hotting up. All the papers this morning had full stories from Conservative headquarters about the decision to destroy the image of Harold Wilson and crucify him as a promise-breaker and crook.' Two days later an article appeared in the *Evening Standard*, the *Express'* sister paper, about Mrs Williams. Crossman found her 'in tears because of a disgusting article about her which appeared in the *Evening Standard*. I tried to cheer her up . . . But Harold had to soothe her till eleven o'clock this evening.' On 19 January,

Crossman dealt with the character assassination campaign at a press briefing: 'I had some luck there, I gather, since at the meeting of the 1922 Committee [meeting of backbench Tory MPs] an hour or two later there were a number of protests made by people who regarded this campaign as a disaster for the Tory Party.' This particular little campaign, however, though indicative of press sniping at Mrs Williams, was just background noise. What really underlay the D-Notice Affair, the Wilson–Wigg secret agenda, was to be found elsewhere.[27]

On 20 December 1966, two months before the Affair began with the *Daily Express* story, Colonel Lohan was approached by Tory MP, Captain Henry Kerby. A former MI6 officer, Kerby had an absolutely safe Tory seat at Arundel in Sussex, and on most issues was very right-wing. But, for reasons that have never been clarified, he was also acting as an informant – mostly on the Conservative Party – to Wigg and Wilson. Wilson had received 'a tip in writing that Lohan, who was strongly anti-Labour, was giving Tory MPs, including himself [Kerby], ammunition for embarrassing parliamentary questions and still more embarrassing supplementary questions mainly on issues affecting defence matters.' Kerby was obviously working both sides of the street. Pincher wrote that Kerby had asked: ' "Come on Sammy [Lohan], what's the latest Whitehall scandal?" ' Lohan then regaled them with a story which I had already heard concerning the alleged sexual exploits of a certain Labour minister who . . . was was having an affair with a lady with Communist leanings'.[28]

Kerby told the story to Wigg who asked for more. They were both playing counter-espionage games. 'Spymaster-General' Wigg was running an agent. Lohan and Kerby met again and had lunch. According to *Private Eye*, Lohan again ran the story, telling 'Kerby that several journalists were making allegations about Lord Chalfont's deep interest in the affairs of Uganda.' (*Private Eye*-speak for extra-marital sex.) In 1977, former Prime Minister Wilson was reported as saying that Kerby had uncovered an attempt by 'a journalist in touch with some hostile individual in the Ministry of Defence' to discredit Lord Chalfont. Who was Wilson thinking of? The journalist could only be Pincher, hence the sustained attacks on Lohan and Pincher in the debates in the House of Commons.[29]

Pincher acknowledges that he heard this story of 'the sexual exploits of a Labour minister'. Lohan, who was in the Special Operations Executive during the war, had been given his own expense account by MI5 who used him as a 'regular informant' and 'conduit' for gossip. Lohan had proposed that 'the matter be made public as part of a campaign to bring down the Labour Government'. With Mrs Williams and the former Prime Minister as sources, Penrose and Courtiour were able to reveal more in 1978. 'There had been a threat to mount a smear campaign against a Labour Minister by a section of the Security Services . . . "Apparently the Security people involved had a photograph of a Minister with a hand on the girl's knee", Sir Harold told the reporters without a trace of humour in his face. "It was taken", he said, "at the White Tower Restaurant . . . Moreover the young lady was said by people in Security to have Communist affiliations".' In fact, before Kerby's tip to Wigg, the allegation against Chalfont had already reached No. 10 from its original source, MI5. They had brought it to the Home Secretary, Roy Jenkins, from whom it went, via Wilson, to his security watchdog, George Wigg. Wigg went to see his friend Chalfont and according to Penrose and Courtiour, 'satisfied himself that the matter had no substance'.[30]

Sir James Dunnett, Permanent Secretary at the Ministry of Defence, was, a month or so before the cable vetting story broke, quite reasonably, told to fire Lohan. He did nothing. Pincher attributes this to the fact that there was 'no easy method of doing this without revealing Kerby's part in the affair existed'. Wigg then tried to use MI5 to find the 'dirt' on Lohan in order to get rid of him. Lohan was kept under surveillance and his telephone was tapped. MI5 were also prepared to smear one of their own and several stories were fed to civil servants on the inquiries, including one that Lohan had 'been involved in an "orgy" in Soho'. MI5 were in a difficult position because it was they who began the smear about Chalfont.[31]

There were many ironies here. Wigg had originally been given this particular post to protect the Labour Party from another Profumo Affair. The Minister for Disarmament, Lord Chalfont, while Defence Correspondent of *The Times*, had been one of Wigg's sources on the Profumo Affair. A former defence adviser to the Liberal Party, Chalfont had the ear of Sir William Haley, editor of the paper, and had largely been responsible for encouraging its highly moral stance on the Affair which had done the Conservatives and Macmillan great damage. Chalfont had enemies inside the secret state for another reason. In December 1966, Richard Crossman had a visit from Chalfont, 'who came to tell me of his alarm at a decision on nuclear weapons which had been taken not at OPD [Defence and Overseas Policy Committee], where I sit, but at a secret committee from which I am excluded. Alun obviously wanted me to treat him as an ally in the battle against the creation of an independent British deterrent.' Chalfont, the firmest of nuclear warriors, was, and remains, an Atlanticist strongly supportive of United States policies which, at the time, saw national, independent – what we might even call parochial – nuclear systems as dangerous and out-dated (and an obstacle to US diplomatic goals). This was not a popular position amongst most sections of the British military/Intelligence establishment.

Lohan was not initially briefed on the GCHQ–NSA dimension – apparently because he hadn't been 'positively vetted', cleared for the information. The GCHQ–NSA intercepts were so sensitive that even the official keeper of secrets was not on the list. Lohan was unable to warn Pincher off with even a hint of the real reasons, because he *did not know* the real reasons. By the time he did it was too late. In any case, Pincher believes that Lohan might well have been wanting to 'deliberately embarrass the government'.[32]

In his 1984 book, *Too Secret Too Long*, Pincher returned to the D-Notice story, this time with the knowledge of the GCHQ–NSA sub-text – and more. He accused Ewart-Biggs of leading an operation 'calculated to ensure that the Radcliffe Committee would be given false testimony by certain Government witnesses . . . a conspiracy to conceal the truth'. The Post Office official, the friend of Pincher's who initially confirmed the story, was persuaded to change his story for the Radcliffe Tribunal – and was prematurely retired. Lohan was now told the truth about the GCHQ–NSA background to the Affair but when he attempted to raise it during the Committee's proceedings he was slapped down by Lord Radcliffe. He was then leaned on to change his story at the Tribunal and 'induced to sign statements which he knew to be untrue'. Lohan retired after an internal civil service inquiry and, for a time, became a cookery writer.[33]

Although it is true, as an anonymous commentator in *Private Eye* pointed out, that the Prime Minister 'succeeded in his original aims . . . to have a mighty bash at Chapman Pincher of the *Daily Express*', the negative consequences were much more important. Most of the media sympathy went to Lohan; Wilson's standing with the press and his Parliamentary colleagues plummeted. For reasons unknown, Wilson chose not to reveal either the GCHQ–NSA aspect, nor Lohan's role in spreading smear stories, to most of his Cabinet colleagues. He did, apparently, let the leader of the Opposition in on part of the sub-text. Crossman noted on 2 July that '[Edward] Heath has been invited to read all the correspondence and will therefore be able to see the case there is against Lohan'. This may explain Heath's comparative reluctance to pursue the affair – as only *Private Eye* seems to have spotted.[34]

In retrospect, the Affair resembled nothing so much as a farce. Wilson was trying to get Lohan fired for spreading smear stories when Pincher got the cable-vetting story, without any knowledge of the GCHQ–NSA connections, and took it – as was his custom – to the Secretary of the D-Notice Committee. At the time, knowing little of the secret sub-text, Lohan gave Pincher the nod, that while the story might be embarrassing, there was nothing specific to prohibit it. Lohan reported back to his intelligence masters who, aware of the sub-text, told him to kill the story – without telling him why it was so sensitive. Pincher declined to take the hint. Meanwhile, back at No. 10, the separate sub-plot, involving plans to fire Lohan, collided with the D-Notice story. Lohan, guilty of muck-spreading, was falsely accused of incompetence in failing to suppress the intercept story. In this, Wilson was advised by Cabinet Secretary Burke Trend, who seems to have encouraged Wilson in Lohan-bashing in the hope of distracting attention away from the serious secrets in the intelligence sub-text. When it all blew up in Wilson and Wigg's faces they were stranded, unable to reveal the sub-text to either of the strands. The permanent government, more concerned about preserving the GCHQ–NSA secret than saving Wilson's face, then leaned on the witnesses to the Radcliffe Tribunal, and faked its report, leaving Wilson out on a limb.

XX

D-NOTICE FALL-OUT

Burke Trend knew all about the secret world . . . he genuinely was a man of
secrets. As Cabinet Secretary he became something of a shop steward for the
secret servants of the state . . . and, naturally enough, became a great
favourite with them.
PETER HENNESSY

WHO WAS TO BLAME for the defeat over the D-Notice Affair? In his
memoir some years later, Wilson accepted the responsibility. To Richard
Crossman, just after the events, he confided that 'the real mistake was made by
not having a lawyer to advise him [Wilson] in drawing up the terms of reference
of the Radcliffe Committee. That was a fatal mistake.' This was also the verdict
of Marcia Williams a decade later. Without her, she felt, behind the locked door
Wilson had been given bad advice: 'In June . . . we saw the end of the D-Notice
affair. At last the Political Office was asked for its views. What amazed us, when
we came to discuss it, was that nobody had thought of having the Government
legally represented at the inquiry that had been set up. Whoever failed to advise
Harold on this bears a heavy responsibility.'[1]

Who is she accusing? Presumably the Cabinet Secretary, Burke Trend. At the
time of the Affair, Crossman believed that it had been Wigg whose advice Wilson
had been taking. Wilson denied it. 'Don't imagine I always take his advice. He
does an awful lot of dogsbody work for me', Wilson told Crossman. 'But surely
you won't deny', Crossman said, 'that it was on his advice that you made the
initial attack on the *Express*?' Wilson replied, 'No, that's quite untrue. I did it on
the advice of Burke Trend.' Crossman was astonished at this, though his
reaction is difficult to understand. Who else but the Cabinet Secretary is a new
Labour Prime Minister, inexperienced in handling security and intelligence
issues, going to ask for advice? (Marcia Williams' comments on the kind of
advice he got seem apposite.)[2]

So how influential was Wigg at this point? It is now impossible to be certain but
Barbara Castle tells us that Wigg was then close enough to the centre to have
written the first draft of the White Paper issued by the Government, disputing

145

the Radcliffe Tribunal report. Apparently, however, *only* the first draft. In his own account of the affair, Wilson attempts a masterful fudge of this entire area – but seems simply evasive on the role of Trend. 'I was not advised, still less pressured, by the then Paymaster-General, George Wigg, to make the charge I did in my parliamentary answer. Nor was I pressed to do so by Sir Burke Trend, the Secretary to the Cabinet who advises the Prime Minister directly on security questions. On the contrary, though he satisfied himself, and me, on the departmental advice he was so clearly given, that the facts were right, he asked me, in the sense of one putting a question to advise against, whether I was really sure that I felt I should make the statement. I said that I was.' This we translate as: having got Wilson to the point of making the attack, Trend covered himself by asking 'Are you sure?' – a device familiar to fans of *Yes, Prime Minister*.[3]

Crossman – in the safety of his diary – was clear about the blame, if only partly informed about what had been done to merit it: 'the criticism . . . lies with the civil servants who allowed Lohan to go on doing a job which was quite beyond him. It also lies with Burke Trend, who wrote a letter recommending that nothing should be done, and with James Dunnett for letting all this fester on.' Marcia Williams was also distrustful of Trend. During the debate on 22 June 1967, Crossman noted in his diaries: 'This evening I got Marcia around to see me. She was utterly miserable about the D-Notice debate which was then going on. She was not being consulted and felt that George Wigg was in complete control. As for Burke Trend, she was convinced that his concern was not to protect Harold but to cover up the Civil Service.'[4]

Mrs Williams was unaware then of the GCHQ–NSA sub-text, the real source of anxiety, Trend was doing his duty as the gate-keeper for the secret state by trying to keep the lid on the intelligence elements in the story. 'Trend', according to Whitehall watcher Peter Hennessy, 'was a great believer in the Anglo-American "special relationship" as a way of shoring up Britain's waning power'. Part of that relationship was the intelligence link and as the 'shop steward for the secret servants of the state', Trend was willing to go to great lengths to protect the flow of information and finance from the Americans. The White Paper stated that exposure of the cable vetting story had caused 'damage, potentially grave, the consequences of which cannot even now be fully assessed'. Mrs Williams was told that 'fifty of our agents were lost as a result of the D-Notice Affair'. Wilson alluded to this in Parliament without giving any details. It was rubbish but without reference to other sources Labour politicians were willing to accept the advice of the 'experts'.[5]

On our analysis, what probably happened was this. The permanent government, via Lohan, had heard that Pincher had got hold of a thread which might unravel the whole GCHQ–NSA intercept secret. Trend was informed. Knowing that Wilson and Wigg were already trying to get rid of Lohan and nobble Pincher, it was a minor matter for him to persuade Wilson that the Pincher story was a terrible threat to national security. That particular lily required little gilding. Trend kicked Wigg and Wilson into action, to suppress not the cable-vetting story but the story behind it.

The ensuing fall-out was serious. Mrs Williams recalls that 'The whole lamentable affair had hung like a heavy cloud over us for many months. It had sapped the energies of the Prime Minister and his morale . . . the cumulative effect of the affair on the Press, sensitive as they were from the Macmillan era about the Vassall Case and Government interference in Press matters, could almost be described as disastrous.' Denis Healey 'thought Wilson's watershed had been the D-Notice affair. Up to that point his judgement had been quite good, but since then he had been very erratic.'[6]

This affair finally ended the relationship between Wilson and Wigg, his main political adviser at this point, though Wigg's reputation in the Party had already begun to fall before the Affair began. The 'old soldier' in Wigg grated on younger members of the Cabinet, who found his obsession with security and leaks absurd, if not dangerous. He was shortly to be eased out of the picture.[7]

Wigg may not have been as important as some believe. His influence on the secret world appears to have been slight. We now have a clearer idea of Wigg's true relationship with the security service. His responsibility for security through MI5's Protective Security Branch brought him into the area of vetting, leaks and, indirectly, scandals. C Branch was very much the unglamorous part of MI5, somewhat on the edge of what the professionals regarded as the important work such as counter-espionage and subversion. It is therefore likely that David Leigh's assertion that Wigg 'set out to cultivate Thistlethwaite and McDonald, the heads of F branch (counter-subversion) and D branch (counter-espionage) respectively', is exaggerated. Trying to cultivate such people is one thing; actually getting anywhere (except lost) with them is another.[8]

Tony Benn, who thought Wigg 'an evil man', was interested in him and asked colleagues about his role. Benn asked Roy Jenkins who as Home Secretary was responsible for MI5: 'Is he authorised by Harold Wilson to do what he likes and does he really control the Security Services?' Roy said: 'Don't worry about Wigg, it is not like that at all. The Security Services don't trust him.' Two weeks later, Benn asked the same question of Otto Clarke, Permanent Secretary at the Ministry of Technology. Clarke replied: 'No, the Security people can't stand him and they don't tell him anything important.'[9]

There are those who believe Wigg's relationship with MI5 was much closer. The Labour MP, Leslie Hale, confided to his diary during the late forties: 'one well informed Minister [Bevan or Wilson perhaps?] says that George Wigg is the Parliamentary secret service agent of MI5, and he does not say it as a joke either.' Denis Healey would not go that far but he has suggested a previous connection with the security service. 'Because [Wigg] was both anti-Communist and anti-Establishment, he became an ideal conduit through which MI5 could exert pressure on the Tory Government over the Philby and Profumo affairs.'[10]

An unofficial 'conduit' maybe, but Wigg was nothing more. MI5 must have had him in their 'enemies' file. There are plenty of reasons for this belief. Although MI5 did leak material during the the Profumo Affair, they got their fingers badly burned and would not have forgiven Wigg for the role which he played in exposing their involvement in it. Secondly, he had been a general gadfly on intelligence and military matters during the Macmillan era; to the extent that 'MI5 had conducted its own inquiries to discover where he derived his information'. Thirdly, he was against Britain's independent nuclear deterrent. And finally, Wigg was distrusted simply for being an associate of Wilson.[11]

That Wilson and Wigg appear to have believed that someone with Wigg's track record – and MI5 must have had files on him dating back to the immediate post-war years when he was part of the grouping that became 'Keep Left' – could 'liaise' with a bureaucracy like MI5 in terms other than those set by the agency is hard to credit. Yet, in the beginning, at any rate, this appears to have been the case. To Chapman Pincher in 1984, Wigg was 'a one-man oversight body, but only for the Prime Minister [and] was quickly "captured" by the security machine.' In his 1991 book, *The Truth About Dirty Tricks*, Pincher goes further: '[Wigg] came to love MI5 even more than he had loved the Army . . . [and] he was . . . an MI5 spy right inside number 10 . . . MI5 made maximum use of him both as a source and an agent of influence'. In his memoir, Wigg was positively rhapsodic about MI5's 'high sense of duty, the quality of their thinking, and keenness of their desire to act within the directives laid down by their political masters'. Wigg admired Hollis as 'a real professional and patriot', he told Richard Deacon. 'Captured' is obviously right.[12]

The D-Notice Affair also resolved the struggle for Wilson's ear between Marcia Williams, along with the rest of the Political Office, and Wigg. Wigg had also become suspicious of Mrs Williams as a source of leaks to the press – one of the areas which, in his view, apparently came under 'security'. The 'Kitchen Cabinet' would pore over the first editions of the papers looking for smear stories, leaks and the source of any information. 'On one occasion', wrote James Margach, political correspondent of the *Sunday Times*, 'when commissioned to discover from which Ministers a number of leaks on Cabinet decisions had emanated, Wigg returned with a list of cuttings, the dates and information that Marcia Williams herself had been lunching or dining with the newspaperman concerned. [Presumably Walter Terry, with whom she was later to have two children.] Wigg also informed Wilson of Mrs William's relationship with a political correspondent and with Harold Davies, Wilson's Parliamentary Private Secretary, pointing out the prima face dangers of the association.'[13]

Wigg's war with Marcia was also Whitehall's war with the idea of the independent Political Office. This was not just a personal battle between Wigg and Mrs Williams. Whoever had been head of Wilson's Political Office in No. 10 during this period would have been under fire. The permanent government did not want independent advice and sources of information inside No. 10. Wigg's fight with Mrs Williams was easily exploited by Whitehall, who recruited Wigg who was 'against allowing her to be privy to secrets to which she was not entitled'. This conflict reached its climax with the D-Notice Affair. Though the Political Office lost that particular battle – upon the cry of 'national security', symbolically and literally, that office found the Prime Minister's door shut in its face – it won the war. Wigg was eased out, pensioned off. His reign as 'Spymaster' had been short and ineffectual.[14]

Over the years, Wigg brooded on the reasons for his ousting from Wilson's inner circle, and gave vent to those feelings in his autobiography which was published in 1972. Mrs Williams managed to obtain an advance copy of the manuscript and through the legal help of Lord Goodman, who had been a close friend of Wigg's (and Wilson's), had references to her removed from the book. Copies of the deleted extracts, however, found their way to Auberon Waugh at *Private Eye*. The editor of Wigg's book was Geoffrey Wheatcroft who happened to be a friend of both *Private Eye* and Waugh. 'Thanks to a calculated indiscretion (mine, of course) it became known that Lord Wigg had hard things to say about Mrs Marcia Williams.' Waugh decided not to publish because 'they were far too boring, even if no problems of copyright had been involved'. It did not stop *Private Eye* from publishing them two years later when Wilson was returned to power. Curiously, the same week that Waugh received the Wigg extracts he was also sent a 'flood of inaccurate information about Mr [Walter] Terry's private life which has been pouring into the office of HP Sauce [Waugh's column] recently.'[15]

Although Wilson was to express privately that 'George's going will be a great relief, you know', the loss of a close confidant meant that Wilson felt himself to be increasingly isolated. The strains of office and of three years' continual defensive action against a hostile Opposition were beginning to tell. 'I don't like the fact but he now sits at the Cabinet table sipping whisky instead of water', Crossman noted. Wilson had confided in Barbara Castle, 'it's the only thing that keeps me going. Fortunately I have a most intelligent doctor who prescribes it for me. It does something to my metabolism.' Most importantly perhaps, however inadequate Wigg's understanding of the intelligence world had been, it was better than that of anyone else around Wilson. With Wigg's departure, Wilson's inner group was left without anyone who understood the intelligence and security services at all.[16]

XXI

BLUNT AND THE 'OXFORD COMINTERN'

All these suicides, they'll ruin our image. We're just not that sort of Service.
MI5 DIRECTOR-GENERAL MARTIN FURNIVAL-JONES

DURING WILSON'S SECOND GOVERNMENT Peter Wright and his colleagues gradually constructed their conspiracy theory of the 'Oxford Comintern', based on old files and the snippets given by Anthony Blunt during the long and repetitive debriefing sessions. From 1967 onwards, elements of this conspiracy theory were used by MI5 to blacken the names of a number of Labour Party members and supporters as 'security risks'. It was often done with destructive effect.

The key year in MI5's understanding of the 'Oxford Comintern' was 1933. In February, the Oxford Union passed the celebrated motion that 'this House will not fight for King and Country', which MI5 regarded as an act of subversion. Shortly after, Bill Younger, an Oxford undergraduate and stepson of thriller writer Dennis Wheatley, was recruited by MI5's agent-runner, Maxwell Knight, to keep surveillance on communist students. That year also witnessed Hitler's consolidation of power in Germany following the burning of the Reichstag, which the Nazis blamed on the Communists. For many socialists and communists in Britain, combating fascism now became top priority. However, the legitimate anti-fascist activities of many respectable, law-abiding citizens were to find their way into MI5's files.[1]

In London the 'Committee for the Victims of German Fascism' was formed. On it were many well-known names such as theatrical impressario Sidney Bernstein, who also provided money for the Commission of Inquiry into the Burning of the Reichstag. Recently released Home Office files from the United States show how these organisations were deeply penetrated by the Special Branch and MI5. According to Peter Wright, Bernstein, who joined the Labour Party in 1917 and was knighted by Harold Wilson in 1969, was 'a very suspicious character and had a file'. In 1925, Bernstein had helped form the influential

'Film Society' which showed 'classic' Soviet films. Special Branch kept the society under surveillance because, as the Beaverbrook press put it, it was 'engaged in furthering the subversive propaganda of the Bolsheviks'.[2]

MI5 was particularly concerned about the activities of the society's London agent, the 'notorious communist' Willi Muzenburg. A Reichstag deputy, Muzenberg escaped Germany following the fire and went to Paris, where he set up offices for a world-wide anti-fascist campaign. There he headed the West European Department for Agitation and Propaganda of the Comintern which was designed to bind the various Communist parties throughout the world into a cohesive revolutionary force. Muzenberg recruited 'Comintern agents' who were essentially political agents; there is little evidence that he recruited 'spies'. To keep an eye on Muzenberg the Soviets planted Otto Katz on him, a Czechoslovakian refugee and former friend of Franz Kafka. In 1929 Katz was invited 'to go to Moscow, ostensibly to discuss theatrical productions, but in fact to be asked to join the Secret Service'. Katz became Muzenberg's contact with the various British anti-fascist groups and, in particular, with Bernstein.[3]

One future Labour Cabinet Minister in contact with the Muzenberg circle was Richard Crossman. In 1931, Crossman met the woman who became his first wife, Erika Gluck, a German communist, who 'was the courier for – and may also have been the mistress of – Willi Muzenberg – Erika and Dick even lived for a time in Muzenberg's Berlin flat'. Crossman's biographer writes that 'Muzenberg took Dick under his wing, possibly even hoping to recruit him to the Communist cause'. The young don rejected this approach and arrived back at Oxford a convinced anti-fascist though 'few people thought him a left-wing figure at all'. The marriage to Erika did not last and in the summer of 1934 he requested a divorce.[4]

According to a former Foreign Office liaison officer with MI6, in 1933 the so-called Trinity communist 'cell' at Cambridge 'gained a powerful adherent in [Donald] Maclean's friend James Klugman, a future historian of the [Communist] party . . . Maclean lost no time in calling on him and urging him to join the party.' Klugman had been Donald Maclean's contemporary at Gresham's public school where other friends, who later became Communists, included Brian Simon, a future President of the National Union of Students, and future Labour MP Bernard Floud. Michael Straight, who already had an MI5 file, arrived the following year. Straight had known the Flouds at the London School of Economics where Bernard's brother, Peter, became 'my first friend . . . He spoke about street fights with the local fascists . . . At Floud's urging, I became a member of the Socialist Club.' In 1935, Straight went to the Soviet Union with Blunt and Simon, close friends of Tess Mayor (who later married Lord Victor Rothschild).[5]

The President of the LSE Students' Union at the time was Frank Meyer, a 'very red politician from America', who was eventually deported. Meyer had been active at Oxford. Sheila Grant-Duff was another on Wright's list of subversives who 'joined the communist October Club when it was formed at the end of 1933 by an American Rhodes Scholar, Frank Meyer'. Members of the October Club included: Anthony Greenwood, Secretary for the Colonies in the first Wilson administration; Jane Rendel, Sheila's friend who became secretary of the New Fabian Research Bureau; and Bernard Floud. As part of the attempt to construct a common front against fascism, the Oxford Labour Club changed its rules in 1935 to absorb the communist October Club. Bill Younger, Knight's infiltrator at Oxford, investigated the Labour Club and the October Club. The Chair of the Labour Club and member of the Communist Party, Denis Healey, later observed that 'many of his [Labour Party] colleagues have not been so open about their pasts'. Healey and his wife, 'an undercover member of the Communist Party' and secretary of the Labour Club, left the Party in 1940 over the Soviet invasion of Finland.[6]

These personal, political links at Oxford were inter-twined with a web of intimate ties which were logged in the Registry files at MI5. Sheila Grant-Duff was a close friend of Goronwy Rees, an intimate of Blunt's, and another viewed with suspicion by MI5. Her best friend was Peggy Garnett, who married future Labour Cabinet Minister Douglas Jay. The Jays and Grant-Duff remained close for the next thirty years. Another friend of Jay's wife was Peter Floud; their respective parents also had a long-standing friendship. The Jays, in turn, were firm friends of Tony Greenwood and Richard Crossman. As we shall see, these files were dipped into by Wright and his colleagues for smears which were based on no more than guilt by association.

In 1936 the anti-fascist struggle began to focus on the problems in Spain. Otto Katz was instrumental in setting up a committee to agitate against the British Government's non-intervention policy. 'As a result, he had been refused re-admission to Britain; but this did not sever his British links, which were strong in the universities. He co-operated with James Klugman at Cambridge and Bernard Floud at Oxford in founding the World Student Committee against War and Fascism, and the latter recruited for liaison a personable young woman from one of the Oxford women's colleges. She came to Paris around the time of Maclean's arrival there and was a good deal closer to Katz than his wife, Ilse, would have wished.' Contemporaries say that Katz 'had a most persuasive way with the ladies'.[7]

Jenifer Williams (later Hart), later Fellow of St Anne's College Oxford, graduated from Somerville College, Oxford, in the summer of 1935. She then became a 'secret member of the Communist Party' and joined the Home Office the following year, where she had responsibilities for monitoring telephone-tapping warrants for MI5. She later revealed that 'her first controller was an Oxford friend. Her second was a British communist. The third was a "rather sinister" central European who 'never revealed his name.' Disillusioned, she claims to have broken contact with him in 1938/9.[8]

In 1937, Sheila Grant-Duff, who had joined the *Observer* as a foreign correspondent, undertook 'an important assignment . . . more directly related to the struggle than a straight newspaper assignment'. Arthur Koestler, representing the *News Chronicle*, had been arrested as a Republican spy, and Grant-Duff was to try to slip into Spain and find out how he was being treated. 'The intermediary with whom all this had been arranged . . . was Otto Katz.' Bernstein helped his friend Katz by donating a portion of his cinema takings to a charity, the Joint Committee for Spanish Relief. As the Second World War approached, MI5 stepped up their surveillance of Bernstein, and when he tried to visit Spain they refused to let him leave the country. In 1940, when he was offered the post of Head of the Film Division within the Ministry of Information, the Ministry's chief, Duff Cooper, was visited by MI5. Cooper was told that he could not employ Bernstein because 'Sidney was known to visit the Russian Embassy every week. With this, they began to outline what amounted to a formal declaration that Sidney was a member of the Communist Party.' Bernstein had never been a member of the Communist Party nor had he visited the Embassy. Cooper told MI5 to get lost.[9]

In 1940, Muzenberg, who had latterly been imprisoned by the French Government, was discovered hanging from a tree. French police believed that he had committed suicide, though it has been consistently alleged that Stalin ordered his assassination. In May, Otto Katz moved to the United States and then to Mexico where he remained throughout the war years. In 1946, equipped with a Czech passport, he left for Prague, where he worked for Soviet Intelligence. Accused of being a British and Zionist agent, he was hanged in December 1952. Six years later, Bernstein went to the Soviet Union, where he learned from former *Times* correspondent Ralph Parker 'more details of the death of his friend Otto Katz. Parker described to him how . . . he had been among those arrested and subjected to the notorious Stalin show trials . . . Pressed to reveal the names of British secret agents Katz had chosen at random the most improbable: Noel Coward and Claud Cockburn.'[10]

At the outbreak of war, Douglas Jay was offered a post as an assistant secretary in the Ministry of Supply. There was an unexplained delay before he was allowed to begin the job, the reasons for which he discovered some years later. 'A very close friend of mine, when he joined MI5 early in the war, found a secret file which cast doubt on my loyalty and patriotism, because I was known to have attended Fabian conferences and was apparently reported by some City source to have sinister "foreign contacts", and was therefore in the eyes of the pre-1939 MI5 a suspicious character.' Jay adds that his 'friend secured the destruction of the absurd file; and so the authorities in their next desperate trawl round the register to find efficient recruits for the industrial effort were no longer confronted with it'. Jay then got his job in the Ministry. In his autobiography, Jay states: 'I shared my pre-war house with Herbert Hart of the intelligence services [and] Jenifer Williams of the Home Office (later his wife).'[11]

Following the war, when Harold Wilson was President of the Board of Trade, he was introduced to Sidney Bernstein by Leslie Plummer, Chief Executive of the *Express* newspapers. Wilson was responsible for protecting the British film industry through quotas on American films. Bernstein, head of the hugely successful Granada Cinemas, was to the left of Wilson but the two got on well and for the first time Bernstein contributed money to the Labour Party. MI5 duly took note. In the mid-fifties Granada Cinemas bid for one of the contracts for independent televison. The setting up of commercial television was a long and often bitter battle. Conservative Party enthusiasm for the new service rested on the belief that the BBC's bias towards the Labour Party had been largely responsible for the Party's 1945 election success. The commercial stations, the Tories believed, tied to the profit motive, would redress the balance. However, Bernstein, a known left-winger, posed a threat. Kenneth Clark, the man responsible for issuing the new licences, reveals that 'Government circles put a good deal of pressure on the Independent Television Authority to turn down Granada's application.' It was later revealed 'that there had been a last minute wavering at the Authority over Sidney's reputed early membership of the Communist Party'. Clark, who knew the Granada boss well, 'made inquires of MI5, and was reassured that Bernstein was not a party member. He threatened to resign if Granada was not given the contract. Objections were withdrawn.'[12]

Bernstein's employment of known left-wingers annoyed the secret state. In 1955, Bernard Floud joined as an Executive, as later did Blunt's friend and wartime intelligence officer, Leo Long, believed by MI5 to have been working for the Soviets. Three years later, 'the *Daily Mail* started a campaign against Granada's "socialism", plaguing Sidney's life by sending reporters round to Mount Street to lie in wait for him outside his flat. Soon complaints from the ITA, and protests from the advertisers, were joined by attacks from the Conservative Party.' During the Profumo Affair and the 1964 General Election particular attention was paid to the Granada flag-ship programme *World in Action*. Right-wing loathing of the programme continues to this day.[13]

During the first Wilson Government, Bernstein's war-time colleague on the Psychological Warfare Board, Richard Crossman, soon found himself under scrutiny by MI5. Crossman had originally been a strong supporter of George Wigg and his views on security. However, it did not take him long to change his mind, telling Barbara Castle that 'Wigg had a disastrous influence on Harold, seeking intrigue everywhere and knowing everything that was going on.' Crossman may have been influenced by the knowledge that he was himself under some suspicion. During 1965 Crossman was investigated by Special Branch, who were interested in what the writer Robert Harbinson has dubbed the 'Gay Establishment'. Anthony Howard writes that 'Dick never sought to conceal the fact that in his early years at Oxford he operated predominantly as a homosexual. Given the circle . . . which he had chosen to infiltrate, it was hardly likely that it would be otherwise.' It is not known if anything came of the 1965 investigation but details of his youthful homosexuality eventually reached the ears of the media. John Junor recalls in his memoirs that 'Stephen Spender always claimed that his own homosexuality started when Crossman had seduced him . . . when they were both schoolboys'. Auberon Waugh referred to 'Crossbum' the 'rather dirty Wykehamist' in his *Private Eye* column in July 1971.[14]

In 1967, after extensive interviews with Michael Straight, Anthony Blunt and some of those whom Blunt named, Peter Wright began to piece together his 'Oxford Comintern' jigsaw. Much of the material found its way into MI5 security briefings. When Wilson started to restructure his Government with a series of ministerial changes, Wright and colleagues on the FLUENCY Committee (the joint MI5–MI6 committee investigating possible Soviet penetration of British agencies) began to 'stir things up' by raising security fears around some of those to be promoted. The conspiracy theory, which MI5's so-called 'Young

Turks' had constructed, expanded when Blunt suggested that Wright talk to Phoebe Pool, a former colleague at the Courtauld Institute. Pool was already 'in the process of a nervous breakdown' and Wright had to use another senior Courtauld figure, novelist Anita Brookner, as a go-between. The 'neurotic' Pool poured out a list of names which Wright then turned into his own version of Angleton's 'sick think'.

Wright interviewed Jenifer Hart, who admitted that Bernard Floud had been her first 'controller' and that she had acted as a 'sleeper' for the Soviets. Wright later said that 'I talked to her a lot and she kept shifting her ground. I am certain that Herbert (her husband) wasn't involved. I think the truth is that she ceased being involved with the Russians when she married in 1941.' It is unlikely that Wright really believed this, especially since it was said that 'Jenifer Hart was another Bentinck Street regular', a reference to the house where members of the 'Ring of Five' met during the war. Wright's thought's would more likely have followed those of a writer on Blunt: 'Herbert Hart, who had "unlimited access" to all Ultra [intelligence] derived from decrypts of the Abwehr traffic, married Jenifer Fischer Williams in 1941 . . . Ultra German intelligence-service reports would have been of intense interest to the Soviets . . . Who shared Hart's office? Blunt!'[15]

Another figure named by Pool was Andrew Cohen, Permanent Secretary at the Department of Overseas Development, where the Minister was Judith Hart, a former member of the Movement for Colonial Freedom. Despite great opposition, Cohen had been a central figure in the post-war period, dismantling Britain's colonial empire in Africa. Cohen's 'progressive outlook' was disliked by many in the permanent government who regarded him as a 'pinko'. Wright crossed Cohen off the list of members of the 'Oxford Comintern' when he died of a heart attack in June 1968.[16]

Mrs Jenifer Hart, according to Wright, identified a trade union official, Arthur Wynn, as a former 'contact'. Wynn was a close friend of Edith Tudor Hart, a former Communist Party member whom Wright accused of being a 'courier' for Kim Philby and the 'Ring of Five'. Wright tried to interview Tudor Hart but she rebuffed him. In what would appear to have been a deliberate 'mistake', Tudor Hart's MI5 file and that of Jenifer Hart were 'mixed together' and used as the basis for a 'trace' which MI5 then used to smear Labour Minister Judith Hart as a 'security risk' (discussed below). In 1968, Wynn was due for promotion to Deputy Secretary at the Board of Trade, a post which required security clearance.[17]

In 1967, when Wilson considered making Bernard Floud, MP for Acton, a junior minister, as a matter of routine he received a security briefing. MI5 already had an extensive file on Floud. In 1948 he had been 'purged' from the Board of Trade, of which Wilson was President, for his membership of the 'Civil Service Communists Group'. By 1953 Floud, according to friends and family, had, like many, rejected his political past and joined the Labour Party. In 1964 he was finally elected to Parliament. 'Wilson was told that Floud, who had been an open communist at Oxford, had been recruited to the Soviet cause by James Klugman, and had recruited others'. Wilson then gave his permission for him to be interviewed by MI5. Floud admitted his past involvement with communism but denied any connection with Soviet intelligence. However, MI5 refused to believe his denial. Peter Wright is adamant that Floud confessed and that he was still in contact with the KGB. 'Floud was definitely not offered immunity. He chose, rather than to talk, to knock himself off. Other things are said but that is the truth.' Michael Straight, the man who had named Blunt, was distraught that he 'may have set in motion the events that led to his death'. In fact Floud had been plunged into a 'suicidal despair' by the death of his wife in January 1967. From June onwards he had been receiving psychiatric treatment, including ECT. The intimidating interrogations by Wright, which took place in the autumn, could only have made the condition worse. Floud killed himself on the night of 9 October.[18]

In 1967, MI5 re-opened the file on Floud's friend, Sheila Grant-Duff, and started a new investigation under a senior counter-espionage officer, Charles Elwell, husband of Ann Glass, the MI5 officer who had started Wright off on this destructive trail. During the war, Grant-Duff married Noel Newsome and worked in the European Section of the BBC. She later married a Frenchman, Michael Sokolov, whom MI5 mistakenly thought to be a 'Russian refugee', and took up farming in Suffolk and Northumberland. MI5 believed Sokolov might be a KGB 'sleeper' waiting to sabotage a local RAF airfield. Part of the investigation included the burglary and surveillance of the couple's farmhouse near Needham Market, which they had in fact left some months before. The real target was almost certainly Sheila Grant-Duff as part of the Oxford circle.[19]

As part of the process of ministerial changes in 1967 Wilson sacked the President of the Board of Trade, Douglas Jay. In September, Jay received a telephone call from Wilson in the Scilly Isles. Rather mysteriously – why the rush? – Wilson asked Jay to meet him at midnight at the station master's office in Plymouth. 'When he emerged from the interview, white and shaken', writes Peggy Jay, 'I knew the blow had fallen – the Prime Minister had sacked him on the Common Market issue.' Whether there was anything more to this decision than Jay's anti-Common Market stance is not known. However, it must have been clear to many, including MI5, that Jay's marriage was in difficulty. It was supposed to have been an open and free marriage, and since 1964 Jay had been having an affair with his personal secretary, Mary Thomas. Did MI5 or George Wigg regard this as a security risk? In 1972, Peggy Jay sought a divorce and Douglas Jay and Mary Thomas married. What is known is that in 1974 MI5 constructed a conspiracy theory involving Jay which was passed on to journalists in a series of smear sheets. This rather strange smear suggested that Jay had co-operated with Wilson in seeking to negotiate trade deals which were advantageous to the Soviet Union. In the late forties, so the smear went, Wilson at the Board of Trade and Jay as Economic Secretary at the Treasury were 'in the critical position(s)' to support one another. According to MI5 there was 'of course, more to that seemingly innocent coincidence'.[20]

Not long after Bernard Floud's suicide, Phoebe Pool followed suit by throwing herself under a tube-train. Furnival-Jones put pressure on Wright to stop the witch-hunt. He is alleged to have told him: 'All these suicides, they'll ruin our image.' At this point on 18 October, MI5 decided to inform the Home Secretary, Roy Jenkins, about the essentials of the Blunt case but in a manner which kept Wilson in the dark. 'I passed this information in writing to the Prime Minister in the form in which it had been given to me', said Jenkins in 1979. It was carefully worded and followed Wilson's statement that he not been told about Blunt in 1967. Jenkins' memo would have gone to the Cabinet Office – and lost. George Young, Deputy Chief of MI6 until his retirement in 1962, commenting on Jenkins' statement, said: 'There is a curious convention in Whitehall – you can inform the Prime Minister without telling him.' The Cabinet Secretary can wait for an opportue moment' which 'may never come'. It would appear that MI5 were attempting to cover their rear in case there was a political row following any possible exposure of Wright's blundering and the suicides. As we shall see, Wilson was not informed about Blunt until 1975.[21]

Despite Furnival-Jones's strictures, Wright and his colleagues did not stop their operation. Wright enlisted the help of Lord Rothschild to try to put pressure on Brian Simon, an old friend from university days. They wanted him to talk about communist friends but he refused – though even this had consequences. In June 1968, Minister of Technology Tony Benn recorded in his diary that 'Purnell, the security officer, sent me a note alerting me to the fact that Brian Simon was an open Communist and that my wife was working with him'. Benn's wife, Caroline, was writing a book with Simon who rang her 'quite regularly from Communist Party Headquarters and I feel sure that they must have been tapping the telephone at the time'.[22]

In August 1967, as part of his government re-shuffle, Wilson told Transport Minister Barbara Castle that he intended promoting Stephen Swingler to Minister of State at Transport, a non-Cabinet post. Swingler was close to Wilson and, while viewed within the party as a highly intelligent and skilled junior minister, was viewed in some quarters as an 'extreme left-winger'. When Castle was moved to Employment the following April, she suggested Swingler as Transport Minister. 'The trouble here, Harold said, was security, Stephen had been doing some "very stupid things".' No evidence was provided and the following day Castle tried again. 'I begged him to put Stephen in my place. Harold said he would check up on the record again and see how black it was but Stephen really had been dabbling in Eastern Europe. He couldn't risk giving Jim Callaghan (who had access to the security records) a weapon against him by bringing Stephen into the Cabinet if Stephen were any way a security risk.' Crossman agreed. Like his brother Randall, an open communist, Swingler had known Crossman at Oxford when he joined the Labour Party in 1933. Swingler was one of the MPs singled out by Gaitskell and Brown in 1961 and had an extensive MI5 file as a 'crypto-communist'. In October 1968, Swingler was finally moved to the Department of Health and Social Security under Crossman. Swingler was still not allowed in the Cabinet, a decision which angered Castle. Crossman notes in his diary that Wilson 'was able to report that Barbara's intervention about Stephen Swingler had been ineffective'. Swingler told the new Transport Minister, Dick Marsh, that 'he was bitterly disappointed because he had expected to become [a Cabinet] Minister'.[23]

While acknowledging that Swingler was 'one of the most successful of our ministers', Wilson's account of the period makes no reference to the security problems which prevented his promotion into the Cabinet. The 'Gentle Rebel', as the *Daily Mail* called Swingler, collapsed, partly through overwork, in his office on 14 February 1968. At his funeral the oration was given by the Prime Minister. Wilson had not been completely taken in by the MI5 assessments of security risks. In the Cabinet re-shuffle of October 1968 the Prime Minister promoted Judith Hart and Jack Diamond, both targeted by MI5.[24]

In July 1967, Wilson had taken the name of Niall MacDermot off the list of members of the Cabinet's defence committee, on the recommendation of, and pending an investigation by MI5. The security services were about to get their revenge for MacDermot's attempt to open up the Philby Affair in 1963, and about to discredit one of the few Labour MPs who had worked for MI5. The last thing which the British secret state ever wants is a Labour minister who not only is a barrister, but also understands its own machinations.

A 'trace' was found on MacDermot's wife, Ludmilla, and she was interviewed in February 1968 by MI5. Both she and MacDermot were then subjected to heavy MI5 pressure – bugging, surveillance, telephone-tapping of their home and offices – the kind of noisy operation that is at least as much concerned with harassing the victim as it is with information gathering. Interrogations were carried out by Wright's close friend, Patrick Stewart, and a female research officer, with Wright listening in another room through headphones. It soon became clear to MacDermot, as a former MI5 officer, that the interrogators were principally concerned about Ludmilla's life in post-war Italy. She had joined the resistance during the war and, following the liberation of southern Italy, had worked on an ad-hoc basis for a Soviet Embassy official, Nikolai Gorshkov, helping to distribute Soviet films. Ludmilla had not known that Gorshkov was a KGB officer and the film distribution business simply his cover.

This information from old war-time Italian files was possibly based on CIA sources. In post-war Italy, the agency spent (by today's money) hundreds of millions of dollars keeping the Italian Communist Party out of office. In charge of those operations was James Jesus Angleton, a chain-smoking paranoid who had gone on to become the head of CIA counter-intelligence, and who was Wright's main US ally in the hunt for the moles. The link is hypothetical, but not implausible. From whatever source, this 'trace' on Ludmilla McDermot arrived at MI5 via MI6 from abroad. MacDermot realised that MI5 'simply will not take the risk of giving clearance to someone who had worked under a KGB officer'. Furnival-Jones prepared a report for Wilson denouncing Ludmilla MacDermot as a 'suspect Soviet agent'.[25]

At a private meeting with a very embarrassed Prime Minister, Wilson asked MacDermot if his wife had ever had access to confidential information; to which MacDermot replied 'Of course not'. Although Wilson was prepared to accept his word and reject their advice, as with Swingler, Home Secretary James Callaghan concurred with MI5 – even to the point of refusing to inform MacDermot, his colleague, of the basis of the accusations against his wife.

In September 1968, MacDermot resigned as Minister of State for Housing for 'personal reasons'. Richard Crossman at Housing recorded that 'He is going to leave parliament to go and earn his living in Geneva.' Twenty years later, when the man sitting listening to his wife through headphones had become world famous, MacDermot told journalists that he had quit when 'MI5 could not be dissuaded from their unjustified suspicions about my wife'; as MI5 never disclosed 'their grounds for suspicion, so we were never able to refute them. Any suggestion that the KGB might have put my wife under pressure is wholly absurd.' MacDermot returned to the Bar and remained in Parliament until the 1970 General Election, when he became Secretary General of the International Commission of Jurists.[26]

This whole unhappy episode, in which MI5 drove a totally innocent minister out of office, finally surfaced in public in 1978 in Chapman Pincher's *Inside Story*: except that the tale had been inverted. Pincher wrote of a 'security scandal which happened . . . during Wilson's first term as Prime Minister . . . [which] would have been highly damaging then had [it] not been kept secret for political reasons'. A minister 'had been required to resign following representations by MI5 acting on information supplied by MI6 from foreign sources. Wilson was given evidence that the minister had placed himself in serious danger of being blackmailed by Soviet bloc Intelligence.' Two years later, with Wright as a source, the story had been significantly changed: now the unnamed minister had resigned 'because he was being subjected to attempted KGB blackmail'.[27]

This episode is a very striking illustration of MI5's thinking on 'security'. Once MI5 are suspicious of someone, that person is effectively convicted. For MI5 'X is a security risk' and 'X *might* be a security risk' are basically synonymous. Ludmilla MacDermot was guilty of nothing more than unwittingly working for a KGB officer's cover job, distributing films – and twenty years previously, at that. Her husband was guilty of nothing more than being married to her! Yet on that basis his political career was halted.

Even Peter Wright occasionally caught a glimpse of the capricious absurdity of his activities. Reflecting on their investigation of Sheila Grant-Duff's husband – guilty of nothing more than his marriage to her – Wright wrote of 'his life utterly changed because of something a man he has never met says in a darkened room on the other side of the world. The quiet rural world of Suffolk colliding with the secret world of betrayal, where there is no such thing as coincidence.' *No such thing as coincidence* – that was the point: all the 'evidence' MI5 had was coincidental, guilt by association. Unfortunately, where those who would challenge the existing order have been concerned, guilt by association will usually suffice. In the entire catalogue of MI5 investigations into Labour ministers, MPs, party members, et al – this massive MI5 trawl that has been catalogued in the last few years – suspicion was transmuted into evidence in only one case, that of Will Owen, discussed below (Chapter XXVII).[28]

For MI5 the only people fit to serve the Crown are those about whom MI5 have no suspicions. On this preposterous axiom does the great wheel of the British state turn.

159

XXII

NUKES

We are very much more closely tied to the Americans than anyone has ever made public.
TONY BENN

NO DOUBT, the Americans were grateful for the way in which Wilson helped to protect the all-important intelligence link between Britain and the United States during the D-Notice Affair. However, Wilson knew that in other areas of the 'special relationship' Britain's motives and committment were regarded by the Americans with some suspicion. Solving the Polaris problem had merely been the beginning of the Labour Party's difficult relationship with the Anglo-American military establishments. Britain's overseas military expenditure was a major contribution to the balance of payments deficit at the heart of the Government's economic problems. At Chequers, in December 1964, 'the weekend of the crunch', the Cabinet took the decision to hold defence spending constant at £2 billion, at 1964 prices – i.e. with expected inflation, an annual minimum cut of between 3 and 4 per cent, perhaps 15 per cent over the full term of the Government. This demanded a serious rethinking of Britain's overseas role and a full-scale review of defence expenditure.

What the Americans wanted most urgently was support in Vietnam. This topic dominated Richard Crossman's account of the report back to the Cabinet given on 11 December 1964 by Wilson and Healey, following their trip to Washington to see President Johnson. 'McNamara had gone out of his way to emphasize the importance of Britain's role East of Suez . . . the President . . . asked [Wilson] outright for a British military commitment [to Vietnam]. Harold had resisted, apart from offering the use of our jungle training team in Malaya and also our teams for anti-subversive activities [presumably IRD] . . . Healey [said] that what they wanted us to do was . . . keep a foothold in Hong Kong, Malaya, the Persian Gulf . . . they think our forces are much more useful to the alliance outside Europe than in Germany.'[1]

For all Wilson's enthusiasm for the Commonwealth and his rhetoric in this period about Britain's world role – the latter, in our view, largely a coded message to the Americans about maintaining British bases East of Suez – in defence and foreign policy the Labour Cabinet had explicitly embarked on the management of decline. It is beyond the scope of this book to consider Labour's management of defence and overseas policy in this period and we will concentrate on certain issues arising from nuclear weapons.

For the British nuclear state, the recognition that Britain would be unable to bear the cost of developing its own nuclear weapons meant increasing dependency on the United States. The Anglo-American nuclear relationship was governed by the 1958 Anglo-American Military Agreement for Co-operation which spelt out the terms for technological transfer. The terms of the agreement were heavily weighted in the Americans' favour: while Britain could not communicate nuclear information to a third party, the Americans were not obliged to consult the British. This resulted in the Labour Government being involved in a series of disputes with its dominant partner and attacked by sections of the British state which regarded the nuclear link with the Americans as essential to Britain's status as a world power.[2]

The 1958 agreement was due to expire in 1968 and its renewal loomed over the nuclear debate throughout Wilson's first period in office. In 1964, though Britain could produce sufficient crude fissile material for nuclear warhead production, it relied on certain crucial materials manufactured in the United States, notably tritium. Although it had been known that tritium was subject to rapid radioactive decay, in the early sixties it was discovered that the tritium ageing problem had been underestimated: nuclear warheads might last as little as five years. The effect of this discovery was to increase annual British demand for tritium and British dependency upon the United States.[3]

Wilson actually alluded to this dependency and the renegotiation of the 1958 agreement during the first Parliamentary defence debate of the Labour Government in December 1964. Deriding Tory claims that the Polaris missiles bought from the United States were a genuine independent British nuclear deterrent, Wilson pointed out that Britain 'would still be dependent after the completion of the Polaris programme in 1968, on the Americans for certain specialised materials essential to the maintenance of our missile force . . . The question is whether after 1968 we shall be in a position to supply all the fissile materials required to maintain the effectiveness of our warheads, having regard to the half-life of those materials and so on.' Angry at Wilson's reference to the tritium problem, Tory MPs tried to smear Wilson as giving away defence secrets. In fact, 'all his information . . . was thoroughly checked by the security service before the speech'.[4]

Acknowledging the illusory nature of Britain's 'independent' nuclear capability raised questions about both the role of Britain's nuclear production and research facilities centred round the Aldermaston weapons development centre, and the need for British testing of nuclear warheads. British tests were terminated after two underground tests at Nevada in July 1964 and September 1965 – a concession to the critics within the Labour Party who saw that the Government had reneged on promises made while in opposition to renegotiate Macmillan's 1962 Nassau Agreement on Polaris. Aldermaston then came under threat as part of the general decline in defence expenditure. The threatened run-down became a cause for major concern within the permanent government which regarded very seriously any threat to reduce still further Britain's contributions to the US–UK nuclear relationship. What may have appeared to be a relatively simple issue of the cost-effective use of scarce scientific resources at Aldermaston, in fact cut through to the heart of the unequal Anglo-American special relationship. The possible cut-back of nuclear research formed the backdrop against which negotiations with the Americans started in late 1967 on the renewal of the nuclear weapons information exchange arrangements.[5]

To Aldermaston's rescue came the 'Soviet threat'. In late 1965, US intelligence began to get information which suggested that the Soviet Union was developing anti-ballistic missiles (ABMs). The hypothetical ABMs (in theory) threatened the 'deterrent' effect of NATO's intercontinental ballistic missiles, and, in particular, allegedly threatened to make the new Polaris missiles redundant before they had become operational. America's response to the 'ABM threat' was to accelerate the development of the next generation of Polaris, the Polaris Mark 3, re-named Poseidon. Britain was to acquire the previous model, Mark 2. In late 1966, a proposed British programme to upgrade Polaris, to make the Mark 2 warhead 'hardened' with 'penetration aids added' so that the missile could cross the anticipated Soviet defensive screen of ABMs, went to the Nuclear Policy Committee, a secret sub-committee of the committee on Overseas Policy and Defence (OPD), from which most of the Cabinet were excluded. Inevitably, with an issue as politically explosive as this, the Polaris improvement proposal leaked.[6]

The Government's Chief Scientist, Solly Zuckerman, did not take the Soviet ABM threat seriously – justifiably, as it turned out – and lobbied Tony Benn and Barbara Castle, both outside the committee, against the proposal. Lord Chalfont, brought into the Cabinet from *The Times* for his anti-independent deterrent views, lobbied Richard Crossman against it. For a government which had already reneged on its pre-election promises to 'renegotiate Nassau', upgrading Polaris was political dynamite to which the only possible political response was delay: Lord Rothschild was appointed Chair of a committee to examine the proposal. In April 1967, Minister of Technology Tony Benn appointed Lord Kings Norton to head an inquiry into staffing at the Aldermaston weapons research centre. Three months later, Kings Norton delivered what the Chancellor of the Exchequer, Roy Jenkins, described as a 'whitewashing document'. In Benn's view, Kings Norton had 'really covered up for Aldermaston, which is heavily overstaffed'.[7]

In June 1967, Defence Secretary Denis Healey formally announced that the Government had rejected the option of buying Polaris Mark 3, Poseidon, from the US; a week later Wilson gave a categorical assurance that the British Government was not interested in the development of new generations of nuclear weapons. In December, the Nuclear Policy Committee, now including Tony Benn as Minister of Technology, considered again the 'big and highly secret issue' of hardening of Polaris missiles, penetration aids and the multi-head missiles. Denis Healey was strongly in favour of hardening, the Foreign

Secretary and the Treasury were against on financial grounds; Chalfont, Wigg and Benn were also opposed. The Atomic Energy Authority argued that 'unless hardening and penetration aids are approved for our atomic weapons, providing work for skilled people at Aldermaston, it would not be possible to keep even the existing Polaris programme going'. No decision was taken and Benn heard nothing more about the issue until 1974: it disappeared even off the agenda of the Nuclear Policy Committee, to be handled in secret inside Whitehall.[8]

On 3 August 1968, Benn received Lord Rothschild's report on the proposed British upgrading of Polaris. He not only 'recommended against further development of our nuclear weapons programme', but went 'outside the terms of reference, not only disagreeing with a lot of what was said in the [Kings Norton] report, but also saying, that in his opinion, it wasn't worth keeping nuclear weapons'. This was too much for the Whitehall mandarins. 'Otto Clark, John Hill and Sir James Dunnett, Permanent Under-Secretary at the Ministry of Defence, cooked up a minute for me to put to Ministers, brushing aside Rothschild and simply saying we ought to run Aldermaston down a bit.'[9]

Even though the major threat to Aldermaston had been largely neutralised, Aldermaston's budget would still be reduced. Wilson's commitment of June 1967 not to develop a new generation of nuclear weapons left Aldermaston carrying out theoretical studies of possible improvements to Polaris to counter the threat apparently emerging from the Soviet ABM system – just enough to maintain an appearance of Britain still being in the nuclear game. This made it increasingly difficult for British weapon designers to justify continuation of the close working relationship with American laboratories at Los Alamos and Livermore. To the Americans it seemed that 'if this was a serious statement of intent by the Labour government there seemed no point in any continued Anglo-American nuclear relationship in the military field.' The 1958 nuclear exchange agreement was up for review in 1968 and the Americans might pull out.[10]

Similar problems were encountered in other areas of defence, the nuclear and high technology field. At a meeting of the Strategic Exports Committee to discuss the sale of computers to the Eastern bloc, Tony Benn was told that the 'Foreign Office were against this because they thought we would be considered unreliable by the US Government'. Another problem arose over the development of 'Acarus', a centrifuge project to enrich uranium. (The technical details are of no relevance here.) In 1966, British, German and Dutch engineers solved the problem which was delaying development of the centrifuge – with American assistance. The centrifuge's nuclear application had been thought impracticable until the Americans invented a special fitting, the so-called Endcap. Minister of Technology Tony Benn was sufficiently excited by the fact that 'Britain could meet its own enriched uranium needs without being so dependent on the Americans' to rush round to tell Wilson the good news at 11.45 p.m. that night.[11]

In November 1968, an agreement was reached between Britain, West Germany and Holland to form a consortium to exploit the centrifuge commercially. Despite having been the Minister responsible for two years, only then was Benn indoctrinated into some of the secrets at the heart of the Anglo-American nuclear relationship. He learned 'that we have an arrangement with the Americans under which we are absolutely tied hand and foot to them, and we can't pass any of our nuclear technology over to them [Holland/Germany] without their [American] permission'. The centrifuge was dependent on the Endcap, which was covered by an American patent. 'Some members of the British Cabinet', Benn recorded in his diary, 'were very concerned because they were afraid that by going with the Dutch and Germans and using an American patent for this purpose we might undermine our nuclear relationship with the US, upon which we depended for the regular supply of nuclear technology, nuclear weapons and, above all, for access to the American international satellite and intelligence systems at the very centre of the so-called Anglo-American special relationship.'[12]

Matters came to a head in June 1969 at a Nuclear Policy Committee meeting when pro-Americans Michael Stewart and Denis Healey opposed Benn. Benn commented in his diary that 'the whole Anglo-American special relationship had boiled down to this Endcap . . . it embraces the whole question of trust in Anglo-American relationships and commercial rivalry versus the old nuclear partnership'. The UK/Dutch/German consortium was put in jeopardy by the 1958 agreement with the United States which forbade giving information to a third party.[13]

Part of Wilson's diplomatic efforts to persuade General De Gaulle to permit British entry into the EEC had been to emphasise 'Britain's ability to contribute its advanced technology'. However, this only helped reinforce 'the fears of those in the United States who believed that Britain was ultimately prepared to transfer nuclear weapons and submarine reactor data to France in order to secure entry'. This anxiety had been triggered by the Government's 1967 decision not to buy Poseidon, one which had been presented to De Gaulle as a 'positive example of Britain's intention to reduce its nuclear ties with the United States'. These suspicions led to 'a series of acute conflicts with the United States which, while they had little direct connection with the military relationship, affected the general atmosphere in which the nuclear exchange agreements were to be amended'.[14]

After much argument and hard bargaining, during which a cut-off of American information on nuclear warhead design was apparently threatened, it had been agreed by September 1968 that the United States would not terminate the agreement. Agreement was reached on tritium supplies, though the protocols remain secret. A similar decision was reached by mid-1968 on submarine fuel.[15]

Opponents of Britain's nuclear weapons programme had their enemies within the secret state and it seems that a number of deception operations were run 'through the judicious use of disinformation and the strict application of the principle that only those who needed to know could be told anything'. Chapman Pincher reveals that by this stage the Defence Ministers under Denis Healey had already 'decided to bar Wigg from access to certain secret information'. Foreign Secretary George Brown was kept in the dark because he was considered a 'security risk'. Others were subject to secret investigations. In a series of letters, Peter Wright conveyed to Pincher a summary of what purported to be Zuckerman's MI5 file. 'Solly Zuckerman had a cottage in the wolds of Essex. It was called "World's End"! He used to hold very odd weekend parties there . . . There were also suspicious left-wing people there . . . Solly had a considerable file in the office and many people were suspicious of him. As you know, he is a South African Jew, with no fundamental loyalty to the UK. A lot of defence decisions were extremely suspect. He was considered untrustworthy basically because he was considered to take decisions popular to the Labour Party, particularly to the left-wing, and not in the best interests of the UK. We never proved any Sov. Bloc connection, but he was certainly a blackmailable character.'[16]

Some officers in the CIA believed Zuckerman's friend and colleague Lord Mountbatten – who relied on Solly's advice – to be 'the perfect target for KGB blackmail', a security risk because of his alleged homosexuality and his left-wing friends, some of whom were alleged to be known communists. A former CIA officer told Richard Deacon that 'if he had been anyone other than Mountbatten, it is almost certain that he would not have survived our positive vetting tests'. Mountbatten was not completely trusted within the Defence departments and his views on the illusory nature of the independent nuclear deterrent were viewed with suspicion. When Mountbatten produced plans to amalgamate the various defence intelligence agencies in the early sixties, 'Tricky Dickie' was accused by those on the right of running down Britain's defence and the smear was spread that he was really helping the Soviets. Lord Rothschild was distrusted by right-wingers because of his pre-war and war-time friendship with members of the 'Ring of Five'. Right-wing intelligence officers on both sides of the Atlantic suspected him of being 'the Fifth Man'. Even the cold-war warrior Lord Chalfont was the subject of an MI5-inspired smear operation in this period, which, from its timing, can only have been because of his position of opposition to the retention, let alone further development, of the British 'independent' deterrent. This operation was at the heart of the D-Notice Affair and is discussed above.[17]

While the permanent government was concerned about leaks and opposition to nuclear policies from Ministers and officials regarded as being on the left of the Government, it turned a blind eye when its major ally, the United States, used its 'assets' to promote its cause. Barbara Castle attended the Cabinet meeting on 6 July 1967 which discussed the White Paper on Defence. 'Harold began by saying he had a telegram from [President] Johnson asking us to go slow on defence cuts East of Suez. This was the second time a foreign power had got to know Cabinet business. In these two cases, being the U.S., it wasn't serious.' It would seem that at least one of Mrs Castle's colleagues was leaking to the Americans.[18]

Chapman Pincher has written that the Labour Party had been 'penetrated for many years by agents of the CIA' and that he knew 'the identity of one former Cabinet Minister who was in regular contact with the CIA'. Political correspondent James Naughtie disclosed that a minister had been subject to a telphone-tapping operation and 'was found – to the surprise of ministers who had served with him – to have been a regular informant to Washington'. According to David Leigh's sources the former MI5 officer Arthur Martin told friends, 'I did hear that _____ was a spy'. An MI5 officer from K branch confirmed to Leigh that 'we knew that _____ was a CIA agent, or if not an agent, at least very close to the Americans' (deletions in Leigh's account). We can reveal that the 'agent of influence' was the Foreign Secretary, Michael Stewart.[19]

Stewart turned out to be the most pro-American of all the former Gaitskellites, supporting US involvement in Vietnam to the bitter end. He had deep personal links with the pro-Vietnam War lobby in Washington. Stewart disliked Wilson because of his 'equivocal attitude during the CND dispute' and 'hostility to Hugh [Gaitskell]' – which puts into an interesting light Edward Short's comment that 'the relationship of Harold Wilson to Michael Stewart . . . was one of great regard and growing reliance – indeed, he probably depended more on his advice than any other minister's'. Short says that 'this was a development which almost everyone in the Government welcomed, for Michael Stewart was a man of considerable wisdom and versatility'. Benn begged to differ. He thought Stewart was 'the most unattractive Cold War warrior, his attitude is a completely transparent plastic bag covering and preserving old Foreign Office policies . . . [they] are still in the Cold War stage and have always got their eyes turned over their shoulders to the United States.'[20]

Twenty years on, despite the collapse of the Cold War and the end of the 'Soviet threat', the Parliamentary Labour Party remains wedded to the link forged with the Americans during and after the Second World War. None of the issues discussed in this and preceding chapters about that relationship have yet made their way out of the left fringe into the main agenda of the Party.

XXIII

WILSON AS CORPORATIST

*In science and industry we are content to remain a nation of Gentlemen in a
world of Players.*
HAROLD WILSON, 1963

DESPITE THE FANTASIES of Peter Wright and his ilk, Wilson was never a
socialist, let alone a communist. From the 1940s onwards he remained true to
the vision of the mixed economy, but one in which 'Private enterprise required
to be guided, instructed, even bullied by the State if the national economy was to
prosper.' This was what he had experienced while in government during and
after the war. Wilson had been the young expert, the man with the slide rule who
had shaken up fuddy-duddy Whitehall during the war, who had sneered at the
City during the Bank Rate Affair of 1957 and 1958 for being run by amateurs,
footling about on grouse moors while Britain was falling behind. 'For the
commanding heights of the British economy to be controlled today by men
whose only claim is their aristocratic connections or the power of inherited
wealth or speculative finance is as irrelevant to the twentieth century as would be
the continued purchase of commissions in the armed forces by lordly amateurs
. . . in science and industry we are content to remain a nation of Gentlemen in a
world of Players.'[1]

The state would force change and settlement. Between 1944 and 1950 Wilson
had experienced the state at its most activist in this country's history. It is
impossible to exaggerate the significance of the lesson about the inefficiency of
the market system learned by Wilson (and others) during the war. However, this
had not made him any sort of socialist. He might occasionally talk of nationalis-
ing 'the commanding heights of the economy' but he had always wanted a mixed
economy. In the Commons in 1949, he boasted that 'Private enterprise has
produced on a vastly greater scale under this Socialist Government than it ever
did when we had a Tory Government.' In 1948, for example, he spoke of ending
'a host of restrictive arrangements in British industry which have had the effect
of frustrating and destroying the operation of that free enterprise which I think
some sentimentalists fondly imagined characterized British industry . . . Com-

167

petition is the public's natural safeguard in any industry which continues on the basis of private enterprise.' These views never altered. They are all to be found in his piece in the *New Statesman* (24 March 1961).[2]

If nothing else, the Party of manufacturing, Labour were enthusiastic readers of the stream of books which appeared diagnosing Britain's 'problem', most famously Michael Shanks' *The Stagnant Society* (1961). Although Wilson frequently used the vague rhetoric of 'science, modernity and technology', he was not afraid to spell out its full implications. Achieving the 'release of energy' he talked of so often – economic growth in the manufacturing sector – would require the state not just to take control of macro-economic policy, but to take it *from* the City of London. In the House of Commons on 11 July 1960, he spelt this out: 'Hon. Members opposite believe that the fulfilment of this release of energy can be left to a system which, in its essentials and institutions, and, above all, in its motivations, has changed little since the Forsytes. Our merchant bankers, our discount houses, our bank parlours, our daily-more-powerful insurance companies all have a job to do, and an important job, but they exceed their function if they claim to be the regulators and the directors of our economy. Our economic development will be safeguarded only when the Government party in the House accepts that, however vital, finance is the handmaiden and not the controller of our economic development.'[3]

During the protracted pre-election period in 1964, it was the more easily digestible rhetoric of science, modernisation and efficiency (bringing meritocratic justice) which dominated Labour's rhetoric. The Party promised that under them, the 'producers' alliance' – between manufacturing industry, the unions and Labour – which in Wilson's view had won the war, would be recreated. Such corporatist ideas were not unique to the Labour Party, of course. A section of the Conservative Party and British manufacturing had learned the same lesson; had, in effect, accepted the post-war social settlement as legitimate. Somewhat to Wilson's irritation, in 1962/3 the Tories took up many of these ideas, setting up the National Economic Development Council (NEDC), a National Incomes Commission and supporting some degree of planning. During 1964, another President of the Board Of Trade, Edward Heath, announced legislation to extend the scope of a number of scientific bodies advocating more industrial research, later the basis of the Ministry of Technology. However, while the Federation of British Industry (the CBI's antecedent), for example, could embrace economic planning, the corporatist Conservatives had to edge slowly towards such notions, taking the rest of the Party, City men and the economic liberals, with them.[4]

At the 1961 Labour Party Conference, Wilson mocked the Conservatives conversion to planning. 'Suddenly last summer planning ceased to be a dirty word in Tory circles . . . it is said they have stolen our clothes. They have not. They have stolen the label sewn into the back of our trousers, but it is only a label, and will be a mighty poor cover for their nakedness.' The corporatist structure which the 1964 Labour Government inherited was only a shadow of the thing itself, the state being allocated little more than a consultancy role.[5]

The intention was radical enough: the power of the Treasury would be broken, the management of the economic and technological acceleration would be handled by the new Department of Economic Affairs (DEA) and of Technology. A Ministry of Technology had been part of the 1964 Labour Party manifesto. It 'was based on the beliefs that Britain's economic problems were largely due to a failure to apply technology sufficiently rapidly in industry, and that a civil technology ministry could help redress the distortions introduced into British technology by defence requirements.' Too much of Britain's research and development was being consumed by the arms industries.[6]

The difficulty was that Wilson was committed to defending the dollar/sterling exchange rate at $2.80, as the *quid pro quo* for American financial support against the City attacks over the deficit. Defending the currency, however, severely reduced the options in other areas – such as increasing domestic economic growth. Substantial deficit-generating activity such as would have been prescribed by the orthodox Keynesian – and such as had, indeed, been attempted by the preceding Conservative Chancellor, Reginald Maudling – would damage the trade balance, and thus the pound/dollar exchange rate. 'Once the decision had been taken . . . the state of the balance of payments and confidence in the economy became the criteria by which the government judged the success or failure of its policy. In these circumstances it was inevitable that the Treasury would retain its dominance over Whitehall because its responsibility for finance and the balance of payments had survived the coming of the DEA.' Although the destruction of the Department of Economic Affairs by the Treasury has been well documented elsewhere, little attention has been given to the detail of that defeat.[7]

It began while Labour was still in opposition. Naively, the Labour Shadow Cabinet had gone along with the so-called Douglas-Home rules, which, in Hennessy's generous view, allowed 'the Opposition access to Whitehall in advance of an election to put their planned changes to the permanent secretaries'. Alternatively, it gives the permanent government advance notice of changes and time to sabotage them. This is what happened to the DEA. The DEA 'blueprint' prepared by the Permanent Secretary at the Treasury excluded any provision for physical essentials (office furniture, telephones, paper etc.). By the time that the staff had actually got their hands on such basics, they found themselves excluded from the information flow from the rest of Whitehall. The urbane Peter Hennessy talks of 'turf fights'. Sabotage of Labour policy is more appropriate.[8]

At the DEA, George Brown gathered around him a group of what used to be called 'progressive businessmen' – Frank Kearton (Courtauld's), George Cole (Unilever), Siegmund Warburg (Warburg's) and John Berkin (Shell). 'This unpublicized body of industrial advisers had an enormous influence on the apparatus we set up'. That 'apparatus' included the most radical of bodies, the Industrial Reorganisation Corporation (IRC), set up in January 1966 and charged with 'promoting industrial efficiency and profitability and assisting the economy of the UK'.[9]

The origins of this body are unclear. In one account, 'George Brown wanted to facilitate company mergers which he felt the merchant banks were neglecting and had the notion of reviving the pre-war Bankers' Industrial Development Company, run originally by Major Albert Pam of Schroder's'. In another, it was based on the example of the Italian Institute for Industrial Reorganisation. In a third, 'its rationale is said to have been some calculations by [Patrick] Blackett, who estimated that, if firms could spend only a certain proportion of their turnover on R and D, then, comparing that figure with the estimated sum of money needed to mount the minimum viable industrial R and D programme, it turned out that relatively few British firms could be expected to do any R and D, and hence most would be technologically backward. The solution was to encourage mergers.' But the radical intentions of its founders were clear. For Harold Wilson the IRC was 'a new and more revolutionary change' which would take the owners of British industry 'by the scruff of the neck and bring them kicking and screaming into the twentieth century'.[10]

The City's response was entirely negative for reasons which follow, and the IRC's £150 million capital could be raised only by the efforts of Eric Roll, Permanent Under-Secretary at the DEA. Sir Frank Kearton, Chairman of Courtauld, was its first Chair and its Director-General was Ronald Grierson from Warburg's. The IRC was independent and answerable only to Parliament through the 'sponsoring' Minister at the DEA. Unlike most parastatal bodies it was independent of the Treasury. The factor which caused most disquiet in the eyes of MPs, according to Lockwood, was its 'power and independence'. While its policy and direction were vague, and its capital base inadequate, its potential power was immense. The IRC Act of 1966 gave it 'the power to do anything . . . which is calculated to facilitate the discharge of its functions'. Seeing the potential power of the IRC to supervise British industry, the Tories labelled it as nationalisation by the back-door and 'fought the proposal up and down the country and made it one of their principal targets in the general election in March'. Those most vehemently opposed to the IRC in 1966 were the Institute of Directors and the Association of British Chambers of Commerce.[11]

Initially, the reality did not justify the cries and alarms of sections of British capital. Ronald Grierson, of Warburg's, the IRC's first Director-General, interpreted the powers narrowly and sought to use the IRC as a 'forum where directors of large companies could discuss their ideas for mergers and reorgan-isations without feeling that they were talking to the Government but knowing that public money could be forthcoming'. Ministers wanted quick action but the board thought that 'research and the establishment of a relationship of trust and confidence with industry should be the priorities'.[12]

The IRC also acted as the Government's 'merchant bank', provided relatively cheap finance and expertise, undercutting the City, threatening its lucrative fees for organising mergers and take-overs. Crucially, unlike the merchant banks, it could intervene against management. 'It seems that the only criticisms from a sectional interest that led to the IRC actually amending its policies and attitudes, rather than acknowledging and accommodating the criticism, came from the City.' Some of the mergers 'incensed City opinion', partly because the IRC 'was flouting convention by introducing the concept of the "bottomless purse" into bid situations.' Also, it disliked the fact that the IRC could keep secret its reasoning for particular industrial mergers. While the CBI leadership was initially not hostile – CBI Director-General John Davies said industry 'was not deliberately against, but it was suspicious' – the whole of the ICI board came out against it, Managing Director Sir Paul Chambers (knighted by Wilson) warning that 'we are getting nearer and nearer to conditions in a planned economy as you have in a Communist state'.[13]

As well as the hostilty to the IRC's potential power to direct British firms, there was another thread, especially in the City. Siegmund Warburg had become the Labour Government's chosen banker and was widely hated for it. Warburg's developed much new business from the efforts of the IRC just as it had during the nationalisation phase of the 1945 Labour Government. Like Wilson with the Bank Rate Affair, Warburg had fallen out with the Establishment of the City in the late fifties for his part in an aggressive take-over bid in what became known as 'the aluminium war'. The battle for control of British Aluminium 'was to a large extent a fight between the "ins" and the "outs" . . . Tube Investments and S. G. Warburg were both companies with an outstanding reputation – but they were both new. The newcomers fought the established City houses at their own game and defeated them overwhelmingly.' Warburg's biographer says that the 'wounds were deep. The attacks had been fierce. Anti-Semitism had never been so evident'. Cromer, Governor of the Bank of England, 'remained angry'. From the outset, Wilson had met with Warburg, using him as an unofficial advisor. The City was 'shocked that a banker could work with the "reds" in this way'. Warburg was also known as the 'émigrés' banker' and was presumably involved with those East European businessmen, friends of Wilson, who were viewed with suspicion by MI5.[14]

The last straw came in the autumn of 1967 with the IRC backing of the General Electric Company's (GEC) bid for the electrical giant Associated Electrical Industries (AEI). With City directors like Lord Shawcross and former Conservative Chancellor of the Exchequer, Reginald Mauldling, AEI was 'very much an Establishment board', which seemed unable to undertake the drastic changes needed to make it profitable. The attempt by GEC and the IRC to rationalise the British electrical industry was vigorously opposed by the board, which was backed by the anti-Wilson grouping collected around Cecil King. A leading AEI director was Lord Renwick, who was a partner of Greenwell's, stockbrokers to Courtauld's and the Queen; Sir Joseph Lockwood on the IRC board was Chair of EMI, which jointly owned a major company with AEI. The financial defence of AEI was undertaken by Baring's, whose partner, former Governor of the Bank of England Lord Cromer, did 'some discreet but potent lobbying on AEI's behalf'. In a bid to beef up the management the Chair of AEI was offered to Lord Beeching. In the end, the defence failed and AEI was forced to concede to the GEC bid.[15]

As its own momentum and pressure from Ministers was turning the IRC into a more active vehicle for mergers, Director-General Ronald Grierson resigned, joining the board of GEC as deputy Chair. Ripples of alarm spread through the boardrooms when the Government proposed the Industrial Expansion Bill which would give the IRC power to buy shares in companies. The CBI's leaders went to Downing Street to tell Wilson that its Council had rejected the proposals entirely and would not even discuss amendments. The IRC became the focus for 'a group of doctrinaire liberals led by Arthur Schenfield (previously executive director) [who] tried to push the CBI into a strongly anti-government stance.' Sir Paul Chambers of ICI and his friends had grown tired of the CBI's general line. 'By starting a new group, they could make a right-wing stand without having to secure the CBI council's endorsement.' This was the notionally independent Industrial Policy Group (IPG) which '[John] Davis was able to pack . . . with more liberal members and ensure that it would play no disruptive role.' Among IPG's members were Chambers, Sir Joseph Lockwood of EMI, and Sir George Bolton, on the 'court' of the Bank of England. Bolton was then starting his role as a major informant for Cecil King, the head of the Mirror Group, who was then engaged in the protracted attempt to bring down the Government, which we discuss below.[16]

In the House of Commons, Chancellor James Callaghan described the IPG as 'potentially sinister' and attributed to it the belief 'that it is impossible for this House of Commons to solve the economic problems with which we are confronted'. Various IPG members pooh-poohed these allegations – Lockwood thought Callaghan had 'gone off his rocker' – but Callaghan was not so far off the mark. At the end of November, on BBC television, Lockwood called for a coalition government after which Parliament would be closed down for six months; and elsewhere in London members of this network were considering how to get rid of Wilson and/or Labour. Many of them were talking to Cecil King.[17]

XXIV

THE CECIL KING COUP

In Britain, we could speak of 'the need for more business-like government' – one can even imply (whether truthfully or not) that the coup is linked with prominent public figures such as newspaper proprietors, big business men or the chairman of a nationalized industry.
EDWARD LUTTWARK,
Coup D'Etat: A Practical Handbook, 1968.

National government is inevitable.
CECIL KING 12/1/68

IN 1966 WITH WILSON OUT of their grasp, safe for the next four years with his large parliamentary majority, the British bankers' machinations began to shift from economic manipulation and pressure, to more covert, political means. With Cromer's departure from the Bank of England, his role as spokesman for the Bank of England and the City was taken up by Cecil King. Although King had begun sniping at the Labour Government through his newspapers, he was still regarded as vaguely 'on Labour's side'. In 1965 he had been appointed a part-time Director of the Bank of England by the Wilson Government. This appointment had major, unintended consequences for Harold Wilson, for King, apparently ignorant of macro-economics, became a captive ear for the bankers. He was also a member of several very important, intersecting circles. King had a number of advantages over Lord Cromer: owning newspapers for one thing; for another, he was able to play public politics, whereas the Governor of the Bank of England could not, or not so overtly.[1]

From mid-1966 onwards, King talked obsessively of an economic crash bringing three million unemployed and social chaos which could be avoided only by that old stand-by, a National Government to 'restore confidence'. Reginald Maulding and Sir Alec Douglas-Home had first tried to foist this on the Labour Government during the first speculative attack in November 1964, following the first Labour budget, and Cromer had persisted with it for the next year and a half. To this 'National Government' idea King added a particular twist: he wanted a National Government with non-politicians, businessmen, drafted in.

173

The first reference to this idea in his diaries is on 24 July 1966 when he met Louis Franck, Chair of the merchant bankers, Samuel Montagu. Franck, who had served with British Security Co-ordination (MI6) and the Special Operations Executive during the Second World War, had been 'on a round of Central Banks – Belgium, Holland, France, Switzerland and Germany . . . at the behest of the Bank of England . . . [and] said that some future government would have to have a large business element. In such a government he foresaw prominent places for [Alfred] Robens and myself.' No wonder that a 'National Government' – with businessmen – appealed to King: centre stage was beckoning. From that point on, the theme crops up regularly in his diaries: a fortnight later, when he asked George Brown about a National Government; again, on 13 August, when Dennis Hamilton, editor of *The Times*, told King that 'both Macmillan and Rab Butler foresee a National Government'. In the following February discussions of this subject are recorded by King with Roy Jenkins, who was not interested, and with Conservative leaders Iain Macleod and William Whitelaw.[2]

From the beginning of 1967, King and *Daily Mirror* Editor Hugh Cudlipp devoted Saturday mornings to seminars on the state of the nation, discussing 'what would happen, and how soon, and who in various activities in the land could be of any use at all when the fabric of the British Way of life broke down'. King took the lead but, according to Cudlipp, on the issues there was a 'basis of wide agreement between us and the cause of no conflict until King convinced himself in 1968 that nothing would be achieved without his personal intervention in national affairs.'[3]

Others were having similar thoughts. The focus of the plotting was a network around Robert Renwick which had formed in the 1950s in pursuit of commercial television. The trio at the centre were Norman Collins, Renwick and C. O. Stanley. Collins had resigned as Controller of BBC Television in 1950 and began campaigning against the Corporation. As well as wide-ranging connections in the radio equipment industry, the financial world and the Institute of Directors, Renwick was an important fund-raiser for the Conservative Party. Stanley was Chairman of Pye Ltd. This trio formed the first commercial broadcasting company, Associated Broadcasting Development Company, and also a campaigning group called the Popular Television Association. It worked closely with the anti-socialist pressure group, Aims of Industry, and the Conservative Central Office, which swopped personnel for the campaign.[4]

In 1967, former Liberal MP and broadcaster Michael Winstanley was approached by a senior ATV executive 'with a plot to break into a television news broadcast and announce the formation of a new political party . . . the Albert Hall had been booked for a mass rally and the holding of this rally was going to be announced on all three TV channels by broadcasters (all known to me [Winstanley] personally) who had undertaken to interrupt their programmes and make the announcement before the programme director had time to pull out the plug'. The organisers, including people who had once been prominent in public life, 'had a lot of money from business behind them'. They wanted 'Wilson removed' to make way for 'a coalition of the centre' – precisely what King's 'National

Government' would have been. Among the organisers of this 'plot', Winstanley was told, were Lord Beeching, Eric Fletcher MP (Deputy Speaker of the House of Commons), 'two obscure Labour backbench MPs', some leading Liberals and Robert Renwick.[5]

Most of this grouping were also part of the King network of the period and we assume that its major figure was Renwick. As chief fund-raiser for the Conservative Party, Renwick was the focal point between British capital and the Tories, one of the key back-room figures of the time. In late July, talking with Lord Mountbatten, Hugh Cudlipp discovered that Mountbatten had already been approached to play a part in some kind of post-democratic regime but had apparently declined because he was too old. Was this the Renwick group, or was there a third, undetected cabal? Apparently unaware of this Renwick cabal, King was working along similar lines. He too was thinking of Mountbatten as the figurehead for his 'Emergency government'.[6]

It should be emphasised that King wanted a coalition of the centre, not a take-over by the right. King had been talking to people like Jo Grimond, Reginald Maudling and Iain Macleod. The Labour Party people he admired were Richard Marsh, (Lord) Alfred Robens, Brian Walden – and, intermittently, Roy Jenkins and Denis Healey. His newspapers had urged readers to vote Labour in both the 1964 and 1966 elections. King's notion of who would run the show after the 'great collapse' was that it would be centrist politicians and 'big businessmen' – the Robens, the Beechings, the Keartons – from manufacturing capital, not the bankers.

King, meanwhile, continued his 'soundings', seeing Iain Macleod on 8 September 1967. 'We discussed possible successors to Wilson and he said he would accept Denis Healey as leader of a Government of National Unity, but doubted whether the Tufton Beamishes of his party would.' (Tufton Beamish was a leading member of the right-wing Imperial faction of the Tory Party.) Roy Jenkins was on King's list, but Macleod hated Jenkins 'because . . . he almost always had the better of Macleod in debate'. Callaghan was a possibility, and Macleod had a growing admiration for the Chancellor: 'The best man they've got is Jim.' William Whitelaw indicated support for Callaghan as coalition leader (28 November), as had Lord Robens the week before. And there was always Lord Cromer, recently removed as Governor of the Bank of England. 'Cromer . . . is obviously contemptuous of the deflationary measures taken so far; does not think they will be carried any further; expects a crisis in April; further devluation in July. I urged him to consider himself as a very possible "outside" minister to come in a National Government.'[7]

Though Callaghan later dismissed King's efforts as 'no more than a piece of amateur theatre', how seriously Labour took King at the time is suggested by the lengths to which they went to buy him off. On 18 September, and again on 24 October, Callaghan had lunch with King and tried to enlist him as a member of the Government. On 28 November, Wilson tried to offer King membership of the Privy Council and a peerage. King would accept only an earldom and Wilson was not prepared to create hereditary earls.[8]

In the New Year King turned to canvassing the Cabinet. Richard Crossman recorded in his dairy on 12 January 1968 having to 'sit there and listen to another lecture on the baseness of our present Government and how good big business-men alone could save the situation'. (This meeting is not mentioned by King.) By the end of January, even someone hitherto as far from King's networks as Tony Benn heard that 'Alf Robens . . . was now evidently playing for the premiership of a theoretical Coalition Government'.[9]

Wilson knew what was going on. 'Substantial sections of the press were engaged again on a "Wilson-must-go" campaign', which Wilson thought 'had the substantial backing of Lord Shawcross [another member of King's circle]. In no time at all the other members of the trinity, Lord Robens and Mr Cecil King, were joining in with demands for a coalition of all the talents – Great Britain Limited – though there were some signs that its leading proponents might not agree on whom the Queen would be advised to send for as Prime Talent.'[10]

Wilson's comment masks his true feelings at the time. Crossman mentioned to Cudlipp 'the depth of Wilson's misery' over the anti-Wilson campaign in the press. Other Cabinet Ministers came to his defence. On 24 January, the Lord Chancellor, Gerald Gardiner, launched a bitter attack on the newspapers for their 'vicious vilification and denigration of the Prime Minister which has really passed all bounds of public decency'. The attacks only fed King's sense of his own self-importance, spurring him on to greater efforts to get rid of Wilson.[11]

On 6 February 1968, Benn was invited to lunch with King for the first time. King offered him gloom and doom from, *inter alia*, Cromer and the US Ambassador, David Bruce, 'who agreed with him [King] that the Government was finished, and others. He even said that Sir William Armstrong at the Treasury was extremely depressed about the outlook. Did he [King] think a Coalition Government was necessary? Yes, indeed he did.' King discussed potential leaders of the coalition. Benn's response was to ring first Peter Shore, then Wilson, as soon as he could.[12]

On the same day a meeting was attended by the following:

- Norman Collins – Deputy Chair of ATV and a major Tory Party fundraiser;
- Eric Fletcher – Labour MP, Deputy Speaker of the House of Commons, one of the original founder members of ATV, Governor of the London School of Economics, and on the Executive Committee of the Fabian Society;
- Ellis Birk – Mirror Group Director;
- Lord Beeching – ICI and Lloyds Bank;
- Lord Watkinson – ex-Conservative Minister for Defence, Director of the Midland Bank;
- Lord Harding – Field Marshal, ex-Chief of Imperial Staff, Director National Provincial Bank, Standard Bank, Plessey.

This was coalition planning – 'Emergency Government' was the expression used.[13]

The next day, 7 February, the journal of the Institute of Directors, *The Director*, called for a 'businessmen's government', suggesting leading roles for Alfred Robens (Director of the Bank of England at this stage), Paul Chambers

(ICI) and Frank Kearton (Courtald's). The same day, trying to 'detach' Crossman from Wilson, Hugh Cudlipp 'made it clear that Cecil King . . . is now convinced that by the summer there will be second devaluation which will be the end of the Labour Government and out of which a national government will come'.[14]

At this point, a group within the Labour Cabinet began to take countermeasures. Tony Benn met with Peter Shore and Thomas Balogh – both close to Wilson – on 8 February, and discussed 'the possibility that the City could be planning a coup against the government'. The next day, together with Shore and Balogh, Benn put his 'conspiracy theory' to John Silkin, the Chief Whip. They 'agreed in general that the press should be alerted to this and that Harold should be told and also that we should prepare some sort of contingency plan'. Two days later, Benn met Crossman, who told him of his meeting on 7 February with Cudlipp who had said 'that we would have a National Government'. Crossman had 'the impression that Jim Callaghan and Denis Healey had been fishing in these waters'.[15]

On 17 February, Benn talked to the journalist (and one time self-confessed MI6 agent) Mark Arnold-Foster and told him something of the Cecil King story. Arnold-Foster 'went away and later rang to tell me that he was interested; he also added one or two things, including that he had been to see Jo Grimond who had been on the phone to Macleod. He thought Jo Grimond had decided he would like a coalition under Roy Jenkins with himself and Macleod.' Benn 'rang Geoffrey Goodman (who) . . . said Denis Healey was pouring stuff into the *Daily Mirror*, including the voting figures on critical issues in the Cabinet, to persuade Cecil King that Harold was weak'. The next day the story, headlined 'Cecil King takes soundings', appeared in the *Guardian*. King's operation had been blown.[16]

The Balogh/Shore/Silkin/Benn agreement that some sort of 'contingency plan' be prepared led to the formation of a small, secret – that is, from the rest of the Cabinet – Cabinet committee MISC 205. Initially it comprised Wilson, Chancellor of the Exchequer Roy Jenkins, Tony Crosland and Peter Shore. Barbara Castle was added in June, thanks to economist Thomas Balogh, who told her about the committee and its 'contingency planning' in May. Balogh was advising Wilson on this. The old 'Bevanite' network from the 1950s was still working.[17]

Within the economic concepts of the time, there *was* a real financial crisis in progress. The year before Wilson had devalued the pound to a lower rate with the dollar, but even this lower rate was proving difficult to sustain. 'In January 1968 Jenkins was confirming privately that virtually no money had flowed back into the reserves and if the Budget failed then another devaluation would be necessary, which he expected to lead to the fall of the government.' On 7 March, Jenkins gave the Cabinet a '*terrifying*' account of the economy not recorded in the Cabinet minutes: 'a second devaluation would occur within the next three months if the budget didn't restore confidence in sterling'. Crossman commented that 'This is exactly what Cecil King had said to me in January . . . Roy is now drawing the conclusion that in such a case the Government couldn't survive'.[18]

There was another flap on 13 and 14 March, another threat to sterling which climaxed with the closure of the London gold market – at the request of the Americans – and the temporary closure of the British banks. The details of this are obscure and irrelevant. What is interesting, however, is the comment on 2 April, by the banker and Labour MP, Harold Lever, to Crossman that the Bank of England had engineered the crisis: 'All that week the Bank of England had known that gold had been pouring out of the country and had done nothing about it. Then, suddenly, the country was faced with the threat of devaluation and the Governor proposed to take no action at all, so that we had to be saved by American intervention. The American request for the closing of the gold market enabled us to have our Bank Holiday and save our gold standard.' Wilson seemed to be hinting at this in a speech on 6 July in which he talked of 'fighting a hostile and embittered Establishment . . . which does not scruple to misrepresent or to distort, an Establishment which is prepared to appeal to those who use money to make money, to do their dirty work for them . . . they are prepared to attack the whole basis of the country's economy, the country's recovery . . . we know and they know what is at stake'.[19]

Against this background, the secret Cabinet committee, MISC 205, produced 'Plan Brutus' in June 1968, ostensibly as a fall-back option in the event of another threatened devaluation. This was fairly astonishing stuff. 'Exchange controls would be imposed on all countries so that all sterling balances held by foreign governments in Britain would be frozen. Import quotas would be imposed on all items except raw materials and basic foodstuffs, there would be crash cuts in defence expenditure and all overseas aid to the Third World would be tied to purchases of British goods. In addition there was "Operation Bootstrap" which involved the compulsory acquisition by the government of all privately held overseas securities (a measure only previously adopted in wartime).'

This was the end of civilisation as the City of London knew it. 'Ministers', comments Clive Ponting, 'realised this package would lead to a major increase in unemployment, austerity at home and a serious disruption of world trade, and were worried about the political consequences for themselves. But they felt they had no choice but to prepare for the worst. The Treasury was told to be ready to implement the plan at seven to ten days notice.' How 'secret', though, is an economic plan which is given to the Treasury to implement? News would have been round the City in no time. It was secret only from the British public and other Cabinet members. Wilson obviously *intended* the bankers to hear of the plan. When Barbara Castle asked him if there was no alternative to 'Plan Brutus', Wilson replied: 'Only multilateral action which we hope will come when they look into the brink and see what we must do otherwise?'[20]

Two months before the formal completion of 'Plan Brutus', Wilson warned the money-lenders about the consequences if they did not support the Government. On 7 April, Cecil King recorded: 'Desmond Donnelly had a piece in the *News of the World* in which there was a paragraph to the effect that a senior Cabinet minister very well in with the Downing St set had said to Donnelly that the Government is going to stick it out and, if it comes to that, pull the whole temple down on top of themselves . . . [Jo Grimond] said the statement was made by Peter Shore at a dinner at Nuffield College, that he made it clear to those listening that he was quoting the P.M. – or, at any rate, reflecting his view.' Wilson was playing chicken with the bankers just as he had in 1965 and 1966. These were psychological operations, only this time, after devaluation, the stakes were higher.

A month later, King had his now famous meeting with Lord Mountbatten on 8 May. Although the meeting was organised at short notice, and then apparently by happenstance, as we have seen, King recorded in his diary contact between the King–Cudlipp team and Mountbatten some ten months before, in 1967. Cudlipp says that the meeting on 8 May was initiated by Mountbatten, who had sent a message that he wanted to see him. They met at Broadlands, Mountbatten's country house. Mountbatten 'was as deeply concerned about the morale and problems of the nation as anyone else, and more than most but, whereas Cecil King's approach to the "forthcoming crisis" was essentially political (chopping down the Rt. Honourable Harold Wilson) and economic (sweeping measures under a new regime in which he would himself be playing a leading role), Lord Mountbatten's approach was more circumspect and philosophical . . . What he was hoping for was massive resurgence . . . I arranged a meeting.'[21]

An interesting group then gathered: King and his loyal deputy Cudlipp; Lord Zuckerman, Wilson's Chief Scientific Officer, who had been trying to prevent the British military establishment upgrading their nuclear weapons; and Mountbatten, suspected by some of the British right of being a Pinko. This was not a gathering of the right but of the centre. Zuckerman was there at Mountbatten's invitation, apparently both as old friend, a source of advice, and as a witness. Lord Brabourne, Mountbatten's son-in-law, distrusted King and telephoned Zuckerman on the morning of the meeting telling him that he had 'to be present to see that nothing unwise happened'.[22]

According to King's account, Mountbatten said that the Queen 'was receiving an unprecedented number of petitions, all of which have to be passed on to the Home Office . . . she is desperately worried over the whole situation'. To Penrose and Courtiour, a decade later, King repeated that but added that 'the Queen had turned to her uncle, Lord Mountbatten, for advice'.[23]

As his guests assembled, Mountbatten knew that there were things afoot. At least two approaches had been made to him to act as the figure-head of a coup. He knew that King was the focal point of one of the groups, and, most important of all, he had the informal authority of the Queen – which he let his guests know. King then delivered a version of his preoccupations at the time – approaching economic collapse and ineffective government, with a Prime Minister no longer able to control events. Public order was about to break down leading to social chaos. There was a likelihood of bloodshed in the streets. Yet *precisely* what King said remains unclear. What is apparently 'agreed' among the participants is that Solly Zuckerman got up and left at that point, saying something along the lines of 'This is rank treachery. All this talk of machine guns at street corners is appalling' – and telling Mountbatten not to have anything to do it, at which point, in the 'agreed' version, the meeting broke up.[24]

What was King actually proposing? That Mountbatten be invited to head a 'coup'? Cudlipp denies that the use of force was envisaged, or that anything resembling a coup was being talked about: 'The only mention of armed forces by Mr King was in the sense that they would be involved in restoring order after the chaos he was expecting.' Cudlipp records King telling him in an earlier scenario that 'before, during, or after this debacle there would be violence and bloodshed in the streets, the docks and factories beyond the strength or patience of the police to subdue or contain'. 'Restoring order' is a coat of many colours. From one point of view, that is precisely what General Pinochet did in Chile. In any case, the use of force was implicit in Zuckerman's remarks as reported by Cudlipp – 'all this talk of machine guns' – and in Zuckerman's reaction. Merely talking about contingencies – 'if and when . . . there are 3 million unemployed and social chaos' – would hardly have provoked Zuckerman's talk of treason or his walking out.[25]

On his own account King was, more or less, talking about what most people would call a coup: 'there might be a stage in the future when the Crown would *have to intervene*; when the armed forces were important' (emphasis added). With their oaths of allegiance not to Parliament, but to the Crown, the military remained beyond the grasp of the political representatives of fractious civil society. The Queen's peace could be restored – by the Queen's peacemakers. King acknowledged to Penrose and Courtiour 'that influential people had spoken of military coups in the 1960s'. Asked if this 'emergency government' proposed by King would be brought in by force, Zuckerman replied: 'I didn't imagine it would be brought in by the Salvation Army.'[26]

What then was Mountbatten's reaction to Zuckerman's outburst and departure? Cudlipp tells us that Mountbatten agreed with him – it 'wasn't on', but Zuckerman wrote in his diary, five years later: 'The fact of the matter is . . . that Dickie was really intrigued by Cecil King's suggestion that he should become the boss man of a "government" '. Zuckerman remarked to Cudlipp, after the meeting: 'I wonder what Dickie would have said if I hadn't been there'; and in his autobiography he claimed that 'For a second or two Dickie tried to restrain me at the door, but as I left the room, I kept repeating, "Throw them out, throw them out" '.[27]

Mountbatten's official biographer attempts to reassure us with this: 'if Mountbatten did hanker after strong leadership and a government of national unity, he never contemplated this coming about except by constitutional means'. However, in Britain's absurd 'unwritten constitution', 'constitutional means' do not rule out what most people would call 'a coup' – democracy is suspended, the military take over. This was pointed out in *The Times* in 1974, when the sabres were being rattled at the third Wilson administration. In some circumstances the British Army could take over and it would not technically be a coup; or would – if this makes any sense at all – be a constitutional coup. The key piece in such a scenario is always the Crown, which can legitimately intervene in the Parliamentary system and 'activate' the army. For all that King and his 'coup' has been largely dismissed as something of a joke, in May 1968 he got to the appropriate member of the Royal Family, the one semi-detached figure with a long history of military service with the state. [28]

Was King, in fact, front man for something more substantial than hitherto acknowledged? There are hints that this might be so. Lord Lambton told *The Times* that 'When this matter was first made public a very senior member of the then government took me aside in the House to say that there was a deal more to the story yet to be told.' In 1981, the paper commented that there were rumours during May 1968 that King 'was a key figure in a putsch backed by senior civil servants, the military and big business'. Penrose and Courtiour were told by one ex-Labour Minister in the House of Lords 'that he had been specifically informed that "military figures" had been waiting in the wings at the time of the Kinnerton Street meeting in May 1968'.[29]

According to David Leigh: 'One senior Army officer at the Ashford Intelligence [Centre], said privately at the time that planning had reached the state of designating the Shetland Islands, in the far north of Scotland, as a home for "internees". Lists of "acceptable" trade union leaders were also being drawn up.' Confirmation of some sort of coup plotting in 1968 came from former MI5 head Furnival-Jones who told Penrose and Courtiour of 'a pretty loony crew' of 'civil servants and military' plotting something in 1968 which was reported to the then Home Secretary, James Callaghan. Furnival-Jones later let slip that a senior military figure had been disciplined. The Prime Minister was never informed about the plotting though he 'had heard rumours from a variety of sources'. There had been a period at the beginning of 1968 when he had talked to Marcia Williams 'about guns' and the possibility of a coup.[30]

The evidence needed to link these fragments together cannot be found, let alone evidence to suggest that King fronted a coup attempt. Yet, if these accounts are true – even if only some of them are true – something was happening. How would a British coup be organised? The likely scenario would doubtless involve sporadic consultations; tentative approaches between the representatives of one circle of the élite and another; the informal networks of clubs; decisions made amidst the serious lunching which lies at the heart of so much of the British élite's activities; and the activation of regimental connections. King's diary and the other fragments show us exactly that process in action.

Whatever is said to have taken place that day in Kinnerton Street, King thought that the hour of his destiny was at hand. The day after the Mountbatten meeting (9 May) he resigned from the 'Court' of the Bank of England. On 11 May he arranged for the *Mirror* to print as its lead story his call for Wilson's departure, headed 'Enough is Enough', in which he fired what he thought was his big gun, his belief that the Government figures about Britain's financial position were being faked. King had been shown 'some secret figures' by Bank of England Director Maurice Allen. Wilson's account of King's *Mirror* action noted that 'we were but a few days from the date when 6-month forward sales of sterling made in the week before devaluation were coming up for settlement. The Bank of England had expressed to the Treasury their concern about monetary movement on that day; Mr King's demarche could not have been worse timed.' Or, perhaps, better.[31]

Had King been trying to generate that final run on sterling which would bring the Government tumbling down? Yes, says Hugh Cudlipp, 'it was now his intention and expectation that the authority of his pronouncement and its timing would bring Wilson down in ignominy and that in the political chaos there would materialise the moment he had prophesied, the final act when he and those names he had written down on slips of paper, revised, testily removed and occasionally restored, would at last be called upon (or call upon themselves) to exercise direct power or indirect influence and save Britain.' King had hoped that this would have 'the titular blessing of Lord Mountbatten'.[32]

XXV

STRATEGY OF TENSION

Conspiracies are necessary for the maintenance of the high police. Hatching them, stifling them, setting up the plot and discovering it, this is the high art of office.
PAUL-LOUIS COURIER, 1820

CECIL KING'S 'COUP' has been largely derided as the fantasies of a megalomaniac. We hope that we have shown that it was more than that; indeed, if Peter Wright is to be believed, it represented considerably more. He says, in *Spycatcher*, that 'feelings had run high inside MI5 during 1968. There had been an effort to try to stir up trouble for Wilson then, largely because the *Daily Mirror* tycoon, Cecil King, who was a longtime agent of ours, made it clear that he would publish anything MI5 might care to leak in his direction. It was all part of Cecil King's "coup", which he was convinced would bring down the Labour government and replace it with a coalition led by Lord Mountbatten.'[1]

Wright's claims about King were dismissed partly because Dame Ruth, King's widow, had told the press that before he died her husband had made a statement that 'As far as I know, I have never had any dealings with anybody from the security services, MI5 or MI6, so it follows that I know nothing about this matter'. This statement had in fact been made some weeks earlier as the result of inquiries by one of the authors, Stephen Dorril, into King's knowledge of the the Profumo Affair. It had nothing to do with the Peter Wright Affair.[2]

The Mirror Group had been co-operating with the intelligence services for years. Managing editor Cyril Morten was a 'friend' of MI6 and employed an MI6 agent as a photographer on the *Mirror*. In *Spycatcher* Wright says that one of the agents of an MI5 Section D4 agent runner was a 'senior executive at the *Daily Mirror* newspaper'. *Private Eye* noted in 1966: 'Unfortunately rumours are now rife that the CIA is contributing funds to the I.P.C.' The rumour may have been generated by the knowledge that King's Mirror Group had assumed financial responsibility for *Encounter* magazine (previously subsidised by the CIA) in 1964. King had visited the United States in 1966 where he had been enthusiastically received by the Johnson Administration including the head of the CIA, Richard Helms.[3]

In 1987, under Parliamentary privilege, Labour MP Dale Campbell-Savours identified 'Mr Harry Wharton' as the 'security controller of Cecil King'. Wharton, whose MI5 job included making links with the press and publishers, especially those who had links with Soviet journalists, denied the allegation. Wharton did say that he had been 'introduced to [Hugh] Cudlipp for [sic] a mutual friend. I occasionally had a drink with him at El Vino's'. Two days later he told a different story. 'I did once meet . . . Mr Hugh Cudlipp, at a meeting of the Paternosters Club at the Wardorf Hotel about 20 years ago, but I did not know Mr King at all . . . I was much too junior to be of concern to the likes of Cecil King.' This indicates, perhaps, that more senior figures dealt with King.[4]

In *The Wilson Plot*, David Leigh found Wright's claim hard to swallow. We do not. King was an enthusiastic intriguer who would have found it irresistible to be on another 'inside track'. We do, however, wonder precisely what 'agent' means to Wright in the case of King. Would someone of King's status have had a conventional 'handler'? Or was it simply that King would have lunch with a senior MI5 person and take (and give) information? This would look like King was 'being run' from the spook side of the fence, and appear to be mere networking (lunching, perhaps) from King's perspective.

The ambiguities in the relationships between intelligence officers and other people are echoed in King's relationship with a number of senior figures in the British Labour movement. At various times King was subsidising Alfred Robens, George Brown, Richard Marsh – all MPs, the latter pair in the Cabinet – and Vic Feather of the TUC. With these men King would have lunch and talk – about politics, the Labour Government, the uselessness of Harold Wilson and so on. People are given money and they tell the donor of the money secrets; at any rate, they divulge information not public. (This is the fascination of King's diaries, of course.) If it is overstating it on present information to describe King as 'running' these men, or to call them 'agents', it is not doing so to any great extent. King may have thought he was running them – especially if he was a conscious agent of MI5's – but Marsh, for example, bit the hand that had been feeding him. When King's conversation turned to talk of replacing Wilson, 'national governments' and so on, Marsh reported this to 'officials'.[5]

No doubt, Wright's view is that MI5's 'stirring up trouble' was part of King's attempt to foist Mountbatten on to a grateful nation, for 1968 was dotted with psychological operations and disinformation, in what looks like a 'strategy of tension', a state-sponsored campaign of social disruption and psychological warfare, which went on long after Mountbatten had declined the proffered role as saviour of Britain. King's Mountbatten gambit was merely one element in this wider strategy.[6]

The origins of the events of 1968 lay in the first major anti-Vietnam demonstration in October 1967. Completely unprepared for the scale of the demonstration, the state authorities had been unable to prevent demonstrators picketing the American Embassy in Grosvenor Square. Special Branch surveillance of the anti-war groups increased. One organiser, Pat Jordan, told Tariq

Ali, 'we were taken by surprise last October. But so were they. This time they have been able to witness all our pre-activities.' The next demonstration was planned for 17 March 1968. Ali thought that some of the strange incidents which took place 'smelt of agent provocateurs'. Posters for the demonstration pasted up around London were overnight overprinted with the words 'COME ARMED'. The *Economist* identified the 'sinister elements' as 'The American group who probably overprinted the organizer's stickers'.[7]

March 1968 also saw the first of the bombings and death threats by what became known as the 'Angry Brigade'. There is no evidence that this had anything to do with the activities of the Angry Brigade of the early 1970s. No one was arrested for these incidents: nor has anyone ever claimed responsibility for them. On 9 April, James Callaghan told the Cabinet that he 'had information that dangerous elements – anarchists and communists – were going to infiltrate the [Aldermaston] march in order to assault Burghfield . . . a home security store full of ammunition and which will have to be defended in order to prevent the ammunition from blowing up'. British communists, in concert with anarchists, stealing munitions? Such preposterous 'information' could only reach the Home Secretary from MI5 and the Special Branch who it is known had infiltrated many of the radical groups.[8]

Four months later, *The Times* reported the existence of a leaflet, a copy of an Economic League bulletin, which asked: 'Are we going to reach the point where the Armed Forces have to step in to unseat the present Government in this country? It is an alarming thought, but what else does one do when a politician refuses to believe that he has been handed his marching orders?' A League spokesman attributed this forgery to the left, but rather gave the game away when he said that 'the forgery is a very clever one . . . the forgers have gone to great lengths to make the bulletin look convincing.'[9]

In 1968, virtually no-one on the tiny 'revolutionary' left, then primarily focused on the war in Vietnam, was even aware of the existence of the Economic League, let alone capable of operating at this imputed level of sophistication. However, given our recent knowledge of the enthusiastic use of forgeries by the security services in the 1970s, it is entirely possible that this effort was also an MI5 stunt. Its central theme, that Wilson had to go, and the Army might have to step in, was precisely the line of the Cecil King group.[10]

Daily Express journalist William Massie has acknowledged that this was 'a particularly busy period' for contact with his MI5 sources. They told him that there was security concern about Wilson's friend, Rudy Sternberg, and gave him 'a full account'. They also told him an outrageous story about Treasury Minister John Diamond who had just been promoted to the Cabinet, claiming that he was a 'womaniser' (See Chapter XV). Chapman Pincher, also on the *Express*, chose June 1968 to use a seven-year-old story about Arthur Bax, the former Press Officer of the Labour Party, accused of being an agent of Czech intelligence.[11]

On 5 September, as the authorities braced themselves for the big anti-Vietnam demonstration then being planned for October, the London *Evening News* and *The Times* published accounts of what they called 'startling plots' to use home-made bombs and plans to seize sensitive installations and government buildings on the path of the march. The *Evening News* ran a story headlined 'Anarchist Machine Gun Factory Discovered'. It was later disclosed that the anarchists were in fact two neo-fascists. These stories had been planted in the press by the Special Branch. Two of the journalists who ran these reports, crime correspondents of *The Times*, Clive Borrell and Brian Cashinella, later wrote of this episode: 'The Special Branch then hatched up their own plot. They decided to "leak" their fears to the press and allow the situation to snowball. Public antipathy would do the rest, they reasoned. Certain Fleet Street journalists, including ourselves, were independently appraised of the situation through "the Old Boy network". It was a story none could refuse coming from such an immaculate source. It was a story which no newspaper could ignore, and as article followed article, public reaction against the march quickly grew. It was a clear case of the media being manipulated by the Special Branch to serve their own ends.'[12]

As a result of this press campaign, public buildings and large offices were protected by specially erected barricades. The *Daily Mirror* installed steel roller blinds to cover doors and windows. Callaghan's comment later, that though 'it was not possible to gauge how serious all this was . . . an agitated atmosphere built up based on very little reliable information, with newspaper reports making the ordinary citizen's blood curdle about the horrors to expect', precisely depicts one strand in a 'strategy of tension'.[13]

Two days before the march, one of the leaders of the Maoists admitted that extremists bent on violence had infiltrated their groups. A forged Vietnam Solidarity Committee leaflet urged demonstrators to take on the police. Someone from the Socialist Student Federation told the press: 'It is a fake and a very clever one . . . the timing of its release is superb.' The next day there was an attempt to blow up the J.F.K. memorial at Runneymede using plastic explosive. Forty-eight hours after the demo at Grosvenor Square a blue van pulled up outside the VSC offices, a man got out and fired at one of the members. The games continued into December. On the 2nd, a bomb destroyed a pipe carrying water to Birmingham. This was preceded by what looks like a fairly clumsy attempt to link Tony Benn to the explosion.[14]

On the 13 December, Tariq Ali, at the offices of the VSC's magazine *Black Dwarf*, received a telephone call asking him if he would be interested in seeing or distributing copies of 'Poster No. 1 – Prepare for Revolution', signed by the 'Militant Trade Union Committee'. Within half an hour of his expressing an interest, 5,000 copies arrived in a taxi. Some on the left recognised these as being a deliberate provocation, 'the outpourings of the extreme Right and not of legitimate Trade Unionists'.[15]

Of the perpetrators of these incidents almost nothing is known. Both *Private Eye* and *Searchlight* carried reports about the shadowy activities of Vic Norris in this period; of far-right groups organised by Norris to cause trouble at demonstrations which would then be blamed on the left. According to *Searchlight*, he had 'intelligence connections'. Though neither report is sufficiently well documented to do more than suggest that some sorts of agents provocateurs were at work, however, in the context of the rest of the 'strategy of tension' being run that year, they cannot be entirely dismissed.[16]

In this atmosphere of 'intoxication' the Cecil King network continued to operate against Wilson. On 7 December there were 'streams of rumours' that the Chancellor, Roy Jenkins, and Wilson were resigning. According to Crossman, the rumours were sent out by telephone from somewhere in the City and then 'cabled back'. The result was another great flight from sterling. Benn commented: 'It really is as Harold feared earlier in the year when Cecil King began firing off his shots.' The next day *The Times* carried a leader from the editor William Rees-Mogg, 'The Danger to Britain', calling for a coalition. Former *Times* editor Harold Evans is quite specific that the paper 'encouraged Cecil King's lunatic notions of a coup against Harold Wilson's Labour Government in favour of a government of business leaders led by Lord Robens.' (Robens was a director of *The Times*.)[17]

Ultimately, the status of the Cecil King 'coup' remains ambiguous. The scattering of incidents we discussed above, apparently the surface signs of a 'strategy of tension', cannot yet be definitely linked to MI5, let alone to some wider conspiracy of which King's networking was a part. However, such a wider conspiracy would hardly come as a great surprise.

XXVI

MORE POLITICAL PLOTS

There was endless talk about Harold Wilson being a liaibility, but it was all talk. As so often, the Prime Minister's position was protected by all the ambitions and jealousies of the contestants, Tony, Roy, George, Jim and Denis. If any two or preferably three had joined forces Harold could have been ousted in 1969.

DAVID OWEN

THE RIGHT OF THE PARTY never stopped thinking about how to remove him. Throughout the year and a half following the 1966 'July crisis' there are glimpses of these manoeuvres. Alan Watkins in the *Observer* recalled 'the days when [he] would come upon him [David Marquand], Dr Owen, Mr Brian Walden and the late John Mackintosh in 1966–7, usually in Henekey's wine bar in Whitehall, all discussing devaluation and the best way to get rid of Harold Wilson'. In August 1966, Tony Benn had noted in his diary that 'Roy [was] working hard with Bill Rodgers, Bernard Donoghue and the old Campaign for Democratic Socialism–Europe Group to take over the leadership of the Party at some stage.' On 10 July 1967, Wilson said to Barbara Castle: 'You know the CDS is active again? . . . The idea is to get Jim into the FO leaving the Chancellorship for Roy.' On the 14th, after talking with Denis Healey, Cecil King noted in his diary that Wilson's 'Ministers and his party are intriguing among themselves for the succession'. By 22 December 1967, Tony Benn, who did not believe at the time that there had been a plot in July 1966, was writing in his diary of 'the junta . . . Roy, George and Michael Stewart and others who were trying to get rid of Harold. Undoubtedly there was an attempt to get rid of him.'[1]

The next identified major attempt after the July 1966 'plot' began in December 1967. Christopher Mayhew talked to Jenkins about removing Wilson, using 'the 1963 Club', the successor to the CDS. A group duly met: (Jack) Diamond, Dick Taverne, Niall McDermot, Denis Howell, Bill Rodgers and Dickson Mabon – all junior ministers – and six unidentified others. They 'declared themselves utterly opposed to Harold'. Mayhew then brought together another group of MPs including Austen Albu, Ivor Richard, David Marquand, Carol Johnson and David Ginsberg. This group 'decided to organise carefully and to follow rigorous rules of security'. They began discreetly canvassing among the Parliamentary Labour Party.[2]

This cabal was to represent more than the attempted removal of Wilson; in essence it approximated what later turned out to be the SDP: 'an alliance of moderate members of all three parties . . . far-reaching constitutional reform, aimed at ending the farce of the present party struggle . . . action along those lines would mean the loss of the left . . . no plans should assume any defections from the Tory Party . . . we could pick up the Liberals for the asking'. They had the plan but not the numbers and had to wait for an issue to mobilise around. Independently of the Mayhew operation 'young MPs on the "radical right" were canvassing in favour of Roy Jenkins for Prime Minister'. Whatever this plan amounted to, the resignation from the Cabinet of Ray Gunter in 1968 'spiked' it, 'infuriating the Jenkinsites'.[3]

The right issue for the Mayhew–Jenkins grouping never arose. Instead the Wilson–Castle proposals on the reform of industrial relations, 'In Place of Strife', came along, splitting the anti-Wilson forces within the PLP. Jim Callaghan made his move for union support by opposing the proposals, 'in almost open rebellion, acting outside Cabinet, holding his own meetings with trade union leaders'. However, the Mayhew group's man, Roy Jenkins, was a strong supporter of the 'In Place of Strife' proposals. Mayhew tried to weld the two camps together. He spoke to Callaghan, who said that he was happy to work with – or under – Roy. By Christmas 1968, however, Mayhew had heard nothing from Callaghan and 'guessed that Callaghan had decided on a different course, that he would win substantial union and party support by vigorously opposing trade union reform and in due course go for the party leadership against both Wilson and Jenkins'.[4]

The Mayhew group eventually decided to move in May 1969. 'If the figures justified it, I was proposing to recommend that Sunday morning's papers would publish a letter to Douglas Houghton [Chairman of the Parliamentary Labour Party] calling for a party meeting to elect a new leader, signed by three middle-rank back benchers. We could then invite all our contacts to write in support of the letter.' The canvassing of the Party still did not suggest they had enough votes and the group split. Some wanted to proceed with or without guaranteed support; others did not – and the whole affair petered out.

Another group, lead by John Mackintosh, not one of those named by Mayhew, canvassed 'signatures for a letter to Douglas Houghton requesting him to call a meeting of the party at which the leadership question would be discussed'. In the accounts in *Private Eye* and by Peter Jenkins the following year, the Mackintosh-led group found 60 MPs willing to sign and another 40 willing to vote against Wilson in a secret ballot. However, 'athough they apparently succeeded in collecting the names of 95 MPs word of the attempted coup leaked out too early for it to stand a chance of success and it was abandoned'. 'Leaked out' is an understatement. *Private Eye* described Mackintosh 'rushing round the Commons, Fleet Street and the Glasgow universities [sic] telling all who would listen'. Among those who were told was Wilson loyalist Richard Crossman, to whom Mackintosh acknowledged 'that he had been one of the main people who caused the sensation about the plot against Harold last week, by taking round his own private poll to see how many MPs would sign a round-robin demanding a special Party meeting for a secret ballot on a vote of confidence'. Also, apparently independent of the Mackintosh initiative, a third group, lead by Willie Hamilton MP, was trying to organise not a mass of signatures, but a select group of heavy-weight backbenchers whose names Douglas Houghton would find it impossible to ignore.[5]

Tory MP Robert Rhodes James adds another element to these manoeuvres: 'In the spring and early summer of 1969 there were serious plots to engineer this situation [i.e. that Wilson be dismissed by the Queen] by means of a Cabinet advice to the Queen.' When this failed to get off the ground, the idea of removing Wilson, not as Prime Minister, but as leader of the Party, via a 'no confidence' vote within the PLP, became the aim.[6]

On 26 March 1969 at a meeting of the Party's National Executive Committee, Callaghan signalled his rebellion against the 'In Place of Strife' proposals by voting against the Party line. Details of the meeting were promptly leaked to the press and appeared the next day, just as Wilson was flying out to Nigeria. Through to 31 March, the newspapers mused on Callaghan's 'defiance' and speculated on what Wilson would do on his return. According to Chapman Pincher: 'In the previous year Callaghan had made several half-hearted attempts to oust Wilson as leader. One of his Cabinet colleagues described to me how he used to go round from time to time counting heads to find out how many would support him.'[7]

With Wilson in Africa, Callaghan tried again. 'One of the RAF officers on the Prime Minister's flight . . . told [Chapman Pincher] how he had to hand Wilson a radio message warning him what was happening back home. The officer was lost in admiration for the way Wilson dealt with the situation while airborne thousands of miles away.'[8]

A week later, on 12 April, Cecil King reported in his diary that Alfred Robens, also subsidised by King, 'told us that he had been approached by an emissary from Transport House who said if the Labour Party is to win the next election they must get rid of Wilson. A small group was being formed with this objective.' Was this the Willie Hamilton grouping? It was not the Mayew plan. Or did it refer to another, as yet unidentified, cabal? We do not know, and in a sense it hardly matters because throughout all these fragments and glimpses, the same names recur. In 1968 *Private Eye* reminded its readers that the plotting began in 1963 when a 'Stop Wilson and Brown Committee' was formed in the flat of Mr Anthony Crosland. Among those present were Douglas Jay . . . and Christopher Mayhew'. By 1969, so common had plotting against Wilson become that *Private Eye* could write of 'the annual attempt at a "May coup" to unseat Mr Wilson'.[9]

Those who have perceived Harold Wilson as 'paranoid' – and this includes many of his Cabinet colleagues, at one time or another – offer as their best evidence his obsession with plots against him. On the evidence we have assembled – and how many other plots existed which have never been reported?

– Wilson was right and they were wrong. From 1966 onwards there was constant plotting by his colleagues. At the heart of it were the Gaitskellites who had never really accepted Wilson as the legitimate leader of the Party. Perhaps Wilson took them too seriously (and perhaps some of his 'obsession' was a pretence on his part); and perhaps a different kind of personality could have ignored them. This, perhaps, will be the conclusion that history arrives at. Be that as it may, plots there certainly were.

Although it was the Gaitskellites in the Cabinet, who were behind most, if not all, of the plotting it is noteworthy, as David Walker points out in his reassessment of the first Wilson Governments, 'how little fundamental disagreement there was about the purposes, indeed the ideology, of the Government . . . Their intense politicking had all to do with position, little with principle'. For them Wilson was the problem, it was entirely personal. As Walker suggests 'for the most part Wilson's colleagues united in their social-democratic sentiment'.[10]

How the Wilson Governments of 1964–70 are assessed depends almost entirely on the political stance of the assessor. To the left within and without the Party, they were a disappointment, even a disaster: socialism had not been advanced; the working class had not moved appreciably nearer to control of the means of production, distribution and exchange; Britain was still a nuclear power, still an ally of the United States. But were such expectations rational? Whatever the British electorate voted for in 1966 it was not the socialist transformation of British society. To the right, within and without the Conservative Party, the Wilson years had been a disaster. The standards of society had been undermined by permissive legislation; increasing welfare benefits had weakened the individual's willingness to stand on his (or her) own feet; the education system was undermined by the spread of comprehensive schools; the profitablity of British industry had fallen; British standing in the world had declined along with its empire and armed forces; and so on. It is not without significance that the Wilson years saw the birth of the New Left *and* the New Right.

Somewhere between those two poles lies something like a rational assessment. In foreign and defence affairs, Labour had managed the decline of the armed forces, the withdrawl from East of Suez and the transition of the rump of Empire to independence without great mishap. For all the traumas of devaluation, sterling crises et al, the six years of Labour administration began with deficits both in the balance of payments and in government expenditure and ended with surpluses in both – having achieved a level of economic growth no less (but also no more) than that achieved by the Conservative Party. Labour built a lot of houses, and enacted a great deal of legislation on fundamental welfare issues such as social security, rent acts, school meals, social services, the expansion of higher education (and the Open University) and so on, which did make a serious impact on the lives of millions of the poor. At the end of the six years, the share of the national 'cake' going to the bottom 20 per cent had risen appreciably. (The measure of this is the fact that the Thatcherite 'counter revolution' had so much to do). It also passed the 'permissive' legislation on personal behaviour – divorce, marriage, family law, abortion, family planning – and sex equality and race relations that so enraged the traditional right. We could go on: the list of legislation enacted in those six years is very long and very impressive. (A quick run-through is provided by N. J. Smith's *A Brief Guide to Social Legislation*, Methuen, London, 1972.)

What Labour under Wilson failed to do was halt British relative industrial decline. British shares of world trade and manufactured goods continued their post-war (post *First* World War) decline. Wilson failed to reconstruct industrial relations, failed to reconstruct the industrial base, failed to seriously reduce the dominance of finance capital on the economic life of the country, failed to reconstruct the British state; in general, failed to achieve the dynamism promised by the Party's rhetoric of science and modernity of the 1962–4 period. Even so, the measure of the Wilson years is that a great deal of what is now taken-for-granted social reality were the products of his Governments.

XXVII

THE CZECH CONNECTION

By now, Harold had no time for MI5. He didn't think anything of them.
LORD KAGAN

ON TAKING OFFICE in 1964, Wilson had sought to defend himself against MI5's attacks by charging George Wigg with overseeing the agency, and by instructing the Director-General, Roger Hollis, to obtain Prime Ministerial permission before investigating any member of the House of Commons or House of Lords. Further, Wilson told Hollis that he was unlikely to consider the allegations of defectors in themselves as the basis for further action by MI5. Such restrictions were largely ignored, of course: in MI5's view their authority came not from politicians but from the Crown. In any case, there are always ways round the politicians' attempts to corral MI5: jobs can be sub-contracted out to other agencies. On the British side there were GCHQ and Special Branch; on the American, the NSA and CIA. Wilson's prohibitions merely meant that MI5 had to be careful.[1]

Wilson's cynicism about defectors does him credit. There is an obvious general problem with them: once in the hands of their new masters, they have a considerable vested interest in telling their hosts what they want to hear and in egging the pudding to boost their 'market value'. This has been demonstrated on a number of occasions, most blatantly by Anatoly Golitsyn.[2]

Such defector issues arose in 1969 when a Czech intelligence officer, Joseph Frolik, defected to the Americans with tales of Czech recruitment of a number of Labour MPs and trade union officials. Precisely whom Frolik identified remains obscure but it is generally accepted that the MPs he named were the Labour members John Stonehouse, Tom Driberg, Will Owen and Barnett Stross.[3]

On investigation, Will Owen was indeed found to have been taking money from the Czechs since the late 1950s, and was tried and acquitted in 1970. In his ghost-written memoir – which we discuss below – Frolik does his best to portray Owen ('Lee') as a major agent, passing over 'top-secret material of the highest military value'. In fact, the closest Owen, as a backbencher, came to handling secrets was his membership of the Commons Defence Estimates Committee, which receives nothing but highly general and carefully sanitised information, most, if not all, of which could be gleaned by reading the non-tabloid press and specialist journals like that of the Royal United Services Institute. Did the prosecution really forget to check that the information Owen was passing to the Czechs was actually classified? Was it simple incompetence? At any rate, Owen's lawyer pointed out that the information Owen was charged with passing over was not secret and Owen was acquitted. To all extents it looks as though Owen – known, apparently, as the Greedy Bastard by his Czech handlers – had been running a successful confidence trick, getting £500 a month from the Czechs for handing over junk. Richard Crossman noted in his diaries at the time: 'How idiotic these Czech embassy people are and how easily they waste their money on bogus information.'[4]

If Owen's information was less than impressive, that provided by the other agent, 'Gustav' – apparently Sir Barnett Stross who died in May 1967 – must have been piffle. Frolik describes him as passing 'interesting information about the domestic and foreign policies of the Labour Party while it was in opposition' – information which could have been obtained by writing to Transport House and asking for it – 'and later, when the Wilson Government came to power, about defence matters'. As 'Gustav' was less important than 'Lee' (Will Owen) on Frolik's own account, and 'Lee' provided nothing of value, what on earth was 'Gustav' actually doing for the Czechs? Stross, a Polish refugee, came to Britain with his parents after the First World War. Before the Second World War, Dr Stross had worked with George Wigg in aid of Czech refugees. After the war he was the founder of the movement which rebuilt Lidice, the Czech mining village destroyed by the Germans in 1942, for which he was honoured by the Czech Government. As Chair of the British–Czechoslovakia Society he used his position to protest against human rights issues in the country. However, this cut little ice with MI5: Stross was on the left of the Labour Party, an émigré and thus a natural target for the security services.[5]

The really explosive allegation made by Frolik concerned the late John Stonehouse. All the right-wing writers on intelligence matters in this country have taken the case against Stonehouse as proven. We do not.[6]

Stonehouse was of interest to MI5 and the CIA because of his position at the Ministry of Technology (MinTech). As the second volume of Tony Benn's diaries for the period illustrate, MinTech was the focus of hostility from the UK–USA military and intelligence because of its role in encouraging exports of high-tech goods to the Soviet bloc at a time when there were still considerable restrictions on such exports. We suspect, but cannot prove, that the real target of the Stonehouse story was thus Benn, not Stonehouse. John Stonehouse had quite a complicated early political career. In one snap-shot he is the very model of the enthusiastic young anti-communist, who helped form the International Union of Socialist Youth, an anti-communist youth organisation later discovered to have had funding from the CIA. Then he is glimpsed in Africa, running an apparently unsuccessful co-operative agricultural venture. In 1959 he contributed two chapters to the collection *Gangrene* (Calderbooks, London, 1959), documenting the brutality of the British in Kenya during the Mau-Mau war. (He was also a member of the Movement for Colonial Freedom.) Stonehouse never referred to his contribution to that book in later years, but it would have opened a file for him in MI5 – if one did not already exist.

Stonehouse became an MP in 1957 after a selection meeting which 'had been "packed" by Co-operative [Party] delegates despatched there by Mrs Stonehouse, his mother, who was a leading Co-op figure'. In 1962, he became President of the London Co-operative Society after a campaign organised by Patrick Dolan Associates. Stonehouse then ran an anti-communist campaign within the Co-operative Society, the 'Democratic Co-operative Alliance', in what he describes in his memoir as a 'war' with the communists. This campaign used PR methods which would be unexceptional nowadays but were then still worthy of comment. 'Press conferences were held, quiet lunches, discreet phone calls and confidential background information was given to any journalist who showed some interest.' Richard Crossman wrote of 'the pretty rough tactics' which Stonehouse used in this campaign in one of the most brutal sketches in his diaries: Stonehouse was 'a kind of dangerous crook, overwhelmingly ambitious but above all untrustworthy'. This view was based on a talk with George Wigg, who also gave the same advice to Wilson, who, in turn, later told Pincher.[7]

At the time of the Owen trial, Stonehouse's former boss, Tony Benn, talked to MinTech's MI5 officer, David Purnell, who told him that Owen had been subverted by the Czechs and asked Benn's permission to talk to John Stonehouse: Stonehouse had had conversations with Robert Husak, the Czech intelligence officer who was running Owen. 'He and John Stonehouse used to talk informally and personally while John was at Mintech. Purnell told me that he had a record of all these discussions.' Where did this 'record' come from? And what constitutes a 'record'? Reports by Stonehouse himself, or MI5 surveillance of the Stonehouse–Husak meetings? In our view, the latter. In his autobiography Stonehouse claimed that, as per MI5 instructions to ministers, he had reported the initial approach from Husak 'through the Ministry's Intelligence Officer [i.e. Purnell] who was then operating under the general supervision of George Wigg'. He also reports Tony Benn saying: 'I'm having lunch with them [the Czechs] all the time and I never make reports about them – do you think I should?' Benn's lunches with the Czechs are probably the tiny thread on which MI5 later hung the smear that he had 'contacts' with Czech intelligence. Stonehouse claimed in 1975 that he knew 'on irrefutable testimony' that his telephone had been tapped since 1968 when he had been responsible for the Post Office.[8]

In most accounts the sequence of events is: Frolik makes allegations in America, these were passed to MI5 and thence to Wilson by the Director-General in person. Frolik was then brought across to Britain and told his story to MI5. Leigh names MI5 officers Charles Elwell, Peter Wright and Michael McCaul as those involved. At the American end, Frolik was being handled by CIA counter-intelligence under James Angleton. The picture is familiar: the Wright–Angleton duo had already played this game with Golitsyn. Wilson was then asked for permission by MI5 to interrogate Stonehouse. Wilson refused, allowing MI5 to interview Stonehouse only with witnesses – himself and his Private Secretary, Michael Halls. It is a lovely example of MI5 apparently obeying Wilson's instructions on seeking his permission before investigating an MP. MI5's Elwell put the Frolik allegation to Stonehouse, who denied it. Elwell admitted to Wilson that they had no evidence other than Frolik, and that, as far as Wilson was concerned, was that.

Purnell's acknowledgement that MI5 had a 'record' of Stonehouse's meetings with Husak is crucially important. If, as we assume, MI5 had Stonehouse under surveillance, the agency not only had no evidence, they knew that there *was* no evidence. If MI5 merely had a report of these meetings from Stonehouse, and had not put the Stonehouse–Husak meetings under surveillance, they were incompetent. The presumption of innocence in Stonehouse's case is over-whelming. The Frolik story did not make operational sense. Frolik claimed that Stonehouse had been sexually entrapped in Czechoslovakia in the 1950s. Were this the case, would the Czechs really send one of their agents to have lunch with him? Would putative agent Stonehouse report his meetings with Husak? Stone-house has been called many things, but stupid is not one of them.

Considering he was intimately involved in this, Peter Wright in *Spycatcher* is uncharacteristically reticent about Stonehouse, merely commenting that he 'was another MP who the Czech defectors claimed was working for them, but after he was interviewed in the presence of Harold Wilson, and denied all the charges, the MI5 objections against him were withdrawn'. Privately, Wright went as far as to say that he was not impressed by Frolik's claims. 'After the initial debriefings defectors want to make some money . . . and reveal or invent more "informa-tion".' If MI5's formal objections were withdrawn, informally they immediately tried to get the press interested in Stonehouse. In 1970, while Stonehouse was still Minister of Post and Telecommunications, Chapman Pincher was tipped off 'by an Intelligence contact' – i.e. MI6; MI5 is Security in this euphemistic world of Pincher's – that 'Stonehouse . . . had been in difficulty with his Prime Minister, Harold Wilson, over a security matter'. If Pincher was plugged into MI6, William Massie, also on the *Express*, was (by his own admission) plugged into MI5. The same year Massie met an MI5 officer and a CIA officer who showed him raw transcripts of Frolik's debriefing in the United States in which Frolik accused Stonehouse of being an agent, and said that Wilson had covered it up.[9]

What actually happened seems fairly clear. Husak was having the occasional lunch with Stonehouse, a junior minister in the Wilson Government. MI5, meanwhile, although tipped off about the meeting by Stonehouse, did nothing to warn him about Husak's identity and let him continue the meetings, using him as a kind of bait. MI5 had already done this with another Labour junior minister, Charles Loughlin, who was at the Ministry of Health (replacing Stross). Loughlin was interviewed by MI5's Dick Thistlethwaite in February 1965 and told him of his relationship with a Czechoslovakian Trade Secretary. Loughlin suggested that MI5 investigate the man and inform him if there was anything he should know about him. Loughlin heard nothing and continued meeting the Czech – though taking the precaution of informing the Minister of Health's private office of the meetings. In 1966 Loughlin was invited to visit Czechoslo-vakia and asked permission to go. (Government policy dictated that before going abroad on unofficial visits Ministers had to seek the permission of the Foreign Secretary.) According to Loughlin, Foreign Secretary Michael Stewart refused, saying that the Czech was an intelligence officer. Loughlin went to see Wilson and reported the events. 'I told him that the Security Service would have a lot of questions to answer as they had knowingly exposed me to an enemy agent for eighteen months. They were fully aware of the danger to myself and to the Government in that I was a member of it and could possibly have been source of embarrassment.'[10]

Other Labour Party members given the MI5 treatment were Wilson's PPS Ernest Fernyhough, and Wilson's close friend Harold Davies, who was 'in tears' because of the smear campaign spread through the bars used by journalists. Probably one of those on the Brown/Gaitskell list given to the security services in 1961, Davies was a natural target. In the mid-sixties, in order to end the Vietnam War, he made an abortive 'peace mission' to Hanoi where he knew some of the senior communists. The mission was deliberately sabotaged by 'one of Wilson's enemies in the Foreign office' who gave the information over lunch at the Reform Club to the *Daily Mail* journalist, Walter Terry. Ray Fletcher, a former defence correspondent and backbench friend of Wigg, had a more serious run-in with MI5, who he was told 'had a file on me'. During the fifties he had been a Trotskyist but later 'repudiated my views in an article in *The Times*'. Fletcher had a long standing interest in Czechoslovakia and supported the pro-Dubček faction which ruled following the Prague Spring of 1968. He had contacts at the London Czech Embassy whom 'it was later claimed were intelligence personnel'. Fletcher says that he 'knew I was running a risk but thought I was safe because I reported all my contacts to Goronwy Roberts at the Foreign Office'. He was later told that MI5 had him under surveillance.

In 1969, Fletcher went to Hungary, where he foolishly had a short affair with a young woman who sent him love letters when he returned to England. He says that 'the letters were intercepted and then MI5 showed them to my wife. They tried to break my nerve and nearly broke my spirit'. The marriage survived, 'just', but his German wife, who was seriously ill, died in 1973. Fletcher, who died in early 1991, said MI5 'were a complete bunch of bastards'. Charles Loughlin, whose experience parallels that of Fletcher, came to believe that he had been set up. 'The Security Service knew what they were doing. They are a law to themselves. They are anti-Labour.'[11]

The events surrounding the Prague Spring saw other Czech intelligence officers defect to the West. Whereas Frolik had a long list of supposed 'agents' in the Labour movement, these more senior officers came virtually empty-handed. Jan Sejna, former Chief of Staff to the Minister of Defence in Czechoslovakia, could only remember the head of Czech intelligence 'boasting that we had enough on one British MP to hang him'. Later he presented the West with his conspiracy theory called 'The Plan', namely the Kremlin's plan to undermine British democracy. Some intelligence officers of the Angleton/Wright outlook even claimed to believe it. Another Czech defector was an Intelligence major, Frantisek August, who worked in the London Embassy between 1961 and 1963, and whose name is consistently joined with Frolik's as proof of the latter's claims of agents within the Labour Party. Although he writes in his memoir that the Labour Party was a target for recruitment, he singularly fails to mention any successes in this area. The only success August acknowledges is that in 1964 the Czechs 'infiltrated' the Board of Trade (BOT).[12]

As we have seen in Chapter VIII, MI5 had been carrying out an investigation into a hypothetical spy in the Treasury and No. 10. With the defection of August and Frolik, who talked of a spy code-named 'Kamen', attention switched to the BOT. According to Pincher, there was a 'clear lead to a former Board of Trade official alleged to have supplied the Russians with information which enabled them to secure better deals to the detriment of Britain's interests. The man later achieved a most important position in Whitehall and was subjected to investigations which came to no conclusion.' According to one account, MI5 had already indentified a spy and Frolik's information only confirmed his existence. Interestingly, during the fall-out from the Blunt debriefings, in 1967 Wright had focused his attention on Arthur Wynn, someone Wright had bracketed with the 'Oxford Comintern'. Wright speaks of 'the problem of Arthur Wynn, who was . . . due for promotion to the Deputy Secretary's job at the Board of Trade, which also required security clearance.'[13]

In one sense, MI5's great coup – a defector naming Labour MPs and a Minister as agents – disintegrated. Owen was acquitted; Stonehouse was acquitted; Barnett Stross – if he was indeed one of those named – was dead; and Tom Driberg knew far too much about MI5 to risk prosecuting. The lack of evidence on Stonehouse, combined with Wright's atypical silence on the subject, suggests another interpretation. By the time that the Frolik allegations had winged their way across the Atlantic in 1969, MI5 had had Stonehouse under surveillance for some years, ever since he reported the first approach from Husak. They knew on the ground that the stories about Stonehouse were fiction, but the Frolik allegation provided them with a weapon to use against Wilson.

In the run up to the 1970 General Election, there is some evidence that MI5 were making serious efforts to gather 'dirt' on Wilson and his colleagues. They renewed their investigation into the 'Oxford Comintern'. The Oxford philosopher Sir Stuart Hampshire, the man who undertook a review of GCHQ in 1965, came under suspicion and was questioned twice by MI5 in 1969 and 1970 respectively. Anthony Blunt's friend Goronwy Rees had told MI5 that Hampshire may have been recruited by the Soviets. This was false. In the same period MI5 investigators began new inquiries into the Bernard Floud case, interviewing some of his relatives.[14]

Between 1968 and 1970 a number of private documents belonging to Wilson went missing from No. 10. The most significant were the 'Mikoyan postcards' sent to Wilson by Sergei Mikoyan, the son of the Soviet Foreign Minister. Mikoyan junior was regarded with suspicion by the security services and the CIA who believed that he was a KGB operative. One postcard, referring to Wilson's 'wonderful daughter', resulted in Wilson's enemies frantically searching Somerset House for this fictitious offspring. Mikoyan had simply mistaken Marcia Williams for Wilson's daughter but anonymous letters and former No. 10 staff helped spread the false rumours. The postcards were later shown in 1974 to Chapman Pincher and *Private Eye*.[15]

Although Marcia Williams' liaison with the journalist Walter Terry and the subsequent birth of two children was a closely guarded secret, news did leak from the small circle of friends who were privy to the knowledge. George Caunt, who was then working for Wigg as a researcher, sought out the birth certificates, which had been registered under the names Williams–Terry and Williams–Field, at Somerset House. These were passed by Wigg to MI5 (apparently to scotch rumours that Wilson was the father). Although newspapers were aware of the Williams–Terry affair, the fear of libel prevented its exposure at the 1970 election, even though anonymous letters were sent to many Fleet .reet journalists, including Pincher. The aura of mystery which surrounded this affair served only to feed later rumours that the children's father was Wilson.[16]

MI5 officers had begun to 'cultivate' current and former staff members of No. 10 to gather material about Wilson, his circle of friends and Marcia Williams. Both Caunt and Wigg were loosely in touch with the security services. David Candler, who worked as a political aide from 1967 until 1970, admits that he had repeated contact with MI5 counter-intelligence officers. Candler picked up gossip about Wilson from the Prime Minister's own Principal Private Secretary, Michael Halls, who in turn was socialising with a number of Wright's colleagues. Candler's gossip eventually turned up at *Private Eye*. Halls was alleged to be worried about the supposed 'security risk' posed by Mrs Williams' children. This came to a head over Mrs Williams' 1969 vetting. MI5 appear to have been using these 'third parties' to push out anti-Wilson smears.[17]

As his diary shows, in the period before the June election Cecil King was still there looking for a 'catalyst', a 'national figure outside politics who could bring our affairs to a head'. Shadow Chancellor Iain Macleod suggested Lord Mountbatten. There were 'urgent' meetings with the same old anti-Wilson crowd – Norman Collins, Lord Renwick, Lord Cromer, Hartley Shawcross, Paul Chambers, George Cole and Joseph Lockwood, all mentioned above – who hoped to issue a 'pronumciamento urging the disastrous consequences of a further five years of Labour'. Lord Geoffrey Crowther, Chair of the Royal Commission on the British Constitution, told the group that he 'could see now no future for democracy nor could he see what would take its place'. Nothing appeared in the newspapers because they were on strike but Lord Cromer did appear on the BBC's *Panorama* programme where he rubbished the Government's economic assessments. According to his obituary in the *Daily Telegraph* 'many thought he turned the tide in the 1970 General Election campaign'.[18]

In the event their assistance was not required to defeat Labour. Against the expectations of most commentators – and the Labour Party itself – Mr Heath led the Conservative Party to victory and a healthy Commons majority.

PART THREE

The Heath Years
1970–74

THE NEXT SIX CHAPTERS are an account of the 1970–4 period, what we have come to think of as the Heath years. We have included this because much of what befell the succeeding Wilson administration of 1974–6 had its origins here. It was in this period that the Wilson–Castle attempts to regulate the trade unions were adopted and imposed by the Tory Party, leading to the most serious outbreak of class warfare – there is no more appropriate term – since the period just after the end of the First World War. The reaction on the right to this gathered in strength during Heath's years to erupt during Wilson's last period in office. Some of the reaction was spontaneous; but much of it was sponsored and guided by the British secret state. In this period there were elements, notably a military and paramilitary tinge to events, not seen during the Labour Governments of the sixties; but many of the threads are familiar, extensions of the attempts by MI5 to portray the Labour Party, and Wilson in particular, as subversive. Under Wilson, MI5 had been inhibited somewhat by the fact that the Government was Labour: with a Tory Government any such tactical inhibitions were unnecessary.

From 1971 onwards the notion that Wilson was a subversive, leading a communist-influenced Labour Party, becomes commonplace on the right. Any proposition repeated often enough begins to sound plausible and this one appears frequently in the following section of the book. It is therefore worth fixing firmly in your mind the fact that this 'subversive' leader of the Labour Party had finally come to grief within his own Party and the wider, supporting Labour movement through his attempts to bind the trade union movement into a tri-partite, corporatist, 'producers' alliance' of the unions, British manufacturing capital and the state. His fundamental ambitions about British society were precisely encapsulated in the title of the White Paper on industrial relations reform issued by Barbara Castle, with his complete support, in 1969: 'In Place of Strife'. Wilson was no class warrior. As we tried to show above, he was never a socialist in any real sense, let alone a communist. The attempt to portray Wilson as a subversive was indeed a Big Lie.

XXVIII

THE DEFECTOR

A curious aspect of the affair was that . . . the British Labour Party launched sarcastic attacks upon the bold action taken by the government in expelling so many Russians. Harold Wilson was particularly scathing in his references to Lyalin, and anxious about the effect upon Anglo-Soviet relations . . . His supporters threw doubt upon the evidence of Lyalin.
CHRISTOPHER DOBSON AND RONALD PAYNE

Of course we know that spying goes on. It goes on between consenting adults so far as advanced nations are concerned.
HAROLD WILSON

IN 1971, MI5 DIRECTOR-GENERAL, Martin Furnival-Jones, outlined to members of the Franks Committee on the reform of the Official Secrets Act the security service's view of Soviet intelligence activities in Britain, and thus, indirectly, the service's considered view of the Labour Party. He told the Committee: 'If the Russian Intelligence Service can recruit a backbench Member of Parliament, and he continues to hold his seat for a number of years and climbs the ladder to a Ministerial position, it is obvious the spy is home and dry. This is certainly one of their objectives.' Furnival-Jones did not reveal whether this had actually happened. We know of no evidence that it had but the implication was there. Was the Director-General thinking of those named by Frolik when he said that Soviet intelligence 'devote a great deal of time and money to the cultivation of people who they think are in an area where they will pick up items of information from the Government table?' He continued: 'What they are hoping to pick up there is not necessarily . . . copies of Government documents but hints as to what they should be looking for in other places.' He believed that the KGB devoted a great deal of effort to this 'profitable' activity. 'The backbench Member of Parliament may give them exactly the kind of information which they are seeking by the more dramatic forms of espionage.' The KGB, he went on, also shows 'a remarkably voracious appetite for party political information'.[1]

When the Committee asked him to comment about the possibility of some MPs being 'intelligence agents for the other side', Furnival-Jones declined because, 'It would involve my having indulged in an activity in which I certainly do not indulge, and that is informing myself of the total circle of acquaintances of every Member of Parliament.' Furnival-Jones was in a delicate position. He could not admit to the Committee that he did so 'indulge' – Wilson had specifically banned such investigations – nor did he want actually to lie to a committee of this significance: hence his tortured answer. We now know – MI5 later admitted it – that Furnival-Jones did order such operations. However, he did reveal to the Committee that MI5 'have a programme which is very extensive, for interviewing people in all walks of life who appear to be being cultivated by a hostile intelligence service'; and he did claim that 'very many Members of Parliament are in contact with very many intelligence officers'. While he was saying this his own officers were cultivating members and former members of Wilson's staff; and in his safe back at the office sat the 'Worthington' file with the results of their research into Wilson and his circle of friends.[2]

In September 1971, a member of the KGB's Department V of the First Directorate, which prepared contingency plans for sabotage operations in the West following the outbreak of war, defected in Britain. That this was MI5's first post-war success in recruiting a Soviet defector perhaps accounts for the way in which his significance as a source was exaggerated. The 34-year-old Oleg Lyalin was a lowly official with the Soviet import–export business RAZNO, based in London. The 'Casanova spy' had been recruited in the spring of 1971 in an MI5 'honeytrap' operation run by K5, the counter-espionage agent-running section, and then run as an 'agent in place'. K5 was eager to pursue the operation even though the use of sex broke Home Office directives. The two key officers involved were Tony Brooks, a former SOE and MI6 officer, and Harry Wharton, the officer alleged to have 'run' Cecil King.

On 30 August 1971, Lyalin was arrested on a drink driving charge, an incident which produced a small note in the next day's *Daily Express*. As he did not have diplomatic immunity his arrest would cause problems – he might be sent back to the Soviet Union – and so MI5 'forced his hand' by threatening to reveal the married man's sexual relationship with his secretary, Irina Teplakova. Although Lyalin supplied details about the sabotage plans – which later helped fuel a whole series of books on the 'Spetnaz [Soviet Special Forces] threat', much of it disinformation – details of the KGB 'order of battle' at the Soviet Embassy, and the names of a few minor spies, he had no information about any KGB penetration of the Labour Party.[3]

MI5's Director-General had been waiting for this moment for many years. MI5 had been compiling a list of the known KGB officers in London. Furnival-Jones persuaded the Heath Government, mainly through the hard-line anti-communist Foreign Secretary, Alec Douglas-Home, to authorise a mass explusion. In all, 105 Soviet officials were expelled in September 1971. KGB defector Oleg Gordievsky, who was station chief in the mid-1980s, says that 'The London residency never recovered from the explusions. Contrary to popular myths generated by media "revelations" about Soviet moles . . . the KGB found it more difficult to collect high-grade intelligence in London than in almost any other Western capital.' Vladimir Kuzichkin, who defected to MI6 in the 1980s from his post in Iran, has also shown that Western intelligence claims of massive recruitment by the KGB were completely false. Officers were instructed not to recruit Britons in their own country but to concentrate on third country nationals. 'The agents of residencies abroad could be counted on the fingers of one hand', claims Kuzichkin. In his time the KGB's S Directorate had 'only two agents in Iran', and in Japan 'a round zero'.[4]

The new KGB Resident from 1972 to 1978, Yakov Lukasevics, 'made little progress in rebuilding KGB operations in Britain'. This is suggested by the absence of expulsions in the rest of the Heath years. MI5 sources later told William Massie of the *Daily Express* that the 1971 expulsion had 'smashed' a 'Soviet conspiracy to control high-level Labour Party decisions'. According to MI5, the 'Czechs handed over their Labour contacts' to the KGB; 'many of their identities were revealed by Frolik'; 'KGB master spy' Ivan Shishkin was sent to London 'to control and maintain "security" on the Labour operation'. It was all garbage. However, some members of the Heath Government believed it. In his autobiography, Attorney General Peter Rawlinson writes: 'Why was there mounted an operation to infiltrate the Labour Party at a time when Harold Wilson had labelled it the "natural party of government"? These expensively trained Intelligence officers were not despatched to London to serve no purpose.' Gordievsky tells us that Shishkin, who was in London from 1966 to 1970, was head of counter-intelligence and the leading expert on the British intelligence community. His job was to infiltrate the security services.[5]

The nonsense about the 'communist cell in Downing St' which was circulated in 1974 and 1975, discussed below, began in 1971 after MI5 'discovered' that the Gannex raincoat manufacturer Joseph Kagan, a fringe member of Wilson's social circle, knew a KGB officer in London called Richardas Vaygauskas, a fellow Lithuanian. Vaygauskas turned up in London in 1969 and throughout the next two years, before he was expelled in 1971, he and Kagan were often seen together. It was not the secret friendship that has often been reported: they played chess together in Lithuanian émigré clubs in London. None the less the Kagan–Vaygauskas relationship generated considerable excitement within K Branch of MI5. Although the information is alleged to have come from Lyalin, MI5 had been interested in Kagan far longer than that and certainly had him under surveillance for a considerable period. MI5 now conducted a major operation against him, recruiting his workers and colleagues as informants, bugging his telephones and undertaking at least one burglary.[6]

The Vaygauskas–Kagan relationship is a fact but almost everything else is a muddle. K Branch believed – or pretended to believe – that Vaygauskas was trying to get to Wilson through Kagan. For this there is no evidence at all and most of what we have learned from recent KGB defectors – Gordievsky and Kuzichkin, for example – makes this very implausible. On being informed of the Kagan–Vaygauskas link, Wilson approached a friend of his in the City of London police, Arthur Young, and tasked him to investigate the two men. Later MI5's Harry Wharton gave a guarded briefing to Wilson about them but did not reveal his private feelings that Kagan was 'a menace' and the ex-Prime Minister's circle of friends were 'an unsavoury bunch'. Wilson later issued a statement 'At no point . . . did [Kagan] raise any matter of government policy with me deriving from his acquaintanceship with Vaygauskas. Nor was he in receipt at any time of classified government information or any other material of the slightest interest to the Russians.' It is more likely that Vaygauskas was interested in Kagan as a fellow Lithuanian, because the latter's relatives were still in that country.[7]

None the less, MI5 now had a KGB 'trace' on Wilson, an invaluable item in their disinformation projects. The game was given away in the notes which Colin Wallace made in 1974 based on MI5 information. He wrote not that Wilson '*was under* KGB control through Vaygauskas', but that Wilson '*could be shown*' to be so through this means. (Just as he wrote that Edward Heath 'could be shown' to be a communist through his connection with Lord Rothschild!) So it was that Vaygauskas-knew-Kagan-who-knew-Wilson became the 'communist cell' in No. 10; its key members were Mrs Williams, Wilson's 'gate keeper', who had the most dealings with Kagan, and Wilson himself – with Kagan the link to the KGB 'controller' Vaygauskas. As we discuss below, at least one other member of the Government was 'located' within this 'communist cell'.

Lyalin's defection, in short, was a convenient peg on which MI5 could try to hang a number of anti-Wilson and anti-Labour smears. The disinformation was leaked out on to the political networks of London – and to some of MI5's media assets. In *Private Eye* on 16 July 1971, while Lyalin was still being run by MI5 'in place', in a piece titled 'Blackmail', Auberon Waugh, wrote that 'Enough is Enough . . . Patriotic Britons will look to the Leader of the Opposition with anxious eyes. At this stage it would be inappropriate for me to say more than that the present Leader of the Opposition seems inadequate to the task with which destiny has entrusted him. However, if Harold Wilson has not resigned from the Leadership of the Labour Party before 30 October this year, I give due warning that my organ, HP sauce, will publish the entire range of information which it possesses on the past and present behaviour of this man.'

Following Lyalin's final defection in September, Waugh announced that 'the thankless task of unmasking the senior KGB agents in high places must remain on the shoulders of your political correspondent . . . The poverty of the late Mr Harold Wilson continues to mystify . . . His latest trip to Moscow can hardly have helped his finances, since he lost his job with Montague Meyer, a firm of timber merchants . . . Nor is it very likely that my old friend Yuri Andropov [then head of the KGB], who heads the timber export business from the Moscow end, was very pleased that Wislon (sic) chose to pose for photographs with a vodka swigging junior clerk in the lingerie exports departments called Oleg Lyalin. It rather lets the side down, don't you know.'

The *News of the World* of 24 October 1971 ran a front page which stated 'Fantastic evidence which suggests that prominent Labour Party figures . . . who died . . . from mysterious symptoms were in fact murdered by Russian killer squads. The evidence has come from the continued interrogation of Oleg Lyalin . . . Incredibly, one name on the list is Hugh Gaitskell. As Labour leader of the Opposition Gaitskell was responsible more than any other leading figure for directing the movement away from communist doctrine at home, and Russian policies abroad. He died in January 1963 from an unknown virus . . . The theory is that . . . in the Labour Movement, right-wingers hostile to communism could be replaced by left-wingers with very different views.'

The discovery of the Vaygauskas–Kagan–Wilson link provided MI5 with the necessary pretext to open an official inquiry into Wilson. This began under Furnival-Jones and was expanded following the appointment of Michael Hanley as the new Director-General in 1972. The operation was aided by the co-operation of the CIA's head of counter-intelligence, James Angleton, who admitted that he was asked by 'MI5 to supply information about Wilson and other people'. This official investigation then 'set about researching the back-grounds of certain key figures' which entailed expanding the already consider-able 'Henry Worthington' and 'Oatsheaf' investigations. It also involved 'bugging' the telephones of friends of Wilson, which contributed to the idea that Wilson himself was under surveillance. When Wilson returned to power, MI5, as we shall see, began to leak the contents of the files in a stream of smears directed against the Prime Minister and his colleagues.[8]

XXIX

SELSDON MAN

Today a 'thin blue line' contains the enemies of society. In the New Year we must be prepared for new outbreaks of industrial intimidation, urban terrorism and political violence. I have called for a special anti-terrorist force and a mobile squad of motorised troops to counter the forces of red fascism which have turned picket lines into storm troops . . .

JOHN BIGGS-DAVIDSON, 1972

THROUGHOUT THE WILSON YEARS, the Tory Party had moved further right; in part because the Tory defeats of 1964 and 1966 had weakened the centrist views in command of the Party, but also because there was nowhere else to go. Wilson had successfully occupied the so-called 'middle ground' of financial orthodoxy – in 1970 Chancellor Roy Jenkins produced a budget surplus of £735 million – and Labour's use of instruments such as the Industrial Reorganisation Corporation had weakened the position of the group within the Tory Party which in the early 1960s had accepted the need for economic planning. 'Freedom' was back on the Tory Party agenda. On 30 January 1970 the Heath Shadow Cabinet met at the Selsdon Park Hotel, near Croydon, to consider the conclusions of the thirty-six working parties which had been formulating policy. The meeting, noted Andrew Roth, 'had elements of a publicity stunt, designed to show the Tories were ready to take over. And to demonstrate that their well-prepared policies were mostly hard-line right-wing.'[1]

For the General Election that year, the Tory manifesto, *A Better Tomorrow*, promised cuts in taxation and public expenditure: 'shirkers and scroungers' would be dealt with; there would be more police, more prisons; the dismantling of most of Labour's corporate structure; and legislation to bring the unions to heel. The 1970 Election turned out to be a strange mirror image of that of 1964, with the Tories taking the role of Labour, offering the electorate dynamism and change. So the Tories took office in June 1970, apparently believing that tax cuts, union bashing and the EEC would produce a climate in which British business would boom. Parts of it did, but the wrong parts.

In 1971 the Government had allowed the Bank of England to relax its rules governing the ratio of deposits to lending. In 1965 – under Wilson – the 'Treasury turned the Bank's general requests to restrain lending into precise arithmetic ceilings on the level of bank advances. The object . . . was to restrain credit growth without raising interest rates.' In 1969, having exceeded their limits, the clearing banks were 'fined' by a reduction in the rate of interest paid on the deposits at the Bank of England. As soon as the Tories came into office, the banks ensured the rules were changed. Given an inch, they then took a mile, 'manufacturing' reserve assets to such an extent that in 1972, one estimate suggests, the money supply measured as M3 (roughly, the notes and coins in circulation plus deposits at banks), rose by 320 per cent. This fuelled the 'fringe' or secondary banking boom, and the inflation of property and housing prices as new mortgages outstripped the supply of houses. Roaring inflation was being built into the system.[2]

The non-specialist media of the day appeared not to notice much of this; they were too involved writing pieces on 'Selsdon Man', the *wunderkinder* of the new 'dynamic Britain', chief among who were Jim Slater and Peter Walker, and their company Slater Walker. From similar lower-middle class backgrounds, Slater and Walker considered British management backward and the City, the 'old money' revealed in the Bank Rate Inquiry a decade earlier, indolent. Slater wrote: 'In many ways Slater Walker was a product of its time, in sympathy at the beginning with the feeling that many British companies badly needed reorganising, that boards of directors were frequently too cosy, self-perpetuating and inefficient, and that the shareholder was given a raw deal. It was also generally thought that we needed a new breed of manager, younger and more meritocratically based than before, and above all we needed a change.' The answer, however, lay not in the Labour Party's corporatist manufacturing alliance but in the therapeutic (if bracing) effects of more aggressive capitalism and exposure to the world economy. Entry into the EEC was top of the agenda.[3]

Clive Irving noted a 'striking irony . . . what Slater and Walker were doing by manipulating the market forces had much in common with what Harold Wilson was trying to do by political means: shock the City of London and shake British industrial management out of its torpor.' Selsdon men would kick-start the country into new prosperity.[4]

By January 1972 Slater's standing was at a peak. The *Daily Telegraph* city editor had called this the period of the 'Slater Walker government'. Slater, in turn, called Heath 'the personification of meritocracy in politics'. Slater knew Heath and was consulted by him on policy matters. Slater-Walker was also a substantial contributor to party funds: from 1969–73 this consisted of over £40,000, with another £19,000 to various pressure groups sympathetic to the Party. Slater-Walker invested Heath's savings. 'Sir William Armstrong [Cabinet Secretary] was packed off to watch Slater in action, to pick up tips about "oomph" which he could apply in Whitehall.' Campbell Adamson remembers a dinner at Chequers when the Prime Minister made much of Jim Slater, 'as if to say to us, the other industrialists, now here is the kind of industrialist I like, he is doing the things you are not doing. He's investing, he's being successful.' It was all a chimera. Almost by accident, it appears, the Government had created perfect conditions for money-lenders and speculators. Money went into property – and abroad – but not into manufacturing. Slater–Walker was, as Slater himself said, a 'maker of money not a maker of things': as soon as the company got big enough Slater tried to get out of 'things' altogether and turn it into a bank, by his attempted merger with Hill Samuel.[5]

Heath apparently thought that all he had to do was create the right conditions and the economy would take off. But what were 'the right conditions'? In 1973, Heath told the Institute of Directors: 'When we came in, we were told there weren't sufficient incentives to invest. So we provided the incentives. Then we were told that people were scared of balance of payments difficulties leading to stop–go. So we floated the pound, then we were told of fears on inflation; and now we're dealing with that. And still you aren't investing enough.' By late 1972 it had all gone wrong. To his credit, the Heath Cabinet stopped in its tracks, looked round and changed economic direction – the infamous U-turn. Tony Benn saw the new post-1972 corporatist Heath regime 'doing the spadework of socialism', demonstrating this in 1974 and 1975: his 'much-criticized forays into the hinterland of British industry in 1974 and 1975 all took place under the imprimatur of Conservative legislation.'[6]

Cecil King's diaries for the period are dotted with apocalyptic visions of British society. For the first time since the 1920s, sections of the British right convinced themselves that the left – the old Communist Party left, and the so-called 'New Left' – working with the British trade union movement, symbolised by Jack Jones and Hugh Scanlon, were a serious threat to the British state and capitalism. Rational or not the network of propaganda organisations linked to the British state and secret state, and funded largely by British capital, began gearing up to meet 'the threat' – as, eventually, did the state itself. Ironically, the increased awareness of, and publicity about, 'the threat' began to convince the tiny 'New Left' groups that 'instead of it being a hobby, which it was, there was a possibility of a real mass revolutionary party'.[7]

As usual, the secret heart of the state was ahead of the game. In 1969, the British Army Land Manual had been significantly revised, giving greater prominence to a possible domestic, counter-subversion role. As the imperial policing role disappeared, the only remaining 'enemy' was the Soviet bloc, frozen in thermo-nuclear stalemate, leaving the the British Armed Forces to train endlessly for a war on the German plains which they knew would never come. This rethink of strategy rested on a radically new, open-ended definition of the key concept of 'subversive': viz. 'People who take action to undermine the military, economic or *psychological morale, or political strength* of a nation and the loyalty of its subjects' (emphasis added). That year, a brigadier in the British Army, Frank Kitson, with experience in counter-insurgency campaigns in Kenya and Malaya, was seconded to Oxford University for a year to read and synthesise the literature on counter-insurgency. His thesis was published in 1971 as *Low Intensity Operations*, and a year later he was given command of a brigade in Belfast to test some of his theories.[8]

In 1970, activists on the Tory right in the Monday Club published a pamphlet entitled *Ireland: our Cuba*, an absurd analogy which, despite the total absence of any evidence, was to become a major plank in the British state's psychological warfare efforts against the IRA. That year, a 'Study of left-wing subversion today', *We Will Bury You*, was published, with contributions from employees of the private domestic anti-subversion organisations which had been marginal on the political scene for over a decade, 'David Williams' of Common Cause, and Harry Welton of the Economic League. Editor Brian Crozier, then in the process of establishing the Institute for the Study of Conflict (ISC), wrote in his introduction, without irony, of 'the new growth industry – the proliferation of subversive groups'. Of actual subversion there was little evidence; but *anti*-subversion was beginning to boom. ISC, Common Cause and the Economic League we will meet again shortly.[9]

Bashing the unions may have seemed a good idea to the Tories when in opposition, jeering at Wilson and Barbara Castle's retreat from the proposals for reform of industrial relations in the 1969 'In Place of Strife', but in office things were more difficult. Conflict with the unions began almost immediately. In the Heath Government's first year it had to declare two states of emergency, in July in response to the first national dock strike since 1926, and in December in response to an overtime ban by the electricity supply workers. Troops were deployed that year during the electricty dispute and during a dispute with refuse collectors in the London borough of Tower Hamlets. On 14 December 1970 Douglas Hurd, then Edward Heath's Private Secretary, sent the Prime Minister a memo suggesting that it was time for a review of the state's emergency procedures.[10]

The climax of this conflict was the miners' strike of 1972. On 8 February 1972, with only a few weeks' coal stocks left, the Cabinet Emergencies Committee decided to declare the third state of emergency of the Heath administration. Two days later came the Saltley depot incident, when the 'flying pickets' of the National Union of Mineworkers, directed by the young, and then nationally unknown, Arthur Scargill, prevented the movement of coke from a depot near Birmingham – 'an event that has haunted contingency planners ever since'. Special adviser to the Chancellor, Brendon Sewill, said of this period: 'The lights all went out and everybody said the country would disintegrate in a week. All the civil servants rushed around saying "Perhaps we ought to activate the nuclear underground shelters and the centres of regional government, because there'll be no electricity and there'll be riots in the streets. The sewage will overflow and there'll be epidemics." '[11]

British industry had begun gearing up for 'the threat'. In January 1972, John Whitethorn, Deputy Director of the Confederation of British Industry, sent out a memo to member companies urging them to increase their funding of five organisations working against 'subversion'. Three of the five were the well-known old hands – the Economic League, Aims of Industry, and Common Cause. Less well known then were the anti-socialist trade union body IRIS and the 1970 creation, the Institute for the Study of Conflict (ISC).[12]

The interesting name was the newcomer, ISC, the latest in a succession of propaganda organisations running back to the CIA operation, the Congress for

Cultural Freedom. ISC began in 1968 when Brian Crozier created within the CIA operation Forum World Features a 'Current Affairs Research Services Centre', which began publishing a series of 'Conflict Papers'. This led to the creation of the Institute for the Study of Conflict in 1970. (Brian Crozier has consistently denied knowing that these operations were funded by the CIA.) As ISC expanded, it recruited personnel from the Information Research Department, the clandestine psychological warfare outfit set up in 1948 by the Foreign Office, and from Forum World Features as an 'independent' research body. With a distinguished list of academic contributors and Council members, ISC had the credentials to open doors that would have remained closed to the older, more overtly anti-Labour outfits such as the Economic League. ISC began a 'long march through the institutions' of the British state, spreading the message of subversion and how, with the help of a concept or two from Brigadier Kitson, it might be countered.[13]

The message had been received at Army HQ. An unnamed British Army brigadier quoted in *The Times* said: 'The whole period of the miners' strike made us realise that the present size of the police force is too small. It is based on the fundamental philosophy that we are a law-abiding country, but things have now got to the state where there are not enough resources to deal with the increasing numbers who are not prepared to respect the law.' *Times* journalist Christopher Walker found officers in the mess talking of 'subversive forces . . . and widespread agreement with the ideas of Brigadier Frank Kitson'. The next day *The Times* devoted two thirds of a centre page to a piece by the then largely unknown Nigel Lawson on 'Communist Influence on Industrial Strife', citing Jimmy Reid, Mick McGahey, Hugh Scanlon, and Ernie Roberts.[14]

In response to these events, particularly the Saltley depot episode, Heath set up a review of the government's Emergency Organisation, which had remained substantially unchanged since its creation by the Labour Government of the 1940s when it faced another apparent 'threat from the left'. The review was headed by Lord Jellicoe (Lord Privy Seal) and John Hunt (Cabinet Office Deputy Secretary). Jellicoe's role ended with his resignation from the Heath Government, an apparent piece of collateral damage from the 1973 'Lambton Affair'. He was replaced by Lord Carrington. Hennessy and Jeffries note: 'Conventional wisdom in Whitehall is that the central government's handling of the 1972 miners' strike was a shambles, that the old Emergencies Organisation, as developed in the late 1940s, . . . finally fell apart when required to tackle the economic and physical consequences of Mr Scargill. This view is directly challenged by some of the excellent quality officials who were involved in it throughout the period. The "shambles" story, they claim, was put about by the Cabinet Office, who took over responsibility for civil emergency planning in the aftermath of the 1972 crisis, in order to justify their imperialism at the expense of the Home Office.' This act of 'imperialism' led to the reconstitution of the Emergencies Committee within the Cabinet Office, renamed, in classic Whitehall euphemese, the Civil Contingencies Unit. Parallel to this, the national 'war plan' was redrawn with greater emphasis on meeting an 'internal enemy' – i.e. the left and the unions.[15]

In MI5, the previously unglamorous F Branch, the domestic counter-subversive unit, began to expand in 1972. Peter Wright reveals that 'early on in his tenure as Director-General, Hanley called a meeting of senior staff in A Branch and F Branch to discuss the changing shape of MI5's priorities. The meeting began with a presentation from Hanley of what he called the "far and wide left". The Prime Minister and the Home Office, he said, had left him in no doubt that they wanted a major increase in effort on this target.'[16]

XXX

BRITAIN'S CUBA

*The arrival of SIS did have one crucial effect . . . this was to mean that . . .
the mounting of covert counter-intelligence operations could be justified as
requirements by the overriding necessity to find a political solution.*
ANTHONY VERRIER

RUNNING PARALLEL to the developing state and freelance parastatal
responses to the 'threat from the left' was the crisis in Northern Ireland. By late
1970, the secret state knew that they had an insurgency on their hands. This
produced old and new responses from its military and intelligence agencies.
Brigadier Kitson, the Army's leading counter-insurgency theorist, began a two-
year tour as Commander of 39th Infantry Brigade in Belfast in 1970. In Belfast,
using methods which he had developed against the Mau Mau in Kenya, he
created the Military Reconnaissance Force (MRF), mixed units of 'turned' or
captured IRA members and British soldiers, on special detachment. In his
memoir, Field Marshal Lord Carver acknowledged the existence of 'surveillance
operations by soldiers in plain clothes . . . initiated by Frank Kitson when he
commanded the brigade in Belfast, some of them exploiting ex-members or
supporters of the IRA, of which I was aware, and for which I had obtained
Ministerial approval.' MRF may have been created for 'surveillance', as Carver
says, but some of its personnel took to shooting Catholics from moving cars, and
eventually two MRF members were actually prosecuted for – but acquitted of –
attempted murder. The fact that the shooting for which the MRF members were
prosecuted happened the day after the Provisional IRA started its June 1972
cease-fire, could have wrecked the move – and the attempts which MI6 were
making to set up peace talks in its wake.[1]

Despite the convention that MI6 operated abroad and MI5 in the UK, and, it
is said, despite the objections of Maurice Oldfield, MI6 had been in Northern
Ireland since late 1970. The service set about penetrating the IRA – and the
Republic of Ireland; and, after the imposition of direct rule from Westminster in
March 1972, they began to arrange talks with the Provisionals. Secretary of State
for Northern Ireland, William Whitelaw met a delegation of the Provisionals in

July 1972. The talks foundered when Whitelaw, faced with competing assessments from MI6 and the Army, chose the Army's (tougher) line, which was rejected by the Provisionals. In retrospect, the meeting was premature. Whatever should have been tried at the point, a face-to-face meeting between William Whitelaw and the Provos, without an agenda, was not it.[2]

In the Irish Republic, MI6 began operations against the Official IRA. They recruited Kenneth Littlejohn, a former Lance-corporal in the Parachute Regiment turned bank robber. Littlejohn and his brother were tasked to obtain intelligence on the Official IRA – and to do bank robberies in their name. Between February and October 1972, the Littlejohns successfully held up banks in the Republic and in Northern Ireland – Kenneth eventually claimed to have committed a dozen robberies – until they were arrested, and eventually imprisoned, in the Republic. Their trial was held in camera and very little information emerged; the idea, it appears, however, was to put pressure on the Republic's Government to take action against the IRA there. It was a classic, if risky, use of the *agent provocateur*. Kenneth Littlejohn eventually escaped from prison and talked to the media.[3]

On 1 December 1972, two bombs went off in Dublin, killing 2 and injuring 73. The Irish Government was then trying to pass tough anti-IRA legislation against considerable opposition. The bombs dispersed the opposition and the bill went through. Though proof is lacking, the fragments of evidence which have surfaced since suggest that the bombs were the final piece in the psy-war campaign against the IRA. This seems to have been too much for the Republic's Government and on 19 December they busted an MI6 intelligence operation in the Republic. MI6 officer John Wyman and his agent inside the Gardai Special Branch were arrested and charged under the Irish Official Secrets Act. Another member of the MI6 network, Andrew Johnstone, was sought by the Irish authorities but never found. It was also alleged that Christopher Ewart-Biggs, later British Ambassador in Dublin, killed by the Provos, was a part of this MI6 network. According to Dublin magazine *Magill*: 'Intelligence services have leaked the word that . . . ' The 'intelligence service' in question was presumably MI5, who made mischief with the Wyman–Littlejohn incidents (because they were MI6 failures). The Wyman–Littlejohn episode and attendant publicity, especially in the Republic, appears to have been a major factor in the permanent government's 1973 decision to replace MI6 with MI5 in overall charge of the intelligence effort in Northern Ireland.[4]

In 1971 the Foreign Office controlled Information Research Department (IRD), comprising the psy-war experts who had worked in the post-war colonial insurgencies, was sent to Northern Ireland. IRD officer Hugh Mooney was seconded to the British Army to set up a psychological warfare unit. This was eventually called Information Policy – the title a Kitsonian euphemism – and it operated under cover of the press office. At Army HQ Lisburn, there was a young civilian workaholic Information Officer, Colin Wallace, 'Army barmy', the only Northern Ireland member of the press office in post when 'the troubles' began. Wallace, first as Press Officer, then as as the leading operator in Information Policy, quickly became the Army's focal point with the world's media who were camped out in the Europa Hotel, Belfast. In 1972, as the IRA began bombing the mainland UK, MI5 also appeared in the province.[5]

Thus, by 1973, the British state had introduced into Ireland its standard counter-insurgency kit, developed in the Empire in the post-war era. The Army, Army under-cover units, Army intelligence, IRD, MI6 and MI5 – and the RUC, RUC Special Branch and the Ulster Defence Regiment – were all jostling each other in this tiny patch, deployed against an enemy whose 'territory' consisted of a handful of housing estates and a strip along the border with the Republic. The Army resented MI6; MI6 and MI5, in turn, were mutual enemies. The Brits did not trust the indigenous police forces because they were almost entirely Protestant; the police did not trust the Brits for the opposite reason. With the exception of MI6, all the forces of law and order distrusted the politicians in London, whom they suspected of being susceptible to the idea of a political deal with the IRA which would 'solve the Northern Irish problem'.[6]

The critical fault-line was between the MI6/Foreign Office end of the secret state allied to the Westminster politicians, on the one hand, and all other agencies on the other. The MI6/Foreign Office axis believed neither that the Labour Party represented the Parlimentary end of a subversive wedge, nor that the IRA was some rough equivalent of the Malay Communist Party. 'From 1971 onwards, SIS officers came to believe that the Provisional Irish Republican Army was a political organisation which could be outwitted, not merely a terrorist organisation which must be destroyed.' After the failure of the 1972 talks, however, this faction of the state was in retreat. During 1973, the hard-liners in HQ Northern Ireland and in London gradually gained the upper hand and took the final step of expanding the category of 'the enemy' to include Westminster politicians – and not just those in the Labour Party.

XXXI

ROTHSCHILD

*Though entirely without foundation . . . just as many people still believe
that some skeleton in Wilson's life will one day be exposed, many also
suspect that Rothschild was not all that he seemed.*
CHAPMAN PINCHER

IN 1973 TWO MI5 OFFICERS approached Maurice Macmillan, then junior
minister at the Department of Employment, 'to complain of the inroads being
made by Communists into the unions. They suggested that MI5 would welcome
the introduction of legislation to curb Communist activites.' Those 'inroads'
were at the heart of the thesis of the ultras in the anti-subversion lobby that
through infiltration of the unions, the CPGB – and thus, ultimately, the Soviet
Union – would gain control of the Labour Party.[1]

During 1973, we get glimpses of the new anti-subversive 'line' being propa-
gated. The Economic League Annual Report for the year noted that 'the greater
demand for detailed knowledge about subversion was reflected in a marked
increase in the number of requests received by the League's Director of
Information and Research to speak at formal and informal meetings at courses
held at MOD establishments'. On 19 September, ex-Army and ISC associate
Richard Clutterbuck was at the West Midlands Engineering Employers' Association, lecturing on 'Revolutionary Politics and Industrial Disputes'.[2]

Proponents of the thesis received a tremendous boost when the Organisation
Sub-committee of the National Executive Committee of the Labour Party
decided to abolish the 'Proscription List' of organisations that were incompatible
with Party membership. This, said the anti-subversion lobby, showed how far
the rot had already spread. The problem for the right was that in 1973 the
Labour left was mostly the Tribune Group. Geoffrey Stewart-Smith, for
example, in his great 1974 'exposé', *The Hidden Face of the Labour Party*, makes
much of the abolition of the Proscription List, but then has to make do with the
Tribune Group – and Judith Hart (Dame Judith as she is now) – as examples of
dangerous villains. In fact, the CPGB's influence on the Labour Party was
virtually nil (nor did it control a single union). The shift to the left within the

Labour Party and the unions during the Heath years was largely a reaction to the Selsdon Man policies, at the centre of which was an attack on union power. The abolition of the Proscription List opened the door not to the Communist Party of Great Britain, which had been in continuous decline since the war, but to the many varieties of entryist Trotskyism, notably the Revolutionary Socialist League (the Militant Tendency) – about whom the likes of Stewart-Smith knew little at the time. The Proscription List comprised mostly CPGB front organisations which, by 1973, were of little political consequence. The list could be abolished because the groups on it appeared to be an irrelevance.[3]

Deeply involved in this anti-subversive activity was Lord Victor Rothschild. The received view of Rothschild is of a cerebal, witty, iconoclastic polymath, rather aloof and dispassionate, a writer of dazzling Whitehall memoranda; most importantly, a liberal. Even without a biography of the man – and his own thin memoirs tell us nothing – it is clear that this impression is inaccurate, at least for Rothschild in the 1970s. Rather, Rothschild was paranoid and given to depression – some of his friends feared he was likely to commit suicide, as had his father when he was a teenager – and increasingly right-wing. He had been in MI5 during the war but had formally left the intelligence field in 1945 and gone into scientific research, notably as head of Shell's Research Department. However, there are the occasional glimpses of him in the post-war intelligence memoirs. To give just two examples. Peter Wright writes of how Rothschild 'maintained his links with British intelligence, utilizing his friendship with the Shah of Iran and running agents for Dick White in the Middle East, especially Mr Reporter, who played such a decisive role in MI6 operations in the 1950s'; Peter Coleman, in his history of the Congress for Cultural Freedom, refers to Rothschild acting as a 'conduit' between MI6 and a magazine MI6 wished covertly to finance, probably *Encounter.*[4]

Wright had been introduced to Rothschild in 1958 by Roger Hollis and was entranced by the breadth of the latter's contacts. 'Victor knew everyone. I met more distinguished people at his house in Cambridge or his flat in London than anywhere else.' According to Wright, turning over to MI5 his technical resources at Shell, Rothschild 'did more than most to secure the modernization of MI5'. In all this we can see a number of themes. There was the appeal of the secret world. Like many others, part-time intelligence work offered to recreate something of the excitement of the war years. Such service to the British secret state was also a way of showing that he had been an innocent friend of Guy Burgess and not, as some on the right suspected, 'the fifth man'. This particular source of anxiety increased sharply when he was told in 1964 that another close friend, Anthony Blunt, had confessed to being a member of 'the Ring of Five'. For Rothschild, this revelation was a blow 'devastating and crushing beyond belief'. Added to which, of course, Rothschild was a Jew, and a Zionist, mixing with an establishment which was fundamentally Arabist. The rumours of his involvement with 'the Ring of Five' also threatened to jeopardise his prized link to the Israeli intelligence service, Mossad.[5]

It was thus not surprising that when Edward Heath appointed Rothschild head of the 'think tank' entitled the Central Policy Review Staff (CPRS), on the advice of Burke Trend, he began to operate a twin-track approach. While the CPRS pottered about with marginalia, Rothschild used his access to the Prime Minister and his installation within the Cabinet Office to become an intelligence activist. CPRS members Tessa Blackstone and William Plowden hint at this in their account of the unit. Peter Wright put it more bluntly: 'Rothschild took a close interest in security, and Heath encouraged him to do so . . . Victor became, in effect, the Lord Wigg of Heath's Government. Once inside the Cabinet Office, Victor teamed up with Dick White, the newly installed Cabinet Intelligence Co-ordinator.' Former MI6 officer, Anthony Cavendish, also reveals that Rothschild was 'very close to Maurice Oldfield', Chief of MI6.[6]

Wright gives one example of Rothschild's interest in security. 'Victor often used to complain to me about the quality of the intelligence reports No. 10 received from F Branch.' They had been receiving better information indirectly from Special Branch. 'In 1972 he told me that Heath had been appalled at a recent Cabinet meeting, which was addressed by Jack Jones and Hugh Scanlon . . . "Ted thought they talked like Communists. I asked F Branch if they had anything, but of course they've got nothing substantial".' Wright says that Rothschild 'knew from gossip that the recent Czech defectors were providing material about trade unions and Labour Party subversion, and began pumping me for details. I told him to minute me formally with a request and I would see what I could do. Later that day I got Victor's minute. "The Prime Minister is anxious to see . . . " ' Wright then drew the files and composed 'a lengthy brief on the intelligence provided by [Czech defectors] Frolik and August'. We know from other sources roughly what the memo alleged: that Wilson, Stonehouse, Scanlon, Jones, Ted Hill *et al.*, were communists and potential or actual agents of the Czech or Soviet intelligence services.[7]

A big Whitehall row blew up. The Cabinet Secretary interviewed Wright. 'Victor relished the row . . . defending the Security Services's right to provide intelligence requested of it by No. 10 Downing St. Philip Allen was outraged by this flagrant flouting of Home Office prerogative.' At the height of the fracas Wright met Heath in Rothschild's room. Rothschild described him to Heath as 'responsible for the briefing on subversion which is currently causing the problem'. Heath replied, 'You should not be indulging in politics, there are mechanisms for this sort of material.' The next day Rothschild told Wright that Heath had 'devoured' the briefing.[8]

We wonder about that. None of this account of Heath's concern about the likes of Jack Jones rings true. Many of the union leaders from this period speak highly of Heath. Other than Wright's version of what Rothschild had reported there is no evidence at all that Heath was ever even slightly concerned about a 'communist menace'. Indeed, the fact that he was insufficiently concerned is one of the things held against Heath by the 'ultras' on the right. It seems obvious to us that Rothschild had used the Prime Minister's name to get the briefing without Heath knowing; he was stirring the pot. In Australia, Wright told the court, 'Victor was always very secretive . . . he loved intrigue and conspiracies and was always engaged in secret deals and arrangements especially with politicians. He loved to exert influence behind the scenes.'[9]

With his access to Heath and the licence given him to roam far and wide throughout Whitehall, little wonder that the senior Home and Foreign Office officials disliked Rothschild, or that they tried to get one of their people in as head of MI5 when Furnival-Jones retired – a move, according to Wright, which was blocked by Rothschild on MI5's behalf.[10]

After 1972, Wright's work for MI5 had been part-time. He had become increasingly concerned about his pension. He had completed only seventeen years in full-time service which meant that his pension would consist of a lump sum of £5,000 and a pension of £2,000 per annum. If he were to die first, his widow, Lois, would receive only half this amount. Wright, therefore, followed up various civil service appeals to try to increase the amount and at the same time, around the end of 1973, sought alternative means of employment. 'It was a bitter blow, and did much to sour my last few years in the Service. Inevitably I thought about the possibility of security work.'[11]

Rothschild offered Wright a job 'moonlighting' for the family firm. In 1971, the leading British Zionists had been given special protection by Scotland Yard following assassination threats by a Palestinian terrorist group, Black September. The guard had long since been removed as resources went to counter the IRA threat in London. The Rothschild family had become increasingly concerned about terrorism and although they had a former Special Branch officer who retained his links to the Branch and their files, Wright would have been a valuable addition. In a letter, which Wright preserved, Rothschild offered to pay him to 'keep himself up-to-date' on terrorist intentions which might endanger members of the Rothschild family or the family firm. Wright would need to 'renew certain acquaintanceships after retirement for the deal to work'. Although attractive, the idea fell through: 'Hanley was unhappy about the proposal.'[12]

Bitter over the pension situation and angry over lack of progress on the molehunts, Wright set his face against the return of another Labour Government under Harold Wilson. He 'encouraged' new Director-General Michael Hanley to study the files 'gathered on Wilson and the Labour Party during the 1960s . . . Elections were in the offing, and it could become relevant again, I told him.' Wright was trying to persuade the cautious Hanley to authorise a full scale investigation into Wilson himself. Hanley looked at the files but told Wright, 'It's like FLUENCY, there's a lot of smoke, but not a lot of fire.'[13]

If Wright was unhappy, so too was Rothschild. His connection with Heath had been damaged. During the miners' strike of 1972 – the moment of supreme crisis as the state saw it – his think tank, had been excluded from the discussions. His problems increased in September 1973. After a meeting with Herman Kahn of an American think tank, the Hudson Institute, Rothschild incorporated some of Kahn's gloomy predictions about Britain's economic future into a speech. Typically, he did not bother to clear the speech with the Cabinet Office and delivered it on the same day that Heath delivered an optimistic (politician's) picture of the future. 'The gloomy forecast by Lord Rothschild contrasted bleakly with the optimism of Mr Heath's speech' and this 'led to a serious but temporary rift between himself and Edward Heath'. Rothschild was dressed down by both Heath and the Cabinet Secretary, Sir John Hunt. There was a 'certain nervousness' in Rothschild's relationship with Cabinet Secretary Hunt and he 'pulled his punches' when dealing with him. Rothschild did not wish to 'jeopardize his contacts with top military people' as he wanted to be involved with defence and international affairs.[14]

Around this time, with his influence within the Heath Government on the wane, Rothschild took his freelance intelligence role a stage further. He introduced Peter Wright to 'a businessman [who] was looking for someone to do security work.' In the original manuscript of *Spycatcher*, Wright records: 'Over drinks [the businessman] talked loosely about needing advice and guidance from someone "in the know" without quite spelling out what he meant, or how much he was prepared to pay for it. Eventually he suggested that I lunch with him and some colleagues at a London hotel to discuss his proposition in more detail . . . His colleagues were a ramshackle bunch. They were retired people from various branches of intelligence and security organisations whose best years were behind them.'[15]

Wright gave some names in the original version. 'David Stirling, the founder of the Special Air Service was there, as was a man named George Young, a former MI6 officer . . . There were others, too, mainly businessmen who seemed thrilled to be in the same room as spies, and did not seem to care how out of date they were.'

The businessman 'came straight to the point. "We represent a group of people who are worried about the future of the country," He intoned . . . they were interested in working to prevent the return of a Labour government to power. "It could spell the end of all the freedoms we know and cherish," he said. "And how do you suppose I can help?" I asked. 'We want information, and I am assured you have it . . . Anything on Wilson would be helpful. There are many people who would pay handsomely for material of that sort . . . Retire early. We can arrange something".'

The next day Wright went to Hanley, told him of the meeting, and offered to 'monitor the group's activities as an agent'. Hanley told him to stay away from the group.[16]

Wright's version of this meeting was leaked to Labour MP Dale Campbell-Savours, who ran the main points of the account and the names through the House of Commons as Early Day Motions in May 1987. He named the businessman as Sir James Goldsmith. In the motion of 12 May, he included the information that 'a copy of a letter sent to him [Wright] by Sir James is now longed [sic] in Whitehall' (presumably, 'is now lodged'). Reaction to the motions was swift and all participants issued denials. Goldsmith dismissed as a 'complete fabrication' any suggestion that he had discussed using intelligence information with the former MI5 officer Peter Wright. He had never been contacted by anybody to join a movement against Harold Wilson when he was Prime Minister. 'I am not in the least upset by it but I am amazed and amused. To the best of my knowledge I have never met Mr Wright . . . There is not an iota of truth in it. The whole thing is complete lunacy.' George Young told the *Guardian* that he had corresponded with Sir James in the early 1970s 'because of his dismay about the Heath government's failure to handle the unions, but he had never met either Sir James or Mr Wright'. David Stirling said 'he had a long standing friendship with Sir James, but he had never met Mr Wright. He had always sought to distance himself from Mr Young.' Just before his death, Sir David again denied to the authors meeting Young.[17]

The alleged meeting took place while Heath was still in office and, clearly, Wright did not use his real name. If Wright invented this meeting, he was making mischief, though his motives are obscure. He certainly picked the right names. As is made plain by Goldsmith's biographer, Geoffrey Wansell, Sir James was at this point quite close to Heath's circle; and a few months later Young, Walter Walker and Stirling were three of the major players in the inter-election period of 1974, which will be discussed below.

XXXII

'THE QUEER WILL BE DETHRONED'

*If anyone ever tried to destabilise a Labour government, George Young
would have been one of them.*
IAN AITKEN

*Sir Harold had once remarked how notoriously extremist and right-wing
the former civil servant was in his passionately held political views.*
PENROSE AND COURTIOUR

WHILE THE STATE was gearing up to meet 'the subversive threat' on the mainland and the crisis in Northern Ireland, the Tory right, feeling betrayed by the economic U-turn, the decision to admit the Ugandan Asian holders of UK passports expelled by Idi Amin, and the defeat at the hands of the miners in 1972, began working against Heath. In the Parliamentary Party, moves against Heath began openly in 1972 when Edward Du Cann was elected Chair of the 1922 committee, a position which was almost invariably given to a backbencher, someone who had never held office. Du Cann had not only held (junior) ministerial office – no. 2 at the Treasury and the Board of Trade under Macmillan – he had also been Chair of the Conservative Party. Nicholas Ridley and John Biffen were elected Chairs of two backbenchers' committees. Noting the appointments in his diary, Cecil King described them as 'men who would stand up to the Prime Minister'. By 1973, even the normally docile Parliamentary Party began showing public dissent. In the second session of that Parliament one or more Tory members voted against the Government in 36 per cent of the divisions; and two-thirds of the backbenchers voted against their own whips on at least one occasion.[1]

Beyond the Parliamentary Party, the revolt centred round the Monday Club, inheritor of a long tradition of right-wing groups primarily concerned with the Empire. The Monday Club had been formed in 1961 by a group of imperial-minded Tories concerned by Conservative Party policies towards Britain's remaining colonies. It acquired the immediate patronage of Lord Salisbury, the leading Tory peer. Though its initial impetus was opposition to Macmillan's policy towards Africa, it soon became the focus of a variety of right-wing tendencies within the Party unhappy at the perceived continuing drift towards the centre. As well as the old imperialist right, the traditionalist conservatives and the economic liberal right, there was what might best be called the nationalist strand which overlapped with both the other tendencies. The nationalists focused on the issue of the growing population of Afro-Caribbean, African and Asian people from the British Commonwealth in Britain, and sought to use it to create a populist political cause and a means of unifying the right. The central figure in this was George Kennedy Young, who retired as Deputy Chief of MI6 in 1961 and joined the merchant bankers Kleinwort Benson. In 1975, based on intelligence sources and information from his contacts in the anti-fascist movement, Wilson indentified Young as one of the 'plotters' against himself and his Government.[2]

Young was introduced into the Monday Club by Tory MP John Biggs-Davidson in 1967. The Tory Party began shifting to the right that year, a move largely triggered by the Race Relations Act, Tory opposition to which was led by Monday Clubber Ronald Bell MP. Bell was also a leading member of the then secret '92 Group' on the right of the Conservative Parliamentary Party. Young's name first surfaced in the media as one of the signatories to a 1967 appeal for funds to meet the legal costs of four members of the Racial Preservation Society charged with inciting racial hatred. On joining the Monday Club, Young set up an 'Action Fund', 'for action throughout the country', using it to hire young, right-wing staff for the Club's HQ, placing his own cadres on key committees.[3]

In 1969, the Monday Club published Young's pamphlet *Who Goes Home?*, in which he advocated repatriation of the black and Asian populations of this country. The club's founder-member, Paul Bristol, resigned when he saw the draft of the pamphlet, which was 'even more extreme than the published version'. Young's destructive course through the Club begins here.[4]

The Club subdivided into subject-based committees and sub-committees, with considerable autonomy. In 1970, the sub-committee on subversion organised a conference on the theme at which the principal speaker was General Giovanni di Lorenzo, a deputy in the Italian Parliament for the neo-fascist party, MSI, and former head of Italian secret service SIFAR. Young had served in Italy at the end of the war and became a specialist in Italian fascist police methods in combatting subversives. He retained a life-long interest in re-establishing a Special Operations Executive-type organisation to fight communism. Di Lorenzo had been heavily involved in the 'Strategy of Tension' in Italy during the late sixties and early seventies and was a leading member of the 'Gladio' network, revealed in late 1990 to have been set up by the CIA to combat communist subversion within Europe. Others in attendance included former ex-FBI agent at the United States Embassy in London, Charles Lyon, who was the London contact for the Robert Maheu Agency which had close links with the CIA, and, allegedly, with British Intelligence. Also there were Sir Robert Thompson, the British counter-insurgency expert who made his name in the campaign in Malaya, and Ian Grieg, a Monday Club founder and Chair of the Subversion sub-committee. It may be no coincidence that in 1970 a 'covert group' called the Resistance and Psychological Operations Committee (RPOC) was set up in Britain very much on the lines of the Gladio network. It is said to have had links with the MOD, the SAS and the Foreign Office's propaganda unit, the Information Research Department.[5]

In 1971 the Monday Club began discreet but open collaboration with the extreme right outside of the Tory Party. The impetus came from the club's Immigration Committee, set up in 1971 at Young's suggestion. Young sat on the new committee, which also included Gerald Howarth, at that time also a member of the Society of Individual Freedom (SIF); Bee Carthew, a former member of the Special Operations Executive; and three MPs, including Ronald Bell. The chairman Geoffrey Baber, a 26-year-old Conservative councillor in Kensington, was an ally of Young and a director of his Action Fund. Baber was also an assistant to Dr Donald Johnson MP at the right-wing publishers, Johnson Publications, one of the few regular advertisers in *Monday World*, the Club's magazine. Johnson was a member of the Society For Individual Freedom, President of the Monday Club's Croydon branch, and a friend of Edward Martell and Henry Kerby MP. All were ex-Liberals who had been directors of Martell's National Fellowship, a forerunner of the Monday Club.[6]

The Monday Club reached its peak in October 1972 when it had 2,000 national members, including 34 MPs, and a reported regional membership of 6,000, though this latter figure has been challenged. Without reference to the Club executive, Young's Immigration sub-committee wrote to all Club branch chairmen: 'Opposition to coloured immigration and lack of proper repatriation arrangements also exercise many of other political views who should be encouraged to lend their support in a campaign, which, when it succeeds, will be of benefit to all.' This gave the green light to local clubs to work with extremist groups such as the National Front. There were even press reports – strenuously denied on both sides as black propaganda – that Young met with NF leader John Tyndall. It was later reported – and also denied – that Young's collaborator, Ross McWhirter, offered to fund some of the extremist groups. In early 1972 this attempt at 'the bridge' between the Monday Club and the further right was exposed in *The Monday Club – A Danger to Democracy*, an anonymous pamphlet which outlined some of the collaboration between Monday Club members and the racist fringe. In it Young was described as 'the single most powerful political figure in the Monday Club . . . responsible for most of the finance'. Much of the pamphlet was clearly based on infiltration of the Monday Club and some of the far right groups. It was sent to MPs and the press, but because of the libellous nature of many of the allegations, little of it reached the mass media. Its authors remain unknown.[7]

Young was adopted in 1972 as prospective Conservative Parliamentary candidate for the then safe Labour seat of Brent East. His agent in the constituency was millionaire David Lazarus, former member of both the League of Empire Loyalists and its successor, the National Front, who 'emerged as the front man for the group of millionaires backing Enoch Powell.'[8]

Young's campaign within the Monday Club climaxed in 1973 with his challenge for the Chair of the Club. This led to a fierce faction fight between

Young's supporters and those of Jonathan Guinness, the incumbent Chair. A rancorous campaign ran, in public, through March and April. The subtext of the campaign was collaboration with groups like the NF. However, Young's personal agenda was nothing less than ridding the Tory Party of Edward Heath. That year, Bee Carthew, an ally of Young's on the Monday Club executive, had her flat burgled and various papers stolen. This burglary was, presumably, the source of the famous Young letter to her in which he wrote that 'the Queer will be dethroned'. This quotation first surfaced in *Private Eye* on 3 March 1974, with 'Queer' misread as 'Queen'. 'The Queer' was Edward Heath.[9]

The Young 'slate' included Bee Carthew, who was Meetings Secretary, and Harvey Proctor, Assistant Director of the Club, who stood for Editor of the Club's journal. The campaign between the Guinness and Young factions produced two forgeries, both apparently from supporters of the Young camp: a forged letter purporting to be from Jonathan Guinness was sent to the 3,000 national members; and an anonymous broadsheet from 'the Conservative Underground Press', in favour of Young, was issued. In the event, Young was defeated and resigned immediately, as did Ronald Bell MP and Young's protégé, Geoffrey Baber. Bee Carthew was expelled and later worked with John Tyndall in the National Front. As many as 150 other members were expelled or threatened with expulsion in the purge which followed Young's defeat.[10]

In retrospect, his challenge was a tactical mistake. With Harvey Proctor in the Club as Assistant Director, Bee Carthew as Meetings Secretary, and his own role in both the Immigration Committee and the Action Fund, Young's faction had taken over the Club in all but name. As it was, his attempt to take complete control led to the downfall of his faction and the decline of the Club within the Tory Party.[11]

With all this bad publicity, the Club became a virtual pariah within the Parliamentary Party. Most of the MPs resigned, those whose primary interest was in economics resurfacing in other new groups. One such was the Selsdon Group, the organising secretary of which was Anthony Van der Elst, who had been employed by Ronald Bell MP, on the recommendation of Young, in the offices of the Halt Immigration Now Campaign, which was being run by Young. A number of Tory MPs, including Nicholas Ridley (SIF member) and Richard Body, switched their allegiance to the Selsdon Group. Richard Body MP was Chair of the Economic Radicals, a 'small, unpublicised group of MPs, Tory candidates and academics' which met regularly in the House of Commons. Body had been in the Monday Club, had stood for Chair in 1972, but had left over the Club's 'wog-bashing image and obsession with darkest Africa'. John Biffen was also a member.[12]

These groups continued the laissez-faire economic tradition which had been kept alive in the Tory Party by groups like the Institute for Economic Affairs and the free-trade, free-market remnants of the pre-war Liberal Party, most spec-tacularly represented by Edward Martell's organisations, such as the Freedom Group. Although none of these ventures had much success at the time in changing Tory Party policy, they are the antecedents of the mid-1970s groups like Ross McWhirter's Current Affairs Press and Self Help, and the National

Association for Freedom. The core supporters and ideas of what became known as 'Thatcherism' can be traced back to these groups and, in particular, the Selsdon Group.[13]

Five weeks after his resignation from the Monday Club, Young was chosen as 'Honorary President' of a 'Tory action group' within West Middlesex Conservative Association, the region in which collaboration between the right-wing of the Monday Club and the further right groups had been most successful. The West Middlesex branch of the Monday Club had been expelled in December 1972 by Guinness. National Front Chairman in 1971/2, John O'Brien, acknowledged that during this period of attempted collaboration between the NF and the Monday Club, the NF's 'best links were with the West Middlesex Club'. This group appears to be the first published reference to the phrase 'Tory action', which was to provide the title for Young's 1975 group, discussed below. It was also his last-sighted connection with 'the bridge' between the Monday Club and the further right.[14]

In his 1972 letter to Bee Carthew, Young acknowledged that the campaign against immigration would fail, and told her he was thinking of 'a wider, national action looking to a more distant future'. Once again the word 'action' crops up. One of the tasks of MI6 officers like Young was the organisation of 'political actions' – i.e covert political operations. The origins of such operations lay with the activities of the war-time Special Operations Executive. This involved setting up front groups, political 'cells', and propaganda units often controlled from a distance by a radio network. In effect, this was what Young was doing – whether successful or not – in the early seventies. He infiltrated his cadres into organisations, manipulated groups and and set up fronts while staying in the shadows. His constant use of 'action' in his British activities was a wink to the intelligence-wise on the Tory right. When *Private Eye* first published this quotation in March 1974, the writer of the piece commented that 'what such a "national action" might involve is anybody's guess'. In fact it had already begun when that was written. Rebuffed after his semi-public campaign on immigration, Young changed tack and returned to what he knew best, forming a clandestine group, the Unison Committee for Action, generally just called Unison. This will be discussed later (see Chapter XXXIX below).

XXXIII

REDS UNDER THE BEDS

O Copeland! My Copeland!
What things must now be done?
What dirty tricks must we employ
Before the prize is won?
O show us, please, your expertise
In tracking down the virus,
With Washington to spur us on
And plumbers to inspire us!
But O Miles! Miles! Miles!
O the rising tide of red!
Teach us the ways of Watergate,
Or see subversion spread!

NEW STATESMAN, 25/1/74

BY LATE 1973, Heath's economic policies were failing. The property and the fringe bank speculation was unravelling; fuelled by the massive expansion of the money supply, inflation was on the up. Heath's expansionist 'dash for growth' – an exaggerated version of the 'go' part of the much derided 1950s and 1960s 'stop-go' policy – would have failed anyway, but it was Heath's misfortune to preside over the 1973 oil price rise, which speeded things up. Sir Gordon White, now Lord Hanson's partner in the United States, was one of the industrialists who 'felt crushed by the Heath government. They unlocked the doors of the banks, lowered interest rates to some ridiculous level and shovelled out money. Then the crash came. I suddenly found that all my shares were practically worthless, that the market had collapsed. So I left.'[1]

Unwilling or unable to tackle the root cause of the inflationary spiral – the financial sector of the economy – Heath (like others before and since) instead took on the unions, and ended up in another confrontation with the miners. The lights began going out all over England, industry went on to a 3-day week, and the British élite groups had a fit of apocalyptic visions at the sight of a Communist trade union leader leader, Mick McGahey of the National Union of Miners, confronting the Government. Heath Cabinet member John Davies was at home in Cheshire that Christmas: 'I said to my wife and children that we should have a nice time, because I deeply believed then that it was the last Christmas of its kind we would enjoy'. Into early 1974 the Heath Government was drifting towards an election. In the background the anti-subversion forces which had been taking root throughout Heath's term finally blossomed.[2]

On 6 January, Tony Benn noted in his diary that 'Heathrow is being defended by rings of Police and the army with tanks. The rumour in the press is that there might be a SAM missile attack as some missiles have disappeared from the Middle East . . . My suspicious mind led me to the possibility that Carrington wanted to get people used to tanks and armed patrols in the streets of London . . . Michael Heseltine rang, saying that they had had tip-offs since Christmas that there would be missile attacks on aircraft as they come into land at London Airport, and that the tanks were there to protect the airport.' Two days later, Benn reported James Callaghan as saying that he had seen Home Secretary Robert Carr, who told him that Heseltine's story was not true. Whatever their purpose, these exercises alarmed both Harold Wilson and Marcia Williams.[3]

In the media, Aims of Industry were running constant scare ads – Stalin behind a smiling mask, for example – in a campaign said to have cost £500,000 in 1974 money. As the February election approached, the context set by the Aims campaign was supplemented by more detailed psychological warfare stories which began appearing in the British press. On 18 January, Christopher Walker reported in *The Times* that, concerned about 'subversion' in Britain, the CIA and NSA were stepping up their operations in the country. The former CIA officer Miles Copeland, who retained close links with the London station, told Walker that MI5 'are restricted and squeamish in your own territory from doing the things that really have to be done to track down . . . subversives'. In 1987, Copeland added that the CIA station 'believed that the Soviets were guiding some of the unions'. On 25 January, Christopher Sweeney, again in *The Times*, ran the first public version of the results of the CIA's debriefing of Czech defector Joseph Frolik, including references to the recruitment of three (unidentified) MPs. During the previous summer, James Angleton and his CIA colleagues had decided to re-activate the Czech defector and agreed to him visiting England where he was allowed to sell his memoirs. Frolik, when he later saw Walker's article in *The Times* on CIA penetration of trade unions, realised that the timing of the visit was critical to the CIA – 'the bell rang'. Cord Meyer, CIA London station chief at the time, denied the Walker story about increased CIA personnel but said nothing about the more important and more damaging Frolik allegations.[4]

The propaganda of the anti-subversion tendency was beginning to take its toll. The Shadow Cabinet, apparently not yet quite under the thumb of the communists, was sufficiently alarmed by the 'Reds under the beds' theme to issue a statement disassociating themselves from the 'wider political objectives' of the miners. Within the state, the Cabinet Secretary, Sir William Armstrong, Heath's right-hand man, became infected with the Red Menace virus. On 27 January, at a conference at Ditchley Park, President of the CBI Campbell

Adamson, who actually knew something about the realities of industrial relations, had the acutely embarrassing experience of being harangued by Armstrong on the ubiquity of communist inflitrators, 'talking about coups and
coalitions'. A week later, Armstrong had completely cracked up. Downing Street
insiders found him 'lying on the floor and talking about moving the Red Army
from here and the Blue Army from there'. Armstrong was removed from office –
to a country retreat owned by Lord Rothschild. When Cabinet Secretaries talk of
coups, under any circumstances, we should take note. Lord Carver, then Chief
of Staff, has gone on record to say that 'fairly senior officers at the Army's
headquarters were talking about the possibility of military intervention during
the miners' strike'. Lord Chalfont said of the time: 'There were some people
behind the scenes . . . who were suggesting that the only answer . . . was a
military government.'[5]

On the 28 January, a full page of the *Daily Telegraph* headed 'Communists Aim
to Dictate Labour Policy', provided a perfect snap-shot of the thinking of the
anti-subversion lobby: the threat was the CPGB's Bert Ramelson, the Labour
Party's abolition of the Proscription List, the miners, Jack Jones, the Transport
and General Workers' Union (which 'recently allowed card-carrying Communists to sit on its 35-man executive'), Hugh Scanlon ('an ex-Communist but his
views remain close to those of King St' – CPGB headquarters), etc. etc.

To meet the 'Threat' there appeared a Saviour. On 1 February, in the *Daily
Express*, Chapman Pincher revealed – 'at George Young's behest' – the existence
of 'The Secret Vigilantes' formed 'to help protect the nation against a Communist takeover [an organisation which] has been quietly organised by former
Service chiefs, senior ex-members of the Secret Service and MI5, [and] has
been recruiting gradually over the last two years.' This was the first public
surfacing of Unison, George Young's 'Committee for Action'. Lest *Express*
readers miss the point of the piece, sharing the page with Pincher was a story
entitled 'Communists – the method and the menace'.[6]

On 3 February, over a page of the *Observer* was devoted to an extract from an
ISC study of 'Sources of Conflict in Industry'. Chosen for publication was the
section which, despite acknowledging that 'no Communist or Trotskyist currently sits on the (TUC) General Council', re-ran the anti-subversion tendency's analysis of the communists-in-unions threat. This was ISC's greatest
propaganda coup. On the 12th, the two one-hour segments of a 'special' on the
KGB broadcast on Independent Television bracketed a Labour Party political
broadcast – a striking piece of programming during an election campaign. Tony
Benn thought the scheduling made it look as if the Labour Party was almost a
part of the KGB.[7]

On 20 February, the London *Evening News* reported a speech by Conservative
candidate George Young. The former MI6 officer claimed 'there were 40 or 50
Labour MPs for whom the Labour label is cover for more sinister roles'. These
were a 'black hand gang', in contrast to 'comrades McGahey, Daley, Buckton
and the overt Red Hand Gang'. The notion that Ray Buckton, General
Secretary of the railway union ASLEF, was some kind of revolutionary says
much about the ignorance of the right. Buckton's telephone had been tapped

since the 1972 miners' strike and he was the target of death threats. His close friend and colleague in the TUC, Clive Jenkins, had the disquieting experience of hearing a bullet smash through his living-room window. Special Branch officers later told Jenkins that informants had reported assassination plots against himself, Scanlon, Jack Jones and Buckton. Armed guards were provided for leading trade unionists. Buckton thought the 'death threats had . . . been engineered to provide an excuse for his being under surveillance'. This was another example of the psychological operations being run in this period.[8]

George Young also spoke of the existence of a dossier held by Special Branch on Reg Freeson, Labour MP and his opponent in Brent East. Freeson's alleged subversive activities appeared to consist of a couple of trips to Communist countries in the 1940s as Chair of the Warsaw Memorial Committee. No one asked how it was that Young had access to a Branch file. Freeson was Jewish (Young called them 'snip-cocks'), and a founder and editor of *Searchlight* the anti-fascist magazine. He would therefore have known a good deal about Young's activities and links to extremist groups in this period.[9]

Beneath the Heath campaign's theme of 'Who rules Britain?', which did not make much of the communist dimension, the anti-subversion tendency were running the hard-core, communist conspiracy version.

MI5 had Wilson under surveillance before the election. Two years later Chapman Pincher was given a copy of a surveillance report from this period. The report, which had come from the registry of MI6, 'was said to be a copy of a progress report on the surveillance of Wilson compiled by another department' – presumably MI5. It was a detailed breakdown of Wilson's movements in the weeks before the February 1974 election. The report also detailed MI5 concerns about Wilson: 'there were strong political overtones showing that the author of the report was opposed to Wilson's re-election as Prime Minister.' The person most likely to have supplied the report was Peter Wright, who may have passed it on to his friend Maurice Oldfield. The expressed concerns were:

– Wilson's 'pro-Israeli stance during his previous premiership because of the danger that, if continued, it would sour relations with Arab states at a time of oil-supply crisis'.
– 'A new Wilson government might increase trade with Russia, leading to greater opportunities for KGB activity in Britain . . . There was mention of the fact that Wilson had previously refused to reduce the number of KGB agents posing as diplomats and trade officals in Britain and had criticized the Heath government for expelling 105 of them.'
– 'Against the advice of the security authorities, Wilson had previously agreed with the Russians to release the professional Soviet spies Peter and Helen Kroger . . . in exchange for Gerald Brooke.' This would in future give the Soviets the precedent to do the same.
– 'There were also fears that a new Labour administration would enforce reductions in the Secret Service as part of the general cuts in public and defence spending of which all government departments had been required to shoulder their share.'[10]

All of these themes turned up later in the year in the information being sent from MI5 in London to Colin Wallace at Information Policy in Ireland, discussed below.

Although the Heath election campaign was run under the heading 'Who rules Britain?', the Conservative leadership declined to dirty its hands with a good deal of the ammunition offered to it. It has been alleged, for example, that as early as 1973 Heath was informed by the CIA that they had established proof of Soviet involvement in the miners' strike. Heath also declined to make capital of the activites of Czech intelligence agents in Britain. Following the expulsion of the 105 Soviet diplomats in 1971, the KGB allegedly shifted their activities to the Czech 'diplomats'. A number had been caught spying and been expelled but Heath refused to allow publicity. 'The Czech situation was drawn to Heath's attention by Julian Amery, who told him that MI5 had proof of blatant abuse of diplomatic privilege by thirteen 'diplomats', including the ambassador, but Heath decided against any public use of it . . . news of the Czech treachery and the thirteen expulsions did not leak out until after the Tory defeat.'[11]

The Tories also declined to use a number of personal smear stories offered to them. In mid-December 1973, the Conservative Party candidate in Jeremy Thorpe's Devon constituency, Tim Keigwin, and his agent had been sent to talk to a doctor who had heard Norman Scott's story of his homosexual relationship with the Liberal leader. The agent passed the information to Conservative Party headquarters. A month later, Scott approached Keigwin himself, told him the story and gave him a written version of it. This was taken to Conservative Party headquarters, but never used, apparently on the advice of the then Chairman of the Party, Lord Carrington. Chapman Pincher admits that he talked with a few friends about the possibility of a 'dirty tricks' media campaign, 'using Mrs Halls' simmering legal action and other genuine topics.' Central Office had been given copies of the birth certificates of Marcia Williams' two children fathered by the journalist Walter Terry. Carrington made it clear to Pincher that he could not go along with the plans. Pincher's friend, former MI6 agent Bruce McKenzie, suggested he put the project to Lord Aldington, who was close to Heath. Aldington was Chairman of the merchant bank Brandts, where the Director of International Department, Anthony Cavendish, was another former MI6 officer. Like his close friend George Young, Cavendish was a Conservative candidate in the February election. In his memoir, Cavendish reveals that he recruited three former MI6 officers to the bank and that from 1973 a frequent lunch guest with himself and Aldington was the newly appointed chief of MI6, Maurice Oldfield. The Prime Minister, through an intermediary, informed Pincher that he 'was going to win the election anyway and wanted to be seen to have won it cleanly'.[12]

After all this drama, the election result was a let-down. It was stalemate; no party had an overall majority. Heath tried to strike a deal with the Liberals to stay in office and failed. Labour, who won the largest number of seats, took over. The anti-subversion campaign had failed.

PART FOUR

1974–76

XXXIV

'DESPERATE TIMES': BETWEEN THE
TWO ELECTIONS OF 1974

*It is difficult to write about those few months without inviting a charge of
paranoia.*
MARCIA FALKENDER

THE GENERAL ELECTION in February 1974 had resolved nothing.
Heath asked 'Who should rule Britain?', to be told by half the voters 'not you,
anyway'. The 'Communist threat' campaign run by the anti-subversion tendency
was not taken seriously. Labour won most seats but not a majority and depended
upon the support of the minor parties, essentially the Liberals: such a political
stalemate would not last long.

Tory hardliners led by Julian Amery were keen to test the legitimacy of the
Wilson Government, believing that every effort should be made to vote down the
Government's legislative programme as laid out in the Queen's Speech. Amery
had information that in the late sixties, when Wilson supported Barbara Castle in
her efforts to reform the trade union laws, the Prime Minister had threatened the
Cabinet with a dissolution of Parliament if they continued to oppose the
legislation. Wilson had apparently consulted Buckingham Palace but had been
told that there would be no dissolution. If the Labour Party could come up with a
leader who enjoyed majority support, he was told, the Government could
continue in office. Using this as a precedent, Amery and Anthony Barber
believed that should Wilson be defeated over the Queen's Speech, she might
then accept whoever could command a Commons majority as Prime Minister. In
the event, the Conservative Party was split on this tactic and Labour won the
division comfortably. Out of this initiative, the theme of 'national unity',
appealing across party loyalties, took shape throughout 1974. By June, one of
Heath's senior colleagues, Peter Walker, was talking about a 'government of
national unity'. This would involve most of the Conservative and Liberal Parties
and, Walker predicted, 'as much as one-third of the Labour Party'. Advocates of
the idea, which held wide appeal among Conservatives, included Amery and his

relative, Maurice Macmillan, who called for 'a ministry of all the talents' – the standard Tory line whenever a Labour Government is elected, though never heard after Conservative victories.[1]

For Harold Wilson, it was 1964 all over again: another General Election could not be far off. In early spring of 1974, Chapman Pincher 'learned that the Tory leadership . . . was frightened that Wilson would launch a snap election in June . . . Tory soundings indicated that the government might be returned with such a majority that some Tory leaders would lose their seats. The election therefore had to be delayed if possible, at least until the autumn and preferably beyond.' The Tories had declined to use smear stories about Wilson, Mrs Williams and Jeremy Thorpe which had been offered to them before the February election. However – 'in late April' – Pincher was visited by 'an emissary of Edward Heath'. The official told him that 'any means of discouraging Wilson from going to the country in June should be brought into play . . . these were desperate times'. Pincher adds that he 'was left in no doubt that they could include the "dirty tricks" which had been rejected just a few months earlier'. The official, wrote Pincher in 1991, who was 'certainly very close' to Heath is 'now an important political figure'.[2]

Pincher's account of his contacts with the Tory Party before and after the February election gives us an important glimpse into the networking between the state, the Tory Party and sections of the media. Pincher openly describes his role as an adjunct to the campaign: 'What was required of me in the main was that I should make use in the *Daily Express* of material in my possession so that other papers would be encouraged to do likewise.' Another glimpse of this network was given to journalist Hugo Young. Later in 1974, Young met a former 'respected politician in the Heath Cabinet'. This 'prince among the wets' intended to stay in politics, he told Young, to get rid of Wilson, whose Government was full of 'Muscovites'. He had seen the files while in government – on Castle, Foot, Benn and Healey. (Labour Cabinet members were refused access to their own files, let alone those on their opponents.) As Young was entering the politician's home, another man was leaving, casually described to Young as 'the chap who kept me informed on these things when I was in government'. This is what the novelist John Le Carré, who as David Cornwell served in MI5 and MI6 in the 1950s and early 1960s, referred to as 'the natural intimacy between the secret services and the Conservative Party'. If a Labour Government were elected, Le Carré said, 'the secret services would be cuddling up with the Conservative Party in exile day and night'.[3]

Wilson and Mrs Williams knew that a smear campaign was in the offing – 'Information of a purely personal kind about various Labour personalities was being brought to the attention of the Tory leadership' – but Mrs Williams attributed this to the Party's 'more powerful, broadly based and over enthusiastic supporters, who wished to see it back in power', rather than the Party itself. In fact, though he had 'no certain evidence that Heath knew of this proposed campaign', Pincher 'was assured by people close to him that he did and had approved it with reluctance'. A game of chicken developed, with the threat of the smear campaign being countered by that of a June election. 'After the weekend of 15th March, when Harold Wilson warned in his High Wycombe speech that the Conservatives' behaviour might force him back to the country, there was another lull.'[4]

Although there is no evidence of this yet, it seems highly probable that the Tory Party's decision to go for dirt was taken by the anti-subversion tendency to mean that they had been given the 'green light' by the Conservative Party establishment to step up their campaign against the Labour Party; but destabilising a government in a democracy like Britain, with British libel laws – and doing it undetected – is a lengthy and complex business. While the Tory Party may have sought to use the threat of smears against Wilson and Mrs Williams to achieve the short-term goal of preventing a June election, the spooks and their allies were preparing a longer game plan. Though many of their operations did not emerge during 1974, the events between the two elections of that year are still so complex that it is impossible to construct a single narrative. We have thus had to break the period down into sections. This is unsatisfactory but unavoidable.

The theme of the period was smears, of which there are several kinds: there are allegations that contain a kernel of truth on to which lies are grafted; there are those which are basically true but which have been slanted in particular, misleading, directions; and there are outright inventions. Though most of the British press were in 1974 loyal supporters of the Tory Party, the libel laws prevented them running the more outrageous smears. These were simply spread as rumour. Marcia Williams recalled 'Talk of close liaisons with KGB colonels, the mysterious East European "benefactors" supposedly bankrolling Harold Wilson's 1974 election campaigns . . . tales of drugs, orgies and nameless vices in mysterious blocks of flats off Baker Street . . . rumours relating to John Silkin and land speculation in South Wales and even more bizarre and fanciful ones about Tony Benn . . . that I was a paid member of the Israeli Secret Service.' Another rumour had it that Wilson had been given a gift of a bag of diamonds.[5]

The first major anti-Labour story to hit the media just after the February election was the story of the 'Wigan alps' – the 'land deals' row. The story has been retold many times and we will only sketch it here. Mrs Williams' brother, Anthony Field, some time Wilson assistant, bought a slag heap near Wigan with the intention of selling off the slag and then developing the land beneath it. This was an entirely routine, arguably even socially useful, piece of speculation, but it was undoubtedly 'land speculation', and, given the Labour Party's dislike of 'speculators', it was an accident waiting to happen. The story had been trundling around just before the February 1974 election and was offered to both the *Guardian* and the *Daily Mail*. Two forged documents appeared, apparently linking Downing Street to the affair. The first was a piece of private enterprise by one of the businessmen involved, invoking Wilson's name in the hope of favourable treatment by a local council; but the author of the second, describing a non-existent Walmsley Family Trust with Wilson as 'trustee', was never identified and looks to us like the work of MI5's forgery department building on the story and the first forgery. Support for the view that this was a planned operation is the testimony of a journalist on the *Jewish Chronicle* who learned the details of the story and the timing of its release some time before it appeared in the press and warned Mrs Williams. Politically the story was bad enough and Wilson made it worse by ignoring his advisers and trying to defend Mr Field's activities in the House of Commons. Joe Haines, then Wilson's press secretary, calculated that 6,000 column inches were devoted to the story.[6]

Although there are signs of leaks from the intelligence services in *Private Eye* all through the Heath years, it was during Wilson's return to power that the magazine began to receive – and print – a lot of intelligence material, primarily it seems, from MI5. The *Eye* was ideal. With its contempt for all politicians and a reputation for printing the unprintable it had established a large and influential readership. The one regular writer for the magazine who is known to have had firm political opinions, Paul Foot, was a member of the International Socialists and despised the Labour Party. If any British media outlet was going to print smear stories about the Labour Party without doing too much checking of the details it was *Private Eye*.[7]

According to Patrick Marnham, a writer on the *Eye*, the first of the intelligence 'information packs' came to the magazine via *The Times*, where 'a reporter on the paper had started to check the allegations, established that they were plausible but then decided that the story would be better handled by *Private Eye*'. The documents which Marnham has allowed journalists to see are very reminiscent in their construction of the type which Colin Wallace was putting together in Northern Ireland, on behalf of Information Policy as part of 'Clockwork Orange' (discussed below). There is the same blend of known facts, intriguing new material, and the subtle insertion of 'black' material (i.e. lies), all of which is held together, or given a 'spin', by the addition of a theme. The theme, Marnham deduced, was as follows: 'The period covered was immediately after the war, when the country was going through a severe economic depression. At the time the United Kingdom suffered from a shortage of foreign currency and manufacturing resources. The few people who could get permission to import heavily rationed raw materials or finished goods were almost bound to be millionaires. The necessary licences were issued by the Board of Trade, and from October 1947 to March 1951 that person was Harold Wilson. It was during his term in office that Wilson first met several of the men who were later to support, and to benefit from, his political career.'[8]

Another journalist at the *Eye*, Martin Tomkinson, recognised the theme and where it led. He had a 'security service contact who hinted that Wilson was far too interested in promoting Anglo-Soviet trade'. As Marnham and colleagues on the *Eye* 'sorted through this material, we were directed back over the years to the Groundnut Scheme, the Lynsky Tribunal, the export to Russia of top-secret Rolls Royce engines, the Leipzig Trade Fair and the opening of the Soviet Trade delegation in London – after a quarry whose name changed on every page. Was it the KGB?' Although Marnham claims that the *Eye* never used the material, with one exception all the smears outlined appeared in the pages of the magazine in the 1974–6 period. The allegations never went as far as MI5 might have hoped but the gradual drip, drip of material on the East–West traders and other businessmen in the Labour Party had its cumulative effect on the portrayal of the

Wilson administration. George Kennedy Young's comment about 'Wilson's gang of spivs' is typical.[9]

One of the documents Colin Wallace kept from his period in propaganda work in Northern Ireland provides strong evidence to the identity of the agency and possibly the individuals responsible for the Marnham documents. On 23 April 1990 Wallace sent to Mrs Thatcher, then Prime Minister, a long letter including a photocopy of an unattributable press briefing, 'Soviets Increase Control Over British Communists'. Produced in the period before December 1973, the briefing included annotations on it in the handwriting of Hugh Mooney, the IRD officer attached to the psychological warfare unit Information Policy. Concerned with the visit to Britain by, and the activities of, a group of Soviet officials, the briefing paper included these passages:

> The Soviet [officials] paid tribute to the excellent contacts built up in the past between British Labour Party activists and the Soviet Trade Delgation in London. In particular they spoke warmly of the work done by Harold Wilson during his four years at the Board of Trade and his help in enabling the Soviet Government to purchase the latest Rolls Royce engines (Derwent and Nene) in 1947 . . .
>
> Needless to say the Soviet visitors forgot to tell their unquestioning hosts that the Soviet Trade Delegation for whom Wilson and his friends had played 'Santa Claus' was the main front for Soviet Intelligence operations in Britain.

The similarities with the *Private Eye* documents that have been revealed are striking. These IRD briefing papers would eventually find their way into the hands of right-wing Tory MPs.[10]

Just after the election, on 22 March, the *Eye* fired its first shot. An article titled 'Supplementary Benefits' listed a number of leading Labour politicians who had taken on directorships when in opposition, who might soon be 'troubled by an old friendship' since many of the companies were now in financial difficulty or under suspicion of fraud. Those listed included James Callaghan, Elwyn Jones, Denis Howell, Denis Healey, John Silkin, Harold Lever, Fred Peart and Lord Brayley.

On 10 April, Wilson told the Cabinet 'there are two other members of the Cabinet . . . who are being pursued by the press. One has been tailed for five years and on the other they have got a dossier two feet thick. They both would be regarded as being in the leadership stakes if I went.' We presume these two were Tony Benn, whose experiences are discussed below, and James Callaghan. Callaghan was vulnerable: of all the Labour leaders he was the one about whom the most convincing smear stories could have been constructed. Rumours of Callaghan's relationship with Welsh money-lender Julian Hodge had started in the early 1960s. Rather like the banker Siegmund Warburg twenty years before, Hodge was another 'outsider' trying to get in among the big players in the City. He was a provincial, based in Cardiff, and a financial supporter of the Labour Party rather than the Tories. Like Warburg, he was hated by the City. Rumours were floated in 1966 that Callaghan had put forward Hodge's name as a possible non-executive director of the Bank of England. Callaghan had, in fact, not done so but 'after the rumour had circulated for a while it was allowed to lapse with the ponderous inference – a satisfying one to many people – that Julian Hodge had been found to be quite unworthy of such an appointment'.[11]

In 1970, Hodge was knighted, reportedly on Callaghan's recommendation, and finally founded the bank he wanted, the Commercial Bank of Wales, in 1972 – not under a Labour Government. George Thomas MP (later Speaker of the House) and James Callaghan were initial share-holders. Callaghan also served as director of the Italian International Bank, which led to calls by Labour backbenchers for his resignation as shadow Foreign Secretary.[12]

Though the relationship between Hodge and Callaghan was explored in *Private Eye* in 1972 and by *Socialist Worker* and the *Sunday Express* a few months before the February election; and though Callaghan had warned Wilson that he expected to get attention because of his connections to the Italian bank and Julian Hodge, nothing appeared during the inter-election period. A full airing was not given until the Labour leadership contest in April 1976. The strange absence of Callaghan from the list of Labour leaders targeted between the two elections is presumably connected to the 1974 view of MI5, as expressed to Colin Wallace, that Callaghan would be a good choice as new leader of the Labour Party because of his role as Parliamentary spokesman for the Police Federation, i.e. he was a safe, conservative, Labour politician who believed implicitly what the secret state told him: in short, who was 'sound'. By 1976, with Mrs Thatcher elected leader of the Tory Party and the anti-subversive lobby clustered around her, a safe conservative was precisely who the ultras did not want leading Labour into the next election.[13]

In June 1974, when it was clear that there would be no early election, Peter Walker organised a dinner in order that Heath could meet one or two leading businessmen. Principal guests were close friends Jim Slater and James Goldsmith. Slater had been Goldsmith's means of introduction to Heath. In 1972, Goldsmith had taken over a number of Slater Walker companies and when, in 1975, Slater Walker itself was ailing, Goldsmith assumed the chairmanship. In the ensuing rescue, Goldsmith invited on to the board his distant cousin Lord Rothschild, with whose family the City financier had previously had business dealings. Goldsmith had generously helped Heath financially with 'a donation of £100,000 to promote the European cause' and underwrote the Centre for Policy Studies which Keith Joseph and Margaret Thatcher were then establishing. The conversation at Walker's home was 'about how to help the Conservative Party win the election that Harold Wilson would clearly be forced to call before the year was out.'[14]

According to his biographer, Geoffrey Wansell, Goldsmith, like Heath, 'shared a distrust of the sometimes ponderous foibles of the democratic process, a suspicion of the English establishment which neither felt quite accepted them, a conviction that they alone might be able to save the nation from the peril that confronted it'. The friendship 'convinced Goldsmith that there could be a political future for him in England'. Heath saw Goldsmith as 'the sort of man he could call on to help with money for particular projects, for research help when he needed it, and who could be relied upon to be as annoyed as he was by the failings of the Tory Party organization'. At the dinner, Goldsmith had been aggressive in his conclusions about the Tory campaigning.[15]

The Heath/Goldsmith friendship was a curious one, since Goldsmith's own politics, even then, were far to the right. 'For most of my life I have despised the established conservative and socialist parties in Britain. I supported the Conservatives, sometimes thinking and hoping that there was a real change, for example the emergence of "Selsdon Man". But usually I had to hold my nose and control my nausea.' Goldsmith's business links put him in close touch with Heath's opponents within the Party. His bankers were Keyser Ullman, chairman of which was Edward du Cann, also Chair of the influential backbench 1922 Committee. Goldsmith, according to arch-enemy Richard Ingrams, held similar extreme right-wing views to those of his friends in what became known as the 'Clermont Set'.[16]

Goldsmith's political ambitions are a barometer by which to read the atmosphere of the period. His increasingly apocalyptic view of the world, partly based on his brother Teddy's ecological warnings, had been given a psychological boost by the stock market fall in 1973. In the City, recalls Slater, 'assets were literally disintegrating before their eyes . . . The market fell to a lower level than during Dunkirk, when many thought that it was unlikely that Britain would survive the war against Germany.' According to Wansell, the golden touch that seemed to have burnished Goldsmith's business in the past decade evaporated as he extended his interest into politics. Friends noticed 'a tiny flame of paranoia that appeared to become a central part of his character'. His company reports were marked by 'elaborate political analysis, couched in grandiose terms, condemning the nature of British society and its relations to commercial enterprise'.[17]

The more direct vision of some members of the City was glimpsed by Simon Winchester, who was researching the death of Lord Lucan, a friend of Goldsmith and probably the most famous member of the 'Clermont Set'. 'The picture which emerged was of a tight-knit group of moneyed men . . . their views of the ultra-right, their bigotry deep-rooted and intense, their intelligence severely limited and their attitudes and behaviour as decadent as thirties' Berlin and as repugnant as seventies' Uganda.' Richard Ingrams writes that 'the slump of 1973 had rather soured the atmosphere there, and Lucan's own ideas had become more and more right-wing. Searching for clues, police had found records of Hitler's speeches in his flat.' Lucan, who despised 'foreigners', would talk openly of 'niggers'. Diary columnist Nigel Dempster called this social set an 'embattled race'. 'The curtain, they know, is halfway down on them but they don't know when the final drop is coming so they've occupied the high ground. They think the scum are baying for their blood so they form clubs to keep the scum out.'[18]

Goldsmith believed that the 'dominant geo-political problem is the imperial and totalitarian ambition of the Soviet Union'. The communist's strategy was 'to infiltrate and progressively to capture the trade unions and Labour Party machinery'. The purpose, he believed, was 'to undermine, destabilise, demoralise and, when the conditions are ripe, to take over'. Lord Lucan's mother, 'the kindly, dry, thoughtful Dowager, secretary of the mild St Marylebone Labour Party', was regarded by the Clermont Set as 'to all intents and purposes a communist', who had been 'trained in Moscow'.[19]

Members of the 'Clermont Set' responded to the events of 1973–4 in a political way. Greville Howard, whose father had served in MI6, had been Goldsmith's personal assistant and then worked for Slater Walker, also acted as Enoch Powell's political secretary. Michael Stoop, a retired company director, volunteered to join David Stirling's 'private army', GB 75 (discussed below). Another Clermont regular, Dominick Elwes, had known Stirling in the sixties during the civil war in the Yemen.[20]

Heath saw Goldsmith again in August regarding ways in which he could help in the upcoming election. 'He would provide advice, look at ways of raising money – he decided to give a dinner for major industrialists at which they would be asked to support the Tory cause – and provide what help he could.' Goldsmith, writes Wansell, 'harboured the dream of a political career, based on a peerage that a grateful Prime Minister would give him after a Conservative Party victory in October 1974, which would bring in its wake a ministerial appointment to allow him to put his theories into practice.' In the end, Goldsmith thought that Heath and his advisers were not tough enough. The experience 'finally left him with the suspicion that the leadership of the Conservative Party were not determined to win'. It would take the security services to organise a real 'putsch'.[21]

XXXV

THE WRIGHT PLOT

Wilson's a bloody menace and it's about time the public knew the truth.
MI5 OFFICER 1974

WHAT WAS PETER WRIGHT, now so firmly associated with the 1974 plotting, doing at this point? There have now been several, apparently contradictory versions of what is known as the 'Wright plot'. The first, partial version appeared in Chapman Pincher's *Inside Story* in 1978. 'Certain officers inside MI5, assisted by others who had retired from the service, were actually trying to bring the Labour Government down . . . One senior MI5 officer had become so incensed by the activities of two particular ministers that he decided it was urgently in the national interest for them to be exposed . . . He was prepared to name the ministers and reveal details of their activities from his knowledge of the files containing evidence against them, some of it derived from undercover surveillance . . . the MI5 officer . . . knew that this action . . . would certainly end his career as a public servant even if he escaped prosecution under the Official Secrets Acts. So he approached a very senior Whitehall personality, whose name I know but whom I will call "Q" to preserve his anonymity. Knowing that he would lose his pension, the officer needed some guarantee of future employment after he had made his sacrifice. He therefore asked Q, whom he knew to be sympathetic regarding the danger of left-wing activity by some ministers, if there was any way of obtaining a job in advance, perhaps in some security role, to ensure that he and his family would have some income.'[1]

In his affidavit to the Australian court during the *Spycatcher* row, Peter Wright cited this passage and identified himself as the dissident officer and 'Q' as Lord Rothschild. Wright described how he had approached Lord Rothschild for a consultancy post as a security adviser in Rothschild's family bank, N. M. Rothschild & Sons.[2]

Pincher again: 'Q [Rothschild] did not attempt to dissuade him. Instead he contacted one of the best known figures in the City on his behalf. This City man, with whom I have discussed the issue and who is also averse to being identified, was keen to get rid of the Labour Government . . . The "City man" took soundings in several large commercial firms. The responses were indentical. Each firm regretfully pointed out that because the power of government was now so extensive it dare not risk employing the officer in any capacity. If the government survived, it might take revenge on the firm for assisting in the exposure and this was a risk the firm could not entertain with the shareholders' interests in mind . . . On being told this by Q the MI5 officer completely lost heart and kept both his silence and his job.' Hard though this is now to believe, this account went unnoticed at the time. Pincher's source for this story, the 'City man', was only to be backed up by the appearance of Peter Wright on the world's media stage.[3]

The story of MI5 plotting against Wilson resurfaced in a long, confused muddle from late 1986 to the end of 1988. Rumours about the manuscript of Wright's book were followed by leaks to the press and Labour MPs, Dale Campbell-Savours in particular, of some of the key allegations said to be in it. Eventually, *Spycatcher* appeared – the most heavily trailed book in history – with some of the leaked material missing. Finally, Wright gave a number of post-publication interviews to journalists, notably John Ware of BBC's *Panorama* and David Leigh, who had done most to run the story in the *Observer*, in which the former MI5 officer appeared to backtrack on some of what he had said privately.

In these various accounts, Wright described three quite distinct plans. Apparent contradictions and confusions have been caused by commentators assuming that Wright was redescribing only one event. The first attempt to bring Wilson down was that which was published by Pincher in 1978. Wright was prepared to go public, name names and describe MI5 operations and suspicions: 'he circulated the information that he was a "patriotic officer" who wished to blow the whistle on treasonable Labour ministers – Wilson himself, Stonehouse, MacDermot.'[4]

When this first scheme of Wright's failed because he was not able to obtain the guarantee of future employment he required, he considered another tactic. He would assemble MI5's files on Wilson and 'show Wilson that we had it. We wanted him to resign. There would be no publicity if he went quietly.' These files comprised the so-called 'Worthington file' kept in the Director-General's safe to which Wright had access. He thought that the MI5 cabal could 'make it clear to him that he was heavily compromised . . . I thought of starting off in [these] terms: "There were a number of us who didn't trust him and the reasons for it were as follows" . . . and I would have produced the documentary evidence . . . I honestly think Wilson would have folded up – he wasn't a very gutsy man.' The 'we' Wright refers to were 'eight or nine colleagues', apparently from MI5's counter-espionage K Branch. Wright would get the files on Wilson from the Director-General's safe: the K branch officers would back him up. In the event, all except one got cold feet.[5]

Finally, in *Spycatcher*, Wright claims he was approached by a group of younger MI5 personnel whom he refers to as 'the boys', and whom we take to be some of the members of F (counter-subversive) Branch recruited during F's expansion during 1972–4. A number of the hardline K Branch members, such as Charles Elwell, had also moved across. They had a plan: in the run-up to the election following that of February 1974, 'selective details of the intelligence about leading Labour Party figures . . . [were] to be leaked to sympathetic pressmen . . . facsimile copies of some files were to be made and distributed to overseas newspapers, and the matter was to be raised in Parliament for maximum effect . . . Word of the material contained in MI5 files and the fact that Wilson was considered a security risk would be passed around.'[6]

In his draft of this section in *Spycatcher*, Wright claims that they intended to 'prime' two MPs to stir things up. 'It was a carbon copy of the Zinoviev letter, which had done so much to destroy the first Ramsay MacDonald Government in 1924.' Dale Campbell-Savours told the House of Commons under Parliamentary privilege that 'those Conservative Members of Parliament, only one of whom is now sitting, acted as conduits for the smear campaign against Harold Wilson which was organised from within MI5 . . . They knew that the information they were receiving came illegally from within MI5 . . . They passed it on in the knowlege that it would destabilise the Labour Prime Minister and his Government.'[7]

Peter Wright had falsely claimed that the MPs were Winston Churchill and Stephen Hastings, an allegation which he later withdrew on BBC's *Panorama* programme. Churchill told the House of Commons that 'I have never at any time worked for or with MI5. Nor have I knowingly even met any individual from MI5. I have certainly never engaged in any conspiracy, treasonable or otherwise, with MI5 or with any of its officers, past or present . . . Furthermore, Sir Stephen Hastings . . . has asked me to state on his behalf that the charges against him are also without foundation.'[8]

This final scheme, excluding the use of the two MPs, is the only one that counts, for a part of this *is what actually happened*. What role Wright played in these operations is unclear. He claims none, that he merely noticed what was happening while he travelled around the world playing out his time before retirement. 'Although the full Wilson story never emerged, it was obvious to me that the boys had been actively pushing their plan as much as they could.' Wright's non-involvement in this plan we might we take with a substantial pinch of salt: why would he back away from this scheme when he was so keen on his own? Nor is it obvious to us that the material that appeared was issuing solely from 'the boys' in F Branch. Much of it – for example, the material gained from the investigation of Kagan and the East–West traders – clearly originated within K Branch.[9]

It would appear that Wright had persuaded the Director-General to re-open the Wilson case. 'Angleton', says Wright, 'was beginning to badger us constantly about Wilson and I told Hanley it would be politic to be seen to be doing something.' Extra support for Wright's position came in May 1974 when a CANZAB conference was held in London which Angleton attended. In December, Angleton was ousted as head of CIA counter-intelligence. However, he, in fact, stayed in office until October 1975. During this period, he was still informing senior CIA officers that Wilson was a Soviet agent. Within MI5's K5 section, with its mixture of MI5 and MI6 officers with close ties to the CIA, there was a small 'Wilson coterie' who continued to harrass Wilson and his friends and colleagues with buggings and general surveillance.[10]

In the next chapters we describe the work of 'the boys' and the other extraordinary incidents in the campaign to bring the Labour Government down.

XXXVI

THE 'COMMUNIST CELL' IN NO. 10

There was a Communist cell right there in the middle of Downing Street.
GENERAL SIR WALTER WALKER

THE FIRST MAJOR TARGET following the February election was Marcia Williams. Around the fact that she was the unmarried mother of two children a web of disinformation was constructed: that she had not been positively vetted; that she had refused to be positively vetted; that she was a security risk; that she had access to documents for which she was not cleared; that the strain of keeping all this secret had contributed to the death of Wilson's Principal Private Secretary, Michael Halls; and, finally, that she was part of a 'communist cell' in No. 10.

As part of this campaign 'one or two [Conservative] backbenchers had already been alerted to ask pointed parliamentary questions'. The first of these was by Wyn Roberts, Conservative MP for Conway and Shadow spokesman on Wales. On 9 April 1974, after a question about the new No. 10 political unit set up under Bernard Donoghue, Roberts asked a supplementary question of Wilson: 'Are all members of the unit paid from public funds? Is this bill justified in view of the party political nature of their work? Have they all been positively vetted? How many members of the Prime Minister's personal political staff at Downing Street are not members of this unit, and have they been positively vetted? Wilson replied: 'Regarding vetting, in 1964 I introduced the requirement that all members of the Prime Minister's staff, whether paid from public funds or not, must be positively vetted.'[1]

Douglas Hurd, who had been Edward Heath's political secretary until becoming an MP at the February 1974 election, returned to this question again a month later on 6 May 1974. Hurd asked the Minister for the Civil Service, Robert Sheldon, 'in which Departments political advisers appointed since 1st March 1974 have so far completed the security vetting procedures appropriate to their function.' Sheldon's reply was that 'the appropriate procedures are being followed in each case'. Hurd's supplementary was more pointed. 'The hon. Gentleman will know that this Question was transferred to him by the Prime

Minister. May we have an assurance covering No. 10 Downing Street . . . that in no case do political advisers have access to highly classified papers or highly classified information until the appropriate procedures are satisfactorily completed?' Sheldon would not be drawn further, merely restating his previous answer. Asked about his questions, Hurd said that he was 'just putting down a marker'. As he was very close to Edward Heath, Hurd's role is further evidence of the involvement of the leadership in the campaign.[2]

As Pincher noted, the questions were 'damp squibs' and 'nothing much happened until May'. Then he went to lunch at a country house in Hampshire on 7 May. 'There were several people there I knew well, including a former senior figure from the Defence Ministry' (Sir Derek Rayner). After lunch Pincher talked of the forthcoming Tory campaign: 'gossip about Wilson and Marcia . . . the affair of the land deals . . . how Tory back-benchers would be trying to accuse Wilson of misleading the House during his defence of Marcia's brother . . . the allegations concerning Marcia's security clearance and how these might become public through a court action being brought by a certain Mrs Marjorie Halls, the widow of Michael Halls, Wilson's former Principal Private Secretary in Number 10. In this connection I also mentioned that Marcia's children would also be mentioned if the case came to court because Mrs Halls was claiming that the efforts involved in concealing them and other matters concerned with them had contributed to her husband's early death from a heart attack.' Unfortunately for Pincher, one of the guests, the historian Martin Gilbert, did not regard Pincher's political gossip as lightly as he himself apparently did. Gilbert wrote to Heath and Wilson giving them the details of what Pincher had said.[3]

The alleged non-vetting of Mrs Williams provides an interesting illustration of the spread and survival of what was, at the time, a completely false allegation. What precisely was the allegation? In Pincher's version it was 'an alleged account of how Halls and other civil servants had been required to issue some sort of waiver over Marcia's second positive vetting in 1969 when she was scared of having to reveal the existence of the children to the security people.' Or was the waiver issued in 1974? 'Mrs Marcia Williams, refused to be positively vetted in 1974. Wilson signed some sort of waiver for her . . . she had been positively vetted in 1964 and 1969.' Same story in the same words – 'some sort of waiver' – but located five years apart.[4]

Joe Haines, Wilson's press officer at the time, states flatly that Mrs Williams refused 'to be positively vetted by the security forces, which was a total and inescapable obligation on everyone who worked in Downing Street.' Although we cannot refute this, it is profoundly implausible, precisely because being vetted was, as Haines says, 'a total and inescapable obligation'. Nor is the story internally consistent. Mrs Williams' 'refusal' was, presumably, because of her two children. But this was no secret by 1974: the birth certificates had been widely distributed. What difference would being vetted make? Finally, the most telling argument against this story is the simple fact that, had it been true, the allegation against Mrs Williams would surely not have been confined, as it was, to rumours and the columns of *Private Eye*. Had there been any evidence, it would have surfaced, and none did.[5]

All we know for sure is that at the time of the original rumours, April/May 1974, the allegation was completely false. Robert Armstrong, the Principal Private Secretary at No. 10, had written to Mrs Williams on 1 May about her vetting, only five days before the fateful Pincher lunch: 'I had been intending to have a word with you about your own position. Your positive vetting ought to be reviewed sometime! But there is no tearing hurry. It is less than five years since the last review. So I thought it would wait until you were back.' Five years was the standard period between reviews, and if the first presumably happened just after the 1964 October election, then October/November 1969 and October/November 1974 would be the five-yearly cycle.[6]

The origins of this nonsense lay in claims made by the widow of Michael Halls, Wilson's Principal Private Secretary. As Wilson's PPS, Halls liaised with the Cabinet Office on security issues, and was friendly with a number of MI5 officers, colleagues of Peter Wright. It appears that MI5 were courting Halls, presumably in the hope of inside information on Wilson and his circle. Since Halls had died in 1970, the story about the 'vetting waiver' attributed to him must be 1969; and this in turn is contradicted by the Armstrong memo of 1974. In 1972 Mrs Halls began two years of fruitless correspondence with the British state, right up to the level of Prime Minister, claiming compensation for the death of her husband, caused, in part, she alleged, by the strain of working at No. 10. When Mrs Halls' claims were finally rejected in 1974, her correspondence with the state – which included her account of her husband's allegations – was given to Chapman Pincher and *Private Eye*. The *Eye* ran large extracts on 4 October 1974. It was Mrs Halls who produced the initial core allegation, that her husband 'regarded [Mrs Williams] as a potential security risk because of her children, and wanted her to be forced to resign.'[7]

The status of Mrs Halls' other claims about her husband's allegations is impossible to evaluate. It is, however, worth noting that in November 1970, just after Halls' death, Cecil King noted in his diary (13 November): 'Lunch yesterday with Baylis of the Stationery Office . . . a friend of his was one Hall [sic], Wilson's Principal Private Secretary, who died recently at an early age. Hall told Baylis that you could not have a nicer boss to work for than Wilson. Baylis said that Hall was very appreciative of his position as the Prime Minister's Principal Private Secretary, but even allowing for that fact, he was loud in Wilson's praises as a most considerate chief.'[8]

As we have seen, the 'communist cell' nonsense began in 1971 after MI5 'discovered' that Joseph Kagan, a fringe member of Wilson's social circle, knew a KGB officer in London called Vaygauskas. Into this fantasy Mrs Williams' two children were incorporated. First, the *fact* of Mrs Williams' two children became the *fiction* that she had not been vetted. Although she had been vetted, certainly up to late 1974, Michael Halls' belief that she should have failed her vetting because of her children, became the false assertion that she had not been vetted in 1969, that Wilson had issued some sort of 'waiver'. The putative reason for Mrs Williams' sensitivity about her vetting was then changed from 'because she wanted to conceal the existence of her two children' to 'because she was a communist agent', part of the 'communist cell' in No. 10.

Having constructed the fantasy 'communist cell', MI5 could populate it. One member so identified was Judith Hart MP. A Bevanite in the 1950s, a member of the Movement for Colonial Freedom and CND, she was also briefly a member of CND's direct action off-shoot, the Committee of 100, which was under surveillance by Special Branch. She had been one of the group of Labour MPs, led by George Wigg, who had campaigned for Wilson in the 1963 leadership contest after Gaitskell's death. Politically slightly to the left of Barbara Castle, she had been made a Privy Councillor in 1967 and had served as Paymaster-General in the second Wilson Government, after the departure of Wigg, without apparently attracting the attentions of MI5.

Hart became of interest to the British secret state after the February 1974 election through her involvement in the debate within the Party about British relations with Chile, an issue which divided the Cabinet and gave the secret state the pretext to investigate and attack some of its more left-wing members. Chile produced within the Parliamentary Labour Party a classic argument of morality and international solidarity versus expediency. During the Heath regime, Chile had placed various military contracts with British companies. Taking office in February 1974, the Labour Cabinet inherited the partially completed Chilean orders which the left of the PLP wanted cancelled. Among government ministers this position was taken by Eric Heffer, then a junior minister under Tony Benn, Judith Hart and Benn himself.

Chile was a very delicate issue for the Labour Cabinet. The Labour Party had approved of the social democratic Allende regime. In 1972, for example, Eric Heffer had visited Chile, taking with him a message for President Allende from Wilson. The overthrow of the Allende regime by the Chilean military, with support from the CIA, outraged most of the Parliamentary Labour Party; and the idea of delivering weapons systems to the brutal regime of General Pinochet was wholly unacceptable to the left wing. On the other hand, British jobs might be lost if the Chilean orders were cancelled. Despite being a junior minister and formally bound by the convention of Cabinet collective responsibility, Eric Heffer delivered a speech critical of the Government's position on the ships for Chile. Judith Hart was considering supporting Heffer and resigning if he got sacked by Wilson.[9]

As usual the Foreign Office and the secret state were cheer-leading US foreign policy and those who opposed their line within the Government became 'enemies'. MI6 Chief Maurice Oldfield had seen Wilson soon after the February election and asked him to withhold 'top-secret information from certain Ministers'. This was on 'security grounds because of the fear that their gossip with left-wing friends might betray sources'. This was a reference to 'communist' friends. Oldfield made sure that the warning was leaked through his MI6 conduits, George Young and Bruce McKenzie. A major part of the US Government's rationale for the overthrow of Allende was the standard line about 'preventing communism', and the permanent government briefings on the issue tried to link opposition to the Pinochet dictatorship to 'communism'. At the Cabinet's Overseas Policy and Defence Committee, Foreign Secretary Callaghan linked opposition to the Chile deal to the Communist Party line: 'It would be a victory for the British Communist Party if these overhauls were stopped.' A fortnight later in Cabinet, he argued that fulfilling the contract was 'a political matter. The Communists were in favour of stopping supplies.'[10]

We have no evidence that Callaghan was getting the communist 'line' from official briefings. However, on 15 July, Benn discussed the left with him and found that 'he knows nothing about the Left at all. Never heard of the ultras, never realised that the Trotskyites were critical of Jack Jones and Hugh Scanlon, of Michael Foot, myself and Eric Heffer as "fake" Left. He simply knew nothing about it.' From which we infer that Callaghan would not know the CPGB line on anything without being briefed on it; and as Foreign Secretary he would receive intelligence briefings from all sectors of the secret state, including MI5. Just two days before that Cabinet meeting, Benn spotted a Walter Terry article in the *Daily Express* 'suggesting that Michael Foot and myself, Judith, Joan Lester, Ian Mikardo and Hugh Scanlon were really trying to work towards an Allende-type Marxist Government in Britain'. As we have seen, Oldfield had been leaking similar information to Pincher, someone the MI6 Chief regarded as 'a contact who could be used to plant leaks'.[11]

In the House of Lords debate on Subversive and Extremist Elements in February 1975, discussed below, Lord Clifford of Chudleigh referred to 'this country being used as a sort of temporary headquarters of Marxist International', citing the example of 'the Chilean Communist Louis Figerra [who] set up a "surgery" for British trade unionists in Transport House on the 7th January which must have official blessing.' Pincher later suggested that the source of the pressure on this area was America: 'The links between some left-wing Labour MPs and foreign revolutionaries like Chilean Marxists, not only allowed to settle in Britain but encouraged to do so, have been investigated by the CIA.'[12]

To back up this communist 'spin' to opposition to the Pinochet Government, the secret state needed evidence. Unwittingly Judith Hart obliged. In search of information on the fate of the left in Chile, not only did she telephone Chile – where her calls would be routinely intercepted by the NSA – she also called the King Street headquarters of the British Communist Party. According to David Leigh, 'MI5's "A" branch were, as usual, tapping the party's phones. The transcript of Hart's innocent contact was excitedly circulated within MI5, and throughout Whitehall.' This contact with King Street would have been added to her earlier 3 March speech at the anniversary celebrations of the Communist Party's newspaper, the *Morning Star*. MI5's assiduous newspaper clippers in F Branch would have spotted the report in the *Morning Star*.[13]

With this exciting double 'trace' MI5 went through their files and found another Mrs Hart with a Communist history. Armed with this 'evidence' MI5 Director-General Michael Hanley went to see Wilson and told him that Mrs Hart might be a security risk. He referred to her calls to Chile, told him that one of her sons was in the Communist Party and 'claimed that there was evidence which might also show that Hart had attended a Communist-backed international peace conference in Warsaw in 1950. Underlying this, it eventually transpired was a 24-year-old blurred photograph from the *Daily Worker*, captioning among others a Mrs Tudor Hart, the wife of a prominent Communist

Party member.' As a result, shortly before the summer recess in 1974, Mrs Hart was summoned to see Wilson. 'In the course of the meeting, Harold Wilson let it be known in a roundabout manner that there was a problem over her security clearance . . . He asked her if she had ever been to Warsaw, and Mrs Hart replied that, apart from a camping holiday in Yugoslavia and one visit to the Soviet Union with a Parliamentary group, she had not travelled to Eastern Europe at all.'[14]

According to Marcia Wiliams this was all the result of a 'truly extraordinary coincidence . . . Security had got hold of the wrong Judith Hart – the other Judith Hart was a lady who not only had the same name but whose career had been similar. More than that, the "wrong" Mrs Hart was married to a man who bore the same Christian name as Judith's own husband!' On this, Mrs Williams gives MI5 more credit than they deserve. The two women did not share the same name; nor did their husbands. One was called Dr Alex Tudor Hart; Judith Hart's husband was Anthony (Tony) Bernard Hart and, despite being a leading member of CND, was a nuclear physicist, at the time working as an Admiralty research scientist. Nor was it a 'mistake' by MI5. This nonsense had started in 1950 when Judith Hart was a Labour parliamentary candidate for Bournemouth West. A Special Branch officer had asked the full-time Labour Party agent in Poole, Freddy Reeves, if Judith Hart had been in Warsaw to attend an international peace conference. Reeves was shown a photograph of a young woman in a copy of the *Daily Worker* of 14 November 1950. There was nothing at all to suggest that this woman was Judith Hart. The actual caption to the photograph read '24-year-old Mrs Tudor Hart, who had accompanied the baton by motorcycle from Dover, seen placing a wreath on the Sheffield War memorial.' She was not named as 'J. or Judith Tudor Hart'; Judith Hart at the time was 26, not 24; and the photograph of a woman almost completely concealed in a leather overcoat, was too indistinct to identify anyone.[15]

According to the *Sunday Times*' Insight team there had been an almighty row between Hanley and Wilson over Hart. 'It seems to have been a foreign agent who sparked the row. On 24 April 1974, Gunter Guillaume, special assistant to the West German Chancellor, Willy Brandt, was arrested as a East German spy. On 6 May, Brandt, a friend of Wilson and a fellow social democrat, resigned ostensibly as a result of revelations about Guillaume. There was no evidence that, in his subsequent interrogation, Guillaume said anything that pointed to Britain. However, 'one high political source in London does maintain that it was in some fashion because of Guillaume that in July, 1974, Hanley presented Wilson with the suspicion that in the early 1950's Judith Hart had been closer that she had admitted to the Communists.'[16]

Brandt was brought down in a plot which involved West German intelligence, MI5 and the CIA, mostly because of his sympathetic attitude towards the East. Peter Wright and James Angleton played roles in his downfall. A refugee from East Germany, Guillaume, who had long been regarded as a security risk, was allowed to stay on Brandt's personal staff 'while inquiries were made, but was to be excluded from access to secret material'. This proved to be a mistake on Brandt's part because the German security service made it appear that the

Chancellor had allowed a security risk access to secret material. At the same time, stories were leaked about Brandt's private life. Brandt later denied he had been subject to blackmail by Guillaume and protested that a smear campaign had been set in motion against him, a notion which official inquiries seemed to endorse.[17]

The similarities with Wilson's problems over Hart are striking. The more Wilson defended his minister, the more 'evidence' MI5 produced. Wilson 'had strong suspicions that there had been a serious error somewhere' but he was in a classic MI5 bind. If he rejected Hanley's case outright he would be accused, as he was with John Stonehouse, of protecting a security risk. So he 'gave instructions that further security checks were to be made on Judith Hart. In the meantime he would take the responsibility of allowing her to carry on as Minister'. In effect, Hart was allowed to 'dangle' with the attendant risk that MI5 would return with another 'trace'. All that then would be required would be a leak that Wilson was protecting Hart as part of the 'Communist cell at No. 10'.[18]

Mrs Hart heard nothing further on the subject during the summer parliamentary recess. Then on the 17 October Wilson sent for her. He told her, 'I can't appoint you back to your Department because I understand you have Communist connections.' Denying that she had been a Communist she did admit she had rung CPGB Secretary John Gollan to cancel an appearance at a Chile meeting – because she would have shared the bill with Jimmy Reid, a Communist! To which Wilson remarked, 'Oh, that's getting nearer the mark.' At which point Hart went back to her office to await a decision. Harold no doubt went back to MI5. At six o'clock Wilson rang to say that 'it was all right'. Later that evening Barbara Castle met her. 'The very idea that anyone could consider her a communist! It was all no doubt to do with her contacts in Chile. Didn't the fools realise there were even more non-communists in gaol than communists? Harold had accepted her assurances, but she was clearly shaken to the core.'[19]

Wilson had indeed accepted her assurances and she did remain as the Minister for Overseas Development, but he had been forced to do a deal with MI5. He had agreed that despite being a member of the Privy Council, she should be positively vetted – a wonderful opportunity for MI5 legitimately to trawl through the Labour Party left-wing. Mrs Hart was also forbidden to travel abroad. This was the restriction placed on John Stonehouse and it indicated that MI5 believed – or pretended to believe – that she might defect, a public mark of her unreliability in their eyes. Thus it transpired that 'in the summer of 1974 London was awash with untrue rumours that Judith Hart was part of the "Communist cell"; and thus the reason for Mrs Hart's statement in the House of Lords debate on Peter Wright in 1988: 'I am one of those who know that the allegations in his book are true.'[20]

XXXVII

CLOCKWORK ORANGE

*When MI5 took over, people like myself, steady regimental officers with a
sense of right and wrong, were replaced by these MI5 characters . . . the
decent people were replaced by very ambitious, mean, nasty people.*
CAPTAIN FRED HOLROYD

IN 1974 WILSON and Merlyn Rees inherited not an agreed, bi-partisan policy
on Northern Ireland with a united state apparatus, but a state machine wracked
not only with the normal bureaucratic 'turf' wars, but split along ideological
lines: wet/dry, hard/soft, destroy/negotiate. Rees, the new Labour Secretary of
State for Northern Ireland, had an inkling of this. During his 'first days in the
province' as Secretary of State, he talked to the General Officer Commanding
Northern Ireland, Frank King, and told him of his 'concern about army
information policy: there has been too much talk in the press of division between
the politicians and the security forces in the days of my predecessors'. The
conversation had no effect. Where the Army's criticisms of the Conservative
Government had been muted, with a Labour Government there were fewer
political or tribal inhibitions. Almost from day one the Army press office at
Lisburn began rubbishing every policy initiative Rees and Wilson came up with:
Rees records the first leak against him from Lisburn only weeks after taking over
and his account is littered with others.[1]

Most important of all Labour inherited the Heath administration's attempt to
set up a non-sectarian government in the province, the so-called Power-Sharing
Executive which had taken office on 1 January 1974 despite the opposition of a
large majority of the Protestant community. The Ulster Protestants had never
accepted the Power-Sharing Executive as legitimate and, three months after
Labour took office, an alliance of Protestant groups calling itself the United
Ulster Unionist Council set up the Ulster Workers' Council (UWC), which duly
announced a general strike, starting on 15 May, which would last until the
Executive fell. In under three weeks the strike had succeeded and the Power-
Sharing Executive had collapsed. At the time there was little critical thought
about how such a remarkable coup had been possible. Only in Robert Fisk's

256

book on the strike a year later was the awkward question asked: what was the British Army actually doing during the strike? Reading between the lines of Fisk's account it was clear that it had tacitly condoned it.[2]

Ten years later Colin Wallace, in Information Policy during the strike, revealed that the Labour Government had been fed with misleading information on the progress of the strike by the Army and civil servants, and that MI5 wanted it to succeed. Wallace's appearance in the British media in 1987 encouraged one James Miller to break cover. Miller had been an MI5 agent inside the Ulster Defence Association, rising to become the UDA's 'intelligence officer'. He told the *Sunday Times'* Barrie Penrose that his MI5 'handlers' instructed him to push the idea of a strike within the UDA.[3]

Despite the fact that no Soviet official of any kind had ever been reported in Northern Ireland, the anti-subversion tendency could not resist the temptation to portray the Northern Irish war as an example of Moscow's 'hidden hand'. The Heath Government's 'surrender' to the unions and the talks with the Provos were seen as aspects of a wider 'subversive' thrust blamed on Moscow's machinations. The resident top MI5 officer at Lisburn, Denis Payne, would give visiting American journalists such as John Barron the standard line of KGB control of the IRA. James Miller's MI5 bosses told him that Wilson was a Soviet agent. The major responsibility for propagating this 'line' was given to the Army Press Office in Lisburn – and the Information Policy unit operating under cover of it. All the strands of the anti-subversion tendency converged on to Information Policy. Between the elections of 1974 the unit became the recipient of the full range of MI5's theories about the subversives, the enemies of law and order – and the 'evidence' they had fabricated to support them. With this material Colin Wallace was instructed to prepare a psychological warfare project code-named 'Clockwork Orange' against the 'enemies within'.[4]

The material which Colin Wallace preserved from his days in Information Policy constitutes the biggest insight into the operations of the secret state ever offered. The revelations of the other MI5 whistle-blowers of the eighties, Cathy Massiter and Peter Wright, though interesting and important, remain merely allegations. The notes Wallace made from the MI5 material, drafts of projects he worked on, and the forgeries supplied by MI5, are primary evidence. Unable to refute this evidence, the secret state had no choice but to try to discredit Wallace in the hope that this would discourage journalists from taking his evidence seriously.[5]

The Wallace material was a snapshot of the operations of 1974 – targets, smears, methods. The story which has emerged since, which has been described in this book, is there in outline. The Wallace material showed that MI5's conception of the state's 'enemies' had extended far beyond the confines of the Labour left and the trade unions, let alone 'the communists' – or even the 'communist cell' in No. 10. The notes showed that MI5 – at any rate the section of MI5 which was providing the information – was not only beyond political control, it was wholly detached from the political system. As Harold Wilson put it in 1987, 'they thought they ran the whole show under the Crown'. Everybody from the Liberal Party leftwards, every sector of the body politic which did not share MI5's fantasies of the subversive menace, was incorporated into that menace: either for us, or against us.

Wallace's notes were hand-written summaries he made of the material supplied by MI5's F Branch between the elections of 1974. Over 70 MPs from all three major political parties were mentioned, most of them in derogatory contexts. The central theme is that the Labour Party in 1974 was under the influence of the Soviet Union: 'It is estimated that between 20 and 30 Labour MPs are members of the Communist Party'. Wallace refers to 'Civil unrest, political violence and industrial disputes in Britain engineered by the Soviet Union through Labour Party activists and left-wing organisations', and concludes that behind the Labour Party's lack of 'moral courage in dealing with the unrest' in Ireland must lie 'deep-rooted causes' – namely, the desire of the Labour Party to see a 'Red Shamrock Irish Workers' Republic'.

The first disinformation project was a document which purported to be a synopsis of a 'confession' made by a senior member of the Provisional IRA, who had become disillusioned by the violence and wished to emigrate to Australia. Part of the confession dealt with meetings between the Provos and Harold Wilson, which took place in Dublin during a cease-fire in 1972. 'The meeting in itself was a dead loss except that evening Wilson was interviewed on RTE and described us as a well-disciplined, tightly-knit force. This was just the boost that our morale needed.' The confession from this non-existent IRA 'defector' was to be released in 1974 with the aim of demonstrating that Wilson had encouraged the Provos to end their cease-fire and to discredit Merlyn Rees' current talks with Sinn Fein and Loyalist paramilitaries. The document was shown to *Sunday People* journalist Len Adams and Gerald Bartlett at the *Daily Telegraph*. The timing was crucial. Bartlett saw the Clockwork Orange document on 10 February 1974, just before the General Election. It was released again in the middle of the October election.[6]

Wallace's notes listed Labour MPs 'who are believed to be communists and who hold positions of influence': Tony Benn, Ian Mikardo, David Owen, Eric Heffer, Judith Hart, Tom Driberg, Barbara Castle, Michael Foot and John Stonehouse. Wilson was at the centre of this, he 'can be shown to be under Soviet control through Dick Vasgauskas', '[he] received approximately £60,000 from East German sources for campaign funds', 'has a friend in the Soviet government', is 'pro Israel' (as well as being pro-Soviet!), 'bowed to the pressure [of the Communist Party members who are MPs] by removing the embargo on CP membership for members of the Labour Party'; was a 'close confidant' of Will Owen MP and 'shielded John Stonehouse'. Also included are many individual allegations, of which the most striking are:

– that Marica Williams refused to be positively vetted;
– that Gaitskell was murdered by the KGB;
– that Edward Heath and Jeremy Thorpe were homosexuals.[7]

MI5 clearly thought that politics was too important to be left to the politicians. Indeed, if the discussion in the notes about whether or not 'they' should embark on 'cosmetic or major surgery' to the leadership of the Tory Party, 'they' seemed to believe that they could control the direction taken by British politics. We quote the key points from Wallace's notes to show how the covert political agenda we have reconstructed from other sources was passed over wholesale to him in mid-1974. Wallace's testimony and these notes and forgeries in particular are the most important evidence that survived the 1970s operations.[8]

XXXVIII

EDWARD SHORT

A senior Callaghan aide told him [Paddy Ashdown] that all politicians were tainted by scandals involving money, sex or drugs – except Jim and Ted Heath. 'What about Jeremy Thorpe?' the young diplomat asked. The aide laughed.

PADDY ASHDOWN

IN MID-JULY 1974 MPs Cyril Smith, James Prior and Eddie Milne, as well as *Private Eye*, the *Daily Mail*, *Time Out*, *Socialist Worker* and Chapman Pincher at the *Daily Express*, all received a photocopy of a bank statement in the name of Edward W. Short, Account No. 312'596 of the Swiss Bank Corporation of Zurich, giving his correct home address. The account was in credit by 163,000 Swiss francs, about £23,000. Pincher immediately sent a copy to Short, then Leader of the House of Commons, who passed it on to the Attorney General; the police were called in to investigate.

In retrospect it is obvious that if anyone on the Labour benches was going to be the victim of a financial smear it would be Edward Short. In the preceding year allegations about his relationship with T. Dan Smith, the business partner of the corrupt architect John Poulson, had emerged intermittently, part of the fall-out from the exposure of the Poulson–Smith relationship. Short had known Smith since the 1930s, and, like Smith, had been leader of the Labour group on Newcastle City Council.[1]

In 1971 T. Dan Smith was found not guilty of corruption involving Wandsworth Council. From then on the corrupt practices of Poulson and Smith began to unravel – and with them the Smith–Short relationship. In psychological warfare terms, Poulson's dealings with a number of Labour local authorities was a gold mine. The first psychological operations use of the relationship was made in 1973 when a forged document was circulated by a clerk at Scotland Yard. It appeared to be an official letter to the Director of Public Prosecutions from the police recommending prosecution of a number of named Labour MPs in connection with Poulson. The document, which named 4 MPs, Ernest Armstrong, Ted Leadbiter, Fred Willey and Roy Mason – received wide publicity,

260

though no names were published at the time for fear of libel. In the summer of 1974 the Scotland Yard man responsible was exposed, though not prosecuted. He retired quietly to Sussex. Only *Socialist Worker* took up this part of the story, made inquiries into his background or his reasons for forging the document.[2]

The first public hint of the Smith–Short connection came in May 1973 when the Young Liberals said that Short had been 'up to his neck' in it and *Private Eye* printed details of Short's (largely unsuccessful) attempt to raise money for Smith when he was facing trial in 1970. Short extracted an apology from the Liberals and told the press that he had never had a business relationship with Smith and denied the fund-raising. Unfortunately for Short, he had revealed details of the fund-raising to friends, word of which reached Smith, who felt 'Short had betrayed a vital confidence'. After Smith revealed the Short connection on the BBC, it was reported in the press on 27 April 1974.[3]

At Smith's trial, begun in late 1973 on charges of conspiracy to corrupt, details of his financial relationship with Short emerged. Most damaging was correspondence from 1963 in which Short, on House of Commons notepaper, acknowledged 'a retainer of £500' from Smith. At his trial Smith said the money had been delivered, in cash, to the Minister's home address; the cash entry was in Smith's books. Short rejected Smith's story. 'At no time was I ever employed by Mr Smith or under any obligation to him. Nor do I believe he ever regarded himself as employing me.' In the view of Ray Fitzwalter, who first uncovered the Poulson Affair, at the minimum 'Short displayed a surprising naivety'. What made the Government's embarrassment over the affair particularly acute was the fact that Short, as Leader of the House of Commons, was then responsible for steering through the Commons legislation introducing the new register of members' interests.[4]

By the beginning of May the Short affair had become front-page news – the *Daily Express* printed the text of the Smith–Short letters from 1963 – and there were allegations of a cover-up, a Watergate-on-Tyne. Wilson counter-attacked, on 2 May accusing Tory newspapers of conducting a smear campaign against Ted Short and announced the setting-up of a Royal Commission on the Press. It was against this background that the forged Swiss bank statement was sent out.

One recipient of the forgery was Eddie Milne, MP for Blyth, whose copy had been left in his House of Commons pigeon-hole in a Commons envelope. Milne was engaged in a long battle with the then spectacularly corrupt North East Labour Party. He had tried to get an inquiry into the links between Poulson and the North East Labour Party but had been frustrated by what he saw as the blocking efforts of the Chief Whip, Robert Mellish, and the Leader of the House, Ted Short. Milne's campaign led to him being removed as the official Labour candidate for Blyth; and in the February 1974 election, standing as Independent Labour, he had achieved the rare feat of defeating the official Labour candidate. Milne had been a good choice as recipient of the forgery. Immediately convinced of the bank statement's authenticity, he went straight to the press. His unpaid research assistant, Ronald Heisler, was less certain, and took a copy of it to a contact at the *Daily Express* for a second opinion. He saw the assistant editor, Paul Hopkins, who had been covering the Poulson–Short affair and who had excellent police contacts. There, Heisler claims, he discovered that Hopkins was unimpressed by the Short forgery: he had already seen the bank statement; a Conservative MP 'had been at the *Express* offices the night before with it'. Hopkins later recalled Heisler's visit but had 'no recollection' of whether the MP was involved.[5]

Both Heisler and Milne were seen by Commander Morrison of the Metropolitan Police, the officer in charge of the investigation, and they told him about the episode involving the MP. To Heisler's surprise, 'the hitherto urbane, even bland Commander Morrison became quite adamant that there was no truth in this story. I persisted in pressing the point, but he brushed it aside, evidently eager to change the subject.'[6]

The *Sunday Express* editorialised at the end of the first week of the forgery story: '[Mr Short] talks of the operation of "one or more dirty tricks departments", of attempts to implicate other senior politicians in engineered scandals. What exactly is Mr Short saying? Whom can he be accusing? Is he suggesting that the Tories may be implicated? . . . Was it a total forgery conceived in a deliberate attempt to smear Labour's deputy leader, Mr Edward Short, and so harm his party's propects at the next General Election? Or does such an account really exist in someone else's name? And if so, whose account is it?' After Wilson described the forgery as 'a characteristic product of the Dirty Tricks Department', Norman Tebbit and George Gardiner, both members of the then still secret 92 Group on the Tory right, led the counter-attack: Gardiner suggested that 'Mr Short had been the victim of a practical joke'.[7]

Commander Morrison went to Zurich at the end of July where he was shown proof of the forgery. The forgery included information which led to two different genuine accounts, one belonging to a Swiss couple, the other to Mr Laurie Crookall, a retired architect living in Northampton. Commander Morrison was told in Zurich that a small reference number on the account statement pointed to Crookall. Police visited and interrogated him on a number of occasions and he repeated his innocence. Crookall was a trade union activist who made no secret of the fact that he had recently joined the Communist Party. Crookall told police that he had worked for the Colonial Government in Aden and Ghana and on leaving Aden in 1967 kept about £3,000 in a Swiss acount to avoid British exchange control problems. For a time suspicion fell on a student who was a member of the International Socialists who visited Crookall. Crookall said that he had left documents around the house which might have been taken. But these leads to the further left were all specious – how would a student IS member get hold of Swiss bank records?[8]

Although in an interview with Commander Morrison on 23 July 1974 Short initially suggested Milne, Heisler and a left group called the Chartist as possible perpetrators of the forgery, he came to believe that the police investigation had been halted because it was known that the forgery was the work of MI5. Although the police took the investigation of the account as far as they could, and were apparently happy to hunt for a left culprit, they did not appear to want to look elsewhere.[9]

With the *Spycatcher* revelations of MI5 operations, Short became certain that

MI5 had been responsible. 'I have no doubt the burglaries at my flat were the work of MI5.' In 1987, his suspicions appeared to have been vindicated. 'Nigel West', Tory MP Rupert Allason, with excellent MI5 sources, asserted that 'this particular incident, one of several involving the leakage of politically sensitive material, came from within K Branch' – home of some of the officers whom Peter Wright had been talking to about removing Wilson. However, within a year Allason had recanted on the Short forgery. During the debates on the Official Secrets bill in 1988, he announced that responsibility for the forgery had 'come down to a group of Socialist Workers in Leicester . . . and the tale of a conspiracy against the Labour Government was sheer fantasy.' 'A group of Socialist Workers in Leicester' appears nowhere in the account of the police investigation supplied to Dale Campbell-Savours MP in 1987 by the Metropolitan Police. The 'fantasy' is Allason's.[10]

Although there is still no proof of MI5's involvement, Colin Wallace's collection of other MI5 forgeries from this period, including a forged bank statement for the Reverend Ian Paisley, make it as close to a certainty as we will come, short of a confession by one of the forgers, that MI5 were the culprits. As *The Times* pointed out in an editorial, having used parts of genuine accounts to make up the forgery, 'the forger must have known that the truth would be established'. It seems an improbable coincidence that one of the genuine accounts revealed turned out to be a member of the Communist Party. It is surely more likely that this was the intention. In the early seventies the Inland Revenue had purchased a list of UK holders of Swiss bank accounts. The most plausible solution appears to be that when the list of Swiss account holders was compared with a list of Communist Party members, the unfortunate Mr Crookall popped up. Then when the forgery was exposed, to add to the initial smear on Short, a 'communist connection' would be exposed and attention diverted from the real forgers.[11]

Because of his prior relationship with T. Dan Smith, Short was a sitting duck for those planning the anti-Labour campaign. The 'Short forgery' was a brilliantly successful smear: for although it was fairly quickly revealed as a forgery – as its perpetrators knew it would – it generated massive headlines in which the important message perceived by the electorate was Short–Labour–crook.

XXXIX

'THE APPREHENSIVE PATRIOTS'

We know the intention of the left-wing activists is to cause chaos.
DAVID STIRLING

Unison is . . . an anti-chaos organisation.
GEORGE KENNEDY YOUNG

MIDWAY BETWEEN the two elections of 1974 occurred what became known as the 'private armies' episode. Its origins lie in the 1972 miners' strike and subsequent rumblings of discontent within the British military which found their way into the columns of *The Times* that year. In late 1973 two complementary movements began: one was press speculation about the possibility of some kind of military coup, which began with Patrick Cosgrave in the *Spectator* in December 1973 and continued later in 1974; the other was the formation of voluntary organisations led by former military and intelligence personnel. The first of these 'private' moves seem to have been made more or less simultaneously in 1973 by a retired soldier called Alexander Greenwood and the late George Kennedy Young. Greenwood began forming an organisation called Red Alert and Young set up the Unison Committee for Action, the 'wider action' he had referred to the previous year in his letter to Bee Carthew.[1]

By 1974 Major Greenwood claimed to have 900 'security vetted' members, who would 'come into action if there was a situation in which no parliamentary government was left . . . the Services would move in to maintain vital services [and] we would be able to come to their assistance'. Red Alert was apparently concentrating on overcoming an anticipated break-down in the telephone system and was later absorbed into Civil Assistance (see below).[2]

Unison was created in 1973 after a group led by George Kennedy Young tried and failed to take over the Royal Society of St George, which one of this group described to the authors as a 'patriotic organisation that wasn't doing anything'. Among the group's members were Young, Anthony Cavendish and Admiral Sir Ian Hogg, the latter later joining Unison. Interestingly, Wilson later expressed his concerns about the Society to Chapman Pincher, presumably because of the presence of Young. Little is known of what Unison was doing during its early months, or, indeed, who were its members. On 1 February 1974, news of the group's existence – though not its name – was leaked by Young through Pincher who told *Express* readers that 'a formidable vigilante group to help protect the nation against a Communist takeover has been quietly organised by former Service chiefs, senior ex-members of the Secret Service and MI5.' The name and personnel would have to remain secret if only because at that time Young was the Conservative Parliamentary candidate in Brent East. According to one member, Unison was set up on the basis of a Special Operations Executive network, 'in the event of unrest'; a type of communications network.[3]

Running roughly parallel to Unison, David Stirling was organising Great Britain 1975 (GB 75). On 24 May he sent out his first 'Round Robin' describing the organisation and its aims. The memo revealed a project – 'a Central Executive committee and a small Central Administrative Bureau are being established in London (working from this office), employing two qualified individuals as paid administrative officers . . . finance is already available' – rather than a functioning organisation. GB 75 was merely one part of a grandiose project whose aim was to regenerate British democracy, defeat the forces of the totalitarian left within and without the Parliamentary Labour Party and reverse Britain's economic decline.[4]

Little attention was paid to the wider aims, however, and attention was focused on GB 75's proposed strike-breaking role. At the outset Stirling was disassociating himself from 'the extreme right-wing and neo-fascists already appearing on the scene' – presumably a reference to Unison. His organisation, he said, must 'give teeth and credibility to the centre'.[5]

He died in 1990 just as we had begun corresponding with him. However, in a letter to us dated 18 October 1990 he wrote: 'I never talked to Young as I thought he was a neo-fascist and did not trust him.' Within the Parliamentary Labour Party he rather comically identified the totalitarian menace as being the Tribune Group!

On 25 June, in Martin Walker's *Guardian* 'Open File', the column in which this corner of British politics was glimpsed most often, Stirling gave vent to his analysis of the political situation – but did not reveal the existence of his organisation. After a weekend in which both Sir Douglas Allen, head of the Treasury and Reginald Maudling had voiced concerns about the survival of Parliamentary democracy, David Stirling told Walker that he 'was approached very informally by some individuals recently who are very concerned about the appalling damage a major strike could do, interruptions of vital services like power, sewage and so on. It was the effect of the Ulster strike and the army's response to that strike, rather than the events of last winter's crisis, which caused their alarm'. This account is a fiction. The Ulster Workers' Council strike did not finish until 29 May 1974 and Stirling's original memo was dated 24 May, while the strike was still in progress. He may have been approached by people concerned at the Ulster strike, but his memo shows that he had been working on this project for some months.[6]

On 29 July Christopher Walker broke the whole story in *The Times*: Unison,

Greenwood's Red Alert, General Walter Walker – then with Unison – and Stirling. General Walker then wrote to the *Telegraph*, triggering off a deluge of letters from that paper's readers who were anxious to help him in his struggle against the encroaching red tide.

According to that *Times* story Unison had 'an inner committee including bankers, businessmen and barristers', of whom only Young, Ross McWhirter, General Sir Walter Walker, Admiral Ian Hogg and Colonel Robert Butler have been identified. Hogg and Young were friends of the late Sir Maurice Oldfield, with whom Young had worked in MI6. Young and McWhirter were the key members. Both had been active in the Society for Individual Freedom and the Monday Club and McWhirter was Chairman of the 1971 Hain Prosecution Fund that raised £20,000 to mount the SIF-sponsored private prosecution of Young Liberal Peter Hain for his role in the campaign against the UK tour by the South African rugby team. Former MI6 officer, and friend of Oldfield and Young, Anthony Cavendish, was identified to one of the authors as a Unison member but denies being a full member, admitting merely attending a handful of meetings. Another 'supporter' was Colonel Ronnie Wareing, who had then recently arrived from Portugal, where he acted as an MI6 'agent'.[7]

Sir Walter Walker was recruited by Young on the strength of a letter of introduction from the late Field Marshal Sir Gerald Templer ('Templer of Malaya'), and Colonel Butler volunteered his services. Though over 70 at the time, Templer was Lord Lieutenant of Greater London, the Queen's represent-ative, and, formally at any rate, in charge of contingency planning – preparations for civil defence and civil disasters – for the area. After active service in counter-insurgency campaigns in Malaya and Borneo, Walker finished his career as NATO Commander-in-Chief Allied Forces Northern Command, 1969–72. After retiring from the Army in 1972 Walker became one of the siren voices warning of the 'communist threat' to Britain and had given talks on this issue to, among others, the Monday Club and the World Anti-Communist League. For Young *et al* a newly retired NATO Commander in Chief was a major coup and, whether Young intended it or not, Walter Walker became the public focus of attention.[8]

A year later, Walker said that Civil Assistance 'fell into my lap'. Quite how this happened is unclear. Civil Assistance began life as the Civil Assistance wing of Unison, then split off. In a letter to one of the authors Walker said he 'never understood what Mr Young's objectives were, he was extremely secretive and I, therefore, decided to keep away from him' – but not initially. In our view it is more likely that, as was put to us by a friend of Young's, after his initial missives to the *Daily Telegraph* Walker received a large quantity of mail from people wanting to join up with him – and Unison just was not that kind of organisation. If Young wanted the 'action' in the group's full title, given his intelligence background and the failure of his overt campaign in the Monday Club, it was covert 'action' that he sought. For whatever reasons – structural, personal incompatibility, or planning by Young – after August 1974 Unison disappeared from the columns of the newspapers and it was Walter Walker and Civil Assistance which became the public face of the 'apprehensive patriots'.[9]

Walker's supporters among the British élite were mostly men of his generation such as the late Lord Mountbatten: 'moral encouragement . . . urged me to take on the Chairmanship of the Burma Star Association and introduced me each year to a member of the Royal Family in the Royal Box at the Annual Reunion at the Albert Hall.' The two individuals he gave most credit to were the former Marshal of the Royal Air Force, Sir John Slessor, his 'main supporter and encourager', and Ross McWhirter, with whom he enjoyed 'close contact and joint planning . . . from the word go', a connection he dated back to 'the 29th June 1972 . . . long before CA, or any other similar organisation, had even been thought of'. On 27 August, Walker wrote to the *Telegraph* again, reporting that 'within three weeks the strength of the support for the organisation more properly called Civil Assistance than Unison, has already reached the figure of at least 100,000'. As the curious circumlocution, 'the strength of the support for' suggests, the figure was a fantasy. In a letter to Kenneth de Courcy, Walker claimed 300 letters a day at this point. More importantly, it was with this letter that the split with Young was announced: the Civil Assistance wing of Unison had become simply Civil Assistance. Walker may have had nothing more to do with Young after August 1974 but the link with Unison, through McWhirter, continued.[10]

With Parliament in its summer recess, the smattering of articles about Unison and Walker had provoked no significant political response. However, on 22 August David Stirling's GB 75 proposal documents, which had been leaked to *Peace News*, were splashed in the *Guardian*, provoking the Minister of Defence Roy Mason to issue a public statement condemning them as 'blimpish bull' and attacking what he called a 'near fascist groundswell'. In a report in the next day's *Times* on the leak, Stirling described GB 75 as an organisation of 'apprehensive patriots' and said that he was resigning as soon as he could find a replacement. On 30 August Stirling sent out his Round Robin No. 2, concerning the leak of No. 1, commenting that he was 'uneasy about the apparently highly militaristic and very right-wing nature of Unison's managment and therefore of that management's long-term intentions.'[11]

What was the right-wing of the Tory Party doing? On the 31 August the existence of a proposal by a group of Tory MPs for a volunteer civilian force to help the police in the 'maintenance of public order' was leaked (deliberately, in our view) to the media. The MP's included Airey Neave, Jill Knight, Angus Maude, Carol Mather and Harold Gurden – a cross-section of the Tory right. Their proposal had apparently been put to Mr Heath and Sir Keith Joseph in July as part of discussions on future Tory Home Office policy. Airey Neave was quoted as saying, 'I think there is widespread anxiety in the country about the question of public order.' Neave was anxious to point out that 'the Conservative proposals had been formulated before the present controversy surrounding the setting up of groups under the control of retired Army officers began at the end of July', in other words before the controversy about the 'private armies' – though surely not in ignorance of the plans of Young and Stirling: the latter, for example, had put his ideas to former Tory cabinet ministers earlier in the year.[12]

According to Peter Wright, Roy Mason asked the Director-General of MI5 to investigate the 'private armies'. The man chosen for this task was Wright himself. It was a clever manoeuvre, since Wright, earlier in the year after his fateful meeting wth Young and others, had suggested to Hanley that he 'continue to monitor the group's activities as an agent, but Hanley thought discretion was a better policy'. Wright now controlled the surveillance, which involved tapping the telephones of Stirling and probably the others in this field. Wright went to see Airey Neave, whom he had already met when investigating supposed communists, about the existence of 'any secret armies in the UK. He [Neave] came out of the interview very well, showing himself to be loyal to the Crown and to British democracy. I do not believe that he was a conspiratorial type of man.' In December 1974, Mason was the victim of an MI5 smear when William Massie in the *Sunday Express* informed readers that the security services were worried about the Defence Minister's private life.[13]

On being exposed in the press, David Stirling had ordered GB 75 to 'stand down' and had suggested to Walter Walker that he 'pipe down' until after the election – which he does seem to have done. Stirling's plans evaporated, his putative organisation not surviving the exposure in the media. In August 1974, he was introduced to the late Frank Nodes, a member of the then Electrical Trades Union (now the EEPTU). Nodes had apparently been an assistant to ETU leader Les Cannon and had helped expose the ETU ballot-rigging by its CPGB leadership, which climaxed in a famous court case in 1962. In 1974, Nodes was in the process of forming what became the Movement for True Industrial Democracy (Truemid). As Stirling's concerns had largely been centred upon the possible disruptive effect of strikes by the engineers (AEU) or electricians (ETU), Stirling saw the value of a merger of the two would-be organisations. Nodes and Stirling were introduced by Michael Ivens, Director of Aims of Industry. Michael Ivens put it thus: 'Frank Nodes and others told David that he was wasting his time and should hand over his money to set up an organisation to promote trade union democracy.' In the end, for all his grandiose plans, Stirling ended up playing no more than the traditional role of financier to the right in the trade unions.[14]

The stated aims of Civil Assistance were 'To alert the British people to the extent and urgency of the danger . . . to provide this government, and any other body that may follow it, with the knowledge that the great body of moderates will support effective steps taken to thwart the intentions of the communists and militant extremists . . . bind men of good will together to oppose violence, law-breaking and political subversion at grass roots level.' As is suggested in the second of those aims, Walter Walker (and his aide, Colonel Robert Butler) were essentially right-wing conspiracy theorists. In response to the letters he received Walker sent back a standard reply which included this: 'a small minority of hard core militants – lackeys of their Russian masters . . . about 10% of all officials of the major industrial unions are Communists or far left revolutionary Marxists. Together with their fellow travellers, they influence substantially the policies adopted at the Annual Labour Party Conferences and hence the content of the Labour Election Manifesto . . . Today there are sinister forces on our very doorstep and were they to succeed Russia would achieve her aim without having to fire a shot . . . All those applying to join UNISON are strongly urged to subscribe to East–West Digest'.[15]

On 30 August in a letter to *The Times* as 'Chief Executive of Civil Assistance', Robert Butler moved effortlessly from the aims of Civil Assistance to the conspiracy theories at the back – and forefront – of his and Walker's minds: 'We . . . realise that the Armed Forces and auxiliary services could not man more than a minimal number of the many plants to maintain even the most inadequate skeletal emergency services in the event of several major unions indulging in concerted strike action. The situation is partly due to the actions of the Labour Government who, in 1968, disbanded the Civil Defence Corps and the Auxiliary Fire Services, and ran down both the Regular and Territorial Armies. The Minister who instituted these reductions did not seem to have the background that I would have looked for when appointing a Defence Minister and has caused many people to question Mr Wilson's ultimate motives.' This last sentence is a clear reference to the notion then current in sections of the right that because he had briefly been a member of the Communist Party, Denis (hammer of the Labour left) Healey was a potential threat. 'Mr Wilson's ultimate motives' was, of course, the subject of much fantasising on the right at this time. Walker also ran this theme. In a 16 April 1975 speech at Petersfield Town Hall he told the audience 'that people in high places had been fraternising and flirting with Russian officials and, therefore, they were now prisoners of their indiscretions.'[16]

When Penrose and Courtiour interviewed General Walker he told them that he had learned from 'reliable sources' that Harold Wilson was 'a proven communist'. His source had been Butler, who was in contact with an 'old friend still serving in MI6'. This officer, whom Butler admitted 'was acting illegally', gave him verbal accounts of secret service files. Another source, a Special Branch officer, informed him that the security services were trying to get Wilson, who 'had £100,000 of Kremlin money via his friend Kagan'. Walker believed Wilson was part of a 'Communist cell' in Downing Street. After all, said Sir Walter, he had seen interviews with Wilson on his return from official visits to the Soviet Union and he had been 'visibly shaking . . . a clear indication that [he] had been compromised in some way by the KGB . . .'[17]

In the super-heated atmosphere between the two elections of 1974, both by their existence and by their activities, the so-called 'private armies' served as amplifiers of the 'threat message' being broadcast on all stations of the right. In Butler and Walker the anti-subversive lobby found perhaps the most explicit public articulations of the 'Red menace' theme of the time.

XL

THE 1974 OCTOBER GENERAL ELECTION

*I have not the slightest doubt that there was a concerted effort to destabilise
the Labour Government in general and Harold Wilson in particular. It
was largely operated through the press . . . 95 per cent of which was were
hostile.*

BARBARA CASTLE

ON 18 SEPTEMBER 1974, Wilson called the General Election for 10
October. At a Cabinet meeting that day 'There was some discussion about
smears, and Barbara Castle said that she had heard that the *Sunday Times* was
going to reveal that Ted Short owned six houses; and Harold said there was a
rumour that his income tax returns had been photocopied, and so on.' That
casual use of 'and so on' says much about the climate within the Cabinet at the
time.[1]

Wilson's office was on 'continuous watch for the warnings of an election
scandal – of which we had been hearing for several months – to bear their fruit.
The most frequently mentioned subject of these stories was the Prime Minister's income tax returns, given added weight by his discovery that some of his tax
papers were missing from his home in Lord North Street.' Tony Benn was
warned that 'a big financial scandal or smear was being prepared against [him]
for the last week of the campaign'. One journalist was taken to an accountant to
be shown material on Benn's financial affairs.[2]

The 'even more bizarre and fanciful stories about Tony Benn' which Wilson
and his close aides heard during the period included the allegation that he had
been smoking cannabis in in a block of flats called Bickinhall Mansions. During
the election, Benn had been telephoned by Harold Wilson, who asked him 'if he
knew anything about Bickinhall Mansions; had he been lured there to a flat to
smoke cannabis?' Bickinhall Mansions had also featured in another curious
incident. One evening, between the two elections of 1974, the handbag of Peggy
Field, Mrs Williams' sister, was stolen from their house. The sisters were

270

telephoned and told that if they wanted it back they had to collect it from – Bickenhall Mansions. Thinking it might be a set-up of some kind – the same address had already figured in rumours – they called the police, who collected the bag, its contents intact, save for a small amount of cash.

Rumours of 'orgies' and other bizarre happenings seemed to have spread far and wide. Unbelievably, one journalist was told that one senior parliamentarian, while fornicating at one of these orgies, stabbed white rabbits. Tony Benn and others came to believe that MI5 were using Bickinhall for 'honeytrap' operations.[3]

In a speech on 20 September, Wilson made his now famous remarks about 'Cohorts of distinguished journalists [who] had been combing parts of the country with a mandate to find anything, true or fabricated, for use against the Labour Party.' The speech had been triggered by an item in Pincher's column in the *Express* that day reporting that Mrs Halls had been promised an *ex gratia* payment for the death of her husband, Michael, Wilson's Principal Private Secretary. The Halls story had been flickering in the background for nearly a year and had formed part of Pincher's conversation in July which had been reported to Wilson by Michael Gilbert. Copies of Mrs Halls' writ, which detailed her allegations, had been distributed by a Conservative MP and had reached No. 10. In July the German magazine *Stern* had published a four-page article, the title of which translated as 'Mrs Marcia [sic] and the power in Downing St', which had included the Halls' allegations. The copies of *Stern* sent to Britain had those four pages removed.[4]

In Northern Ireland, one of the documents supplied by MI5 to Information Policy was a pamphlet alleging that Heath was a homosexual. A copy found its way to Tony Benn just before the election. 'Someone there showed me a very expensively printed colour booklet entitled "I challenge Heath", which attacks Ted Heath in the most scurrilous and disreputable way, and alleges he is a homosexual. It was written by the woman, Karen Cooper, who threw ink at him when he was in Brussels to sign the Treaty of Accession to the Common Market, and she had tried to get Ken Coates to publish it as a trailer to her book which is due out soon. It was filthy, and in it the author alleged she was a member of the Labour Party, so one wonders whether it wasn't really designed to damage us.'[5]

Two weeks before the election, Benn commented in his diary: 'I just don't think this is going to be an ordinary Election. I think something very big is going to blow up on us.' In the event no massive bombshell landed, partly, it seems, due to the intervention of Richard Briginshaw, General Secretary of the printing union NATSOPA, who later told Tony Benn that he had 'foiled attempts by the *Daily Mail* and the *Daily Express* to print smear stories against Labour during the Election simply by threatening to stop the presses.'[6]

There was an attempt at another Edward Short-type 'Swiss bank account' smear. Just before the election, the *Evening Standard* in London had been given what purported to be evidence of Harold Wilson's bank account with the International Credit Bank of Geneva. An ICB bank card, bearing Harold Wilson's signature on it as account-holder, was given to the paper. Convinced that it was a forgery, the *Standard* refused to use it, and called the police. In fact, the account was genuine and this unforeseen reaction by the *Standard*'s editor delayed the appearance of the story until after the election (see the following chapter).[7]

The Conservative Party had no more luck running their last minute disinformation story. On the day before polling day, a number of newspapers were given the story that 'on that very afternoon Sir Claus Moser, the government's chief statistician, had made a devastating statement during a lecture to postgraduate students at Southampton University. This was to the effect that while Denis Healey, the Chancellor, was claiming that inflation was down to 8½ per cent, it was in fact much higher and would soon be up to 25 per cent.' Chapman Pincher was telephoned at about 6 pm in his office 'by a Tory official, who is no longer there'. Pincher's Conservative Party informant 'said that he was sure of his facts, suggested that this could make a good story for election eve. It would have been sensational had it been true but a call to Sir Claus' office, which was on the point of closing, showed that he had been in Geneva for the past three days and had given no lectures in Southampton.' Pincher believed that the Party official 'had been hoaxed himself but it was a dangerous story to put about and I learned from Sir Claus' office that calls about it had been received from other newspapers. Had we printed the story, which Heath knew nothing about, and Labour had lost the election it would have gone down in history as another Zinoviev letter.' This disinformation attempt was based on information originally supplied by James Goldsmith to the Tory Party. 'When Denis Healey, Labour Chancellor of the Exchequer, had claimed during the campaign that inflation was going down, he had provided detailed research to contradict him.' Unaware of the attempt to plant the story, Goldsmith felt that the information 'had not been properly used. He had been left to predict that food prices would soar upwards himself, when he felt the issue could have had a dramatic effect on the election result.'[8]

The election came: and for all the paranoia and anxiety on the right, for all the attempts to establish smears, the Government survived – just. Labour's share of the vote was up 2 per cent on the February figure but their overall majority was only 3 seats.

Yet, extraordinary though the period was, it did not quite come to the climax which some in the Labour Cabinet feared it would. This is because, while a political party such as the Tories operated on a short time-scale – starting in April to prevent an election being called in June – for the professionals, running such a campaign and doing it properly, i.e. in such a way that the operators are not exposed, is difficult, time-consuming and slow. Cranking up a smear campaign to remove a government in the space of a few months really cannot be done when there is no material to use and everything has to be invented. This is an important point: the material did have to be invented: the Wilson Cabinet was not full of communists; there was no communist cell; there were no orgies in Baker Street. It appears that the spooks, having taken over just after the February election, embarked on a serious, long-range campaign. Wallace was not given the MI5 material in 1974 with a deadline attached – produce for use by, say, September. The evidence is pretty clear that once the spooks got the political nod of approval many of the really serious moves did not begin to show fruit until 1975. Most importantly of all, the evidence – especially from Wallace – is that the secret state and its allies had embarked not just on a campaign against the Labour Government, but against the whole of the liberal-left of British politics. The ambition shining nakedly through Wallace's version of MI5's thinking between the elections of 1974 is nothing less than the realignment of British domestic politics along hard right lines.

XLI

WATERGATE POLITICS

We don't have Watergate politics in Britain.
RON HAYWARD, LABOUR PARTY GENERAL SECRETARY, 1974

THE SECOND LABOUR election victory of October 1974 did not end the anti-Labour campaign; if anything, the campaign intensified. At the end of November 1974, Labour MP John Stonehouse disappeared in Miami, flying to Australia under a new identity after faking his own death by drowning. A colleague of Tony Benn noticed that the last written question Stonehouse had asked before he disappeared was requesting the statistics on death by drowning. Benn thought 'it was a most extraordinary coincidence – or else very mysterious'. Exactly two months before Stonehouse's disappearance, *Private Eye* had revealed that two Labour MPs were under investigation by the Special Branch for their connections to the Czech Embassy. *The Times* mentioned that Stonehouse 'had been under surveillance by MI5'.[1]

In the hiatus between his disappearance in 1974 and later arrest in Australia, Stonehouse was variously accused of being a CIA, a Czech (by Joseph Frolik) and an MI6 agent. The fragments of information available on all the accusations were inconclusively chewed over in *Time Out* and *Private Eye* during this period. At the time of his trial, Stonehouse suspected his troubles had been the work of Pakistani intelligence. He had been targeted because he was a friend of Bangladesh. Just before his death, at the height of the Peter Wright revelations in 1987, Stonehouse claimed to have been one of the victims of MI5's dirty tricks.[2]

Upon his disappearance, Stonehouse's alleged connection with the Czech intelligence service was relaunched: a statement in the name of Joseph Frolik was issued on 15 December. Two days later, Harold Wilson took the unusual step of reading a statement to the House of Commons in response to press speculation. Wilson told the Commons, *inter alia*, that 'following its investigations the Security Service advised me at that time that there was no evidence to support the allegations . . . had there been a scintilla of evidence in 1969, my right hon. Friend would not have remained a member of the Government'. On 20 December, Conservative MP Teddy Taylor, briefed by someone with

274

knowledge of the Frolik allegations, asked the Prime Minister 'which other Members of Parliament were named by the Czechoslovak defector . . . and whether the allegations about these Members were also investigated and proved to be unfounded'. Wilson stone-walled him.[3]

Frolik's allegations surfaced again in a House of Lords debate on 26 February 1975, initiated by Lord Chalfont, concerning 'Subversive and Extremist Elements'. During the course of the debate Chalfont, Viscount Colville of Culross, the Earl of Kimberley, Lord Gisborough and Lord Clifford of Chudleigh revealed a surprisingly detailed knowledge of the (tiny) British extra-parliamentary left, listing at least eleven obscure groupings. Lord Clifford revealed that he had received advance notice of the publication of the ghost-written Frolik memoir, remarking that 'there will be mentioned three fairly well-known people as having supplied information to the Czechs'.[4]

Running parallel to the Stonehouse story at the end of 1974 and beginning of 1975 was the story of Wilson's account with the London branch of the International Credit Bank of Geneva (ICB), mentioned in the previous chapter. ICB had been set up in 1959 by Tibor Rosenbaum, a leading light in the world Zionist movement, and appears to have been a semi-detached Israeli Government laundry for money into and out of Israel. ICB had run into difficulties and had closed its doors in July 1974. The *Evening Standard*, which had been sent Wilson's ICB bank card before the October General Election, but convinced it was a forgery, had refused to use it, now got its consolation prize. On 1 November 1974, echoing the Edward Short Swiss account story earlier that year, it reported: 'Among those who have had their private accounts temporarily frozen at the London branch of a Swiss bank is the Prime Minister, Mr Harold Wilson.'[5]

The account had been opened in July 1973 with an initial deposit of £1,500 made by Wilson, personally. Joe Haines told the press that the money – none of which had been spent – was to be used to help pay for Wilson's Private Office while in opposition. The donor was a friend of Arieh Handler, head of the London branch. Handler told the *Sunday Telegraph*: 'It seems a certain staff member was treated to get information out of him.' The *Sunday Times* recycled a *Private Eye* story on the failure of the ICB, filled it out a little, confirming the Mafia angle. The detectives investigating the burglaries of Wilson and Lord Goodman were told to look into it, but no-one was ever charged and the interesting questions of who 'treated' the ICB employee – and how they knew who to 'treat' – was never answered.[6]

Private Eye used ICB as the peg on which to hang a list of possible donors of the £1,500 – Joseph Kagan, Rudy Sternberg, Sigmund Sternberg, Eric Miller, Lord Kissin, Montague Meyer – the people about whom the magazine had been receiving information from MI5. The *Eye* returned to the story two months later, with a piece about Sternberg and the Plummers: 'It would be reasonable . . . to suggest that Sir Rudy placed the money in this bum bank because of his interest in shipping East European Jews to Israel. The ICB was used by the Israelis to pay for this operation.'[7]

Thus emerged one of the sub-themes of MI5's campaign against Wilson, the notion that he was too close to the Israelis, and was working the 'Bar-Mitzvah Circuit'. This allegation subsequently appeared in books by Chapman Pincher and Andrew Roth; in *Private Eye* in describing Mrs Williams as the 'Zionic Woman'; and, in 1987, in the MI5 response to the allegations of MI5 plotting. Mrs Williams claimed that it was even put about that she was an Israeli agent.[8]

In what looks like an attempt to resurrect the Stonehouse story, in the spring of 1975, MI5 officers travelled to the United States to re-interview Frolik. The unnamed officers poured poison into the former Czech intelligence officer's ears about 'a senior member of the Board of Trade in past years (i.e. Wilson)' who had been 'successfully subverted'. With the knowledge that there would be substantial media interest in his forthcoming memoirs, MI5 wanted him to drop hints about Wilson. In September, Peter Wright asked Lord Rothschild to inform Chapman Pincher that another Czech defector, Frantisek August, would be in the country for a secret visit. August, who was also interested in publishing his intelligence memoirs, would be able, said Rothschild, to give Pincher 'a most interesting story concerning the activities of a well-known Labour MP . . . it was said that this MP was not just an agent of Czech intelligence but an officer of the KGB.' August claimed to have 'run' Stonehouse but his memoirs, when finally published, made no reference to this 'fact'.[9]

During the summer, MI6 chief Maurice Oldfield appeared to want to stir the pot further. MI6 released into MI5's hands an old picture of Wilson which showed the moustachioed Secretary of Overseas Trade, as he then was, in Moscow, in the company of a young woman. This completely innocent photograph was presented with the rider that the source was Soviet. Oldfield's friend Anthony Cavendish would appear to have known of its existence. In his memoir he writes: 'Wilson travelled a great deal . . . to Warsaw Pact countries. This may be one of the facts which so worried MI5. One is forced to ask, therefore, what action would the KGB take if they had evidence of some theoretical indiscretion on the part of a British prime minister. There could be no consideration of approaching the PM directly or indirectly. What the KGB would probably do in such circumstances, therefore, is to pass what they had to . . . MI6, secure in the knowlege that it would cause chaos.' It did not cause chaos but it did cause great excitement within the 'Wilson coterie' inside MI5. However, the most probable source was one of the MI6 recruited East–West traders or even a member of Wilson's party to the Soviet Union. What was important for the anti-Wilson brigade was the Soviet angle, which they then exploited.

The photograph story appears to have had a wide circulation. In June 1975, Auberon Waugh, in *Private Eye*, writing about Wilson talks of 'the matter of some photographs that had come into my possession'. Later, in the *Spectator*, in a way which evaded the libel laws, Waugh laid out the entire scenario. Wilson and Mrs Williams are photographed in compromising circumstances by Soviet security agents. The 'Prime Minister has been an agent of the Soviet Union – albeit an unwilling one – throughout his entire period of office'.[10]

The smear campaign continued elsewhere, using the traditional technique, called 'surfacing', of trying to plant stories in overseas media and then 'importing' them back into Britain as 'news'. In America, smear stories about Heath,

Thorpe, Wilson, Williams and other Labour and Liberal MPs, were offered to news agencies in September and October 1975. Copies of letters from Jeremy Thorpe to Norman Scott from the early 1960s were on offer – presumably part of the package that Bureau of State Security (BOSS) agent, Gordon Winter, had collected for the South Africans; a copy of which had been deposited with the *Sunday People* just before the General Election in February 1974. This is what Peter Wright described as the plan of the group of younger MI5 officers who approached him, but it is significant that these smear stories extended to the leaders of all three parties – as had the information from MI5, sent to Colin Wallace in Northern Ireland in 1974.[11]

XLII

THE ASSAULT ON BENN

*There is little evidence that MI5, or anyone else in Britain outside the hard
Left, ever took Benn seriously, but the CIA may have done so.*
CHAPMAN PINCHER

PINCHER, as on so many things, is just plain wrong. The permanent government took Tony Benn very seriously indeed. No other politician, besides Wilson
himself, was to suffer such a sustained and vicious campaign of
vilification and dirty tricks. In October 1974, Benn was appointed Secretary of
State at the Department of Industry. In this field, the Labour Manifesto for the
February 1974 election had talked of a National Enterprise Board (NEB) – in
Tony Benn's words, 'a channel for public funds into industry which would also
allow for the acquisition of some prominent companies that occupied a key role
in the economy' – and planning agreements (then in vogue in France) with major
companies. These concepts were clearly a continuation and extention of the
Industrial Reconstruction Corporation (IRC) set up by George Brown and
Wilson in the sixties. In the brief hiatus between the two 1974 elections, the
bitter opposition which the IRC had aroused in the sixties was revived even more
strongly against the NEB. After the October election the NEB proposals
produced a torrent of hostility against Benn.[1]

Permanent Secretary at the Department of Industry Sir Anthony Part had
greeted Benn on his first day with the words: 'I presume, Secretary of State, that
you do not intend to implement the industrial strategy in Labour's programme.'
Not so, Benn did indeed intend to implement the strategy. As the campaign
against Benn developed into early 1975, Harold Wilson faced a classic Labour
Party dilemma. Benn argued that he had the right to implement the Manifesto
commitments in his field: the Manifesto was party policy. Against this view,
Wilson was leading a Government which had a majority of only 3 in the
Commons. Further, he was leading a Cabinet few of whose members actually
supported the Manifesto commitments on industrial strategy. Benn was thus in a
very weak position; and when he began showing an interest in workers' co-
operatives, his Permanent Secretary 'finally declared war with his minister. In

January 1975, Part threatened, as chief accounting officer, to dissociate himself from the programmes of assistance Benn was proposing, and report them to the Public Accounts Committee. Wilson picked up the opportunity immediately, and from this point Benn's socialist industrial policies and his tenure of the department were doomed.' Once Part was clear that Benn no longer had the backing of the Prime Minister, he was able to use 'the circuit of power that connects top civil servants with the Prime Minister through the Cabinet Secretary.'[2]

As well as the radical drift of his thinking about the control of the industrial base, Benn was also starting to challenge the secret state. A Tory MP informed him that a constituent had her application to join the civil service rejected by MI5. When Benn pushed for the reason he found that it was primarily because she read the *Morning Star*. This fact, said the security service, 'may well indicate an attitude of mind, which on a security connotation, may cause some unease. We would therefore prefer to err on the side of caution.' Ten days later, Benn raised similar questions about the case of a radical Catholic who was being barred by MI5 because of his membership of a putative CPGB front organisation. Benn commented at the time: 'I felt that even raising this issue would probably get me in bad odour with the Secret Service, but I have no alternative, otherwise I'm simply copping out.'[3]

Similar issues arose over Benn's proposal to appoint Transport and General Workers' leader Jack Jones to the National Enterprise Board. Initially Jones was rejected on security grounds; Benn refused to accept this decision and eventually MI5 relented. Benn commented: 'The point is that they dare not put me in a position where I might minute the Prime Minister saying that Jack Jones is regarded as a security risk.'[4]

In early 1975, the campaign against Benn by the media was joined by the secret state. The timing is interesting. In January, his Permanent Secretary had 'declared war' and the following month began the most extraordinary campaign of harassment any major British politician has experienced. While this is not provable by any means, it does look as though there is a clear causal connection between withdrawal of Prime Ministerial support, the open hostility from the Whitehall mandarins and the onset of covert operations. Benn's telphones were tapped, his house was bugged and he was under open surveillance. 'Journalists' were camped out in flats next door and facing his house. His domestic refuse was daily being stolen by a man in a Jaguar car. The family received more than a dozen calls or visits from 'journalists' inquiring about the health of his children. These veiled threats were also accompanied by a string of death threats, beginning with one from 'Red Flag 74', a pseudo-gang which was active in October/November 1974. In various calls to the media, person or persons unknown described RF74 as a 40-strong break away faction from the International Marxist Group and claimed the credit (sic) for a series of attempted and successful bomb attacks, including the Guildford and Birmingham pub bombings. These claims were not taken seriously.[5]

MI5 had to find or create 'a trace', a connection between Benn and a subversive organisation, in order to legitimise their campaign. In Northern

Ireland, Colin Wallace had already been given information that Benn had 'connections to Czech intelligence'; but while suitable for use in briefing foreign correspondents ignorant of the realities of British politics, this was of no value in the domestic context. One attempt at a trace appears to have been made: a leak of information from Benn's department to the *Morning Star*. 'In a flash,' Benn, 'saw that this could be a dirty tricks campaign to demonstrate that the Department of Industry was leaking . . . it is a way of implying that the Labour Government, particularly me, gives information to the *Morning Star*, this would explain why only the *Morning Star* received the information.' This analysis appeared to be confirmed two days later when, during a debate in the Lords on Subversive and Extremist Elements, Viscount Culross said: 'I have no idea . . . whether there is any truth in the suspicions that the most recent leak from the Department of Trade [sic. Industry] has anything whatever to do with a dirty tricks department on the Left Wing which has somehow infiltrated the Civil Service.'[6]

The secret state's major focus of attention, however, was on linking Benn to the Institute of Workers' Control (IWC). The IWC was regarded on the right as a subversive organisation. In the 1970 anthology *We Will Bury You*, both Harry Welton of the Economic League and the pseudonymous 'David Williams' of Common Cause counted IWC as part of the 'subversive threat'. IWC was largely the brainchild of Ken Coates, a former Communist. He joined the Labour Party in 1961 and had been President of Nottingham Labour Party before being expelled. Though ostensibly about the supposed increasing Trotskyist influence in the local party, the underlying reason for the explusion was the dispute between a right-wing controlled council and the left-wing city party. Coates was expelled for expressing continuing criticism of the Party's leadership and programme. Two of his leading critics later defected to the Conservatives. It was later admitted that the National Executive Council had acted against natural justice and he was re-admitted in September 1969.[7]

On 26 February 1975, Lord Chalfont initiated and made the opening contribution to the Lords debate on Subversive Elements. Chalfont referred to IWC as having 'very considerable significance . . . [its] fringe meeting at the last Labour Party conference . . . was addressed by a Cabinet minister, who not only paid a tribute to the work of the Institute for Workers Control but actually claimed to be a member of it.' Just in case we had not guessed who he was referring to, he added: 'I hope that those whose business it is to consider the current Industry Bill will ponder with care the activities of the Institute for Workers' Control.'[8]

Six months later, 'Ken Coates rang [Benn] to say that Lord Chalfont had asked the Institute for Workers' Control to participate in an Anglia Television programme based on the article by Tom Stacey called "The Road to Communism".' Coates refused and Anglia offered £2,000 to the Bertrand Russell Press, which prints IWC publications, to film them at work. This was an enormous sum and it made Benn 'wonder whether British Intelligence is involved in an attempt to make it a big expose of revolutionaries in Britain'. The cash in 1974 terms is way beyond the normal budget of any documentary team we have ever heard of and though the involvement of 'British Intelligence' is unproven, the availability of that kind of money does suggest supplementary funding from somewhere. The anti-subversive lobby's Brian Crozier was among those who appeared in Chalfont's television psy-war programme, *It Must Not Happen Here*. Broadcast in January 1976, it 'purported to show that the Communist Manifesto was being implemented bit by bit in Britain. Bert Ramelson, Stuart Holland, Ken Gill and others were named and then Frank Chapple, Reg Prentice, Lord Hailsham, Brian Crozier of the Institute for the Study of Conflict, Woodrow Wyatt and Chalfont himself all spoke in support of this view. At the end, Chalfont produced a check sheet to show that out of the ten points of the Communist Manifesto we had already met seven.'[9]

On 9 June 1975, after the referendum on Britain's membership of the EEC, Wilson removed Benn from the Department of Industry and transferred him to the Department of Energy. Nine months later, Benn learned that some months before his eventual ousting, Wilson had told Joe Slater, former Wilson PPS, that he had to get rid of Benn 'because of all his Trotskyite connections'. Benn assumes it is the connection to Coates and the IWC. 'What on earth could this mean, other than that Harold is so stick-in-the-mud that he thinks if you have contact with Ken Coates, this is a Troskyite connection.' Wilson may not have thought this but MI5 certainly would. Wilson had alluded on several occasions to Benn's 'Nottingham Guru'. 'I wondered how Wilson knew about me,' says Coates. He now believes that the source may have been Harry Newton, the IWC treasurer since 1971, who, Cathy Massiter revealed, had been infiltrated into the ISC by MI5.[10]

It is an irony of this period that the only person who would have shared Benn's paranoia about spooks at the time was Wilson himself; but their relationship had become so strained that this did not happen. Indeed, when Wilson revealed some of his anxieties a couple of years later, Benn – to judge from his diaries – was among the sceptics, and showed curiously little interest.

XLIII

TALKING OF COUPS

It was a time of paranoia. Rich men made plans to shift their money abroad. A stockbroker moored a motor boat on the south coast, laden with provisions, so as to make his getaway when the revolution came. Industrialists met secretly to discuss what was to be done, paid private armies to train in the West Country. Establishment cabals muttered that what we needed was a Strong Man: . . . there was talk of . . . the Duke of Edinburgh leading a government of national unity.
GODFREY HODGSON

AFTER THE OCTOBER 1974 ELECTION, Walter Walker soldiered on, trying to create his nation-wide Civil Assistance network, anticipating the cataclysmic show-down at any time. In January 1975, however, the British Military   Volunteer Force quit, its leader, Paul Daniels, quoted as saying that 'General Walker was too right-wing'. By this time Walker's moment had passed. The media was no longer interested. The frenzied campaign between the two elections, designed to prevent a Labour Government, had neither failed nor succeeded: Wilson had won the October election but had not won a workable majority. A government with a majority of 3 was hardly going to usher in the dawn of socialism – even if, as some on the right believed, its leader was a Communist and the Tribune Group was really the Trojan horse of totalitarianism. Just as Walker began getting access to the serious money men in the City of London, Mrs Thatcher and her small group of right-wing supporters centred around Airey Neave captured the leadership of the Tory Party. From then on, Walker's correspondence with his friend Kenneth de Courcy provides a rare glimpse of the networking of the right. Here we see the evidence of the interlocking of the City, the Tory Party and members of the security services, notably MI6. During 1975, these men were meeting secretly. Exactly what they were planning is not completely clear on present evidence, but the snippets we do have suggest the formation of a 'businessmen's government' to take over in the result of a major breakdown in society, perhaps as the result of a coup instigated by the Army.[1]

The 'businessman's government' theme was a variation of the old 'nation before interest theme' which had been trotted out on a number of occasions during the Wilson Governments of the sixties as well as between the elections of 1974. This theme was present in both the content and rhetoric of the Tory Manifesto in October 1974. 'Putting Britain first', 'no narrow partisan spirit', 'the nation's crisis should transcend party differences' were the phrases which Barbara Castle thought worthy of her diary.[2]

The first glimpse, after the October election, of renewed agitation from within British business comes in January 1975 when Frank Taylor, head of the construction company Taylor Woodrow, wrote to Joe Kagan. Taylor, whose company has long been (and remains) a major financier of the Tory right, asked Kagan to join an unnamed group to 'save Britain' by helping to prevent the communists and fascists taking over. That he should approach Kagan, given MI5's feelings about the man, is surprising, but Kagan's closeness to the Prime Minister was obviously pertinent. It also indicates that MI5's security fears about Kagan were not taken seriously by the City.[3]

On 18 March 1975, General Walker wrote to de Courcy about 'a very interesting lunch with Angus Mackay Charrington, Michael Ivens (Aims for Industry) and Nigel Neilson, who was Onassis' PR representative in this country . . . Charrington is going to arrange a series of similar working lunches in order to introduce me to influential people in the City and in industry.' A month later, Walker had lunch in the City sponsored by Julian Tennant, Chair of C. Tennant and Sons Ltd. It was attended by representatives of Consolidated Goldfields, Anglo Eastern Bank, Lazard Brothers, M and G Unit Trusts, Cazanove, Cater Ryder and Co. Ltd, Sir Berkeley Gage, ex-Ambassador and former Chair of the Latin America British National Exports Council, and, from the Tory right, Nicholas Ridley MP, a member of the Selsdon Group. In a report to de Courcy, Walker described 'Ridley . . . talking in riddles . . . It seemed to me that what he was trying to convey, but hadn't the guts to say so openly, was that the only hope for this country would be a military coup.' George Kennedy Young was also running around the City and the Tory Party, organising meetings at the Carlton Club with right-wing MPs and businessmen, drumming up support for some kind of action. He asked Walker to 'attend an informal reception on April 30 to be given by Sir Frederick Bennett MP, for members of Unison and associated groups, to meet his "Right Wing Group" of some 20–30 MPs.' Since 1970, Bennett had been chairman of the Society for Individual Freedom parliamentary group.[4]

It was probably through this group that in late 1974 or early 1975, 'Young with others, with the backing of Airey Neave, rapidly organised a network throughout the constituencies to support [Mrs Thatcher].' This was 'Tory Action' which was formed when it became clear that Edward Heath would be challenged for the leadership. Young later claimed that Tory Action received the encouragement of the Chair of the influential backbench Tory 1922 Committee, Edward Du Cann, who was also a member of the so-called 'Milk Street Mafia', a key group in making Margaret Thatcher leader of the Conservative Party. DuCann denies having anything to do with Tory Action.[5]

At the beginning of April, David Stirling wound up GB 75 and formally launched his 'anti-extremist counterforce' within the trade unions, Truemid. Its council quickly established links with the Industrial Research and Information Service and the Economic League. Money was raised from City sources. John Henderson of the stockbroking firm Cazenove helped to raise more than £10,000. When the full-time chairman, Syd Davies, left he told the press that Truemid 'is not the organisation I set out to create. It has become extremely right-wing. It is a Frankenstein monster.'[6]

On 1 May, Walker lunched with the board of British and Commonwealth, arranged by Walker's main supporter and encourager, Marshal of the Royal Air Force Sir John Slessor, a neighbour of his at the time. A cheque for £10,000, and promises of more, arrived next day. Cayzer wrote to him: 'I see the Army, the Police and such a body as Civil Assistance, standing between the wreckers and the vast majority of the people of this country who want to live in peace and who are reasonable people. The Conservative Party will have to re-write its policy. Too long it has been a pale shadow of Socialism, and I am afraid expedience has always been the rule of the day rather than principle.'[7]

Later in the month, a most curious meeting took place. Mike Molloy, assistant editor of the *Daily Mirror*, had dinner with Sir Val Duncan, head of the mining conglomerate Rio Tinto Zinc, together with Bill Deedes, editor of the *Daily Telegraph*, and Bruce Page of the *Sunday Times*, Lord Robens and Alan Protheroe from the BBC. Since the mid-sixties, when Cecil King promoted the idea of a coalition government, Lord Robens had been the prime candidate for the role of leader of a 'government of the talents'. 'There were also a couple of staff officers who had worked with Field Marshal Montgomery. Val Duncan had called them in to head off the revolution. He said, "When anarchy comes, we are going to provide a lot of essential generators to keep electricity going, and we invited you, the Editors, to tell us if you can maintain communications to people, then the army will play its proper role".' Molloy cannot remember much more, but he says that he and Bruce Page sat there rather bemused. When they were asked if they could 'keep the presses rolling', they answered 'not without union support', which more or less finished it as far as they were concerned.[8]

In what looks like a comment on the meeting and the surrounding events, the *Daily Telegraph* reported on 22 May that 'as well as supplying uranium, copper and other metals, Rio Tinto Zinc is also in a position to furnish a coalition government should one be required.' This reflected the presence on the RTZ board of a number of leading politicians and establishment figures. Former Foreign Secretary Lord Carrington joined in 1974, as did Lord Sidney Greene, former General Secretary of the NUR and past President of the TUC. Also on the board were Lord Byers, a senior Liberal peer, and from May 1975, former Labour Foreign Office Minister Lord Shackleton became the company's deputy chairman. Val Duncan, who had been the driving force in the RTZ's astonishing growth from an obscure company in Spain to one of the world's leading mining corporations, was suitably well-connected. He had been a pre-war member of the 'Castlereagh' dining club, whose members included Airey Neave and SOE member Peter Wilkinson, the latter an experienced intelligence official who in

1972 had been made Co-ordinator of Intelligence and Security in the Cabinet Office. He retired in 1976.[9]

At the end of May, David Stirling stirred the pot. He was known to be planning psychological warfare operations to create a suitable atmosphere, perhaps to panic Wilson and his friends. On one occasion, with some of his SAS friends, Stirling made a reconnaissance of the House of Commons with a view to flooding the lower floors with sewage from the Thames, apparently as a symbolic statement on the current state of the Government. That month, when a couple of minor operators, John Banks and Dave Tomkins, advertised for mercenaries, Stirling offered them a contract to fight *against* white-ruled Rhodesia. In his book on mercenaries, Anthony Mockler commented that 'the whole scenario sounds like a farrago of imaginative nonsense'. A 'carefully organised' recruiting meeting did take place in a London hotel on 27 May 1975 with 120 would-be mercenaries. The meeting's occurrence soon leaked to the press. By June, over 200 men had allegedly been selected and a second meeting was arranged, through Stirling, on 25 May, at a hotel near Heathrow airport. From there a small group would fly out to Zambia to join black Zimbabwean guerrillas. The meeting ended in farce and the police had to be called to stop the drunken brawl which developed, at which point, the 'Paymaster', presumed to be Stirling, pulled out. Mockler comments that 'later Banks and Tomkins and their associates began to suspect that the "mission" had never been intended to take place at all'. Wilson later told reporters that he 'took the mercenaries seriously'. Presumably referring to the July meetings, Wilson continued: 'if one could hire mercenaries it wouldn't be difficult to have a couple of thousand men in Horse Guards. It could do an awful lot of damage before the troops came in. If the troops came in.'[10]

On 7 July 1975, former chairman of Cunard Sir Basil Smallpiece and his successor, Victor Matthews, were approached by an Army officer then with the Home Office. They were summoned to a meeting to talk about Cunard. Matthews recalled 'an Air Marshal at the time telling me about the need for the forces to take power'. Managing director of the Cunard line John Mitchell 'met three Army and secret service people' who made it perfectly clear that he was being asked to take part in a *coup d'état*. Mitchell was asked to put the QE2 at the Army's disposal, apparently to be used as a floating prison for the Cabinet. This was reported to Sir Michael Carey, Permanent Secretary at the MOD, who told Mitchell that the matter had been 'an exercise which had been dealt with'.[11]

One week later, Unison hove into view for the last time. G. K. Young gave a story to Pincher which graced the front page of the *Express*, 'An Army On Riot Alert'. 'An anti-Chaos organisation . . . is on alert to step in if there is a national emergency over the economic crisis . . . [There is] an emergency radio network . . . a secret air organisation, with its own planes and airfield . . . Arrangements have been completed for the production and distribution of a broadsheet newspaper.' Unison claimed to have a direct link with Buckingham Palace, giving them access to 'the still extensive executive powers which derive directly from the Crown'. Young was quoted as saying that 'The Queen appoints Lord Lieutenants and they can swear in constables. Members of Unison could therefore be sworn in as constables with their powers'. The 'Palace link', from this context, was probably through Lord Templer, who was then Lord Lieutenant of Greater London, appointed by the Queen, and who had recommended Unison to General Sir Walker. The Palace denied any such link. What did this amount to? A Unison member told us it was an attempt to make the organisation look more impressive than it actually was, a 'shot across the bows' of the Wilson Government. Unison had access to a couple of light planes, and they did, apparently, do a few wireless drills, but a national organisation? Of that there is no evidence. Whatever Young was, he wasn't stupid. His network, for example, never seriously believed that Harold Wilson was a Soviet agent; nor did it believe that the revolution, which it professed to fear, was imminent. Unison, *qua* anti-chaos organisation, was a cover for something else.[12]

In 1975, the military historian John Keegan was at Sandhurst and heard Cecil King tell a group of (unimpressed) officers about the need for the armed forces to act to save the country. 'I had no doubt', Keegan said, 'I was listening to a treasonable attempt to suborn the loyalty of the Queen's officers.'[13]

Such was the general atmosphere at the time. Were the events described above isolated incidents, psychological operations, or was there something more sinister underlying them? The evidence does not yet exist for an answer to be given. A leading member of the anti-subversive tendency at that time, Brian Crozier, said in 1991 that 'There was an interest in certain circles in the Army in countering [the threat from the left] and I know that a great deal of consideration was given to it.' There was, for example, an 'elaborate contingency plan which Army officials in Belfast recall seeing.' It was drawn up in Northern Ireland in the aftermath of the Ulster Workers' Council strike of May 1974, presumably with the help of Peter England, a Home Office official responsible for MI5 and Civil Contingencies in Northern Ireland. The plan drew on the 'transition to war' blueprints which already existed for a Soviet conflict. The scenario went: 'another strike in Northern Ireland would require a flow of supplies across the North Sea. The mainland ports might be crippled by sympathetic strikes, and this would require the introduction of protective "control zones" around them. Meanwhile, terrorist attacks could be expected from groups like the Baader–Meinhof gang as British troops were withdrawn by plane from Germany. It would be necessary to guarantee their passage, as well, and this would require a "control zone" around Heathrow airport . . . British passenger lines "including the QE2", would be immediately requisitioned by the military.'[14]

This is reminiscent of the sudden appearance of the Army at Heathrow, initially in January 1974, followed by further troop deployments in June, July and September. Of the first Heathrow alert, junior Home Officer Minister in the Heath Government Lord Colville stated that 'the Commissioner of Police for the Metropolis sought government authority to put into operation the contingency plans for the use of police and troops to defend Heathrow against terrorist attack.' At the time, Marcia Williams had taken the incidents lightly but she later remembered Wilson 'saying that the troops could be used in another way by turning them around . . . they could turn and get a situation, a very frightening situation where the alert itself could trigger off a plan for a coup.'

Tony Benn was told by Major-General Bate, Commander of the National Defence College, that there had been a 'movement called PFP – Philip for President. The paras were supposed to be involved, and some movement of troops in Northern Ireland was contemplated.'[15]

What do these fragments amount to? We do not know. It seems clear that there would be far-reaching contingency plans, in which the 1974 experience in Northern Ireland would loom large. Even though the Army and MI5 were happy to allow the Ulster Workers' Council strike to succeed, there were lessons to be drawn from the dispute, especially the way in which it shut down power supplies; and the next time the strike might be from the left, not the flag-waving super Brits of the Protestant ghettos of Northern Ireland. Our guess would be that on the fringe of a rehearsal of these contingency plans, some people tried to hi-jack the exercise and run it for real. The reaction of Sir Michael Carey, Permanent Secretary at the MOD, when told of the 'Cunard plot', that it was 'an exercise which had been dealt with', suggests this possibility.

More prosaically, the focus of attention for the right became the National Association for Freedom (NAFF). NAFF rose out of the brief period of intense organisation and agitation by a number of middle-class 'protest' groups formed in 1974 or early 1975. NAFF was formally launched on 2 December 1975 in London but the planning had begun in July. It had sprung out of a lunch meeting between Michael Ivens, Director of Aims of Industry, and Lord De L'Isle, former Governor General of Australia. This had been arranged by Colonel Juan Hobbs, then with British United Industrialists, the major laundry of money from British capital into political projects. The urbane Mr Ivens claims the credit for much of the early recruitment of names willing to appear on the letter-head. On the other hand, Chris Tame, who worked for NAFF in its early days, described it as the successor to Ross McWhirter's organisation Self Help, 'a second try' after that body had been 'hi-jacked' by the racist Lady Birdwood. In its personnel, activities and attitudes, NAFF was a fusion of the anti-subversion tendency, middle-class protests being articulated through rate-payer and self-employed groups and the right-wing of the Tory Party.[16]

Bearing the message of the anti-subversion tendency were Robert Moss and Brian Crozier (of Forum World Features and Institute for the Study of Conflict fame). The publication of Moss's apocalyptic (and entirely misjudged) *The Collapse of Democracy* was timed to coincide with the public launch of NAFF. John Gouriet, NAFF's first administrator, described later how 'we felt that 1975 and the years that followed were really a watershed in British politics . . . down the slippery slope towards communo-socialism [sic] and a satellite state of the Soviet Union at its worst'. A month after its inaugural July 1975 meeting, NAFF arranged for the anti-subversion tendency's leading press adjunct, Chapman Pincher, to lecture on 'the grave dangers facing Britain'. By now, the reader should have some idea of what he thought they were.[17]

Though NAFF soon acquired the sponsorship of Monday Club members Jill Knight and Rhodes Boyson, Airey Neave, plus Winston Churchill and Nicholas Ridley, who were all then in Mrs Thatcher's Shadow Cabinet, Chris Tame says the Council was little more than a 'notepaper job', the organisation being run by an inner group of Ivens, Gouriet and Moss. Seed money, says Tame, came from Aims and 'the usual people' – notably the construction firms McAlpine and Taylor Woodrow. NAFF, in Tame's view, was basically 'a shambles'. None the less, it almost immediately became the focal point of the Tory right. Other groups which had appeared during 1974 melted away. NAFF had political support from the Tory Party; it had the financial support of the stalwarts among British industrialists who support the right; it had the support of key members of the state/private sector interface in the anti-subversion tendency; and the aims in its Freedom Charter were couched sufficiently widely to please almost every section of the right-wing. Most important of all, they had the support of the leader of the Tory Party, Margaret Thatcher, who addressed NAFF's inaugural 'subscription dinner' in January 1977.[18]

In its first eighteen months, NAFF initiated a series of what an intelligence officer would have called 'political actions': legal actions against strikes, propaganda about 'scroungers', and 'Marxists' in the Labour Party – and, most spectacularly, its strike-breaking intervention in the strike at the Grunwick factory. These brilliantly successful psychological operations gained them oceans of favourable coverage in the Tory press, anticipating (and to some extent setting) the agenda for the Conservative Government of 1979. If the Heath Government of 1970–2 was the Slater Walker Government, the first Thatcher administration was the National Association for Freedom Government.[19]

Although it is beyond the scope of this book it would not be too far off the mark to say that Thatcherism grew out of a right-wing network with extensive links to the military-intelligence establishment. In our view Mrs Thatcher's rise to power was the climax of a long campaign by this network which included a protracted destabilisation campaign against the Labour Party during 1974–6. The outlines of a concerted campaign to discredit other parties, to engineer a right-wing leader of the Tory Party and then a right-wing government is visible.

CODA: THE CONSTITUTIONAL COUP

> *The monarchy is the instrument of secretive, centralised power. It is the notion of the Crown that allows MI5 to burgle your home and bug my phone.*
> TONY BENN

During 1975, there was talk in Tory clubland of the 'collapse of democracy' and the need for some kind of action. Often the talk turned towards the idea of a coup. As in 1965, during the Rhodesian crisis, in the 1967 Winstanley affair, the 1968 Cecil King/Mountbatten talks and in a number of plans advanced in 1974, the essential requirement for those tempted to become British 'Colonels' was the backing of the Crown. In all the fragments we have about putative coups in this country, the Royal Family in some form is always included in the planning. As the conspirators knew, in Britain's absurd un-written constitution lies the legal basis for a constitutional coup. Peter Wright was clear where the loyalties of his colleagues lay. 'I certainly didn't, and most people in MI5 didn't have a duty to Parliament. They have a duty to the Queen . . . It's up to us to stop Russians getting control of the British government.'

The Labour Party, with the notable exception of Tony Benn, has generally been happy to place its trust in what it sees as a benign British state. An interesting light was thrown on this general area in the late seventies during the debate on Clement Freud's proposed Freedom of Information Bill. In Cabinet, Benn made the awkward discovery that its only other supporters were social democrats – Bill Rodgers, David Owen and Shirley Williams. They, unlike many of the 'socialists' – who thought such concerns wholly middle-class and of little importance – were more realistic about the problems posed by Britain's absurd constitution. At a meeting of the Devolution Committee held at Chequers, Roy Jenkins gave Benn his definition of Sovereignty. 'Sovereignty in Britain belonged to the Sovereign, whose power went to the Cabinet to exercise, and the Cabinet has succeeded in exercising sovereignty to the extent that it has successfully manipulated Parliament and the electorate.'[20]

A general consensus holds that because the Queen has not been known to exercise her Prerogative Powers, their mere existence gives no cause for concern. Her powers are generally seen as being illusory, largely symbolic and, therefore, without substance. However, as we have shown, there have been many people in positions of authority who have based their actions on the belief that there is some substance to the Royal Prerogative. For instance, Peter Wright justified the burglaries and bugging that he did on the basis that he was a crown servant and, therefore, protected by the Royal Prerogative, something agreed in the past by successive Home Secretaries.

'The truth is,' suggested Conservative historian Lord Blake, 'that the power of the crown has quite properly in an era of democratic party politics become an emergency power – to find a Prime Minister when a national crisis arises in which the ordinary party usages prove inadequate, to guard against a reckless unnecessary general election at a time of grave economic peril, and perhaps in an extreme case to force a general election if a government for partisan reasons attempts to break the rules of the constitution and prolong itself in office. These powers are not the less important for being rarely used.'[21]

Former Conservative Attorney General Lord Rawlinson is well aware of these residual powers. 'If ever corrupt or revolutionary Ministers are intent on imperilling the whole concept of the unwritten British constitution and on destroying the existence of Parliamentary government and constitutional monarchy, then there does exist in the constitutional armoury, normally locked by convention, a weapon of last recourse for ultimate use by the Sovereign upon her sole responsibility.'[22]

Rawlinson does not spell out precisely what this means or how it might be achieved, but as a last resort the Crown still has a prerogative power to direct the use of troops. This is exercised through the Queen's Regulations by the Defence Council. Leading constitutional lawyer S. A. De Smith, noting the executive power which this gave the Council (which hardly ever meets), stated: 'it cannot mean that troops can lawfully be ordered to do whatever the Crown thinks fit whenever it thinks fit to maintain internal security, irrespective of what necessity requires.' We would argue, however, that this is precisely what it does mean. A coup in this country can be legal, heralding in an Emergency Government backed by law.[23]

'The Manual of Military Law' defines the situations in which the military may be called to aid the civil powers. They would include a National Emergency, intimidation of workers, unlawful assembly, riot and insurrection. In the last case, if this was in general defiance of the government of the country, 'the military would have a duty to act, under law, in these situations whether or not ordered to do so by the government.' In these circumstances, under the provisions of the Emergency Powers Act, effective power would reside with an executive and parliamentary control of that executive would be forsaken. The 1964 Emergency Powers Act allowed troops to be used in industrial disputes and disasters on the authorisation of only two members of the secretive Defence Council, thereby by-passing Parliament. Whether this might include a Mount-batten type-figure acting on behalf of the Crown is not known, but on the basis of the various coup scenarios proposed during the Wilson years it seems highly likely.[24]

XLIV

WHAT DID WILSON KNOW?

*Maurice Oldfield . . . said that there's a section of MI5 that is unreliable
. . . he said he was going to bring it out . . . I never heard any more.*
HAROLD WILSON

BY THE SPRING of 1975, Wilson knew that something was going on. He had already decided that a 'Dirty Tricks Department' was operating against him but had few concrete leads; and, most importantly, no-one to whom he could entrust an investigation. MI5, the logical candidate for the job, were his chief suspects. As Lady Marcia Falkender told *Observer* editor Donald Trelford in 1977: 'The only people qualified to provide the evidence, and present the case for an inquiry, were the same people who are part of the thing that is wrong. So the Prime Minister couldn't do that.'[1]

As well as his (and his colleagues') experience of the various smear campaigns which had taken place, Harold Wilson had received other information about the plotting against him that we know of – and, presumably, received more than we are aware of. Between the two elections, for example, he had received three tip-offs. Historian Martin Gilbert had written to him in May 1974, recounting conversations he had heard at a party with, *inter alia*, Chapman Pincher. Pincher had relayed what he calls 'this gossip' about the 'Communist cell' in Downing Street; but Gilbert told Wilson that MI5 had been given as a source. A member of the Labour Party in London, Bob Griffith, wrote to Wilson between the elections telling him that smear stories had been published in a newsletter in Canada.[2]

A third warning came from playwright Jimmy O'Connor, whose TV play, *A Tap on the Shoulder*, about a corrupt businessman who was close to Labour Cabinet ministers, was broadcast in August 1974. O'Connor was approached by Henry Kerby MP, who had seemingly turned against Wilson, a well-known right-wing journalist, and a member of the Heath Cabinet. Assuming that O'Connor's play was based on a real incident, all three were looking for dirt on Wilson and there was talk of O'Connor making a lot of money for the right information. O'Connor rebuffed them, instead writing to Wilson's Press Office reporting 'a conspiracy against the Wilson Government'.[3]

Wilson was also probably aware of the Norman Scott allegations about Jeremy Thorpe. It seems highly likely to us that Wilson had known of these for many years: a number of his Cabinet colleagues in the sixties – David Ennals, Frank Soskice and George Thomas, for example – had dealt with the 'Scott problem'. Wilson was apparently told again in 1974. BOSS agent Gordon Winter had delivered his dossier of tape recordings of Scott and letters from Thorpe to Scott to the *Sunday People* newspaper the week before the February 1974 election. Winter later discovered that Sydney (later Lord) Jacobsen, then head of the IPC Group which owned the *People*, had copied the entire dossier and taken it to Wilson.[4]

Added to his knowledge of attacks on himself and his colleagues, a private detective and former MI5 officer, Ralph Matthews, reported to the Labour Party that the telephones in their headquarters, Transport House in London, were bugged. Doing some electronic 'sweeps' nearby for another client, Matthews picked up conversations in the Party's HQ. Wilson and those around him were also being burgled and bugged.[5]

In 1977, Wilson told reporters that there had been more than a dozen burglaries at his home and offices and at those of his professional advisers. In his submission to the Royal Commission on the Press in April he added that 'seven burglaries of the homes of my staff took place in the three months before I announced my resignation of the premiership'. Wilson himself had been burgled eight times. These sensational claims, compared to the infamous Watergate burglary, received scant investigation by the British press. In fact, Wilson's estimates were on the conservative side.

Between the two elections in 1974, a burglary took place at Wilson's home in Lord North Street during which personal tax papers were stolen. These were later shown to *Private Eye* but were deemed to be of no interest. Another took place at a room in Buckingham Palace Road where Wilson stored personal papers. Tax documents, personal letters, photographs and tape recordings relating to his exchanges with President Nixon and the Rhodesian Premier, Ian Smith, were taken. There was a burglary at Marcia Williams' London home. She also had two break-ins at her country home at Grange Farm, Great Missenden, at the beginning of 1975.[6]

In 1974, there were two break-ins at the offices of Lord Goodman, Wilson's chief legal adviser. This led the *Sunday Mirror*, following a series of burglaries at the offices of solicitors involved with Wilson, to ask 'Is this the work of a Dirty Tricks Department?' Goodman hadn't any notion why he was burgled 'until much later, when I discovered that they had been searching for documents that might in some way incriminate Harold Wilson. We had no such documents. I don't think any such documents existed.' 'They', Goodman discovered, were a 'few cowboys in MI5 . . . who saw in Harold Wilson a danger to their whole scheme of life'. In the seventies, one author declined James Goldsmith's offer of a 'handsome fee', use of any number of researchers and indemnity against his legal costs, if he would write a 'no-holds-barred' biography of Goodman. One

Conservative Parliamentary candidate told us that he did hear of 'financial smears' being directed against Goodman in the middle seventies.[7]

During the year, there were two burglaries at the London flat of Edward Short, when personal papers were taken. A Special Branch contact informed us that the offices of Lord Houghton and Joe Kagan were entered and documents copied. Bernard Donoghue, Wilson's Chief Policy Adviser, suffered three burglaries. In October, Tony Crosland was burgled. Benn took note – 'a regular burglary they say, without political significance, though that may or may not be the case.' John Allen's mother told Tam Dalyell 'how they were burgled in extraordinary circumstances several times over that period – and John was known to be living at home'. In 1975, break-ins took place at office of a lawyer acting for Anthony Field, brother of Marcia Williams, and later at Field's home. Another victim was Jean Denham, who once worked in the press office at No. 10. There were two burglaries at the home of the late Michael Halls, Wilson's former PPS at No. 10. Lord Brayley, the disgraced Army Minister, was also burgled.[8]

In March 1976, Geoffrey Goodman, who was running the Counter-Inflation Unit inside No. 10, told Tony Benn that 'Something strange is going on.' There had been three burglaries at his house. 'All his papers had been gone through. He is certain it was political.' Goodman also thought Joe Haines, the Prime Minister's Press Secretary, was preventing him from 'seeing really sensitive documents. The security officer comes and pokes around my office from time to time and asks questions that could only come from Joe Haines. I know my phone is tapped.' Haines had made it clear to Goodman that he wanted the Counter-Inflation Unit wound up. Later, the Prime Minister asked Goodman round to Lord North Street where Wilson was very secretive and, after telling him to continue with the Unit, said: 'I won't tell Joe Haines you have been here.' Benn wondered why Wilson had to operate 'conspiratorially against Joe Haines!' Had Haines been told something by security? Goodman had an MI5 file because of his membership of the Fleet Street Forum of Socialist Journalists in the fifties. An MI5 officer told him: 'If you go on with the Forum, you are going to find it very hard to get work.'[9]

In October 1976, Yorkshire Television's contracts department was 'burgled and papers examined'. Wilson was due to appear on a David Frost special about British Prime Ministers. Frost publicly announced the fact but not one newspaper reported the break-in. Shortly before Easter 1977, a break-in took place in Wilson's study at his home in Buckinghamshire. The haul consisted of personal letters, bank statements, and the typescript of a book of a former colonial judge, concerning his dealings with agencies of the South African Government. At the same time, documents relating to South Africa were taken and other papers were rifled through at Marcia Williams's country house.

The police carried out an investigation of the burglaries and some files were recovered by a well-known Soho figure, Nicky Nichols, who paid £2,500 to a stranger to get them back for the Prime Minister. Two years later, Maurice Henn, a businessman who ran a private delivery service, and Khalail Waifai, a Lebanese stationery salesman, were charged with the Buckingham Palace Road burglary. However, no one else was charged for the countless break-ins. Although suspicion at one time fell on South African agents as the perpetrators, we understand the police came to the conclusion that MI5 were the culprits. Because relations between MI5 and the police were so strained at this stage an intermediary was used, a Sunday newspaper journalist with excellent contacts with MI5. The results of this approach are not known.[10]

However imperceptible at the time, other influences were pushing in Wilson's direction and provided further support for his concern about dirty tricks. Britain was not the only 'democratic', 'western' country in which the secret state had been playing politics. As we now know, throughout 1974 similar events were happening in Australia and New Zealand – and, most spectacularly. in the United States, where the secret history of the CIA and FBI activities in the post-war period was unravelling in the wake of the Watergate affair. The November 1974 issue of the *Washington Monthly* contained an article by ex-US State Department official John Marks on how CIA personnel under light cover at US Embassies could be identified. A young American journalist, Mark Hosenball, working for the London radical magazine, *Time Out*, came back from a visit to the States with a copy and, with a fellow staffer, Phil Kelly, began applying Marks' methodology to the London Embassy. Other journalists, notably Martin Walker of the *Guardian*, were also on the story, but in the end only *Time Out* published the names which Hosenball and Kelly had identified. CIA ideological defector Philip Agee was also then in London, finishing off his memoir *CIA Diary* (published by Penguin in July 1975), and under surveillance. He worked with the journalists hunting the CIA, claiming later that they had collectively identified sixty-two CIA personnel attached to the US Embassy in London. With the CIA's role in Chile fresh in the memory, left-wing Labour MPs were unhappy at the discovery of a CIA presence in Britain and an Early Day Motion was organised in the House of Commons calling for their expulsion. *Private Eye* claimed that the identity of some of the CIA personnel had been confirmed by 'DI-6 (sic) frothing at the mouth over the CIA's cavalier interpretation of the agreement which says that the CIA can follow and spy on anyone in Britain as long as DI-6 (sic) is kept informed.'[11]

The CIA in Britain were suddenly newsworthy; even the *Sunday Times* carried a profile of the London CIA station chief, 'Cord Meyer Superspook', on 15 June 1975. A week later, the whole spook-hunting enterprise moved up a gear. *Time Out* 'blew' the London-based CIA propaganda operation, Forum World Features.[12]

In the midst of this exposure of intelligence misdeeds, on 7 August, with Parliament in recess, Wilson had lunch with his publisher and friend Lord Weidenfeld, who told him that 'the whole of London was now awash with talk about the "Communist cell" in Downing St.' This proved to be the last straw.[13]

Chapman Pincher has muddied the waters surrounding this event, claiming it was the Martin Gilbert account of the 1974 lunch at which Pincher spoke which triggered the Prime Minister's fears about MI5. Wilson was, in fact, roused to action by a dinner party held in August. In an excerpt in the *Express* for his forthcoming book, *Inside Story*, Pincher reported that 'during a private dinner a young and well-known Tory MP was discussing the Communist connections of certain Labour Ministers. He is alleged to have left the table to telephone me for confirmation that Wilson and Lady Falkender were among the suspects.' In 1978, Pincher said that he recalled no such call, 'but the MP is said to have returned with my confirmation'. Thirteen years later, Pincher's account had changed. 'The Tory MP Winston Churchill, who had been present at the dinner, had telephoned me about it that same evening to seek my opinion about the "Communist Cell in Number Ten". I had told him that this was a completely garbled account of something I had said [at the Gilbert lunch] and was untrue, as far as I was aware.' By now his memory of the telephone call had cleared but it was Pincher who was giving the garbled account. Also present at the dinner was Churchill's wife Minnie, who told her friend Lord Weidenfeld what had been said. 'There had been an MI5 officer there who had spoken very freely.' Weidenfeld then told Wilson 'that he heard that certain officers of MI5 considered the Prime Minister himself to be a security risk'. In the *Pencourt File*, Wilson adds that the talk was of a 'Communist Cell'. 'They were saying that I was tied up with the Communists and that MI5 knew. The arch link was my political secretary Marcia [Williams]. She was supposed to be a dedicated Communist!'[14]

Wilson's account, recorded on tape only a year after the event, sounds the most convincing and fits in with our knowledge of MI5 operations against him in the previous year. In December 1974, Winston Churchill had written to Wilson to warn him that 'your friend Sir Joseph Kagan should be informed that his houseguest, a delightful Russian, Victor Lessiovsky, is a senior serving officer in the KGB.' Churchill cannot recall from where he obtained this startling piece of information. However, the 'notorious' Lessiovsky was of interest to MI5. The former assistant to United Nations Secretary-General, U. Thant, who left New York in 1973, was regarded by some US intelligence authorities as the double agent FEDORA. Right-wing MI5 officers, such as Peter Wright, and James Angleton at the CIA disagreed. They believed that FEDORA was a triple agent who was still operating on behalf of the Soviets. It was thus in MI5's interest to discredit Lessiovsky. The *Daily Mail* ran a piece on the Soviet official Lessiovsky, who had been denounced in John Barron's recently published book on the KGB as a senior KGB officer.[15]

'After Lessiovsky's withdrawal from New York', writes Brian Freemantle in his book on the KGB, 'the Russians made a visa application for him to enter Britain. Warned by MI5 of Lessiovsky's activities, the Foreign Office refused.' Lessiovsky is alleged to have flown into London Heathrow in 1974, and then made his way north to Kagan's Lake District mansion, Eusemere. The KGB officer was trailed there by MI5 officers who then, apparently, lost their prey. Tony Brooks, the MI5 officer who had been investigating Kagan for about four years, tried to discover Lessiovsky's whereabouts but only picked his trail up again when two days later the Russian flew out of Heathrow. Although he readily admitted meeting a number of Soviet trade officials, whom he assumed could be KGB officers, Kagan denied ever meeting Lessiovsky.[16]

MI5 officers explained away this rather baffling episode to David Leigh as a

KGB 'provocation' – 'a sinister presence designed to throw suspicion on Kagan and hence on Wilson'. It is more likely that Lessiovsky's visit was used by MI5 to discredit the Soviet official by portraying him as an active KGB officer [i.e. running agents] and use his presence to form another 'trace'. Lessiovsky had replaced Vaygauskas in MI5's demonology. MI5 'Watchers' from the 'Wilson coterie' now put Kagan under tighter surveillance and when a Soviet official or KGB officer, Boris Titov, visited his London flat, the place was bugged. On one occasion, Marica Williams telephoned Kagan while Titov was in the room. In this manner, MI5 constructed a No. 10–Kagan–KGB link – the 'Communist cell'. When this was inserted into the dinner party gossip circuit Wilson was informed that Mrs Williams was the 'arch link' and a 'dedicated communist'.[17]

Wilson, now armed with a substantial body of circumstantial evidence that MI5 were behind the dirty tricks campaign, called in MI6 Chief, Maurice Oldfield. The Prime Minister put it to Oldfield that there was a conspiracy by elements of the British secret state – essentially MI5 – against him in particular and the Labour Government in general. 'Oldfield', Wilson told journalists Penrose and Courtiour (and Penrose's bugged briefcase), 'said that there's a section of MI5 which is unreliable . . . he said he was going to bring it out . . . I never heard any more.' Both Cavendish and the late George Kennedy Young suggest that Wilson went further, inviting MI6 to investigate the campaign against the Labour Party – in effect asking MI6 to investigate MI5. Oldfield, on Cavendish's admittedly third-hand account, declined, telling Wilson: 'You have the wrong man in me, Prime Minister'.[18]

Oldfield's reaction, as reported by Wilson, that he would 'bring it out' is more plausible. One of the unacknowledged rules of the British intelligence 'game' is the concealment of internecine conflict. If the opportunity to attack MI5 was welcome, it would have to be done deniably, at arms length. Within those rules, Oldfield's confirmation of Wilson's suspicions about MI5 was a profoundly hostile act. Oldfield could have pleaded ignorance: domestic affairs was not within MI6's brief. With the post-Watergate exposure of the CIA, 'Oldfield and Hanley were terrified by the pace of events abroad, fearful above all that some of the revelations would spill onto their own services.' All those joint operations with the Americans since the war might be revealed. A curious and angry Prime Minister was the last thing the spooks wanted. Yet Oldfield confirmed Wilson's suspicions about MI5.[19]

For MI6, Wilson's unprecedented intervention in the affairs of the secret state was well timed. MI5 and MI6 had been bureaucratic rivals since the end of the Second World War – as the books by Wright and Cavendish demonstrate. This endemic conflict had erupted less than two years before over control of the intelligence side of the war in Northern Ireland. MI6 had been in overall control of the intelligence situation there since 1971, but in late 1973, in a bureaucratic coup still unexplained, MI5 had taken over. Wilson's anger at MI5's activities against him was thus a bureaucratic weapon of major proportions for MI6's Maurice Oldfield: and for all the image we have been given of him as a genial, civilized 'George Smiley' sort of figure, Oldfield had already made this kind of move against MI5. A year before, in mid-1974, MI6 FLUENCY Committee member Stephen de Mowbray had warned Oldfield that he was going to No. 10 to spill the beans about Hollis. Oldfield did not stop him. On Wright's account MI5 Director-General Michael Hanley saw this as 'Bloody Maurice interfering again. How can he let one of his officers prance around to Downing Street and wash all our linen without asking me . . . it's intolerable.'[20]

The day after hearing Wilson's allegations about MI5, Oldfield went straight to Peter Wright, with whom he had been dining regularly. Wright's account of this meeting in *Spycatcher* is worth quoting at some length.

'He returned the conversation to Wilson. "How high had feelings been running in there?" he asked. He kept hearing all sorts of rumours. I was noncommittal. "Most of us don't like him. They think he's wrecking the country." Maurice was clearly preoccupied with the subject, because he returned to it again and again. "You're not telling me the truth," he said finally . . . "I was called in by the Prime Minister yesterday," he said, his tone suddenly changing. "He was talking about a plot. Apparently he's heard that your boys have been going round town stirring things up about him and Marcia Falkender, and Communists at No. 10 . . . I need to know everything. Look what's happening in Washington with Watergate. The same thing will happen here unless we're very careful." I ordered another brandy and decided to tell him everything I knew. When I had finished describing the plans of the previous summer he asked me if Hanley knew. "No," I replied, "I thought it best just to forget the whole thing".' Oldfield told Wright that he wanted him to go back to the office and tell Hanley everything. Wright continues: 'When I saw Hanley the next morning, he went white as a sheet . . . he was learning that half of his staff were up to their necks in a plot to get rid of the Prime Minister . . . "There will have to be an inquiry, of course," said Hanley.'[21]

This is perhaps the most remarkable passage in *Spycatcher*. The Personal Assistant of the Director-General of MI5 is 'regularly' dining with the head of MI6? Why would Wright spill the beans to the organisation he sneers at all the way through his book? At this point, Wright had known for three years that he was not going to get a full pension from MI5 (because MI5 refused to recognise his pre-MI5 employment as contributing towards it, despite – on Wright's account – having said they would); and, further, he believed that MI5 was suppressing the discovery of the Soviet 'mole' in MI5, Roger Hollis, the climax of his life's work, the event which would ensure Wright's place in (secret) history. Had Oldfield not recruited him, 'turned' him? Had Wright not 'defected' to MI5's arch-enemy, MI6?

With Oldfield's confirmation, Wilson then brought in Hanley and put the allegation to him. Forewarned by Wright that Oldfield had confirmed Wilson's fears, Hanley did not deny the allegation but claimed, in Wilson's account to Pincher, 'that only a small number of right-wing officers were involved'. Hanley retaliated against MI6 as best he could by telling Wilson of the involvement of George Kennedy Young, ex-MI6 and a close friend of Oldfield, in the right-wing machinations.[22]

A fortnight after Hanley and Oldfield were confronted by Wilson, the focal point of the CIA hunt in Britain, *Time Out*, received a reported 1,500 pages of photocopied documents from the files of the Institute for the Study of Conflict (ISC), discussed above. The documents were stolen, or leaked by a member of ISC's staff. (There were no signs of a break-in at ISC, but a decent burglar could have done it without leaving traces.) The *Time Out* journalists overcame their initial suspicions that this windfall was a fake designed to discredit them, and published a pair of lengthy articles.[23]

ISC grew out of the CIA's Forum World Features and was largely staffed by former employees of the MI6/Foreign Office psychological warfare outfit, the Information Research Department (IRD). ISC was, in effect, a response to the political pressure upon IRD created by Labour Governments. IRD had already been subject to a review and subsequent pruning under the Labour Government in the sixties, and could reasonably expect more attention. ISC was a quasi-independent alternative. 'Blowing' ISC focused attention away from MI5 on to MI6 and the CIA, and was, we presume, a retaliation by MI5 for Oldfield's confirmation of Wilson's suspicions about them.[24]

Although MI5 had admitted that a number of disgruntled officers were behind the dirty tricks, the campaign did not cease. Obviously it was in their interest to discover exactly what the Prime Minister knew about their activities and what action he intended to take. In July 1977, Joe Haines, who was now at the *Daily Mirror*, wrote an article: 'Why Wilson thought No. 10 was bugged.' Haines dismissed the idea, claiming 'it was all based on the discovery of a "bug" which turned out to be a light picture fitting.' Wilson had thought for some time that he had been bugged and now with Oldfield's confirmation of the MI5 plotting he was convinced that it was true. His offices and home were swept by a debugging expert who was said 'to have come from a private firm'. Wilson could not trust the official agencies to do the job.[25]

In late July 1975, James Goldsmith was introduced to Wilson through the friendship of Lady Annabel Birley and Marcia Williams. One result of this rather bizarre relationship was that, according to Wilson, the financier offered the services of 'a large number of "buggers", I mean "de-buggers", not "buggers"' to 'sweep' No. 10 and later a number of Wilson's private residences. Personnel came from Diversified Corporate Services (DCS), which was one of a number of 'front' companies set up in 1970 by MI6 officers, including John Farmer, who later joined Kleinwort Benson, and his son-in-law, John Pilkington, who had been involved in the abortive sanctions campaign against Rhodesia. Its head was Colonel Alan Pemberton, an Establishment figure who had been Templer's aide-de-camp in Malaya and had links to Buckingham Palace. He was said to have had excellent banking connections and DCS undertook security work for merchant banks. Covertly it undertook bugging operations for MI6 which needed an arm's length approach for freelance activity. Coincidentally, one of DCS's personnel, Major 'Freddy' Mace, had been a covert entry specialist at the Intelligence Centre at Ashford, where a mock-up of 10 Downing Street had been constructed. One of the DCS employees appointed in 1975 was Colonel Peter Goss, former Head of Army Intelligence in Northern Ireland. He was also working part-time in the Cabinet Office on the Joint Intelligence Staff. Goss had been privy to the Clockwork

Orange project on which Colin Wallace had worked. Clearly Wilson knew none of this background. Duncan Campbell comments that 'it is hard not to wonder about the value of assistance from firms so closely associated with the secret services themselves'.[26]

Was Wilson bugged? The circumstantial evidence strongly indicates that he was. Duncan Campbell stated in 1980 that 'together with MI5, the Diplomatic Telecommunications Maintenance Service (DTMS) was responsible for the bugging of Harold Wilson at Downing Street and Westminster'. The DTMS, which is a specialist branch of GCHQ, is the unit most involved in bugging work. Electronic detection facilities are installed by a Post Office security team, which, as *Spycatcher* shows, is closely tied to MI5. MI6 sources told Pincher that the bugging did take place. However much Pincher may ridicule his sources on other issues concerning the plotting against Wilson, he has not produced any reason why MI6 should lie on this matter. It is clear that Pincher did not really believe the denial later issued by Callaghan (discussed below, in Chapter XLVIII).[27]

When Wilson sold his house in Lord North Street in 1979 to William Rees-Davies, the Tory MP found 'some very sophisticated telephonic equipment in the house'. This would have been normal for any Prime Minister but Rees-Davies, who himself had experience of having his telephone tapped, also claimed that when he undertook alterations they discovered a 'positive swarm of bugs'.[28]

In the final months of 1975, after Wilson had seen Hanley about the plotting, MI5 introduced a new security scare into No. 10. They raised the alarm that there was was a traitor within the Cabinet Office itself. Wilson was softened up for this final smear. In the early summer, the Cabinet Secretary, John Hunt, finally let him into the secrets at the heart of MI5's molehunt. Hunt told Wilson of the immunity deal given to Establishment traitor Anthony Blunt, and then he learned that Graham Mitchell, former deputy head of MI5, had come under suspicion and had prematurely retired from the service. He was also told about the Trend Report which concerned Roger Hollis, though it is not clear whether the Prime Minister was ever given real names, or merely the code-names given during the molehunts. Wilson remarked to Mrs Williams: 'Now I've heard everything! I have just been told that the head of MI5 himself may have been a double agent.'[29]

By briefing the Prime Minister on the unmasking of Blunt and the various molehunts, a suitable atmosphere was created whereby information would reach Wilson that his entourage had been infiltrated by the communist left. Wilson had previously dismissed MI5's warnings about security risks as right-wing paranoia. However, if the security service itself could be penetrated perhaps the fears were genuine. MI5 leaked false information that a high-ranking Government official, closely associated with Wilson, was suspected of being the 'fourth or fifth man'. 'He was thought to have been recruited by the Soviet Intelligence Service while a young student at Cambridge', so the smear ran. When Wilson was informed of his identity, he asked Marcia Williams: 'If he is the fourth man can we trust each other now?'[30]

This was the final piece in the construction of MI5's 'Communist cell' at No.

10. It had Wilson shaken. He acknowledged that he had helped the man's career against the advice of some of his colleagues. Further, there was supposed to be a family link to Wilson's close friend Beattie Plummer, who had been regarded as a Soviet bloc 'agent' by the security services. Rumours about the official reached the close circle of senior civil servants at the Treasury, Foreign Office and other key departments. A former Labour Minister, who had turned to the right and was hostile to Wilson, also heard the rumours. The smear was directed against (Sir) Kenneth Berril, head of the Cabinet Office 'think tank', the Central Policy Review Staff (CPRS). When reporters Penrose and Courtiour interviewed Berril in the Cabinet office it was immediately clear that this was an MI5 smear. Berril, a graduate of Trinity College Cambridge, had had no connection with any intelligence organisation or the 'Ring of Five' and could not have been the fourth man. MI5 had a file on Berril going back to his days at the London School of Economics, where he had apparently been linked to a radical magazine. In 1947, he joined Sir Stafford Cripps' economic planning staff and at Cambridge was part of a group which included Nicholas Kaldor. In MI5's blinkered view Berril was thus a 'suspect' left-winger.

The CPRS was regarded by the right as one of those 'hidden, indirect influences in favour of the USSR'. The first head was 'a controversial figure in a controversial job' – Lord Rothschild. Rothschild had also been a close friend of Beattie and Dick Plummer. In the forties, Rothschild, on Plummer's recommendation, was a generous financial contributor to the left-wing paper *Tribune*. In 1971, Auberon Waugh, in *Private Eye*, ran the smear that Rothschild was having trouble with his positive vetting because it revealed that he 'was once a member of the Communist Party'. Waugh later dismissed suggestions that Lord Rothschild could be a Soviet agent as preposterous. However, Berril, according to Richard Deacon, 'had been a much more controversial choice'.[31]

The atmosphere among the Wilson circle in the final months of 1975 was one of paranoia. Rumours were reaching the Prime Minister and his closest advisers, in particular Marcia Williams, about Liberal leader Jeremy Thorpe. There was a general feeling that the rumours were being spread by Wilson's enemies in an orchestrated attempt to destabilise the Government. Labour's working majority was dependent upon Liberal Party support. But who was responsible this time – South Africa?

XLV

BOSS

Those that have known the former Prime Minister will know that he has a great capacity for illuminating the truth long before it becomes apparent to other people.
JAMES CALLAGHAN, MAY 1976

ON 18 SEPTEMBER 1975, a month after Wilson talked to Oldfield and Hanley, an advertisement appeared in *Time Out* seeking 'adventurers'. The ad had been placed on behalf of Faoud 'Fred' Kamil, a security officer for the Anglo-American Corporation. Kamil had made his reputation by reducing the pilferage of diamonds at Anglo-American's South African mines. He was paid by results and his success made him a wealthy man. Around 1970, he became involved in a dispute with Anglo-American, believing that they owed him a lot of money. (The details are of no interest here.) The company refused to pay and Kamil began to wage a kind of guerrilla warfare on it. At one point, Kamil and some associates hi-jacked a plane which they believed was carrying a senior Anglo-American executive. Their information was wrong and Kamil and his colleagues were imprisoned in Malawi.[1]

In December 1975, John Malcolm, one of those recruited via the *Time Out* advertisement, contacted Kenneth Wyatt, whom he had met in prison – Wyatt was there for handling pornographic films – and recruited him to Kamil's cause. Wyatt was flown out to Spain to meet Kamil in January 1976. Kamil told him about his struggle with Anglo-American and, more importantly, showed him some documents purporting to be the 'blueprint' for the destruction of the Liberal Party. This 'blueprint' included the framing of Young Liberal leader Peter Hain for bank robbery and the smearing of Jeremy Thorpe. Kamil told Wyatt that the file had come into his possession via penetration of Anglo-American's security by an associate of his. Wyatt was sent back to Britain to tell this to Peter Hain, the Young Liberal leader, who was then preparing for his trial on a charge of robbing Barclay's Bank in Putney in October.[2]

The 'South African dimension' in British domestic politics had been flickering off and on in the background since the early 1970s. In January 1975, junior

Home Officer Minister Lord Harris had written to the South African Ambassador in London warning that the British Government 'would take the necessary action' if official South African agents were found to be involved in political burglaries. This letter was presumably the political response to evidence of BOSS operations in Britain. Wilson told Chapman Pincher that MI5 had supplied this information to the Cabinet Office: 'There had been suspicions that people used by BOSS had been paying attention to certain black Commonwealth diplomats in London.' This was the first official, if secret at the time, governmental acknowledgement that the agents of South Africa's Bureau of State Security (BOSS) were active in Britain – something which had been known by the black African groups in exile in London and their British supporters for over ten years and which occasionally was reported by the liberal British press.[3]

At the end of January 1976, Peter Hain had told Jeremy Thorpe that the journalist and suspected BOSS agent Gordon Winter was involved in promoting the allegations about Thorpe which were being made by Norman Scott. Hain had learned this from a journalist at the *Daily Mirror*. Hain's information coincided with the appearance in court in Barnstaple of Norman Scott and the first public airing of his allegations about Jeremy Thorpe. The Scott allegations had finally surfaced. Although it is impossible to work out precisely how far back the various intelligence agencies had first learned of these, they had been in the possession of various branches of the British state since the mid-sixties, the Conservative Party had been given them just before the February 1974 General Election, and Wilson had begun hearing the rumours in early 1975.[4]

The day after Scott's brief appearance in court at Barnstaple, Mrs Williams told Wilson: 'Harold you've got to save Jeremy.' With a working majority dependent upon Liberal support, Wilson hardly needed telling. On 30 January a briefing was given to the *Daily Mirror* and the next day's front page lead was on Gordon Winter, 'Thorpe's Hunter Exposed: Man Who Tried to Wreck the Liberals'.[5]

On 3 February 1976, Wilson met Thorpe and said he would attribute the Scott allegations to South Africa. The same day, Peter Hain's mother received a call from Fred Kamil's envoy, Kenneth Wyatt, who wanted to talk about her son's forthcoming trial. Hain and Wyatt met the next day and Wyatt told him about Kamil, his dealings with Anglo-American, and, more importantly, about a South African Government plot to smear the Liberal Party. Unconvinced by Wyatt, who had no evidence to support his tale, Hain did nothing.[6]

A week later, Wilson made another counter-offensive move, sending his friend George Weidenfeld to the US with a letter to Hubert Humphrey, bypassing the British spooks, with questions to put to the CIA. This was unprecedented, announcing to the CIA (and Humphrey) that he did not trust his own intelligence people. Wilson asked:

– about an American 'doctor', a Dr Erskine, who was friendly with Peggy Field, Marcia's sister and Mrs Wilson's secretary, and a businessman called Grenfell-Jones, suspected of undertaking surveillance on the Wilson circle;

- for 'enlightenment concerning the general extent of CIA activities in Britain over recent years';
- if any British politicians had been involved in the Lockheed bribes affair;
- and if CIA money had been used to arm the British mercenaries sent to Angola.[7]

Little thought has been given to this act by Wilson. At first glance it looks naive – did he really expect to get an answer? Though Prime Ministers – especially Labour Prime Ministers – have little contact with the secret services, it is inconceivable that Wilson could be this innocent. Instead, we have to ask how it would have been 'read' in Langley. As a veiled message from Wilson telling them that he was on to them? A warning? A challenge? At any rate, the then Director of the CIA, George Bush, thought it important enough to fly over and make the appropriate denials and concede, regretfully, that the CIA had indeed funded the Angolan mercenaries.[8]

On 18 February, a week after Wilson's extraordinary message to America, Kenneth Wyatt, Malcolm and three other people were arrested in England and charged with conspiracy to demand money with menaces from Anglo-American. At this point, with apparent confirmation of at least part of Wyatt's story, Hain wrote a memo to Thorpe on Wyatt's allegations. Four days later, on 22 February, news of the Wyatt approach to Hain was given to Peter Gladstone-Smith of the *Daily Telegraph*, a journalist who had worked closely with Labour MPs Paul Rose and James Wellbeloved on BOSS stories in the past. Gladstone-Smith put out the story in the last paragraph of a rewrite of the *Express* piece about the hunt for Kamil for his role in 'an international terrorist plot in London against Mr Harry Oppenheim [head of Anglo-American]'. Two days later, 24 February, Hain's report on the Wyatt conversations reached Wilson, via Thorpe.[9]

In the Commons on 9 March 1976, in response to a planted question from James Wellbeloved asking if Wilson had any evidence about the involvement of South African agents in the 'framing' of leading Liberal Party members, Wilson replied that he had 'no doubt that there is strong South African participation in recent activities relating to the leader of the Liberal Party', but had 'no evidence that the South African government or agencies or agents have any connection with these unsavoury activities'. He added, giving what with retrospect is a clear hint about the threat to himself and Edward Heath, that 'Anyone in this House concerned with democracy will feel revolted with the fact that we have to face this sort of thing in so far as the leaders of any party or of all parties are concerned.'[10]

Meanwhile the press had been briefed, for, together with the parliamentary report of this statement, the next day's *Guardian* carried pieces in which Norman Scott recounted his relationship with Gordon Winter and Winter's attempts to get the story published since 1971, as well as a detailed account of the Wyatt allegations about the plan for 'The Disruption of the Liberal Party'. This report also confidently asserted that the Wyatt material had been given to MI6, who 'investigated it and confirmed its plausibility'. We have been unable to confirm this but, if true, it looks like another attempt by Wilson to enroll MI6 against

MI5. For, as his comments to Penrose and Cortiour showed, Wilson knew very well that it wasn't just BOSS who were active.

In the next issue of the *Sunday Telegraph*, Gladstone-Smith reported that as well as an alleged report compiled by MI6 there was one by MI5, who had produced 'a dossier . . . [which] accused South African business interests of employing secret agents and mounting an operation to discredit the Liberal Party. The dossier was the basis of Mr Wilson's Commons statement last week.' This 'MI5 dossier' alleged South African involvement in the Hain frame-up, in the circulation of smear stories against Cyril Smith, in the 'revival' of the Scott–Thorpe allegations, and in the procuring of a pornographic film which included a Liberal MP's daughter, as well as providing evidence that an 'attempt is to be made to smear 5 more prominent Liberals before the next election'.[11]

This 'MI5 dossier' sounds like an invention by Gladstone-Smith, a peg on which he could hang the interview he had conducted with Wyatt almost two weeks before on 3 March. Almost all of the content of this 'dossier' is referred to by Wyatt in that interview. There is, however, one notable addition to the material, namely reference to 'false allegations against Cyril Smith the Liberal Whip, [which] were circulated in his home town of Rochdale'. Wyatt did not apparently name Smith. Gladstone-Smith's reference to 'South African business interests' is also striking. Interviewing Wyatt, what Gladstone-Smith heard about was not BOSS, but Anglo-American security police. For others, for example the *Guardian* of 29 April, Kenneth Wyatt and Anita Sassin, another member of Kamil's 'gang', were 'part of Kamil's evidence of a BOSS plot against the Liberal Party in general'. BOSS is referred to both in the Anita Sassin interview – 'BOSS and Anglo-American work together' – conducted by Paul Rose MP, and in some of the anonymous letters which Kamil was sending to politicians (including Wilson) at this point.[12]

There is, thus, no mystery about the basis for Wilson's Commons statement. He had known about Winter's role in the Thorpe–Scott affair since 1974, when he was told by Sydney (Lord) Jacobsen, at the Mirror Group. The simultaneous arrival of the Kamil–Wyatt allegations with the Thorpe–Scott story's reappearance was merely more of the same. Whether or not Wilson actually had the 'conclusive evidence' about South African involvement which he claimed to Barbara Castle barely matters. 'South Africa' was a useful short-hand, almost a metaphor, for the other forces he knew were at work against him. His problem was that the evidence he did have was about MI5's activities against him; but this he felt unable to use.[13]

PART FIVE

1976–79

XLVI

RESIGNATION

*The message I received from a very senior member of MI6 [was] that I
would not be wasting my time trying to find out why Wilson resigned
because there was 'something of a mystery there'.*
CHAPMAN PINCHER

ON 16 MARCH 1976, Wilson stunned the political world by announcing his
intention to resign. In *The Wilson Plot*, David Leigh suggests that Wilson's
decision was taken just after his confrontation with Michael Hanley over the
plotting. We are left to infer that the two events are in some way linked. Leigh is
not alone in finding something unexplained in Wilson's resignation. Anthony
Cavendish, for example, wrote in his memoir: 'I believe that there was something
that triggered Wilson's abrupt resignation, and it is related to something about
which no outsider knows all the details . . . if something came into Maurice's
[Oldfield] hands relating to the Prime Minister of the day, his duty would be
clear, he would show it to one of three people: the Prime Minister himself, the
Cabinet Secretary or his immediate boss, the Foreign Secretary. I believe from
things Maurice said that something may have come into his hands and that he
showed it to the Foreign Secretary, James Callaghan.' For Chapman Pincher,
grazing on fields not so far from Cavendish, the resignation was 'the biggest
mystery of post-war politics'.[1]

Alas for those seeking a mystery, there is none. From the three people closest
to Wilson during his last two years in office, Bernard Donoghue, head of his
Policy Unit, Marcia Falkender (Williams), and Joe Haines, his Press Secretary,
there is unanimity about what actually happened. 'In the late 1960s, he had
already indicated that if he won a further election, he would want to stay as leader
and Prime Minister for a further two years only. Those close to him, therefore,
knew that if Labour had been returned in the election of 1970, he would have
probably resigned in 1972: when they went into Downing Street with him in
1974 they were equally aware that his intention was to resign in 1976 – unless
prevented by crisis.'[2]

When Donoghue joined Wilson in March 1974, he was told 'to arrange two years' leave from the London School of Economics because he [Wilson] would retire in the spring of 1976 on reaching his sixtieth birthday'. Joe Haines confirmed this in a letter to the *Guardian* in 1987. Further evidence – were any needed – comes from Tony Benn's driver, Ron Vaughan, who told Benn in April 1975 that Wilson had arranged for all future Prime Ministers to have their own car and chauffeur for life. The drivers in the car pool had concluded that 'the crafty bugger must be preparing to get out, and then he'll have a car for life'. The closest connection we can get to the 1975 meetings in August with Oldfield and Hanley is October that year when Wilson instructed Haines and his Principal Private Secretary, Sir Kenneth Stowe, to draw up a resignation timetable. This timetable foresaw Wilson resigning on 5 April 1976 – which, as Haines noted, is what he did.[3]

Why did Wilson resign? There is no single overriding factor. Centrally, he was tired and disillusioned with the business of holding together the warring factions inside the Party. He had been under continuous assault by the media and the secret state for over a decade and to cope with the stress he had begun drinking rather a lot. A part of him had been a reluctant politician – had it not been for the war he would have remained an academic – and he wanted to write books. Mary, his wife, had never enjoyed being married to a politician and he wanted to spend more time with her and his family. On top of all that, he believed that politicians really ought to leave office when they reached 60: after that they became stale and repetitive. Essentially, perhaps, the job had ceased to be any fun.[4]

Wilson's resignation was thus a secret and a surprise, but not a mystery. Far from the activities of the spooks influencing his decision to resign, it was his intention to go which influenced his actions towards the spooks. Confronting Oldfield and Hanley, going over their heads to the CIA, was the act of someone who knew he was going and could, therefore, afford to take some risks. Wilson was de-mob happy.

Because Fred Kamil never did produce any evidence, because his little band of conspirators were arrested shortly after Wyatt and Sassin were interviewed, and because the Kamil episode dribbled off into other South African 'connections' which appeared to be nonsensical – those involving André Thorne and 'Colonel Cheeseman', discussed below – the Kamil allegations were dismissed. Yet there was rather more to them than was given credit at the time. Reading the original interviews with Wyatt and Sassin, what is striking about them is the modesty – and incomplete nature – of their allegations. The *Sunday Times*, in its rubbishing of the entire episode, suggested that Wyatt had invented the story 'in some convoluted reasoning, to protect himself from a serious charge' – i.e. the conspiracy with Sassin, Kamil and others to blackmail Anglo-American. Wyatt, however, spoke of the 'plot' before he was arrested and charged. It is clear that both Sassin and Wyatt did see some kind of documents. Gordon Winter confirms that BOSS did indeed have files on leading members of the Liberal Party, and Wyatt's allegations contained a number of striking details about the plot against the Liberals which very closely resembled the information Colin Wallace had been handling in his post as psy-ops officer in Northern Ireland.[5]

The motives of Fred Kamil in this period remain unclear. In his biography, he glosses over the whole business. However, it is possible to assemble the incomplete evidence we have in several ways. The simplest explanation is that Kamil was as he appeared, i.e. a self-interested mercenary, using the 'files' not to expose the plot, but as further pressure on Anglo-American. When journalists did track him down in Spain he refused to talk about the 'political plot', instead he talked only of his grievance against Anglo-American. The 'plots' were a brilliantly effective enticement for the media. This, however, presupposes that the 'plot' documents were genuine, and this strikes us as unlikely – if only because we find it hard to believe that BOSS would actually produce a 'blue print' for the sabotage of a party, complete with easy-to-understand 'The Disruption of the Liberals Party' heading. It seems more likely that Kamil was simultaneously furthering his dispute with Anglo-American and playing a part in the BOSS operations, using fabricated documents (describing a genuine operation!) to 'brief' Wyatt and Sassin on 'the plot'. For, if nothing else, to warn of a 'smear campaign' alerts the media to the existence of smears (whether true or false). The information brought back by Sassin and Wyatt did indeed warn of a smear campaign, but also – particularly in the case of Wyatt – communicated the nature of the smears to the British media. The acid test is that Kamil never did deliver any of these 'documents' – and he could have done so in a dozen easy ways. Even if under surveillance, getting material from Spain to London is not impossible. If the documents were genuine, why did he not just send Wyatt and Sassin back with copies of them?

No longer Prime Minister, Wilson continued trying to nudge the British media into action. A month after his resignation, on 8 May, in a speech in Halifax, he hinted that Labour as well as Liberal MPs were the target of smears. Four days later, he gave the parliamentary journalists another hint, talking again about dark forces in British politics, and contacted Barrie Penrose, then with BBC TV. Penrose took another BBC journalist, Roger Courtiour, along to the first meeting with Wilson. Although both Courtiour and Penrose had been working on the South African connection, and both had worked on South African stories in the past, they were not Wilson's first choice. He had already hinted to the editors of the *Observer* and the *Guardian* about mounting an investigation – without success. To Penrose and Courtiour, Wilson voiced his suspicions about MI5, told them in particular of the 'Communist cell' story of the summer before and his conversations with Oldfield and Hanley, and offered to be a clandestine source for the two journalists if they would investigate it. Wilson saw himself as 'the big fat spider in the corner of the room'. In talking to Penrose and Courtiour the 'big fat spider' had broken the Official Secrets Act, his Privy Council oath and, in effect, decided to take the spooks on.[6]

While Pencourt (as Penrose and Courtiour quickly became known in a snide echo of Woodstein – Woodward and Bernstein, the *Washington Post* journalists who investigated Watergate) went back to their bosses at the BBC with this extraordinary news, two disinformation hares had been set loose. The opening moves of the first project had begun six weeks earlier on 12 March. A 20-year-old youth, André Thorne, had gone to the *Guardian* and reported that in 1975 he had taken part in the making of a pornographic film with 'a prominent politician'.[7]

On 15 May, Peter Hillmore of the *Guardian*, who had been reporting on the 'South African connection', wrote a long piece about Thorne, the blue film, the South African Embassy and an unnamed British politician. Hillmore commented in his piece that 'Such tales are relatively common at the moment.' Gordon Winter provides the further detail that the film was said to involve a Liberal MP, dressed as a scoutmaster, interfering with young boys. Thorne claimed that he had been approached by the South African Embassy about obtaining a copy of it. Hillmore went with Thorne to the South African Embassy, had an inconclusive talk with the Embassy official concerned, and published a piece which carefully suggested that while they did not have any evidence, Thorne seemed to them to be telling the truth. The opening sentence of Hillmore's piece began: 'The *Guardian* has discovered a direct link between a South African diplomat and a leading British politician.' In fact the story did not live up to that opening sentence. Moreover, the whole affair was to backfire.[8]

André Thorne went to the *Sunday People* and told them that he had made up the whole story. Much derisory comment on the *Guardian* then followed in the tabloid press. The South African Embassy released an edited version of the interview with Hillmore, which appeared to refute his version of the meeting. Scotland Yard was called in, concluded that Thorne's allegations were groundless and, despite the *Guardian* printing the entire, unedited – and uninteresting – text of the conversation with the Embassy official, the story imploded, just like the Kamil episode. Yet, as with the Kamil case, on close examination there was much about Thorne's story which made it possible for journalists to accept it initially. To give just two examples: Thorne accurately described the room he claimed to have met the Embassy official in; and he did receive some money from the Embassy after a visit there. Gordon Winter says he was told by BOSS that the whole thing was mounted by the Bureau, not to get the South Africans involved, but to launch the smear story about the MP. Thorne himself had embroidered the story with the South African official angle, not appreciating that this would change the way it looked to the press. Thorne's approach had been intended as a part of the BOSS operation to smear the Liberals, amplification of the blue movie–MP element in Kenneth Wyatt's original allegations. Happily for the South Africans, however, it 'seriously discredited efforts to expose any South African plot'. However, for Pencourt, worse was to follow, almost immediately.[9]

On 17 May, two days after the Thorne episode appeared in the *Guardian*, Pencourt learned from Peter Hain that a former British intelligence agent, apparently with evidence of a smear campaign, had approached the Liberal Party. The next day Pencourt found the identity of the source and beat the Liberals to him. Claiming to be have been a Lieutenant-Colonel, Frederick Cheeseman duly informed Pencourt that he had seen dossiers on British politicians, including Jeremy Thorpe, in BOSS headquarters. Two days later, after much checking of these allegations, a Cheeseman interview went out on BBC TV. Unnoticed at the time, a Nicholas Comfort piece appeared in the *Daily Telegraph* on the same day, reporting that 'persistent efforts have been made in recent months to discredit leading members of the three major British political parties by planting derogatory stories about them on news agencies in Washington.'[10]

Like the Thorne story, Cheeseman's 'revelations' imploded when he told the *Daily Express* that it was all a hoax. Another bout of tabloid derision was aimed at the journalists trying to work on the 'South African connection'. Penrose and Courtiour commented that they 'were being subjected to the same process as the *Guardian* over André Thorne'. Fortuitous in the case of Thorne, but apparently deliberate with Cheeseman, the 'process', according to Colin Wallace, was a psychological warfare technique called the 'double bubble', which 'contains a second dimension in deception and not only deflects attention from the main target but "bursts" leaving the investigator doubting everything he has un-covered so far'. In fact, as only the *Sunday Telegraph* had the intelligence to note at the time, Cheeseman's claims had been substantiated.[11]

In that *Sunday Telegraph* piece, the Thorne/Cheeseman affair had been portrayed as 'an elaborate South African plot aimed at discrediting the British media'. In our view the episodes involving Kamil, Wyatt, Sassin, Thorne and Cheeseman were part of the same operation. By the end of the episode the existence of smear stories about the Liberals – and some of their content – had been broadcast by the media but the 'South African connection' had been discredited and abandoned by all but a handful of the British journalists. Discrediting 'the South African connection', not the media, had been the objective. The ridicule heaped on the *Guardian* over André Thorne was merely a bonus.

By March 1976, a month before his planned resignation, Wilson knew that there were serious plots against him. He had the evidence of his own eyes and ears – the deluge of smears and gossip that had accompanied the 1974 Government: the 'private armies' episode; rumours of coups; a number of known tip-offs, discussed above; others we must reasonably presume we have not heard of. He had received confirmation from Oldfield and Hanley that MI5 were involved and had already sent a message via Weidenfeld to the CIA; and on the next day, 11 February, he had heard of the 1968 Cecil King 'coup plot' from Lord Zuckerman. At this point, Wilson was the man in the William Burroughs aphorism, the paranoid who really was the only one who knew what was going on. More, he had a problem: what could he actually do about it? The people who should investigate such things for the PM, MI5, were at the centre of the plots.[12]

Wilson's behaviour in this period is quite intelligible (and intelligent). He was planning to resign. He did not have access to independent sources of informa-tion and had the political problem of ensuring a smooth transition to his successor and maintaining the Government with help of the Liberals. The Kamil/Hain material about the 'South African plots' provided the basis for a political gamble, a defensive hare about the Liberals and South Africans which might just conceivably provoke some journalists into digging into the anti-Labour campaigns; and, more importantly, which might postpone Thorpe's political demise until after Wilson's long-planned resignation. In a remarkable passage in *The Pencourt File*, Wilson revealed something of what he thought might have happened had Thorpe resigned in February or March 1976, just before his planned resignation: 'They would have linked my going with his. There was a double scandal, they would have said his homosexual partner the Prime Minister, or something like this.' From what we know of the kinds of smears being run at the time, this is exactly the story which would have been spread.[13]

XLVII

'THE BIG FAT SPIDER'

We were naïve. We didn't know anything about the intelligence services.
We didn't know what it all meant. Who did then? It was completely foreign
to us.
BARRIE PENROSE

AFTER HAVING THEIR fingers burned by Cheeseman, Penrose and
Courtiour went back to the cuttings library, to discover that there was more there
than they had realised, some concerning Norman Scott. Wilson had told them of
letters from Scott's lawyer which talked of 'a visit to South Africa and his being
paid large sums of money'. They met Scott on 20 May and, to their surprise, he
immediately handed over his files, after a quick perusal of which 'the two
reporters began to suspect they were seeing the tip of an enormous iceberg'. But
it was not the one Harold Wilson had in mind. From this point on, the central
focus of their investigation shifted away from the activities of the intelligence
services on to the Scott–Thorpe story. It was not their fault. If investigating the
intelligence services in this country is difficult now, it was infinitely more so in
1976 and 1977. Wilson had actually told them very little of substance and none
of his leads produced anything useable. The one really solid lead they discovered, the existence of the attempts to plant smear stories about Wilson,
Heath, Thorpe et al. in news agencies in the United States, came to nothing.
The packet of material sent to them by the head of the agency Edward Von
Rothkirk disappeared *en route* and the agency was then burgled and suffered an
'incident' which destroyed the relevant files. In striking contrast to the long
succession of dead ends they experienced trying to research the intelligence
component of the story, there was Scott, co-operative, handing them files of
material. It is hard to imagine any journalist in 1976 not behaving the way
Pencourt did.[1]

Their research on Scott–Thorpe did not, however, please the BBC's senior
managers. The editor of TV news told them: 'You've produced extraordinary
information but you're like puppy dogs who keep bringing back sticks. These
sticks always seem to have some connection with Thorpe.' As they recounted

their first conversations with Wilson, the BBC's Director, Sir Charles Curran, had commented that 'almost everything fitted'. Not long before, Curran had heard about 'a rift within British intelligence'. That Curran had heard of this is not suprising. The BBC's long relationship with the Foreign Office would ensure that its higher executives had access to intelligence information. Curran's comment suggests he knew of the split between MI5 and MI6: his subsequent behaviour suggests he had taken the side of MI6, for the BBC's management first tried to steer the journalists away from the Scott–Thorpe story; and when that failed, they tried to take over the project, asserting BBC rights to the material.

The 'rift' Curran mentioned seems to have been reflected within the BBC's hierarchy. The only senior member reported by Penrose and Courtiour as enthusiastic about their research was deputy editor of TV News Alan Protheroe, who was a part-time Information Officer in the British Army. A decade later, Protheroe blocked transmission of the first BBC interview with Colin Wallace. The Pencourt–Wilson investigation leaked from the BBC right from the beginning. Reports of its progress went to BOSS, that we know of (and presumably to MI5), and to Paul Foot at *Private Eye*, resulting in a series of detailed stories shadowing and mocking Pencourt's investigation. The dispute between Pencourt and the BBC dragged on through August to the end of September when the relationship was severed.[2]

Running parallel to the Wilson–Pencourt–BBC investigation, the spook-hunting story which began in 1975 continued to grow. Most alarming for the British permanent government, the initial interest in the CIA had expanded to include their British counterparts. After their articles on Forum World Features and ISC, in May 1976, *Time Out* published Mark Hosenball and Duncan Campbell's ground-breaking essay on signals intelligence, 'The Eavesdroppers'. One or two left-wing Labour MPs began working on the fringes of this little group of researchers.[3]

In November 1976, Philip Agee and Mark Hosenball were served with deportation orders on grounds of 'national security'. Round them formed the Agee–Hosenball Defence Committee which campaigned not only for their right to stay in this country, but also against the CIA and covert operations in general. In February 1977, the Committee's members began to experience the full-range of break-ins and thefts of documents which are now the hall-mark of MI5/Special Branch offensive operations. The trigger for this campaign was a letter to the Committee by John Berry, a former corporal in signals intelligence, who wanted to publish his knowledge of the secret world. On 18 February, the day the deportations of Agee and Hosenball were confirmed, journalists Crispin Aubrey and Duncan Campbell from the Defence Committee had their first meeting with John Berry – at the end of which all three were arrested and charged with offences under the Official Secrets Act.[4]

In retrospect it is striking, if not surprising, how many of the people involved with Agee were subsequently attacked by the intelligence services. Convenor of the Agee–Hosenball Committee, Phil Kelly, was the subject of an MI5-generated smear which described him as a KGB asset. John Berry, Crispin

Aubery and Duncan Campbell were brought to court but eventually acquitted of offences under the Official Secrets Act in what became known as 'the ABC trial'. Mark Hosenball was deported. Paul Rose MP, who spoke for Agee at the Tribunal which deported him and who had been active in the hunt for BOSS operations since 1970, was smeared in a forged CIA dossier about him circulated in 1977. Labour MP Tom Litterick, who had been asking awkward questions about British and American intelligence operations, and who had appeared for the defence in the prosecution of Aubery, Berry and Campbell, was smeared in May 1977 when fifteen national and local newspapers carried an account of Litterick's alleged failure to provide for his family after separation from his wife. Litterick sued them all, and won.[5]

Meanwhile, the campaign of denigration against Wilson continued. In February 1977, Joe Haines added fuel to the fire with the publication of his memoir of life at No. 10, *The Politics of Power*. Haines' serious comments about British political life were largely ignored by the press which (unsurprisingly) concentrated on one chapter in which Haines described the influence – largely malign, in his view – of Mrs Williams. This provided the context for the *Sun* to publish what purported to be extracts from a forthcoming memoir by another of Wilson's retinue in the 1960s, George Caunt. On 18 February, *The Times* recycled Caunt's account of disputes between Wilson and Mrs Williams during the 1966 election campaign. After Robin Day had asked Joe Haines, on BBC's *Panorama*, who had paid the bills for Wilson's Private Office while in opposition, the *Daily Mail* devoted almost two pages to the story of the fund that had been set up in 1970 to pay its cost. The trustees were Lord Wilfred Brown, Lord Fisher, Sir Rudy Sternberg, Lord Goodman and Arieh Handler of the International Credit Bank. The next day, the *Daily Telegraph* rehashed the *Mail* story, but with a sting in the tail, reporting in the final paragraphs that 'the intriguing question of whether Lady Falkender had access to Cabinet Secrets – Sir Harold Wilson's and Lady Falkender's recollection are that she did not – appeared to be answered yesterday when it was reported that a minute was in existence giving her the authority to see Cabinet documents'. Four days later (22 February), the *Sun* published this 'minute', a 1965 letter from then Principal Private Secretary Derek Mitchell to Wilson which had been 'hoarded by George Caunt', who by this time had been recruited by MI5. According to Pincher, Caunt also named Lady Plummer as one of the people of whom MI5 were suspicious.[6]

On 22 and 28 March 1977, Pencourt briefed Mrs Williams on their research so far. At their story of the alleged Liberal Party murder conspiracy against Scott *et al*, Mrs Williams blanched. By this time Wilson had abandoned his role as 'the big fat spider in the corner'. At the beginning of May, there were more meetings with Mrs Williams. 'If it all came out she said, "He [Wilson] said it would, of course, be helping the South Africans".' She reported that Lord Goodman did not want Wilson to even read Pencourt's information on the alleged conspiracy to murder Norman Scott lest he be subpoenaed as a witness in court proceedings. It was 'better if Harold didn't see you again', she advised them.[7]

On 14 May 1977, *The Times* published, in full, Wilson's statement to the Royal Commission on the Press (apparently written by Joe Haines). This is a remarkable document whose full import was never considered at the time by a media and political culture which had persuaded itself that Wilson was paranoid about the press. To anyone who reads this page-long account of smears and harassment now, it is immediately clear that Wilson had cause to be paranoid. Although quite extraneous to the Royal Commission on the Press, Wilson also took the opportunity of listing all the burglaries he and those around him had suffered. At this stage he still felt unable to mention publicly his anxieties about the intelligence services.[8]

Pencourt, meanwhile, having left the BBC, had sold the serialisation rights to their forthcoming book to the *Observer*. Wilson's fears about MI5 finally emerged in public on 17 July when the *Observer* ran the first of several extracts based on Penrose and Courtiour's 'notes' of their conversations with Wilson. These included:

– the whispering campaign in 1975 about 'the Communist cell';
– Lord Weidenfeld's visit to Hubert Humphrey with a message to the CIA;
– MI5's 'confusion' of Will Owen with David Owen, and Judith Hart with Mrs Tudor Hart.

The cat was finally out of the bag.

XLVIII

WHITEHALL GAMES

Harold Wilson is absolutely paranoid.
DAVID OWEN AND MERLYN REES, 1977

Harold is just a Walter Mitty.
JAMES CALLAGHAN, 1978

IN RESPONSE to the *Observer* revelations of Wilson's allegations about MI5, Labour MP Gwilym Roberts asked Prime Minister James Callaghan in a written parliamentary question on 26 July 1977, 'if he will move to set up a Select Committee to examine in detail the operation and structure of the counter-intelligence services'. Callaghan's answer was 'No'. Two days later, Pincher ran his 'Wilson was bugged at No. 10' story in the *Express*. Pincher claimed initially that he had been 'touched off' by the *Observer* story. In fact, he had been given the story in 1976 by Bruce McKenzie, who, Pincher suspects, got it from Maurice Oldfield. This was the second big leak he had been given by MI6 which supported Wilson – and attacked MI5. The year before, after Wilson resigned, MI6 had leaked to Pincher an MI5 report which not only included details of MI5 surveillance on Wilson just before the February 1974 General Election, but expressed some of MI5's objections to Wilson.[1]

Pincher says of this period that Oldfield 'was most anxious to assure the new Prime Minister, James Callaghan, that his department had not been involved in any nefarious activities and he was not averse to any non-attributable publicity making that clear'. On the basic political principle of 'my enemy's enemy is my friend', Oldfield was making trouble for MI5; and what better way than to support Wilson's allegations which were directed against that service. In Chapter 15 of *A Web of Deception*, Pincher not only denies getting anything 'directly from MI5' but says his intelligence sources were MI6 – Oldfield himself, using Bruce McKenzie as insulation, a cut-out. Pincher describes McKenzie, a neighbour of his, as 'an extraordinarily well-informed Kenyan politician and a close friend of Sir Maurice Oldfield'; but he was also an MI6 agent of long standing. McKenzie, says Pincher, gave him information on the plot, and the story of the bugging of No. 10. Pincher took the story about the MI5 plot to Oldfield, who confirmed it. With one of the great understatements in this entire saga, Pincher calls this act of Oldfield's 'a mild deception operation to impugn MI5'.[2]

On 2 August 1977, Colin Wallace wrote to Wilson asking for an appointment to see him. It was two years since Wallace had lost the job he loved in Northern Ireland to these MI5/MI6 machinations, and had begun to realise that some – only some – of the projects he had been working on there had been illegal and unconstitutional. The reply came from Mrs Williams: Wilson was on holiday until September, would Mr Wallace put the details of what he wanted to discuss in a letter? Wallace did put some of them in a letter but heard nothing more. By this time Wilson was in retreat.[3]

The *Observer* articles, the escalation from Wilson's vague talk a year before of South African business interests to naming MI5 and describing some of their activities, produced widespread disbelief – and the inevitable political counter-attack. In another striking coincidence, Pincher's *Express* story on the bugging of No. 10 appeared the day that Conservative MP Peter Blaker (ex-FO), as a means of attacking Wilson, initiated a House of Commons debate on the security services. Blaker accused Wilson of shaking 'public confidence in the security services', breaching the Official Secrets Act and his oath as a Privy Councillor. (All of which are true, of course, and a measure of Wilson's actions.) To Conservative MP Stephen Hastings (ex-MI6), the *Observer* articles were 'an attempt, conscious or otherwise, to confuse public reaction and to discredit the security services'. He described Wilson as 'positively paranoic' (sic), and ran some of Frolik's allegations through the House, promising that 'a version of the book is soon to be published in the United States and that the information that it contains will be fuller than was allowed by our libel laws.' In other words, it would contain the names of Frolik's 'agents' in the Labour Party and unions. Hastings topped this off with the suggestion that Wilson and/or the *Observer* was working for the KGB: 'Could it be – and it would be consistent with the known tactics of the KGB – that it was worried about the publication of such a work [i.e. Frolik's book] and that an attempt to counter its effect by confusing the issue in the manner that I have described was behind the articles in the *Observer*?'[4]

In this debate, the permanent government – under nominal Labour control – gave its first reply through junior Home Office Minister Dr Shirley Summerskill. Noting that the 'arrangements' [for accountability to Ministers] had been 'reviewed and further improved only last year', she was 'authorised to assure the House that on the basis of these arrangements my right Hon. Friends [i.e. Home Secretary Rees and Prime Minister Callaghan] are confident that the service concerned [MI5] is carrying out its duties within the limits laid down in the directive to the Director-General issued in September 1952 and which remains in force.'

Dr Summerskill's statement did not satisfy the Conservatives and, eventually, Prime Minister Callaghan was called to the Commons late on the morning of 29 July. Mrs Thatcher, leader of the Opposition, asked if 'any request [had] been received from the Government to make a statement on the matters which have previously been raised concerning allegations made against the security services?

We think it vital that such a statement be made before the Summer Recess for the confidence and morale of the security services and because it would appear that there may, on the face of it, be some infringements of the Official Secrets Act.'[5]

Callaghan replied: 'A great many matters are being written and spoken about at the present time, but there is very little hard fact, as far as I can see. If anyone who has any information about what has taken place cares to place it before the appropriate authority – who in this case would be the Home Secretary – then, of course, the matter would be looked into. As to the present situation, I am quite satisfied with the arrangements at No. 10 and what is going on in the security services . . . My responsibility is to make sure that these matters are now properly conducted. That I have done.'

Just after the debate, 'Callaghan had telephoned Wilson several times late at night to say that he might not be able to avoid a security inquiry because of the atmosphere in the Commons.' Mrs Williams thought Callaghan was 'baiting' Wilson. To 'read' this correctly it must be remembered that an inquiry was what Wilson had wanted; but now any inquiry would include his breaches of the Privy Council and (perhaps) the Official Secrets Act. Two days after Callaghan's statement to the House, in the *Observer*, 31 July, Wilson called for an inquiry into the allegations of electronic bugging at No. 10 reported by Pincher, while simultaneously making light of them and denying that he ever believed them to be true![6]

On 23 August, with Parliament in recess, Whitehall tried to find a form of words which would make the story go away. A statement was issued in Callaghan's name. 'The Prime Minister has conducted detailed inquiries into the recent allegations about the security service and is satisfied that they do not constitute grounds for lack of confidence in the competence and impartiality of the security service or for instituting a special inquiry. In particular, the Prime Minister is satisfied that at no time has the security service or any other British intelligence agency or security agency, either of its own accord or at someone else's request, undertaken electronic surveillance in 10 Downing Street or in the Prime Minister's room in the House of Commons.'

Presumably conducted by Cabinet Secretary Sir John Hunt, this cannot have been much of an inquiry. Callaghan set it in train after Wilson's comments in the *Observer* on 17 July and issued his statement five weeks later. Pincher checked this 'inquiry' and found that 'questioning had been limited to the Cabinet Secretary and . . . the Directors-General of MI5 and MI6, the chief of GCHQ and the Co-ordinator of Intelligence'. In a letter, 2 August 1976, to Peter Wright in Tasmania, MI5 Director-General Michael Hanley remarked on 'the recent examinations' which 'the firm' had passed. Wright heard that this 'examination' had been done by 'a member of the Security Commission [who] was called in to make a private inquiry for the Cabinet Office' – thus revealing another piece in the Whitehall intelligence mechanism.[7]

Callaghan's statement is a classic piece of Whitehall 'economy with the truth'. Had the statement been written with the aim of being clear and informative it would have said something like this: 'We did not examine any of Wilson's allegations but we did have a look at the Chapman Pincher story in the *Daily Express* and the people we spoke to deny it.' By not specifying what the 'recent allegations' were it gave the impression that an inquiry had been held into Wilson's wider allegations. This was reinforced by putting the specific denial of bugging in a separate paragraph. In fact, as Merlyn Rees, the then Home Secretary, began telling the House of Commons in 1987, 'We were not inquiring into the allegations which are now being made by Wright and others, we were inquiring into alleged electronic devices at Number 10.'[8]

Even so, in Callaghan's statement the security service was not praised or reaffirmed in any way; it was not even completely cleared. The statement merely stated that 'the recent allegations do not constitute grounds for lack of confidence in the competence and impartiality of the security service or for instituting a special inquiry'. Though some way short of a ringing endorsement, this mendacious statement has done more than anything else to impede attempts to get at the truth, being trotted out on every occasion since to demonstrate to (mostly Labour) MPs that there had been an inquiry which had cleared MI5. Whatever had transpired in 1976 and 1977, there is no evidence that the allegations against MI5 were subjected to detailed investigation.

These statements ended any lingering hopes Wilson might have had of getting a decent inquiry, let alone the Royal Commission 'to examine the accountability of the Security Services' which he had talked of with Penrose and Courtiour a year before. Whitehall, the permanent government, was dealing with it, in-house. 'By the autumn of 1977 . . . Sir Harold had also felt questioning pressure from the Cabinet Office. Officials wanted to know what exactly he had told Penrose and Courtiour.' Roger Courtiour remembers talk of Wilson being prosecuted for breach of his Privy Council Oath if he persisted in his allegations. We find it difficult to believe that Wilson ever seriously believed he would get a Royal Commission. He was a constitutional sophisticate, if nothing else, and the idea that 'the Crown' would appoint a Crown inquiry into one of its central secrets was an absurdity he would never have believed, no matter how angry or stressed. Nor did Wilson ever publicly campaign for such a Royal Commission, even when given the perfect context – the *Observer* articles, the Commons debate – in which to do so. Wilson may have been disappointed when Callaghan had not publicly set up an immediate inquiry, but he can hardly have been surprised.[9]

In late 1977, Penrose and Courtiour, anxious not to be portrayed as simply adjuncts of the Labour Party, contacted the Tory Party and played the tapes of their conversations with Wilson in the House of Commons to a group of Tory MPs, including Airey Neave (ex-MI6), Norman Tebbit, Cranley Onslow (ex-MI6), Peter Blaker (ex-FO) and Ray Whitney (ex-IRD) – men either close to Mrs Thatcher or from the permanent government. After hearing the Wilson tapes Blaker tried again. On 7 November, he asked Callaghan to refer Wilson's talk with Penrose and Courtiour and the *Observer* to the Attorney General. He quoted Callaghan's statement in August as demonstrating that Wilson was talking nonsense: 'There can seldom have been such a sharp rap over the knuckles by a new Prime Minister of the same party.' Blaker then wrote to Wilson. Wilson's reply, reprinted in full in *The Pencourt File*, offers a revised –

and false – version of the whole of his contacts with Penrose and Courtiour. Wilson was now in total retreat. Once again, having been the victim of the machinations of the security and intelligence services, Labour was on the defensive.[10]

In the early morning of 14 December 1977, after an all-night Commons sitting at the end of a parliamentary session, former MI6 officer Stephen Hastings finally ran some of the details of the Frolik allegations through the Commons, naming Ted Hill, Jack Jones, Richard Briginshaw, Ernie Roberts and Hugh Scanlon as 'agents' of Soviet or Czech intelligence. Hastings' pretext for trying this again was a letter from Frolik (being run by the CIA) to Joseph Josten (funded by MI6 but in this exercise being run by the CIA). This little operation was completed the next day when *The Times* added to their report of Hastings' remarks the night before the fantasy that: 'The key passage in the letter written by Mr Frolik to a friend in London, stated that three months after Sir Harold, as Prime Minister, made his statement in the Commons in December 1974, to the effect that Mr Stonehouse was not a spy, he had sent a high official of MI5 to apologise to Mr Frolik.'[11]

The next day, Callaghan refused Peter Blaker's request that Wilson's conversations be reported to the Attorney General and dismissed Frolik: 'The general allegations have been floating around since January 1974 . . . and have been investigated in the past . . . These matters were looked into two or three years ago and recently Mr Frolik has been embroidering the original story he told when he was debriefed.'

Into 1978, the Tories kept the story running. Cranley Onslow wrote to Callaghan about the statements attributed to Wilson in *The Pencourt File*, urging that the Security Commission undertake a full inquiry. On 20 February, Callaghan replied to Onslow that: 'So far as I can see, there are no significant statements about matters of national security in this book of which the authorities were not aware when I issued a statement on allegations about the Security Service on 23 August last. I have nothing to add.' This is another masterpiece of Whitehall writing. By linking 'national security' and his statement of 23 August 1977, the impression is given that the inquiry he described investigated matters of 'national security' – when all it did was ask the heads of the British intelligence and security services if their people had been bugging the Prime Minister. Further, the criterion of 'significant statements about matters of national security' is simply a means of avoiding the content of Wilson's allegations. To be worthy of consideration, this statement says, a proposition would not only have to pertain to 'national security' (undefined) but do so 'significantly' (undefined). The Callaghan statement of the year before made no mention of 'national security': it was added here.[12]

Although these various statements emanating from No. 10 were designed to obfuscate rather than illuminate, looked at carefully it is apparent that there had been serious political fall-out from Wilson's charges; but it had been kept discreetly hidden away inside the permanent government where the Home and Foreign Office mandarins tried to use the trouble to assert their control over the intelligence and security services.

Something happened in 1976 – Dr Summerskill referred to a 'review' that year, presumably the same one that Hanley referred to in his letter to Wright. During the debate following Mrs Thatcher's Prime Ministerial statement on Anthony Blunt in 1979, James Callaghan described, but did not date, a meeting he had attended while Prime Minister with heads of MI5 and MI6, the Cabinet Secretary and the PM's Private Secretary (presumably Hanley, Oldfield, Sir John Hunt and Sir Kenneth Stowe, respectively). They discussed the Soviet war-time penetration (Philby *et al*), 'the nature of the procedures for positive vetting . . . the management and recruitment of the two services [i.e. MI5 and MI6] . . . the Home Secretary did change the nature of recruitment into the Security Service and the way it was conducted . . . [we discussed] the question of whether any of the recent Soviet defectors who had come across had been planted . . . Finally we went over once more *the most important question of all, which was whether grounds existed for continued suspicion in the Security Service*' (emphasis added). This is the only occasion on which Callaghan ever acknowledged that something untoward had been going on within MI5. We do not know what the changes he referred to consisted of – and Lord Callaghan declined to tell us – but something had been done and Callaghan could not resist letting the House of Commons know that he had been involved.[13]

Whether connected to these events or not, the Information Research Department was disbanded in April 1977. It had been pruned in 1964, 1968 and 1970; and, in 1976, Permanent Secretary at the Foreign Office Sir Michael Pallister set up an inquiry by Sir Colin Crowe. 'As a result of his report Labour Ministers became aware of IRD's approved list of British contacts. They . . . were alarmed, according to several government sources, with the political complexion of a handful of them including Mr Brian Crozier'. The list was pruned by Foreign Secretary Tony Crosland and his successor, David Owen, authorised the outfit's disbandment. The Foreign Office had good reason to dislike the semi-detached IRD – which was neither Foreign Office nor MI6. On occasion IRD was running its own foreign policy, at variance to that of the Foreign Office. In 1976, also closed down were the Resistance and Psychological Operations Committee and the Information Policy Unit, both of which had access to IRD.[14]

These piecemeal changes culminated in proposals, apparently from within Whitehall, to tighten central control of both MI5 and MI6. Throughout 1978, there were leaks to that effect. These began – where else? – in *Private Eye*, on 17 February 1978. The *Eye* reported that Hanley (head of MI5) and Oldfield (head of MI6) were to 'quit in a sensational shake-up of the government Intelligence apparatus. The Whitehall mandarins, who believe that both MI5 and MI6 should be placed under tight civil service control, have yet to give up the battle to place "amateurs" in charge of both services.' A month later, the *Eye* reported that 'confidential' letters had been sent out under the signature of Callaghan aide Tom McCaffery to 'alert key newspapers' that the heads of MI5 and MI6 were going.[15]

For some time, it appears, Callaghan, or at any rate people within the Cabinet Office acting in Callaghan's name, had been trying to bring MI5 and MI6 under the Office's control. 'Speculation mounts over Callaghan's clean sweep at the top of his intelligence hierarchy. Whitehall claims that he intends to establish a Directorate of Central Intelligence – American-style – with the man in charge reporting directly to the Prime Minister . . . Callaghan is said to have lost patience with this clumsy set-up and has picked a key civil servant to mastermind the new centralised Intelligence group.'[16]

Both Richard Deacon, in his biography of Maurice Oldfield, and Oldfield's friend Anthony Cavendish, in his memoir, refer to these ideas of placing MI5 and MI6 under the control of the Cabinet Office. These proposals were abandoned, however: 'In the end Oldfield was able to smile quietly and feel reasonably satisfied. His own choice [Arthur Franks] was ultimately selected as Director-General of the SIS and the Service was untouched by gimmicky changes in its unwritten constitution.'[17]

What lay behind these decisions has never been made public. One hypothesis would be that, faced with this threatened accretion of power by the Cabinet Office, the mandarins at the Home Office and Foreign Office combined to resist the proposals. This appears to be the sub-text behind the comment of Foreign Secretary David Owen to Tony Benn on 30 November 1978: 'Whatever you do don't recommend [to Callaghan] the centralisation of security under the Prime Minister; it is much better to have the power diffused in the hands of the Foreign Secretary and the Home Secretary, with the Prime Minister keeping an eye on it.' That has the authentic ring of departmental interests. The only published comment at the time was in *Private Eye*: 'The Prime Minister's decision to appoint Arthur Temple Franks . . . is now recognised as a major defeat for the Whitehall establishment. Senior officials in the Foreign and Commonwealth Office, who were strongly supported by other civil service mandarins, used their considerable influence to promote several candidates from the diplomatic world. They were anxious to return the Secret Service to its original departmental status – once under strict Foreign Office control. It now reports directly to Downing Street through the Cabinet Office.'

This is a curious paragraph containing significant errors – or disinformation. MI6 did not then – and does not now – report 'directly to Downing Street'. In so far as there were any formal structures, MI6 reported to the Foreign Office and the Foreign Secretary. It was to *achieve* 'reporting directly to Downing Street' that lay behind the notion of a centralised intelligence service controllable by the Cabinet Office.[18]

Keep power diffuse, don't centralise – that would be a line that most of the denizens of the secret permanent government would follow if the alternative meant being controlled from the centre by the Cabinet Office. If the permanent government saw off the threat of centralised Cabinet Office-controlled intelligence services, there was still a price to pay for the chaos and political embarrassments of the preceeding five years. MI6, which had never come under criticism, was allowed to continue with an 'insider', Arthur Franks, at its head: but, in 1979, ex-Foreign Office man Howard Smith, who had worked with Callaghan in Northern Ireland, was appointed as the new Director-General of MI5 and Oldfield was sent to Northern Ireland as Intelligence Co-ordinator – an MI6 officer had been appointed over the heads of MI5 who had been in charge of the Northern Ireland intelligence operation since late 1973. In the bureaucratic war between MI5 and MI6 which had rumbled through the 1970s, it was MI6 which seemed to have come out on top.

In 1979, with the right-wing Tory Government of Mrs Thatcher in office, the intelligence–military alliance which had worked so hard to achieve this reversal of the direction of British politics had one major collective problem: keeping their activities over the previous decade secret. Unfortunately, there were two witnesses to some of these events, Colin Wallace and Peter Wright, who between them provided the background information to unravel this long sorry story of deceit.

XLIX

PETER WRIGHT

Peter Wright is a shit.
LORD ANNAN

IN 1979, PETER WRIGHT had retired to Tasmania, his theories about Hollis still secret, still rejected by most of his colleagues. In 1980, his relationship with Lord Rothschild was renewed when Rothschild brought him to Britain and put him in contact with Chapman Pincher. As he told the Australian court, Wright, not surprisingly given Rothschild's track record, assumed that he was being drawn into 'a deniable operation'. For his part, Pincher denies this but assumes that Wright meant an MI5 operation. This, as he points out, is an absurd idea, contradicted by Wright's belief that their project had to be kept secret from MI5, who would suppress it if they learned of it. But did Wright mean an MI5 'deniable operation'? Wright was a friend of Maurice Oldfield, as was Rothschild. On his own account, Pincher had been receiving information from Oldfield in the mid-1970s and was friendly enough with Rothschild to have gone on holiday with him. If this was a 'deniable operation', as Wright believed, and if there was a sponsoring body, it was MI6 not MI5.[1]

Retiring as Chief of MI6 in 1978, Oldfield played at being an academic at Oxford University for a year, then was persuaded to take the post of Northern Ireland Intelligence Co-ordinator, tasked primarily to stop the faction fights between the British state's forces in the province. MI5, which had been in overall command of the Northern Ireland intelligence operation since late 1973, did not take kindly to Oldfield, from MI6, being appointed over them. There was the matter of Oldfield's political activities in the MI5/MI6 bureaucratic wars a few years before. Oldfield had allowed one of his officers (de Mowbray) to inform Downing Street of the FLUENCY committee's suspicions about Hollis; via Bruce McKenzie, Oldfield leaked the 'Wilson was bugged' story and the 1974 MI5 report on surveillance of Wilson to Pincher; and he confirmed Wilson's suspicions about MI5. It is probably not an exaggeration to say that in 1979, Oldfield's re-emergence from retirement made him MI5's number one target. On 9 November 1979, *Private Eye* reported that Oldfield's appointment 'has revived the once-bitter rivalry between MI6 – the Secret Intelligence Service – and the Security Service . . . MI5 men claim that the Oldfield appointment is merely the latest example of Downing Street's bias against their service'.

Oldfield's arrival in Ireland in 1979 triggered a smear campaign against him, assumed, if not yet proven, to be the work of MI5. This was a success, resulting in the withdrawal of Oldfield's positive vetting in April 1980. Oldfield then retired, ill, from Northern Ireland in June that year.[2]

That much we know. What we *suspect* is that thinking of a way to hit back at MI5 for the smear campaign, Oldfield turned to the bitter, disillusioned Peter Wright, who had begun informing Oldfield on MI5's internal politics in 1975, if not earlier. Oldfield contacted their mutual friend Rothschild to act as go-between and reactivate Wright. (If this sounds like a Le Carré plot, so much the better: Le Carré was in MI6.) In September 1980, Rothschild suggested that Wright should expand a manuscript of 10,000 words which he had written into a book with the help of Pincher. The Wright–Pincher collaboration, *Their Trade is Treachery*, revealing the Roger Hollis saga (and much more besides) duly appeared in 1981.

This, at any rate, is how the events could be construed; but with Oldfield and Rothschild dead, this will never be proven or disproven. The argument against this hypothesis would have to start by explaining what Rothschild's motives were in lighting the fuse of the Peter Wright bomb, if not those we suggest. After a life-time of service on the secret corridors of Whitehall, Rothschild already knew first-hand of the corrosive effects on MI5 of the molehunts – and what their public impact would be. Why, after a life-time of discretion was he suddenly conspiring to break the Official Secrets Act? There is no evidence that he actually believed Wright's theories about Hollis, or shared Wright's estimation of their importance.

Rothschild and Oldfield were very close friends. When the allegations of the latter's homosexuality finally surfaced, leading to Oldfield's confession of homosexual activity when a young man, Oldfield discussed his position with only three people: Sir Robert Armstrong, Anthony Cavendish – and Victor Rothschild. Cavendish, to whom we owe this information, wrote in the same paragraph that he was 'intrigued' by 'Victor Rothschild's involvement in the Wright allegations', wondering if the 1987 public revelation of Oldfield's homosexuality was 'timed to take the heat off the Wright case?' More likely, in our view, it was simply revenge by MI5 for Oldfield's role in unleashing Peter Wright on them.[3]

The threat of revealing Oldfield's alleged homosexuality and the emergence of Wright's allegations look like a linked sequence. In October 1979, when Oldfield took over in Ireland, the smear stories began. After reading an Auberon Waugh column in *Private Eye*, which suggested that Oldfield was homosexual, Commissioner of the Metropolitan Police Sir David McNee telephoned John Junor at the *Sunday Express*. McNee, convinced that Oldfield was homosexual, informed Junor that he had information from a Special Branch officer, who had been guarding Oldfield's home at Marsham Court, about young boys visiting the flat. McNee had given this information to Home Secretary William Whitelaw, and Cabinet Secretary Robert Armstrong. In March 1980, Oldfield's vetting was reviewed after 'reports were received' while he was Security Co-ordinator. He confessed – though to what is in dispute – and his positive vetting was withdrawn. (Then, bizarrely, he was allowed to carry on as Security Co-ordinator until June.)[4]

On 12 June, the same month that Oldfield left Northern Ireland, Peter Wright wrote to Rothschild that he was 'writing a book whose tentative title is "The Cancer in our Midst". It is about the penetration of our society by the Russians and how the Soviets have used it to manipulate us to achieve their ends.' This would form the basis of Pincher's *Their Trade is Treachery*. Two days later in the *Spectator*, Auberon Waugh wrote a half-serious article titled 'Lord Rothschild is Innocent'. Revealing the links between Rothschild and the Cambridge Comintern, Waugh added, tongue in cheek: 'Any suggestion which might be implied that Lord Rothschild could even have been under suspicion by MI5 as a Soviet agent is so preposterous as to belong to the world of pulp fiction.' According to Pincher, this article left Rothschild 'deeply perturbed'. Rothschild then wrote to Wright in Australia: 'Things are starting to get rough. I cannot see that it would be a breach of the Official Secrets Act for you to put on a piece of paper, but not to send to anybody, a detailed account of your relationship with me, including all details.' Wright's memorandum, 'Victor Rothschild's help since 1951 to the Security Service', was designed to show that Rothschild could never have been the 'Fifth Man' and had, in fact, been a loyal subject and friend to the security services.[5]

In July, Rothschild replied to a request from Pincher for information on the Hollis Affair. He tried to dissuade the journalist from pursuing it. 'I am inclined to think one should let the dogs lie without comment.' In the space of a month, Rothschild had changed his mind. In August, 'out of the blue', Wright received instructions from Rothschild to travel to England. At Cambridge, Wright drew up Rothschild's loyalty memorandum – which could have been written in Australia – and his host read his manuscript. Rothschild thought it 'very good' and suggested a ghost writer, Chapman Pincher.[6]

On 5 September 1980, Rothschild introduced 'Philip' (Wright) to Pincher and as a result of this meeting *Their Trade is Treachery* was produced. Interestingly, Rothschild never communicated with Wright thereafter and, according to Pincher, 'distanced himself from the project totally'. His role was complete. In December 1980, a copy of the synopsis had been placed in the hands of Oldfield's successor at MI6, Sir Arthur Franks. The project was allowed to go ahead partly because other journalists were known to be on to the Hollis story and Pincher was regarded as having 'safe hands'. Or so it is said; at least one other explanation suggests itself. The rest of the story we know.

In late 1986, news of Wright's forthcoming book, *Spycatcher*, and some of its key allegations, began to surface in the British media; this, linked with Colin Wallace's complementary allegations, exploded in the early months of 1987. On 23 April, the Oldfield homosexuality story, which had been drifting around the fringe media of the Irish Republic, notably in Ireland's equivalent of *Private Eye*, the *Phoenix*, was announced by Mrs Thatcher to the House of Commons. The *Sunday Times* in Britain, and the radical magazine *Hibernia* in the Republic of

Ireland, then carried versions of the same incident in a restaurant toilet in Northern Ireland said to have revealed Oldfield's homosexuality. (Oldfield was said to have got drunk and made a pass at a man in a toilet: a preposterous story which, upon investigation by Channel Four News' Robert Parker, proved to be entirely fictitious – but a stunningly successful posthumous smear nevertheless.)[7]

When, in 1986, we first wrote about the events surrounding the campaign against Wilson (*Lobster* 11: 'Wilson, MI5 and the Rise of Thatcher'), largely influenced by Colin Wallace's information, we focused on the role of MI5. As the later sections of this book have shown, however, the situation was more complex than that. It is now apparent that the covert operations against the politicians of this country in the late sixties and early seventies were woven into, and became a tool in a fierce bureaucratic conflict between MI5 and MI6.

The background to that conflict was the shrinking overseas post-war British Empire. By the time Labour took office in 1964, relative economic decline and the forces of colonial liberation in the Empire, where both MI5 and MI6 had been operating, was producing pressure on overseas budgets and the security services. MI5 found their imperial security role being reduced and MI6 moving into some of what had been their territory, notably in Africa. In this process, it was always MI5 who were on the defensive, and their apparently incompetent handling of the various security scandals of the Macmillan era did nothing to help. The trans-Atlantic dissatisfaction with MI5 eventually produced the secret American Grey–Coyne inquiry into British security procedures in 1965. While the CIA's Angleton failed in his attempt to use the report to engineer a CIA take-over of MI5, MI6 were more successful, subsequently getting themselves on to joint MI5/MI6 operations like the FLUENCY committee and the counter-intelligence unit K5.

This erosion of MI5's bureaucratic 'turf' continued when MI6 was put in overall charge of the intelligence war in Northern Ireland in 1971 by Edward Heath. Insult was added to injury when IRD (the Information Research Department), a Foreign Office/MI6-oriented outfit, was added in 1971, to run the psychological war. On the mainland UK, MI6's incremental expansion into MI5's territory continued with the formation of the nominally 'freelance' anti-subversive activities of the Institute for the Study of Conflict, largely staffed by former IRD employees, and its rapid penetration of the institutions of the state – the military and police, for example – where once MI5 had the exclusive franchise. The ensuing vicious faction fight in Northern Ireland has been described by two of its victims, Colin Wallace and Fred Holroyd.

Yet even this analysis is too simple. Although sometimes it makes sense to write of 'MI5' and 'MI6', as if they are unitary bodies, they are composed of politically diverging factions just like any other large bureaucracies. When David Stirling was asked by one of the authors in 1987 if the sub-text to the 'Wilson plots' was a conflict between MI5 and MI6, he said no, it was factions, with 'ghost figures' floating about, bridging the gaps. Further complexity is added by the attempts of the senior civil service figures in the Home and Foreign and Commonwealth Offices who liaised with MI5 and MI6 to use the 'turbulence'

(Colin Wallace's word) in the security services to assert their authority over their secret servants. We have done no more than sketch in that struggle, and there is much work to be done in this area.

What is clear, however, is that from 1973 onwards, joining the main assault on the 'subversive threat' by MI5 personnel, were individuals who were either former members of MI6 and IRD, or have been associated with them – what we might call its affiliates – the personnel of ISC, and various media allies. What we see is a number of right-wing MI6 personnel, who had a significant input – the evidence does not yet exist to put it more strongly – into the private armies' episode, the election of Mrs Thatcher to leader of the Tory Party, and the formation of the National Association for Freedom.[8]

The anonymous *Private Eye* correspondent who portrayed the enormous leak of Institute of Study of Conflict documents in 1976 as an expression of the conflict between 'freelance' anti-subversives and MI5 got it half right. Crucially – and misleadingly – absent was the point that the 'freelancers' were ex-MI6/ Foreign Office people. Into this conflict walked Harold Wilson; and a Prime Minister can be a very useful weapon for the skilled intelligence bureaucrat. Wilson put the allegation of MI5 plotting to Oldfield, who confirmed it and then leaked material supporting it to Pincher. When Wilson put Oldfield's allegation to MI5 Director-General Michael Hanley, he attempted to minimalise MI5's role, and, it appears, told Wilson instead to look at George Young, formerly of MI6. But it was MI5 which got the attention.

George Kennedy Young does look crucial in this period, and Peter Wright has said as much to journalists; but much of the detail is missing. All we have are glimpses of Young drifting around in the background, a facilitator, apparently involved at the beginning of things, then slipping out of the picture. Just before his death in 1990, Young wrote an autobiographical sketch which he sent out to one or two people who would write his obituary. In it there are two major items missing in the account of his known political activities in Britain since leaving MI6: his attempted coup at the Monday Club, and Unison. What is he telling us by omitting those but including, from this period, Tory Action? *Searchlight* magazine claimed that 'Tory Action was originally . . . the kernel of the Tory Party caucas which put forward Margaret Thatcher for the leadership of the Conservative Party'; but there is little to support this view beyond the claims of Young himself, and the extraordinary storm which hit the BBC in 1984 when *Panorama* had the temerity to focus on Tory Action in its survey of the far-right fringe of the Tory Party in the programme 'Maggies' Militants'. Quite clearly an extremely sensitive nerve had been touched – but precisely which one remained unclear.[9]

If Young looks crucial in this period, so does the Institute for the Study of Conflict network. At this time Mrs Thatcher 'was receiving intelligence briefings from a free-lance group' until Oldfield intervened and got Prime Minister James Callaghan to agree to to allow her to have official briefings. Although unwilling to reveal who composed this group, Chapman Pincher did confirm that one of them 'was associated with' the Institute for the Study of Conflict. Brian Crozier declined to confirm or deny to us that it was him. His ISC associate Robert Moss was writing speeches for Mrs Thatcher in this period, as well as acting as the first Director of the National Association for Freedom. After 1973 the ISC network joined a European–American network of conservative think tanks and political pressure groups which helped re-launch the Cold War with the Soviet bloc and, along with it, the election of appropriately Cold War governments in the UK and USA.[10]

At root here is the widespread acceptance of the idea, carefully fostered by MI6 itself, that MI6 do not operate within the UK – do not 'play at home' to use the vernacular. It is becoming increasingly clear that this is a lie. When Stephen Dorril and Anthony Summers re-researched the Profumo Affair in 1987, they found MI6 everywhere, then slipping away just before the denouement, leaving MI5 to be embarrassed. More recently, George Blake revealed in his memoir that MI6 (like the CIA) had recruited extensively within Britain – especially within the British media – in the 1950s. What we suspect is that, in keeping with the MI6-generated stereotypes of the clumsy, rather down-market MI5 and the sophisticated, up-market MI6, while MI5 blundered about with crude smear campaigns, the right-wing of MI6, working to a longer game plan and, using deniable, 'private' assets, were engaged in a more subtle series of 'political actions' to shift the Conservative Party and the electorate to the right.

CONCLUSION

It is a matter of when, not whether, Harold Wilson's historical reputation
will recover . . . There is material for revisionists.
DAVID WALKER

SINCE 1978, LORD WILSON has said (and written) almost nothing about
the events we have described in which he was the central figure. In 1981, he used
the publication of Gordon Winter's *Inside BOSS* to make a final call for an
investigation into the activities of BOSS in Britain; after that he gave only a
couple of brief press interviews in 1987 in which he said nothing of note. His
silence is understandable. His attempt at mounting a private investigation a
decade earlier, with Penrose and Courtiour, had backfired when its existence
leaked (probably from the BBC's senior management); and lacking both political
support from the Callaghan Government and hard information to back up his
allegations, he was unable to respond to the political counter-attack generated by
the Tory Party and the state itself when his allegations were made public. As the
cliché has it, he had raised his head above the parapet only to have it nearly blown
off. Added to which, worn out by his years in office, he has suffered a number of
serious illnesses, and has been losing his memory. As is absolutely typical, Lord
Wilson's deteriorating memory has become the subject of rumour: from different sources we have heard versions of the story – commonplace, apparently, at
Westminster – that his memory loss was the result of a botched anaesthetic. In
one version it was an accident; in another it was the long arm of the secret state
reaching out to shut him up.[1]

The climate is right for a major revision of Wilson. In a way that the present
leadership of the Parliamentary Labour Party has singularly failed to do, Wilson
caught the public imagination in the mid-sixties. Despite (or because of) the
absence of the ubiquitous pollsters to describe peoples' attitudes, Wilson had
the 'feel' of the times. By any standards, he was a brilliant politician. Holding the
Labour Party together – in itself a minor miracle – he won four General
Elections, two of them in the face of a media assault against him and his party

unparalleled in post-war British history. Twice his governments inherited, and largely rectified, the economic mess left behind by Conservative Governments.

Wilson embodied the radical end of the wartime social contract, which not only saw that a dynamic mixed economy demanded a producers' alliance, but also saw that such an alliance could not succeed with an ascendant City of London. The extraordinary hatred that Wilson provoked on the British right was not irrational: Wilson was a serious threat; he knew who the 'enemy within' actually was. And they knew that he knew; 'they' – the banker in the City with the elder brother in MI6 and a cousin in the Army – 'they' knew that Wilson, virtually alone among Labour leaders of his generation, had pulled aside the whisps of mystification which hid the British Establishment and seen the power of finance capital at its heart. Faced with the first Thatcher administration, Wilson would have had no difficulty identifying it as a front for the City of London, its policies what used to be called 'a bankers' ramp', in the more robust Labour discourse of days gone by.

A decade of Conservative Party 'freedom' has produced the destruction of a quarter of the manufacturing base, a credit-fuelled boom, the collapse of private saving (and massive expansion of private debt), with a government-induced slump at each end of the period. Though his name is still unmentionable, Wilson's corporatist model of the British economy is now routinely advocated in the economic pages of the non-Tory press in this country. As we were writing this, the John Major-led Conservative Party began distancing itself from the 'freedom' of its predecessor, proclaiming its belief in 'the social market'. (But then Major's Cabinet is dominated by survivors of the Heath Government, who never actually believed in 'freedom' but kept their mouths shut during the Thatcher period.) Eventually, even the British electorate may notice that the successful industrial European economies have some form of corporatist structure at their heart.

Wilson remains the only senior politician of any stripe to challenge the secret state while in office. He did not have enough information and, if Pincher's *The Truth About Dirty Tricks* is to be believed, his first ally in this struggle, George Wigg, had been 'turned' by MI5 and run against him. Even so, his efforts continue to influence the British political agenda to this day. Would we have witnessed the extraordinary events surrounding Colin Wallace and Peter Wright between 1987 and 1989 without Wilson's allegations in 1977? That the British secret state is now permanently on the political agenda of this country is almost entirely due to Wilson's tenacity, his courage, and, most of all, his ability to ignore the longest, sustained campaign of vilification against a major politician in British history. (The campaign against Tony Benn would come a close second.)

Yet he is still perceived by the political classes in this country as a great failure, a man who promised much and delivered little; who had an overwhelming Parliamentary majority and did nothing with it. Such views underestimate both the scale of the opposition which Wilson faced beyond the Commons and the conservative nature of the Parliamentary Labour Party. The right may have conjured up a subversive, fellow-travelling PLP; the truth is that there was only ever a small minority of the PLP who had even the remotest notion of what a socialist Britain might look like, let alone a plausible means of getting there.

Wilson's great mistake was to share so little of the political sub-text with the rest of the Labour Party. For much of the time, what he was actually trying to do was known to hardly any of the PLP, let alone the wider Labour movement (much less the British electorate). Was this in his character? The notion that Wilson was a rather solitary figure recurs in practically all the memoirs of the period. Or was his distrust of his colleagues merely a rational assessment of the faction-ridden nature of the Labour Party he had inherited, riven by the domestic anti-communism which plagued the party in the fifties? As he put it once, he was 'a Bolshevik Prime Minister with a Czarist cabinet'. How much of the blame lies not with Wilson but with his Cabinet colleagues, who were, more or less continuously, caballing against him? Was he, perhaps, trying too hard to imitate the American Presidential-style of government – but without either the equivalent powers or informal networks of support. Wilson, like others of his generation, may have been rather too smitten by the model presented by John F. Kennedy. There seems to us to be some truth in all of these suggestions; indeed, any one of them, considered together with the series of problems which his governments encountered, might be explanation enough. With Wilson, the problem is not finding an explanation, it is that there are too many of them: his behaviour is over-determined.

That he and the governments he led are now so widely perceived as failures seems to us to be the clearest possible example of how public perception can be radically altered by the media. The campaign of denigration against him (and the Labour Party in general) succeeded in severely distorting the perception of him and his governments. After fifteen years of being told that Wilson – essentially a Liberal whose radical tinges were more than balanced by his love of the monarchy and the 'unwritten' British constitution – was a crook, a red, a union stooge, unpatriotic, a Walter Mitty and a threat to the British way of life, the electorate was prepared for the Orwellian disinformation which emanated during the Thatcher administrations: promising to 'put Britain back to work' yet tripling unemployment; proclaiming economic triumph where there was actually economic disaster; proclaiming 'financial rectitude' while permitting the biggest credit explosion in our history; claiming to have 'rolled back the frontiers of the state' while erecting an increasingly centralised and authoritarian system; and finally claiming to have 'put the Great back in Britain' – by war, imperial pretensions and American military power – while thousands of its citizens slept on the streets of our cities.

After a decade of Thatcherite 'success' we would welcome a return to Wilsonian 'failure'.

NOTES

CHAPTER I: 'THE BOY WONDER'

1 L. Smith, pp. 18 and 122.

2 *Listener*, 29/10/64; Roth, *Walter Mitty*, pp. 61–2.

3 Thus collapse the fantasies of Dr Kitty Little. In a letter to the Speaker of the House of Commons 1/5/87, Dr Little described joining a 'study group' comprising of former Oxford Communists who 'went underground' and joined the Oxford University Labour Club. She went to Oxford in October 1940 and attended this study group, claiming that 'the leader of the group [was] Harold Wilson'. In October 1940, Wilson was doing war work. If there was such a group, Dr Little has got the wrong Wilson. In 1977, Dr Little appeared as 'Ridgeway consultants' at the Windscale nuclear inquiry where she submitted a document outlining her conspiracy theory about Wilson. It was later passed to Chapman Pincher, who took it to Wilson, upon which the latter claimed that Little had 'got it wrong, it was "Tom Wilson".' See Pincher, *Inside Story*, p. 29, telephone conversation with Little, 1989.

4 Hennessy, *Whitehall*, p. 104; *idem*, *Cabinet*, p. 70.

5 Foot, *Wilson*, p. 41.

6 *Daily Telegraph*, 14/10/44.

7 Glees, p. 332.

8 Kay, p. 41.

9 L. Smith, p. 164.

10 Foot, *Wilson*, p. 63; HOC *Hansard*, 20/4/50.

11 Wilson, *Memoirs*, p. 99.

12 Foot, *Wilson*, p. 62.

13 Deacon, *C*, p. 53.

14 Van den Heuvel was known as 'Z' and was responsible for recruiting businessmen and journalists. See Anthony Cavendish and further details in review of his book in *Lobster* 15.

15 On Rosebaud: Kramish, p. 250. On Hambro: West, *The Friends*, p. 23 and Foot, *Wilson*, p. 63. On Maxwell: Haines, *Maxwell*, Chapter 4, 'Berlin, Barter and Books'.

16 Leigh, p. 41; Pincher, *Inside Story*, p. 52.

17 Leigh, p. 47 quoting Foreign Office documents.

18 Thomas, *Armed Truce*, p. 298. Letters from (Lord) Hugh Thomas, 25/6/88 and 11/8/88.

19 Leigh, pp. 50, 51 and 113; *Daily Telegraph*, 28/8/50; Marnham, *Trail of Havoc*, p. 97; 'Trade that may Disturb E.R.P. Programme', *Guardian*, 1/7/48.

20 Northedge, p. 225.

21 Kay, p. 38.

22 Wilson, *Memoirs*, p. 121.

23 Wheen, p. 122. Thomas, *Strachey*, Chapter 16, 'The Groundnuts Affair'.

24 On the Lynsky Tribunal, see Barron, and John Gross, 'The Lynsky Tribunal' in Michael Sissons and Philip French (eds.), *Age of Austerity, 1945–51*, Penguin, 1964.

25 *The Times*, 2–3/5/74; Pincher, *Inside Story*, p. 347.

26 D. Smith, p. 143.

27 *Daily Express*, 3/4/51.

28   Roth, *Walter Mitty*, p. 148; Kay, p. 70.

CHAPTER II: 'NYE'S LITTLE DOG'

1   Goodman, p. 75.

2   Richter, p. 137.

3   Wilson, *Memoirs*, pp. 132–3.

4   Figures of the sales of the Bevanite group's publications have to be treated with caution as it was the custom of many unions to order bulk purchases of pamphlets, many of which were never actually sold. This point was made to us by Andrew Bennett MP. Hunter quoted M. Jenkins, p. 159; *News Chronicle*, 5/8/52 cited M. Jenkins, p. 161. See Hunter, pp. 47–8 on expulsion campaign.

5   Hunter, p. 65; *The Times*, 6/10/52; Crossman, *Backbench Diaries*, p. 329, 19/5/54.

6   Brockway, p. 164. 'Conspiracy' acknowledged by Wilson, *Memoirs*, pp. 138–9. On the Union of Democratic Control, see Swartz. The UDC was a pressure group set up during the First World War to campaign against secret diplomacy. MI5 regarded the UDC as 'fellow-travellers'. Wilson wrote a pamphlet for them in the fifties.

7   Crossman, *Backbench Diaries*, p. 196.

8   *Ibid.*, pp. 409–10.

9   M. R. D. Foot, 'A Comparison of SOE and OSS', RUSI, 1987, p. 162. Godson meeting, P. Williams, *Gaitskell Diaries*, p. 384.

10   See Blum for best survey of CIA intervention. Braden in Smith, *OSS*, p. 368.

11   Beginnings have been made by Weiler, Schneer and Carew on the history of US involvement in the Labour Party.

12   Peck, Winslow, *The AFL–CIA*, in Frazier (ed.), pp. 238–43. On the CIA connection to the international trade union movement see Roy Godson in which he tried to obfuscate the AFL–CIA connection, Kwitney p. 345. Jack Anderson and Drew Pearson 1967: cited in Peck p. 257. See also Radosh, chapter titled 'Lovestone Diplomacy'. From 1954 Lovestone's CIA case officer was James Angleton, who 'allowed his most loyal friends in British Intelligence to read items that Lovestone had culled from the United Kingdom, where he had good contacts with the TUC and the Labour Party.' Mangold, pp. 293 and 384.

13   Fletcher, various sources; see also Christopher Lasch in Barnton Bernstein (ed.), *Towards a New Past*. Lasch is deeply, and in our view properly, hostile to this operation, but for more sympathetic, and more detailed accounts see Dittberner, Chapter 3, and, most recently, Coleman.

14   Fletcher, pp. 59–60.

15   Haseler, p. 68. There is no evidence that *Socialist Commentary* was funded by the CIA, though this would hardly be a surprise.

16   D. Jay, p. 244. On CIA links: see Cooper, p. 343, Roosevelt, p. 469 and Brown, p. 147. When diplomatic relations broke down between Britain and the United States following the Suez debacle, MI6 approached Healey to met with a CIA representative to help restore the intelligence link. Healey, p. 173.

17   Bissell quoted in 'CIA and the Labour Movement,' *Militant*, 1982.

18   Some indication of the close relationship between Watson and Labour Attaché Joe Godson is suggested by the fact that Watson's daughter married Joe Godson's son Roy. Crane: Cassandra in the *Daily Mirror*, 1/10/57; Minkin, p. 400; Benn, *Diaries*, vol. 3, p. 420.

19   During 1974 Shawcross became an unlikely lunch guest at *Private Eye* 'where he guardedly talked about Wilson's social connections in the old days at Montague Meyer'. Leigh, pp. 50, 60 and 248.

20   Hughes, p. 123; Wilson, *In Place of Dollars*, quoted in D. Smith, p. 147.

21   See Wilson, *Memoirs*, pp. 143–4, Kay, p. 24. Wilson had developed excellent 'unofficial' channels to the Soviet leaders. He was the only senior British politician who actually knew G. N. Malenkov, Stalin's successor.

22   Foot, *Wilson*, p. 111.

23   *The Times*, 8/9/53 and 23/3/54, cited in Glen Alden Smith, p. 263. On the problems with the US, see Cahill, Chapter 2, 'A History of Secrecy'.

24   *Sunday Times*, 5/10/69, quoted in Haines, p. 150.

25   Leigh, p. 160.

26   *The Times*, 10/1/58; Summers/Dorril, p. 125; Wright, p. 120.

27   Blake, pp. 183–6. The British businessman Greville Wynne, who met MI6's ace spy Oleg Penkovsky on a trade delegation to the Soviet Union and was later to act as his 'cut-out', was helped in his East–West trade

activities by Airey Neave, a right-wing Tory MP with excellent contacts in MI6. Neave 'approved his appointment'. Wynne, p. 111.

28 Pearson/Turner, p. 267. Profile of Sternberg in *The Director*, July 1962.

29 Milczynski, p. 243; Heath, cited in Stewart-Smith, p. 50; President of the BOT, cited in Deacon, *British Connection*, p. 234.

30 Cited by Ian Waller, 'Pressure Politics', p. 12, in *Encounter*, August 1962. Donnelly had written a book promoting East–West trade for the right-wing Institute of Economic Affairs.

31 Sternberg blamed the problems on the West Germans who want 'to keep the whole thing to themselves'. *Daily Mirror*, 14/3/62.

32 Haines, *Maxwell*, p. 220.

33 D. Cameron Watt, p. 145.

CHAPTER III: REDS

1 Wilson, *Memoirs*, p. 173.

2 M. Foot, p. 483; J. Campbell, *Bevan*, p. 335. Although we report this received account of Bevan's 'conversion', there had been a two year run-up to it. It was not quite as 'instant' as it has been portrayed.

3 M. Jenkins, p. 286; Crossman, *Backbench Diaries*, p. 331.

4 *Tribune*, 21/2/58; Crossman, *Backbench Diaries*, p. 673.

5 Crossman, *Backbench Diaries*, p. 815.

6 *Ibid.*; Mikardo, pp. 130–1; Shaw, p. 93.

7 Shaw, pp. 120 and 314.

8 The 15 who raised their heads above the parapet included Maurice Foley, Richard Leonard (Crosland's PPS 1964–70), Bryan Magee, Dick Taverne and Shirley Williams. Others involved were Austen Albu, Desmond Donnelly, Roy Mason, Reg Prentice, Alf Robens, Denis Howell and Philip Williams (Gaitskell's biographer). Haseler, p. 209.

9 Wilson, *Memoirs*, p. 181.

10 *Ibid.*, pp. 181–2.

11 S. Crosland, p. 104.

12 Crossman, *Backbench Diaries*, May 1957, p. 581.

13 Roth, *Walter Mitty*, p. 195.

14 Howard, *Crossman*, p. 233.

15 S. Crosland, p. 102.

16 Goodman, pp. 70 and 278; P. Williams, *Gaitskell Diaries*, p. 616.

17 Crossman, *Backbench Diaries*, pp. 884–5; *The Times*, 19/10/60.

18 Haseler, pp. 211, 217 and 219; Fletcher, p. 62. In his autobiography, Forte's comments on Gaitskell are quite illuminating. 'Though I am not and never have been a Labour supporter . . . I also believe passionately in the Welfare State . . . In order to fulfil its obligations to the less well-off, the country must be prosperous, and in my opinion prosperity can only be achieved through free enterprise. This is why I supported Hugh Gaitskell in his fight against a section of his party's attempts to impose a high degree of nationalisation on British industries.' Forte, p. 81.

19 Richter, pp. 144–5.

20 *Ibid.*, p. 151. On the history of IRIS and Common Cause and their links to the Americans, see 'In A Common Cause', in *Lobster* 19.

21 S. Crosland, p. 104.

22 P. Williams, *Gaitskell Diaries*, pp. 394 and 651; According to Lewis Minkin, 'the organisation was never very coherent. And was never very large. At its height in 1958 there were approximately 1,000 members and in 1961 at the height of the factional conflict only four effective area groups.' Minkin, p. 35.

CHAPTER IV: LOOKING OVER HIS SHOULDER

1 *Socialist Commentary*, November 1961. John Stonehouse was very active against the left in the Co-operative movement. In 1962, he was elected President of the London Co-operative Members' Organisation following an expensive campaign run by a former member of the war-time Office of Strategic Services (OSS) and CIA, Patrick Dolan. Dolan had the backing of Hambros Bank. In 1963, Stonehouse operated through a right-wing grouping, the Democratic Co-operative Alliance, which set out to defeat the left in

Co-operative elections. See *Time Out*, 20/12/74, *Private Eye* No. 109, 19/2/66, and No. 182, 6/12/68. Aiden Crawley, a right-wing Labour MP who resigned to join the Tories in 1957, published in the *Sunday Times*, in 1962, a series of articles entitled 'The Hidden Face of Communism' on communist fronts and influence in the Labour Party. Crawley worked in Intelligence during the war. See his autobiography, *Leap Before You Look*, Collins, 1988.

2 See P. Williams, *Gaitskell*, p. 937, n. 124, for mention of Davies and Driberg, and p. 939 n. 169 and 170 on numbers. According to Lord Harris of Greenwich, who was close to Gaitskell, the former Labour leader thought Driberg had been involved with the KGB. Pincher, *Dirty Tricks*, p. 112. Leigh, p. 114.

3 During the inquiry into the Vassall case Pincher produced a letter dated 17/11/56, from the Services Press and Broadcasting Department. 'My dear Pincher, I have seen a copy of MI5's note of appreciation, with the signature of Rees and Morley, and have added my own on this . . . As I told you, the heads of MI5 know of the *Daily Express* co-operation and of your own part in the matter. This is all to the good. Very many thanks again. Sincerely yours . . . ' When asked if that was a typical letter, Pincher replied: 'Of several, yes.' HMSO Cmnd. 2037, p. 62.

4 Gaitskell would appear to have had a back-channel to MI5 through his old friend and former colleague in the Special Operations Executive, Robin Brook. See P. Williams, *Gaitskell*, pp. 933, n. 14, 161 and 461–2; Pincher, *A Web of Deception*, p. 100; *idem, Inside Story*, p. 22.

5 Viscount Cyril John Radcliffe, 1961 'Security procedures in the Public Service', Report of the Committee Session 1961–2, Cmnd. 1681, xxvii, HMSO, 1962.

6 Shaw, pp. 120 and 59; Labour Party Conference Report 53, cited in Shaw, p. 315.

7 Statement on the Findings of the Conference of Privy Councillors on Security (March 1956) Cmnd. 9715; Wright, pp. 54/5.

8 Wright, pp. 55/6; *Independent*, 25/11/90.

9 Pincher, *A Web of Deception*, p. 100; McGovern, pp. 212–4. McGovern's was a strange political journey from the days as a radical member of the Independent Labour Party to the fifties and a supporter of Moral Rearmament. The continuing thread was a militant anti-Stalinism.

10 Pincher, *Inside Story*, pp. 25–6, also, Bunyan, pp. 165 and 169–70. Leigh p. 69. On Driberg, see Masters, pp. 168–78; Pincher, *A Web of Deception*, p. 100, and *idem, Trade is Treachery*, p. 244.

11 Pincher, *Inside Story*, p. 23.

12 *Ibid.*; telephone conversation with Mrs Bax, 6/11/90.

13 Telephone conversation with Mrs Bax 6/11/90. Bax moved to the Oxford University Press in 1962. He established the Publicity Office for the Borough of Enfield in 1966 and worked there until 1969 when he joined the *Enfield Weekly Herald*. He died at Christmas, 1989.

14 Leigh, p. 82. See P. Williams, *Gaitskell*, pp. 425–9, for background on Gaitskell's illness.

15 Leigh, p. 82, quoting Dr Somerville.

16 Thomas, *Mr Speaker*, p. 85.

17 HOC *Hansard*, 'Official Secrets Bill', cols. 1082 and 1087–8, 25/1/89.

18 M. Jenkins, p. 48. Hugh Jenkins referred to the Equity campaign in his play *View to a Death*, broadcast on BBC Radio Four in 1988. See H. Jenkins, pp. 18–24.

19 C. Jenkins, p. 45.

20 Benn, *Diaries*, vol.1, 6/7/63, p. 39. Ray Gunter and Braddock later became directors of Securicor. Sir Tom Williamson of NUGMW was another Securicor director. He was also involved with Common Cause. In 1968 Gunter became a director of IRIS. On Mathews see *Private Eye*, 17/9/66. In May 1964, Mathews was instrumental in promoting the Common Cause publication of a 50-page booklet listing 180 alleged 'fellow-travellers' and communists. The accuracy of the Common Cause list is indicated by the inclusion of Lord Boyd Orr and Bertrand Russell! See, for example, *Sunday Times*, 31/5/64. C. Jenkins, pp. 49–51. Jenkins was a natural target for the Americans as he was at the time Chair of the British Cuba Committee and had been to Cuba where he met Castro and other 'communists'. Both Browns, Ron and George, later joined the SDP.

21 Roth, *Walter Mitty*, p. 284.

22 Brown in Crossman, *Backbench Diaries*, p. 1022; *Sunday Times*, 31/7/77; Penrose/Freeman, p. 445.

23 BBC Radio 3, *The Wilson Years*, 31/10/90.

CHAPTER V: 'SICK THINK'

1 Wright, p. 362.

2 Martin, p. 108' Golitsyn was 'professionally incompetent', Deriabin quoted Mangold, p. 63.

3 *Ibid.*, p. 195. When he left the CIA, Jameson was retained by the agency as a consultant through the Jameson

Institute, having responsibilities for bringing together Soviet bloc defectors and Western journalists for the dissemination of authorised briefs.

4   Ranelagh, p. 564.

5   West, *Molehunt*, p. 12; Brook-Shepherd, p. 169. Although, the Russian word *'Pyatyorka'* was never uttered by Golitsyn, he had heard the phrase, 'Ring of Five', in 1955, from a colleague who had served in London in the early fifties. However, he knew absolutely nothing of Philby.

6   Knightley, pp. 302–3; Ranelagh p. 564; Corson/Trento, p. 91. Ray Rocca became Golitsyn's new case officer.

7   Epstein, p. 41; Corson/Trento, p. 75.

8   Corson/Trento, p. 75; Martin, p. 110; Knightley, p. 308; Ron Rosenbaum in *Harper's Magazine*, October 1983.

9   Leigh, p. 79; Corson/Trento, p. 238. 'Martin was a close friend of Angleton's', Mangold, p. 68.

10 Epstein, p. 71. In fact, Golitsyn was MI5's *only* defector since the war.

11 See West, *A Matter of Trust*, Chapter 7 and *Molehunt*, Chapter 2. In the Intelligence pecking order, the Chief of MI6 is regarded as the superior of the Director-General of MI5.

12 Wright, pp. 315–6 and 170.

13 Leigh, pp. 81–3.

14 Leigh, pp. 82–3; Wright, pp. 362–3; Pincher, *Trade is Treachery*, p. 78. See also Harris/Paxman, pp. 88–94. British intelligence had used biological weapons in assassination attempts including, it is believed, that against Reinhard Heydrich (the grenade fragments had chemical traces), in May 1942, and against President Nasser in 1956.

15 Penkovsky: Epstein, p. 80, presumably based on information supplied by de Mowbray: MI6 counter-intelligence developed its own analysis that Penkovsky had come under Soviet control early on. Verrier, *Through the Looking Glass*, p. 208. Soviet Union/China split, and Harriman, see Pincher, *Too Secret*, p. 475. 'We put the proposition that Harriman was a spy to him because there was someone in the US BRIDE [Soviet war-time radio traffic] who would appear to be Harriman. This was what provoked Golitsyn to tell his story of Harriman to Angleton.' Wright correpondence quoted in Leigh, p. 84. Harriman was not liked by the British Establishment, probably because he was a long-established East–West trader.

16 Epstein, p. 73; West, *A Matter of Trust*, p. 147.

17 Martin, pp. 110, 170 and 190.

18 Brook-Shepherd, pp. 172–3; Cavendish, p. 8; Pincher, *Trade is Treachery*, p. 295.

19 One member of the panel: 'he simply posited that the split was a fake. He couldn't conceive it being anything else . . . it was strictly a hypothesis, very forcefully presented . . . he got angry and overbearing because we didn't agree with him.' Martin, pp. 150 and 200. Harry Rositzke, another senior CIA officer on the panel, says 'that if one started from a common sense point of view then the whole thing was ridiculous.' Knightley, pp. 304–5.

20 Leigh, p. 85; Wright p. 363.

21 Epstein, p. 81; Rodin and 'Korovin', see *ibid.*, pp. 286–8, Freemantle, p. 78; Andrew/Gordievsky, p. 386.

22 Epstein, p. 81.

23 Martin, p. 250; Brook-Shepherd, p. 173; Wright, pp. 363–5.

24 Deacon, *C*, p. 138; Martin, p. 199; Corson/Trento, pp. 91 and 98.

25 Epstein, p. 106. The Loop was a method which Angleton thought the Soviets used but it could apply to any intelligence organisation.

26 Epstein, p. 108. Golitsyn's book *New Lies for Old* was eventually published in 1984 by Bodley Head after Stephen de Mowbray had persuaded an old school friend of its merits; this despite the fact that the million-word manuscript which Golitsyn had completed by 1968 appeared to even a close supporter like de Mowbray as a 'mishmash of ungrammatical repetitive gobbledegook.' Knightley, p. 305. It appeared with a forward signed by Arthur Martin, de Mowbray, Scotty Miler, former chief of operations in CIA counter-intelligence and firm Angleton supporter, and Vasia Gmirkin, a CIA Sino-Soviet expert. In a letter to the *Independent*, 7/2/90, the redoubtable anti-communist Brian Crozier was still displaying faith in the book. 'The author forecast all the major recent developments . . . the evidence is very strong that Gorbachev's "new thinking" was an ambitious deception operation which went wrong because of the advanced decay of an unreformable system.'

27 West, *Molehunt*, p. 38; Penrose/Freeman, pp. 429–30.

CHAPTER VI: SMEAR!

1   Ali, p. 33; *Independent On Sunday*, 8/4/90. Letter from Neal Ascherson, 17/5/90. Walden was PPS to the Chief and Financial Secretary at the Treasury, 1964–6. Rodgers was Parliamentary Under-Secretary of State at the Department of Economic Affairs.

2 Conversation with David Leigh; Ali, p. 33; Leigh, p. 68; interview with Philby in *Koduma*, USSR, 13/10/71, reprinted in *Lobster* 16.

3 Pincher, *Inside Story*, p. 246; Leigh, p. 68.

4 'This was the eleventh visit to the country [Russia]', Howard/West, p. 47.

5 *Private Eye*, 19/9/75; *Spectator*, 19/6/76.

6 *Daily Telegraph*, 18/1/64; Farr, p. 113; R. Churchill, p. 171.

7 Roth, *Walter Mitty*, pp. 304–5; *Private Eye* No. 72, 18/9/64.

8 *Private Eye*, 7/8/73; Pincher, *Inside Story*, p. 31. Special Branch were probably seeking dirt. Brown was visiting a prostitute during this period – information acquired by Stephen Dorril while researching the Profumo Affair.

9 *Evening Standard Magazine*, 11/1/90. That summer also saw one major attempt by the press to generate a Profumo-like scandal via the Krays. On 12 July 1964, the *Sunday Mirror* splashed its front page with a story alleging a homosexual link between a peer and one of the Kray twins. The German magazine *Stern*, not restrained by the British libel laws, published details and an innocent photograph which showed the Tory Lord Boothby seated on a sofa with Ronnie Kray. Boothby wrote a 500-word open letter to *The Times* on 2 August denying he was a homosexual or that he had any kind of relationship with the gangsters. The *Mirror* withdrew the charges and paid Boothby £40,000 in compensation. Boothby later felt guilty about accepting the money, possibly because he was bisexual. Wheen, p. 352. See Junor, pp. 52–3 for tittle-tattle on Boothby and young men.

One fact, which had been officially denied, was true. The police had been conducting an inquiry into the Krays since early 1964. The Krays became dangerous when they started meeting politicians and their 'unusual social connections had all been duly noted . . . their backstairs influence at all levels of society' had echoes of the American Mafia. The Krays were put under intense surveillance by Scotland Yard – an operation in which MI5 showed a great interest. Former MI5 staff told Duncan Campbell, 'one particularly valuable source of information about MPs and peers was a large archive of telephone intercepts which were operated against the Kray family and their associates. Through these, MI5 were able to learn fact and gossip alike.' Of particular interest was gossip on sexual matters. Tom Driberg was one Labour Party figure who attended Ronnie's parties 'where rough but regular compliant East End lads were served like so many canapes'. Given Driberg's links to MI5, and the fact that he 'managed to avoid any unpleasant publicity for his friendship with the Krays', we can only guess at his true role in this episode. It is interesting to note that the one victim of the surveillance, Boothby, was an East–West trader. Were MI5 behind his exposure? Pearson, p. 169; *New Statesman*, 21/10/88; Wheen, p. 350.

10 *Private Eye* No. 68, 24/7/64 and 72, 18/9/64.

11 Pincher, *Inside Story*, p. 246; *Private Eye*, 2/10/64; Junor, p. 144; Roth, *Walter Mitty*, p. 288.

12 *Private Eye* No. 72, 18/9/64; Roth, *Walter Mitty*, p. 182; Castle smear in *Monochrome* No. 20, October 1987; Leigh, p. 178; Wheen, p. 12.

13 *Private Eye* No. 73, 2/10/64 and 74, 16/10/64; Pincher, *Inside Story*, p. 246.

14 Junor, p. 143; Miss Cartland, 'I just do not remember the sequence of events', letter to authors 26/10/90; Howard/West p. 194.

CHAPTER VII: THE SPECIAL RELATIONSHIP

1 See van der Pijl, Quigley, Shoup and Minter for details. Quigley's revelations showed that the Council on Foreign Relations and the Royal Institute for International Affairs were, originally, virtually fronts for the (then) secret Round Table group, set up by Lord Milner, using money left for the purpose in Cecil Rhodes' will. As the network expanded in the 1920s and 1930s, with similar institutes being created throughout the 'white' Commonwealth, the control from the centre diminished. By the end of the Second World War, the network had become so ramified, and the economic and strategic aims of the primary members, the US and the UK, so antithetical, that it had lost its pre-war cohesion. The most accessible summary of this thesis is 'The Rhodes-Milner Group', Jan Nederveen Pieterse, in *Lobster* 13. Quigley's revelations have yet to be internalised by most academic historians of the period.

2 The similarity of view and frequency of social intercourse across the Atlantic has led some on the American right to see this as evidence of a global British–Round Table–Fabian conspiracy. See for example Eustace Mullins. The Neustadt letter was found in the Kennedy Presidential Archive in Boston by John Booth, to whom our thanks. Richard Neustadt is now married to SDP funder member, Shirley Williams

3 Details and background of the various treaties can be found in, for example, Richelson and Ball, especially Chapter 7.

4 Healey, p. 238. On Bilderberg see Peter Thompson, 'Bilderberg and the West', in Sklar (ed.). Bilderberg looks like an MI6 initiative, initially. See also the interview with Healey in *Tribune*, 26/10/90.

5 On the Chiefs' opinions, see Zeigler, Chapter 42; the debate is in Pierre, pp. 192–3. In his autobiography Denis Healey notes that 'It is easy to forget that in the fifties and sixties both sides were much more

concerned with the political, economic and military arguments about the wisdom of diverting Britain's scarce defence resources to the maintenance of a strategic nuclear force.' Healey, p. 241.

6   Zeigler, p. 561.

7   Wigg's memoir, pp. 209–12, contains a caustic account of the period from Sandys' 1957 defence review through the Blue Streak and Skybolt debacles; Crossman, *Backbench Diaries* p. 667.

8   The Kennedy administration contained at least twenty Rhodes Scholars. Simpson, p. 160, citing H. Kissinger, *The Whitehouse Years*, Weidenfeld and Nicolson/Michael Joseph, 1979, p. 90.

9   S. Bayliss, p. 80.

10 *Evening News* cited by Wilson in *Purpose in Politics*, p. 169.

11 Healey, p. 244; Horne, in Louis/Bull (eds.), p. 95.

12 Verrier, *Through the Looking Glass*, p. 257; Healey, p. 245; Wilson, *Purpose in Politics*, p. 201.

13 See for example his speeches from 27/4/60 onwards in Wilson, *Purpose in Politics*, p. 167. The quote is from *ibid.*, p. 178.

14 *Ibid.*, pp. 214–5.

15 Horne, *Macmillan*, p. 683. According to Mangold (pp. 85–6) Golitsyn mentioned the Sino-Soviet split, a KGB mole within the CIA, that Gaitskell had been murdered, that Wilson was probably a KGB asset, and that MI5's Graham Mitchell was probably a KGB agent. The list was delivered by Archie Roosevelt to Sir Roger Hollis, who sent McCone a cable in reply to the five queries: 'No. No. No. No. No.' Leigh, pp. 85–6. Although there is no evidence of this, it would be a reasonable guess that Elder meant not the International Socialists but the Socialist International. Like so many of the manifestations of social democracy (known inside the CIA as the NCL, non-communist left) after the Second World War, the SI was probably funded by the CIA's more liberal wing through its International Organisations Division. Knowledge of the funding would have been kept on a 'need to know' basis. The CIA, like any big organisation, had many factions within it, and the European social democrats, funded by one wing of the CIA, were regarded with suspicion by right-wingers in the agency such as Angleton.

16 Horne, *Macmillan*, p. 535.

17 *Economist*, 12/9/64.

18 First appearances might indicate that Chalfont, whom we now know as the firmest of nuclear warriors, had gone soft, but he was really undertaking a delicate balancing act. Chalfont was, and remains first and foremost, an Atlanticist strongly supportive of United States policies on nuclear weapons. Chalfont was defending the American position which saw national independent systems, rather than NATO controlled ones, as dangerous and out-dated. Chalfont has often been associated with the CIA. In 1978 a pamphlet called the *CIA INSIDER* appeared which named him as a CIA agent, along with Chapman Pincher, Brian Crozier and Geoffrey Stewart-Smith. This was dismissed as a KGB forgery, which it almost certainly was, by Pincher, who reproduced part of it in the photographic section between pp. 160–1 of his *The Secret Offensive*.

19 Wigg later charged Healey with 'intellectual arrogance and with living in a world of bizarre fantasy'. *The Times*, letter 20/2/69. Williams/Reed, p. 169; Wilson, *Labour Government*, pp. 68–9; Castle, *Diaries*, vol. 1, 12/1/68; Malone, p. 16. See Bayliss (ed.), p. 140, Chichester/Wilkinson, p. 9 and Dockrill, p. 86.

20 Freedman, *Britain and Nuclear Weapons*, p. 32; Williams/Reed, p. 31; Healey, p. 302.

21 Hennessy, *Whitehall*, p. 188.

22 Hennessy, *Cabinet*, p. 149.

23 Interview with Bates in 1986 by Anthony Summers.

24 *Ibid.* Johnson on Wilson and Mrs Williams, see George Ball, p. 336 and Hennessy, *Whitehall*, p. 189. CIA memo, Helms to Bundy, 30/11/64. Thanks to Michael Crick who supplied it.

25 Malone, p. 18. CCF links; see Coleman, pp. 185–6. 'Oatsheaf' confirmed by Angleton himself who told the journalist and his unofficial mouthpiece, Edward J. Epstein. See Epstein, p. 81. This is also confirmed by Wright and Mangold, pp. 74–5.

CHAPTER VIII: WILSON AND THE SPOOKS

1   Wilson, *Labour Government*, p. 312. Was Wilson told that Philby was a triple agent, i.e. working for us? It is the only scenario that makes sense.

2   Horne, p. 465.

3   HOC *Hansard*, 23/7/63.

4   On Kerby: Deacon, *With My Little Eye*, p. 172 and *History of British Secret Service*, pp. 338–44. Pincher, *Inside Story*, pp. 101–9 and *Trade is Treachery*, pp. 246–8. *Spectator*, 6/12/86; and *New Statesman*, 5/12/86.

5 Telephone conversation with Ray Fletcher, 24/10/90.

6 Pincher, *Inside Story*, p. 28; Benn, *Diaries*, vol. 3, 30/3/73, p. 15.

7 HOC *Hansard*, col. 872, 17/6/63; HOC *Hansard*, col. 50, 17/6/63.

8 West, *Molehunt*, p. 25; Macmillan informed, see Horne, *Macmillan*, p. 466; West, *A Matter of Trust*, p. 171.

9 Mid-fifties campaign, see Bunyan, p. 166. Benn Levy was one of the few Labour MPs to have worked in MI6 during the war.

10 Quoted in Lord Denning's Report, September 1963. Cmnd. 2152. (HMSO 1963).

11 HOC *Hansard*, col. 872, 16/12/63; Pincher, *Too Secret*, p. 426.

12 HOC *Hansard*, col. 875 and col. 979, 16/12/63.

13 D. Williams, *Not in the Public Interest*, p. 169. The Maxwell–Fyfe directive had been written casually over lunch by the Conservative Home Secretary. Successive Home Secretaries were entitled to write their own but none did – another example of Labour politicians' exaggerated deference to the British state and its unwritten constitution.

14 Hennessy, *Whitehall*, p. 655; *New Statesman*, 21/10/88.

15 Benn, *Diaries*, vol. 1, p. 172.

16 Pincher, *Too Secret*, p. 464.

17 Wilson, *Labour Government*, pp. 388/9; HOC *Hansard*, 'Telephone Tapping', col. 635 and 639, 17/11/67; HOL *Hansard*, 'Telephone Tapping (Peers)', col. 337, 14/2/67.

18 Pincher, *Too Secret*, p. 465.

19 Wilson, *Labour Government*, pp. 34–5.

20 Leigh, p. 91.

CHAPTER IX: WIGGERY-POKERY

1 Short, p. 31.

2 Wilson, *Labour Government*, p. 35.

3 Wigg, p. 317; Short, p. 31.

4 Wigg, p. 308; Short, p. 32.

5 Pincher, *Too Secret*, p. 464.

6 See Ian Gilmour review of Alistair Horne's biography of Harold Macmillan in *London Review of Books*, 27/7/89.

7 Short, p. 32; HOC *Hansard*, 'Paymaster-General', col. 1186, 12/11/64 and Leigh, p. 96.

8 Pincher, *Too Secret*, p. 464; Wilson, *Labour Government*, p. 35; Wigg, p. 323; Benn, *Diaries*, vol. 1, 3/7/63, p. 37.

9 Franks Committee, 1972, vol. 3: *Oral Evidence*, p. 245; Pincher, *Inside Story*, p. 246; Wigg, p. 323.

10 West, *A Matter of Trust*, pp. 164–5; Deacon, *With My Little Eye*, p. 221.

11 Wilson, *Labour Government*, p. 35; Pincher, *Inside Story*, p. 167; Short, p. 32.

12 The later Radcliffe Report recommended that positive vetting should be carried out every five years, though there have never been enough investigators to carry out the job properly or consistently. HOC *Hansard*, col. 775, 23/1/89. Aitken was a leading member of Quintin Hogg's leadership campaign.

13 Benn, *Diaries*, vol.1, p. 182; Pincher, *Inside Story*, p. 166.

14 Wilson, an arch monarchist, appeared to believe that the MPs' oath of allegiance was enough: 'I do swear by Almighty God that I will be faithful and bear true allegiance to Her Majesty Queen Elizabeth II, her heirs and successors according to law. So Help Me God.' Pincher, *Inside Story*, p. 167; Hennessy, *Whitehall*, p. 349; Benn, *Diaries*, vol.1, p. 122; HOC *Hansard*, col. 60, 16/1/89. Whether this means that the Privy Council Office organises its own vetting process, or has a secret relationship with the security services, is not known.

15 Pincher, *Inside Story*, p. 167; Benn, *Diaries*, vol.1, p. 175.

16 Silkin, p. 76; Short, p. 61. Destroying the 'dirt book' was honourable, but it might have later proved a useful weapon against the Tory smear tactics.

17 Benn, *Diaries*, vol. 1, pp. 302–3; Leigh p. 97.

18 Short, pp. 32 and 196–7.

19 Pincher, *Inside Story*, p. 245 and Ponting, p. 177; Pincher, *Dirty Tricks*, p. 74; Robertson p. 43; Interview with Barrie Penrose, November 1990.

CHAPTER X: THE KITCHEN CABINET

1 M. Williams, p. 281.

2 *ibid.*, p. 23; Short, pp. 14–15.

3 M. Williams, p. 282; Benn, *Diaries*, vol. 1 pp. 182 and 194; *Independent*, 28/4/87, Peter Jenkins, 'Skeletons in a crowded cupboard'; Short, p. 76.

4 Benn, *Diaries*, vol. 1, p. 194.

5 Barrie Penrose, interview 15/11/90. Marcia Williams, discovered Wigg's big secret some years later: Leigh, p. 109.

6 HOC *Hansard*, 'Security', 12/11/64.

7 M. Williams, pp. 47 and 283; Ponting, p. 178; Wilson, *Governance of Britain*, p. 117.

8 S. Crosland, p. 170; Margach, *Abuse of Power*, p. 141.

9 Doig, *Westminster Babylon*, p. 202.

10 Crossman, *Diaries*, vol. 1, p. 350; Short, p. 91.

11 Short, pp. 17–18.

12 Castle, *Diaries*, vol. 1, p. 280. The clan consisted of Dick Crossman, Barbara Castle, Tony Benn, Peter Shore, John Silkin, Tommy Balogh, Judith Hart and Marcia Williams. Wigg, p. 315; Benn, *Diaries*, vol. 1, 2/11/65, p. 345; Short, pp. 248–9.

13 M. Williams, p. 257; Roth, *Walter Mitty*, p. 24.

14 *News of the World*, 20/2/77; *Sunday Times*, 19/7/81.

15 Benn, *Diaries*, vol. 1, 19/2/65, p. 223; Crossman, *Diaries*, vol. 1, p. 363; Benn, *Diaries*, vol. 1, 2/11/65, p. 345.

16 Short, p. 173; Wilson, *Governance of Britain*, p. 117.

17 Short, p. 76; Roth, *Walter Mitty*, p. 24; *Private Eye*, 17/5/74, deleted extracts from Wigg's book.

18 Short, pp. 32 and 76.

19 *Ibid.*, p. 15.

20 *Ibid.*, pp. 248–9.

CHAPTER XI: WILSON AND THE BANKERS

1 Longford, p. 270.

2 Falkender, p. 92. Still a good short account of the Bank Rate affair is Ferris.

3 Ferris' account makes very interesting reading in the glow of the 'big bang' in the City, and the erection of 'Chinese (i.e. imaginary) walls' of the type described by Lord Cobbold. Ferris, pp. 139–40. Roth, *Walter Mitty*, p. 223.

4 Ferris, p. 155. In 1967 Wilson repeated these opinions to Kenneth Harris in response to the question 'One hears sometimes that you aren't trusted in the City. Why not?' Harris, *Conversations*, p. 285; cited in Roth, *Walter Mitty*, p. 224.

5 Maudling, p. 116.

6 Edinburgh speech, cited in Ponting, p. 72; TUC speech, cited in Brandon, p. 3.

7 Maudling, p. 116.

8   For a contemporaneous Labour view of Maudling's role in the attack see Shore, pp. 122–3.

9   Attali, p. 239.

10   Newton/Porter, pp. 151–2.

11   Ponting, p. 46. There is a good account of these talks with the US authorities in Eric Roll's memoir pp. 144–7. See also Ponting, p. 44.

12   Brandon, pp. 36–7; Short, p. 37.

13   Lord Cromer was George Baring. In 1967 he became Chairman and Managing Director of Baring Brothers & Co., one of the City's oldest merchant banks. There is an extremely complex network which could be traced here. For example: Managing Director of Baring's since 1955 was Hon. John Baring, who married the daughter of Lord (Robert) Renwick, a key figure in the anti-Labour plots of 1967 and 1968, discussed below. In 1942 Lord Cromer married Hon. Esme Harmsworth. 2nd Daughter of Viscount Harmsworth. Cecil (Harmsworth) King's mother was the daughter of Alfred Harmsworth – King, *Diaries*, vol. 1, p. 55. During the war Guy Liddell, head of MI5's B Division, recruited Sir Edward Reid Bt, a Director of Baring Bros (1926–66), Liddell's first cousin by marriage. He became B Division's expert on financial affairs, an important figure in the City, President of the Institute of Bankers 1962–4. West, *A Matter of Trust*, p. 284. Richard Norton-Taylor (*In Defence of*) adds: 'MI5 has a "plant" in the Bank of England. The agencies also have informal links with merchant bankers and businessmen', (p. 57).

14   Wilson, *Labour Government*, pp. 61–2.

15   Heatherington, p. 105. This version of events is confirmed, in part, by Wilson himself. See Wilson, *Labour Government*, p. 66.

16   Loan, see Wilson, *ibid.*, p. 66; Foot, *Wilson*, p. 159.

17   Hirsch, p. 129.

18   Attali, pp. 232–3.

19   Cited in Ponting, p. 51.

20   Castle, *Diaries*, vol. 1, 11/12/64.

21   King, *Diaries*, vol. 1, 14/10/65.

22   *Ibid.*, 5/8/65, p. 28 and 30/6/66, p. 74.

23   Ponting, p. 53. *Private Eye* (8/1/65) carried a piece describing 'Wilson's Russian deal . . . the possibility that a trade deal might be made with the Russians which would actually get Britain off the hook in its trade balance deficit, and in consequence profoundly affect domestic policies all the way from Bank Rate to wage "restraint". ' Evidence of this being anything more than a Wilsonian fantasy is nil. None of the memoirs of this period, from Government members, including Wilson, mention this. It was probably a plant by Wilson or someone close to him, a part of the game of bluff and double-bluff he was playing with the Bank of England: co-operate or I'll look East. Something very similar happens in Chris Mullin's thriller *A Very British Coup*.

24   Brandon, p. 79.

25   Attali citing *ibid.*, p. 243.

26   Attali, pp. 241–4. This received an ironic echo in 1991 with the British support for US intervention in the Gulf against Iraq.

27   Crossman, *Diaries*, vol. 1, p. 161.

28   King, *Diaries*, vol. 1, p. 27; Brandon, p. 94.

29   Wilson, *Labour Government*, pp. 173–4.

30   Brandon, p. 103.

31   King, *Diaries*, vol. 1, p. 173. Cromer is there with King, still thinking of how to lose Wilson the election in 1970. *ibid.*, pp. 329–30.

CHAPTER XII: 'RHODESIAN DISTRACTIONS'

1   The Rhodesian Front contained a substantial minority of hard-core conspiracy theorists, one of whom, Ivor Benson, was briefly 'Adviser to the Government' in the Rhodesian Government Information Services. Barber, p. 256.

2   Horne, p. 389; K. Young, *Rhodesia*, p. 107; 'Southern Rhodesia', Minister of Defence Denis Healey was told,

'had powerful armed forces and we had no reason to believe that they would not fight us if we attempted to intervene'. Healey, p. 332. His choice of 'we had no reason to believe they would not fight', rather than the simpler 'we were told they would' is interesting.

3 'There is little doubt that Gutteridge was expressing the views of the British Ministry of Defence at this period.' K. Young, *Rhodesia*, p. 331. Indeed, what other source could have provided such detailed information? Denis Healey was on friendly terms with the RIIA. He had been on the Council of Chatham House, the publishers of *The World Today*, since 1946. Healey, p. 119.

4 Flower, pp. 41 and 51.

5 Healey, p. 332 and *Guardian*, 11/4/81. Mr Healey declined to expand on these published fragments to us. Verrier, *Zimbabwe*, p. 262.

6 Flower, p. 49.

7 Rex quoted in Loney, p. 141.

8 Penrose/Courtiour, p. 298. Additional information from Barrie Penrose, interview November 1990. This account has a curious ring of truth, for when in the Rhodesian Army in the late 1970s Fred Holroyd found there that many of the older (white) officers felt an oath of loyalty not to 'the Crown' but to the Queen Mother personally.

9 Penrose/Courtiour, p. 317; *Sunday Times*, 29/3/81.

10 Denis Healey called Wilson's statement 'insane' in the TV programme *End of Empire*, Channel Four 1987; and Wilson later acknowleged to Cecil King that it was a mistake. Healey, p. 51 and King, *Diaries*, vol. 1, p. 45. The 'military difficulties were exaggerated in consequence of a combination of prejudiced military advice and the political reluctance of the Labour Government to risk civilian casualties, which would have exaggerated the already strong "kith and kin" arguments espoused by a largely hostile press.' David Owen cited in Loney, p. 142.

11 Obituary of Gibbs by Patrick Keatley, *Guardian*, 7/11/90.

12 Castle, *Diaries*, vol. 1, p. 69.

13 On sources of the advice see Bailey, p. 130 and Berridge, p. 151. Former civil servant Dudley Seers, in Thomas (ed.), p. 97, blames the Department of Economic Affairs.

14 Bailey, pp. 110–16; R. Hall, p. 116.

15 Healey, p. 303. For Martin Bailey 'Wilson listened to those advisers who were telling him what he wanted to hear . . . the British Government as a whole became over-confident that South Africa and Portugal would respect the embargo'. Bailey, p.131.

16 Bailey, pp. 131–9; K. Young, *Rhodesia*, p. 413; Pincher, *Inside Story*, p. 16. Pincher was unable to recall the source of this information. Letter to the authors, 12/12/90. Reports would have reached Wilson from the Joint Intelligence Committee where the source of the information is masked.

17 Sedgemore, p. 20.

18 Verrier, *Zimbabwe*, p. 156. 'SIS in Rhodesia duly reported the flow of oil by road and rail from South Africa.' Verrier, *Looking Glass*, p. 263.

19 K. Young, *Rhodesia*, p. 135. This view is also expressed by Hudson, pp. 62–3, but is unsourced.

20 Verrier, *Zimbabwe*, cites co-operation over operations in Kuwait. p. 154.

21 Wilson, *Labour Government*, p. 256; Flower, p. 63: emphasis added. Penrose/Courtiour, p. 228. Windrich suggests that a contributory factor was Wilson's ignorance of African, colonial and Commonwealth affairs: 'Once in Government his main source of advice on Rhodesia was the the Commonwealth Office, policy-making having shifted from its previous sources – Transport House, the Commonwealth Colonies Group of Labour MPs, the Fabian Commonwealth Bureau – to the Whitehall Establishment. While Mr Wilson (as were his senior ministers) was well equipped with party political advisers on other subjects, none were then provided for Commonwealth or African affairs.' Windrich, pp. 48–9.

CHAPTER XIII: WAR BY OTHER MEANS

1 Verrier, *Zimbabwe*, pp. 112–13. 'Nairobi was the regional MI5 headquarters during these years of advancing African independence and it was there that Security Liaison Officers (SLOs) met to plan the continued support of key figures and the training of nascent intelligence and security services. An SLO from MI5 was stationed in Salisbury operating on a declared basis with FISB [Federation Intelligence and Security Bureau] . . . [South Africa] also co-operated with British Army intelligence throughout the entire region south of the Zambezi, including Angola and Mozambique. British regular soldiers known as Field Service Intelligence Officers (FSIOs) operated under the High Commission cover. South Africa's departure from the Commonwealth in May 1961 made no difference to this liaison. It continues today.'

2   Flower, p. 11; Verrier, *Zimbabwe*, p. 117. K. Young, *Rhodesia*, p. 48, comments that, presumably as a result, 'Walensky [was] reputed to have the best intelligence in Africa.'

3   Flower, p. 81.

4   Crossman, *Diaries*, vol. 1, p. 393 – the exact date of this conversation is unclear.

5   K. Young, *Rhodesia*, p. 419. 'To the Foreign Office's Information Research Department and the BBC was left the doubtful honour . . . of providing or transmitting material designed to reassure the loyal and bid them to be of good cheer.' Verrier, *Zimbabwe*, p. 156. St Johnston, p. 176. Duncan Campbell, *New Statesman*, 4/7/80; Flower, pp. 81–2. The first director of the Zambian Broadcasting Company was Michael Kittermaster, said to be seconded from the British Central Office of Information. Kittermaster was presumably also from the IRD. Joyce, p. 365 and K. Young, *Rhodesia*, p. 354. Zambia also joined the propaganda war, running in London 'a covert publicity exercise . . . Central Africa Research Office, which sent out bulletins to MPs, universities and public libraries . . . These bulletins were . . . careful imitations, in both typography and style, of briefing papers put out by the Foreign and Commonwealth Office.' R. Hall, pp. 51–2.

6   Flower, p. 69.

7   *Ibid.*, p. 104; *Daily Telegraph*, 30/3/66. Colvin had worked for MI6 before the war.

8   Flower, p. 103.

9   *Independent*, 7/9/87.

10   Pincher, *Inside Story*, p. 246; Ian Hancock interview with Flower, 4/2/82. Flower quoted in the *Independent*, 7/9/87. Wilson described the Tudor Rose pamphlet as 'an anonymous and electorally illegal document, issued under the name of the 'White Rose' organisation from an accommodation address in London but printed in Rhodesia, [which] was circulating in Hull North with urgent pleas that the recipient should vote against the Labour candidate'. Wilson, *Labour Government*, p. 258.

11   Skeen, p. 39.

12   Bloch/Fitzgerald, p. 187; Fairer-Smith intended joining Colonel Edward Askew, ex-Palestine CID, then running a business investigation bureau, 'Tel Peda', in Rhodesia, *Observer*, 29/12/71. Rose, pp. 163–4 and Winter, p. 307.

13   On Fairer-Smith and his network in the UK see Bloch/Fitzgerald, p. 187; Rose, pp. 163–9, Winter, p. 308. Blackburn, allegedly Rhodesian SAS, *Private Eye*, 28/11/75. Labour MP Paul Rose identified four of the 70 South African agents said to be in the UK. On Richardson, see Parker, *Rough Justice*, pp. 285–7. It was later suggested that the South Africans had asked Richardson to bug Wilson. He denied the accusation. On 'Kruger' see HOC *Hansard*, cols. 650–5, 15/12/71. Details of trial in *Daily Telegraph*, 27/5/67, *Sunday Telegraph*, 18/6/67, and *The Times*, 26/7/67.

14   British co-operation with Rhodesian and South African intelligence is one of the sub-themes of Gordon Winter's *Inside Boss*. *Observer*, 19/12/71. Winter describes such a 'warning' visit by Special Branch, p. 416.

15   Penrose/Courtiour, p. 98.

16   Flower, p. 91.

17   *Ibid.*, p. 58.

18   Flower, p. 64. Verrier's claim that 'the limitations of SIS activities within the Federation – in practice, Southern Rhodesia -would rob Whitehall and its masters of critical intelligence about UDI factors in 1964 and 1965' just won't wash. Verrier, *Zimbabwe*, p. 117.

19   See Flower, pp. 90–1 and Pincher, *Inside Story*, p. 108. Kerby's friend, the White Russian George Knupffer, also went to Rhodesia. Flower hints that Knupffer – 'a kind of modern-day Keynes with a Soviet connection' – was some kind of MI6 agent. In 1975, Knupffer published his *The Struggle for World Power* (Plain Speaker Publishing) on the dust jacket of which he says of himself 'For over 30 years he worked closely with the late Captain Henry Kerby.' To judge by this publication and his association with racists like Lady Birdwood in the 1970s, Knupffer was just another dotty global conspiracy theorist. Or was this a cover? From Thayer, p. 101: 'Knupffer is the founder of a new sect in Britain called the Right Party, a group of small size and no influence which has ties with some right-wing organisations in the United States. The party is anti-Communist, anti-Capitalist, anti-Income-Tax, and anti-foreigner. It is pro-OAS, pro-Salazar, pro-Franco, and pro-Absolute Monarchy.' Extracts from Kerby's report to Wilson were published in the *Sunday Times* on 13/2/77.

20   Roth, *Heath and Heathmen*, p. 194; K. Young, *Rhodesia*, pp. 510–11.

CHAPTER XIV: BLUNT

1   Penrose/Freeman, pp. 430 and 439.

2   Wright, pp. 213–14.

3 Penrose/Freeman, pp. 410–11. Michael Straight also continued to see MI5 officers in London when he came across the Atlantic for business trips.

4 Pincher, *Too Secret*, p. 374; Boyle, p. 408.

5 Boyle, pp. 480–1; HOC *Hansard*, col. 424, 21/11/79. Elwyn Jones wasn't informed until 1974 and then by Silkin. At least one senior figure in the DPP's office, Sir Theobald Mathew, who died in February 1964, suspected Wilson of being a Soviet agent. Information from Dr Kitty Little, letter to Bernard Weatherill, Speaker of the House of Commons, 1/5/87.

6 Elwyn-Jones, p. 64. Elwyn Jones was in Vienna at the same time as Philby, Gaitskell and others.

7 See obituaries on Gardiner in the *Independent* and the *Guardian*, 10/1/90. Elwyn Jones and Gardiner died within months of each other. On bugging, see *The Profession of Intelligence*, part 5, BBC Radio Four, 10/2/82. Also, the *Guardian*, 29/5/81, and Knightley, p. 351. The tap would have been there if only to make sure that he had not heard about Blunt.

8 Benn, *Diaries*, vol. 1, 29/9/65. Frank Soskice, Home Secretary in 1964, was a right-wing conservative-minded Minister and ardent anti-communist. The son of a White Russian, Soskice also had a Russian wife, possibly enough in itself to make sections of MI5 regard him as unreliable. Moorehead, p. 123.

9 Wright, p. 188. Arthur Martin and Elwell had served in the Far East. Such officers were known inside MI5 as the 'Malay Mafia'. On Maxwell and communist infiltration see Masters, p. 186.

10 Wright, p. 236; Penrose/Freeman, p. 431.

CHAPTER XV: SPOOKS TWO

1 Short, p. 32; Summers/Dorril, pp. 270/1. Interview, Charles Bates 1986. Bates had undertaken the report when John McCone was head of the American Atomic Energy Authority. John Kennedy later made McCone head of the CIA.

2 HOC *Hansard*, 21/5/65; West, *A Matter of Trust*, p. 170.

3 Photographs were produced of the meetings which four years later found their way to the *Sunday Times*, 7/12/69. Roberts has alleged to researchers that a set of obscene photographs (negatives) were dropped through his letterbox with a note from Soupert asking him to bring them to their next meeting. Roberts claims the photographs portrayed Labour MP Bernard Floud, Conservative MP Anthony Courtney, and Roger Hollis, Director-General of MI5, in sexually compromising positions. The *People* and the *Sunday Times*, 28/2/65.

4 See *Private Eye* for details, 1/4/65. MI5's D Branch (counter-espionage) carried out an investigation into the background of the defence barrister Jeremy Hutchinson QC. Roberts believes that Hollis scuppered the case in order to cover up the existence of the embarrassing photographs.

5 Courtney's wife was a former MI5 secretary. He was a close friend of 'C', Sir Stewart Menzies, and had been involved in running MI6 agents into the Baltic states after the war.

6 The 'affair' took place one month after MI5 had used Pincher to publish details of KGB 'honeytrap' operations in the *Daily Express*. The 5 April 1961 article had been targeted at businessmen who would attend this Exhibition. Greville Wynne, the contact for Penkovsky, was also enticed by a KGB 'swallow' at this time but avoided her. Courtney, p. 117. See Hyde, p. 295 and Courtney, pp. 132 and 135–6. If the Roberts/Kodak story is true then British security authorities already had in their possession (a year before) pornographic photos relating to Courtney.

7 Courtney, pp. 131–49; *Observer*, 28/8/77. Wigg agreed with H. Montgomery Hyde who believed the 'somebody' was 'almost certainly Tom Driberg who was acting as double agent'. Driberg was hardly 'someone in a high position' and correspondence with Mr Hyde shows that this was merely speculation. Hyde, p. 294; Letter, 31/3/88; Wigg: Pincher, *Dirty Tricks*, p. 82. The target may have been Roger Hollis. It was common knowledge in London's small intelligence community, that the head of MI5 was having an affair with his secretary. Hollis was under investigation by the 'Gestapo' and was being left out of major decisions in the office, even to the extent that information was kept away from him. 'A former MI6 officer has confirmed to me that concern arose about Hollis, who had a long affair with his secretary in MI5 . . . The only public allusion to this situation was made by Anthony Courtney, the MP who was framed by the KGB . . . Courtney pointed out at a public meeting that Hollis had put himself in a blackmailable position, which was known to many people, he had been allowed to continue in high office.' Pincher, *Inside Story*, p. 93.

8 *Private Eye*, No. 102, 12/11/65. The *Eye*'s editor, Richard Ingrams, later apologised for the Courtney reference. 'That was a clear case where we were wrong to do as we did since we were really playing the KGB's game.' *Observer*, 28/10/90.

9 *Observer*, 28/8/77; Andrew Wilson letter to authors 21/1/86.

10 The true indentity of FEDORA has never been established. FBI sources mischievously suggested KGB

officer Victor Lessiovsky, though Chapman Pincher, presumably with Wright as a source, proposes Vladimir Chuchukin, indentified by John Barron as a KGB disinformation officer at the UN. Pincher, *Too Secret*, p. 609 and Barron, *KGB*, p. 212. Mangold (p. 370) says that FEDORA 'was a KGB colonel who worked in New York under a cover as a scientific and technical officer on the permanent staff of the United Nations'.

11 *Sunday Times*, 21/1/90.

12 Pincher, *Too Secret*, pp. 423–4 and *idem., Inside Story*, p. 247.

13 Pincher, *Too Secret*, p. 337. 'American officials [James Angleton] decided as long ago as the early 1970s that TOP HAT was a Soviet plant who was passing on mostly false information . . . As TOP HAT, he passed Soviet secrets to the United States until the mid-1970s, but then the CIA concluded that he was a Soviet "dangler" . . . American intelligence agencies still believe Polyakov was a double agent whose main loyalty was to the Kremlin.' *Sunday Times*, 21/1/90. According to Mangold (pp. 370 and 386) both FEDORA and TOP HAT were both bona fide defectors. MI5 had been informed that TOP HAT was the source for Bossard in order to protect the true source, NICK NACK (pp. 318/9).

14 *Sunday Times*, 21/1/90; Wright, p. 274.

15 Benn, *Diaries*, vol. 2, 11/1/68, p. 11 and 29/5/68, p. 181.

16 In revealing the Gray/Coyne report to Wright, Angleton was returning a favour. Patrick Stewart, one of Wright's colleagues, had earlier sent a copy of MI5's damage assessment report on the Bossard case. Stewart added a one-word memorandum which read 'Help!'. Wright, p. 306. According to Wright: 'The CIA intended making a direct approach to Harold Wilson, along with the American Ambassador in London, David Bruce, to, brief him on the findings . . . Cram opposed the approach to Wilson, yet Helms and Angleton insisted he begin sounding out George Wigg, Wilson's security adviser.' *Ibid.*, pp. 274–5.

17 West, *The Friends*, pp. 167–8; Wright, p. 275.

18 *Guardian*, 27/1/78, and *Observer*, 20/12/81. *Time Out*, 20/6/75. See *Lobster* 11 for full background on Forum World Features.

19 Leigh, p. 104; Pincher, *Too Secret*, pp. 425–6 and 78.

20 Pincher, *Too Secret*, p. 78. The 'professional advice' came from Hollis, although in the twelve months during which Wigg knew the Director-General there could have been only a few meetings: Hollis was abroad for a good deal of the time making his farewells to Commonwealth intelligence colleagues. Deacon, *With My Little Eye*, p. 278; Benn, *Diaries*, vol. 1, p. 284.

21 Pincher, *Trade is Treachery*, p. 248; *idem., Dirty Tricks*, p. 95. Kerby's role still remains unclear and with Kerby and Wigg both dead, may never be clarified.

22 Wright, pp. 291, 343 and 275.

23 Pincher, *Trade is Treachery*, p. 32 and West, *Molehunt*, p. 38. FLUENCY's membership included Anne Orr-Ewing, Evelyn McBarnet, an MI5 researcher to Martin, MI5 Soviet expert Patrick Stewart, Terence Lecky, de Mowbray and later Christopher Phillpotts from MI6.

24 Leigh, p. 80. Dick White, according to one story, tried to get rid of de Mowbray but Phillpotts intervened to save his friend.

25 Wright, pp. 276 and 307; Leigh, p.104. Another consequence of the Gray/Coyne review was that Angleton 'ensured that all important communications with British intelligence went through him personally, by-passing the London station.' At the first CANZAB conference in Australia, the chief guest was Golitsyn, who had just been re-employed by MI5 at a standard rate of £10,000 per month. Wright reveals that Angleton regarded CANZAB as 'the first decisive step in creating a unified Western intelligence command capable of challenging the Soviet Bloc'. p. 307.

CHAPTER XVI: MI5 AND THE WILSON CIRCLE

1 Epstein, p. 81. Angleton set up a Special Investigation Group, a super-secret unit which investigated a number of world leaders. Mangold pp. 280–2 and 75.

2 *Ibid.*, p. 81.

3 *Ibid.*, p. 82; Wright correspondence. Leigh, p. 156; Pincher, *A Web of Deception*, p. 102.

4 Pincher, *A Web of Deception*, p. 101, and *idem, Trade is Treachery*, p. 255.

5 *Sunday Times*, 19/7/81; Wright correspondence. Leigh, pp. 119 and 160. Wright had been put on the trail of Kagan by the Rothschilds. Pincher, *Trade is Treachery*, p. 255.

6 Leigh, p. 109. The existence of this file alone gives the lie to the claim that the investigations only began after

Wilson came to power. It would therefore be wrong to suggest, as Leigh does, that Wigg 'stimulated the compilation within MI5 of the "Worthington file" '.

7 *Sunday Times*, 19/7/81; *The Times*, 4/5/77; Colin Wallace document 'Political and Security implications regarding the disclosure of security classified information to assist in the the investigation of the allegations relating to the Kincora Boys' Hostel, Belfast', March 1982, p. 8.

8 Wright, p. 291.

9 *Ibid.*, p. 364.

10 Epstein, p. 82. Our assumption would be that they were Sternberg and Beattie Plummer. Angleton did not learn about Kagan until the early seventies – Leigh, p. 200.

11 Epstein, p. 82.

12 Leigh, p. 110.

13 *Spectator*, 16/5/87.

14 *Private Eye*, 2/9/77.

15 Franks Committee, 1972, pp. 244–8.

16 *Sunday Express*, 14/2/88. This photograph and accompanying material given to William Massie presumably came originally from either MI6 – or the CIA. *Private Eye*, 2/8/77.

17 Pincher, *Inside Story*, p. 346; Deacon, *The British Connection*, p. 238. In a tribute to her when she died in 1972, Wilson wrote: 'She was a founder-member of the Agricultural Export Council and travelled widely, especially in Eastern Europe, promoting the sale of farm products . . . She was passionately devoted to improving East–West relations not so much by speeches and organised movements as by personal relations . . . A great hostess . . . but above all, a loyal and understanding friend.' *The Times*, 5/6/72.

18 Howard/West, p. 47; Deacon, *The British Connection*, p. 239. Throughout his career Wilson was linked to people he had met on one or two occasions.

19 Leigh, p. 118. Another Tory MP and former MI6 officer, H. Montgomery-Hyde told us Sternberg was 'highly suspect'. Letter, 31/8/88.

20 Leigh, pp. 118 and 191.

21 *Sunday Telegraph*, 3/5/87; Pincher, *Inside Story*, p. 255; William Massie, quoted in Leigh p. 192.

22 Leigh, p. 116; *Listener*, 6/8/87. Masterman had been Douglas-Home's tutor at Oxford and 'as late as 1965 . . . was still confiding his doubts and inner feelings . . . in Sir John'. K. Young, *Alec Douglas-Home*, p. 21. A second more likely indirect source was MI6 for whom he had Ministerial responsibility during his tenure as Foreign Secretary; a direct source possibly being Dodds-Parker. The information appears remarkably similar to that which Dodds-Parker knew and which was peddled by Conservative Central Office during the 1964 election campaign.

23 See Leigh, pp. 116–19.

24 Dodds-Parker, p. 195.

25 Pincher, *Trade is Treachery*, p. 247; See *Spectator*, 22/11/86 and 6/12/86. The smear began when Kerby denounced the Polish defector Goleniewski as a KGB plant. Deacon, *Russian Secret Service*, p. 342.

26 *Private Eye*, 2/9/77. So began the allegation of a 'Communist cell in No. 10' which was to haunt Wilson in his third term in office during 1974–6.

27 Short, p. 204.

28 *Ibid.*, p. 204; Leigh, p. 143.

29 *Ibid.*, p. 143; Short, p. 204; Crossman, *Diaries*, vol. 1, 20/2/66, p. 462.

30 Benn, *Diaries*, vol. 3, 17/1/75, p. 303. Leigh, p. 144. It is possible that MacDermot had responsibilities at the Treasury for the 'secret vote' which funded the security services.

31 *Sunday Telegraph*, 3/5/87.

32 *Private Eye*, 2/9/77.

33 *Sunday Telegraph*, 3/5/87; Hollingsworth/Norton-Taylor, p. 190. *Guardian*, letter 13/1/88.

CHAPTER XVII: POLITICAL PLOTS

1 David Owen records how in May 1966, as a new MP, he attended his first meeting of the 1963 Club, which 'was really the CDS'. K. Harris, *Owen*, p. 39. Owen reports that at the time he did not even know what the

CDS was, but had been a fan of Gaitskell's, so was happy to join. See also P. Jenkins, p. 110. The CDS in 1969 'remained in existence, although only about twenty now attended its meetings'.

2 A good, explicit account of the 'sterling crisis' is Samuel Brittan, especially Chapter 8.

3 An interesting account along these lines is, Stephen Blank, 'The Politics of Foreign Economic Policy', International Organisation, Vol. 31, 1977.

4 Butler/Pinto-Duschinksy, p. 13.

5 Castle, *Diaries*, vol. 1, p. 145. During a conversation on the Monday, the 18th, with Home Secretary Roy Jenkins, Crossman told Jenkins: 'Harold is working against you, telling us anti-Europeans that anyone who wants to devalue the pound is trying to do so as a practical way into Europe.' Crossman, *Diaries*, vol. 1, p. 574.

6 Castle, *Diaries*, vol. 1 25/7/66. Such contact with Callaghan is not recorded in King's diaries of the period. Castle told Wilson: 'If you read something in the *New Statesman* this week . . . ' See her diary entry for 25/7/66, last line, and *New Statesman*, 29/7/66.

7 Benn, *Diaries*, vol. 1, 6/8/66, and 12/9/66, p. 472.

8 Castle, *Diaries*, vol. 1, 7/10/66.

9 The Terry–Marcia Williams relationship was supposed to be a secret, but it had reached the ears of Wigg, who duly informed Wilson. See Margach, p. 151. *Daily Mail*, 10/10/66.

10 Donnelly, p. 67; Wigg, p. 334; Crossman, *Diaries*, vol. 1, p. 575; Callaghan, p. 199.

11 S. Crosland, pp. 170–2. On Harris, see also J. Campbell, Jenkins, p. 99.

12 Beloff, p. 213. Letter from Lord Jenkins of Hillhead, 18/1/90.

13 Susan Crosland quoting the economist Robert Nield, p. 174. Anne Fleming: In 1961, for example, she wrote to Evelyn Waugh: 'I understand from Mrs Donaldson that all your children and you dote on Mr Gaitskell? . . . I sometimes walk with him in remote parks, he wears dark spectacles and tells me his problems while my mind wanders.' Amory, p. 281. See also *ibid.*, pp. 381–2. There is also a splendid line about the exposure of the CIA funding of *Encounter*, again to Nicolas Henderson: 'There's an awful fuss going on about *Encounter*, it appears that Stephen Spender did not know it was financed by the CIA, very rum for everyone else did.' *ibid.*, pp. 384–5.

14 Crossman, *Diaries*, vol. 1, p 575 and vol. 2, p. 70. The *Daily Express* chipped in on the 18th with a report that Denis Healey and the service chiefs were ready to resign en bloc if there were any further cuts in the defence budget.

15 Benn, *Diaries*, vol. 1, p. 545; S. Crosland, p. 174; Crossman, *Diaries*, vol. 1, p. 574; Castle, *Diaries*, vol. 1, 18/7/66.

16 Castle, *Diaries*, vol. 1, pp. 147–8; Castle noted in her diary on the 31 July that she could 'see clearly what George meant about secret commitments Harold has made to Johnson.' King, *Diaries*, vol. 1, pp. 79 and 78.

17 D. Jay, pp. 367–8. King, *Diaries*, vol. 1, 20/1/66, p. 56. Jay lists a series of quotes from King's diary to show King's influence on Wilson's EEC thinking but misses out (or simply missed) this 20 January entry.

18 One of the interesting sub-themes of this period is Wilson's apparent belief that some of the pressure on the pound was coming from the French. If De Gaulle knew that there was this kind of Wilson–Johnson agreement, one that neither party could publicly acknowledge, he might well have been tempted to have a dig at it.

19 S. Crosland, p. 173.

20 Alexander/Watkins, p. 127; *Observer*, 17/7/66 – this section of Donnelly's speech is omitted from his extensive quotes from it in his memoir. Donnelly had been one of Brown's leading supporters against Wilson in the contest for the leadership. Andrew Roth reports Donnelly in the 1950s acting as an informant for the Gaitskellites within the Bevanite group, Keep Left. Mackintosh, p. 434. The then editor of the *Spectator*, Nigel Lawson, summarised his understanding of the 'plot' on 14 October after it had surfaced in the newspapers: 'certain Gaitskellite members of the Cabinet . . . the attempt was thoroughly amateurish . . . the plotters choice of successor was James Callaghan . . . the dastardly conspiracy was revealed to the Prime Minister by . . . George Wigg.'

21 King, *Diaries*, vol. 1, 26/6/66, 10/8/66 and 13/8/66.

22 Cabinet voting, according to King, who got it from Brown.

23 On Wilson's paranoia, see Healey, p. 336: 'Inevitably (after 1966) his persecution mania finally turned his nightmares into reality'; Abse, pp. 264–5: 'his capacity to interpret policy discussions as personal plots'.

Notes

CHAPTER XVIII: 'RED PLOT': THE SEAMEN'S STRIKE

1 *Time and Tide*, 28/9/65.

2 Crossman, *Diaries*, vol. 1, p. 445.

3 *Economist*, 15/1/66.

4 Crossman, *Diaries*, vol. 1, p. 529. The rise would have given the seamen just over £60 for a 40-hour week (until then a 56-hour week).

5 HOC *Hansard*, 20/6/66; Crossman, *Diaries*, vol. 1, p. 544.

6 *Guardian*, 25/6/66; *Observer*, 26/6/66, quoted in *Private Eye* No. 119, 8/7/66. Another name gleaned by the Special Branch was NUS member John Prescott, then a student at Hull University and now Labour Shadow Transport spokesperson. He had been warned by researchers at the BBC's *Panorama* programme that Wilson was about to name him. *Guardian*, 28/6/89.

7 Benn, *Diaries*, vol. 1, p. 439. Meeting with Heath: Leigh, p. 106 and Pincher, *Inside Story*, p. 137; Wilson, *Labour Government*, p. 302.

8 Gunter later denounced the building workers strikes' as a 'Red plot . . . an unholy alliance of communists and trotskyists to ruin the social democratic movement'. In 1967, he said 'The Communists are planning a winter of discontent', for which there was 'abundant evidence'. Jack Jones, pp. 145–6 and Foot, *Wilson*, p. 191; Castle on the MI5 reports: 'To begin with, the material is always mighty thin and most of it would be obvious to an informed politician . . . take Jack Jones: I don't need a Security Service to tell me that he succeeded in giving the impression he was more militant than [Hugh] Scanlon, or that he hadn't been in direct contact with the Communist Party during the dispute'. *Sunday Times*, 12/12/76.

9 Wilson, *Labour Government*, p. 308; Pincher, *Inside Story*, p. 136; Benn, *Diaries*, vol. 1, pp. 519–20; *Guardian*, 28/6/89; *Private Eye* no. 153, 8/7/66; interview with Penrose/Courtiour, quoted in Leigh, p. 105.

10 Short, pp. 278 and 215.

11 Crossman, *Diaries*, vol. 2, p. 131; Wilson, *Labour Government*, p. 388.

12 HOC *Hansard*, cols. 634–41, 17/11/66; Wilson, *Labour Government*, pp. 388–9; *The Times*, 18/11/66; M. Williams, *No. 10*, p. 183. The Tories 'Colonel Blimp', Tufton Beamish, used the debate as an opportunity to raise other matters. He wanted to know how Wilson squared the MPs' immunity from phone-tapping with the fact that he was 'Chairman of the Labour Party in 1961, when, it is said, at least a dozen Labour Members had their loyalty investigated by the Special Branch, including having their telephones tapped at the request of the Labour Party?' Referring to what was in fact the Gaitskell/Brown initiative, Wilson said he knew nothing of any such request. HOC *Hansard*, col. 336, 14/2/67.

CHAPTER XIX: THE D-NOTICE AFFAIR: WILSON FIGHTS BACK

1 Wilson, *Labour Government*, p. 478.

2 *Ibid.*, p. 481.

3 Pincher, *Inside Story*, p. 231.

4 Pincher acknowledges in *ibid.*, p. 243 that while DDPR Lohan had leaked information – on instructions – to him. Pincher read to Lohan's predecessor at the D-Notice Committee 'every story I wrote whether I thought it offended a D-Notice or not'. *Ibid.*, p. 231.

5 Cited in Headley/Aynsley, p. 42.

6 *Daily Telegraph*, 16/6/67. On 20/2/67, Liberal MP Peter Bessell, alleged agent of MI5 and the CIA, introduced an anti-tapping Bill in the House of Commons.

7 Crossman, *Diaries*, vol. 2, pp. 244–5.

8 This admission is in King's diary entry for 25 June 1967, a summary of the D-Notice Affair which is oddly missing from his diary while it was going on.

9 M. Williams, *No. 10*, p. 160.

10 *Ibid.*, p. 152.

11 Hedley/Aynsley, pp. 11 and 15; Wigg, p. 348.

12 Bamford, pp. 329–30 and Fitzgerald/Leopold, pp. 85-6.

13 This was an Act to Amend the Official Secrets Act 1911 – known as the Official Secrets Act 1920.

14 Hedley/Aynsley, pp. 23 and 20. Another potential embarrassment was that the British cables and GCHQ intercepts were being fed into the NSA's illegal MINARET operation which began in October 1967. This involved keeping a watch-list of American 'subversives' and anti-war protesters. It was not until 1975, when the Justice Department conducted a full-scale inquiry, that details of British co-operation were revealed. On this see Bamford, p. 331 and 'Minaret intelligence': Department of Justice Report on Inquiry into CIA-related Electronic Surveillance Activities, 30 June 1976, p. 160; also West, *GCHQ*, pp. 248–9 and Campbell, *Unsinkable Aircraft Carrier*, p. 164.

15 Bamford, pp. 333–6 and Fitzgerald/Leopold pp. 94–5.

16 Wright, p. 247.

17 Quoted in Bamford, p. 336.

18 *The Times*, 2/2/67; Pincher, *Inside Story*, p. 38.

19 *Private Eye*, 23/6/67; HOC *Hansard*, col. 2029, 22/6/67.

20 HOC *Hansard*, col. 2061, 22/2/67. Pincher writes: 'He [Lawson] came into my office from the street, so the information did not come to me from MI5 or any other official source.' *Dirty Tricks*, p. 90. However, the biographical clues offered by Lawson to Ensor suggest a possible intelligence connection, perhaps MI5.

21 M. Williams, *No.10*, p. 152.

22 Crossman, *Diaries*, vol. 2, p. 394.

23 HOC *Hansard*, col. 2090, 2/2/67; Crossman, *Diaries*, vol. 2, p. 394.

24 HOC *Hansard*, 'Press and Broadcasting Committee (Colonel Lohan)', cols. 257 and 260–1, 27/6/67.

25 Hedley/Aynsley, pp. 52–3; HOC *Hansard*, 'D-Notice', col. 2032, 22/6/67.

26 *Observer*, 26/2/67.

27 Crossman, *Diaries*, vol. 2, pp. 197, 201 and 204.

28 Pincher, *Inside Story*, p. 234.

29 *Private Eye*, 18/2/67; *Sunday Times*, 13/2/77.

30 Pincher, *Inside Story*, p. 234. Lohan may have had a personal axe to grind. *Private Eye*, 13/10/67, reported that Chalfont and Lohan had fallen out while Chalfont was with *The Times* when Lohan gave Chalfont some false information about a story. Penrose/Courtiour, pp. 234–5. On 10 June 1974, Auberon Waugh in his *Private Eye* column published the following. 'I have not been able to sleep for several nights worrying whether Lady Falkender will be able to call her children "Honourable". This dignity is reserved for children of certain degrees of the peerage, born in wedlock. If Lord Chalfont, for instance, had been sowing his wild oats around (a most preposterous suggestion), the resulting offspring would not be entitled to this distinction.' Pincher, *Inside Story*, pp. 236–7.

31 Wigg's researcher, George Caunt, told Pincher that he had seen transcripts of Lohan's telephone calls. *Dirty Tricks*, pp. 91 and 94, and *idem, Inside Story*, pp. 236 and 239.

32 Pincher, *Inside Story*, p. 240, and *Dirty Tricks*, p. 93.

33 *Idem., Too Secret*, p. 590 and *Dirty Tricks*, p. 94.

34 *Private Eye*, 23/6/67 and 13/10/67; Crossman, *Diaries*, vol. 2, 2/7/67; Mrs Williams comments that 'we were able to sustain the Prime Minister . . . when a suggestion was made that it would be a good idea to ask the Leader of the Opposition to see all the documentation so that he could have full knowledge of all the security aspects.' *No. 10*, p. 160. Meaning, we take it, that she was able to sustain the PM in *resisting* the suggestion. Added to the Wilson quote in this paragraph, this suggests that Heath *was not* informed of the GCHQ–NSA sub-text.

CHAPTER XX: D-NOTICE FALL-OUT

1 Crossman, *Diaries*, vol. 2, 10/7/67, pp. 418–19; M. Williams, *No. 10*, p. 160.

2 Crossman, *Diaries*, vol. 2, pp. 418–19.

3 Castle, *Diaries*, vol. 1, p. 266; Wilson, *Labour Government*, p. 481.

4 Crossman, *Diaries*, vol. 2, p. 405. Concerning the Trend letter, we have no other information.

5 Hennessy, *Whitehall*, p. 215; Leigh, p. 108. The same line – 'lives at risk' – was used when Labour Home Secretary Merlyn Rees expelled the former American CIA officer Philip Agee. Rees privately told MPs that

'lives are at stake'. Rees told Liberal leader David Steel: 'Agee is directly responsible for the death of two our agents behind the Iron Curtain.' This was also untrue. Agee, *On the Run*, p. 174.

6 M. Williams, *No. 10*, p. 160; King, *Diaries*, vol. 1, p. 169.

7 On 9/11/67 Crossman was at lunch when 'I first heard the rumours that George Wigg was to go to the Lords and become the head of the Horse-race Betting Levy Board. Later I got the fact from Harold . . . [who] explained to me that Anthony Head had been offered and had refused the job. This gave George his chance and if he didn't take it now he would miss it for ever. "Anyway, I think it's the right time for him to move on." This confirmed the impression I'd got that afternoon from Trevor Lloyd-Hughes that George didn't really want to go and had to be pushed, but in a nice way.' Crossman, *Diaries*, vol. 2, pp. 554–5. Roy Jenkins gave Wigg the news and 'expressed the hope that I would accept the post'. Wilson was 'kind enough to express concern at the prospect of my departure but, all in all, the choice seemed pre-ordained.' Wigg, p. 360

8 From the context, Leigh's source is Alex McDonald. Leigh, pp. 89–90.

9 Benn, *Diaries*, vol. 1, 22/2/67 and 1/3/67, p. 489.

10 Schneer, p. 223; Healey, p. 303.

11 Pincher, *Inside Story*, p. 245. The Army Bureau of Current Affairs and the Workers' Educational Association in which Wigg had been prominent before and during the war were regarded with suspicion by MI5. See Pincher, *Traitors*, p. 70.

12 Pincher, *Too Secret*, p. 588; *idem, Dirty Tricks*, p. 77; Wigg, p. 323; Deacon, *With My Little Eye*, p. 221. Pincher claims that Wigg 'regularly informed on Number 10 and all its inhabitants to MI5' (*Dirty Tricks*, p. 77). In his fictional book *Dirty Tricks*, Sidgwick and Jackson, 1980, (p. 56), an MI6 Chief says that 'One of the best runs we ever had was in Harold Wilson's day. MI5 had a steady informer on the Downing Street staff and they used to send us copies of all of his reports – details of where the Prime Minister went, who he saw . . . Marvellous stuff.' In the sixties, Pincher had intended to collaborate with John Drew on a political novel about the Labour Party. Drew is described by Pincher as a 'senior under-secretary in the Defence ministry, who had been a contact of mine.' He decided to 'retire prematurely . . . after Labour achieved office in 1964'. Drew 'had been in charge of the Intelligence side of defence issues, especially that part involving cover-plans.' During the Second World War he had worked closely with MI5. The book's thesis was that since a communist agent could have become head of MI6 [Philby] it was possible for 'a crypto-communist MP to become Defence Minister or Prime Minister'. To be called 'Achievement of Arms' they wrote 30,000 words describing the actions of a Prime Minister dedicated to helping the Soviet Union. Of course the programme was described as being similar to that of the Labour Party under Wilson. 'After six months we abandoned the project because as fast as we wrote a chapter the Labour government actually did what we predicted.' Pincher, *Inside Story*, p. 288/9. The story was resurrected in the fictional *Dirty Tricks*, where 'Albert Henderson, the British Prime Minister, is an agent of the Soviet Union!' p. 24.

13 Margach, p. 151. Walter Terry was Parliamentary Press Lobby and political editor of the *Daily Mail*. His relationship with Marcia Williams was a closely guarded secret. It is also worth noting that Wigg produced a list of meetings between Marcia and other people. Who did the leg-work on this? Presumably, MI5, who were keeping the Wilson–Mrs Williams team under surveillance for other reasons.

14 Roth, *Walter Mitty*, p. 24.

15 *Spectator*, 12/2/72; *Private Eye*, 14/1/72, 17/5/74.

16 Crossman, *Diaries*, vol. 2, p. 564; Castle, *Diaries*, vol. 1, p. 79.

CHAPTER XXI: BLUNT AND THE 'OXFORD COMINTERN'

1 Masters, p. 60. Younger reported back either to Knight or his tutor at Christ Church, J. C. Masterman, who in the Second World War chaired MI5's Double Cross Committee. He was later recruited to MI5 as a full-time officer and wrote novels under the pseudonym 'William Mole'.

2 On Special Branch surveillance, see for example Costello, pp. 168–71; Moorehead, p. 26.

3 Deacon, *Russian Secret Service*, p. 229; Moorehead, p. 106. There are a considerable number of versions of the spelling of Muzenberg's name, we have used the simplest, changing the other versions found in quotations.

4 Howard, *Crossman*, pp. 33–4. Crossman was regarded by some in the Labour Party in the thirties as a fellow-traveller of the Germans. This was later resurrected by Auberon Waugh in *Private Eye* in the early 1970s. *Ibid.*, p. 44. The marked similarities with Kim Philby, who came back from Vienna with a communist wife in the same period, cannot have escaped MI5's notice.

5 Cecil, pp. 17–25; Straight, p. 49.

6 Meyer was possibly deported because he had identified an MI5 informer at the LSE, a former Indian policeman. Meyer later turned to the right and testified to the Un-American Activities Committee giving them a long list of all his old communist friends. Grant-Duff, p. 35; Foot, *Wilson*, pp. 31–2; Williams/Reed, pp. 25 and 37.

7 Cecil, p. 56.

8 *Listener*, 28/7/89.

9 Grant-Duff, pp. 148–9; Moorehead, p. 108. Around this time, Bernstein became a close friend of future Labour MP, Ian Mikardo. Later in the war, Bernstein worked for the Psychological Warfare Board with Richard Crossman, who was attacked by right-wing Tories while undertaking his propaganda work. Anthony Eden had to assure them that Crossman was neither a Bolshevik nor a Fascist. Howard, *Crossman*, p. 92.

10 Costello, pp. 661–2 n. 36 and 297–8; Moorehead, p. 276. Parker, a former member of the Special Operations Executive, had defected to the USSR in the late forties where he married a Russian ballerina.

11 D. Jay, p. 106. Labour Minister Hugh Dalton noted in his diary (14/10/43) a party at the Gaitskells' with the Jays. Also present was Jenifer Hart, 'now at Home Security and very intelligent as well as attractive, with whom I swap stories of the relations of civil servants to each other and to ministers'. B. Pimlot, *Dalton Diaries*, p. 652.

12 Moorehead, p. 218.

13 *Ibid.*, p. 261.

14 Castle, *Diaries*, vol. 1, p. 158; Howard, *Crossman*, p. 24; Junor, p. 53.

15 Penrose/Freeman, p. 447; Costello, p. 401.

16 *The Times*, obituary of Cohen, 19/6/68.

17 Wright, pp. 265–6 and 249; Pincher, *Too Secret*, p. 168.

18 Pincher, *Too Secret*, p. 384. Wright's belief that Floud, who worked in intelligence during the war, was in contact with the KGB may be based on the curious episode when he claimed that an MI6 contact had told him that the naval diver 'Buster' Crabb had been captured by Soviet intelligence. 'MI5 officers believe [Floud] was in contact with the KGB at the time.' (Ibid., p. 236). Penrose/Freeman, p. 445; Straight, p. 56.

19 Wright would later claim that the investigation had been instigated as a result of a lead given by Golitsyn. This was almost certainly untrue but was the way of introducing a 'trace'. Wright, pp. 170–1.

20 P. Jay, p. 95; see Marnham, *Trail of Havoc*, p. 96, where Jay's name has been deleted from the smear sheet. Jay told us that he was mystified why MI5 should believe this, though in the light of the Peter Wright affair, he is not surprised. Telephone conversation with Douglas Jay, December 1991.

21 Wright, p. 267; *Daily Telegraph*, 22/11/79; *Daily Express*, 19/11/79. Young, one of the ex-intelligence officers who thought Wilson was a security risk, added that he would have been 'hesitant' about informing the Prime Minister. In 1977, Young wrote to an intelligence friend that 'At one point under Wilson there were five ministers of the Crown whose membership of the Communist Party of Great Britain is not known to have been renounced and over-lapping with them other ministers whose ultimate alliance is outside Britain.' Pincher, *Inside Story*, p. 28.

22 Wright, p. 267; Rothschild intervention: Wright memorandum 'proving' Rothschild was not the 'fifth man'; Benn, *Diaries*, vol. 2, 10/6/68, p. 290.

23 Castle, *Diaries*, vol. 1, pp. 289, 422 and 531; Crossman, *Diaries*, vol. 2, 17/10/68; Marsh, pp. 126–7. Inevitably, Randall Swingler, who had been a Communist Party member and, during the war, editor of a communist arts magazine, had an MI5 file. This family link was probably enough in the eyes of MI5 to condemn his brother Stephen as a 'security risk'.

24 Wilson, *Labour Government*, p. 777.

25 Leigh, pp. 147–9.

26 *Ibid.*, p. 149; *Observer*, 10/5/87 and 17/5/87; Crossman, *Diaries*, vol. 2, 17/10/68. It is (just) possible that the security-conscious Crossman was 'babysitting' Swingler and MacDermot.

27 Pincher, *Inside Story*, p. 17 and *idem*, *Trade is Treachery*, p. 253. Notice even in the second version there is still not even an actual blackmail, merely 'attempted blackmail'.

28 Wright, pp. 171–2.

CHAPTER XXII: NUKES

1 Crossman, *Diaries*, vol. 1, pp. 94–5. 'The United States, after trying for thirty years to get Britain out of Asia, the Middle East, and Africa, was now trying desperately to keep us in: during the Vietnam War it did not want to be the only country killing coloured people on their own soil.' Healey, pp. 280–1.

2 The consequences of the relationship are skimmed over in less than a page in Freedman, *Britain and Nuclear Weapons*, p. 42.

3 'Tritium plants had been built in Britain, linked to the operations of the Windscale and Calder Hall reactors, but the unit costs of producing the gram quantities required for nuclear weapons were much greater than equivalent figures for American output, which was being produced at annual levels of several kilograms in the much larger American plants at Savannah River.' Simpson, p. 130.

4 HOC *Hansard*, cols. 701–3, 17/12/64; Shrimsley, pp. 112–13.

5 One of Wilson's sub-themes in the speech to the Labour Party conference, which included his famous remark about the 'white heat of technology', had been that too much of Britain's research and development effort was being absorbed by the nuclear programme.

6 Crossman, *Diaries*, vol. 2, p. 49; Castle, *Diaries*, vol. 1, p. 306; Benn, *Diaries*, vol. 1, p. 517, note 5. See also Healey p. 313. The sexual connotations of the language here – 'hardened', 'penetration aids' – are amusing.

7 Benn, *Diaries*, vol. 1, p. 483; Castle, *Diaries*, vol. 1, p. 306; Crossman *Diaries*, vol. 2, p. 49. Chalfont (and Zuckerman) hated Denis Healey whom he described as 'a thug'. Benn, *Diaries*, vol. 2, pp. 246, 56, 130 and 115.

8 Benn, *Diaries*, vol. 1, 15/12/67, p. 513; Benn, *Diaries*, vol. 2, 5/4/68. 'This was the last I heard of the matter until the 1974 Labour Government when Harold Wilson made casual reference to a "refurbishing" programme, which must have been an early version of the Chevaline project and was approved by Jim Callaghan without consulting the Cabinet.' Benn, *Diaries*, vol. 1, p. 517.

9 Benn, *Diaries*, vol. 2, pp. 97 and 115–16.

10 Simpson, p. 193.

11 Benn, *Diaries*, vol. 2, p. 89 and *idem.*, vol. 1, p. 507. While all this took place under the heaviest security with Benn getting numbered sheets marked 'Top Secret: UK eyes only', the *New Scientist* published a full description of the centrifuge. 'The only thing that was secret was that we knew it could be done'. *Ibid.*, p. 509.

12 Benn, *Diaries*, vol. 2, pp. 127 and 41.

13 *Ibid.*, p. 182. In November, for reasons that do not seem to have ever been made public, Healey withdrew his objections and the Americans agreed to the transfer of the Endcap technology, embodied in the Treaty of Almelo, signed 4/3/70.

14 Simpson, pp. 184–5, and 171.

15 The Anglo-American military nuclear relationship was gradually revitalised from 1972 onwards by Britain's entry into the EEC and the decision to start development of a new Polaris warhead and the related commitment to recommence explosive testing. 'The Labour government was close to making a decision to initiate a formal feasibility study [of upgrading Polaris] when it was replaced by Mr Heath's Conservative one'. A feasibility study was authorised in 1970 followed by a project definition phase in 1972. *Ibid.*, p. 173.

16 Pincher, *Dirty Tricks*, pp. 277 and 86; Benn, *Diaries*, vol. 1, p. 511; Leigh, p. 160.

17 On Rothschild and the right, see Stephen Dorril and Morris Riley, 'Rothschild, the right, the far-right and the fifth man' in *Lobster* 16. On Mountbatten see Deacon, *The Greatest Treason* and *With My Little Eye*.

18 Castle, *Diaries*, vol. 1, pp. 273–4.

19 Pincher, *Inside Story*, pp. 28 and 159; *Guardian*, 6/5/87; Leigh, p. 96. Information on Stewart from David Leigh. Pincher has also claimed that a second CIA 'agent of influence', 'now dead, was a senior Cabinet minister'. While another CIA agent was still believed to be in the Labour Cabinet as of 1977. The second was probably Tony Crosland who would have developed CIA links through his work with the Congress for Cultural Freedom in the fifties. The identity of the latter is not known but presumably was one of those who left for the SDP. A fourth alleged CIA agent left the Labour Government in 1970, turned against the Labour Party and was active in the House of Lords on security issues. Pincher declined to identify this agent to us.

20 Stewart left the Government in 1970 when he accepted a peerage. 'Dean Rusk and I . . . were alumni of St. John's college.' Stewart, pp. 153 and 122; Short, p. 33; Benn, *Diaries*, vol. 2, p. 228.

CHAPTER XXIII: WILSON AS CORPORATIST

1 Foot, *Wilson*, p. 110; Speech to Annual Conference 1963, cited in Wilson, *Purpose in Politics*, p. 28. It is one of the ironies of recent British history that the economy which most closely approximates to the ideal of the majority of the British Labour movement is Germany – the one society that was seriously reconstructed by the still corporatist British state in the years after the war.

2 The best short account of the 1944–50 period is Newton/Porter, Chapter 5; HOC *Hansard*, 11/4/49 and 22/4/48.

3 Quoted in Wilson, *Purpose in Politics*, p. 51.

4 Young/Lowe, p. 13. The FBI's President, Sir Peter Runge, told an audience in Reading in 1964: 'Simply leaving it to the market will not suffice', cited in Blank, *Identity and Government*, p. 222. On the Tory Party relationship with economic planning, see Gamble/Walkland, especially pp. 112–18.

5 Gamble/Walkland, p. 116.

6 Gummett, p. 45.

7 Newton/Porter, p. 154. It is important to recognise that it was a defeat, not a failure. DEA: George Brown's own account in his *In My Way*, Chapters 5 and 6, and Hennessy, *Whitehall*, pp. 180–191.

8 Hennessy, *Whitehall*, pp. 183–5.

9 Brown, *In My Way*, p. 94.

10 Attali, pp. 250–1; Broadway, p. 62. Broadway worked for the Economic League; Gummett, p. 47; Wilson, *Labour Government*, p. 263; Wilson cited in Young/Lowe, p. 93. Blackett was the Chief Scientific Adviser at MinTech. He had held no significant government posts since 1947, when, virtually alone within Whitehall, he argued against the British development of nuclear weaponry.

11 Young/Lowe, p. 111; Wilson, *Labour Government*, p. 264; Gummett, p. 47. Appointees to the IRC included: Berkin, Shell Transport; Lockwood, EMI; Schon, Marchan Products; Stokes, Leyland Motors; Wheeler, AEI; Clapham, ICI and Boxhall, Lindustries.

12 Young/Lowe, p. 91. IRC participated in the setting up of the computer firm ICL, Chrysler's stake in Rootes, the merger of GEC and English Electric, and later of BMC and Leyland. A short account of its activities is in Beckerman (ed.), pp. 189–94, and Broadway, pp. 63–4 and 129.

13 'It is impossible to deny that IRC financial activity distorted the capital market', Young, p. 71. See also *ibid.*, pp. 115 and 80; Davis, pp. 52 and 78.

14 Bull/Vice, p. 68; Attali, pp. 214, 240 and 201.

15 Jones/Marriott, Chapter 15, 'The Battle for AEI'. The inter-locking directorships in this area and the connections to the Cecil King network are too intricate to be described in full here. However, a few are suggestive. George Brown was later made Productivity Counsellor at Courtauld's where other directors included Rab Butler and Lord Eccles. Eric Roll went to work for Warburg's in 1967 and was also made a director of *The Times* and the Bank of England. Shawcross was a director of EMI.

16 Davis, p. 55; Newton/Porter, p. 157; Davis p. 80; Blank, *Identity and Government*, p. 234. IPG's formation was announced in *The Times*, 12/10/67, its personnel listed in *The Times*, 23/11/67.

17 *The Times*, 23/11/67 and 18/12/67.

CHAPTER XXIV: THE CECIL KING COUP

1 Why King had become disillusioned with Wilson is neither intelligible nor important.

2 King, *Diaries*, vol. 1, 24/7/66, 10/8/66, 13/8/66 and 22/2/67.

3 This section taken from Cudlipp, pp. 302–4.

4 Tinker, pp. 142 and 175.

5 The plot was first revealed on Granada TV's *What the Papers Say*, 9/4/81. Information from Winstanley, letters to authors, April and May 1989.

6 'From the moment we first met in 1966, King repeatedly tried to get me to conspire against Wilson, and to promote me as a leader of the Labour Party or of a Coalition Government. He finally accepted that I was not interested and turned his attention instead to Mountbatten', Denis Healey, p. 337. Renwick was a leading member of the right-wing Society of Individual Freedom which campaigned for liberal free-market ideas.

7 Meetings in King, *Diaries*, vol. 1, at dates given; Jenkins-Macleod in Watkins, *Brief Lives*, p. 77. Beamish thought Healey was untrustworthy because of his communist past.

8 Callaghan, p. 205; Cudlipp, p. 345. This Wilson offer to King was later leaked to Walter Terry, then political editor of the *Daily Mail*, 31/5/68.

9 Benn, *Diaries*, vol. 2, 2/2/68.

10 Wilson, *Labour Government*, p. 625.

11 Cudlipp, p. 309.

12 Benn, *Diaries*, vol. 2, 6/2/68.

13 Personnel in King, *Diaries*, vol. 1, 7/2/68 and 9/2/68. Fletcher and Beeching had apparently been part of the previous year's television cabal.

14 The Institute of Directors at this stage was flourishing again after a period of decline. It had 32,000 members in 1959, 420 in 1948 – Labour Party pamphlet, *Talking Points*, No. 16, on the IOD., 1959. IOD's revival, like the formation of Aims of Industry in 1948, was a response to the perceived threat of the Labour movement in Britain. Leading figures in the IOD at this time were (Lord) Robert Renwick, a Director of ATV and part of the group gathered around King, Lord Watkinson and Paul Chambers. As mentioned above, Renwick was also a major fund-raiser for the Tory Party. In the year 1968–9 Conservative Party (known) income from all donations was £1,414,000 which was a rise of about £800,000 on normal non-election years. Taking into account inflation, it was the only year in the 1950–70 period that such a rise took place. See *Independent*, 16/1/89. See also Crossman, *Diaries*, vol. 2, p. 669.

15 Benn, *Diaries*, vol. 2, pp. 32–3.

16 Benn was already suspicious that Arnold-Foster was some kind of a spook.

17 Castle, *Diaries*, vol. 1, p. 462.

18 Ponting, p. 372; Crossman, *Diaries*, vol. 2, p. 695.

19 Closure of British banks, Wilson, *Labour Government*, pp. 640–4; Crossman, *Diaries*, vol. 2, p. 764. Wilson's speech is reproduced in full in his *Labour Government*, pp. 687–8.

20 Ponting, pp. 373–4. Ponting gives no sources for this section, even though some of the material is in Castle, *Diaries*, vol. 1, for the period. See index references to MISC 205. *Ibid.*, vol. 1, p. 463.

21 Cudlipp,'The So-called "Military Coup" of 1968', *Encounter*, September 1981. This version of Mountbatten's thinking is also in Ziegler. Interestingly, 1968 was the year when the decision was made that the Prince of Wales should be invested at Caernarvon, an event which revived media interest in the monarchy. As a result a television film was produced on the Royal Family which, historians have noted, 're-launched' them into mass consciousness. 'By universal consent its success marked a new rapproachment between Crown and People', Tom Nairn, p. 217. There was also a major television series on the life of Lord Mountbatten.

22 Zuckerman, p. 463, also Ziegler, p. 659. William Evans, Mountbatten's personal valet, backs up the distrust of King but also disputes the 'official' version of events. He claims that it was King who requested the meeting and that the two had met the day before the meeting at Broadlands. At that meeting, Mountbatten told Evans, who was in the next room, that King had suggested that he 'organise a coup'. Evans, pp. 125–6.

23 Cudlipp, *Encounter*; Penrose/Courtiour, p. 318. King later told *The Times*, when the story emerged in 1981, that he had not included this in his published diary as he regarded it as confidential, 'especially the part about the Queen'.

24 King painted a picture of an England which corresponded with his memories of the Easter rebellion in Ireland in 1916. He told Cudlipp that 'if civil war could break out in Dublin in 1916 why couldn't it flare up in . . . London in . . . 1968'. Cudlipp, p. 303. According to Cudlipp, *Encounter*, the 'agreed' version is that agreed between Cudlipp and Zuckerman.

25 Cudlipp, *Encounter*; Cudlipp, p. 303.

26 Penrose/Courtiour, p. 318.

27 Ziegler, pp. 659–61; Zuckerman, p. 464.

28 Ziegler, p. 662; *The Times*, 16/8/74. One of the attractions of an 'unwritten constitution' is the fact that none of the brute realities have to be actually spelled out, but as far as we can tell, the necessary conditions for such a 'constitutional coup' would include the breakdown of civil order, as happened in Northern Ireland, and, if the approval of Parliament was lacking, the consent of the Monarch, to whom, rather than to Parliament, the Armed Forces owe allegiance.

29 *The Times*, 7/8/87 and 3/4/81; Penrose/Courtiour, p. 316.

30 *Leigh*, p. 158; *Sunday Times*, 29/3/81 and 5/4/81. It remains unclear if this 'plot' had any connection with the King–Mountbatten talks. Callaghan refused to talk about it in 1981 and makes no reference to it in his memoir. Penrose/Courtiour, p. 317; interview with Barrie Penrose November 1990.

31 King's diary first records the idea of the figures being 'faked' on 30 June 1966 – with the interesting footnote that the faking was being done 'thanks to the co-operation of the Americans'. King was shown the figures on 14 April 1968, just under a month before the *Mirror* piece (and the 'coup' meeting). Wilson, *Labour Government*, p. 669.

32 Cudlipp, p. 341.

CHAPTER XXV: STRATEGY OF TENSION

1 Wright, p. 369.

2 *The Times*, 29/4/87.

3 Morten in Summers/Dorril, p. 151; Wright, p. 309; *Private Eye*, No. 125, 30/9/66; *Encounter: International Herald Tribune*, 10/5/66; Helms: King, *Diaries*, vol. 1, 6/9/66.

4 *Guardian* 28/4/87 and 2/5/87; *The Times*, 4/5/87. During 1966–7, Wharton served in Nigeria where King had extensive newspaper interests. Wharton's colleague, Tony Brooks, had been attached to Mountbatten's 1966 inquiry into the prison escape of MI6 traitor George Blake. In 1979, following Mountbatten's assassination, Brooks acted as MI5 liaison officer with the press.

5 King, *Strictly Personal*, p. 130: 'In 1954 both Alfred Robens and George Brown were planning to leave politics and return to work . . . So I arranged for them to be paid £500 a year, later increased . . . I later did the same thing for the same reason for Richard Marsh.' See Marsh, p. 154. Feather: King, *Diaries*, vol. 2, p. 235, and Benn, *Diaries*, vol. 3, p. 383.

6 In Italy in the 1960s and 1970s the techniques included: the infiltration and manipulation of left-wing organizations, in particular the Maoist groups of the time; a programme of *intoxication* (poisoning) operations designed to sow dissension within the groups; and terrorist bombings and attacks launched under leftist cover. Such techniques were widely used by right-wing intelligence and security forces in Europe in the late 1960s and early 1970s. On this see Bale, *Lobster* 18.

7 Ali, pp. 177–8.

8 Angry Brigade: *Searchlight*, 118 and Bunyan, p. 48; Crossman, *Diaries*, vol. 2, p. 768; Infiltration: Borrell/Cashinella, p. 41.

9 *The Times*, 13/8/68. On 17 August 1968 Cecil King handed over the entire front page of the *Daily Mirror* to Tariq Ali. It provided an opportunity for another attack on Wilson and the Labour Party, this time from the disaffected young. It also helped King 'stir things up'.

10 See Foot, *Wallace*, appendices for examples of forgeries.

11 Leigh, p. 159. The *Daily Express* eventually ran the Diamond story in 1988. Pincher, *Inside Story*, p. 26.

12 According to *Searchlight* 118, the two neo-facists were the Olliffe brothers of the National Socialist Group. Borrell/Cashinella, p. 20.

13 For *Daily Mirror*, see Laurie, p. 124; Callaghan, p. 258.

14 *Guardian*, 26/10/68 and 27/10/68; Ali, p. 219; Benn, *Diaries*, vol. 2, pp. 131–2.

15 See p. 7 of the anonymous 1972 pamphlet, *Monday Club – A Danger To British Democracy*, which cites other examples of forgeries, though not in 1968.

16 *Searchlight* 117 and 118; *Private Eye*, 31/1/69. Norris, according to *Searchlight* claimed 'that he had important connections with counter-subversion agencies'. He also boasted of 'his ability to cause havoc on the left', a claim that has to be treated with caution. Norris later gained notoriety when it was learned that his investigative firm 'Contingency Services' had been involved in the surveillance of Sizewell nuclear objectors. One of the objectors had been Hilda Murrell, whose death is thought to have been the result of a botched attempt to search her house. During the 1960s Norris is reported to have had his own group called the Salvo Society, though what this amounted to is unknown, and was active in the Friends of Rhodesia and Anglo-Rhodesia Society. See *Essex County Standard*, 18/11/68, for background of plot by right-wing extremists led by Norris.

17 Crossman, *Diaries*, vol. 2, 9/12/68. This 'streams of rumours' is the classic 'surfacing' technique as practised by the now defunct Foreign Office/MI6 psychological warfare department, the Information Research Department (IRD). Information is planted abroad, then re-imported as 'news' from a foreign source. Benn, *Diaries*, vol. 2, 8/12/68; Evans, p. 284. Robens was a strong advocate of a Council of State in times of crisis (in which both Houses of Parliament would be merged, enabling a peer to be Prime Minister). King, who wrote a column for *The Times*, was seen at the paper's office on 9 December, *Private Eye*, 20/12/68.

CHAPTER XXVI: MORE POLITICAL PLOTS

1 *Observer*, 2/10/88; Benn, *Diaries*, vol. 1, p. 465; Castle, *Diaries*, vol. 1, p. 275; Benn, *Diaries*, vol. 1, 22/12/67.

2 All Mayhew quotes in this chapter are from his *Time to Explain*, Chapter 15. Mayhew, Diamond, Taverne, Rodgers, Mabon, Owen, Marquand and Jenkins all later joined the SDP.

3 P. Jenkins, p. 113; *New Statesman*, 7/3/75.

4 S. Crosland, p. 203; 'The Mayhew-led affair which trundled through 1968 and 1969 was not very serious because it depended on Roy Jenkins and he was prepared to wound but hesitant to go for the kill. I fear, a constant.' Letter from David Owen to authors, February 1990.

5 *Private Eye*, 23/5/69; Butler/Pinto-Duchinsky, pp. 42–3; Crossman, *Diaries*, vol. 3, 8/5/69, p. 482. Mackintosh was suitably vague about this episode in his discussion of it in his *The British Cabinet*, p. 135, where his own role is not included. P. Jenkins, p. 112.

6 Rhodes-James, pp. 70–1. His principal source was John Mackintosh – letter to authors, December 1990.

7 Pincher, *Inside Story*, pp. 361–2. Pincher's 'cabinet colleague' source was probably George Brown, a source for much of his information on the Labour Party. See e.g. Pincher, *A Web of Deception*, p. 126.

8 *Ibid.*, pp. 361–2.

9 *Private Eye*, 16/2/68. See also S. Crosland, pp. 115–7; *Private Eye*, 9/5/69.

10 Hennessy/Seldon (eds.), David Walker, 'The First Wilson Governments 1964–70', p. 200.

CHAPTER XXVII: THE CZECH CONNECTION

1 On Wilson, MI5 and defectors' allegations, see Pincher, *Too Secret*, p. 599.

2 Almost as spectacular was the illustration by 'Victor Suvorov'. In 1980, the pseudonymous Suvorov wrote *The Liberators* (Hamish Hamilton), an account of his time in the Red Army. *The Liberators* portrayed the Soviet army as a chaotic, brutal, drunken, incompetent shambles – about as threatening to NATO as a large rice pudding. This evidently did not please his hosts in the British armed forces who were bent on stoking up the Cold War. A year later 'Suvorov' published a second book, *Inside the Soviet Army* (Hamish Hamilton), in which the chaotic shambles of the previous book had been transformed into the fearsome, threatening Red Army beloved of NATO propagandists.

3 In his recent book, *KGB*, Christopher Andrew says that the identification of Stross 'remains highly implausible', but declines to say why. (pp. 434–5).

4 Frolik, p. 97; Crossman, *Diaries*, vol. 3, p. 913.

5 Frolik, p. 97; Stross, obituary, *The Times*, 15/5/67.

6 Andrew hedges his bets: he recycles the Frolik allegations but cautions that 'there is no hard evidence that Stonehouse had more than occasional dealings with Czech intelligence'. *KGB*, p. 433.

7 CIA funding: *Private Eye*, 6/12/68, quoting *Le Monde*, 4–5/8/68. Roth, *Walter Mitty*, p. 217, for the 'packed' meeting. Dolan worked in the Office of Strategic Services (OSS) during the war and, possibly, in the CIA after it. Stonehouse's association with Dolan is practically all there is of 'the evidence' which has lead some to believe that Stonehouse was actually CIA. Dolan died in 1987. See the obituary in the *Independent* 12/1/87. On Stonehouse's PR methods, see the *Spectator*, 10/5/63. Crossman, *Diaries*, vol. 3, p. 339.

8 Benn, *Diaries*, vol. 2, 12/3/70, p. 252; Stonehouse, *Death of an Idealist*, pp. 89 and 148. One of the forgeries Colin Wallace preserved from his days with Information Policy in Northern Ireland was a pamphlet 'authored' by Denis Healey, Stan Orme and Tony Benn. Next to Benn's name, in Wallace's handwriting, was the comment 'links with Czech intelligence'. See also Foot, *Wallace*, p. 74.

9 Wright, p. 362; Wright telephone conversation with Morris Riley, 10/5/86; Pincher, *Inside Story*, pp. 111–12. This probably came indirectly from Wright. In his correspondence he admitted leaking Stonehouse material to Pincher. See the *Observer* 16/10/88. Leigh, p. 193.

10 *New Socialist*, May 1985. Telephone conversation with Loughlin, December 1990.

11 Ray Fletcher, telephone conversation with Stephen Dorril, 24/10/90; *Independent*, 28/1/91; *New Socialist*, May 1985.

12 Sejna, Chapter 14 on 'The Plan for Britain'. Speaking to US Senate committees August said that the Czechs had recruited 'several members of the British Parliament' and that one MP was pressured when they discovered some of his personal secrets.

13 Deacon, *British Connection*, p. 229; BOT, see August, p. 79; Pincher, *Too Secret*, p. 472; Wright, p. 266.

14 Penrose/Freeman, p. 447; Leigh, pp. 135–6.

15 Pincher, *Inside Story*, pp. 33 and 252.

16 *Ibid.*, p. 250.

17 Leigh, pp. 196/7.

18 King, *Diaries*, vol. 1, pp. 259 and 329–32. Obituary of Lord Cromer in *Daily Telegraph*, 18/3/91.

CHAPTER XXVIII: THE DEFECTOR

1 Franks Committee on the Reform of the Official Secrets Act, 1972, pp. 252–3 and 246–7. It presumably did not cross Furnival-Jones' mind that there is nothing illegal in KGB officers – or anybody else – talking to backbench MPs, none of whom have access to classified information. During the *Spycatcher* Affair in 1987, Peter Wright expressed to the court in Sydney his belief that Soviet bloc intelligence officers cultivated politicians by getting them young and building them up. Wright, who claimed to be 'the authority on this', said that he had 'discussed the whole of this with [Furnival-Jones]'. R. V. Hall, p. 154.

2 Franks, pp. 250 and 252.

3 Pincher, *Too Secret*, p. 468; *Daily Express*, 31/8/71; Leigh, p. 186. Lyalin 'blew' two Greek Cypriot brothers who had access to no sensitive material, and a Malayan called Abdoolcader, who was able to supply the numbers of cars used by MI5. This supports the testimony of KGB defector, Kuzichkin, that the KGB's unwritten rules say that officers abroad should 'concentrate [their] attention on representatives of third countries.' Kuzichkin, p. 106.

4 Andrew, *KGB*, p. 436; Kuzichkin, pp. 116, 104 and 106.

5 Gordievsky in Andrew, *KGB*, p. 436–7; *Daily Express*, 16/10/88; Rawlinson, p. 213. Of course it can be argued, no doubt will be argued by some on the right, that both Gordievsky and Kuzichkin are false defectors, sent to the West to spread reassuring lies about the incompetence of the KGB.

6 'Secret friendship': *Observer*, 9/8/70; confirmation from MI5 officer Tony Brooks in Leigh, p. 188.

7 Leigh, p. 190. On Kagan/Vaygauskas see *ibid.*, Chapter 9; Pincher, *Trade is Treachery*, p. 254. Young at one point introduced Vaygauskas to the Commissioner of the Metropolitan Police.

8 *Sunday Times*, 3/5/87; *Sunday Telegraph*, 3/5/87.

CHAPTER XXIX: SELSDON MAN

1 On the origins of the pro-planning group within the Tory Party see Gamble/Walkland, pp. 114–17. On the 36 working parties: Rhodes James, p. 112; Roth, *Heath*, p. 206.

2 Moran, pp. 48 and 70.

3 Slater, p. 256.

4 *New Statesman*, 8/2/74. In his 1974 book, Clive Irving's chapter on Slater Walker is titled 'Busting up the League of Gentlemen; the Hustlers, the Strippers, and the Importance of Not Being Wet'. The analogy with the Thatcher years is exact, right down to the use of 'wet' and 'dry'. A reasonable introductory guide to Slater Walker and the expansion of the 'fringe' banking sector is Michael Clarke.

5 Raw, p. 346; Irving, p. 110; Whitehead, p. 93; In 1972 the export of capital actually doubled. Gamble, p. 225. Slater was to write that the 'Conservative Government's easy money policy was the final major single influence on the company, and we took advantage of it to the full while the climate was favourable.' Slater, p. 256.

6 Whitehead, p. 96.

7 King apocalyptic visions: Edwin Plowden of Tube Investments (21/7/70), Vic Feather (10/11/70), Arnold Weinstock (21/4/71), Alf Robens (26/10/71), Sir John Stevens (22/5/72) and Lord Shawcross (26/10/73) all predicted an authoritarian future for Britain. Paul Foot quoted in Whitehead, p. 207.

8 See *State Research*, vol. 2, p. 20–1. It is noteworthy that this did not write of a 'society and its citizens'. Kitson is discussed in more detail in Chapter XXX on Northern Ireland.

9 *We Will Bury You* published by Tom Stacey though described in one of Geoffrey Stewart-Smith's catalogues as 'a Common Cause publication'.

10 This section is taken from Steve Peak's excellent *Troops in Strikes*. Troops were later called in during the 1972 dock strike and the 1973 Glasgow fire brigade strike.

11 Hennessy/Jeffries, p. 234; Whitehead, p. 76. See also Sewill's comment: 'At the time many of those in positions of influence looked into the abyss and saw only a few days away the possibility of the country being plunged into a state of chaos not so very far removed from that which might prevail after a minor nuclear attack. If that sounds melodramatic I need only say that – with the prospect of the breakdown of power supplies, food supplies, sewerage, communications, effective government and law and order – it was the analogy that was being used at the time. This is the power that exists to hold the country to ransom: it was fear of that abyss which had an important effect on subsequent policy'. Hennessy/Jeffries, p. 235.

12 See *Morning Star* 31/1/76 for the leaked memo. On the Economic League, see Hollingsworth/Tremayne; on Common Cause and IRIS see *Lobster* 19, 'In A Common Cause'.

13 This section is largely based on *Time Out*, 5/11/75. Detailed in *Searchlight* 18 special issue 'The Men in the Shadows'.

14 *The Times*, 23/5/72. Significantly, perhaps, Walker was allowed to quote officers' names and rank. *The Times*, 24/5/72. Lawson was on the Board of the Society for Individual Freedom at the time.

15 Jellicoe, in fact, had nothing at all to do with the Lambton scandal. He had never met the prostitute Norma Levy. His name 'had come to the notice of the police while they were investigating the Lambton situation.' Pincher, *Inside Story*, p. 276. Hennessy/Jeffries, p. 136. Lambton's use of Levy had come to the attention of both MI5 and MI6 through 'contacts' among London prostitutes and nightclub owners. However, Lambton was allowed to carry on the liaison for at least six weeks. The police later charged him with possession of illegal drugs. It is entirely consistent with what we know of the bureaucratic struggles within Whitehall that Jellicoe's name was deliberately fed to the police. *State Research*, vol. 2, 'The Hidden System', p. 21.

16 Wright, p. 360.

CHAPTER XXX: BRITAIN'S CUBA

1 On the MRF see, most recently Heather. Carver, p. 429. Carver thought highly of Kitson and wrote the foreword to his *Low Intensity Warfare* – the ultimate 'good review'. Best account of MRF actions is Murray; also Faligot, pp. 31–5 and Dillon/Lehane, Chapter 15.

2 Cecil King noted in his diary that 'there is a civil servant called Burroughs who lives in a hotel in Belfast distributing generous hospitality. His role in not clear.' King, *Diaries*, vol. 2, p. 57. This was Ronald Burroughs, previously spotted in Nigeria during the Biafran war. On the talks see Verrier, *Looking Glass*, p. 314; Bishop/Malle, pp. 224–9.

3 The best account is now in Murray, pp. 75–91. Still useful is Bloch/Fitzgerald, pp. 218–20. On the history of use of *agent provocateurs* in Britain see Porter.

4 Faligot, p. 108. At one point MI5 used the British Army's Information Policy Unit's printing facilities to reprint the Clann nah Eireann pamphlet on the incidents, *The Littlejohn Memorandum*. Information from Colin Wallace.

5 Wallace and his activities were first described, under transparent disguises, in Kevin Dowling's 'novel', *Interface Ireland*, Barrie and Jenkins, London, 1979. The book was withdrawn soon after publication after the publisher received a writ. On the novel see 'Information Policy in Fiction' in *Lobster* 17. The best factual account of the unit and its work is in Foot, *Wallace*.

6 There was a considerable degree of bi-partisan policy-making in the 1970s. Wilson and Shadow Northern Ireland Secretary Merlyn Rees may have believed they could do the job better than Heath and Whitelaw, but they hardly claimed to do it differently. Whitelaw had talked to the Provos; so had Wilson. Verrier, *Looking Glass*, p. 6.

CHAPTER XXXI: ROTHSCHILD

1 Pincher, *Inside Story*, p. 334. Macmillan had been in one of the 'secret armies', I.S.9, during the war with Airey Neave, and was later on the board of one of the IRD front companies.

2 The relationship between MI5 and the Economic League is unclear. Campbell/Connor (p. 289) quote a former RAF officer who claimed that in 1970 he had attended a lecture on subversion given at MI5's Gower St building by a League official and discovered that the League actually had a desk in MI5's offices in Gower Street. See also Hollingsworth. *Socialist Worker*, 20/10/73. A major distributor of the literature of the anti-subversion lobby was Geoffrey Stewart-Smith, MP for Belper 1970–4. Stewart-Smith crops up in a variety of groups from the early 1960s: the Foreign Affairs Circle, founded in 1962, which became UK affiliate to the World Anti-Communist League; *East–West Digest* ('funded by some well-wishers in British industry', letter to authors 21/12/87); Foreign Friends of NTS (*Peace News*, 32/2/68); and his Foreign Affairs Publishing Company.

3 A typical reaction to abolition of the list is Pincher, *Inside Story*, p. 327. The anti-subversion lobby view, incidentally, was shared by some in MI5, including Peter Wright, who thought the 1972 decision to shift resources on to F Branch was a mistake. How far this is simply internal politics and how far a genuine political evaluation by Wright is not clear. See Wright, pp. 359–60. In a forthcoming book the *Encyclopedia of Espionage*, Wright claims that the growth of F Branch and its targeting of groups such as CND looked 'more and more like a Gestapo'. He did not take the 'threat' from the left seriously. 'The Socialist Workers' Party and Workers' Revolutionary Party, despite their frightening names, were about as dangerous as a pond of ducks'. *Independent*, 29/3/91.

4   See for example Hennessy, *Whitehall*, pp. 222–35 for the standard view of Rothschild. Wright, p. 348 and Coleman, p. 146.

5   R. V. Hall, p. 44; Wright, p. 117. On suspicions of Rothschild see Stephen Dorril and Morris Riley, 'Rothschild, the right, the far-right and the Fifth Man', in *Lobster* 16. Penrose/Freeman, p. 151. To Peter Hennessy he said of the Blunt revelation: 'I lost confidence in my ability to judge people. Let me be quite crude, I would not put my hand in the fire that you are not a Soviet agent, Peter.' BBC Radio 3, 20/5/84. Zionism: At the time of the Six-Day War in 1967 Rothschild had organised a fund-raising dinner. Thirty of Britain's leading Zionists contributed an astonishing seven million dollars. *Daily Express*, 10/6/67. Rothschild also administered the EJRMG Foundation, the Israeli interests of the late Baron Edmond Rothschild. Mossad: The Mossad defector Ostrovsky claims that the Israeli intelligence service had 2,000 of what might best be called intelligence 'auxiliaries' in London alone. See Ostrovsky/Hoy, p. 86.

6   Hennessy *Whitehall* p. 223. Rothschild had been picked because in the sixties he had been commissioned to do a report on Aldermaston. Accounts vary as to what this consisted of. One version, quoted above, describes it as a survey of Aldermaston's staffing levels. Another, in the account of the Central Policy Review Staff by Plowden and Blackstone, describes him as doing a report on security at Aldermaston. Whichever is true, he had apparently convinced Trend that he was a reliable Whitehall 'insider'. Rothschild's intelligence activities: 'Jobs could be done for Prime Ministers which never formed part of the CPRS's offical work programme, and which sometimes were not admitted by the head of the CPRS to any or some of his colleagues. Some of Rothschild's forays into areas of defence and foreign policy fell into this category, as did work on Northern Ireland.' Blackstone/Plowden, p. 45; Wright, p. 348. Rothschild seems to have been the only individual, other than the Cabinet Secretary, who had complete right of access to the Prime Minister. The relationship with Oldfield was so close that when the Chief of MI6 resigned it 'was discussed only with (Robert) Armstrong, Rothschild and Cavendish'. Interview with Anthony Cavendish, November 1990.

7   Wright never considers the possibility that the reason F Branch had 'nothing substantial' is that there *was* nothing substantial. Wright, pp. 366–7. Part of Wright's account of Jack Jones is reproduced in Leigh, p. 204.

8   Wright, p. 366.

9   See for example the comments of Len Murray quoted in Whitehead, p. 108. Mr Heath declined to discuss such matters with us. R. V. Hall, p. 50.

10 The Rothschild-as-Heath's-George-Wigg analogy begins to look plausible, for it was Wigg who helped MI5 block Wilson's attempt in 1965 to appoint his friend Eric St Johnston as head of MI5.

11 Wright, p. 366.

12 Leigh, p. 225. On the terrorist threat, see Dobson/Payne, p. 44; also Colin Smith. Wright, p. 367. Rothschild's concerns about terrorism were vindicated when, on 30 December 1973, the international terrorist, 'Carlos', shot 'Teddy' Sieff at his home. Sieff miraculously survived. Sixty-eight-year-old Sieff was President of Marks and Spencers and honorary vice-president of the Zionist Federation of Great Britain.

13 Leigh, p. 244.

14 Former think-tank members Blackstone and Plowden suggest that had Rothschild not been excluded, 'the CPRS would have been much better placed to deploy its members' views on the handling of the strike; and that had some attention been paid to these views, the Government's conflict with the miners could have been resolved, the February 1974 election avoided, and the administration saved' (p. 55). Saving the Heath administration was not the primary aim of sections of the British state at this point. *The Times*, 26/9/73. Blackstone/Plowden, pp. 35 and 63.

15 Wright, p. 367.

16 *Ibid.*, p. 368.

17 Details of the motions on 7 and 12 May and subsequent denials, in the *Guardian* and the *Independent* on 8 and 13/5/87. Wright also alleged that Young had sent him a postcard which referred to the meeting.

CHAPTER XXXII: 'THE QUEER WILL BE DETHRONED'

1   King notes the significance of the Du Cann election in his *Diaries*, vol. 2, 23/11/72, p. 247.

2   According to Peter Wright, Young was fired by the new MI6 Chief, Dick White. Just before his death in 1990 Young wrote an account of his life which was sent to various obituarists. This was published in full in *Lobster* 19. 'Benson' was Sir Rex Benson, cousin and life-long friend of former MI6 Chief Sir Stuart Menzies. Benson had been Military Attaché to Washington from 1941–4 – a critical post – and became a leading, though rarely mentioned, member of MI6. A measure of Benson's centrality to the British Establishment was the memorial service for him in St Paul's Cathedral when he died in 1968. See Cave Brown, pp. 34–6 and 629. John Stonehouse went to Kleinworts for help with his own banking enterprise in the early

seventies. The talk of the boardroom over the cocktails and roast beef lunch was about the unions, their leaders and the communists who were controlling them. Stonehouse, *Death of an Idealist*, p. 120. Wilson received information from anti-fascist activists in Birmingham and probably from Israeli intelligence. Wilson seemed to be particularly concerned about Young's links with fascists in Brighton and the Hancock family who were important printers of extreme right material. Information from Barrie Penrose, December 1990.

3 On the '92 Club' see Tebbit, p. 96–7. Biggs-Davison, who died in 1988, is reported to have worked in India in the late forties as an intelligence officer and later in Parliament as an MI5 agent (though we can't confirm this). Like Young, he was a member of another right-wing group of this period, the Society for Individual Freedom. *Private Eye*, 19/1/68. Another signatory of the 1967 appeal was Mary Howarth. The appeal's address was that of the former HQ of the League of Empire Loyalists, at this juncture about to become one of the founding elements in the National Front. Walker, *NF*, p. 118.

4 Rhodes James, p. 206.

5 In 1964 Di Lorenzo attempted to seize power in Italy through a presidential-type coup. Plan Solo was to have concluded with the assassination of premier Aldo Moro. Di Lorenzo was involved with the Rose of Winds organisation which controlled the carbinieri (of which he was commander) as a secret parallel army within the armed forces with the aim of neutralising subversives. Former war-time SOE operative in Italy, John McCaffery, who became the Hambros Bank representative in Italy after the war, was involved. *Private Eye*, 23/8/74: On McCaffery see Christie, p. 16. On the 'strategy of tension' see Christie, and Bale in *Lobster* 18. Greig was the author of the 1968 manual on Soviet fronts, *The Assault On the West*, published by Geoffrey Stewart-Smith's Foreign Affairs Publishing Co. Smith is discussed below. On the RPOC see Pincher, *Daily Express*, 18/7/77.

6 Howarth is now an MP. His mother was Mary Howarth of the Immigration Control Association and later a member of the NF. Cathew was a prominent member of the short-lived Powellite Association, she later joined the NF. Walker, *NF*, p. 124. Johnson, p. 149. One of the books Baber had been responsible for was Erika Johnston's *'The Other Side of Kilimanjaro'*, which described her experiences in David Stirling's Capricorn Society in Kenya. Johnson published many books by right-wing Tories, including Monday Club members Commander Anthony Courtney and John Biggs-Davidson MP. Some of these books, especially those on Africa, had been arranged through the public relations firm the O'Brien Organisation, which acted as a lobbyist in the 1950s and 1960s for a wide variety of right-wing causes and regimes. On the Toby O'Brien PR organisation, see Pearson/Turner, Chapter 16. The National Fellowship aimed to 'use its influence to persuade the Conservative Party to govern with greater courage and to abandon its present leanings towards pink socialism' – *Labour Research*, February 1962. It was anti-nationalisation, anti-communist, anti-union, pro-immigration control.

7 Walker, *NF*, pp. 125 and 130; see also Martin Webster in *Spearhead*, May 1973.

8 *New Statesman*, 6/4/73; Walker, *NF*, p. 126. Powell, in the event, would have nothing to do with the group who wished to build an organisation round him. Cosgrave, p. 338. On Powell and the Tory right see Rhodes James, pp. 204–9.

9 The *Sunday Telegraph* (25/3/73) described the Young faction as 'a powerful group of newcomers [which] plans to convert the club to a "populist movement" which will openly challenge Mr Heath and the Conservative leadership . . . drawn mainly from the 6000 members in the branches who outnumber the 2000 to 3000 in the national club.' On collaboration see e.g. the late Peter Gladstone-Smith, who had links both to the anti-Young faction and elements in the British Jewish community who were alarmed at the developments, in *Sunday Telegraph*, 8/4/73. The *Financial Times* commented that 'much of the Club's present troubles date back several years when it first became the chief weapon of the Anglo-Rhodesian Society'. Burglary: *Sunday Times*, 22/4/73. The Young letter in its entirety was subsequently published in *Searchlight*'s 1976 issue 'The Men in the Shadows'. Young's homophobia is clearly expressed in his autobiographical sketch, 'The Final Testimony of George Kennedy Young', printed in *Lobster* 19, in which his activities in the Monday Club are conspicuous by their absence.

10 *Financial Times*, 16/4/73. Harvey Proctor, Conservative Party candidate for Hackney and Shoreditch 1974, member of SIF, member of the SW London Monday Club branch whose chairman was Roy Bramwell, a property developer and leading member of the Immigration Control Association. Proctor, Mrs Anna Bramwell and a young unemployed actor, Tony Van der Elst, worked at Club HQ. Van der Elst had been brought in to work on repatriation proposals and the Halt Immigration Now Campaign. Walker, *NF*, p. 126. Forgeries see Malcolm Stuart, source unknown, probably *Daily Telegraph*, 10/4/73 and 3/5/73; also *Financial Times*, 13/4/73.

11 There are some on the British right who have seriously considered the proposition that Young's real, concealed, aim was to smash the Monday Club.

12 Deputy Chair of the Selsdon Group was the CBI's deputy director of economics, Dr Barry Bracewell-Milnes (member of the SIF and later involved with Tory Action). Funds came from Young's friend and SIF member, Sir Ian McTaggart, the property developer whose company offices at 55 Park Lane provided a base for the SIF and other Young and McWhirter backed operations, including Freedom Under the Law, Anti-Common Market Campaign and the Prosecute Hain Campaign. Interestingly funds (probably from McTaggart) for the SIF stopped in 1973, perhaps to be directed into these other operations. Selsdon Group: *Observer*, 29/4/73 and *Socialist Worker*, 1/9/73.

13 Martell's groups included the Free Press Society (1955), the Peoples' League for the Defence of Freedom (1956), the Anti-Socialist Front (1958), the National Fellowship (1962) – the whole amalgamated in 1963 as the Freedom Group. In 1960 Martell even began a right-wing newspaper, *The New Daily*.

14 *Guardian*, 12/6/73 and *Willesden and Brent Chronicle*, 22/6/73. *Daily Telegraph*, 24/5/73; Walker, *NF*, p. 125.

CHAPTER XXXIII: REDS UNDER THE BEDS

1 Attallah, p. 600.

2 Cited in Lindsay, p. 107.

3 In *The Pencourt File* (p. 241) Mrs Williams is quoted as saying that Wilson said to her: 'Have you ever thought that all that could be used in a different way?'

4 AIMS: an example is in the *New Statesman*, 15/2/74. *Guardian*, 6/5/87; Leigh, p. 212; Meyer, pp. 170–3.

5 See Benn, *Diaries*, vol. 3, 30/1/74, p. 101; Whitehead, pp. 109–10; Hennessy, *Whitehall*, p. 240; *Guardian*, 5/3/80, a speech given at the Cambridge Union by Carver, 4/3/80. Chalfont in Whitehead, p. 211.

6 Four days later Auberon Waugh played back the Unison story in an entry in his diary in *Private Eye*: 'The first meeting of the Chapman Pincher Vigilantes group to smash the working class was held at the White Tower in Charlotte Street. Our membership is largely composed of MI5 men and senior officers of the armed services, so I fear I cannot reveal their names. But I can reveal that the bill for wine and food came to £66 a head, kindly paid by a gentleman from the American Embassy whose name I never caught.' Unison, if it was anything, was right-wing MI6: Waugh's sources were probably MI5.

7 Benn, *Diaries*, vol. 3, p. 107.

8 Buckton was told by a Special Branch officer that his phone was bugged. See Benn, *Diaries*, vol. 3, p. 5. Assassination plot: C. Jenkins, p. 160 and Benn, *Diaries*, vol. 4, p. 527.

9 Young and Freeson, see *Private Eye*, 8/3/74. Freeson would certainly have had an MI5 file. He was a member of the NCCL and Vice-President of the Campaign for Democracy in Ulster, both of them targets of the security services.

10 Pincher, *Inside Story*, pp. 29–31. At the 1975 Labour Party Conference, Tony Benn talked to Bryan Stanley of the Post Office Engineering Union about the 1974 election. Stanley believed 'the Tories were engaged in a widespread surveillance campaign involving the telephone tapping of activists in the trade union movement and the Labour Party, as well as in the Communist Party. The aim was to prepare a general dossier so that, in the run-up to an Election, he [Heath] could blacken the character of his political opponents and get public opinion on his side.' Benn, *Diaries*, vol. 3 p. 441.

11 Pincher, *Inside Story*, pp. 158 and 55–6. See also Stephen Dorril, 'Five at Eye' in *Lobster* 17. Leak it did. The *Eye* reported (6/9/74) 'The cloak and dagger atmosphere which had been hanging around the Czech Embassy in London may be ending. In recent months 9 Czech diplomats have suddenly returned home. Now the Ambassador himself, Dr Miroslav Zemla, will bring the total to 10, though his departure will not be undignified and he observed the usual diplomatic protocol by giving his goodbye party at the Embassy last week.' There followed a number of detailed snippets on the activities of the Czech Embassy – see *Private Eye*, 20/9/74.

12 Penrose/Courtiour, pp. 203–8; Pincher, *Dirty Tricks*, pp. 120–1; *idem., Inside Story*, p. 41; Cavendish, pp. 134 and 138.

CHAPTER XXXIV: 'DESPERATE TIMES': BETWEEN THE TWO ELECTIONS OF 1974

1 Cosgrave, pp. 363–4; Halcrow, pp. 69–70.

2 Pincher, *Inside Story*, pp. 41–2 and *Dirty Tricks*, pp. 122 and 125. Rumours which Pincher describes as 'considered worthy of development' at this time include Mrs Williams' two children, allegations that there had been problems over her positive vetting and 'aspects of Wilson's reaction to the land deals row' which had broken just after the election.

3 Pincher, *Inside Story*, p. 42; *Guardian*, 18/12/88. Young declined to name the 'respected politician in the Heath Cabinet' to us. Le Carré, in the *Independent*, 3/1/91. George Kennedy Young provides yet another glimpse of the way in which intelligence activities are a natural part of this area of political life. He told one journalist that 'he'd been able to work out pretty well everything about the *Spectator*, except one loose end. – "Who's running [Geoffrey] Wheatcroft?" ' *Guardian*, 16/5/90.

Notes

4 Falkender, *Downing Street*, pp. 132–3; Pincher, *Inside Story*, p. 42.

5 Compiled from Falkender, *Downing Street*, pp. 133 and 141, and *Mail on Sunday*, 3/5/87. The Silkin stories appeared in the *Daily Telegraph* 'on the profits on land deals by the family company of John Silkin, a Labour minister – illustrated, with slogans like 'property speculator' and 'profiteering'. Doig, *Corruption*, p. 200. The 'East German money for Wilson' and 'KGB colonels' themes were among the material sent by MI5 to Colin Wallace in Northern Ireland during this period.

6 Best short account is in Doig, *Babylon*, pp. 205–14. Roth, *Walter Mitty*, p. 40. *Jewish Chronicle* journalist, information from Barrie Penrose. Haines, p. 202. Commentators are agreed that Wilson made things worse by trying to defend the indefensible. That a different response by Wilson would have reduced the ensuing press onslaught is only an assumption. On 20 March, there was the curious attempt to kidnap Princess Anne. One Ian Ball held up the Princess in her car in The Mall, shooting her personal detective, her chauffeur and a journalist, Brian McConnell, who was passing and tried to intervene. Ball was arrested almost immediately, confessed, adjudged insane and detained in a psychiatric hospital, where he has remained since. See the *Sunday Times* 17/9/89. Although Ball had been arrested within ten minutes of the attack, two days later *The Times* received a letter claiming the credit for the attack from 'the Marxist Leninist Activist Revolutionary Movement'. Despite the transparently phoney title of the group, *The Times* headlined it on its front page 'Left wing group in Mall attack, letter claims' (22/3/74). Between the elections of 1974, any excuse would do if it might damage the left. One result of the attack had been increased security within No. 10 which increased the level of paranoia felt by Mrs Williams and Wilson, already rising following the Army security operations at Heathrow. On this see Penrose/Courtiour, p. 241.

7 As we have seen a number of anti-Wilson people, including former colleagues Candler, Wigg and Caunt, were already leaking material to the *Eye*. There were also a number of MI5-linked lunch guests, notably Tom Driberg and Henry Kerby, who had earlier supplied gossip. More serious was the presence of journalists such as William Massie, with his admitted access to MI5 and CIA information. The possible intelligence links of the chief author of anti-Wilson stories, Auberon Waugh, are described in *Lobster* 17. The British left has never taken *Private Eye* seriously enough. In our view from about 1971 it has been one of the most important British political journals. The surprising alliance between Harold Wilson and James Goldsmith which led to Wilson knighting him in 1976 is entirely explained by their mutual loathing of *Private Eye*. The published citation for James Goldsmith's knighthood – 'for services to ecology' – is an in-joke about Goldsmith's assault on the *Eye*.

8 See Marnham, Chapter 7. Marnham has failed to respond to telephone and letter inquiries and has remained silent about the indentity of *The Times* journalist or whether he holds other pages other than the three he reprints in his book.

9 *Guardian*, 15/5/87; Marnham, Chapter 7. See *Lobster* 17 for examples of the *Eye*/Wilson stories. Young comment in *Lobster* 19. There is little evidence that Wilson knew half the people he was alleged to be in league with. Most were nodding acquaintances or were guests for formal dinners. He still had few close friends.

10 Like a barium meal we can trace the course of the briefing document, 'Soviets Increase Control Over British Communists', round the intelligence-connected British right. In July 1976, Airey Neave contacted Colin Wallace, who gave him material which concentrated on the alleged communist links of the IRA. On 7 August, the *Daily Telegraph* reported: 'The allegation of Communist involvement in Northern Ireland is a new theme for Mr Neave, who has long criticised the government's handling of the situation there.' On 11 September Neave spoke in Northumberland where he said that the IRA had 'increasingly Marxist aims . . . for which Cuba is the model'. See Foot, *Wallace*, pp. 119–21. Five days before, the *Telegraph* published an article ' "Cubans and Czech agents" forment Ulster strife', a review of a pamphlet by John Biggs-Davidson MP, entitled 'The strategic implications for the West of the International links of the IRA in Ireland' (Foreign Affairs Research Institute). Biggs-Davidson was at that time the Conservative Party's deputy shadow Minister for Northern Ireland, under Airey Neave (both were members of FARI). It is clear from the quotations published that Biggs-Davidson had had access to an early, unrevised version of the above briefing paper. In the 1980s Biggs-Davidson became President of the British Anti-Communist Council (BACC). In March 1988 issue of *Asian Outlook*, we find BACC Chairman Peter Dally writing: 'It is perhaps worth recalling that when, during the Korean war, the UN and their allies, including UK and US troops, were being attacked by Moscow supplied MIG fighters, it was the British who had so obligingly supplied the original Rolls Royce jet engines. We British wanted to make a friendly trade gesture to that nice "uncle Joe Stalin".'

11 Benn, *Diaries*, vol. 3, 10/4/74, p. 137; *Private Eye*, 2/5/76. See also O'Sullivan, p. 63 and *Private Eye*, 28/4/67. O'Sullivan, p. 88. 'Vilifying Hodge was an easy means of vilifying James Callaghan . . . because of their well-known association personally and, following Callaghan's term as a director of [Hodge's] the Commercial Bank of Wales . . . Some reference to the Callaghan connection was almost invariably made whenever Hodge and his mortgages were under discussion in the media.' *Ibid.*, p. 94.

12 O'Sullivan, p. 112. George Thomas' agent said 'You cannot be a socialist and sit on the board of a private commercial bank . . . we expect it of Jim but not of George.' No allegations were ever made against Thomas.

13 *Private Eye*, 'Julian et Jim', 2/6/72. Callaghan warning, see Falkender, *Downing Street*, p. 133. We do not wish to be seen as in some way defending Hodge or the relationship with Callaghan. Hodge was just a money-lender in a hurry who took advantage of the cheap money/few controls policy during the Heath years. But he

was no more obnoxious than any others. For the MI5 link see, for example, *Private Eye*, 2/4/76 and 16/4/76. The MI5 link is, of course, speculation and it is possible that the appearance of the anti-Callaghan stories in 1976 had nothing at all to do with the spooks.

14 Wansell, pp. 111, 113 and 110. 'Jimmy Goldsmith, the London financier, was brought in to reorganise the Rothschild food business.' Cowles, p. 243.

15 Wansell, pp. 110–13. Interestingly, most of these statements were deleted from Wansell's re-write of his book, as was this passage. 'He advocated the consideration of limiting immigration into Britain . . . if we continue to avoid facing the facts then very soon we will be heading for disaster . . . Chaos would ensue and out of the disorder would emerge a new kind of order' (pp. 114–15).

16 Goldsmith, p. x; *Private Eye*, 17/8/79 and 4/4/75. The Keyser managing director, Roland Franklin, was the bank's nominee on the board of Goldsmith's main company Cavenham.

17 Slater, p. 197; Wansell, pp. 88 and 107.

18 Winchester, p. 161; Dempster quote in *ibid.*, p. 163; Ingrams, pp. 18–19.

19 Goldsmith, pp. vii, 5 and 39; Marnham, p. 51.

20 Ingrams, p. 26; Marnham, pp. 49–50 and 17. In September 1965, an RAF officer, John Curtis, was court-martialled for apparently passing documents to Elwes that were pertinent to the Civil War in the Yemen. Britain was officially neutral in the war but Colonel David Stirling was helping Royalist forces. Elwes was in some way also helping Stirling, though the facts of the case are obscure.

21 Wansell, pp. 111–12. Goldsmith 'believed for a while that Heath would be returned to power by the end of 1975; he even had a bet with "Tiny" Rowland to the effect: but the dream faded rapidly'. 'Goldsmith, along with Jim Slater and Roland Franklin, bet Rowland £10,000 that Edward Heath . . . would be back in power by the end of 1975.' *Ibid.*, p. 112 and Ingrams, p. 117.

CHAPTER XXXV: THE WRIGHT PLOT

1 Pincher, *Inside Story*, pp. 16–18.

2 This is repeated in Wright, p. 377. See also West, *Molehunt*, p. 75.

3 Pincher has refused to identify the 'City man' other than that he was 'exceptionally eminent and greatly respected' and that he was 'a peer and former politican of great distinction, who was then an important figure in the City'. *A Web of Deception*, pp. 18 and 130.

4 Leigh, p. 224. The fact that Wright is talking here of the period before any of the events surrounding the Stonehouse affair took place indicates that MI5 were indeed behind that particular furore. Although no smears about MacDermot actually appeared in this period, it is an interesting coincidence that it was at this point that Lord Elwyn Jones happened to to tell Benn about the MacDermot case – perhaps indicating that there was background noise about MacDermot. See Benn, *Diaries*, vol. 3, p. 304.

5 BBC1, *Panorama*, July 1988; Leigh, p. 246. The Labour MP Dale Campbell-Savours named two of this group of K Branch officers in the House of Commons in 1987. They were Tony Brooks and Harry Wharton, closely involved with the operation against Kagan.

6 Wright, p. 369. The material that was being transmitted to Colin Wallace in Northern Ireland during this period came via F Branch officers.

7 HOC *Hansard*, 'Security Services', col. 783, 15/12/86.

8 Churchill also named in Leigh, p. 238. HOC *Hansard*, 'Allegations', col. 35, 12/1/87. Biographical note on – *Winston Churchill*, grandson of his namesake, son of the Conservative MP Randolph Churchill. Randolph had been one of the original members of the SAS and was a life-long friend and 'comrades-in-arms' of David Stirling. Member of Whites, the Monday Club, the Anglo-Rhodesian Society and the 92 Club. Not so bright right-winger, part of the Julian Amery coterie, PPS to Amery at Housing (1970–3) and Secretary of the Conservative backbench Foreign Affairs Committee 1973–6. Had an interesting career in the sixties as a journalist visiting many trouble spots in the world. *Sir Stephen Hastings*. Member of the Monday Club, Council of the Anglo-Rhodesia Society, 92 Club. Colleague of David Stirling having served in the Western Desert and the SAS. See Cowles, p. 191. Former MI6 officer who served in Cyprus at the time Peter Wright was there. Elected to Parliament in November 1960. His father was a respected MP in Rhodesia. Julian Amery sponsored his first appearance in the House of Commons. In 1965, with Julian Amery and former MI6 officer, Cranley Onslow, Hastings launched a campaign against the cancellation of the aircraft TSR2. A close friend of Christopher Phillpotts the MI6 officer who as we have seen, as head of Counter-Espionage, was heavily involved in the molehunts of the late 1960s with Peter Wright (*Daily Telegraph*, 24/4/85). Served with Phillpotts in Paris, replaced by Tony Brooks. Friend of Stephen de Mowbray, who was responsible for the genesis of the Trend report.

9   Wright, p. 370.

10 *Ibid.*, p. 376; Corson/Trento, p. 99; Leigh, p. 215.

CHAPTER XXXVI: THE 'COMMUNIST CELL' IN NO. 10

1   Pincher, *Inside Story*, p. 42.

2   Marnham, *Trail of Havoc*, p. 105.

3   Pincher, *Inside Story*, pp. 43–4. Rayner, a director of Marks and Spenser, had been looking at efficiency in the MOD. In 1977, he was made a member of the Security Commission. Pincher, *Dirty Tricks*, p. 124. In Leigh's version, at the lunch 'Marcia Williams had been accused of leading a Communist cell in Downing St.' Leigh, p. 249.

4   Pincher, *Inside Story*, p. 45; *Sunday Times*, 31/7/77.

5   Haines, p. 218. Haines is hardly a dispassionate source on Williams, whom he disliked intensely.

6   Penrose and Courtiour were shown the memo. Penrose/Courtiour, p. 324.

7   Leigh, p. 196.

8   King, *Diaries*, vol. 2, p. 59.

9   Benn, *Diaries*, vol. 3, 10/4/74 and 14/4/74.

10 Pincher, *Dirty Tricks*, pp. 102 and 137; Benn, *Diaries*, vol. 3, pp. 146, 1/5/74 and p. 155, 16/5/74.

11 Pincher, *Dirty Tricks*, pp. 102, 137 and 148.

12 HOL *Hansard*, col. 893, 26/2/75; Pincher, *Inside Story*, p. 158.

13 Leigh, p. 229. Geoffrey Stewart-Smith noted this speech in his 1979 pamphlet, *The Hidden Face of the Labour Party*.

14 Pencourt/Courtiour, pp. 236–8. Calls to Chile: on BBC 2's *Newsnight* in December 1986 Joe Haines said that Wilson had 'sent for transcripts of telephone calls between Chile and Judith Hart' – clearly implying that Wilson had been told of such calls, and that the calls had been taped, presumably by GCHQ or the NSA.

15 Falkender, *Downing Street*, p. 252; Penrose/Courtiour, pp. 237–8. In fact, MI5 had actually amalgamated bits of the files of two or three other 'Harts', J. Tudor Hart, Edith Hart and Jenifer Hart.

16 *Sunday Times*, 31/7/77.

17 Leigh, pp. 230–1.

18 Penrose/Courtiour, p. 236.

19 Benn, *Diaries*, vol. 3, 17/10/74, pp. 242–3; Castle, *Diaries*, vol. 2, 17/10/74.

20 Castle, *ibid.*; Benn, *Diaries*, vol. 3, p. 392; Leigh, p. 228; HOL *Hansard*, 16/3/88.

CHAPTER XXXVII: CLOCKWORK ORANGE

1   Rees, p. 46. Leaks: see, for example, *ibid.*, pp. 57, 81, 84, 122–3, 234–5, 302 and 306. Early on Rees managed to convince himself that the leaks 'stemmed not from the top but from those lower down the line in the information services who were not aware of the evolving discussions and agreements reached with senior officers' – a remarkable view of how an Army operates, which survived a public attack on his policies by GOC Frank King. See the *Sunday Times*, 20/4/75. The most detailed account of the Army's campaign of leaks and misrepresentation against Wilson and Rees is in Foot, *Wallace*, especially Chapter 2.

2   This may explain why Fisk's book, *The Point of No Return*, (Methuen, 1975) received so little attention and has subsequently been so hard to find.

3   Wallace allegations originally in 1984 document given to Stephen Dorril in November 1985; Miller in the *Sunday Times*, 22/3/87. Unfortunately, after talking to Penrose, Miller disappeared and has never surfaced since. Miller's allegations have never been effectively challenged.

4   Barron visit, information from Colin Wallace. In London in 1974 to publicise one of his KGB books, Barron addressed the Monday Club's Sub-committee on Subversion.

5   The campaign against Wallace was discussed by us in *Lobster* 14 and 15, and in more detail in Paul Foot's book. Wallace's notes, the paper and the ink used, were forensically dated to 1974 by Britain's leading 'paper and ink man', Dr Julius Grant, for the *Observer* and Channel Four News in 1987.

6   Document sent by Wallace to Mrs Thatcher, 23/4/90; ITV, *This Week*, 29/4/90.

7   Among the supporting material Wallace received were a number for forged documents, leaflets, pamphlets and bank statements. Some of these have been reproduced at the rear of Paul Foot's book *Who Framed Colin Wallace?* Others from the same period but which had not been distributed to Colin Wallace were sent anonymously to Robin Ramsay in 1989. The whole collection were published as a pamphlet, *Forgery*, by the Labour Campaign for Reform of the Intelligence and Security Services, PO Box 102, Hull. Despite wide distribution to the British media, no notice was taken of these extraordinary documents. One of the documents supplied by MI5 was a pamplet alleging that Heath was a homosexual. A copy found its way to Tony Benn in 1974 just before the election in October. Benn at Transport House, Bristol: 'Someone there showed me a very expensively printed colour booklet entitled "I challenge Heath", which attacks Ted Heath in the most scurrilous and disreputable way, and alleges he is a homosexual. It was written by the woman, Karen Cooper, who threw ink at him when he was in Brussels to sign the Treaty of Accession to the Common Market, and she had tried to get Ken Coates to publish it as a trailer to her book which is due out soon. It was filthy, and in the author alleged she was a member of the Labour Party, so one wonders whether it wasn't really designed to damage us.' Benn, *Diaries*, vol. 3, p. 230, 29/9/74. The status of this pamphlet is unresolved. Karen Cooper did exist and did throw the ink at Heath. However, whether she actually produced this pamphlet is unknown. She is said to have moved to Sweden where she died.

8   The notes were first discussed in detail by Robin Ramsay in *Lobster* 13 and most of them have been reproduced at the rear of Paul Foot's *Who Framed Colin Wallace?*, though in being reduced to fit the page size they have become rather difficult to decipher.

CHAPTER XXXVIII: EDWARD SHORT

1   Fitzwalter/Taylor, p. 28. By the early 1960s Smith had become one of the major political figures in the North East. Using finance provided by Poulson, Smith then set up a number of PR firms which employed local councillors and council officials. This arrangement did no harm to the Poulson firm's chances of getting local government contracts.

2   Doig, *Corruption*, p. 150; Foot, *Wallace*, pp. 75–6. Foot speculates that this was the work of MI5.

3   Fitzwalter/Taylor, p. 236.

4   *Ibid.*, pp. 65, 99, 199, and 240.

5   Ronald Heisler, Statutory Declaration made before a solicitor, 28/5/87.

6   *Ibid.* Hopkins was never interviewed by the police.

7   *Sunday Express*, 21/7/74; *The Times*, 3/8/74.

8   *Observer*, 26/7/87.

9   There is some support for Short's view from his enemy Milne. At Commander Morrison's request Milne went to see him in November 1974. When Milne arrived for the appointment, Morrison pretended that he did not know why Milne was there (Milne, p. 198). Robin Ramsay interviewed Ronald Heisler twice in 1987 and found him a completely credible witness.

10   *Sunday Times*, 3/5/87. Short had been burgled twice in the months before the forgery appeared. West, *Molehunt*, p. 76. HOC *Hansard*, 'Official Secrets Bill', cols. 506 and 1134, 21/12/88.

11   *The Times*, 1/8/74. Inland Revenue list, Milne, p. 200. Chapman Pincher, *Inside Story*, p. 189, charmingly claims that 'I have always suspected that the forged document purporting to be a Swiss bank account held illegally by Edward Short was a KGB-inspired device to discredit the British Government through one of its senior ministers.' Quite how this squares with the contemporaneous notion among Pincher's circle that the Government was being run by the 'Communist cell' in No 10 escapes us.

CHAPTER XXXIX: 'THE APPREHENSIVE PATRIOTS'

1   Lord Mountbatten, while Defence Chief, is said to have organised a 'Unison' discussion group for senior officers to discuss wider political issues.

2   *The Times*, 29/8/74.

3   Wilson was informed of the Royal Society of St. George. See Pincher, *Inside Story*, p. 135.

Notes

4 This memo was leaked to *Peace News* and later reprinted in both the *Guardian* and the Workers' Revolutionary Party collection, *Britain's State Within a State*. The project included proposals to institute a written constitution and make society and industry more ecologically conscious. Stirling told *The Times* that GB 75 was financed by 'two individuals in Jersey'. One turned out to be the arms dealer, Geoffrey Edwards, a friend of Chapman Pincher; the other, Charles Wackett-Evans, was chair of a company called Aviation (Jersey) Ltd. – linked to Slater Walker – which was found guilty in 1976 of exporting military equipment to South Africa. See *The Times*, 23/8/74 and *Private Eye*, 25/6/76.

5 Biographical note on *David Stirling*. In 1941, Stirling founded the SAS. Fellow members included Stephen Hastings, future MI6 officer, other Conservative MPs Carol Mather and Randolph Churchill (father of Winston S.). Stirling was captured by the Germans and imprisoned in Colditz with Airey Neave and MI5 officer Charles Elwell. In the fifties, Stirling set up and ran the Capricorn Africa Society, a classic (but failed) attempt to co-opt the leaders of the African nationalist movements in the British African colonies; Capricorn had the backing of the Commonwealth Office and funding from international banks. In Kenya, he became a close friend of Bruce McKenzie, the Minister of Agriculture and MI6 agent. At the beginning of the sixties, Stirling recruited former SAS troops for mercenary operations in support of Royalist forces in the Yemen. This MI6 arm's length operation had been initiated by George Young. See *Lobster* 19 and *Anarchy* 37. Three years later, Stirling set up the companies Watchguard and Kulinda which provided bodyguards for leaders of whom the British Government approved. They were essentially fronts. His co-director was Colonel John Woodhouse, who, as commanding officer of 22 SAS, had worked closely with Walter Walker in Borneo in the mid-sixties. Stirling also set up a commerical television company, Television International Enterprises, with funding from Lord Thomson of *Times* newspapers. Stirling had friends across the whole spectrum of the secret state and moved easily across the boardrooms of the City.

6 From a man who was shortly to bemoan loudly the media's discovery of GB 75, talking to Martin Walker of the *Guardian* so freely does not make a lot of sense. Stirling was running up a flag for all to see.

7 Hogg has written to the papers on Unison's behalf, as did Butler, briefly, in 1974. McWhirter stood as a Conservative in the 1964 election, but had earlier been a member of the League of Empire Loyalists. McWhirter worked with Lady Birdwood for a time, in the short-lived organisation, Self Help. They fell out, apparently when Lady Birdwood's racism was revealed – information from Chris Tame. According to *Searchlight* 144 and the anonymous 1972 pamphlet *The Monday Club, a Danger to Democracy*, it was McWhirter who was involved in negotiations with Tyndall of the National Front and was a general source of funding for the far-right. Gordon Winter, who had infiltrated the anti-tour campaign for South Africa's Bureau of State Security (BOSS), was told by his controller, A. H. Bouwier, that McWhirter and Young were senior British intelligence, i.e. MI6, operatives in the SIF. Winter, Chapter 27, covers this period.

8 See *Observer*, 4/9/77 for Walker's recruitment; Butler, conversation with Robin Ramsay in 1987. In his autobiography, Denis Healey praises Walker for his role in Malaya and Borneo but describes him as a disaster at NATO (p. 290). Walker's talks, see *Private Eye*, 23/8/74. Walker had arranged to talk at the Monday Club through Bee Carthew as early as July 1972 for his 19/9/72 talk on 'The Growing Russian Threat' see Document 10 in *Searchlight* 18, special issue: 'The Men in the Shadows'. Some of his correspondence with Monday Club Meetings Secretary and George Young ally Bee Carthew were among the documents stolen in the 1973 burglary of Carthew's flat which surfaced in that issue of *Searchlight*. Young's recruitment of Walker revealed some of the factional divisions within the far-right. This is inferrable from the Jane Pelling letters, reprinted in 'The Men in the Shadows'. In February 1974 Jane Pelling wrote to Ian and Isobel Greig. Of the Pincher article (referred to above) she wrote 'have discerned that GY [George Young] is "head boy" '. She referred to contact between Walker and Young ('the dreaded one'), and urged the Greigs to use Geoffrey Stewart-Smith to warn Walker off, having already tried to do so herself 'last September', i.e. 1973. Document 8, *Searchlight* 18.

9 Walker acquiring Civil Assistance, in a letter of 17 July 1975 to Kenneth de Courcy. De Courcy's papers, including his correspondence with Walter Walker, have been deposited in the Hoover Institution in California. We are grateful to Dr Pauline Henri for a copy of that correspondence. It should be noted here that this analysis of Young's role is denied by one of his friends during this period, who told us that Young simply wanted to be a 'right-wing political figure' and created Unison as 'a political platform'. This was true of his Monday Club activities but not of Unison, unless a 'secret political platform' makes sense. Perhaps, given the clandestine nature of much of the British right's activities, it is just intelligible.

10 Others named by Walker as his supporters were: Field Marshal Sir Claude Auchenleck, Admiral Varyl Begg, Lord Peyton (formerly John Peyton MP), the Duke of Westminster, Lord Boyd, and Sir Alexander Abel-Smith. Unison link: information from an unpublished Walker letter to editor of the *Sunday Times*, 27/7/87, and letter to authors 7/2/86. The quotation about McWhirter is from a circular to Civil Assistance's Regional and County Co-ordinators, December 1975, just after McWhirter's assassination by the IRA.
In August Walker had talks with the leadership of the newly-formed National Association of Rate-payers' Action Groups (NARAG) and the National Voluntary Civil Aid Serices (NVCAS) but neither group was willing to associate formally with Civil Assistance. *The Times*, 26/8/74 and *Daily Telegraph*, 13/8/74. On this episode see also Nugent/King, especially Chapter 2. Other than Major Greenwood's Red Alert, the only other organisation which did join up with Civil Assistance was the British Military Volunteer Force, led by a Mr Paul Daniels. It is alleged to have had 1,367 members at the time. Members had included former SAS officer, Mike Calvert, a friend of Young's, and Lady Birdwood, 'who was once accused by Egypt of gun-running to Yemeni royalists' – i.e. when Stirling was organising mercenaries for the operation. A profile of the organisation is in the *Sunday Times*, 23/4/72. For the link with Walker, see *The Times*, 24/8/74.

11 Lord Mason of Barnsley, as he is now, did not reply to our inquiries about this episode.

12 *Guardian*, 23/8/74. Mather had served with Stirling in the desert with the SAS. Post-war, he held various military intelligence posts and was one of the few MPs to attend the funeral of Maurice Oldfield.

13 Wright, p. 368 and Leigh, p. 224. Bugging of Stirling – see Stirling obituary note in the *Independent*, 19/11/90. Neave – see Leigh, p. 224. Biographical note on *Airey Neave*. In 1942, Neave joined the P15 section of MI9, the escape organisation controlled by MI6. After escaping from Colditz, Neave was a leading member of IS(9), a secret unit attached to SHAEF. After the war he was a barrister and rather anonymous Conservative backbench MP. However, he was generally regarded as a psychological warfare expert. He continued to be involved with MI6 and émigré Polish groups: his wife had served in the Polish sections of the Special Operations Executive and then joined MI6. In the early fifties, Neave was in the Territorial Army version of IS(9) which later evolved into the 23rd SAS regiment (TA). The 23 SAS (V) was formed in London in 1959 but then transferred to Birmingham. It was formed from an existing unit, 'The Joint Reconnaisance Unit (TA)' which in turn had originally been known as the Joint Reserve Prisoner of War Intelligence Organisation (TA); and before that IS(9). It had squadrons in the more important industrial centres and could provide a means of monitoring social unrest.

14 Walker claims that Stirling asked him to take over GB 75; Stirling denied this (letters to the authors). Walker perceived Stirling's apparent plans to break strikes as being more extreme than his and refused. For Nodes, see the obituary note on Stirling in the *Independent*, 17/11/90. About Mr Nodes we know almost nothing. There is no reference to him, for example, in the recent official, massive history of the ETU by John Lloyd.

15 Walker's correspondence with de Courcy is dotted with Walker's comments on right-wing nonsense, Phylis Schafley, Frank Capel *et al*. *East–West Digest* was an authorless anti-subversion magazine produced by Geoffrey Stewart-Smith.

16 On Butler's career and views see Leigh, pp. 218–22. Petersfield speech in letter to de Courcy, 20/4/75.

17 Leigh, pp. 221–2 and 218; Pencourt/Courtiour, pp. 245–6.

CHAPTER XL: THE 1974 OCTOBER GENERAL ELECTION

1 Benn, *Diaries*, vol. 3, 18/9/74, p. 226. The tax returns had been given to *Private Eye*.

2 Haines, p. 212; Benn, *Diaries*, vol. 3, 25/9/74, p. 228; accountant reference, interview with Barrie Penrose, November 1990.

3 Benn, *Diaries*, vol. 3, p. 244; on the handbag story, see Dalyell, *Misrule*, p. 129.

4 Haines, p. 213 and Pincher, *Inside Story*, pp. 46–7. Pincher describes the main points of the writ in *ibid.*, p. 45–6. Specific evidence of the 'cohorts' is thin. However, one of the authors learned that *Daily Mail* journalists did turn up at the *Huddersfield Examiner* looking for dirt.

5 Benn, *Diaries*, vol. 3, 29/9/74, p. 230. The status of this pamphlet is unresolved. Karen Cooper did exist, did throw the ink at Heath. However whether she actually produced this pamphlet is unknown.

6 *Ibid.*, vol. 3, 18/9/74, p. 227 and 8/4/75, p. 362. Briginshaw was himself subsequently smeared in *Private Eye*, 18/8/78.

7 *Standard* news editor quoted in the *Guardian*, 2/1/75.

8 Pincher, *Inside Story*, p. 48; Wansell, p. 112.

CHAPTER XLI: WATERGATE POLITICS

1 Benn, *Diaries*, vol. 3, 25/11/74, pp. 272–3; *Private Eye*, 20/9/74; *The Times*, 16/12/74.

2 See *Time Out*, 20/12/74 and 2/1/75. MI6: 'Stonehouse's work in Africa, in Pakistan and in Bangladesh as a minor intelligence man for the British MI6', *Private Eye*, 30/4/76. Pakistani intelligence: Stonehouse, *My Trial*, pp. 171 and 206; *Daily Telegraph*, 7/8/87.

3 HOC *Hansard*, cols. 1354–7, 17/12/74 and col. 711, 20/12/74.

4 The groupings were the Workers' Revolutionary Party, International Marxists Group, International Socialists, Labour Research Department, Institute for Workers' Control, the Free Communications Group, Socialist Labour League, Workers' Fight, Big Flame, International Research Group, Nalgo Action Group etc. Viscount Colville had been Minister of State at the Home Office, 1972–4, in which capacity he would have liaised with MI5. Lords Guisborough and Clifford were both former Deputy Lord Lieutenants of English counties, part of the generally invisible alternative power-structure of this society which by-passes Parliament altogether and sits waiting for the breakdown of the parliamentary structure. Clifford, HOL *Hansard*, cols. 892–3, 26/2/75. As we discuss later, the Stonehouse allegation resurfaced in 1976 when the

Notes

Frolik material was run through the Commons by Stephen Hastings (ex MI6); and again in 1978 when Cranley Onslow (ex MI6) tried to persuade Prime Minister Callaghan to refer the Stonehouse case to the Security Commission. See Pincher, *Inside Story*, p. 114.

5 *Guardian*, 2/1/75: 'the bank's central function has been to channel foreign money into the Israeli financial system'. See also Naylor, pp. 235–6. ICB seems to have been willing to launder money from, *inter alia*, Meyer Lansky and Bernie Cornfeld's Investors Overseas Services. *Private Eye*, 18/10/74. *Standard* news editor, quoted in the *Guardian*, 2/1/75.

6 Funding the Wilson office: this was before the Leader of the Opposition received the so-called 'Short money', expenses paid by the state to enable the Opposition to maintain an office. *Sunday Telegraph*, 3/11/74; *Sunday Times*, 3/11/74 and *Private Eye*, 18/10/74. Detectives: *Daily Telegraph*, 4/11/74.

7 See Marnham, especially Chapter 7; *Private Eye*, 15/11/74 and 10/1/75.

8 Pincher, *Inside Story*, and Roth, *Walter Mitty*. *Private Eye*, 2/3/79. Robert Porter, *Sunday Telegraph*, 3/5/87. Mrs Williams' claims, *Daily Mail*, 3/5/87. Wilson's sympathy for Israel was hardly a secret. After he retired Wilson wrote a book about Israel, and Williams (Falkender) devotes one chapter of her *Downing Street in Perspective* to an account of their pro-Israeli attitudes.

9 Leigh, p. 240; Pincher, *Inside Story*, p. 114 and *Dirty Tricks*, p. 135.

10 See *Lobster* 15 for fuller background and the *Spectator*, 19/6/76.

11 'Surfacing': Former IRD head Ray Whitney used the term in a piece in the *Sunday Telegraph*, 3/7/88. The point of running a news agency such as Forum World Features lay precisely in the ability to 'surface' an item in one of the agency's features – as well as serving as 'cover'. Smear stories, Penrose/Courtiour, pp. 303–4.

CHAPTER XLII: THE ASSAULT ON BENN

1 Benn, *Diaries*, vol. 3, p. 113.

2 *Guardian*, 16/1/91, obituary of Sir Anthony Part. Part retired in 1976 from the Department of Industry to various directorships including one with Lucas Aerospace. In 1982 Benn told Hugo Young: 'You're quite right in saying that a Permanent Secretary who thinks that a Prime Minister doesn't approve of a minister's policy will then undermine that minister . . . In 1974 I was faithful to the manifesto upon which [I] had been elected. Therefore you had the power of the Permanent Secretary uniting with the power of the Prime Minister who was . . . uncommitted to the manifesto.' Young/Sloman, pp. 29–30.

3 Benn, *Diaries*, vol. 3, pp. 296–9. On p. 299 Benn reproduces the text of the note he received from the security service about this woman. As far as we are aware this is the first time such a document has ever been published. See also 26/1/75, p. 308 and 10/2/75, pp. 313–14.

4 *Ibid.*, 13/2/75, p. 318. Benn was also becoming increasingly concerned that the CIA might be attempting to destabilise the Government. 16/2/75, pp. 318–19 and 28/2/75, pp. 332–3.

5 It should be emphasised also that this claim concerning the timing of covert operations is based solely on the evidence in Benn's diary. It is clearly possible that the spooks had been on his trail before early 1975. If so, the campaign became overt – visible – in early 1975. The first reference to RF74 is believed to be 24/10/74 when a man who claimed to be a member claimed responsibility for five recent bombings in England (Deutsch/Magowan p. 156). The Provos later issued a statement saying that RF 74 had nothing to do with them and had no connection with the Republican movement (*ibid.*, p. 168). On RF 74 see, for example, Peter Shipley, 'Friends of Terror in Britain', *Spectator*, 30/11/74. A recent look back at RF 74 is in *Black Flag*, 23/1/89 where it is suggested, without evidence, that it was the National Front. From Benn's *Diaries*, vol. 3: 8/11/74 death threat from RF74, others on 23/2, 1/3, 17/4 and 16/5/75: bugging and surveillance; 2/3, 29/7 and 25/11/75; harrassment by 'journalists': 30/4, 1/5, 6/7 and 23/10/75; rubbish being stolen, 29/7/75. It was notable that none of the reviews we saw of this volume of Benn's diaries referred to this campaign.

6 Benn, *Diaries*, vol. 3, 24/2/75, p. 323; HOL *Hansard*, col. 842, 26/1/75.

7 IWC – Welton: It 'contributes to the subversive operations aimed at destroying our present way of life.' 'David Williams': 'the Trotskyist-inspired . . . neo Communist-penetrated'. On Coates's struggle with the Labour Party, see Shaw, pp. 83–8.

8 HOL *Hansard*, col. 832, 26/2/75.

9 Benn, *Diaries*, vol. 3, 6/9/75, p. 431 and p. 501. We have not seen this programme. Chalfont, former Labour Minister for Disarmament, had resigned from the Labour Party in September 1974, creating a minor news item. Noting that Chalfont had apparently left the party to join Dick Taverne's little Social Democrat splinter, Tony Benn commented that it was 'a *Times* plot of some kind so far as the timing is concerned'. (*ibid.*, 22/9/74, p. 228). On p. 433, Benn provides evidence of the links between Taverne and Rees-Mogg, the *Times*' editor.

10 *Ibid.*, p. 547; *Guardian*, 28/2/85.

CHAPTER XLIII: TALKING OF COUPS

1   Daniels: *Daily Mirror*, 2/1/75. In a letter to de Courcy on 19/12/74 Walker listed his committee, most notably Nigel Morris, former head of Special Branch in Singapore, and Alexander Greenwood, founder of Red Alert. Others, as of December 1974, were Peter Burnard, Brigadier Peter Hinde, Stephen Winkworth and Rupert Russell, none of whom we have heard of before or since. In February, Walker paraded 60 of Civil Assistance's leaders in the Church of St Lawrence of Jewry in London, among the 23 ex-army and ex-naval officers were one general, six brigadiers and nine colonels. The Vicar of that church was among the founder members of the National Association for Freedom a few months later. *Morning Star*, 26/2/75.

2   Castle, *Diaries*, vol. 2, pp. 188–9.

3   Letter in the possession of Geoffrey Seed.

4   Letters to de Courcy 18/3/75 and 2/5/75. Young and Carlton Club, see *Searchlight* 7, September 1975. Sir Frederick Bennett wrote novels with titles like *Reds under the Bed* and was senior director with Young of the bank Kleinwort Benson. He was also a director of Commercial Union Assurance, where a retired MI6 officer with long experience in the Middle East, Ellis Morgan, was political and economic adviser. Bennett was a member of the Bilderberg group and later, along with Airey Neave, of Geoffrey Stewart-Smith's Foreign Affairs Research Institute. In 1972, at Chapman Pincher's behest, Bennett in Parliament named Arthur Bax, who was supposed to have been in contact with Czech intelligence. Pincher, *Inside Story*, p. 26.

5   Formation of Tory Action: *Scotsman*, 4/2/84 and *Lobster* 19. Tory Action member and some time political ally of Young, Gerald Howarth, was an 'aide' of Du Cann's. *Guardian*, 16/2/84 and *Searchlight*, May 1984. The Tory Action mailing list included Norman Tebbit, a member of the 'Gang of Four' which organised the Thatcher election campaign, and John Biffen, member of the Selsdon Group, though this may mean nothing. *Private Eye*, 24/2/84 and *Daily Mirror*, 1/2/84.

6   See *State Research*, 13, 1979, pp. 127–8.

7   Letter to de Courcey 20/5/75. With this money, Walker appointed the first full-time official of CA. It had taken ten months to get this far. Unfortunately, by this time the entire venture was dying: Walker could not even find an individual willing to be Controller for each English county. In his December 1975 circular to Regional and County Co-ordinators he reported that he was 'extremely disappointed with the progress of recruitment'. The English middle-class were proving difficult to motivate with the threat of an unknown crisis at an unknown point in the future.

8   Meetings: Benn, *Diaries*, vol. 3, 11/3/76, p. 531 and *Independent* magazine, 25/3/90. Telephone conversation with Molloy, January 1991. William Deedes declined to add to our knowledge of this curious episode. In 1976, Robens gave the Ashbridge lecture, published as 'Managing Great Britain Ltd.', in which he condemned Labour Party decisions to nationalise the banks, insurance companies, finance houses and other forms of state control. He said that in 'the constituency Labour Parties the militant left-wing is triumphant'. Robens called for 'five years of a Council of State, comprised of all parties and of none, and of the Trade union and business world . . . The country needs today good, efficient business management.'

9   During the 1974–5 period, RTZ contracts for Nambian Uranium were under review by the British Government. From 1973, Labour Party policy was to terminate the contracts, which resulted in the secret state manoeuvring to ensure that the policy failed. See 'The Rossing File: The Inside Story of Britain's Secret Contract for Namibian Uranium' by Alun Roberts, CANUC, no date but probably 1980. A leading shareholder in RTZ at the time was the Queen. It is interesting to note that one line of inquiry made by investigative researchers in 1976, when Wilson made contact with journalists, was a supposed nuclear/ South Africa link in the plot against the former Prime Minister. This may have been connected to the 'West German slush funds' mentioned by Wilson to Penrose and Courtiour. According to the journalists involved, the inquiries had only just begun when the Agee/Hosenball case (see Chapter XLVII) drew their attention away from Wilson's claims. Telephone conversation with Mark Hosenball December 1989.

10   Information on the flooding idea from Barrie Penrose; Mockler, pp. 212–19.

11   *Sunday Times*, 22/3/87 and *News on Sunday*, 3/5/87.

12   *Daily Express*, 14/7/75; Palace denial, *Guardian*, 15/7/75.

13   *Daily Telegraph*, 21/4/87.

14   Crozier, Radio 3, *Cock-up or Conspiracy*, 13/2/91. Leigh, p. 223.

15   Penrose/Courtiour, pp. 241 and 315. Benn, *Diaries*, vol. 4, p. 283. No specific date was given for this attempted coup.

16   On the middle-class protest groups, which included the Middle Class Association, National Federation of the Self-Employed, National Association of Ratepayers' Action Groups, National Association of Self-employed, and Association of Self-Employed People, see Nugent/King. Formation of NAFF, Michael Ivens letter to *New Statesman*, 29/7/77 and letter to authors. Telephone conversation with Tame, 1987.

17   The military/intelligence input into NAFF is striking. As well as Crozier and Moss (NAFF's first Director), who are widely regarded as intelligence 'assets', NAFF's Council also contained Stephen Hastings (ex-

MI6), Sir Gerald Templer and Sir Robert Thompson, both of whom made names for themselves in the counter-insurgency campaigns in Malaya, and MI6 agent the late Joseph Josten. Gourier statement, Whitehead, p. 213. Gouriet, like so many on the anti-subversion tendency, put his fantasies about the Soviet threat out in fictional form. See the unreadable Gouriet, 1981. Gouriet was also a former member of Self Help. Pincher – the quotation is from NAFF's own minuted account of the meeting, *New Statesman*, 15/7/77.

18   The demise of Stirling's grandiose plans to bring salvation to the nation was finally signalled by the inaugural meeting of Movement for True Industrial Democracy (Truemid). On Truemid see 'The anti-Scanlon guerrillas', *Guardian*, 8/10/75 and 'The Bosses Union', *Leveller* 17, 1978. In Stirling's leaked GB 75 Round Robin, the introductory paragraph had referred to the threat posed by the militants in two unions, the AEU and ETU: and Truemid did attempt to intervene in the 1975 elections in both unions. Walter Walker sent out his last letter to his regional controllers (the Civil Assistance middle management) in October 1976, bemoaning the failure of the Civil Assistance/NAFF negotiations. NAFF pleased everybody but the racists. NAFF were never overtly racist, to their credit, and though *Searchlight* did their best to link NAFF and the British racists, they merely showed that they'd failed to understand the ideological variations on the British right. See *Searchlight* 29, 31 and 33.

19   A list of these actions in included in a profile of NAFF in *Labour Research*, August 1977.

20   Benn, *Diaries*, vol. 3, 17/1/75, p. 303. According to the *Guardian* (3/1/90) the Queen is better informed than most ministers. It revealed that she 'receives every Cabinet paper as well as unamended weekly reports drawn up by the Joint Intelligence Committee in the Cabinet Office. This privilege is shared by the Prime Minister, the Foreign Secretary, the Defence Secretary, the Home Secretary and the Chancellor of the Exchequer, which suggests that sovereignty resides with these key Cabinet Ministers. 'It is said that her private secretary, Sir William Hesltine, communicates regularly – in the traditional green ink – with "C", the . . . head of the Secret Intelligence Service.' Quite why the Queen should have this privilege has not been disclosed, nor why 'C' should receive his seals of office from her personally. As was pointed out in the *Spycatcher* trial in Sydney, MI6 does not officially exist, though it may have a secret charter bestowed on it by the Crown.

21   'The Crown and Politics in the Twentieth Century', in Murray-Brown, p. 24. Blake's view was based on lengthy correspondence in *The Times* by eminent constitutionalists in 1950 including Sir Alan Lascelles, the King's Private Secretary.

22   Rawlinson. 'Dissolution in the United Kingdom', *The Parliamentarian*, vol. LVIII, No. 1, January 1977.

23   *State Research* 14, quoting S. A. De Smith 'Constitutional and Administrative Law', 1977, p. 501. The responsibilities of the Defence Council were laid out in a White Paper in 1963 when Mountbatten was Chief of Staff and Zuckerman Chief Scientific Adviser.

24   Bunyan, p. 275; *State Research* 14, p. 15.

CHAPTER XLIV: WHAT DID WILSON KNOW?

1   Penrose/Courtiour, p. 399.

2   MI5 source: Pincher, *Inside Story*, pp. 43–4 and *A Web of Deception*, p. 95. Griffith wrote to Harold Wilson reminding him of the Canadian newsletter smears in 1987 after the Peter Wright story made the headlines. Wilson replied (25/3/87): 'I had forgotten the Canadian incidents and was glad to be reminded.' Robin Ramsay interviewed Griffiths in 1987 but unfortunately he had not retained a copy of the newsletter in which the smear material had been published.

3   O'Connor, letter to Dale Campbell-Savours MP, 15/12/86.

4   'Scott problem', see Penrose/Courtiour, pp. 105 and 125. Winter in *Lobster* 18.

5   *The Times*, 4/10/74.

6   See *The Times*, 14/5/77 and 4/5/87; Penrose/Courtiour, pp. 223–4. Dalyell, *Misrule*, p. 129. There would appear to have been some burglaries at the time of the Poulson inquiries. Geoffrey Rhodes, Labour MP for Newcastle East and former PPS to Crossman at the Ministry of Housing, claimed that Crossman prepared a dossier on local government corruption which eventually he sent to 'the proper authority'. Crossman was also keeping his diary and, after a burglary at his home, he had told Rhodes: 'They've gone and pinched some of my damned tapes. They're so confidential they're dynamite.' Three other tapes on the way to his publishers had also apparently been wiped clean. Crossman (and Rhodes) died soon after and his wife disclaimed any knowledge of the tapes. Fitzwalter, pp. 237–8.

7   Attallah, p. 285; *Independent on Sunday*, 8/7/90 and private information.

8   Burglaries: Short – *The Times*, 20/12/75 and 4/5/87, *Guardian*, 4/5/87 and *Sunday Today*, 3/5/87. Donoghue – *Newsnight*, BBC2, December 1986. Crosland – Benn, *Diaries*, vol. 3, p. 448. Field, Denham, Halls – Dalyell, *Misrule*, p. 129. Brayley – *Sunday Times*, 4/7/76.

9 Benn, *Diaries*, vol. 3, 15/3/76, p. 534 and 17/10/77, p. 231.

10 Penrose/Courtiour, pp. 223–4. We were informed that in the late seventies one Fleet Street editor, at a meeting with trainee MI5 officers, was told by a former Director-General that MI5 had indeed carried out a campaign of burglaries and buggings against Wilson when he was Prime Minister.

11 The New Zealand story has yet to be put together. New Zealand journalist, Owen Wilkes, is currently working on it and has supplied enough fragments for us to make this assertion. The overthrow of Gough Whitlam is best described in John Pilger's *A Secret Country* (1989). The radical American *Ramparts* magazine encapsulated this in the title of one of its big articles during this period: 'From Dallas to Watergate. *Washington Monthly* article, 'How to spot a spook', reprinted in Agee/Woolf. Agee, *On the Run*, p. 120. *Private Eye*, 4/4/75. We have been unable to confirm this. The use of DI-6 for MI6 and DI-5 for MI5 occurred quite widely in the mid-1970s after somebody in the secret state apparently decided to put it about that they had been renamed.

12 'Meyer', reprinted in Agee/Woolf. *Time Out*, 20–26/6/75. One of the leaked Institute for the Study of Conflict documents, discussed immediately below, is a copy of a 9/7/75 letter from the ISC's Director of Studies, Iain Hamilton, to the editor of the *Irish Times*. Hamilton described the *Time Out* article as 'wholly untrue, tendentious, malignant, and politically-motivated rubbish . . . ' and refers to documents he has which 'could destroy *Time Out*'s "disinformation operation" . . . and particularly undesirable connections of one or two of the spooks who concocted the original fabrication.' The *Time Out* story was based on information originally picked up accidentally in America by the TV programme, *World in Action*, and, as far as we are aware, is entirely accurate. On the genesis of the Forum story, see Steve Weissman, 'CIA Makes the News', in Agee/Woolf.

13 Leigh, p. 249.

14 *Daily Express*, 2/10/76. Pincher, *Dirty Tricks*, p. 137 and *Inside Story*, pp. 43–4. Penrose/Courtiour, p. 9.

15 Letter quoted in Leigh, p. 237. Wright came to believe that Lessiovsky was not FEDORA. Pincher, *Too Secret*, p. 609. Barron, p. 26.

16 Freemantle, pp. 128–9; Kagan denial: *Sunday Times*, 19/7/81.

17 Leigh, pp. 243–4. Penrose/Courtiour, p. 9.

18 *Ibid.*, pp. 9–10. The meeting with Oldfield has been confirmed by Oldfield's friend, Anthony Cavendish (Cavendish, p. 165). After doubt was cast on the existence of this meeting, in a letter to the *New Statesman*, 14/7/78, Penrose and Courtiour reported that their conversations with Lord Wilson were taped and the quotes attributed to him in *The Pencourt File* were verbatim. Cavendish intro., pp. ix and 163.

19 Wright, p. 377.

20 Foot, *Wallace*, pp. 40–1. Wright, p. 377. See also the account of the de Mowbray incident in West, *Molehunt*, pp. 98–9.

21 Wright, pp. 370–1. Oldfield seems to have been interested in this area before he was called in by Wilson. In late 1974 and early 1975, an actor we have talked to was friendly with a woman who had been one of Kagan's mistresses. At a party he met an old schoolfriend, who, it turned out, worked in Whitehall. Some weeks later he was invited to dinner with Oldfield at Lockett's restaurant. He can now no longer remember anything of what they talked about, though it it certainly was not politics. We can only assume that Oldfield was interested in the actor *qua* friend of the former mistress of Kagan, perhaps with a view to recruitment. Oldfield's address, home and work numbers appear in the actor's diaries for 1974 and 1975. As for Oldfield being gay, the actor reported that not a trace of it showed, even after alcohol.

22 Pincher, *Inside Story*, p. 19. Because he was alive when it was published, *The Pencourt File* did not name Young, though the authors gave a large hint on p. 10. That Wilson claimed to have learned of Young from Hanley was confirmed by Roger Courtiour: interview September 1990.

23 We were unable to find any of the original documents referred to by *Time Out*. Bloch and Fitzgerald wrote of 'files removed from the offices of research director Peter Janke' (p. 99). In fact, many of the remaining documents from this cache that we did trace were office file copies of letters from ISC Director Iain Hamilton. The trawl was wider than Janke, and, given the irrelevance of many of the documents, entirely unfocused. *Searchlight* 18 also published some of the ISC documents but included in with them other documents which come not from ISC's files but from other operations, e.g. a good deal of private correspondence between members of 'the bridge', the groups which liaised between the right fringe of the Tory Party and the British neo-fascists, some of which were obtained after burglaries at their homes. This mix of documents has caused some confusion. See for example 'A Duff Inquiry', *Private Eye*, 15/5/87, in which the *Searchlight* documents are still attributed to the ISC leak.

24 In *Private Eye* 7/1/77, an anonymous correspondent wrote: 'Suspicion persists among the Institute's men that the job was done by professionals, that is, by the moderates in British intelligence who felt that the freelance anti-subversion work taken on by the institute ought properly be left to MI5 . . . These "moderates" were one faction in the British spook world split down the middle between those who insist on remaining loyal and responsible to the government and those who say that the Red Menace can only be effectively dealt with if intelligence experts are allowed to "freelance" in anti-subversion work.' The use of 'moderates' and

Notes

'freelancing' is misleading. In the *Washington Post* on 22/12/75, its London correspondent, Bernard Nossiter, stirred the pot a little more, claiming that 'Fleet St relies on the SIS [MI6] secret vote to keep its correspondents in the field these days.' In his 1978 book, *Britain: a Future that Works*, p. 188, footnote, Nossiter apologises for a previous article on intelligence matters, but conspicuously does not withdraw this one. The post-war recruitment of large numbers of journalists by MI6 is described by George Blake in his memoir.

25   Pincher, *Inside Story* p. 34.

26   Penrose/Courtiour, p. 225. *New Statesman*, 22/2/80, and company records. Goldsmith continued to have interests in this area. In the mid-eighties, he had a financial interest in Zeus security, whose directors included Vice-Admiral Ian Hogg of Unison and Gerald Howarth, a close friend of Goldsmith who later funded his libel action against the BBC.

27   *New Statesman*, 22/2/80.

28   *Daily Express*, 13/3/88.

29   Pincher, *Dirty Tricks*, pp. 128–9.

30   Penrose/Courtiour, pp. 321–3. The totally unjustified smear operation against Berril began when a lecturer at Cambridge University contacted MI5 following a series of domestic disputes which had allegedly involved Berril.

31   Deacon, *The British Connection*, pp. 252–3; *Private Eye*, 4/9/87 and 16/7/71; *Spectator*, 14/6/80; Blackstone/Plowden, p. 31. The real controversy began in late 1975 when the think tank proposed an inquiry into diplomatic representation abroad. Even before the Foreign Secretary, James Callaghan, had announced the inquiry, leaks were made to the press. The *Daily Mail* on 29 December 1975 announced that 'Think Tank report angers FO'. It alleged 'a major row between the Foreign Office and Downing Street about manning levels – and the shock waves are still rippling'. The secret report would demand extensive cuts in the most expensive and overloaded diplomatic service in the world. Until the Review of Overseas Representation was published in 1977, the Foreign Office organised a rubbishing campaign against the members of the 'think tank'. See Blackstone/Plowden on the FO campaign. The Review also involved a secret report on MI6 representation abroad which was never made public. See Hennessy, *Whitehall*, p. 269. Two staffers with the necessary security clearance undertook the research – presumably David Young from the MOD and Tony Hurrell from the Overseas Development Ministry – Blackstone/Plowden, p. 160.

CHAPTER XLV: BOSS

1   See Kamil for the details.

2   Kamil told Wyatt – *Guardian*, 10/4/76, and text of an interview with Wyatt conducted by the late Peter Gladstone-Smith.

3   *Evening Standard*, 11/3/76; Pincher, *Inside Story*, p. 367–8. That South Africa's covert operations had finally appeared as a footnote to the political agenda was largely the result of the work of two Labour backbenchers, Paul Rose and James Wellbeloved, who had collected information on BOSS operations and presented it to Home Secretary, Reginald Maudling. See Paul Rose, Chapter 11. The role of BOSS is one of the major threads in this period.

4   Hain told Thorpe – Hain, p. 128. First public airing – this also coincided with the publication of a report on the collapse of the so-called 'fringe bank', London and County, of which Thorpe was a director. He had been mildly criticized for his inactivity. We have not closely examined the actual sequence of events which led him to court, but it is entirely possible that this gradual exposure of Scott's allegations was tightly organised. This was suspected by Mrs Williams. See Penrose/Courtiour, pp. 324–5. Rumours in early 1975, *ibid.*, pp. 206–7 and 325. See *New Statesman*, 29/6/79, on MI5 knowledge of Thorpe's homosexuality as far back as 1960. MI6 knew about the Thorpe/Scott affair since at least 1971 when Winter's documents were photographed by MI6 operative Lee Tracey. Interview with Tracey, 24/1/82. Andrew Newton, who shot Scott's dog, claimed in 1990 that he had been paid by MI5 for his involvement in the Thorpe trial. *The Times*, 3/3/90.

5   Chester, p. 244; Van den Bergh, the head of BOSS, told Winter that Wilson had personally placed the story in the *Mirror*. Winter, p. 453.

6   C. Smith, pp. 193–4. As Cyril Smith put it: 'If the South African allegations were a calculated red herring, one can only assume that Harold was eager for the Liberal Party to hold on to its vote-catching. It was, of course, the Liberals who had given Labour power in the previous two elections.' Hain meets Wyatt, Hain, pp. 125–6. Asked in July 1990 if he had any further thoughts on this episode, Hain made the point that it is hard now to grasp just how extraordinary Wyatt's claim about a plot to wreck the Liberal Party seemed at the time. Had Wyatt merely reported that BOSS had framed him, said Hain, it would not have seemed too surprising – that suspicion was already in his mind. But at that point there had never been a suggestion of anything as big as an attempt to wreck a whole party's leadership. Hence, in part, Hain's initial scepticism.

7   Compiled from Pincher, *Inside Story*, pp. 20–1 and *Dirty Tricks*, p. 139. Attempts were made to link Harold

Wilson and George Brown to the Lockheed scandal. See *Private Eye*, 17/9/76, for a short piece about 'Pointer' and 'Powder'. On 10 June 1976, Reuters put out a telex saying that 'Pointer' and 'Powder', allegedly codenames for Wilson and Brown, had appeared in a code book as part of the Lockheed story. No British papers printed the story. The telex is reproduced in *Lobster* 17. In August 1976, Ernest Hauser, a former sales executive for Lockheed, claimed that 'an unnamed Cabinet Minister' had been bribed to the tune of $1 million. The money had allegedly been delivered to the minister in cash in four suitcases by Lockheed officials.

8   Wilson also by-passed MI6 with this, not just MI5.

9   Arrests, *Daily Express*, 19/2/76. *Sunday Telegraph*, 22/2/76 and Hain, p. 128.

10 *The Times*, 10/3/76. To Barbara Castle, earlier in the day, he had said that he had 'conclusive evidence that South African money has been involved' but would 'have to say the South African Government isn't involved, because we need their help over Rhodesia.' Castle, *Diaries*, vol. 2, p. 677.

11 Hain's version of this 'dossier' sounds more like the truth. 'Mr Wilson, I gather, had the security services confirm that there might be some substance in it.' *Guardian*, 27/4/76. In *Inside Story* (p. 371), Pincher attributes to Cyril Smith MP the rumour that Smith was alleged to have masturbated a horse.

12 We have a copy of the notes Gladstone-Smith made of his interview with Wyatt and a transcript of the Paul Rose interview with Sassin.

13 Wilson later told Pincher that his Commons charge was 'based on information given to him via the Cabinet Office from MI5 . . . There had been suspicions that people used by BOSS had been paying attention to certain black Commonwealth diplomats in London', he said. 'As regards Thorpe, MI5 could not say the South Africans were guilty but could not say they were innocent either. There had also been one or two suggestive articles in the South African papers, so I felt justified in going ahead.' (*Inside Story*, pp. 367–8.) This is curious. In part it is just Wilson misleading Pincher; but the piece about the activities against black diplomats rings true, and sounds like the basis for the warning which Lord Harris had given the South African Government some months before. As for MI5 being unable to say the South Africans were innocent or guilty, if true, this is another example of MI5 lying to Wilson, for they knew perfectly well about Winter's role. Winter has told us that he had dealings with MI5 people in London, although he declined to name them. He would say, however, that they were not the people named as a result of the Wallace–Wright revelations in 1986/7. In the *Independent* (2/5/87) it was claimed that a Cabinet Office inquiry was begun in early 1976 into allegations of subversion against Labour and Liberal Party leaders. The inquiry was apparently completed just after Wilson resigned, and its conclusions are understood to have been handed over to Cabinet Secretary Sir John Hunt. It is said that it found no evidence that BOSS was operating against British politicians. Well, as Mandy Rice-Davies famously said during the Profumo Affair, they would, wouldn't they? In 1978, James Callaghan told Tony Benn that 'plainclothes men' were keeping surveillance on members of BOSS in Britain 'to find out which meetings they were attending'. Benn is suitably sceptical. Benn, *Diaries*, vol. 4, p. 378.

CHAPTER XLVI: RESIGNATION

1   Leigh, p. xi; Cavendish, p. 165; Pincher, *Inside Story*, p. 356. Pincher also has James Callaghan playing a role, though in this version Wilson resigned because of the 'absolute necessity for some deal with the Liberals of some other Parliamentary group . . . [and] Wilson was irrevocably opposed to such a deal.' In Pincher's version, this extra factor enabled Callaghan 'to push Wilson into a political corner and, though resisted for a while, this extra pressure proved too much on top of the medical fear, the supplications of Mary, the wear and tear of the years and the problems of running a minority government containing a restless group of Left extremists making insistent demands' (p. 362). In his 1991 *Dirty Tricks*, Pincher retracts all this. In *Inside Story*, Pincher was given the nod about the 'mystery' of Wilson's resignation from an unnamed MI6 source – from the context, either Bruce McKenzie or George Kennedy Young – both of whom would have got it from Maurice Oldfield.

2   Falkender, *Downing Street*, p. 3.

3   Donoghue, p. 86; Benn, *Diaries*, vol. 3, 25/4/75; *Guardian*, 1/5/87. Donoghue also confirms the existence and timing of this timetable (p. 87).

4   Writing books: Crossman, *Diaries*, vol. 3, p. 899. In his *Dirty Tricks* Pincher speculates about Wilson's alleged fear of premature senility; but speculation is all it is.

5   *Sunday Times*, 15/5/77; Winter, pp. 472–3.

6   Halifax speech, Pincher, *Inside Story*, p. 370. Details of their previous work on the area, Penrose/Courtiour, pp. 18–19. Wilson conversations, *ibid.*, pp. 9–15.

7   *Guardian*, 15/5/76.

8   Winter, p. 468.

9   *Ibid.*, p. 469; Hain, p. 131.

10 Penrose/Courtiour, pp. 44, 49 and 54. Edward Von Rothkirk, head of one of the news agencies who had received the material, told journalist Nicholas Comfort about this at a lunch, the first time they met. Letter from Comfort to authors, 23/12/87.

11 'Double bubble', Hain p. 132. *Sunday Telegraph*, 23/5/76. Gordon Winter also confirms Cheeseman's original allegations and *bona fides*, Winter, pp. 472–3.

12 'Coup plot': Penrose/Courtiour, p. 316. After the meeting with Zuckerman, Marcia Williams described Wilson as 'absolutely bursting with it'.

13 Penrose/Courtiour, p. 394. Colin Wallace's material shows that Wilson's assessment was correct.

CHAPTER XLVII: 'THE BIG FAT SPIDER'

1 Penrose/Courtiour, pp. 68 and 71; and (agency material disappearing) 409. Penrose and Courtiour knew they were under surveillance: a police contact of Courtiour's warned them. It seems clear that once they began their investigation an operation would have been mounted to frustrate it.

2 *Ibid.*, p.170. This antipathy to stories about Thorpe is presumably explained by the prejudice within the BBC – and elsewhere in the serious media – in favour of the Liberals. *Ibid.*, p. 38. Protheroe: *ibid.* p. 171. Protheroe blocking Wallace: *Sunday Times*, 5/4/87. Just before this event we predicted to the *Newsnight* journalist who interviewed Wallace that Protheroe might do this. 'The BBC isn't like that', we were told. According to Wallace, Protheroe, in his capacity as a TA Army Information Officer, was given a guided tour of the Information Policy Unit under cover of the Army press office in Northern Ireland. BBC leak to BOSS, Winter, p. 457. *Private Eye* leaks, see, for example, *Private Eye*, 17/9/76, 1/10/76, 29/10/76, 29/4/77 etc. Foot was named as the author of most of these stories to us by then *Eye* editor, Richard Ingrams. It may only be coincidence that one of the BBC executives closely involved in the investigation had been at school with Foot. On Sir Charles Curran's views about investigative journalism, BBC reporter Tom Mangold wrote in the *Listener* (5/3/81): 'In conversation with the late Director-General, Sir Charles Curran, I learned how strongly he felt that clear lines had to be drawn beyond which the investigative journalist wandered at some peril. For example, he regarded as improper any originating investigation into the background of the Jeremy Thorpe story. His opposition rested on the firmly held view that the primary task of the BBC reporter, news or current affairs, was to report it straight.' We would place a small bet that an analysis of the output of BBC TV news or current affairs under Curran would show that this 'firmly held view' was selectively applied. In the 1960s Curran was named in the Soviet media as being an MI6 agent, an allegation for which no evidence was provided at the time nor has appeared since.

3 In the pilot issue of the *Leveller* in January 1977, Margareta Ramsay was named as an MI6 officer. Among the co-authors of the piece was Mark Hosenball. The *Leveller* came to loom large in the demonology of the right-wing media allies of the intelligence services. In the dreadful De Borchgrave and Moss novel, *The Spike*, the *Leveller* appears as the *Digger*, part of a global KGB conspiracy to manipulate Western opinion! The growing consciousness of the activities of the security and intelligence world is one of the interesting themes of Tony Benn's diaries in this period.

4 'Offensive operations' here means operations which are not concealed, whose aim is harassment and intimidation as well as information-gathering. Details of the operations are in Aubrey, pp. 56–60. Also see Aubrey for details of the meeting and subsequent arrest and trial.

5 Kelly smear, see 'Destabilising the Decent People', *New Statesman*, 15/2/80. The MI5 smear story was foolishly committed to paper by *Searchlight* journalist Gerry Gable in a memo to his then superiors at London Weekend Television. To our knowledge, Gable has never explained this action. Phil Kelly was editor of the Labour weekly, *Tribune*, 1987–91. Rose smear, see *Time Out*, 19/8/77, 'Argen – Spies for Sale'. Litterick libel victory, Press Association report, 10/7/80. If this report was actually carried in any newspaper the cutting does not appear in the Press Association library file on Litterick.

6 Caunt's book, trailed as *Who Goes Home?*, never appeared. We have been unable to find the 'report' of 18/7/77 referred to by the *Telegraph*. 'Hoarded by Caunt': Roth, *Walter Mitty*, p, 196. Caunt recruited by MI5 in *Today*, 13/7/87. Caunt names Plummer in Pincher, *Inside Story*, p. 346. Caunt may be the source that Pincher alludes to in his 1980 novel *Dirty Tricks*, p. 56, 'MI5 had a steady informer on the Downing Street staff.' This, as we have seen, could also apply to George Wigg.

7 Penrose/Courtiour, pp. 334 and 396–7. Mrs Williams even reported Lord Goodman speculating that Penrose and Courtiour were being funded by South Africa.

8 A good example of how mistaken even the well-informed serious British journalists were about Wilson is the otherwise excellent Andrew Roth: 'The difficulty Wilson had in distinguishing between what was demonstrable fact and what he believed to be true was dramatically illustrated during his transition from Prime Minister to backbencher. He used one of his last question times as Prime Minister to assert that South African interests were responsible for the blackguarding of Jeremy Thorpe and for his consequent retirement as Leader of the Liberal Party. He repeated this insistently at his farewell speech to the Parliamentary Press Club at luncheon. Quite naturally, political journalists assumed that he made his allegation on the basis of secret intelligence sources. In fact, British Intelligence had been quite unable to

find evidence to underpin his suspicions . . . It was not the first time he had blurred the boundary between reality and his doubts or hopes . . . His fury about their [Pencourt's] failure to prove his suspicions produced suggestions of MI5 "plots" against him.' *Walter Mitty*, p. 50.

CHAPTER XLVIII: WHITEHALL GAMES

1 Pincher, *Inside Story*, p. 33; *idem, Web of Deception*, p. 95; MI6 leak: *idem., Inside Story*, pp. 30–1.

2 Pincher, *Web of Deception*, p.127. The late Malcolm McDonald, erstwhile governor of Kenya, told the authors of *British Intelligence and Covert Action* that McKenzie had been recruited by MI6 in 1963, if not earlier. See Bloch/Fitzgerald, p. 153. An account of Bruce McKenzie's involvement in the Entenbe rescue is in Pincher's *Inside Story*. Pincher adds another interesting twist: when McKenzie died, in a sabotaged plane, it was Harold Wilson who wrote his obituary for *The Times*, never used because it was too vituperative about the regime of Idi Amin. See Pincher, *Web of Deception*, p. 201. In his 1991 *Dirty Tricks*, Pincher finally acknowledges that McKenzie was an MI6 agent.

3 His letter should be in Wilson's papers, which are in store. However, if we were running MI5, as soon as Wallace mentioned this letter to the press in 1987 we would have removed it, just as they (someone, anyway) removed from the British Parachuting Association files Wallace's free-fall licence details, and from Arun District Council his personal file.

4 HOC *Hansard*, especially cols. 1215-18, 28/7/77. Oh, the irony (and the absurdity) of this charge being hurled at the *Observer*, one of the best sources of cover MI6 ever had in the media.

5 HOC *Hansard*, col. 1373, 29/7/77.

6 Pincher, *Dirty Tricks*, p. 150.

7 Callaghan was quoted in the *Guardian*, 23/3/87, saying that 'My inquiries in 1977 . . . were based on stories published at the time by the *Observer* newspaper.' In his 1980 novel, *Dirty Tricks*, one of Pincher's MI6 characters says: 'There was a bad leak in this building . . . Somebody gave a journalist details of one of the reports MI5 sent us and he published them along with a claim that Wilson had been bugged. There was quite a nasty inquiry by Callaghan.' (p. 56) The report, which we discussed in the Reds under the Beds chapter, was obviously deeply embarrassing for the inquiry as it was direct confirmation of the anti-Wilson bias of some MI5 officers. Who gave the report to MI6? At the time of the inquiry Callaghan told Benn: 'Pincher's links with the services ended five years ago (1973).' Healey said: 'There was a man at MI5, an extreme right-winger, feeding Pincher with stories until he retired or resigned.' Benn, *Diaries*, vol. 4 pp. 379 and 290. This sounds like Peter Wright, who probably gave the report to MI6 and which was then passed by Oldfield on to Pincher. Pincher, *Inside Story*, p. 37; Wright, p. 372.

8 *Independent*, 17/3/87.

9 Penrose/Courtiour, p. 410. 'From his Political Secretary the reporters heard that the former Prime Minister had been disappointed that Mr Callaghan had not set up an immediate enquiry. He had expected his successor would rally quickly to his support.' *Ibid.*, pp. 401–2.

10 *The Times*, 8/11/77. Playing the tapes – information from Roger Courtiour.

11 HOC *Hansard*, cols. 508–15, 14/12/77.

12 On 15/7/78, Tony Benn recorded in his diary that 'On the platform at the Durham Miners' Gala, Jim said to me: "The Tories are going to try and create a lot of scandal before the Election. They are trying to dig up the story about Stonehouse and the Czechoslovak Government and hoping to drag Harold into it".'

13 HOC *Hansard*, cols. 506–7, 21/11/79. Benn's diaries for this period reveal Callaghan, Home Secretary Merlyn Rees, and Foreign Secretary David Owen, as apparently astonishingly complacent and naive about the intelligence and security services, all of them assuring Benn that they were in complete control. Callaghan: 'Its all under Ministerial control' (25/10/78); Rees: 'I want you to know that I am in complete charge of the security services, twenty-four hours a day, and nothing is done without my approval' (1/11/78); Owen: 'I took complete control of security, just like Merlyn' (30/11/78). Benn, *Diaries*, vol. 4.

14 IRD closure, see the *Guardian*, 27/1/78. In 1983, former ambassador Hilary King gave an example of what he called IRD's 'corrupt dissemination of "misinformation" which happens to suit our current prejudices', in a letter to *The Times*, 9/3/83. David Owen: 'Of course there is anxiety about security being in the hands of unsuitable people. For example the Tory MP for Wycombe, Ray Whitney, who is terribly right-wing, was the head of the FO's Information and Research Department before it was wound up.' Benn, *Diaries*, vol. 4, 30/11/78.

15 *Private Eye*, 17/3/78. Accidentally – or deliberately – one of the papers informed was the CPGB's *Morning Star*. See Deacon, *C*, p. 209.

16 *Private Eye*, 17/3/78.

17 Deacon, *C*, pp. 208–9. 'As the time for Oldfield's retirement drew near, controversy about who his successor

should be was fuelled by considerable argument as to whether there should be an overhaul of the Intelligence Services . . . some advisers who had the ear of the Prime Minister, James Callaghan, believed there were arguments in favour of a more positively Foreign Office figure. One or two other unofficial advisers had talked about the need for "tidying up" the Intelligence Services and setting up a Directorate of Central Intelligence rather on the American model, with a supremo who reported directly to the Prime Minister.' *Ibid.* 'Maurice [Oldfield] already knew that the Government were considering appointing an intelligence supremo in the Cabinet offices.' Cavendish, p. 151.

18 Benn, *Diaries*, vol. 4, p. 40; *Private Eye*, 15/9/78. The author of this piece confused 'report' with 'control'. MI6 did send its reports to the Joint Intelligence Committee, which is in the domain of the Cabinet Office, but control remained where it had always been.

CHAPTER XLIX: PETER WRIGHT

1 Pincher, *Web of Deception*, pp. 7 and 2.

2 MI5 smear: Oldfield's friend, Anthony Cavendish, suggests this in his *Inside Intelligence*, but offers no evidence. See, also, Deacon, *C*, p. 242. It is an indication of the state of the MI5/MI6 rivalry that Oldfield, who had stomach cancer, also suspected that he might have been poisoned.

3 Cavendish, intro., p. xvi.

4 Junor, p. 257, and Pincher, *Traitors*, p. 112.

5 Pincher, *Web of Deception*, pp. 3–4 and 9; *Spectator*, 14/6/80.

6 Pincher, *Web of Deception*, p. 6 and note 9, p. 196; R. V. Hall, pp. 45–7.

7 Pincher, *Web of Deception*, p. 34.

8 Oldfield's relationship with all this is unclear. He was certainly engaged in the conflict with MI5, and was friendly with Young and Sir Ian Hogg in Unison (and Cavendish); and did know about the organisation. When asked what Oldfield's views of Unison were, a friend of his told us that 'he neither approved nor disapproved'; but neither did he attempt to shut it down.

9 Young's autobiographical sketch was printed in full in *Lobster* 19; *Searchlight* 144, June 1987.

10 Pincher, *Dirty Tricks*, p. 40; ISC link with Mrs Thatcher, telephone conversation with Pincher, February 1991. ISC and the European network is described in David Teacher's essays on ISC's links to the Pinay Circle in *Lobster* 17 and 18. This fascinating subject is beyond the scope of this book.

CONCLUSION

1 A version of this is included in Chapman Pincher's *Dirty Tricks* (1991). The loss of memory is real and not an excuse to dodge the press. In 1986 we were told by a senior Labour MP that there was little point in taking Colin Wallace's allegations to Wilson because his memory was going. The MP had been at a meeting where Wilson had read the same page of his speech twice.

BIBLIOGRAPHY

ABSE, Leo, *Private Member*, London, MacDonald, 1973
AGEE, Phillip, *CIA Diary*, Harmondsworth, Penguin, 1975 – *On the Run*, London, Bloomsbury, 1987
AGEE, Phillip and Wolf, Louis, *Dirty Work: the CIA in Western Europe*, London, Zed, 1978
ALEXANDER, Andrew and Watkins, Alan, *The Making of the Prime Minister*, London, Macdonald, 1970
ALI, Tariq, *Street Fighting Years*, London, Collins, 1987
AMORY, Mark (ed.), *The Letters of Anne Fleming*, London, Collins Harvill, 1985
ANDREW, Christopher and Gordievsky, Oleg, *KGB: The Inside Story*, London, Hodder and Stoughton, 1990
AUGUST, Frantisek and Rees, David, *Red Star Over Prague*, London, Sherwood Press, 1984
ATTALI, Jacques, *A Man of Influence: Sir Siegmund Warburg 1902–82*, London, Weidenfeld and Nicolson, 1986
ATTALLAH, Naim, *Singular Encounters*, London, Quartet, 1991
AUBREY, Crispin, *Who's Watching You?*, Harmondsworth, Penguin, 1981

BAILEY, Martin, *Oilgate*, London, Coronet, 1979
BALL, George, *The Past Has Another Pattern: Memoirs*, New York, W. W. Norton, 1982
BAMFORD, James, *The Puzzle Palace: America's National Security Agency and its Special Relationship with Britain's GCHQ*, London, Sidgwick and Jackson, 1982
BARBER, James, *Rhodesia: The Road to Rebellion*, London, Oxford University Press/Institute for Race Relations, 1967
BARON, Stanley Wade, *The Contact Man: Sidney Stanley and the Lynskey Tribunal*, London, Secker and Warburg, 1966
BARRON, John, *KGB; The Secret Work of Soviet Secret Agents*, London, Corgi, 1983
BAYLIS, John (ed.), *British Defence Policy in a Changing World*, London, Croom Helm, London, 1977
BAYLIS, Stephen, *Anglo-American Defence Relations 1939–84: The Special Relationship*, London, Macmillan, 1984
BECKERMAN, Wilfred (ed.), *The Labour Government's Economic Record: 1964–70*, London, Duckworth, 1972
BELOFF, Nora, *Transit of Britain*, London, Collins, 1973
BENCE, David and Branson, Clive, *Roy Jenkins: A Question of Principle?*, London, Moat Hall, 1982
BENN, Tony, *Diaries*, London, Hutchinson: (vol. 1) *Out of the Wilderness 1963–7*, 1987; (vol. 2) *Office Without Power 1968–72*, 1988; (vol. 3) *Against the Tide 1973–6*, 1989; (vol. 4) *Conflicts of Interest 1977–80*, 1990

BERNSTEIN, Barton J. (ed.), *Towards a New Past: Dissenting Essays in American History*, New York, Vintage, 1968

BERRIDGE, Geoff, *Economic Power in Anglo-South African Diplomacy*, London, Macmillan, 1981

BISHOP, Patrick and Malle, Eamonn, *The Provisional IRA*, London, Corgi, 1989

BITOV, Oleg, *Bitov's Britain*, London, Viking, 1985

BLACKSTONE, Tessa and Plowden, William, *Inside the Think Tank*, London, Heinemann, 1988

BLAKE, George, *No Other Choice*, London, Jonathan Cape, 1990

BLANK, Stephen, *Identity and Government in Britain: The Federation of British Industry in Politics 1945–65*, Westmean, Farnborough, Saxon House, 1973

BLOCK, Jonathan and Fitzgerald, Patrick, *British Intelligence and Covert Action*, London, Junction/Brandon, 1983

BLUM, William, *The CIA: A Forgotten History*, London, Zed, 1986

BORRELL, Clive and Cashinella, Brian, *Crime in Britain*, London, Routledge and Kegan Paul, 1975

BOULTON, David, *The Lockheed Papers*, London, Jonathan Cape, 1978

BOYLE, Andrew, *The Climate of Treason*, Coronet, 1980

BRANDON, Henry, *In the Red*, London, Andre Deutsch, 1966

BRITTAN, Samuel, *Steering the Economy*, Harmondsworth, Penguin, 1971

BROADWAY, Frank, *State Intervention and British Industry 1964–8*, London, Kay and Ward, 1969

BROCKWAY, Fenner, *Towards Tomorrow*, London, Hart-Davis, 1977

BROOK-SHEPHERD, Gordon, *The Storm Birds: Soviet Post-War Defectors*, London, Weidenfeld and Nicolson, 1988

BROWN, Anthony Cave, *The Secret Servant*, London, Sphere, 1989

BROWN, George, *In My Way*, London, Victor Gollancz, 1971

BULL, George and Vice, Anthony, *Bid for Power*, London, Elek, 1961

BUNYAN, Tony, *The History and Practice of the Political Police in Britain*, London, Quartet, 1977

BUTLER, Michael and Pinto-Duchinksy, Michael, *The British General Election of 1970*, London, Macmillan, 1971

CAHILL, Kevin, *Trade Wars: The High-Technology Scandal of the 1980s*, London, W. H. Allen, 1986

CALLAGHAN, James, *Time and Chance*, London, Collins, 1988

CAMPBELL, Duncan, *The Unsinkable Aircraft Carrier*, London, Paladin, 1986

CAMPBELL, Duncan and Connor, Stephen, *On the Record*, London, Michael Joseph, 1986

CAMPBELL, John, *Roy Jenkins: A Biography*, London, Weidenfeld and Nicolson, 1983 – *Nye Bevan and the Mirage of British Socialism*, London, Weidenfeld and Nicolson, 1987

CAREW, Anthony, *Labour Under the Marshal Plan*, Manchester University Press, 1987

CARVER, Michael, *Out of Step*, London, Hutchinson, 1989

CASTLE, Barbara, (vol. 1) *The Castle Diaries 1964–70*, London, Weidenfeld and Nicolson, 1984; (vol. 2) *The Castle Diaries 1974–6*, London, Book Club Associates, 1980

CAVENDISH, Anthony, *Inside Intelligence*, London, Collins, 1990

CECIL, Robert, *A Divided Life: A Biography of Donald Maclean*, London, The Bodley Head, 1988

CHESTER, Lewis, Linklater, Magnus and May, David, *Jeremy Thorpe: A Secret Life*, London, Andre Deutsch/Fontana, 1979

CHICHESTER, Michael and Wilkinson, John, *The Uncertain Ally*, London, Gower, 1987

CHRISTIE, Stuart, *Steffano Delle Chiaie: Portrait of a Black Terrorist*, London, Refract, 1984

CHURCHILL, Randolph S., *The Fight for the Tory Leadership*, London, Mayflower-Dell, 1964

CLARKE, Michael, *Fallen Idols*, London, Junction, 1981

COLEMAN, Peter, *The Liberal Conspiracy*, New York, The Free Press, Collier/Macmillan, 1989

COOPER, Chester, *The Lost Crusade*, London, MacGibbon and Kee, 1970

CORSON, William R., Trento, Susan B. and Joseph J., *Widows*, London, Macdonald and James, 1989

COSGRAVE, Patrick, *The Lives of Enoch Powell*, London, The Bodley Head, 1989

COSTELLO, John, *Mask of Treachery*, London, Collins, 1988

COURTNEY, Commander Anthony, *Sailor in a Russian Frame*, London, Johnson, 1968

COWLES, Virginia, *The Rothschilds: A Family of Fortune*, London, Weidenfeld and Nicholson, 1973 – *The Phantom Major: The Story of David Stirling and the S.A.S. Regiment*, London, Fontana, 1970

CRAWLEY, Aidan, *Leap Before You Look*, London, Collins, 1988

CROSLAND, Susan, *Tony Crosland*, London, Coronet, 1982

CROSSMAN, Richard, *The Diaries of a Cabinet Minister*, (Janet Morgan, ed.), London, Hamish Hamilton and Jonathan Cape: (vol. 1) *Minister of Housing 1964–6*, 1975; (vol. 2) *Lord President of the Council and Leader of the House of Commons 1966–8*, 1976; (vol. 3), *Secretary of State for Social Services 1968–70*, 1977; *Backbench Diaries*, 1981

CROZIER, Brian, (ed.), *'We Will Bury You': Studies of Left-Wing Subversion Today*, London, Tom Stacey, 1970

CUDLIPP, Hugh, *Walking on the Water*, London, The Bodley Head, 1976

DALYELL, Tam, *Misrule*, London, Hamish Hamilton, 1987 – *Dick Crossman: A Portrait*, London, Weidenfeld and Nicolson, 1989

DAVIS, William, *Three Years Hard Labour: The Road to Devaluation*, London, Andre Deutsch, 1968

DEACON, Richard (Donald McCormick), *A History of the British Secret Service*, London, Frederick Muller, 1969 – *A History of the Russian Secret Service*, London, Frederick Muller, 1972 – *The British Connection*, London, Hamish Hamilton, 1979 [withdrawn] – *With My Little Eye: The Memoirs of a Spy-Hunter*, London, Frederick Muller, 1982 – *'C': A Biography of Sir Maurice Oldfield, Head of MI6*, London, Macdonald, 1985 – *The Greatest Treason*, London, Century, 1989 [withdrawn]

DEUTSCH, Richard and Magowan, Vivien, *Northern Ireland 1968–74: A Chronology of Events, Volume 3, 1974*, Ireland, Blackstaff Press, 1975

DILLON, Martin and Lehane, Dennis, *Political Murder in Northern Ireland*, Harmondsworth, Penguin, 1973

DITTBERNER, Job L., *The End of Ideology and American Social Thought*, USA, UMI Research Press, 1979

DOBSON, Christopher and Payne, Ronald, *The Carlos Complex: A Study in Terror*, London, Hodder and Stoughton, 1977 – *The Dictionary of Espionage*, London, Grafton, 1986

DOCKRILL, Michael, *British Defence Since 1945*, Oxford, Blackwell, 1989

DODDS-PARKER, Douglas, *Political Eunuch*, London, Springwood Books, 1986

DOIG, Alan, *Corruption and Misconduct in Contemporary Politics*, Harmondsworth, Penguin, 1984 – *Westminster Babylon*, London, Allison and Busby, 1990

DONNELLY, Desmond, *Gaderene '68*, London, William Kimber, 1968 – *The Nearing Storm*, London, Hutchinson, 1968
DONOUGHUE, Bernard, *Prime Ministers and British Central Government*, London, Jonathan Cape, 1987
DRIVER, Christopher, *The Disarmers: A Study in Protest*, London, Hodder and Stoughton, 1964
DUFF, Peggy, *Left, Left, Left*, London, Allison and Busby, 1971

ELWYN-JONES, Lord, *In My Life*, London, Weidenfeld and Nicholson, 1983
EPSTEIN, Edward Jay, *Deception: The Invisible War Between the KGB and the CIA*, London, W. H. Allen, 1989
EVANS, Harold, *Good Times, Bad Times*, London, Coronet, 1984
EVANS, William, *My Mountbatten Years*, London, Headline, 1989

FALIGOT, Roger, *The Kitson Experiment*, London, Zed/Brandon, 1983
FALKENDER (Williams), Marcia, *Inside Number 10*, London, Weidenfeld and Nicolson, 1972 – *Downing Street in Perspective* London, Weidenfeld and Nicolson, 1983
FARR, Diana, *Five at 10: Prime Ministers' Consorts Since 1957*, London, Andre Deutsch, 1985
FERRIS, Paul, *The City*, London, Pelican, 1962
FISK, Robert, *The Point of No Return*, London, Methuen, 1975
FITZGERALD, Patrick and Leopold, Mark, *Stranger on the Line: The Secret History of Telephone Tapping*, London, The Bodley Head, 1987
FITZWALTER, Raymond and Taylor, David, *Web of Corruption: The Story of John Poulson and T. Dan Smith*, London, Granada, 1981
FLETCHER, Richard, *Who Were They Travelling With?*, Nottingham, Spokesman, 1977
FLOWER, Ken, *Serving Secretly: An Intelligence Officer on Record: Rhodesia into Zimbabwe 1964 to 1981*, London, John Murray, 1987
FOOT, Michael, *Aneurin Bevan Vol. 2*, London, Paladin, 1975
FOOT, Paul, *The Politics of Harold Wilson*, Harmondsworth, Penguin, 1968 – *Who Framed Colin Wallace?*, London, Macmillan, 1989
FORTE, Charles, *Forte: the Autobiography of Charles Forte*, London, Sidgwick and Jackson, 1986
FRAZIER, Howard, (ed.), *Uncloaking the CIA*, London, Free Press/Macmillan, 1978
FREEDMAN, Lawrence, *Britain and Nuclear Weapons*, London, Macmillan/Royal Institute of International Affairs, 1980
FREEMANTLE, Brian, *KGB*, London, Michael Joseph, 1983
FROLIK, Joseph, *The Frolik Defection*, London, Leo Cooper, 1975

GAMBLE, A. M. and Walkland, S. A., *The British Party System and Economic Policy 1945–83*, Oxford, Clarendon, 1984
GAMBLE, Andrew, *The Conservative Nation*, London, Routledge and Kegan Paul, 1974
GLEES, Anthony, *The Secrets of the Service*, London, Jonathan Cape, 1987
GODSON, Roy, *American Labour and European Politics*, New York, Crane, Russack, 1976
GOLDSMITH, James M., *Counter Culture*, London, privately published, 1985
GOLITSYN, Anatoli, *New Lies for Old*, London, The Bodley Head, 1984 and Wheatsheaf edition, 1986
GOODMAN, Geoffrey, *The Awkward Warrior, Frank Cousins: His Life and Times*, London, Davis-Poynter, 1979
GOURIET, John, *Checkmate Mr President*, Glasgow, William Maclellan, 1981
GRIFFITHS, Robert, *S. O. Davies – A Socialist Faith*, Wales, Gomer, 1983

GUMMETT, Philip, *Scientists in Whitehall*, Manchester University Press, 1980

HAIN, Peter, *A Putney Plot?*, Nottingham, Spokesman, 1987
HAINES, Joe, *The Politics of Power*, London, Coronet [revised edition], 1977 – *Maxwell*, London, Futura, 1988
HALCROW, Morrison, *Keith Joseph: A Single Mind*, London, Macmillan, 1988
HALL, Richard, *My Life with Tiny*, London, Faber and Faber, 1987
HALL, Richard V., *A Spy's Revenge*, Harmondsworth, Penguin, 1987
HARRIS, Kenneth, *David Owen*, London, Weidenfeld and Nicolson, 1987 – *Conversations*, London, Hodder and Stoughton, 1987
HARRIS, Robert and Paxman, Jeremy, *A Higher Form of Killing*, London, Paladin, 1983
HASELER, Stephen, *The Gaitskellites*, London, Macmillan, 1969
HEDLEY, Peter and Aynsley, Cyril, *The D-Notice Affair*, London, Michael Joseph, 1967
HEALEY, Denis, *The Time of My Life*, London, Michael Joseph, 1989
HEATHERINGTON, Alastair, *Guardian Years*, London, Chatto and Windus, 1980
HENNESSY, Peter, *Cabinet*, Oxford, Basil Blackwell, 1986 – *Whitehall*, London, Secker and Warburg, 1989
HENNESSY, Peter and Jeffries, Keith, *States of Emergency*, London, Routledge and Kegan Paul, 1983
HENNESSY, Peter and Seldon, Anthony, (eds.), *Ruling Performance*, London, Basil Blackwell, 1989
HEREN, Louis, *No Hail, No Farewell*, London, Harper and Row, 1970
HIRSCH, Fred, *The Pound Sterling*, London, Victor Gollancz, 1965
HOLLINGSWORTH, Mark and Norton-Taylor, Richard, *Blacklist: The Inside Story of Political Vetting*, London, Hogarth Press, 1988
HOLLINGSWORTH, Mark and Treymayne, Charles, *The Economic League*, London, National Council for Civil Liberties, 1989
HOLROYD, Fred and Burridge, Nick, *War Without Honour*, Hull, Medium, 1989
HORNE, Alastair, *Macmillan 1957–86; Vol. 2 of the Official Biography*, London, Macmillan, 1989
HOWARD, Anthony, *Crossman: The Pursuit of Power*, London, Jonathan Cape, 1990
HOWARD, Anthony and West, Richard, *The Making of the Prime Minister*, London, Quality Book Club, 1965
HUDSON, Miles, *Triumph or Tragedy?*, London, Hamish Hamilton, n.d., *c.* 1980s
HUGHES, Emrys, *Sydney Silverman: Rebel in Parliament*, London, Charles Skilton, 1969
HUNTER, Leslie, *The Road to Brighton Pier*, London, Arthur Baker, 1959
HYDE, H. Montgomery, *A Tangled Web*, London, Futura, 1986

INGRAMS, Richard, *Goldenballs*, London, Coronet, 1980
IRVING, Clive, *True Brit*, London, Jonathan Cape, 1974

JACKSON, Robert J., *Rebels and Whips*, London, Macmillan, 1968
JAMES, Robert Rhodes, *Ambitions and Realities*, London, Weidenfeld and Nicholson, 1972
JAY, Douglas, *Change and Fortune*, London, Hutchinson, 1980
JAY, Peggy, *Loves and Labours*, London, Weidenfeld and Nicolson, 1990
JENKINS, Clive, *All Against the Collar*, London, Methuen, 1990
JENKINS, Hugh, *Rank and File*, London, Croom Helm, 1980
JENKINS, Mark, *Bevanism: Labour's High Tide*, Nottingham, Spokesman, 1979
JENKINS, Peter, *The Battle for Downing Street*, London, Charles Knight, 1970
JOHNSON, Donald, *A Doctor Reflects: Miracles and Mirages*, London, Johnson, 1975

JONES, Jack, *Union Man*, London, Collins, 1986
JONES, Robert and Marriott, Oliver, *Anatomy of a Merger: A History of GEC, AEI and English Electric*, London, Pan, 1970
JOYCE, Peter, *Anatomy of a Rebel: Smith of Rhodesia*, Salisbury [Rhodesia], Graham, 1974
JUNOR, John, *Memoirs: Listening for a Midnight Train*, London, Chapman, 1990

KAMIL, Fred, *The Diamond Underworld*, London, Allen Lane, 1979
KAY, Ernest, *Pragmatic Premier: An Intimate Portrait of Harold Wilson*, London, Leslie Frewin, 1967
KELLNER, Peter and Lord Crowther-Hunt, *The Civil Servants: An Inquiry into Britain's Ruling Class*, London, Macdonald, 1980
KING, Cecil, *Strictly Personal*, London, Weidenfeld and Nicolson, 1969 – (vol. 1) *Diaries 1965–70*, London, Jonathan Cape, 1972; (vol. 2) *Diaries 1970–4*, London, Jonathan Cape, 1976
KNIGHT, Derrick, *Beyond the Pale*, Leigh, CARAF, 1982
KNIGHTLEY, Phillip, *The Second Oldest Profession: The Spy as Bureaucrat, Patriot, Fantasist and Whore*, London, Andre Deutsch, 1986
KRAMISH, *The Griffin*, Boston, Houghton Mifflin, 1986
KUZICHKIN, Vladimir, *Inside the KGB*, London, Andre Deutsch, 1990
KWITNEY, Jonathan, *Endless Enemies*, New York, Congdon and Weed, 1984

LAURIE, Peter, *Scotland Yard: A Study of the Metropolitan Police*, Harmondsworth, Penguin, 1972
LEIGH, David, *The Wilson Plot: The Intelligence Services and the Discrediting of a Prime Minister 1945–76*, London, William Heinemann, 1988
LINDSAY, Kennedy, *Ambush at Tulleywest*, Dundalk, Dunrod, 1980
LLOYD, John, *Light and Liberty: the History of the EEPTU*, London, Weidenfeld and Nicolson, 1990
LONEY, Martin, *Rhodesia: White Racism and Imperial Response*, Harmondsworth, Penguin, 1975
LONGFORD, Elizabeth, *The Pebbled Shore*, London, Sceptre, 1988
LOUIS, William Roger and Bull, Hedley (eds), *The Special Relationship: Anglo-American Relations since 1945*, Oxford, Clarendon, 1980
LOUIS, William Roger and Owen, Roger, (eds.), *Suez 1956: The Crisis and its Consequences*, Oxford, Clarendon, 1989
LUTTWAK, Edward, *Coup D'État: A Practical Handbook*, London, Allen Lane, 1968

McGOVERN, John, *Neither Fear Nor Favour*, London, Blandford, 1960
McKAY, Peter, *Inside Private Eye*, London, Fourth Estate, 1986
MACKINTOSH, John P., *The British Cabinet*, London, Stevens and Sons, 1977
MALONE, Peter, *The British Nuclear Deterrent*, London, Croom Helm, 1984
MANGOLD, Tom, *Cold Warrior: James Jesus Angleton, the CIA's Master Spy Hunter*, London, Simon and Schuster, 1991
MARGACH, James, *The Abuse of Power*, London, Star, 1979
MARNHAM, Patrick, *The Private Eye Story*, London, Fontana, 1983 – *Trail of Havoc: In the Steps of Lord Lucan*, London, Viking, 1987
MARSH, Richard, *Off the Rails*, London, Weidenfeld and Nicolson, 1978
MARTIN, David C., *Wilderness of Mirrors*, New York, Ballantine, 1980
MASTERS, Anthony, *The Man Who was M*, Oxford, Blackwell, 1984
MAUDLING, Reginald, *Memoirs*, London, Sidgwick and Jackson, 1978
MAYHEW, Christopher, *Time to Explain*, London, Century Hutchinson, 1987

MEYER, Cord, *Facing Reality*, London, Harper and Row, 1980

MIKARDO, Ian, *Back-Bencher*, London, Weidenfeld and Nicolson, 1988

MILCZYNSKI, J., *The Economics and Politics of East–West Trade*, London, Macmillan, 1969

MILNE, Edward, *No Shining Armour*, London, John Calder, 1976

MINKIN, Lewis, *The Labour Party Conference*, London, Allen Lane, 1978

MORAN, Michael, *The Politics of Banking*, London, Macmillan, 1984

MOOREHEAD, Caroline, *Sidney Bernstein: a Biography*, London, Jonathan Cape, 1984

MULLINS, Eustace, *The World Order: A study in the Hegemony of Parasitism*, Staunton, VA, USA, Ezra Pound Institute of Civilization, 1985

MURRAY, Raymond, *The SAS in Ireland*, Dublin, Mercier, 1990

MURRAY-BROWN, Jeremy (ed.), *The Monarchy and its Future*, London, Allen and Unwin, 1969

NAIRN, Tom, *The Enchanted Glass: Britain and its Monarchy*, London, Radius, 1988

NAYLOR, R. T., *Hot Money and the Politics of Debt*, London, Unwin Hyman, 1987

NEWSLINE, *Britain's State Within a State*, London, New Park Publications, n.d., *circa* 1981

NEWTON, Scott and Porter, Dilwyn, *Modernisation Frustrated*, London, Unwin Hyman, 1988

NORTHEDGE, F. S. and Wells, Audrey, *Britain and Soviet Communism: The Impact of a Revolution*, London, Macmillan, 1982

NORTON, Phillip, *Dissension in the House of Commons 1945–75*, London, Macmillan, 1975 – *Conservative Dissidents*, London, Temple Smith, 1978

NORTON-TAYLOR, Richard and Hollingsworth, Mark, *Blacklist: The Inside Story of Political Vetting*, London, Hogarth, 1988

NOSSITER, Bernard, *Britain: a Future that Works*, London, Andre Deutsch, 1978

NUGENT, Neill and King, Roger (eds.), *Respectable Rebels*, London, Hodder and Stoughton, 1979

OSTROVSKY, Peter, and Hoy, Claire, *By Way of Deception*, New York, St Martin's Press, 1990

O'SULLIVAN, Timothy, *Julian Hodge: A Biography*, London, 1991

PARKER, Robert, *Rough Justice*, London, Fontana, 1981

PEAK, Steve, *Troops in Strikes*, London, Cobden Trust, 1984

PEARSON, John, *The Profession of Violence: The Rise and Fall of the Kray Twins*, London, Weidenfeld and Nicolson, 1972

PEARSON, John and Turner, Graham, *The Persuasion Industry*, London, Eyre and Spottiswoode, 1965

PENROSE, Barrie and Courtiour, Roger, *The Pencourt File*, London, Secker and Warburg, 1978

PENROSE, Barrie and Freeman, Simon, *Conspiracy of Silence: The Secret Life of Anthony Blunt*, London, Grafton, 1986

PIERRE, Andrew, *Nuclear Politics*, London, Open University Press, 1972

PIMLOTT, Ben (ed.), *The Second World War Diary of Hugh Dalton 1940–45*, London, Cape, 1986

PINCHER, Chapman, *Inside Story: A Documentary of the Pursuit of Power*, London, Sidgwick and Jackson, 1978 – *Their Trade is Treachery*, London, Sidgwick and Jackson, 1981 – *Too Secret, Too Long: The Great Betrayal of Britain's Crucial Secrets and the Cover-up*, London, Sidgwick and Jackson, 1984 – *The Secret Offensive: Active Measures: A Saga*

of Deception, Disinformation, Subversion, Terrorism, Sabotage and Assassination, London, Sidgwick and Jackson, 1985 – *Traitors: The Labyrinths of Treason*, London, Sidgwick and Jackson, 1987 – *The Spycatcher Affair: A Web of Deception*, London, Sidgwick and Jackson, 1987 – *The Truth About Dirty Tricks*, London, Sidgwick and Jackson, 1991
POCOCK, Tom, *Fighting General: The Public and Private Campaigns of General Sir Walter Walker*, London, Collins, 1973
POLLITT, Christopher, *Manipulating the Machine*, London, Allen and Unwin, 1984
PONTING, Clive, *Breach of Promise: Labour in Power 1964–70*, London, Hamish Hamilton, 1989
PORTER, Bernard, *Plots and Paranoia*, London, Unwin Hyman, 1989

QUIGLEY, Carroll, *Tragedy and Hope*, New York, Macmillan, 1966

RADOSH, Ronald, *American Labour and US Foreign Policy*, New York, Random House, 1969
RANELAGH, John, *The Agency: The Rise and Decline of the CIA*, London, Weidenfeld and Nicolson, 1986
RAW, Charles, *Slater Walker: An Investigation of a Phenomenon*, London, Andre Deutsch, 1977
RAWLINSON, Peter, *A Price Too High*, London, Weidenfeld and Nicolson, 1989
REES, Merlyn, *Northern Ireland: A Personal Perspective*, London, Methuen, 1985
RICHTER, Irving, *Political Purpose in Trade Unions*, London Allen and Unwin, 1973
RITCHELSON, Jeffrey T. and Ball, Desmond, *The Ties That Bind*, London, Unwin Hyman, 1990
RITCHIE, Richard (ed.), *A Nation or No Nation? Enoch Powell: Six Years in British Politics*, Kingsmead, Surrey, Elliot Right Way Books, 1978
ROBERTSON, Geoff, *Reluctant Judas*, London, Routledge and Kegan Paul, 1976
ROLL, Eric, *Crowded Hours*, London, Faber and Faber, 1985
ROSSER, David, *A Dragon in the House*, Wales, Gomer, 1987
ROOSEVELT, Archie, *For Lust of Knowing*, London, Weidenfeld and Nicolson, 1988
ROSE, Paul, *The Backbencher's Dilemma*, London, Frederick Muller, 1981
ROTH, Andrew, *Heath and the Heathmen*, London, Routledge and Kegan Paul, 1972 – *Sir Harold Wilson: Yorkshire Walter Mitty*, London, Macdonald and James, 1977 [withdrawn]

SAMPSON, Anthony, *Anatomy of Britain*, London, Hodder and Stoughton, 1962
SCHNEER, Jonathan, *Labour's Conscience: The Labour Left 1945–51*, London, Unwin Hyman, 1988
SEDGEMORE, Brian, *The Secret Constitution*, London, Hodder and Stoughton, 1980
SEJNA, Jan, *We Will Bury You*, London, Sidgwick and Jackson, 1982
SHAW, Eric, *Discipline and Discord in the Labour Party: The Politics of Managerial Control in the Labour Party, 1951–87*, Manchester University Press, 1988
SHORE, Peter, *Entitled to Know*, London, McKibbon and Kee, 1966
SHORT, Edward, *Whip to Wilson*, London, Macdonald, 1989
SHOUP, Laurence and Minter, William, *Imperial Brain Trust: the Council on Foreign Relations and United States Foreign Policy*, London, Monthly Review Press, 1977
SHRIMSLEY, Anthony, *The First Hundred Days of Harold Wilson*, London, Weidenfeld and Nicolson, 1965
SILKIN, John, *Changing Battlefields: The Challenge to the Labour Party*, London, Hamish Hamilton, 1987
SILVER, Eric, *Victor Feather*, London, Victor Gollancz, 1973

SIMPSON, John, *The Independent Nuclear State: The United States, Britain and the Military Atom*, London, Macmillan, 1986

SKLAR, Holly (ed.), *Trilateralism*, Boston, USA, South End, 1980

SKEEN, Brigadier Andrew, *Prelude to Independence: Skeen's 115 Days*, Cape Town, Nasionale Boekhandel, 1966

SLATER, Jim, *Return to Go: My Autobiography*, London, Weidenfeld and Nicolson, 1977

SMITH, Colin, *Carlos, Portrait of a Terrorist*, London, Sphere, 1976

SMITH, Cyril, *Big Cyril*, London, W. H. Allen, 1978

SMITH, Dudley, *Harold Wilson: A Critical Biography*, London, Robert Hale, 1964

SMITH, Glen Alden, *Soviet Foreign Trade*, London, Praeger, 1973

SMITH, Leslie, *Harold Wilson: The Authentic Portrait*, London, Hodder and Stoughton, 1964

SMITH, Richard Harris, *OSS: The Secret History of America's First Central Intelligence Agency*, California, University of California, 1972

STEWART, Michael, *The Jekyll and Hyde Years*, London, Dent, 1977 – *Life and Labour*, London, Sidgwick and Jackson, 1980

STEWART-SMITH, Geoffrey, *No Vision Here: Non-Military Warfare in Britain*, London, Foreign Affairs, 1965

ST JOHNSTON, Eric, *One Policeman's Story*, London, Barry Rose, 1978

STONEHOUSE, John, *Death of an Idealist*, London, W. H. Allen, 1975 – *My Trial*, London, Star, 1976

STRAIGHT, Michael, *After Long Silence*, London, Collins, 1983

SUMMERS, Anthony and Dorril, Stephen, *Honeytrap: The Secret Worlds of Stephen Ward*, London, Weidenfeld and Nicolson, 1987

SWARTZ, Marvin, *The Union of Democratic Control in British Politics During the First World War*, Oxford, Clarendon, 1971

TEBBITT, Norman, *Upwardly Mobile*, London, Weidenfeld and Nicolson, 1988

THAYER, George, *The British Political Fringe*, London, Anthony Blond, 1965

THOMAS, George, *Mr Speaker: The Memoirs of The Viscount Tonypandy*, London, Century, 1985

THOMAS, Hugh, *John Strachey*, London, Eyre and Methuen, 1973 – *Armed Truce: The Beginnings of the Cold War 1945–6*, London, Sceptre, 1988

THOMAS, Hugh (ed.), *Crisis in the Civil Service*, London, Anthony Blond, 1968

TINKER, Jack, *The Television Barons*, London, Quartet, 1980

TODD, Judith, *The Right to Say No*, London, Sidgwick and Jackson, 1972

TOMKINSON, Martin and Gilliard, Michael, *Nothing to Declare: The Political Corruptions of John Poulson*, London, John Calder, 1980

TURNBULL, Malcolm, *The Spycatcher Trial*, London, Heinemann, 1988

VAN DER PIJL, Kees, *The Making of an Atlantic Ruling Class*, London, Verso, 1984

VERRIER, Anthony, *Through the Looking Glass: British Foreign Policy in the Age of Illusions*, London, Jonathan Cape, 1983 – *The Road to Zimbabwe 1890–1980*, London, Jonathan Cape, 1986

WALKER, Martin, *The National Front*, London, Fontana, 1977

WANSELL, Geoffrey, *Sir James Goldsmith: The Man and the Myth*, London, Fontana, 1982

WATKINS, Alan, *Brief Lives*, London, Hamish Hamilton, 1982

WATKINSON, Harold, *Turning Points: A Record of our Time*, London, Michael Russell, 1986

WATT, D. Cameron, *Succeeding John Bull: America in Britain's Place 1900–75*, Cambridge University Press, 1984

WAUGH, Auberon, *Four Crowded Years: The Diaries of Auberon Waugh*, London, Andre Deutsch, 1976 – *The Diaries of Auberon Waugh 1976–85*, London, Andre Deutsch, 1985 – *The Trial of Jeremy Thorpe*, London, Michael Joseph, 1980

WEBBER, G. C., *The Ideology of the British Right Wing*, London, Croom Helm, 1986

WEILER, Peter, *British Labour and the Cold War*, California, Stanford University Press, 1985

WEST, Nigel (Rupert Allason), *A Matter of Trust: MI5 1945–72*, London, Weidenfeld and Nicolson, 1982 – *Molehunt: The Full Story of the Spy in MI5*, London, Weidenfeld and Nicolson, 1987 – *The Friends: Britain's Post-War Secret Intelligence Operations*, London, Weidenfeld and Nicolson, 1988 – *GCHQ: The Secret Wireless War 1900–86*, London, Weidenfeld and Nicolson, 1986

WHEEN, Francis, *Tom Driberg: His Life and Indiscretions*, London, Chatto and Windus, 1990

WHITEHEAD, Philip, *The Writing on the Wall*, London, Michael Joseph, 1985

WIGG, Lord, *George Wigg*, London, Michael Joseph, 1972

WILLIAMS, David, *Not in the Public Interest: The Problem of Security in Democracy*, London, Hutchinson, 1965

WILLIAMS, Geoffrey and Reed, Bruce, *Denis Healey and the Politics of Power*, London, Sidgwick and Jackson, 1971

WILLIAMS, Phillip, *Hugh Gaitskell: A Political Biography*, Oxford University Press, 1982

WILLIAMS, Phillip (ed.), *The Diary of Hugh Gaitskell 1945–56*, London, Jonathan Cape, 1983

WILSON, H. H., *Pressure Group: The Campaign for Commercial Television*, London, Secker and Warburg, 1961

WILSON, Harold, *Purpose in Politics*, London, Weidenfeld and Nicolson, 1964 – *The Labour Government 1964–70*, London, Weidenfeld and Nicolson, 1971 [pbk. Penguin, 1974] – *The Governance of Britain*, London, Weidenfeld and Nicolson, 1976 – *Final Term: the Labour Government of 1974–76*, London, Weidenfeld and Nicolson, 1979 – *Memoirs: The Making of a Prime Minister 1916–64*, London, Weidenfeld and Nicolson, 1986

WINCHESTER, Simon, *Their Noble Lordships*, London, Faber and Faber, 1981

WINDRICH, Elaine, *Britain and the Politics of Rhodesian Independence*, London, Croom Helm, 1978

WINTER, Gordon, *Inside BOSS*, Harmondsworth, Penguin, 1981

WOODHOUSE, C. M., *Something Ventured*, London, Granada, 1982

WRIGHT, Peter, with Greengrass, Paul, *Spycatcher*, Australia, William Heinemann, 1987

WYNNE, Greville, *The Man from Odessa*, London, Robert Hale, 1981

YOUNG, G. K., *Subversion and the British Reposte*, Glasgow, Ossian, n.d., *circa* 1985

YOUNG, Hugo and Sloman, Anne, *No, Minister: An Inquiry into the Civil Service*, London, BBC Books, 1982

YOUNG, Kenneth, *Rhodesia and Independence*, London, Dent, 1969 – *Sir Alec Douglas-Home*, London, Dent, 1970

YOUNG, Stephen with Lowe, A. V., *Intervention in the Mixed Economy: The Evolution of British Industrial Policy 1964–72*, London, Croom Helm, 1974

ZIEGLER, Philip, *Mountbatten*, London, Guild, 1985

ZUCKERMAN, Solly, *Monkey, Men and Missiles: An Autobiography 1946–88*, London, Collins, 1988

INDEX

This index includes the material in the notes. References to that material consists of two n umbers – e.g. *12/3*. The number of the left of the oblique line is the chapter number; the number or numbers to the right of the oblique line that of the note(s). For example, *12/3,7,9* means chapter 12, notes 3,7 and 9. The acronym 'FNU' which appears occasionally below means 'first name unknown.'

Index

Index